The Archaeology of Human Origins

THE ARCHAEOLOGY OF HUMAN ORIGINS

Papers by Glynn Isaac

EDITED BY
BARBARA ISAAC

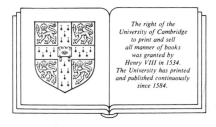

*The right of the
University of Cambridge
to print and sell
all manner of books
was granted by
Henry VIII in 1534.
The University has printed
and published continuously
since 1584.*

CAMBRIDGE UNIVERSITY PRESS
CAMBRIDGE
NEW YORK   PORT CHESTER
MELBOURNE   SYDNEY

Published by the Press Syndicate of the University of Cambridge
The Pitt Building, Trumpington Street, Cambridge CB2 1RP
40 West 20th Street, New York, NY 10011, USA
10 Stamford Road, Oakleigh, Melbourne 3166, Australia

First published 1989

Printed in Great Britain at the University Press, Cambridge

British Library cataloguing in publication data

Isaac, Glynn L1. (Glynn Llywelyn), 1937–1985
The archaeology of human origins: papers
by Glynn Isaac.
1. Prehistoric archaeology
I. Title II. Isaac, Barbara
930.1

Library of Congress cataloguing in publication data

Isaac, Glynn Llywelyn, 1937–85
The archaeology of human origins.
Bibliography: p.
Includes index.
1. Man, Prehistoric. 2. Man – Origin. I. Isaac, Barbara. II. Title.
GN741.I85   1989   573.3   88-28519

ISBN 0 521 36573 2

ST

Contents

Illustrations

Tables

Foreword

MARY LEAKEY

In his introduction John Gowlett has paid tribute to the many aspects of Glynn's tragically short career. My contribution in this brief foreword is on a more personal basis, of shared experiences and enjoyable discussions on problems arising from interpretation of Acheulean sites and other related topics. A number of long-held fallacious beliefs were swept away in the course of our conversations. Glynn's presence in the field of East African prehistory was a source of inspiration and an incentive to approach issues with a greater clarity of mind.

It was always stimulating and interesting to visit Glynn when he and Barbara were excavating at Olorgesailie, Peninj or East Turkana. This was particularly true at the time I was digging at Olduvai Gorge myself, since the sites often presented similar problems requiring the same techniques of excavation and recording, and shared ideas helped towards interpreting the evidence.

Glynn maintained a cheerful optimism about his work on the Acheulean, believing that, in spite of the paucity of information we were usually able to extract, a time would come when the puzzles would be resolved. Chief among these, of course, was the riverine context of so many East African Acheulean sites. His optimistic attitude was in marked contrast to my despondency when I began to dig the Acheulean sites at Olduvai after the splendid undisturbed stratigraphy of the Oldowan sites in Bed I. I remember him telling me emphatically that I must learn to live with the Acheulean if I hoped to complete my programme of excavation at Olduvai. He was right and I did eventually.

There are many reminiscences I can recall of experiences and expeditions shared with Glynn and Barbara; for example, a visit we made to Ethiopia to see the site of Melka Kunturé shortly after it had been discovered by Gerard Dekker. There were occasions, too, when Glynn visited Olduvai and I had the benefit of his advice and critical examination of the sites I was working.

Glynn was a prolific writer and one tends to forget the number of important and thought-provoking papers he wrote over the years. To collect the most significant and reprint them in this volume under one cover is most valuable and also provides an important record of the changing attitudes, over the years, to the study of early man, his environment, his lifestyle and his tools.

Acknowledgements

Barbara Isaac and Cambridge University Press are grateful to the original publishers of Glynn Isaac's papers included in this volume for permission to reprint them here. The photographs in chapter 8 are reproduced by permission of Peter Kain and Richard Leakey.

Cambridge University Press also acknowledges with thanks a grant from the Peabody Museum of Archaeology and Ethnology, Harvard University.

The writings of Glynn Isaac, 1937–85

*Paper reprinted in this volume

Monographs, articles and papers

Undated   *A Guide to the Olorgesailie Prehistoric Site*. Nairobi: National Museums of Kenya.

1964   Olorgesailie: a study of the natural history of a middle Pleistocene lake basin. *Proceedings of the East African Academy, First Symposium, Makerere University College, June 1963*, 141–3. Nairobi: Longman for the East African Academy.

With A. B. Isaac. Layer by layer, the history of man is being uncovered in eastern Africa. *Africana* 1: 34–6.

1965   An annotated list of the most important palaeontological (mammalian) and archaeological assemblages associated with the Rift Valleys of Kenya. *East African Rift System*. Proceedings of a seminar sponsored by the Upper Mantle Committee and UNESCO: 44–9. Nairobi: University College.

The stratigraphy of the Peninj Beds and the provenance of the Natron Australopithecine mandible. *Quaternaria* 7: 101–30.

1966   The geological history of the Olorgesailie area. *Actas del V Congreso Panafricano de Prehistoria y de Estudio del Cuaternario 2*, 125–33. Edited by L. D. Cuscoy. Santa Cruz de Tenerife: Museo Arqueologico.

The middle and later Stone Age in Africa. *Prelude to East African History: a collection of papers given at the first East African vacation school in Pre-European African history and archaeology in December 1962*: 43–50. Edited by M. Posnansky. London: Oxford University Press.

New evidence from Olorgesailie relating to the character of Acheulean occupation sites. *Actas del V Congreso Panafricano de Prehistoria y de Estudio del Cuaternario* 2: 135–45. Edited by L. D. Cuscoy. Santa Cruz de Tenerife: Museo Arqueologico.

Olorgesailie: an investigation into the natural history of early men. *Prelude to East African History: a collection of papers given at the first East African vacation school in Pre-European African history and archaeology in December 1962*: 40–2. Edited by M. Posnansky. London: Oxford University Press.

With J. D. Clark, G. H. Cole and M. R. Kleindienst. Precision and definition in African archaeology: implications for archaeology of the recommendations of the 29th Wenner-Gren symposium, 'Systematic Investigation of the African Later Tertiary and Quaternary', 1965. *South African Archaeological Bulletin* 21: 114–21.

1967   The stratigraphy of the Peninj Group: early Middle Pleistocene formations west of Lake Natron, Tanzania, *Background to Evolution in Africa*: 229–57. Edited by W. W. Bishop and J. D. Clark with contributions by A. W. Gentry, R. L. Hay, L. S. B. Leakey, T. Reilly and B. Verdcourt, Chicago: University of Chicago Press.

*   Towards the interpretation of occupation debris: some experiments and observations. *Kroeber Anthropological Society Papers* 37: 31–57.

1968   Traces of Pleistocene hunters: an East African example. *Man the Hunter*: 253–61. Edited by R. B. Lee and I. DeVore, with the assistance of J. Nash-Mitchell. Chicago: Aldine.

With C. M. Keller. Note on proportional frequency of side- and end-struck flakes, *South African Archaeological Bulletin* 23: 17–19.

1969   Studies of early culture in East Africa, *World Archaeology* 1: 1–28.

1970   With A. B. Isaac. *COWA Surveys and Bibliographies, Area 12, No. IV, 1969, Equatorial Africa: A Commentary and Annotated Bibliography*: 2, 11p. Boston, Mass.: Department of Sociology and Anthropology, Boston University.

With A. B. Isaac. *COWA Surveys and Bibliographies, Area 14, No. IV, East Africa: A Commentary and Annotated Bibliography*: 4, 26p. Boston, Mass.: Department of Sociology and Anthropology, Boston University.

1971*   The diet of early man: aspects of archaeological evidence from Lower and Middle Pleistocene sites in Africa, *World Archaeology* 2: 278–99.

*   Whither archaeology? *Antiquity* 45: 123–9.

With R. E. F. Leakey and A. K. Behrensmeyer. Archaeological traces of early hominid activities, east of Lake Rudolf, Kenya. *Science* 173: 1129–34.

1972*   Chronology and the tempo of cultural change during the Pleistocene *Calibration of Hominoid Evolution: Recent Advances in Isotopic and other Dating Methods Applicable to the Origin of Man*: 381–430. Edited by

W. W. Bishop and J. Miller, assistant editor S. Cole. Edinburgh: Scottish Academic Press.

Comparative studies of Pleistocene site locations in East Africa. *Man, Settlement and Urbanism*: 165–76. Edited by P. J. Ucko, R. Tringham and G. W. Dimbleby. London: Duckworth.

*   Early phases of human behaviour: models in Lower Palaeolithic archaeology. *Models in Archaeology*: 167–99. Edited by D. L. Clarke. London: Methuen.

The identification of cultural entities in the Middle Pleistocene. *Congrès Panafricain de Préhistoire, Dakar 1967: Actes du 6e Session*: 556–62. Edited by H. J. Hugot. Chambéry: Imprimeries Réunies de Chambéry.

Some experiments in quantitative methods for characterizing assemblages of Acheulian artefacts. *Congrès Panafricain de Préhistoire, Daker 1967: Actes du 6e Session*, edited by H. J. Hugot, 547–55. Chambéry: Imprimeries Réunies de Chambéry.

With R. E. F. Leakey. Hominid fossils from the area east of Lake Rudolf, Kenya: photographs and a commentary on context. *Perspectives on Human Evolution*, vol. 2: 129–40. Edited by S. L. Washburn and P. Dolhinow. New York: Holt, Rinehart and Winston.

With II. V. Merrick and C. M. Nelson. Stratigraphic and archaeological studies in the Lake Nakuru basin, Kenya. *Palaeoecology of Africa* 6, for 1969–71: 225–32.

With K. W. Butzer, J. L. Richardson and C. Washbourn-Kamau. Radiocarbon dating of East African lake levels. *Science* 175: 1069–76.

1974   Stratigraphy and patterns of cultural change in the muddle Pleistocene. *Current Anthropology* 15: 508–14.

With A. Brock. Paleomagnetic stratigraphy and chronology of hominid-bearing sediments east of Lake Rudolf, Kenya. *Nature* 247: 344–8.

With G. H. Curtis, Age of early Acheulian industries from the Peninj Group, Tanzania. *Nature* 249: 624–7.

1975   Sorting out the muddle in the middle: an anthropologist's post-conference appraisal. *After the Australopithecines*: 875–87. Edited by K. W. Butzer and G. Ll. Isaac. The Hague: Mouton.

Stratigraphy and cultural patterns in East Africa during the middle ranges of Pleistocene time. *After the Australopithecines*: 495–542. Edited by K. W. Butzer and G. Ll. Isaac. The Hague: Mouton.

Edited with K. W. Butzer, assisted by E. Butzer and B. Isaac. *After the Australopithecines*, xv, 911p. The Hague: Mouton.

With A. B. Isaac. Africa. *Varieties of Culture in the Old World*: 8–48. Under the editorial supervision of R. Stigler. London: St James Press.

1976   The activities of early African hominids: a review of archaeological evidence from the time span two and half to one million years ago. 482–514. Edited by G. Ll. Isaac and E. McCown. Menlo Park: Benjamin.

A brief report on Quaternary stratigraphy in Kenya. *INQUA Subcommission for African Quaternary Stratigraphy* 6: 57–66. Berkeley: Department of Anthropology. (Cyclostyled.)

* Early hominids in action: a commentary on the contribution of archaeology to understanding the fossil record in East Africa. *Yearbook of Physical Anthropology for 1975*: 19–35.

Early stone tools – an adaptive threshold? *Problems in Economic and Social Archaeology*: 39–47. Edited by G. de G. Sieveking, I. H. Longworth and K. E. Wilson. London: Duckworth.

East Africa as a source of fossil evidence for human evolution. *Human Origins: Louis Leakey and the East African Evidence*: 120–37. Edited by G. Ll. Isaac and E. McCown. Menlo Park: Benjamin.

From East Africa: fragments of man's prehistory. *The Listener* 95: 379–80.

Perspectives on Human Evolution: East Africa and Paleoanthropology. Menlo Park: Benjamin. (Series of 100 slides and handbook.)

Plio-Pleistocene artifact assemblages from East Rudolf, Kenya. *Earliest Man and Environments in the Lake Rudolf Basin*: 552–64. Edited by Y. Coppens, F. C. Howell, G. Ll. Isaac and R. E. F. Leakey. Chicago: Chicago University Press.

Researches in the area formerly known as 'East Rudolf': a commentary and classified bibliography. *Palaeoecology of Africa* 9, for 1972–4: 109–22.

* Stages of cultural elaboration in the Pleistocene: possible archaeological indicators of the development of language capabilities. In *Origins and Evolution of Language and Speech*: 275–88. Edited by S. R. Harnad, H. D. Steklis and J. Lancaster. New York: New York Academy of Science.

Traces of early hominid activities from the Lower Member of the Koobi Fora Formation, Kenya. *Les Plus Anciennes Industries en Afrique*: 7–23. Edited by J. D. Clark and G. Ll. Isaac. Nice: Union Internationale des Sciences Préhistoriques et Protohistoriques. (IXe congrès, colloque V.)

With A. Brock. Reversal stratigraphy and its application at East Rudolf. *Earliest Man and Environments in the Lake Rudolf Basin6*: 148–62. Edited by Y. Coppens, F. C. Howell, G. Ll. Isaac and R. E. F. Leakey. Chicago: Chicago University Press.

Edited with J. D. Clark. *Les Plus Anciennes Industries en Afrique*, 216p. Nice: Union Internationale des Sciences Préhistoriques et Protohistoriques. (IXe congrès, colloque V.)

With J. W. K. Harris. The Karari industry: early Pleistocene archaeological evidence from the terrain east of Lake Turkana, Kenya. *Nature* 262: 102–7.

With R. Leakey. East Rudolf: an introduction to the abundance of new evidence. *Human Origins: Louis Leakey and the East African Evidence*: 306–32. Edited by G. Ll. Isaac and E. McCown. Menlo Park: Benjamin.

Edited with E. McCown. *Human Origins: Louis Leakey and the East African Evidence*, xiii, 591p. Menlo Park: Benjamin.

With J. W. K. Harris and D. Crader. Archaeological evidence from the Koobi Fora Formation. *Earliest Man and Environments in the Lake Rudolf Basin*: 533–51. Edited by Y. Coppens, F. C. Howell, G. Ll. Isaac and R. E. F. Leakey. Chicago: Chicago University Press.

Edited with Y. Coppens, F. C. Howell and R. E. F. Leakey. *Earliest Man and Environments in the Lake Rudolf Basin*, xxi, 615p. Chicago: Chicago University Press.

1977   *Olorgesailie: Archaeological Studies of a Middle Pleistocene Lake Basin in Kenya*, xvi, 272p., 60 plates, 73 illustrations, 29 tables. Assisted by Barbara Isaac, Chicago: Chicago University Press.

*   Squeezing blood from stones: comments on the importance of Australian data for the promotion of realism in 'Stone Age' studies. Notes towards discussion of general issues and of issues raised by contributions. *Stone Tools as Cultural Markers: Change, Evolution and Complexity*: 5–12. Edited by R. V. S. Wright. Canberra: Australian Institute of Aboriginal Studies.

1978   The archaeological evidence for the activities of early African hominids. *Early Hominids of Africa*: 219–54. Edited by C. J. Jolly. London: Duckworth.

Early man reviewed. *Nature* 273: 588–9.

The first geologists: the archaeology of the original rock breakers. *Geological Background to Fossil Man: Recent Research in the Rift Valley, East Africa*: 139–47. Edited by W. W. Bishop. Edinburgh: Scottish Academic Press for the Geological Society of London.

Food-sharing and human evolution: archaeological evidence from the Plio-Pleistocene of East Africa. *Journal of Anthropological Research* 34: 311–25. (The Harvey lecture series 1977–8.)

*   The food-sharing behavior of protohuman hominids. *Scientific American* 238 (4): 90–108.

The Olorgesailie Formation: stratigraphy, tectonics and the palaeogeographic context of the middle Pleistocene archaeological sites. *Geological Background to Fossil Man: Recent Research in the Rift Valley, East Africa*: 173–206. Edited by W. W. Bishop. Edinburgh: Scottish Academic Press for the Geological Society of London. (Accompanied by a colour map of the Olorgesailie Formation, prepared from the original map by R. Shackleton and A. B. Isaac with the assistance of G. Ll. Isaac.)

With J. W. K. Harris. Archaeology. *Koobi Fora Research Project*. Vol.

1: The Fossil Hominids and an Introduction to their Context 1968–1974: 64–85. Edited by M. G. Leakey and R. E. F. Leakey. Oxford: Clarendon Press. (Volume also includes Preface by R. E. F. Leakey and G. Ll. Isaac, v–vi.)

1979   The philosophy of archaeology. *Analytical Archaeologist: Collected Papers of David L. Clarke*: 15–20. Edited by his colleagues. London: Academic Press.

Edited with R. E. F. Leakey. *Human Ancestors: Readings from Scientific American*, vi, 130p. San Francisco: W. H. Freeman.

1980   Casting the net wide: a review of archaeological evidence for early hominid land-use and ecological relations. *Current Argument on Early Man: Proceedings of a Nobel Symposium Organized by the Royal Swedish Academy of Sciences and held at Bjorkborns Herrgard, Karlskoga, Sweden 21–27 May 1978, Commemorating the 200th Anniversary of the Death of Carolus Linnaeus*: 226–51. Edited by L.-K. Konigsson. Oxford: Pergamon for the Swedish Academy of Sciences.

The emergence of man. *Nature* 285: 72. (A report on a Royal Society and British Academy meeting.)

With J. W. K. Harris. Early Pleistocene site locations at Koobi Fora, Kenya. *Proceedings of the 8th Panafrican Congress on Prehistory and Quaternary Studies*: 205–7. Edited by R. E. F. Leakey and B. A. Ogot. Nairobi: The International Louis Leakey Memorial Institute for African Prehistory.

With J. W. K. Harris. A method for determining the characteristics of artefacts between sites in the Upper Member of the Koobi Fora Formation, East Lake Turkana. *Proceedings of the 8th Panafrican Congress on Prehistory and Quaternary Studies*: 19–22. Edited by R. E. F. Leakey and B. A. Ogot. Nairobi: The International Louis Leakey Memorial Institute for African Prehistory.

With D. P. Gifford and C. M. Nelson. Evidence for predation and pastoralism at Prolonged Drift: a pastoral Neolithic site in Kenya. *Azania* 15: 57–108.

*   With H. Bunn, J. W. K. Harris, Z. Kaufulu, E. Kroll, K. Schick, N. Toth and A. K. Behrensmeyer. FxJj 50: an early Pleistocene site in northern Kenya. *World Archaeology* 12: 109–36.

1981   Analytical archaeology. *Antiquity* 55: 200–5. (A review article on *Analytical Archaeology* by D. Clarke, London: Methuen, 1978.)

*   Archaeological tests of alternative models of early hominid behaviour: excavation and experiments: *Philosophical Transactions of the Royal Society of London*, Series B, 292, 177–88.

Hoe leefden onze voorouders? *De Evolutie van de mens: de speurtocht naar ontbrekende schakels*: 184–203. Maastricht: Natuur en Techniek.

*   Stone Age visiting cards: approaches to the study of early land-use patterns. *Pattern of the Past: Studies in Honour of David Clarke*:

131–55. Edited by I. Hodder, G. Ll. Isaac and N. Hammond. Cambridge: Cambridge University Press.

Edited with J. D. Clark. *Las Industrias mas Antiguas*. Mexico: Congreso Union Internacional de Ciencias Prehistoricas y Protohistoricas, 146p.

With D. C. Crader. To what extent were early hominids carnivorous? An archaeological perspective. *Omnivorous Primates: Gathering and Hunting in Human Evolution*: 37–103. Edited by R. S. O. Harding and G. Teleki. New York: Columbia University Press.

* With J. W. K. Harris and F. Marshall. Small is informative: the application of the study of mini-sites and least-effort criteria in the interpretation of the early Pleistocene archaeological record at Koobi Fora, Kenya, *Las Industrias mas Antiguas*: 101–19. Edited by J. D. Clark and G. Ll. Isaac. Mexico: X Congreso Union Internacional de Ciencias Prehistoricas y Protohistoricas.

Edited with I. Hodder and N. Hammond. *Pattern of the Past: Studies in Honour of David Clarke*, 424p., 11 plates, 99 figs., 31 tables. Cambridge: Cambridge University Press.

1982   The earliest archaeological traces. *The Cambridge History of Africa. Vol. 1: From the Earliest Times to c. 500 B.C.*: 157–247. Edited by J. D. Clark. Cambridge: Cambridge University Press.

1983   Aspects of the evolution of human behaviour: an archaeological perspective. *Canadian Journal of Anthropology* 3: 233–43.

* Aspects of human evolution, *Evolution from Molecules to Men*: 509–43. Edited by D. S. Bendall. Cambridge: Cambridge University Press.

* Bones in contention: competing explanations for the juxtaposition of early Pleistocene artifacts and faunal remains. *Animals and Archaeology. Hunters and their Prey*: 3–19. Edited by J. Clutton-Brock and C. Grigson. Oxford: British Archaeological Reports International series 163.

Early Stages in the Evolution of Human Behaviour: The Adaptive Significance of Stone Tools, 32p., 13 figs. Amsterdam: Stichting Nederlands Museum voor Anthropologie en Prehistorie. (60th Kroon Lecture.)

1984*   The archaeology of human origins: studies of the Lower Pleistocene in East Africa, 1971–1981. *Advances in World Archaeology* 3: 1–87.

With E. Kroll. Configurations of artifacts and bones at early Pleistocene sites in East Africa. *Intrasite Spatial Analysis in Archaeology*: 4–31. Edited by H. J. Hietala, with editorial contributions by P. A. Larson, Cambridge: Cambridge University Press.

1985*   Ancestors for us all: towards broadening international participation in paleoanthropological research, *Ancestors: the Hard Evidence*: 346–51. Edited by E. Delson. New York: Alan R. Liss.

The first human economy. *Homo: Journey to the Origins of Man's History: Four Million Years of Evidence*: 56–9. Venice: Cataloghi Marsilio.

1986*   Foundation stones: early artefacts as indicators of activities and abilities. *Stone Age Prehistory: Studies in Memory of Charles McBurney*: 221–41. Edited by G. N. Bailey and P. Callow. Cambridge: Cambridge University Press.

With M. Cartmill and D. Pilbeam. One hundred years of palaeoanthropology. *American Scientist* 74: 410–20.

1988   With J. M. Sept. Long-term history of the human diet. *The Eating Disorders: Medical and Psychological Bases of Diagnosis and Treatment*: 29–38. New York: PMA Publishing Corporation.

In prep.   Assisted by A. B. Isaac. Monograph on the archaeology of the Koobi Fora region, East Turkana. Oxford: Clarendon Press.

Reviews, comments and forewords

1967   Review of *Southern Africa during the Iron Age*, by B. M. Fagan. New York: Praeger, 1966. *American Anthropologist* 69: 776.

1969   Review of *Kalambo Falls Prehistoric Site*. Vol. 1, by J. D. Clark with contributions by G. H. Cole, E. G. Haldemann, M. R. Kleindienst and E. M. van Zinderen Bakker, Cambridge: Cambridge University Press, 1969. *Azania* 4; 175–7.

Review of 'Culture traditions and environment of early man', by D. Collins, in *Current Anthropology* 10: 267–96. *Current Anthropology* 10: 305–7.

1971   Review of *Aboriginal Man and Environment in Australia*, edited by D. J. Mulvaney and J. Golson. Canberra: Australian National University Press, 1971. *Mankind* 8: 162–4.

Review of *The Emergence of Man*, by J. Pfeiffer. New York: Harper and Row, 1969. *Current Anthropology* 12: 379–80.

1972   Review of *Olduvai Gorge*. Vol. 3: *Excavations in Beds I and II 1960–1963*, by M. D. Leakey. Cambridge: Cambridge University Press, 1971. *Antiquity* 46: 242–4.

1979   Review of *People of the Eland: Rock Paintings of the Drakensberg Bushmen as a Reflection of their Life and Thought*, by P. Vinnicombe. Pietermaritzburg: University of Natal Press, 1976. *American Anthropologist* 81: 145–7.

1980   Review of 'Time and place: some observations on spatial and temporal patterning in the later Stone Age sequence in southern Africa', by J. Parkington, in *South African Archaeological Bulletin* 35: 73–83. *South African Archaeological Bulletin* 35: 96–8.

1981   Foreword to *The Biology of Love*, by S. L. W. Mellon, vii–x. San Francisco: Freeman.

The early development of protohuman sociocultural behaviour, a comment on 'The origin of man' by C. O. Lovejoy, in *Science* 211: 341–50. *Quarterly Review of Archaeology* 2(1): 1.

1982   Early hominids and fire at Chesowanja. Letter to 'Matters Arising'. *Nature* 296: 870.

Life in the Pliocene: the primacy of gathering. A comment on *On Becoming Human* by N. M. Tanner. Cambridge: Cambridge University Press, 1981. *Quarterly Review of Archaeology* 3(1): 1.

1983   Art of indoctrination. A review of *The Creative Explosion: an Enquiry into the Origins of Art and Religion*, by J. E. Pfeiffer. New York: Harper and Row, 1982. *Nature* 302: 764–5.

Review of *Bones: Ancient Men and Modern Myths*, by L. R. Binford. New York: Academic Press, 1981. *American Antiquity* 48: 416–19.

1984 The loss of robusticity transition. A review of *The Mousterian Legacy: Human Biocultural Change in the Upper Pleistocene*, edited by E. Trinkaus, Oxford: British Archaeological Reports, 1983. *Quarterly Review of Archaeology* 5(2): 3

Review of *In Pursuit of the Past: Decoding the Archaeological Record*, by L. R. Binford. New York: W. W. Norton, 1983. *American Scientist* 72: 90–1.

1985 Using isotope chemistry to detect prehistoric diet. A report on 'Isotope assessment of Holocene human diets in the southwestern Cape, South Africa', a letter by J. Sealy and N. van der Merwe in *Nature* 315: 138–40. *Nature* 315: 98–9.

Introduction

JOHN GOWLETT

Ideas are the most powerful inspiration of human behaviour. Once conceived and launched they can take flight and soar on, far beyond the temporal bounds of the person who inspired them. This is of the very essence of culture, and a subject near to the heart of Glynn Isaac, who devoted many years to studying human origins and evolution. But ideas can become buried, like an artefact covered by sediments. Hence the importance of republishing this collection of Isaac's papers, which bring together in a series many of the most penetrating thoughts conceived within the domain of human evolution.

A principal purpose of this introduction must be to stress that this is not just a collection for Palaeolithic archaeologists. Isaac's ideas about the variation of archaeological evidence in time and space have a far wider relevance, and should be made readily available to others – to archaeologists of all periods. Many recognized Glynn's pre-eminence in his particular area, but were perhaps less inclined to study a field so far from their own, and to reapply his thoughts toward their own work. His work, indeed, has a relevance beyond archaeology – in the life sciences, earth sciences, and anthropology in its broadest sense. As he wrote, 'In the study of human evolution, the distinctions between archaeology, human palaeontology and evolutionary biology are steadily breaking down' (chapter 3). Separate as these fields tend to remain in the nature of their primary data, Glynn's mind was able to embrace them all, and scientists of the various disciplines in their turn recognized this wide-ranging contribution.

To a larger extent, then, the chapters can speak for themselves; but the truism is not quite true. Each represents a careful formulation of thoughts and facts over a limited period. Here are eighteen such capsules of thoughts scattered along 25 years of a career. The articles are a selection of a particular genre; mainstream scientific archaeological papers, of various levels of formality. As such they cannot provide their own complete context; although they are very suitable for general reading, they are addressed to particular problems. In some areas, particularly those concerned with model-building in early hominid evolution, there is a clear evolution of ideas in the successive chapters. Other chapters represent views which

Glynn would scarcely have changed, if at all. Wide-ranging as his themes are, we must remember too, that limited space restricts this volume to include less than half of his published papers. These were ably selected by Barbara Isaac for their special interest – a daunting task since the material omitted would itself be the basis for a considerable career.

Inevitably there are overlaps in the chapters, but it is hardly necessary to make much of the conventional explanation, that the subjects are treated from different angles; the differences of substance in the chapters far outweigh any similarities. More pertinent, and leading in to the following point, is that there are gaps – papers covering some aspects of Isaac's work that could not be included here, for example, detailed stratigraphic studies and site reports.

The chapters, indeed, represent just one strand in a career which, like many others in archaeology, was ultimately based on the inspiration derived from a few major pieces of fieldwork. Carried out over periods of years, these contributed the kind and quantity of data which it is logical to publish eventually in the form of monographs. In the twenty-five years of his career Glynn Isaac undertook and carried through three such major projects, all based in East Africa: the excavations at Olorgesailie, the subject of his doctoral dissertation, and which he published as a monograph (Isaac, 1977b); East Turkana, the monograph of which was largely complete in manuscript when he died (Isaac, in prep.); and Peninj, west of Lake Natron, where he carried out fieldwork in the early 1960s, and where he had begun to return in recent years.

Without labouring the point, it is worthwhile to bear in mind the context of the selected chapters in terms of their broader relationships – with the major pieces of fieldwork, and with Glynn's other works, larger and smaller, such as introductions to edited volumes, and book reviews. It is equally important, at the same time, to trace some of the external factors, of chance, luck and personality which helped to shape the thoughts of a most able and kind man in the course of his journey through life.

When Glynn Isaac began work at Olorgesailie in 1961, shortly after graduating from Cambridge, concepts of the Pleistocene world were changing rapidly. The discoveries made by Louis and Mary Leakey at Olduvai Gorge were central in this change. In 1959 and 1960 for the first time artefacts and early hominid remains were found together, and the results of potassium-argon dating gave a far longer time scale for Pleistocene man than had been conceived – about 1.8 million years (Evernden and Curtis, 1965).

Merely by being in East Africa, Isaac was in the right place at the right time. He was able to assimilate the currents of thought, and test ideas in active excavation, at a time when all was in a state of flux. His background and character, however, made him uniquely well suited to take on board this new state of affairs and its many implications. He had grown up in South Africa, and had the great benefit of a first degree with a broadly based training in the natural sciences, zoology, geology and archaeology; from Cape Town he had gone to Cambridge. There he studied Palaeolithic archaeology at a time before the 'New Archaeology' as we now know it had taken shape, but nevertheless at a time of rapid changes in view. Statistical approaches to artefact studies were in vogue; the radical approaches to economic archaeology favoured by Eric Higgs were in gestation. In his writing Glynn acknowledges Charles McBurney as a mentor, but it is also fair to note that he came to Cambridge with his experience sufficiently broad to make a critical appraisal; and that much of the benefit which he derived was in interchange of ideas and methods with fellow undergraduates, for example with Derek Roe in artefact measurements; with David Clarke especially in the realms of archaeological theory; and with many others in morning breaks at the now-vanished Hawkins' coffee house.

Glynn had the opportunity to take on the work at Olorgesailie partly because Louis and Mary Leakey were fully occupied elsewhere; the Acheulean had become overshadowed by the new importance of the Oldowan. In comparison, the Acheulean was late in time, difficult to date, and lacking in hominid remains. This shade, however, gave him space to work. It seems certain that the Olorgesailie phase not only laid the foundations for his later theoretical work and research strategies, but also allowed some of his most signal contributions to Palaeolithic research in general, in particular those concerned with the theory of typology, studies of artefact form, and pioneering work in taphonomy.

The Olorgesailie results were presented in his doctoral thesis (1968b), by which time he had already published around ten papers, several of them on Olorgesailie; and then in a condensed and partly revised form in the Olorgesailie monograph (Isaac, 1977b). Four of the papers reprinted here go back to the Olorgesailie stage of his work, and are entirely or largely antecedent to the influence of East Turkana.

The Kroeber paper (Isaac, 1967b) is a document whose implications should be signalled loudly in the late 1980s. It shows how deeply concerned Glynn was with factors of taphonomy, at a time before the word was even in use. Experimental work was going on elsewhere, concerned with the factors affecting the preservation of bone (e.g. Brain, 1967a), but studies of artefact transport had hardly started. Perhaps, following its republication here, this paper will be cited more often as one of the outstanding pioneering works in its field.

Similar concerns with taphonomy, here mentioned by name, can be seen in the 'diet' paper of 1971 (chapter 10). It is clearly recognized that 'dispersal and destruction by scavengers may obscure or bias the record'. The paper is perhaps the first to treat densities of stone artefacts and bones as separate variables, and forward-looking in its appreciation that, in warmer parts of the world at least, 'hunting has seldom if ever been in any exclusive sense the staff of hominid life'.

Another early paper, the 'models' paper of 1972 (chapter 1), reads as freshly and crisply now as when it first appeared. The debate about recurrent artefact variation, which contrasts the possibilities of 'different cultural traditions' and 'different activities', is treated in a masterly fashion. Isaac argues that '*stochastic models* may provide an important alternative to phylogenetic or activity difference models' (p. 22). His ideas of the 1970s are every bit as relevant for the 1990s.

Much the same can be said for the review paper on 'chronology' (chapter 2), but here of course more has changed, and one can only be amazed by how much he got right. There are of course revised dates and new sites: the reader has the opportunity to compare the site appendices of this and Isaac's 1984 paper (chapter 5). Brief mention should be made alongside these early articles, of the *World Archaeology* paper of 1969, a review now clearly dated, but one of the first examples of clear and balanced adjustment to the new long time-scale (Isaac, 1969).

A major turning point of Glynn Isaac's career came with his move to Berkeley, and the start four years later of investigations at Lake Rudolf (now Turkana) in Kenya. At Berkeley Isaac joined J. Desmond Clark in the Department of Anthropology. There followed a long and warm association, highly profitable to studies of African prehistory. This was a relationship of common aims and sympathies, rather than of shared fieldwork, but it was no less useful on that count for studies of human origins. Exploration work at East Turkana (formerly East Rudolf), 600 km north of Olorgesailie, was begun by Richard Leakey in the late 1960s. The discovery of artefacts in a tuff dated, as it then seemed, to 2.6 million years was of first importance. Dr Mary Leakey initially examined the finds, but her commitments at Olduvai were too great to allow her to take on the new site. Glynn Isaac was the obvious person to collaborate in the new archaeological research programme. His fruitful co-leadership with Richard Leakey was to last for more than ten years. By 1972, the year when the famous '1470' hominid cranium was found by Richard Leakey's team, archaeological investigations were also well established. Isaac stood at the centre of a team, not only of excavators, but of research students who were able to pursue as specialists the research questions which he had played a large part in formulating.

Once more, the new finds opened up a new vista of time, a world for conceptualiz-

ing: that of pre-Olduvai hominids. Here there appeared to be an extra three-quarters of a million years of tool-using creatures, who could not be assumed to have even the basic attributes of humanlike behaviour observed at Olduvai. The lower density of finds, and the somewhat simpler artefacts, strengthened this appearance.

Hence, it was possible to start thinking afresh about the archaeological evidence for earliest man. The first fruits of this thinking appear in the two essays published in 1971 and 1972 (chapters 1 and 2), reaching their developed form soon afterwards (chapter 11). The ideas were expressed at two levels: the nature of the archaeological record now uncovered; and the models of earlier human evolution that can be built upon it. Key features of the latter are the concepts of 'home-bases' and the importance of 'food-sharing'.

In the meantime the East Turkana dating had gradually become open to question. The first doubts were expressed because of apparent discrepancies in faunal dating with the Omo series. The issues were fully aired at a conference held in Nairobi in September 1973. Glynn Isaac was a co-editor of the proceedings (published as Coppens *et al.*, 1976), and it fell to him to edit and introduce the Geology and Geochronology section. His introduction (Isaac, 1976c) shows once more his ideal of an objective scientific approach; he frames several crucial questions, including the pertinent inquiry, 'What has caused the great scatter of apparent K/Ar ages determined for several of the East Rudolf tuffs?' Characteristically he plotted out all the results in a readily comprehensible diagram.

By 1976 the early dates had been revised, and it had been established that the early East Turkana sites, like those of Olduvai, are about 1.8 to 1.9 million years old. There is a certain irony in this redating; in particular the appreciation that the actual date is almost irrelevant to the archaeology. The important point is that early in the 1970s, freed from an excessive dependence on Olduvai, a new style of thinking had been liberated.

The size of the exposures and the remoteness of East Turkana contributed to this revised view. They gave the space for new approaches, and a vision of the early hominids not dependent on Olduvai and its overpowering wealth of data. The new dimensions of thought are echoed in the section headings of this book. Questions of diet, function of artefacts, non-random distribution of sites in the landscape, all these presaged in the work at Olorgesailie were now developed.

Turning over in Glynn's mind, hinted at in the earlier papers, were questions about artefact transport; questions about association and the distortion of evidence; questions about how landscape was used. His approach to these problems was formally scientific. Amid the welter of potential evidence, one had to select questions that were capable of definite treatment, that might be made to yield answers. A partial list of the completed research topics of Berkeley graduate students supervised by Isaac speaks volumes for what was achieved:

S. Ambrose Holocene environments and human adaptations in the Central Rift Valley, Kenya (1984)

J. W. Barthelme Later Stone Age archaeology of the region east of Lake Turkana, Kenya (1980; published revised as Barthelme 1985)

R. J. Blumenschine Early hominid scavenging opportunities: insights from the ecology of carcass availability in the Serengeti and Ngorongoro Crater, Tanzania (1985)

H. T. Bunn Meat-eating and human evolution: studies on the diet and subsistence patterns of Plio-Pleistocene hominids in East Africa (1982)

T. Cerling Palaeochemistry of Plio-Pleistocene Lake Turkana (1977)

D. P. Gifford Observations of modern human settlements as an aid to archaeological interpretation (1975)

J. W. K. Harris The Karari Industry: its place in African prehistory (1978)

Z. M. Kaufulu The geological context of some early archaeological sites in Kenya, Malawi and Tanzania; microstratigraphy, site formation and interpretation (1983)

H. V. Merrick Change in later Pleistocene lithic industries in eastern Africa (1975)

K. Schick Processes of Palaeolithic site formation: an experimental study (1984)

J. Sept Plants and early hominids in East Africa: a study of vegetation in situations comparable to early archaeological site locations (1984)

C. Sussman Microscopic analysis of use-wear and polish formation on experimental quartz tools (1985)

N. Toth The stone technologies of early hominids at Koobi Fora, Kenya: a technological approach (1982)

A. Vincent The underground storage organs of plants as potential foods for tool-using early hominids (1984)

The two joint papers included in this book, Bunn *et al.* and Isaac *et al.* (chapters 8 and 9) are just two of the many products of the collaborative approach fostered at East Turkana.

The new perspective formed through this work itself helped to raise the doubts about archaeological interpretation that others have since harnessed as the basis for criticizing 'established' theory – ironically sometimes in fields where Glynn

himself had laid the foundations of critical (but not destructive) analysis. His surveys and analyses were objective enough to pinpoint weaknesses in theory and practice. On occasion opportunistic critics would then comment upon these, as if they had been the first to notice the problem.

Eminence inevitably attracts some criticism, but in this case there were undoubtedly other factors at work. Glynn Isaac's fieldwork and his interpretations were so central to knowledge of human evolution that they attracted enormous interest. As the field opened up, the greater American involvement in it led to more publications, more cross-fertilization, more involvement. All this happened at a time of great general change in archaeology as well as human palaeontology. There were rivalries in the search for hominids; the development of the New Archaeology, ethnoarchaeology, taphonomy... all engendered a more critical view of archaeological data. When specialists in several disciplines work in the same area, material that at one time might have seemed exclusively archaeological will inevitably become just as much their concern.

Very little in the critical interchanges was directed at Glynn Isaac in any personal sense, but the range of his ideas was so great that any novel viewpoint would be almost bound to disagree with him in some way. Mary Leakey (1971) doubted the likelihood that sandy channels were foci of occupation; Richard Gould (1980) was disinclined to accept the validity of home-bases. Amid the generally enhanced debate on human origins and the status of early archaeological material, the most directed of the criticisms were those of Lewis Binford. Binford himself traces these back to his review of the Olorgesailie monograph 'Olorgesailie deserves more than an ordinary book review' (the title itself a testimonial), though he followed up with several later forays (Binford 1977b, 1981, 1984, 1985).

It is right to mention these, not because they necessarily carry any great weight, but because they are now part of the history of the subject, and because of Glynn's own attitude towards critical examination. It is plain even from his earliest papers that he felt an obligation to operate at the highest levels of scientific thought – those in which partisan emotion is discarded as a vehicle of judgement. He believed in the competition of scientific ideas, and their evaluation under test over as long a period as necessary. In this, no doubt, he followed T. H. Huxley, Karl Popper and Thomas Kuhn, but more than many of us he was willing to live up to the implications of the doctrine. Glynn Isaac's frequent citations of Binford, and his reviews of the Binford books, show that he held many of his (unchosen) combatant's views in high regard, and was keen to see them further disseminated.

Binford's criticisms may be summarized here, since some of Isaac's later papers clearly refer to them. The critique was made at two levels (broadly corresponding with the two levels of Glynn's own writing, mentioned earlier):

(1) that Glynn, pioneering archaeologist as he was, had ignored the question of 'association'; that he could not justifiably go on to higher levels of interpretation, until, for example, it was conclusively demonstrated that assemblages of stone artefacts and bones were related as a result of hominid activity, rather than through subsequent natural rearrangement.

(2) that Glynn's general model of hominization lacked any theoretical basis, and was a 'just-so' story.

Here is not the place to embark on detailed justification or refutation, nor is it necessary. The critique was shaped from 1977 to 1981, giving Glynn plenty of time to formulate his responses, which appear implicitly or explicitly in his later papers (e.g. chapter 5). Then again, if in doubt, the reader is urged to examine carefully the earlier Isaac papers, to see whether or not the finer issues were appreciated.

The criticism, ironically, was started off by a piece of 1960s work, published in final form in the 1970s. The word 'association' scarcely appears in the Olorgesailie monograph, as Glynn had largely been concerned with the other side of the turning coin: 'rearrangement'. Nothing can hide the fact that questions of association were weighed most carefully at East Turkana from the beginning. As a privileged observer in the field, I recall plainly how the question of association was made central by the work of Diane Gifford (Gonzalez) in 1971–2, in the field of ethnoarchaeology. She noted spurious apparent associations of recent hearths and animal bones – observations which were fully appreciated by Glynn Isaac. Hence, Isaac's suggestion that the points argued by Binford (1981) had largely been anticipated, and the fullness of his answers in Isaac (1984–chapter 5). Glynn Isaac's reviews of Binford's books give an insight, in return, to his feelings (Isaac, 1983b, 1984).

On the second major issue, models for the earlier stages of human evolution, Glynn had the advantage of being a moving target. Undoubtedly the prime mover in the evolution of his ideas was his own intelligence and experience, coupled with the steady acquisition of new facts from his own excavations and many other sources. Thus he came to reshape his ideas, and along with them the terminology of home-bases and food-sharing, which he felt had come to evoke the wrong images (see chapter 4). It is unlikely that he was troubled by the notion that his models lacked theoretical justification; he was very well aware of both their strengths and limitations.

There is no need to dwell further on the cut-and-thrust of archaeological debate. Nevertheless, we can descry benefits in the challenges, which probably led to fuller statements of particular evidence than might otherwise have been the case. This goes especially for demonstrations of refitting of stone artefacts, and work concerned with cut-marks on bone.

Isaac's determination to build up a corpus of clearly recorded information stands out. As he said early on (Isaac, 1971 – chapter 17), 'It seems undeniable that the prime responsibility of any scholarly discipline must be to maintain its factual basis in good order.' We owe him this debt to his responsibility – to ensure that no new myth shall emerge, that Glynn Isaac and his students were there in East Africa, working away industriously towards amassing facts from sites, without considering a research strategy. These chapters show clearly that the research strategy was all-important, equally in their content and in their dates of conception and writing. Indeed, the original grant proposals preceding the investigations would make the same point.

The full account of the East Turkana work will appear elsewhere (Isaac, in prep.). The papers reprinted here include a wealth of related ideas and data, in total presenting a vivid picture of modern archaeology in action. After East Turkana, and moving to Harvard, Glynn Isaac had begun to organize new research at Peninj, where he had first worked with Richard Leakey twenty years before, and had discovered very early Acheulean sites (Isaac, 1967a). Just a hint of the possible importance of the new work appears here in a modest summary (chapter 5), and a diagram (chapter 15). He had intended to carry out further studies of early hominid land-exploitation, developing earlier work (cf. chapter 7).

The subject of human evolution is perhaps the broadest of archaeology, since it is broader than archaeology itself. It is appropriate, then, that the collected papers are completed by two on the broadest of issues: the future of archaeology, and the need for wider international participation in palaeoanthropological research. Though it appears almost last (chapter 17), 'Whither Archaeology?' is an early paper. Again, it is astonishingly fresh and topical. The last chapter (18) reflects Glynn's awareness of his own educational privilege, and his desire for a greater equality.

If the reader possesses just this book as knowledge of its author, he or she cannot fail to be struck by the power of human culture – which allowed this one person in such a relatively short life to build up and carry with him such a complex wealth of information. But this was no ordinary man. It is one thing to make comments on his academic breadth, quite another to talk about the man. He gave unstintingly to his wife, family and friends of all races. Many of them, I know, knew him far better than I did; the mark of their esteem is well enough shown in the numbers of books and papers dedicated to his memory.

The beauty, and most poignant quality, of culture is that, once recorded, a man's output is not lost with him; it does not lose its value. Here, then, is immense food for thought. Glynn would have been the first to admit that he could not have completed so much without Barbara Isaac beside him. The coherent arrangement and editing of these papers is her effort. In them his vigour lives on.

I

The archaeology of human origins

1

Early phases of human behaviour: models in Lower Palaeolithic archaeology

This essay is about experiments with various lines of interpretation in that vast segment of prehistory that is commonly termed 'Lower Palaeolithic'. It is convenient to make use of the models metaphor, which archaeology borrows from other sciences, because the word has qualities of flexibility and vague but stimulating suggestiveness (cf. Piggott, 1959; Renfrew, 1968, 1969; Trigger, 1969, 1970; Clarke, 1968).[1] In Palaeolithic archaeology as in other sciences it is now recognized that 'facts' are never reported without some frame of reference, some notion of how things work. This essay is concerned with these frames of reference, whatever they may be called.

Although Lower Palaeolithic studies share many interpretational problems with the archaeology of other periods, there are highly distinctive features that arise, in particular from the following circumstances:

1. The fact that profound changes occurred not only in the cultural systems but in the neurophysiological system, especially the brain, which supported them.
2. The vast span of time that is involved.
3. The very low density in space and time of sites providing useful information.

A major challenge facing Lower Palaeolithic archaeology is the delineation of stages and processes in the evolution of the human capacity for culture. Realistic organization of theoretical concepts and research strategy depends in large measure on recognizing that available evidence amounts to a very sparse scatter of samples. As in all archaeology the pattern perceived from a single Palaeolithic occurrence relates only to a sample portion of the total culture of the former occupants, while in turn the total culture of the occupants is a sample only of the total space-time segment concerning which inferences are to be made. For example, the material recovered from the Olorgesailie Acheulean sites is comprised of stone artefacts and utensils, together with bone food refuse. Each of these probably represents only a small fraction of equipment and diet respectively, while material culture and subsistence arrangements in turn were only components of the total behavioural system formerly in operation at the particular sites. Within the activity range of the hominids using the Olorgesailie lake basin the sites represent only those patterns appropriate to the valley floor (Isaac, 1968a). The behaviour of the Olorgesailie Acheuleans was probably not identical with those at nearby Olduvai, let alone with those at more distant sites such as Torralba. Thus we have to recognize that even in comparatively favourable cases such as the Olorgesailie sites, we are dealing with a highly biased subsample of something that was already only a small sample of Middle Pleistocene culture. When, as in Lower Palaeolithic studies, material culture is comparatively simple, preservation is often indifferent, and the space-time sample densities are very low, these problems become acute. Theoretical considerations taken on their own might tempt us to abandon the whole pursuit, were they not tempered by the empirical demonstration that good Lower Palaeolithic sites have high intrinsic interest and that some regularities in technology and economy do emerge and do seem worth more careful investigation.

In designing research, the density of samples is usually adjusted in relation to variability in the properties about which inferences are to be made. However, in a situation where overall sample density is irrevocably low, the choice of variables to be stressed must be adjusted instead.

There is at present some sense of crisis with regard to models in Palaeolithic archaeology (cf. Bordes and Bordes, 1970; Binford, 1968a; Sackett, 1968; Mellars, 1970; Isaac, 1971a [this volume, ch. 10]). This stems in large measure from dissatisfaction with historical (i.e. ideographic) approaches and from growing unease over assumptions of regularity in the transmission and expression of material culture traditions. Various workers are experimenting with alternative lines of interpretation, sometimes involving the allegation of morphological regularities induced by functional determinants – such as the specific exigencies of butchery. Most new studies are more concerned with process than narrative.

The development of attitudes and theory

Palaeolithic archaeology could have no suitable status as a legitimate research field until the antiquity of man was recognized. Pre-Darwinian European thought patterns prevented even perceptive men who had observed stratified Lower Palaeolithic tools from making any real sense out of their finds. John Frere had reported that his discovery of handaxes deeply buried, and in association with fossil bone, tempted him 'to refer them to a very remote period indeed; even beyond that of the present world . . .'[2] Frere did not pursue his find, but a little later the eccentric Boucher De Perthes made a succession of similar discoveries and, though he himself lacked a coherent scheme into which his results could be fitted, he insisted in effect that his facts should not be disregarded just because they could not be accommodated in current 'models' (Daniel, 1950:59; Heizer, 1969:69–109). However, before the issues had received wide attention the enunciation of the theory of evolution by descent with modification through natural selection (Darwin, 1858, 1859; Wallace, 1858) effectively circumvented the antiquarians' dispute by making it an integral part of a much larger one. The theory of evolution established as one corollary hypothesis the proposition that the ethnographic and historic complexity of culture must have grown from a state of effectively zero material culture. Not only could the new paradigm tolerate the discovery of very ancient artefacts; it demanded them! The challenge met with a ready response and a wealth of artefactual evidence for man's antiquity came flooding in (Gaudry, 1859; Lyell, 1863; Lubbock, 1865; Evans, 1872). Within a few decades the belief arose that the features of stone tools could be used to demarcate stages in the evolution of culture – or at least technology (de Mortillet, 1883; Sollas, 1911). Those concerned with Lower Palaeolithic archaeology during the nineteenth century were preoccupied with considerations of artefact morphology and stratigraphy. Although there was little or no explicit discussion of the mechanisms of cultural development, it appears from nineteenth-century writings and from the legacy they left to twentieth-century scholarship that subconscious models were adopted, which were closely allied to the evolutionary principles of contemporary biology. The implicit rules of interpretation can be reconstructed as follows:

1. Each phase, or culture, is demarcated by a distinctive stone tool kit, and conversely each distinctive stone tool assemblage must derive from a significantly different phase, or culture.
2. Specific resemblances between assemblages from successive stratigraphic zones must result from a continuous chain in the transmission of craft tradition. That is to say that alleged patterns of similarity linking assemblages of different ages must be due to the former existence of 'phyla' of culture.

The rules were applied to impressions of the morphology of artefact assemblages in a way closely analogous to the operations of a palaeontologist engaged in recognizing taxonomic identity, affinity and phylogeny from the morphology of fossils. Indeed as Sackett (1968:67) has remarked, many writers report on their material as though the models really involved the notion that the stone tools formed sexually active, breeding populations with a phylogeny of their own! These assumptions of stability and of regularity in lineages of change were a reasonable part of the first approximations of Lower Palaeolithic prehistory; but now that the magnitude of Pleistocene time is better understood and great variability has been observed, uncritical retention of them constitutes an escape from the realities of having to deal with very low sample density. They are attractive because they enable what might otherwise appear as a bewildering scatter of instances to be transformed to a hypothetical culture history; but the details and processes of such histories have proved to be illusory.

Now, although few modern prehistorians are as naive as might be implied by this caricature, these principles of interpretation have only very recently been formally challenged and the great bulk of Palaeolithic research continues to appear as though it rests on these unverified assumptions. Of course, in confronting these tacit rules of interpretation, we are not dealing with neat true or false propositions. Common sense and the experience of ethnography all combine to show that resemblances between items of material culture are often correlated with degrees of interconnectedness, and the converse. However, all resemblances or differences need not be so determined, and the dangers are particularly acute when tool forms are simple and the space-time sample density is very low.

Initially, and in conformity with the organic model of material culture evolution, there was an expectation that the stages would be universal. Further, technological progress was treated as though it was an intrinsic and inexorable tendency in human evolution. Results accruing from research into areas outside western Europe gradually persuaded scholars to abandon this model in favour of one involving more complex mechanisms such as regional differentiation and migration.

The recognition of regional differentiation in Palaeolithic archaeology helped to give its development as a discipline the historical orientation it has retained until very recently. The first objective in study became the taxonomy of tools and assemblages, which was avowedly undertaken in order to establish 'culture histories', or ideographic narratives, of changing artefact design through space and time. Through most of this century work has tended to be descriptive and there was little attempt to establish processual models which would facilitate explanation of the detail that began to be compiled. Rather dramatic particularistic explanations were offered for a few allegedly gross differences in artefact sets. These sometimes involved racial or specific differentiation of the hominids – as in the case of the replacement of Neanderthal makers of Mousterian industries by the 'Neanthropic' men of the Upper Palaeolithic (e.g. Burkitt, 1933; L.S.B. Leakey, 1934; McBurney, 1960; Howell, 1965). In other cases, distinctions between ecogeographic zones were offered as partial explanations, as in the case of Clacton and Acheulean industries (e.g. McBurney, 1950; Collins, 1969). Neither the racial nor the geographic models and the theories based on them are held up for mockery, but it must be pointed out that little has been done to bridge the gulf between the descriptive nature of reports on the material evidence and the sociological, ecological or behavioural implications of the models.[3]

In summary, during its first 100 years Lower Palaeolithic archaeology developed unconsciously into a historical pursuit without any well-defined concern with economics, sociology, or the processes underlying the details of culture change. Stone artefacts were important at the outset because of their ubiquity and their usefulness in demonstrating the antiquity of man. Abundance and fascination have kept them as the prime focus of research, but a reaction against excessive reliance on them is now apparent. Beginning some twenty years ago and intensifying over the past decade, there has been a growing awareness that 'occupation sites' rather than stone artefacts might constitute the most informative evidence to survive from Lower Palaeolithic times.

Concern with occupation sites

'Occupation site' is here used as a loosely defined term, which denotes archaeological situations in which artefacts occur in spatially patterned sets, which may be indicative of activities other than stonecraft and which are sometimes associated with food refuse and other organic traces. There are isolated instances of the study of the contextual implications of such occurrences prior to 1940 (e.g. Worthington-

Smith, 1894; Commont, 1908; Cerralbo, 1913), but in general the modern research drive can be said to have begun with M. D. and L. S. B. Leakey's excavations at Olorgesailie in 1943. The 'floors' then exposed were visited by delegates to the Pan African Congress on Prehistory in 1947, and subsequently similar work on an expanded scale followed elsewhere in Africa: for example, Kalambo (J. D. Clark, 1954, 1969), Olduvai (L. S. B. Leakey, 1963b; M. D. Leakey, 1967, 1971), Isimila (Howell *et al.*, 1962). Later comparable work has been done also in Eurasia: for example, Torralba-Ambrona (Howell, 1966), Latamne (J.D. Clark, 1966), Vértesszöllös (Kretzoi and Vértes, 1965), 'Ubeidiya (Stekelis, 1966), Terra Amata (de Lumley, 1969b), and High Lodge. There is a growing number of such field studies. This reorientation of research effort has stemmed from the belief that the rare, well-preserved sites provide far more useful information than a myriad of distorted artefact assemblages which lack significant contextual evidence. The first two decades of this movement have been exploratory. At the outset no one had any very clear idea of what might turn up on a series of Lower Palaeolithic occupation floors. Though a general sense of optimism about the utility of such investigations prevailed, the questions that were to be answered by the data recovered were by no means clearly formulated.

Palaeolithic archaeology is not alone in having diversified itself by turning from preoccupation with typology and assemblage taxonomy to consider also settlement patterns, economic systems and subtle traces of social arrangements. Studies of the post-Pleistocene prehistory of Europe took a very early lead in this direction (J. G. D. Clark, 1954; Fox, 1948; Childe, 1935). Palaeolithic archaeology has also participated in the recent resort to quantitative methods. Some of the consequences of quantitative experiments are discussed below in the section dealing with models for the interpretation of artefacts.

Models inspired by comparative studies of behaviour

Prehistory derives research problems in part from observation of features in existing archaeological data, but questions also arise as a result of concern with the development of behaviour. Particularly, the growth of field studies of animal behaviour has resulted in fresh interest in aspects of early hominid activity and organization (e.g. DeVore and Washburn, 1963; Morris, 1967; Tiger, 1969). Many authors have been especially concerned with possible evolutionary consequences of hunting as a means of subsistence. This is a matter that can be investigated by archaeological means (Isaac, 1971a [This volume, ch. 10]).

Ethnography is widely regarded as being of crucial importance as an aid to interpreting the Palaeolithic (cf. J.D. Clark, 1968; Isaac, 1968a), but what is borrowed is usually a specific analogy. In the scale of concepts discussed in the introduction this is usually a hypothesis or a theory rather than a model. The use of such parallels implies a vague sense of equivalence in the processes of culture regardless of time differences. As Binford (1968a:17) has pointed out, this is both useful and dangerous. Carried to an extreme it would limit our exploration of prehistory to the terms of ethnography, whereas presumably we practise archaeology in part out of the conviction that it will give information on different, antecedent cultural conditions. This caveat is especially important for the formative phases comprising the Lower Palaeolithic, since they must surely have included intermediate conditions of a kind that no longer exist among either men or primates. Ethnographic analogy has been extensively discussed in recent years and is not pursued here (e.g. various essays in *Man The Hunter*, edited by Lee and DeVore, 1968).

Field studies have demonstrated that animal behaviour is made up of a highly complex set of components interrelated as an integrated system, which mediates between physiology, ecology and society. The most promising models for interpreting the evolution of human behaviour are thus systems models. These enable us to consider how selection pressure would act on genetic and cultural innovations to bring about far-reaching biological and sociological changes. Given appreciation of the high degree of integration commonly exhibited by behavioural systems, we can recognize that changes in one component necessitate or facilitate changes in others. Analogy with the cybernetic phenomenon of 'feedback' now appears to be an indispensable means of discussing the interrelations of aspects of evolving behaviour.

Versions of hominid evolutionary processes have often rested implicitly on additive models involving seriatim accumulation of components by chain reaction. For example, a version envisaged in the writings of Elliot-Smith (1927) can be summarized as follows:

1. Development of enlarged brain.
2. Tool manufacture.
3. Bipedal stance.
4. Cultural elaboration.

The discovery of the Piltdown hoax, the recognition of the Australopithecines and the archaeological evidence from Bed I at Olduvai Gorge have all combined to render this specific hypothesis untenable, but revised formulations involving comparatively simple additive models remain current. For example, several authors, including Campbell (1966) and Pfeiffer (1969), appear to have envisaged something like the following chain of developments:

1. Shift to open country habitat.
2. Bipedalism and tool use.
3. Tool manufacture.
4. Small game hunting.
5. Cooperative big game hunting.
6. Division of labour and the bonding of family units.
7. Enlargement of the brain.
8. Language and cultural elaboration.

This is in some ways an unfair caricature of what was a very useful first approximation of a complex transformation process. However, the discovery that several of these behaviour patterns are present at least in incipient degrees in the repertoire of wild chimpanzees necessitates revision of the models (Goodall, 1964;

Lancaster, 1968). Integrated growth is a better analogue than chain reaction. Thus I would favour models involving concurrent development with mutual reinforcement of adaptive advantages by matching changes in all components, and from this stance I would argue that hunting, food sharing, division of labour, pair bonding, and operation from a home base or camp, form a functional complex, the components of which are more likely to have developed in concert than in succession (Isaac, 1972e [This volume, ch. 2]). It is easy to see that tools, language and social cooperation would fit into the functional complex as well, and very likely had equally long developmental histories within the overall system.

The findings of comparative studies of mammal behaviour have become a source of inspiration of palaeoanthropological reconstructions. Generalizations about arboreal behaviour, savannah behaviour, carnivore behaviour or seed-eating behaviour can function as components of models, which in turn generate theories explaining the transformation of ancestral anthropoid organization into hominid systems (e.g. Washburn and Lancaster, 1968; Reynolds, 1966; Fox, 1967; Morris, 1967; Schaller and Lowther, 1969; Jolly, 1970). Of particular value in developing such models are observations on the same species under differing ecological conditions (e.g. Crook and Gartlan, 1966; Gartlan and Brain, 1968).

Theories based on the results of comparative studies have an interest and intellectual validity of their own, but ultimately they must remain speculative if they are not tested for consistency with palaeontological and archaeological facts. Since the hypotheses involve retrodictions of the distribution and nature of potentially discernible traces of various kinds of behaviour, they can be tested against the archaeological record.

In practice the nature of surviving traces places restraints on the components which can presently be included in models designed for testing by palaeoanthropological research. In Table 1.1 I have attempted to summarize inferences currently feasible on the basis of Lower · Palaeolithic archaeological evidence

Table 1.1.

Archaeologically observable phenomena	Possible interpretations
Location and density of sites and relicts	Aspects of demographic arrangement, land use and ecology
Site sizes and internal structure	Estimates of community size and aspects of organization
Seasonality and duration of occupation	Patterns of movement and aspects of economic strategy
Food refuse and faeces	Aspects of diet and subsistence practices
Introduced materials	Range of movement or contact
Artefact forms	Aspects of role in economy/society Level of complexity of material culture rule systems (in part) Propagation patterns of material culture traditions (historical, geographic and sociological implications)

without intending to define limits as to what will eventually be possible. It is already established that each of these lines of behavioural reconstruction is possible, when conditions of preservation are suitable. However, many classes of evidence are in fact only very rarely available. No site or site complex is yet known where all of these kinds of inference have simultaneously been possible, and it is apparent that studies must proceed in the hope that interpretable regularities will be found in an opportunistically accumulated patchwork of information.

The interpretation of artefact sets

Stone artefacts constitute by far the most abundant trace of Pleistocene hominid activity. In varying versions of prehistory, aspects of their characteristics are used as indices of technological elaboration, as markers of culture-historic connections, as indicators of diverse economic activities and as clues to the nature of socio-cultural systems. Now it is probable that the importance of stone artefacts relative to other kinds of evidence has been exaggerated, but it is also clear that they constitute a source of evidence rich enough to demand the development of refined analytical systems. 'Models' are involved in the description and analysis of artefacts as well as in interpretation (Neustupný, 1971). Concepts and assumptions with regard to 'typological' and morphological treatment of artefacts are discussed in Sackett (1966), Clarke (1968), Isaac (1972c) and elsewhere. The attention of this essay is focused on models that facilitate the interpretation of the results of comparative operations.

Distinctive features that appear to be emerging from comparative studies of Lower Palaeolithic stonecraft can be summarized as:

1. 'Conservatism' in the sense of prolonged failure of tool kits to transcend certain limits of technology, typological composition and morphology.
2. Great variability in the specific permutations of attributes within the conservative limits.

The conservatism is widely seen to be explicable in terms of neurophysiological limitations of early hominids and or supposed resistance of primitive culture to change, but variability has met with a wider range of interpretational responses. On logical grounds it would appear that the morphology of a stone tool is governed by the interaction of (1) the physical properties of the stone being employed, and (2) the 'intentions' (design concepts) and the motor habits of the craftsman. The design concepts themselves are presumably related in turn to two kinds of determining influences: first, the functional requirements of the tool will place limits on the range of forms that would be effective; secondly, systems of transmission of traditions provide a craftsman with a set of technical and morphological patterns that are functionally adequate and socially acceptable. The traditional tool patterns may be few in number, and embody only simple rules with wide tolerances – as is apparently the case among stone-tool-using aborigines of the Western Australian deserts (Gould, 1968). In contrast, some late prehistoric stone tool kits give the impression of involving fairly numerous distinct 'patterns', each with comparatively low variability. The archaeological record probably documents a gradual oscillating rise in the maximum level of design complexity through time, but methods of measuring this have not yet been devised (Isaac, 1972e [This volume, ch. 2]).

Fig 1.1 summarizes diagrammatically the supposed system of determinants affecting artefacts. Differential emphasis on the importance of two of the above listed determinants of stone tool morphology has given rise to distinct schools of thought in the interpretation of the results of comparative study. Each school stresses one factor in the models it uses to 'explain' variations (differences) among stone artefact assemblages.

1. Traditional or 'phylogenetic' models assume tremendous inertia in craft transmission systems so that successive generations of craftsmen are tightly bound to particular patterns. Where instances of marked diversity among contemporary assemblages are detected, variants are liable to be explained as the products of distinct 'phyla' of culture, that is, separate, coexistent systems of cultural transmission. This is the conventional approach to Palaeolithic archaeology, which has already been discussed (cf. Warren, 1926; Breuil, 1932; Leakey, 1934; Bordes, 1950a, 1953, 1961a; Collins, 1969, 1970).

2. 'Activity variant models' differ from traditional models by assuming that functional requirements exert an influence on assemblage character, which creates variety and which commonly transcends differences in the degree of culture-historic interconnectedness. It is further supposed that distinctive tool kits for specific tasks must have existed, and the variety among stone artefact assemblages can often be explained as the results of differing intermixtures of the 'tool kits'. Extensive concern with this kind of model is fairly recent (cf. J.D. Clark, 1959; Kleindienst, 1961; Binford and Binford, 1966, 1969).

The two schools advocating these models are engaged in 'competition' generally

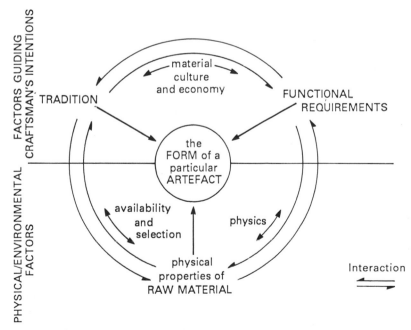

Fig. 1.1. Diagrammatic illustration of physical, economic and cultural factors influencing the morphology of a particular stone artefact. The factors interact.

involving attempts to attack the credibility of interpretations based on the models of their 'opponents' (e.g. Bordes and Bordes, 1970; Binford and Binford, 1966, 1969; Collins, 1969; Mellars, 1970). Logically there is a niche for a third school, which advocates the physical properties of raw material as the primary determinant of variation. However, although all parties recognize the influence of this factor, there has been little formal attempt to use it as a major basis of explanation.

Both of these contending 'schools' make assumptions of regularity: 'tradition' is seen as providing tight constraints and long-term constancy; in the other case 'function' is seen as a binding determinant which gave rise to prolonged constancy of complex, patterned variation. However, there are possible solutions to the problem of variation that do not assume constancy and regularity. For instance, if we accept that there may be wide tolerances for the morphology of tools with equivalent functions, and that 'tradition' itself may be subject to change through time and space, then it becomes apparent that stochastic models may provide an important alternative to phylogenetic or activity difference models (Binford, 1963; Isaac, 1969:19). A stochastic model allows for 'random walk'[4] drift of 'craft norms' within the constraints of functional and technological limits. It should be apparent that these lines of explanation are not mutually exclusive. They can and should be combined into composite models which involve all of these 'mechanisms' as variable components.

In seeking to explore the applicability of these models for explaining artefact variation it is useful to partition the observable diversity of samples (assemblages) between three categories:

1. The first category is composed of regular differences between sets of assemblages, each of which can be related to time and/or space divisions. These sets are the entities of orthodox culture history or archaeological taxonomy (Fig. 1.2).

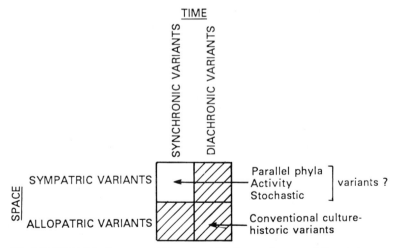

Fig. 1.2. Diagrammatic representation of possible time and space relations between pairs (or sets) of varying archaeological occurrences. Conventional entities of archaeological taxonomy involve the recognition of more or less consistent differences between assemblage variants, which are either separated in time (diachronic) or in geography (allopatric) or both. Debate concerning the relative applicability of parallel phyla, activity difference and stochastic models arises in cases of synchronic and sympatric assemblage variants.

2. The second category is composed of consistent differences between definable sets of assemblages which do not appear to be restricted to specifiable subdivisions of time or to definable regions, but are legitimately believed on some positive evidence to have been associated with different activities.

3. The third category is composed of the residuum of variability which cannot be associated with time, space or activity factors on the basis of existing evidence.

Each of these three categories of variance is fairly directly associable with one of the three aforementioned models.

Now for the Lower Palaeolithic this division of variability is a difficult procedure to follow because for many regions, such as Europe, the sites yielding evidence of variation are geographically scattered and the precision of chronological control is low. It simply is not feasible to isolate many assemblage sets from segments of space and time which have anything like the same order of magnitude as the space-time coordinates of Late Pleistocene or Holocene cultures. The overall situation in East Africa is worse, since we have fewer samples from a larger area and a longer time span. However, during my work in East Africa I became aware that the subcontinent offered opportunities of an almost experimental nature for clarifying the nature of variation among at least some Middle Pleistocene occurrences.

The overall space-time density of excavated Middle Pleistocene assemblages from East Africa is appallingly low – less than one sample per 10,000 years per 1,000,000 km^2; but local sample densities in the 'lake basins' for which the region has become archaeologically famous, are much higher (Fig. 1.3). Site complexes like those at Olorgesailie, Olduvai, Isimila and Kalambo provide situations where assemblage variation can be studied in relation to very restricted spatial limits and reasonably well-controlled time spans. The pattern and magnitude of variation in each of these microcosmic experimental situations can then be compared with the overall variation in the whole Acheulean series from the subcontinent – that is, from the one million year long, 1.75 million km^2 macrocosm.

If the range of variation of each of the several microcosms proved to be much smaller and more tightly clustered than the total range, then one might conclude that a succession of distinctive localized and time-restricted 'cultures' has existed within the region – even though the available sample densities were inadequate for one to resolve the culture history in full. However, comparative operations employing either percentage frequency of categories or averages for the size and shape indices of tool forms indicate that, for many variables, the localized 'short-term' sets are almost as varied as the whole series (see Figs 1.4 and 1.5 for examples). These experiments thus run counter to expectations implicit in traditional culture-historic or culture-evolutionary thinking. What do numbered stage divisions such as those formerly employed in the Somme, Morocco or Olduvai mean if a penecontemporaneous set shows almost as much diversity as a markedly diachronic series? Whatever models we employ in seeking to account for variation in East Africa, it is clear that they must be able to cope with behavioural systems which involved the abandonment of markedly different stone artefact sets at sites within a single valley during a time span that is at least very short by comparison with the whole Middle Pleistocene.

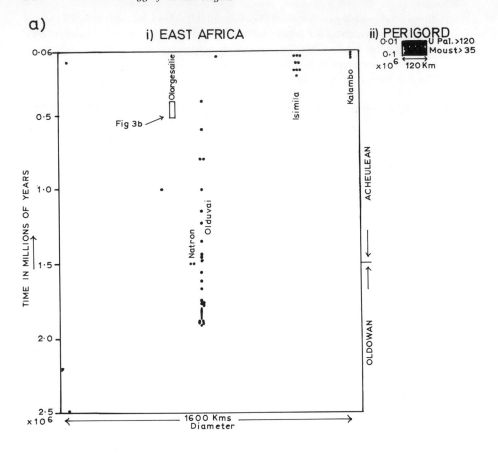

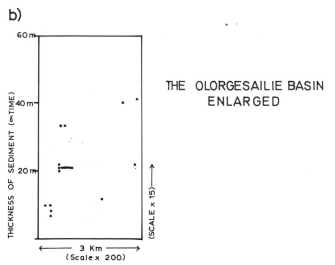

THE OLORGESAILIE BASIN
ENLARGED

The conventional culture-taxonomic entities of archaeology show allopatric and/or diachronic relations with each other (Fig. 1.2). Very few of the observed patterns in these experiments can be meaningfully partitioned into such culture-historic entities, but a choice between a variety of other models remains. Parallel phyla models can be applied, if they are used to generate theories involving prolonged territorial interdigitation by differing cultures all over East Africa. This line of interpretation would be rendered particularly credible by evidence that each of the allegedly stable non-blending cultural lineages was associated with a genetic-ally isolated species of hominid, and such evidence is being tentatively advanced for Beds II and IV at Olduvai (M. D. Leakey, personal communication).

Hitherto the most popular model for explaining the observed pattern has been that involving activity differences (J.D. Clark, 1959; Posnansky, 1959; Kleindienst, 1961), but this depends in part on personal predispositions and there have been no rigorous tests. Among other alternatives I think that stochastic models have also become worthy of consideration: some aspects of pattern in the morphology of tools at Olorgesailie actually suggested cultural drift to me during my laboratory studies before I had considered 'random walk' as an important process.[5]

One might have expected that the growing corpus of carefully excavated Lower Palaeolithic 'occupation sites' would have provided critical evidence for testing the utility of activity variation models, but this is not yet true. For most of the sites excavated and reported we do not have certain indications of any specific activities that characterized them, and in very few instances has localization of subsidiary tool kits within a floor even been claimed (cf. Freeman and Butzer, 1966).

The only activity for which evidence external to tool morphology is fairly widely distributed is butchery – and, by extension, hunting. Desmond Clark has put together comparative data which indicate that instances of impoverished tool kits dominated by smallish, rather informal tools, including scrapers and denticulates, have been found associated with butchery sites of all ages from Oldowan to Later Stone Age (Clark and Haynes, 1970). However, some sites at which carcasses were undoubtedly cut up do show wider ranges of forms, which include large bifaces – for example, Torralba, Ambrona (Howell, 1966; Freeman and Butzer, 1966), Terra Amata (de Lumley, 1969b), Olorgesailie DE 89 B (Isaac, 1968a). I still remain uncertain as to whether the butchery facies envisaged by Clark is in fact representa-tive of the total kit used in the process of dismemberment, or whether it might be the impoverished residue left after elaborate and perhaps less dispensable tools such

---

Fig. 1.3(a). A diagrammatic representation of archaeological sample densities in relation to space and time. Data for the Lower Palaeolithic of East Africa are contrasted with those for the Middle and Upper Palaeolithic of the Perigord, France. Each dot represents a significant, excavated occurrence. Space is represented by the horizontal dimension of each rectangle, which is drawn proportional to the diameter of the region. Time is represented by the vertical dimension (modified after Isaac, 1972e [this volume, ch. 2]). (b) An enlargement of part of the East African sample series–the occurrences within the 'microscosm' of the Olorgesailie lake basin. The scales are enlarged by factors of 10 (time) and 375 (space). Low density and unequal spacing remain apparent. Of the greatest value for studies of variation is the set of seven spatially clustered and penecontemporaneous sites.

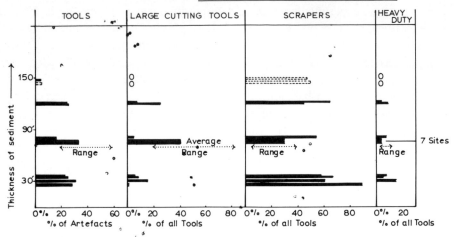

A. OLORGESAILIE VARIATION IN TOOL CLASS % IN RELATION TO STRATIGRAPHY

B. VARIATION AT OLORGESAILIE COMPARED WITH THE RANGE FOR EAST AFRICA

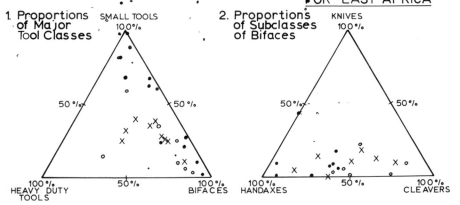

1. **Proportions of Major Tool Classes**

2. **Proportions of Subclasses of Bifaces**

• Olorgesailie   X Isimila   ○ Kalambo   · Other

Fig. 1.4. A graphic representation of analysis of variation in the percentages of major categories of artefacts. 'A' shows variation among the Olorgesailie occurrences in relation to thickness of accumulated sediment (∞ time). 'B' uses ternary diagrams to compare variation in the Olorgesailie 'microcosm' with the range observable in a wider series of East African occurrences (after Isaac, 1968b).

as handaxes had been taken away for continued use. Neither at Olorgesailie (Isaac, 1968a) nor Olduvai (M. D. Leakey, 1971) is there any clear evidence of regular relationships between the frequency of either large tools or small tools and the density or species composition of bone refuse.

The evidence from Central Australia suggests that great care is necessary in interpreting a local set of discarded stone tools as the complete set used in any

A. <u>OLORGESAILIE - VARIATIONS IN SIZE FORM – INDICES ETC.</u>
<u>IN RELATION TO STRATIGRAPHY</u>

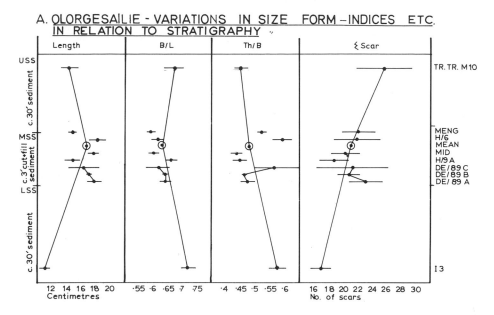

B VARIATION AT OLORGESAILIE COMPARED WITH THE RANGE
FOR EAST AFRICA

MEAN LENGTH

MEAN BREADTH/LENGTH RATIO

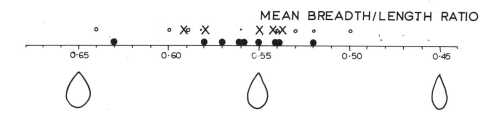

MEAN THICKNESS/BREADTH RATIO

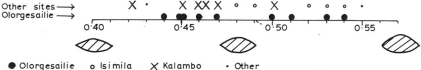

● Olorgesailie   o Isimila   X Kalambo   · Other

Fig. 1.5. Graphic representation of analysis of variation in the numerical measures of biface morphology. 'A' shows variation in relation to sedimentation. Weak time trends with 'oscillations' are reflected in relative thickness (Th/B) and in the number of trimming scars (ξ Scar) but length and relative elongation (B/L) appear to vary erratically in the series (see Isaac, 1969). 'B' provides graphic representation of the extent of variation in the Olorgesailie 'microcosm', compared with a wider range of East African occurrences.

operation. The scraper form called 'purpunpa' by the Ngatatjara people, but now more widely known as the 'tula adze flake', is carried everywhere by men, hafted to their spear throwers. It is used in many places for shaping wood or cutting things. In many of these places other ad hoc stone forms may be made (or selected) and immediately discarded. However, worn-out 'eloura adzes' would be discarded only in places where fire, mastic and stone were available to permit their leisurely replacement. The activity documented would be spear thrower repair, not eloura flake usage (cf. Thomson, 1964; Gould, 1968).

The extent of variation between assemblages from the floors of the sedimentary basins containing the East African site complexes makes it clear that if activity patterns determined the variation then the activities represented were not specific to gross ecological divisions of the terrain such as uplands, woodlands or plains. A variety of kits were abandoned within the range of micro-environments pertaining to lake or riverside floodplains. Recognition of this restriction on appropriate activity theories does not preclude differing seasonal pursuits, the division of labour by sex and age, the exploitation of differing localized resources, and so on, from having been determinants of diversity in the tool kits. However, as yet we lack specific evidence for any of these – and, given the evidence for 'stylistic' variability in the morphology of sets of artefacts which seem very likely to have been functionally equivalent, I am very inclined to think the activity variation model may hitherto have enjoyed undue appeal. Schemes that have been put forward sometimes smack rather of a Rand Corporation 'Design for Palaeolithic living'. While it may be flattering to envisage our ancestors as having been equipped with a tool for every need, it is disquieting to learn what a broad range of basic functions can be accomplished with poorly differentiated stone tools of the simple kinds reported for the Bindibu and Ngatatjara of Central Australia (Thomson, 1964; Gould, 1968).

While the testing of various activity difference hypotheses should continue with vigour, it seems to me that we should seriously consider that an appreciable proportion of the variation not yet accounted for by time, space and activity differences may be a residuum generated by stochastic change. That is to say the result of local band-specific 'drifts' in craft norms, both with regard to 'style' in standardized forms such as handaxes, and with regard to assemblage composition. As envisaged here such drift might accumulate over several, even many generations and lead to quite widely divergent craft manifestations. However, the micro-traditions involved would be unstable and would lose their identity in new short-term directions of drift. This is an equilibrium basin model (Clarke, 1968:51) of the processes underlying assemblage patterning in the East African Middle Pleistocene and it has the attraction that it helps account for the conservatism shown with regard to gross technological and typological features, while also accommodating variation and permutation among the components. A simple mechanical analogy for the pattern would be the trajectory of a ball-bearing in a bowl being tilted or vibrated in a random fashion.

Stochastic or 'random walk' change is of course in some sense a non-explanation:

it is a residue of variation which defies attempts to see persistent patterns or trends. As such it should be treated as a null hypothesis: never proven and persistently re-examined as fresh data accrue.

Stochastic models of the kind I envisage may also have implications with regard to the socio-culture systems that underlie drifting craft idiosyncrasy. Binford (1963), Owen (1965) and Deetz (1965) have all pointed out that demographic arrangements, residence and marriage exchange systems affect craft and culture transmission. I have argued elsewhere (Isaac 1968b, 1972e [this volume, ch. 2]) that the persistence of the basic features of Acheulean stone-tool assemblages over large parts of three continents during approximately a million years may be connected with features of the cultural transmission systems as well as with neurophysiological limitations on the craftsmens' 'inventiveness'. The model treats relations between bands or communities as a communications system. It is conceivable that a widespread low density network lacking in mechanisms for preventing the equalization of information content between neighbouring nodes would have great inertia to fundamental changes (cf. Owen, 1965), while a more tightly knit network involving culturally determined differentials in the rate of information exchange might engender localized partial isolates, which, on occasions, might be more prone to the acceptance and exploitation of innovations (Fig. 1.6). This process may have the same kind of importance for cultural change as isolating mechanisms have in genetic evolution.

Now the Lower Palaeolithic might legitimately be characterized as a situation involving a low density network of population (bands) with considerable variability in the permutations of a very restricted number of artefact traits, while the Late Pleistocene and Holocene are perhaps characterized by higher population densities, greatly increased numbers of traits and increasingly diverse regional combinations of these traits. It is tempting to suggest that the contrast arose from changes in the communications network of the kind schematically formulated in Fig. 1.6. In addition to possible changes in population densities this model accommodates the development of cultural arrangements conducive to differential rates of communication. Paradoxically, fully developed, effective language may, by virtue of the complexity of its rule systems and the arbitrariness of its vocabulary, have led to the establishment of intelligibility barriers. This model is speculative at present, but can be applied and tested against archaeological data. It gives comparative study of patterns of cultural drift some positive interest, whereas otherwise it would have only the negative value of raising objections to traditional culture-historic lines of interpretation.

In suggesting that the development of linguistic barriers may have had an important influence on the rate and characteristics of cultural change and diversification, I do not wish it to appear that another kind of parallel phylum theory is advanced. Linguistic and cultural isolates were, to judge from history and ethnography, almost certainly not stable over any great length of time. Inasmuch as they were segments of culture involving at least several generations of relatively numerous closely interacting humans, they may have constituted a mechanism for

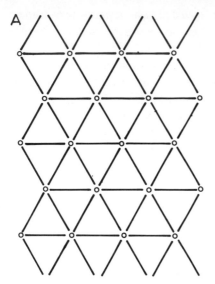 

Fig. 1.6. Diagrammatic representation of differing systems of interaction between human groups. Line thickness denotes increasing frequency of exchanges. (A) depicts a low-density arrangement in which linguistic and cultural factors do not create differentials in the extent of interaction and in which there is a constant tendency toward equalization between nodes. (B) represents a hypothetical situation of higher density in which linguistic and other cultural factors affect interaction frequency. Short-term 'partial cultural isolates' result.

readier development and establishment of innovations, which might have been lost or rejected in a more diffuse situation.

The data presented by Smith (1966) and by Wendorf and co-workers (1968) on the late Pleistocene artefact assemblages of the Nile valley constitute a possible example of correlation between demographic pressures and an allegedly complex pattern of contemporaneous and successive cultural differentiation. Comparative studies and further internal research on the Nile evidence will be necessary to check this.

Time series

Progressive change was long a universal assumption for all Lower Palaeolithic sequences, but instances where both the stratigraphic sequence and quantitative evidence for persistent trends of change have been adequately reported are in fact remarkably rare. At Olorgesailie I detected weak trends towards reduction in the relative thickness of bifaces and increase in the number of flake scars resulting from the process of shaping them. These trends are known to have been operative in differentiating the Upper Acheulean from the Lower (Isaac, 1969:18), but there is room for a great deal of random oscillation within a general drift of change which lasted almost a million years (Isaac, 1969, 1972e [this volume, ch. 2]), and indeed the Olorgesailie series shows such fluctuations (Figs. 1.4a and b).

Collins (1969:274) has presented a seriation table for Acheulean industries from Britain. It is claimed that the serial sequence is not only concordant for various apparently independent variables such as handaxe form, proportion of Levallois flakes, and numbers of scrapers, but it is in accord with stratigraphic evidence documenting a span from Late Holstein to Mid-Riss. The stratigraphic evidence is not defended in detail and we have no secure means of assessing the length of time involved in the alleged series, or its duration in relation, say, to the time span represented by individual site complexes in Africa such as Isimila and Olorgesailie. This does seem to be an example of persistent regional trends through a segment of Lower Palaeolithic time. Other examples have emerged from M. D. Leakey's study of the Olduvai sequence (1971).

Derek Roe (1968) has compiled an unprecedented body of metrical data relevant to morphological patterns in handaxe assemblages in Britain. The series is believed to span a time range from 'Mindel' to 'Early Würm', but unfortunately very few of the sites are dated with any security. Roe did not attempt seriation with his numerical data. Because he became convinced that at least two parallel phyla were represented ('pointed tradition' and 'ovate tradition'), he chose to use his numerical data for setting boundaries on classificatory classes. Fig. 1.7A shows mean values computed by Roe, arranged on three-dimensional graphs. A rather striking pattern emerges, and consideration of those sites that are dated may suggest that a time trend in changing forms does run through the series. If so, it is a complex recurved trend. Further work on the dating of sites is necessary to check this. Fig. 1.7C shows a similar graphic representation of the Olorgesailie sites and such other East Africa Acheulean sites as have been measured. It can be seen that the range of variation in handaxe form at Olorgesailie is much less than the total for British Lower Palaeolithic sites, although the scatter is larger than might be expected on traditional grounds for a penecontemporaneous set.

Statistical findings and methodology

Detailed treatment of either statistics or other aspects of methodology lie beyond the scope and ambitions of the essay. However, it should be pointed out that very close, though not necessarily very clearly recognized relations exist between paradigms, models and research procedures.

It seems to me that the 'statistical' movement, which began to be felt in Palaeolithic archaeology about twenty years ago and which has intensified over the past decade, started with the vague assumption that quantitative data would help bring into sharp focus some of the features of prehistory that were rendered fuzzy by differences between individual intuitive perceptions. Research proceeded as though it was expected that percentage inventory tables would group into statistically homogeneous sets, while measures and attribute counts would cluster around statistical norms which could be used to characterize segments of culture.

In many areas of research, such as French Palaeolithic studies, the formal use of statistics other than the computation of percentages and indices has been avoided

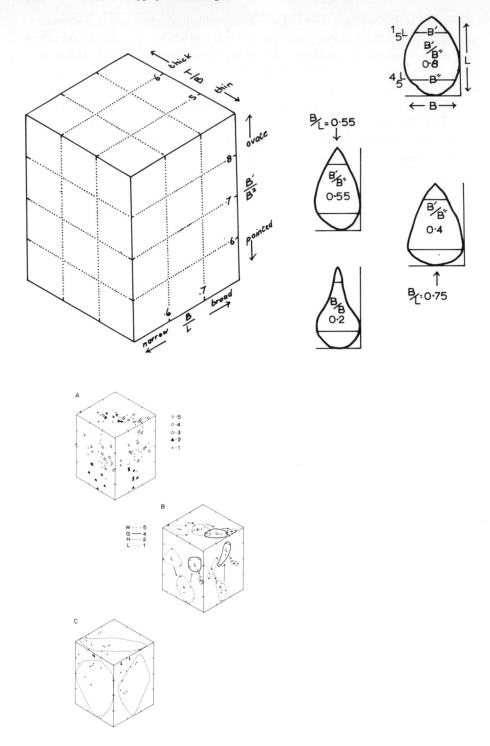

by reversion to a 'second-order' typology involving arbitrarily ordered graphic representations of the percentage values. This may have been a wise act of restraint since conventional statistical testing where applied has produced what are initially bewildering rather than clarificatory results.

In my own experiments on the Olorgesailie site complex, both per cent frequency values and many metrical attributes of individual samples from a highly restricted space-time segment failed to behave as random deviants varying about a common norm such as is implied in traditional views of cultural taxonomy (Isaac, 1968b, 1969). Analogous departures from expectations were demonstrated by Sackett (1966) when he tested the clustering of scraper attributes in relation to a current system of typological classification.

It now seems very likely to me that the numerical parameters of distinct archaeological occurrence will commonly fail to group into sets which behave as random sample deviants with respect to an inferable norm. This means that conventional statistical tests of significance have a minimal role in inter-site comparisons. We are plunged directly into pattern recognition operations, which have

---

Fig. 1.7. Differences in biface form have been numerically defined by three ratios between linear measurements (Roe, 1968):

B/L relative elongation

B^1/B^2 degree of 'pointedness'

T/B relative thickness

If the mean values of these form defining ratios for each assemblage are plotted against the axes of a three-dimensional Cartesian graph, then an array of points in space reflects variations in 'mean form'. Because of the difficulties of drawing and examining three-dimensional graphs, the effect has been achieved by plotting the points on the faces of an imaginary cube containing the three-dimensional array. 'A', 'B' and 'C' are isometric projection drawings of these cubes. On each face there is a bivariate scatter, but the combination of these enables the overall array to be visualized.

'A' shows the total array for the thirty-eight British Acheulean sites measured and reported by Roe (1968). Sites for which stratigraphic data permit a tentative age classification (largely based on Roe) are shown with distinctive symbols.

In 'B' the tentatively dated assemblages only are shown, with rings drawn around the allegedly time-related sets. Arrows show shifts in mean form which are indicated if one accepts that the time sets are valid and representative – which is highly uncertain. The trace represented in the graph shows zigzag oscillations in degree of pointedness (B^1/B^2) and an erratic drift in the direction of reduced relative thickness (T/B) and reduced relative elongation (B/L).

Roe gives warning that time/stratigraphic relations among the sites are poorly known and this graph should therefore be treated with the utmost caution. It is presented here for its methodological interest rather than as a securely established instance of long-term trend and oscillation in artefact morphology. A more detailed explanation and discussion of the graphic method and its results is in preparation for publication elsewhere.[6]

'C' shows variations in the same indices for the samples from the microcosm of the Olorgesailie basin. The dotted encircling line indicates, for comparison, the overall range of variation in the British series.

Key

1 (l) Possibly pre-'Hoxnian interglacial' occurrences (Lowestoft)

2 (H) Full 'Hoxnian' occurrences

3 Possible late 'Hoxnian'/early 'Gipping' occurrences

4 (G) Post 'Hoxnian' but pre-'Würm' occurrences

5 (W) Probable 'Würm' occurrences (Mousterian of Acheulean tradition)

more in common with numerical taxonomy and multivariate analysis than with conventional biometry and the classic statistics of contemporary sociology and economics, a conclusion writ large in D. L. Clarke's *Analytical Archaeology* (1968) but otherwise not clearly articulated.[7] Presumably there is a level in material culture where numerical values that define morphology do behave as random deviants about population norms, but this has seldom been investigated. We do not know whether it generally exists at the level of the products of individual craftsmen, or at the level of the products of a craft community such as a craft lineage or a short-term regional social interchange network. Careful ethnographic study of this problem is a matter of urgency (Isaac, 1972e [this volume, ch. 2]). Whatever the socio-cultural level normally involved, it is one that we must recognize as largely beyond the power of Lower Palaeolithic archaeology to resolve because of the low sample density normally achieved under even optimal conditions.

Conclusions: strategy and priorities

As already indicated, many of the interpretational problems of Lower Palaeolithic archaeology, as distinct from Late Palaeolithic and post-Pleistocene studies, stem from differences in sample density amounting to many orders of magnitude. We probably have fewer significant site samples from the whole of three continents during the first 2 million years of the archaeological record than we have from the 20,000 years of the Upper Palaeolithic of France alone. This means that our ability to resolve all but the most gross culture-historic episodes and/or culture-geographic entities is diminished to the point where conventional culture history is probably not feasible, and in any case is certainly not very informative. Since perception of systemic features is often obscured by preoccupation with the ephemeral local idiosyncrasies that are important for the culture historian, I argue that our efforts are best directed toward the search for regularities in the data that are indicative of widespread states and of major evolutionary trends.

The significance of this strategy is twofold. First, it seems reasonable to suppose that gross features of evolutionary development, such as levels of craft competence, or levels of socio-economic organization, are liable to have been much more stable than the details of artefact forms: they are thus more likely to reveal intelligible regularities, perceptible even with a low density of sample coverage. Secondly, even if it was practicable to record 2 million years of culture history over three continents in the degree of detail hitherto achieved in cases such as the Upper Palaeolithic of France, summary narrative records alone would fill several libraries–and would be incredibly boring.

It is in the nature of science (Kuhn, 1962) that proponents of the various possible models must compete in order to establish the relative utility and acceptability of their ideas. This process is certainly evident in present-day Palaeolithic studies.

There is widespread dissatisfaction with the conventional assumption of regularity and stability in the transmission of the details of craft tradition. As a consequence elaborate attempts at culture taxonomy and culture history appear futile.

However, the alternative that has been most vigorously espoused has involved the assertion that long-term regularity exists in the functional determinants of stone industries (e.g. Binford and Binford, 1966:291). This view has been advocated largely on the basis of complex 'multivariate' patterning in the covariation of type categories. There exists as yet very little empirical, contextual evidence showing that particular tool kits were really discrete entities associated with specific activities. It seems to me that the assumption of regularity in functional determinism is just as dangerous as the assumption of regularity in culture history. In both instances regularities have to be recognized and demonstrated by reference to a given body of data.

In conclusion I will restate my conviction that there is good reason to believe that stone tool morphology has in part been erratically determined, and that the study of occupation sites and their contents seems more promising than preoccupation merely with artefact assemblages. While comparisons of artefact sets remain important, it seems likely that there will be a shift towards emphasis on behavioural system models, which facilitate the interpretation of site locations, food refuse, site size and site character as well as artefact morphology.

Notes

1 It appears from the growing volume of abstract literature that controlling ideas with very broad applicability may be termed paradigms, while more specific lines of interpretation may be styled as models (Chorley and Hagget, 1967:26–7, 35, based on Kuhn, 1962). Models as used in this essay relate to ideas about processes rather than to specific accounts of particular situations or transformations. Thus 'activity differentiation' is a possible label for various related models (interpretative principles), whereas, for example, the actual explanation of a distinctive stone industry at Broken Hill (J.D. Clark, 1959) is not a model but a hypothesis, which involves the conjunction of a model and a specified situation.

  The term 'models' is a piece of jargon, albeit useful jargon. It should be appreciated that some authors who do not use the term are writing about thought categories that are closely allied to those being called 'models'; for instance, Binford (1968a) in a cogent essay, 'Archaeological perspectives', uses the labels 'interpretative principles' and 'explanatory propositions' to convey concepts that Clarke (1968) would probably have classified as models.

2 J. Frere (1800), quoted from Daniel (1950:27).

3 In his doctoral thesis on 'The tools of Neanderthal Man' (Cambridge University, 1948), McBurney did report systematic quantitative tests, but these have never been published.

4 The concept of 'random walk' change is probably implicit in much of the ideographic or narrative treatment of post-Pleistocene prehistoric material culture; what may be new is explicit, or nomothetic, concern with stochastic change as an important process (cf. Clarke, 1968:448).

5 A comment by Dr L. S. B. Leakey at the 4th Pan African Congress on Prehistory shows that his perception of the same phenomenon entirely preceded the statistical work that demonstrated its reality. I quote: I am quite sure that from Acheulean times onward and probably even earlier, the assemblages at any given living site was very considerably

influenced by the tool makers of that particular home and their skill. I am perfectly certain you can find, in places like Olorgesailie, on exactly the same horizon, from the same year, with an accumulation of tools made by one family, another by another family; because X was more clever than Y or because X had rather different ideas as to what he wanted than Y, the two things are completely contemporary of the same culture, of the same sub-culture. Yet statistically they are completely different to look at. (Mortelmans and Nenquin, 1962:127).

6 Isaac, 1977b:245–9, Appendix F. [Ed.]

7 In a series of as yet unpublished experiments C. B. M. McBurney has found that a harmonic system of internal correlations may characterize a series of related assemblages even when individual parameters fluctuate in an erratic fashion (personal communication).

Acknowledgements

The development of many of the ideas expressed here has stemmed from discussions with former mentors such as the late A. J. H. Goodwin and C. B. M. McBurney – as well as from exchange with such present colleagues as J. D. Clark, F. C. Howell, M. D. Leakey, R. J. Rodden, D. A. Roe, J. R. Sackett, S. J. Washburn and my wife. Between completion of the first draft and the final typescript I read L. R. Binford's contribution to the volume, and also attended a seminar on the East African Acheulian organized by C. M. Keller in Ubrana, Illinois. Both of these encouraged some sharpening of emphasis but no changes in content were undertaken.

My wife has helped with the preparation of the essay and has drawn the diagrams. Tom Lengyel has clarified the text by thoughtful editorial work.

2

Chronology and the tempo of cultural change during the Pleistocene

Introduction

In the past two decades, a variety of geophysical techniques have been developed whereby the passage of time in prehistory can be measured. The data which have accumulated as a result of the application of these techniques affect not only historical perception of cultural changes but also interpretation of the processes by which the human species came to be as it now is.

Geophysical measurements suggest that previous estimates of the total time span of the Pleistocene archaeological record were too short by a factor of three or four. They further show that during the earlier part development was extremely slow: there were immensely long periods within which little or no change can be detected, while in contrast the late Pleistocene was generally characterized by increasingly rapid rates of change both of an adventitious or stylistic, and of a definitely progressive, nature. Pleistocene evolution has involved concurrent development of a neurophysiological mechanism (the brain), of rule systems by which the brain has been programmed (culture), and of information content (culture and technology). Since feedback relationships prevailed amongst these, it is perhaps predictable that the capabilities of the combined systems should show geometric growth properties; but more accurate data are needed to define the pattern satisfactorily. A subsequent portion of this paper is devoted to scanning the archaeological record for significant, measureable variables which can be plotted against chronometric measurements and used to gain more closely analytic information with regard to rates of change in behaviour.

An understanding of the use to which archaeologists put geophysical dates involves the recognition of two complementary, interrelated lines of endeavour: (1) to unravel a narrative of human culture and activity through the time span prior to written records; and (2) to resolve the *processes* by which culture has changed and the mechanisms by which more generalized primate behaviour patterns have been transformed into the varied and complex behaviours of the modern human species.

The documents of archaeology are fossilized traces of human behaviour in the form of artefacts and structures, food refuse and modifications to the environment. However, since these traces are incorporated in fragmentary stratigraphic successions, and since they are scattered over wide areas, independent geophysical dating methods are of critical importance for providing sharp resolution of true sequence and for providing a numerical time scale against which changes in culture can be charted.

Archaeologists, like palaeontologists, use geochronometric data in a number of ways. Dates are used to correlate and arrange in sequence series of archaeological occurrences, where conventional lithostratigraphic or biostratigraphic evidence is incomplete or uncertain. With the decline of faith in global palaeoclimatic correlations, geophysical dating has come to be regarded as by far the most reliable way of establishing relations between major biogeographic regions. The equally important use of dates for the measurement of rates of change is one to which they have scarcely been put, because there has been little agreement about measurable changes in behaviour that could be calibrated.

Patterns in the association between geochronometry and archaeology

Figure 2.1 shows diagrammatically the frequency distribution of isotopic age determinations that are in direct stratigraphic association with Pleistocene archaeological material. It is immediately clear that the great majority of dates stem from the last 3 per cent of the record. It is only for the time span within which C^{14} dating is applicable that numerous dates with a broad geographic distribution ensure high chronological resolution.

On the other hand, at the base of the Pleistocene, three important East African archaeological localities have provided a comparatively large number of dated samples so that the chronometry of that end of the archaeological column is moderately well established. Between these two extremes in the span of human behavioural evolution there are very few chronometric data, and much of what exists is of uncertain validity. The Appendix provides a list of important archaeological dates greater than 60,000 years that are currently available, and a commentary on aspects of their circumstances and acceptability. The need for palaeochronometric data in the time range 100,000 to 1,000,000 years is clearly evident. As will emerge in discussion below, critical changes in the tempo of cultural evolution appear to have begun around 100,000 years ago. It seems likely that new dating techniques – or great technical development of existing ones – will be necessary to achieve satisfactory resolution in this crucial segment of the archaeological column.

In Fig. 2.2, the data from Fig. 2.1 have been used to compile a tentative chart showing the chronology of gross archaeological divisions as indicated by radiometry. Taken singly, many of the age determinations shown in these figures can be discounted as in some respects unreliable or unconfirmed; however, considered together they form a pattern with the strong implication of a need for reconsidera-

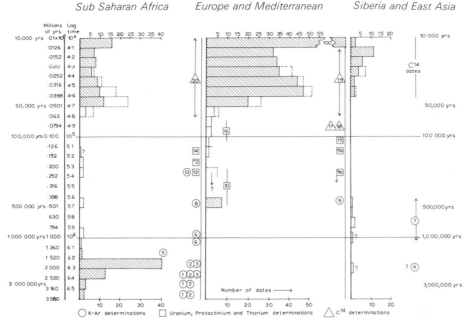

Fig. 2.1. Frequency distributions of isotopic age determinations for materials in direct strati-graphic relationship to Pleistocene archaeological occurrences. The frequency distribution is shown in equal intercepts along a logarithmic transformation of the time scale. The numbers refer to items in the Appendix which supplies additional information and sources. The radiocarbon data are probably reasonably complete, but in the absence of systematic lists of Th/U, K/Ar, etc. dates, there may have been omissions. Hatching denotes high potential reliability. Dotted portions of columns indicate 'greater than' dates. An arbitrary value of ten thousand (10^5) C^{14} years B.P. has been used as the upper boundary of the Pleistocene, while the precise age of the Plio-Pleistocene boundary has been deliberately left vague, though a value of between 2.5 and 3 million K/Ar years is considered a reasonable estimate (cf. Savage and Curtis, 1970: 225).

tion of currently accepted versions of Pleistocene chronology (e.g. Oakley, 1966: 291–5; Howell, 1965: 55; Bordes, 1968: 135). In particular it appears likely that the duration of the Middle Pleistocene and associated Acheulian or chopper/chop-ping tool industries has been severely underestimated. Unfortunately there are very few age determinations for early Middle Pleistocene strata, but in these biogeo-graphic provinces the upper limits of the Lower Pleistocene have been dated to the time span between 2.0 and 1.5 million years. In Africa at Olduvai, the aeolian tuff or Lemuta Member of Bed II is estimated to be *c.* 1.7×10^6 years old. This has for some time been arbitrarily taken as the local boundary between Lower and Middle Pleistocene (Appendix item 3; Curtis and Hay in Bishop and Miller, 1972). The Humbu Formation date for early Middle Pleistocene fossil and artefact assemblages is in accord with this (Appendix item 6). In Europe a series of dates on volcanics associated with Villafranchian faunas span the time between 3.8 and 1.9×10^6 (Bout, 1969; Savage and Curtis, 1970). Savage (personal communication) considers that the Le Coupet date of 1.9 is close to the upper boundary of the Villafranchian. (For further details and discussion see Appendix item 21). In North

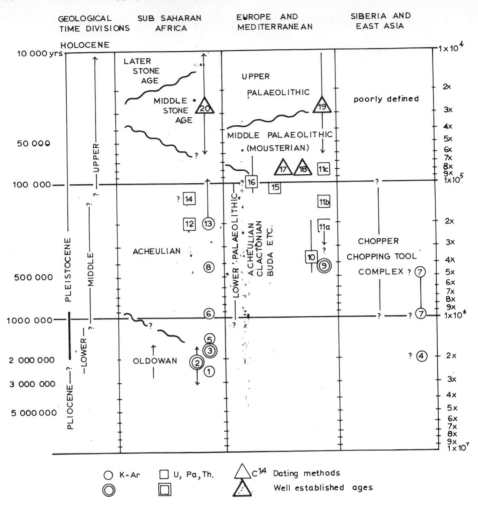

Fig. 2.2. Gross culture-stratigraphic entities are shown in relation to a logarithmic time scale. Numbered points refer to data as shown in Fig. 2.1 and as documented in the Appendix. Especially well-established dates or series of dates are shown by symbols drawn with double lines.

America the transition between the late Pliocene and Lower Pleistocene Blancan faunas and the Middle Pleistocene Irvingtonian faunas is estimated to have taken place between 2.0 and 1.7 $\times$ 10^6 years ago (Savage and Curtis, 1970). Estimates of 0.5 to 0.6 $\times$ 10^6 years for early Middle Pleistocene strata have been current, but appear to be incompatible with the collective implications of radiometric data, and this paper assumes that the boundary between the Lower and the Middle Pleistocene definitely lies between 1.0 and 1.7 million years.

All known Lower Pleistocene artefact occurrences can be assigned to the Oldowan Industrial Complex (M. D. Leakey, 1966, 1967) and a time range of 2.5 or 3 my to *c.* 1.5 my is indicated for these industries. In Africa and possibly in circum-Mediterranean Eurasia, the oldest occurrences assignable to the Acheulian

Industrial Complex fall very early in the Middle Pleistocene; that is to say, *c.* 1.0–1.5 mya. The Eurasian chopper/chopping tool complex, including the Choukoutien, Buda and Clacton industries, is certainly in part coeval with the Acheulian, although the lower time limit for it is undefined.

In Eurasia, industries with a Mousterian aspect start to appear in a poorly dated time range somewhat prior to 0.1×10^6 and had largely replaced the Acheulian and chopper/chopping tool complex by *c.* $0.08–0.07 \times 10^6$.[1] In Africa, the changeover from Acheulian industries to 'First Intermediate' and 'Middle Stone Age' industries probably occurred slightly more recently in the range $0.07–0.05 \times 10^6$ (see Appendix item 20). The change between the Mousterian (Middle Palaeolithic) and the Upper Palaeolithic industrial complexes of Eurasia occurred within the range of C^{14} dates and is securely dated to the span $0.04–0.03 \times 10^6$ years (Appendix item 19).

Correlation problems

The Eastern or Gregory Rift System is a source of hominid fossils and archaeological sites that is unparalleled anywhere in the world for the richness of evidence and for the length of time represented. Because the lower and middle portions of the regional sequence are also better dated than any other, it has been used in this paper as a standard of reference; however, a variety of problems in correlations with other palaeoanthropological successions do exist.

Problems are perhaps particularly acute with regard to Europe for which a much shorter version of Middle Pleistocene chronology has become firmly entrenched. Although much more detailed stratigraphic information exists for Europe than for Africa, the great increase in estimates for the overall span of the Pleistocene make it necessary to consider the possibility that resolution is in fact less complete than has generally been supposed. In particular the practice of dating occurrences by assigning them to one of a limited set of glacial or interglacial episodes involves the assumption that the total sequence and characteristics of such fluctuations are already known. In Africa, a comparable former assumption has proved to have been very misleading (Cooke, 1958; Flint, 1959; Howell in Bishop and Miller, 1972).

Only a very restricted number of European Lower Pleistocene ('Villafranchian') palaeoanthropological occurrences are in any way credible (e.g. Grotte du Vallonet: see Howell 1966), but there are numerous 'Middle Pleistocene' archaeological sites, and some hominid fossils, the stratigraphic nomenclature of which has been brought into great confusion by the common failure to distinguish between lithostratigraphic, time-stratigraphic, biostratigraphic and climatostratigraphic concepts. Very often the same term does undistinguished service in all these guises.

The only K/Ar determinations in direct lithostratigraphic association with European Middle Pleistocene archaeological material are the seven dates with a mean value of 0.429 ± 0.007 my for the 'tuff with black pumices' below the Acheulian industry at Torre in Pietra. The fact that this site had hitherto been assigned to the 'Penultimate Glaciation', for which no such high antiquity has generally been supposed, underlines the need for careful revision. Particulars of other European Middle Pleistocene dates not associated with artefacts are given in Appendix item 21.

The important long-term archaeological stratigraphy of the Maghreb and the Moroccan littoral (Balout, 1955; Biberson, 1961) strongly suggests that the Lower and Middle Pleistocene cultural sequence of at least part of the Mediterranean basin is similar to that which has been dated in East Africa. However, the Th/U dates for the upper part of the Moroccan succession do not help to resolve either the correlation problems or the questions of the overall length of the Middle Pleistocene (see Appendix item 11).

Other important palaeoanthropological occurrences which lack direct geophysical indicators of age are the Transvaal australopithecine breccias. These have long been assigned to a time range that spans an appreciable segment of the Lower and the Middle Pleistocene (e.g. Cooke, 1963). This remains reasonable on palaeontological and palaeoanthropological grounds (e.g. Howell, 1967: 475). Taungs and the Makapansgat Limeworks deposit may well be older than Olduvai and perhaps even than Koobi Fora and much of Omo (Shungura), and hence may document a non-stone-tool manufacturing 'stage'. The status of the Sterkfontein breccias has become more problematic. The artefact assemblage from the extension site 'Middle Breccia' has a decidedly Middle Pleistocene aspect (Mason, 1962b; M. D. Leakey, 1970b). Such authorities have suggested that the Middle Breccia may not be very different in age from the hominid-bearing 'Lower Breccia'. If this is confirmed it will prove that at least this fossil population of *Australopithecus africanus* was part of a separate, genetic line which was not ancestral to Lower or Middle Pleistocene forms assigned to the genus *Homo*. The excavation of a trench linking the type site and the extension site is urgently needed, as is the development, if possible, of geophysical measures of age for this kind of deposit. Swartkrans and Kromdraai seem clearly to be of Middle Pleistocene age, though more precise estimates are difficult. estimates are difficult.

The hominid-bearing deposits of Java have also long posed correlation and chronological problems – as witnessed by differences between Hooijer (1962) and von Koenigswald (1962) regarding placement of the Lower Middle Pleistocene boundary in the area. Stratigraphic studies and K/Ar measurements are currently in progress by G. Curtis, working in collaboration with Jacob and others. Preliminary results appear to be in good accord with the long chronology indicated by East African dates (see Appendix items 4 and 7).

The study of ocean cores may be expected to assist in the resolution of some of these problems, though as yet they seem also to pose many fresh questions. The implications of Emiliani's studies (e.g. 1958, 1963) appears to be that a graph of $0^{16}/0^{18}$ ratio fluctuations during any segment of Pleistocene times looks rather like the edge of a saw; that is to say, that climatic stratigraphy may be much more complex than the classic four glacial system indicates. The biostratigraphic data (species counts, coiling directions, and so on) of Ericson and Wollin (e.g. 1968) also show complexity, but purport to be divisible into climatostratigraphic divisions corresponding to four sets of glacials. The dates assigned to these on the basis of geomagnetic reversal chronology are in remarkable accord with the chronology adopted in Fig. 2.2 on the basis of K/Ar dates associated with archaeological material; but a hasty marriage of such disparate data would be unwise.

Culture history and palaeoanthropological resolution

Formulations of narrative versions of prehistory have hitherto been comprised of two principal ingredients: (1) developments in technology and (2) culture history. This latter can be characterized as a kaleidoscopic view of chronological and geographic patterning amongst classifiable palaeocultural entities. Prehistoric cultures are defined in terms of recurrent associations of characteristic artefact forms. The content and validity of any version of a segment of culture history will depend on (1) the number, distribution and size of archaeological samples available; (2) the nature and suitability of the technological and typological analytical systems used to subdivide and characterize the range of artefact samples involved; (3) the taxonomic system used to express patterns of resemblance and differentiation amongst the assemblages (see Bishop and Clark, 1967); (4) the degree of chronological resolution achieved amongst them.

Sampling, typology and taxonomy are topics that fall largely outside the scope of this paper. Various recent works discuss aspects of these questions (e.g. Willey and Phillips, 1958; Bishop and Clark, 1967: 821–75; D. L. Clarke, 1968).

The problem of archaeological resolution is central to this essay and can now be taken up. Fig. 2.3 provides graphic representation of archaeological sample densities in relation to space and time in two selected areas. Each dot represents a significant, excavated site. The vertical axis of each frame represents time; the horizontal axis represents space. Not all significant excavated sites are firmly dated, so that the positioning of some plots is in part arbitrary.

The diagram shows that studying human behaviour in the Pleistocene is like looking through a telescope backwards – detail is only readily available close to the observer. Perhaps 95 per cent or more of the documents come from the last 2 to 5 per cent of the time span, while sample densities for the Lower and Middle Pleistocene are extremely low. Yet recent research shows that there is high archaeological variability in the same early time period (Kleindienst, 1961; Howell and Clark, 1963; Howell, 1966a; Collins, 1969; Isaac, 1972d). We have therefore to recognize that in methodological terms we face a tough situation: a small sample thinly spread and highly varied. As a consequence, it would probably be wise for Pleistocene archaeologists and geochronologists to recognize that detailed culture history of the kind that engrosses many of their Holocene colleagues is simply unattainable, and to turn their attention to the investigation of more fundamental aspects of early prehistoric life such as economy and socio-cultural systems.

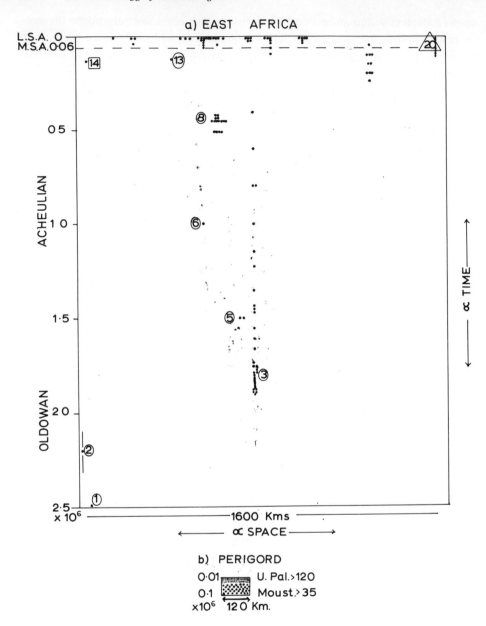

Fig. 2.3. A diagram illustrating aspects of archaeological sample densities in relation to space and time. Two areas are represented: (a) East Africa (Kenya, Uganda and Tanzania): (b) the Perigord in France. The former is chosen because of its prime importance for Lower and Middle Pleistocene chronometry and prehistory. The latter probably has the highest density of excavated Pleistocene sites anywhere in the world. The vertical axis of each rectangle represents the time scale indicated by available dates.

Trends in the evolution of culture

In the absence of conventional culture historic goals, students of Early Pleistocene prehistory need to organize their work around other kinds of rationale. The most important of these involves recognition that the evolution of human behaviour and of culture as a whole resulted in profound changes in the systems that underlie the superficialities of the short-term regional differentiations that comprise culture history. Consequently experimentation should be initiated in order to establish distinctions between systemic and adventitious features in the Pleistocene arch-aeological records. The problems imposed by low-sample density can be amelior-ated by pooling significant items of evidence into a series of sets each representing major geographic provinces and broad but well-established time zones. The sets can then be analysed for essential internal homogeneity with regard to systemic features and, where appropriate, can be contrasted so as to establish major evolu-tionary patterns in space and time.

Neither the archaeological nor the geochronological data are as yet in a state to allow of anything more than a pilot study along these lines, but a tentative survey of patterns in the broad relationships between potentially measurable archaeologi-cal variables and the time scale currently suggested by geophysics has been under-taken. The urgent need for better chronological control will be very apparent.

The archaeological record can perhaps usefully be scanned for indications of trend and systematic change in regard to a number of aspects of culture and behaviour:

1. Geographic distribution and ecological range.
2. Subsistence patterns.
3. Material culture systems.
4. Social group size and organization.

In the survey that follows much of the data presented is uncertain or liable to strong bias; however, the tentative formulations of pattern have been set out in order to get away from purely culture historic versions, and in order to pose some of the crucial evolutionary questions that archaeology and geochronology ought to tackle.

Expansion of geographic and ecological range appears to be indicated by available data. Lower Pleistocene traces of tool-making hominids are effectively confined to Africa, though it may well prove that hominid populations in fact occupied the entire tropical and warm temperate regions of the Old World, with the possible exceptions of the forested regions of Africa. By the early Middle Pleistocene, cool temperate Eurasia had certainly been colonized by hominids (e.g. Choukoutien (Kurtén and Vasari, 1960), Torralba (Howell, 1966a)) but the first demonstrable adaptations to fully arctic types of biome are not documented before the Upper Pleistocene.

Towards the end of the Upper Pleistocene, hominids effectively filled the con-tinents of the Old World and at that time the Sahara and the forests of western Africa were occupied. Hominids then also spread out into Australasia and the New World, completing the process of geographic and ecologic expansion. The total number of hominids must certainly have increased during this process of expansion and there are signs that densities were at least locally much higher by the end of the Pleistocene (cf. Wendorf, 1968; Binford, 1968b; Hole and Flannery, 1967).

Subsistence patterns. However great our interest in studying archaeological records of the behaviour of non-human primates, our efforts may be frustrated. The formation of an archaeological record depends on the manufacture of durable tools, and on the accumulation of food refuse at home base localities where food has been transported for sharing. For all practical purposes shells and bones are the only forms of refuse liable to survive from the early Pleistocene, so that meat-eating is also a prerequisite for the formation of a normal archaeological occupation site. Amongst the primates, these behaviours have become important only in the Hominidae, and the archaeological study of behavioural evolution consequently begins only after intensification of these activities had reached a critical level.

Bed I at Olduvai preserves traces of the oldest archaeological situation that has yet been studied in detail. The sites at Olduvai indicate that toolmaking, hunting and the sharing of meat at a home base was already established by 1.86 ± 0.13 million years ago (Curtis and Hay in Bishop and Miller, 1972; Isaac 1969). The antecedents of this behavioural arrangement are not yet known in detail. As indicated in the Appendix items 1 and 2, the current Omo and Koobi Fora research-es probably extend the record of toolmaking back to between 2 and 3 million years ago. The accumulation of bone at occupation sites appears to be documented also at Koobi Fora, though the only excavated site shows very low densities.

We might expect to deduce trends in effectiveness of hunting and the dietary importance of meat from samples of information on bone refuse from different gross time-space division with regard to: (a) gross abundance of bone refuse; (b) the range of species represented; (c) the relative preponderance of any one or more species and/or age category (degree of specialization).

However, patterns are not yet clearly established and attention should be drawn to the existence of many factors that distort bone refuse as a record of diet and hunting practice (Brain, 1967b; Isaac, 1971a [this volume, ch. 10]).

Data regarding density and abundance of bone have not as yet been reported sufficiently systematically to support any worthwhile overall numerical assess-ment. Within Africa, available information does not suggest any marked contrast between Early, Middle and Late Pleistocene sites, though some Holocene sites show very high densities that may in part relate to more sedentary habits. However, African sites in general appear to contrast with Eurasiatic sites of equivalent age, many of which show more impressive accumulations of bone (e.g. Middle Pleis-tocene: Torralba, Choukoutien, Vértesszöllös; and Upper Pleistocene: Saltzgitter Lebenstedt, Solutré, Dolni Věstonice). Certainly the Late Pleistocene populations of northern Eurasia appear to have achieved hunting success on an unprecedented scale. The data may thus imply a space-time trend towards increasing dependence on hunting, as opposed to gathering, with encroachment northward into cool temperate areas, and in those areas perhaps some as yet unmeasured increase in efficiency through time. However, Klein (1969a: 224) claims that as yet no significant distinction between the Mousterian and the Upper Palaeolithic can be demonstrated either with regard to gross abundance or specialization.

Hominids appear throughout the record as eclectic hunters, though at high latitudes some populations appear to have subsisted by the hunting of one or a few species (J. G. D. Clark, 1954). Instances of specialized success with particular species are first known in the Middle Pleistocene and this may have significance for recognizing a qualititative advance in hominid predatory organization (Isaac, 1971a [this volume, ch. 10]).

Shell middens make their first appearance in several regions during the Late Pleistocene, the earliest dated instance being the *c.* 70,000–80,000 year old shell accumulation at the Haua Fteah (McBurney, 1967: 99. See Appendix item 17). The middens, together with the first specialized apparatus for preparing gathered plant foods such as seeds and grains, have been taken to indicate exploitation of particular food resources on a more intense scale than ever before (cf. Braidwood and Howe, 1962).

Material culture systems. Archaeological attention has hitherto been focused extensively on artefacts, although until recently these were treated as culture-historic markers rather than as functional parts of operative systems. Various workers have shown that patterns preserved in artefact assemblages may be analysed in various subtle ways so as to provide evidence for the reconstruction of aspects of economy or social organization (e.g. Deetz, 1965; Binford and Binford, 1966, 1969; D. L. Clarke, 1968; Isaac 1972d).

Fig. 2.4 presents a generalized view of the rate of change in material culture systems as expressed by the relative durations of gross culture stratigraphic divisions (technocomplex division of D. L. Clarke, 1968). In order to obtain a more analytic perception it is necessary to start compiling a variety of quantitative data concerning artefact assemblages that seem likely to have relevance in assessing the evolution of craft capabilities and technological systems rather than to the specifics of culture-history.

There is some evidence to suggest a rise in the *gross abundance and maximum densities of artefacts* on archaeological sites through time. Among the factors involved may be the following: increasing sedentary habits, an increase in the importance of tools in hominid behaviour, and a tendency for stone-tool knapping to become an habitual hominid pastime, or all of these.

Increases in the *maximum levels of finesse and refinement* in artefacts were achieved at different time periods. These somewhat subjective terms can sometimes be measured and the trend firmly defined as, for instance, in the development of refinement shown by hand-axe forms through the long time span of the Acheulian (cf. Isaac, 1969: 17 and Fig. 3). It must be stressed that it is a rise in the maximum attainment that can be observed with certainty; the overall level is harder to assess. Thus some Late Acheulian assemblages are refined, others are very crude, but no Early Acheulian assemblages are yet known to be refined in the same degree as some late ones.

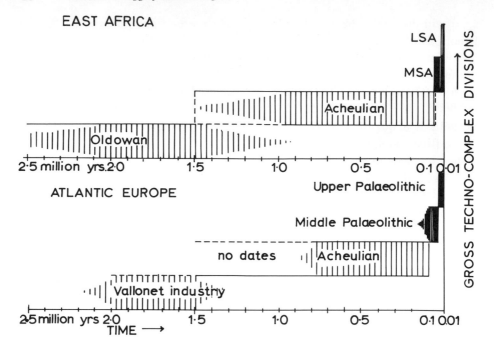

Fig. 2.4. Diagrammatic representation of decreasing time duration of successive major culture stratigraphic or technocomplex entities.

Coordination of mind, hand and eye is involved in the execution of a design on irregular raw material. The specificity and complexity of the design and the degree of precision with which it is imposed in manufacture are potential indices of levels in the technical capabilities of the evolving brain, as well as of degrees of elaboration of cultural rule systems. Unfortunately archaeologists have only just begun to devote attention to the task of analysing artefact assemblages so as to measure characteristics such as design specificity and standardization (cf. Sackett, 1966; Movius *et al.*, 1968; Hodson *et al.*, 1966; Isaac, 1972c).

The number and degree of standardization of 'types' constitute interrelated properties of artefact assemblages that are also logically related to refinement and precision of execution of individual form classes. These properties are potentially measurable and although, as already stated, effective methods of analysis have not yet been developed or applied, there are some possible indicators of evolutionary pattern (Fig. 2.5).

The number of type categories found necessary, and feasible, for the analysis of assemblages of different ages may be a crude index of the actual number of tool modalities that were rendered distinguishable as a result of design separation and manufacturing precision on the part of their makers. Once again it is the maximum number of 'types' documented at any given time level that is under consideration. Ethnography provides ample evidence that material culture does not uniformly express the capabilities of man. However, the technological capacity of mind and culture cannot have been less than that required for the maximum level of material culture complexity evident at a particular gross time period.

Fig. 2.5 shows the numbers of categories regularly used (that is, in actual inventory tables) in analysis of artefacts from selected gross culture-stratigraphic entities, each from a different segment of Pleistocene time. The numbers are plotted in relation to the time scale.

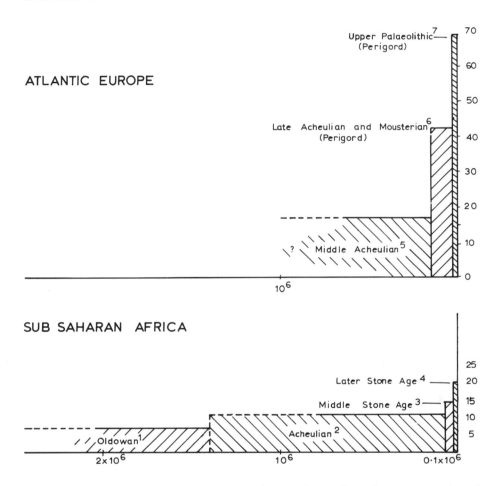

Fig. 2.5. Diagrammatic representation showing the numbers of categories used in the characterization of stone industries in relation to their age. The numbers plotted are taken from tables or figures that summarize the inventory of an assemblage. This diagram is deliberately contentious inasmuch as there is little agreement about what constitutes a 'significant type category' as opposed to an arbitrary division of a single modality (Isaac, 1972c). Many workers would undoubtedly subdivide the early material more extensively. However, the diagram represents a *de facto* classificatory situation which *may* reflect indirectly changes in the complexity of rule systems. It certainly emphasizes the need for systematic study of the problem. Sources: (1) M.D. Leakey (1967: Fig. 1, but excluding hammerstones, utilized etc.); (2) Kleindienst (1961, Figs. 3 and 4); (3) J.D. Clark (1975); (4) Sampson (1967: 227); (5) Howell (1966a: 135); (6) Guichard (1965: 456); Bourgon (1957); (7) de Sonneville-Bordes (1960; Tables 25 and 39).

Rapid and radical change in the maximum levels of artefact differentiation during late Middle and Upper Pleistocene time may be implied, but this requires verification by the development of methods designed specifically to discern modal categories and to measure degrees of standardization.

Recent studies have demonstrated that a very wide range of tool forms is characteristic not only of the Late Pleistocene, but of very early industries such as those of Olduvai Bed I or Vértesszöllös. In view of this it should be stressed that the implication of Fig. 2.5 is not so much that the range of forms has undergone dramatic expansion through Pleistocene time, but that the degree of standardization and the maximum complexity of rule systems governing design changed drastically, particularly in the Upper Pleistocene. This point can be illustrated qualitatively. Supposing an Oldowan assemblage and a European Upper Palaeolithic assemblage are laid out side by side. It may be found that the range of forms of working parts overlaps extensively – in both there are convex and concave scraping edges, there are delicate boring and 'graving' points, and so on. However, it will also be found that in the Upper Palaeolithic assemblage there will be several series comprised of numerous pieces that replicate one another very closely and may show signs of a common design principle in operation through the whole process of their manufacture. In the Oldowan assemblage such series would be largely or entirely absent. The tools, however delicate, generally appear to have been made in an *ad hoc* fashion on any suitable flake or fragment that was to hand.

The extent of discernible *differentiation between the material culture systems of different regions* appears to increase greatly during the Pleistocene. Truly distinct palaeocultural (industrial) entities in the Middle Pleistocene appear to be few in number and each one spans a vast duration of time and may have distribution covering parts of several continents; whereas distinct Late Pleistocene industrial (culture-stratigraphic) entities are very numerous, and they generally occupy restricted geographic areas and are of comparatively short duration.

Fig. 2.6 illustrates the appearance of this pattern by plotting the number of discrete palaeocultural entities that are currently recognized as having had allopatric coexistence in successive divisions of Pleistocene time in Africa. The taxonomic basis for definition of these entities is at present under heavy criticism (e.g. Bishop and Clark, 1967: 871–5), but revision is likely to raise the number of Upper Pleistocene entities and hence exaggerate rather than demolish the pattern represented.

It should be clear that archaeological resolution is an important contributory factor. We are able to distinguish details in the Late Pleistocene differentiation that could not be apparent for much earlier periods. However, there are qualitative differences in the Late Pleistocene pattern. These, with the impressive gross quantitative differences, combine to reassure one of the reality of a phenomenal increase in the extent of significant geographic differentiation. Working out the details of the change will require thoughtful development of archaeological measures of distinctness and finer chronometric resolution.

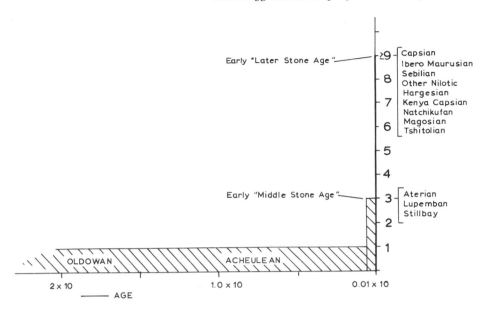

Fig. 2.6. Diagrammatic representation of increasing numbers of distinctive stone industries during the Pleistocene in Africa. Each step in the diagram represents a *minimum* number of verified entities at specific time lines: Early M.S.A. at *c.* 30,000 years, and Early L.S.A. at 11–9,000 years. (Partly based on J.D. Clark, 1970, Fig. 1). The Developed Oldowan is tentatively regarded as a facies rather than distinct cultural 'tradition' and is not shown separately. The diagram cannot be regarded as rigorous since exploration is unequal and the taxonomy of industries is at present in a state of flux. Similar patterns can be recognized in Eurasia but the complexity of the literature and lack of agreement on taxonomy make graphic representation even more difficult.

Closely associated with the geographic fragmentation of material culture systems is the phenomenon of increasingly rapid change in the specifics of artefacts. Very often the changes appear to be in large measure of a stylistic nature rather than being in themselves progressive. However, it is suspected that the acceleration in the rate of change, the extent of local differentiation and the degree of artefact standardization can be considered together as symptomatic of a great increase in the complexity of cultural rule systems; and since the complexity of rule systems is liable to have been limited in large measure by the efficacy of the communication system, these changes may imply that during the Upper Pleistocene, language crossed a critical threshold in its information capacity and precision of expression. Concomitant socio-political changes may also have been involved (see Isaac, 1969; and brief discussion below).

Technological adaptation and efficiency

As yet we know so little about the specific functioning of Pleistocene artefacts that it is very difficult even to discuss changing levels of efficiency or the development of special adaptations to particular environments. However, there can be little doubt that increases in both have been extensively involved during the Pleistocene. A major difficulty in this matter is the virtual absence of fossilized wooden or fibre artefacts.

Richard Lee has argued that containers are *the* basic human technological invention, since division of labour and the sharing of gathered vegetable foods depend on portable baskets, trays or sacks. Observation of primates in the wild makes it clear that they are simply unable to carry any appreciable quantity of vegetable food about, and that this limitation is often inconvenient to them. This draws attention to another point of evolutionary significance in the adoption of hunting as a partial means of subsistence: namely that meat is naturally containerized and readily transportable, and is very likely to have been the first commodity to be shared on an economically important scale (cf. Hewes, 1961).

As already indicated, we may infer that the sharing of meat was established by 1.8 mya at Olduvai, and perhaps is evident in some degree even earlier at the Koobi Fora sites east of Lake Rudolf (Appendix item 1). Whether or not the gathering of plant foods in containers was a part of the behavioural organization at that time remains to be determined.

Stone artefacts have a well-established record going back at least 1.8 million years in Bed I at Olduvai; and if the indications at Koobi Fora (R. E. F. Leakey *et al.*, 1970; Isaac *et al.*, 1971) and Omo (Chavaillon, 1970; Howell in Bishop and Miller, 1972) are accepted, then their manufacture had begun by 2.5 or 3 million years ago. It seems entirely probable that the manufacture of stone tools arose following a longish but unmeasured period of intensification in the use and preparation of simpler tools of the kind now known to exist within the natural repertoire of chimpanzee behaviour. However, the status of archaeological evidence for pre-stone fracture tool-use and manufacture, such as is claimed for the osteodon-tokeratic 'culture' of Makapan, is uncertain and controversial.

The Pleistocene manufacture of stone tools depended from the outset on empirical appreciation of the principles of conchoidal fracture; 'discovery' of these principles may well have functioned as a threshold, making possible immediately a broad range of chopping, scraping and drilling forms. As previously mentioned, such a broad range is known in the earliest well-documented stone artefact assemblages (see above and M. D. Leakey, 1967). The breadth of the form range in these industries is thus not necessarily proof of long-term evolutionary antecedents. Subsequent changes with regard to complexity of design specificity and the differentiation of assemblages have already been discussed, but there are some technical features in the stratified record of stone tools that may deserve mention as being indicative of rising technological 'levels'.

Two important, highly systematized methods for securing flakes *sensu lato* with largely predetermined forms have been recognized in the Pleistocene record; namely the Levallois and the prismatic blade methods. In general these show homotaxial culture-stratigraphic sequence over large areas with 'Levallois' and related methods preceding elaborate blade techniques. In the east Mediterranean, the complex and controversial 'Pre-Aurignacian' phenomenon constitutes an ex-

ception (Rust, 1950; Howell, 1961: 12; McBurney, 1967.) The fully developed
Levallois method had antecedents extending well back into Middle Pleistocene
Acheulian industries (Biberson, 1961; Sohnge *et al.*, 1937) and also into non-
Acheulian industries (Bordes, 1950a). The Levallois method (Bordes, 1968: 27–31;
Howell, 1965: 112) involves organized predetermination of a desired flake form
prior to separating the flake from its parent core. As such it documents directly a
degree of conceptualization not unequivocally evident in Oldowan or early Acheulian industries. The method was frequently practised in Europe during the Upper
Pleistocene from *c.* 100,000 to 35,000 B.P.; and in Africa the method was highly
characteristic of some, but not all, 'Middle Stone Age' industries during the time
span *c.* 60,000 to 10 or 20,000 B.P.

The blade core method (Howell, 1965: 113) can in some ways be regarded as a
special extension of the prepared core methods just discussed. It involves the
production of extremely enlongate flakes[2] generally with parallel sides and parallel
longitudinal patterns of primary ridges. The cores are characteristically fluted
cones, cylinders or slabs. The method can perhaps be regarded as more efficient
than any other on the following grounds:

1. The number of preparatory acts per flake is greatly reduced relative to most
   Levallois methods. Once a skilled craftsman has established an appropriate core
   edge angle and a parallel ridge pattern, he can produce dozens of blades in a very
   short space of time.
2. The degree to which a series of blades may be standardized so as to form a
   replicating series is unparalleled in the products of any other stone-working technique.
3. The length of cutting edge produced per unit weight of stone is unequalled by any
   other method.

Blades can be produced by direct percussion, by the use of a punch, or by pressure
– with ascending degrees of delicacy and precision respectively. In the technical
sense of flakes with length greater than twice breadth, blades can occur in small
numbers in stone industries of all ages. However, industries involving the production of very large numbers of parallel-sided blades are unknown before the Upper
Pleistocene, and are very rare and localized prior to *c.* 40,000 B.P.; but by 30,000
years ago, the debitage of most industries in Western Asia, Europe and round much
of the Mediterranean basin was of this kind; and the industries are classified as
Upper Palaeolithic. Various more or less dramatic theories have been put forward
to account for the rapid technological changeover. Hypotheses include the spread
of waves of the allegedly genetically superior 'species' *homo sapiens* (e.g. Breuil,
1912; Garrod, 1938; McBurney, 1960: 35), but comparatively little attention has
been devoted to the notion that the transition was rendered relatively abrupt by the
rapid diffusion of an invented technique, namely the use of a punch to facilitate
blade production. This would have acted as a threshold in change, radically
transforming technology without any prolonged intermediate stages being
involved.

However this may be, the rise to prominence of blades in stone technology is in
part associated with a great acceleration in design complexity and in the degree of

cultural differentiation that has already been discussed. Also at this time there appear the first elaborate bone tools and the first examples of graphic art. These innovations have often been taken to document the 'dawn of self awareness' (see J. G. D. Clark, 1970).

Another detectable landmark in the rising level of technology may well have been the advent of composite tools. It is possible that the increase in the design precision of small tools that appears to have occurred in some areas around the beginning of the Upper Pleistocene may have been associated with the practice of hafting. Mulvaney (1966) discussed a possibly analogous transformation of stone industries in Australia 5–6,000 years ago.

It seems very likely that one factor involved in the mounting regional diversity of culture has been increasingly specific adaptation to regional differences in environments; but this is very hard to measure from available archaeological documents. We can see clearly, for instance, that the behaviour that fits such peoples as the Pintibu to survive in the Central Australian deserts is not closely bound up with special artefacts. Subsistence strategy that depends on intimate knowledge of seasonal change and of the location of key resources at particular times is crucial to survival but could not be deduced from the material culture. Thus idiosyncratic tool items such as Solutrean lance heads, Aterian points or Lupemban core axes may brand distinctive cultural traditions that formerly involved complex local adaptations, but yet the type fossils may in no way be indicative of those adaptations.

Social group size and organization

Of all the aspects of hominid behaviour for which archaeology may eventually be able to measure change through time, group size and organization is the one for which data are at present least readily available. This is partly a consequence of practical and methodological problems, but more particularly is due to lack of research interest in the problem, a situation that, happily, is now changing.

As various authors have shown, area of camp site and number of occupants are roughly in proportion to each other (e.g. Cook and Heizer, 1965). However, very few Pleistocene sites have been dug in a way that enables one to assess (a) the total area of the former occupations, and/or (b) whether the area over which archaeological remains are scattered is the result of more than one partially overlapping occupation.

A site often used as a model for this kind of investigation is Star Carr, an early Holocene hunting camp in Yorkshire (J. G. D. Clark, 1954) which had a diameter of *c.* 15 m and was estimated to have been occupied by a group of 25 to 30 men, women and children. The '*Zinjanthropus*' Oldowan site FLK I at Olduvai (M. D. Leakey, 1967; Isaac, 1969: 9), the DE/89 Acheulian site at Olorgesailie (Isaac, 1968a) or Latamne (J. D. Clark, 1967, 1969b) and the Mousterian camps at Saltzgitter-Lebenstedt (Butzer, 1964) and Molodova I (Klein, 1969b) are all of the same order of magnitude. Many rock shelters occupied by Mousterian groups are of similar sizes (Binford in Lee and DeVore, 1968: 247). The indications, for what they are worth, are that through most of the Pleistocene there was little or no progressive or systematic change in the order of magnitude of hominid 'residence groups'. Archaeology does perhaps document the beginnings of local trends to enlargement during the Late Pleistocene. For example, sites such as the Upper Palaeolithic camp of Dolni Věstonice in Czechoslovakia had a diameter of *c.* 50 m and is estimated to have been occupied by 100 to 120 persons (Klima, 1962). Site sizes of this order of magnitude or larger became more common in the Holocene, even in cases where agriculture was apparently not involved (e.g. Eynan: Perrot, 1966).

It is possible also that the contrast between the patterning of variation in culture during the Middle Pleistocene and the Upper Pleistocene might be related to changes in socio-cultural organization at levels involving sets of bands and communities. Variability in the Middle Pleistocene is very considerable (Kleindienst, 1961; Howell, 1966a) but yet even under circumstances where archaeological resolution is optimal, the kind of patterns of differentiation through time or between regions does not appear to occur to anything like the extent observed in the Upper Pleistocene. The pattern seems in part to be a random walk pattern (Isaac, 1969). It seems probable that this contrast may be due to important differences in the systems by which culture was transmitted in each time period. During the Middle Pleistocene individual communities may have been linked by marriage, exchange, and so on, to other groups through a vast web of contacts that extended over large areas without the existence of culturally determined zones of low frequency of interaction. In contrast, during the Upper Pleistocene, systems may have come into existence in which local regional groupings of communities interacted preferentially with one another and set up partial cultural and ethnic boundaries around themselves.

This later kind of system would be much more closely similar to that observed in the ethnographic present, where one of the most prominent features of culture is its division into innumerable partial isolates, each maintained for some duration, not only by geographic but also by cultural mechanisms such as language differences and marriage rules (see Fig. 2.7). This contrast between two hypothetical states of cultural systems needs to be examined and tested against archaeological and anthropological evidence. Its interest lies in its consistency with the pattern of increasing regional fragmentation of culture that seems to be so marked and which has already been discussed.

Clearly the reason for the changeover, if such there was, between the systems, was probably related to the rising complexity of cultural rule systems which in turn would have been involved in a feedback relation with brain development. The more specific and detailed rules became, and the more 'information' that could be involved in culture, the greater was the opportunity for internal isolating mechanisms to be developed. Other factors such as increasing population densities and changing settlement patterns may also have influenced the hypothetical transition. It seems possible that vast diffuse and unsegmented networks of cultural contact

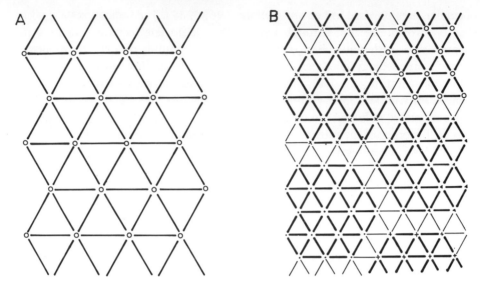

Fig. 2.7. Graphic representation of the contrast between (A) low-density demographic systems without marked culturally determined differences in interaction frequencies, and (B) higher-density systems in which preferentially higher interaction frequencies may occur amongst communities belonging to a common social, cultural or linguistic set.

might allow of idiosyncratic local variation in cultural minutiae while having high inertia to structural change (Owen, 1965). On the other hand the individual partial isolates of the culturally segmented contact network might well have had greater initial receptivity to systemic change and thus have provided a local base where innovations could be established and from which they could spread. It is tempting to see an analogy here with the role of isolating mechanisms in genetic evolution. While the development of these isolation mechanisms cannot, even if proven, be regarded as the *cause* of the rising tempo of cultural change during the Upper Pleistocene, they might be viewed as an important part of the mechanism.

Summary of pattern

Despite the many deficiencies of the archaeological and chronometric data presented, there seems to be convergence of implications with regard to the tempo of change: namely that the rate of development in systemic aspects of culture was initially very slow, and only became rapid during the last 5 per cent or less of the 2.5 my archaeological record. During vast spans of Lower and Middle Pleistocene time, very little measurable change occurred. By contrast, during the comparatively brief time span of the Late Pleistocene, change and differentiation became increasingly rapid and involved important accumulation of innovations and apparently profound modifications to the system itself.

The form of graphic representation used may have created the illusion of a smooth geometric growth trend line, but in fact available data do not enable us to decide whether the development in complexity followed a steady curve or was episodic in one of a number of fashions. Certainly technology appears to have been subject to episodic change involving thresholds as well as to some more steady trends.

Plotting the trajectory of the evolution of this culture-brain system now requires archaeological research with fresh emphasis on systemic features, and more intensive geophysical research into the chronometry of archaeological documents. As indicated in Fig. 2.1, dates are extremely sparse between 10^5 and 10^6 years, while the need for development of refined chronometry covering the initial period of rising tempo, $0.05–0.15 \times 10^6$, is particularly urgent.

Process and relations with biological evolution

As already mentioned, feedback relations surely prevailed between cultural and genetic aspects of human evolution; however, within the total complexity changes in two biological systems can be singled out as crucial to understanding the pattern of development.

First, adaptation to a bipedal stance and gait was very probably a necessary concomitant of a behavioural system that depended heavily on tool use and food sharing. The fossil record shows that the transformation to effective bipedalism was already well under way in at least some hominids at the time when archaeology attests the oldest known regular tool manufacture, hunting and home-base usage. As specified above, such a behavioural system is distinctive of man and constituted the adaptive base from which the full complexity of modern human culture and society has arisen.

Geochronometric data have added greatly to our understanding of human evolution by showing that for vast spans of time this basic social adaptive system existed apparently without the kind of cultural elaboration that is now a universal feature of human behaviour. As Lancaster (1968: 64) has pointed out, the 'hominids of the Early Pleistocene should not be thought of as merely forms transitional to man. They were highly successful, judging by their wide geographic distribution, and they lasted without major changes in either anatomy or tool tradition for a long time'. Lancaster (1968) and Washburn (1967) both suggested the need to revise views expressed earlier (e.g. by Washburn, 1960; Oakley 1957; and others) that treated tools as *the* critical formative ingredient in human evolution. The fundamental hominid behavioural system, which involved tools, hunting, food-sharing and division of labour, seems to have come into partial equilibrium as a potentially stable adaptive mechanism; however, it also created new selection pressures relating to emotional restraint, and the storage and transmission of information. As a consequence, a second biological system, the brain, underwent enlargement and profound evolutionary change. Brain size is only a very crude indicator of change in neurophysiology and experimental research shows that the human brain is not merely an enlarged version of the brains of other hominoids (e.g. Washburn, 1960; Geschwind, 1965; Robinson, 1967). The fossil evidence makes it clear that the earliest artefacts and hunting camps belonged to relatively small-brained hominids (Holloway, 1970; Tobias, 1965a); however, the considerable extent to which even these brains had already undergone reorganization can best be judged from the fossilized evidence for increases in the importance of culture and socialization.

Studies of tooth eruption sequences in the australopithecines by Mann (1968) strongly suggest that maturation was retarded relative to that in other non-human primates. Very probably the adaptive significance of this was in part an extension of the period of easy socialization and high learning receptivity. Presumably this was an important part of the feedback system which allowed selection pressures to establish a trend towards enlargement and further modification of the brain.

We are not yet in a position to plot brain size in relation to time or to cultural evolution, nor is it clear whether the trend-line will be rectilinear, curvilinear or will show episodic increments. The available data imply some pattern of steady increase and do not suggest a marked acceleration of the kind implied by data indicative of increasing cultural complexity, so that a one-to-one relationship between brain size and culture seems unlikely to be discovered.

It is often stated or implied that the great elaboration of culture evident in the Upper Palaeolithic is associated with the appearance of anatomically modern man, *Homo sapiens sapiens*. This is a taxonomic description of the change and does not define the process at all. It would seem possible that the apparently geometric or hyper-geometric growth rate in culture over the last 40,000 to 50,000 years has been dependent on attainment of a critical threshold in the capabilities of the joint brain-culture system.

We do not know yet whether the genetic changes that led to the crossing of that threshold finally occurred within hominid populations as a whole in consequence of universal selective pressures, or whether the final genetic changes occurred in local populations to be followed by population expansion and partial population replacement in other regions. Many models are possible involving both genetic and cultural components. Language in particular may have been involved in the transition: it is at least conceivable that rudimentary language systems were developed during the Lower and Middle Pleistocene, but had only limited potential information content. Perhaps, after brain evolution had proceeded far enough, more effective systems of syntax and grammar could be 'invented', and that these being cultural, not genetic, spread fairly rapidly bringing about the radical changes in material culture and in socio-cultural systems that are positively documented by the archaeological record of the Upper Pleistocene.

This hypothesis has the great disadvantage of being beyond direct tests of validity. Scientific studies of cultural evolution will in general require to be much more closely tied to the material facts of archaeological remains, but it is at least important to keep in mind the immense significance of behavioural systems that are not directly incorporated in the fossil evidence.

Conclusion

In order to achieve a first approximation with regard to the tempo of change in Pleistocene culture, this paper has avoided extensive technical discussion of the many uncertainties that exist with regard to Pleistocene chronometry. Other papers in this volume [Bishop and Miller, 1972] discuss the inherent strengths and weaknesses of the three geochronometric methods from which the chronology adopted derives (i.e. K/Ar, Th^{230}/U^{234} and C^{14}). Not all of the numerical values of this chronology should be regarded as securely established, but it seems probable that geophysical measurements made during the past one or two decades do provide for the first time valid indications of the relative duration of different segments of Pleistocene time.

The validity of the patterns outlined here depends not so much on the individual dates assigned to the Lower and Middle Pleistocene sites as on the hypothesis that most of the measurable change in cultural complexity is confined to the last 3–5 per cent of the total Pleistocene record.

Progress in understanding the evolution of culture must depend on the acquisition of suitable comparative data from samples that range widely in space and time. This review has attempted to emphasize some archaeological variables which may reflect systemic changes in culture and which can be expressed as quantities which changed in relation to a numerical time scale. Since archaeologists have hitherto been largely preoccupied with adventitious or idiosyncratic features in their material it has often been necessary to present unsatisfactory and uncertain data. Careful research will undoubtedly lead to revisions and amplifications, but in the meantime the pattern indicated by available data may help to bring into focus some of the most urgent research problems facing the Pleistocene archaeologist and to emphasize the critical shortage of geochronometric data in some segments of the record.

Acknowledgements

This paper draws on wider sources than can be represented by the bibliography of the original paper or text notes. In particular I would like to acknowledge a general indebtedness to friends and colleagues such as W. W. Bishop, K. W. Butzer, J. D. Clark, H. B. S. Cooke, G. Curtis, R. L. Hay, F. C. Howell, C. M. Keller, J. Lancaster, L. S. B. Leakey, M. D. Leakey and R. E. Leakey, D. Savage, and S. L. Washburn, with all of whom information and ideas have been exchanged during the past few years. Cooke, Curtis, Howell, Hay and Washburn read a draft of the paper and gave advice. My wife helped inestimably by discussion, by editorial work and by drawing the figures.

APPENDIX

Notes on pleistocene age-determinations in direct lithostratigraphic relationship with archaeological occurrences[3]

Late Tertiary hominid occurrences

The following East African localities have yielded fossils but no stone tools and may represent a phase of hominid behavioural evolution prior to regular stone tool manufacture:

Fort Ternan	Late Miocene	$c.\ 14 \times 10^6$ yrs
Ngorora	Early Pliocene	$>9 \times 10^6$ yrs
Lothagam	Pliocene	$?4\text{--}4.5 \times 10^6$ yrs
Kanapoi	Pliocene	3.75×10^6 yrs
Chemeron Beds	Late Pliocene	$>2.0 \times 10^6$ yrs

At Fort Ternan, a battered cobble and depressed fractures on bones are claimed as possible evidence of tool use (L.S.B. Leakey, 1968), but sufficient evidence is not yet available for evaluation. The hominid status of *Kenyapithecus* is also questioned by some authorities.

The dating and fossil contents of these hominid-bearing late Tertiary strata are discussed extensively in other papers in this volume [Bishop and Miller, 1972]. They may indeed document a behavioural phase prior to regular stone artefact manufacture, however it should be borne in mind that the recognition of low densities of Oldowan artefacts probably requires specialist searching and test excavation. Thus the negative evidence cannot yet be accepted as conclusive.

Lower Pleistocene artefact or hominid occurrences

Stone tools have been reported from various parts of the world, from strata which on palaeontological grounds are regarded as being of Lower Pleistocene age, or even of Late Pliocene age. Occurrences for which stratigraphic context and significant palaeontological evidence corroborates the claims of antiquity are listed below. (Numbers in parentheses refer to appendix items which give more detailed information.)

Koobi Fora beds (1)	East of Lake Rudolf	Kenya
Shungura Formation (2)	Lower Omo Valley	Ethiopia
Kanam beds	Kavirondo Gulf	Kenya (L.S.B. Leakey, 1935)
Olduvai Gorge (3)	Bed I Formation and lower portion of Bed II	Tanzania
Kanyatsi?	Semliki valley	Republic of Congo (de Heinzelin, 1961)
Atlantic Morocco	Various localities	Morocco (Biberson, 1961)
Ain Hanech	Uppermost part of the St Arnaud group	Tunisia (Balout, 1955)
Grotte du Vallonet	Cave deposits	Southern France (Howell, 1966)

In addition fossil hominids of possibly Lower Pleistocene age have been found without clear evidence of associated stone tools from the following:

Taungs	Cave breccias, South Africa (see
Sterkfontein type site (?)	discussion in the text)
Makapansgat Limeworks deposits	

Djetis Beds (4)   Java
Usno Formation (Plio-Pleistocene)   Lower Omo valley (for K/Ar
                                                   dates see Howell in Bishop
                                                   and Miller, 1972)

I.*Koobi Fora stratigraphic unit II A (Kenya)*. Oldowan industry.

K/Ar dating: the best estimate on the basis of six determinations by different methods is 2.61 ± 0.26 my (Fitch and Miller, 1970).

Newly explored strata east of Lake Rudolf have provided the oldest acceptable geophysical age determinations in unquestionable association with an excavated artefact assemblage (R.E. Leakey *et al.*, 1970; Isaac *et al.*, 1971). As such this is a critical document and is discussed in detail.

Excavations in a very hard discontinuous tuff bed have yielded a total of 35 stone artefacts and manuports, which were definitely not intrusive. The artefacts are associated with a series of localities lying along the course of one or more palaeo-stream channels which were filled with highly tuffaceous sediment and which are stratified within the unit hitherto known as 'Koobi Fora II A'. At one of two excavation localities, FxJj 1, the stone forms a low density scatter, *c.* 2 per sq. m, along with broken-up bone remains; an occupation episode, albeit of low intensity, seems to be indicated.

The tuffaceous sediments contain rounded and sub-rounded pumice pebbles and cobbles. Sanidine crystals from these provided the most suitable dating material. Fitch and Miller obtained age determinations by several variations of method:

(a) conventional K/Ar age determination on:
     Leakey I B1 Pumice whole rock   3.02 ± 1.6 my
     Leakey I B2 extract of feldspar crystals   2.37 ± 0.3 my
(b) total degassing $^{40}Ar/^{39}Ar$ age determination on the same two samples respectively   3.45 ± 1.2 my
     2.64 ± 0.29 my
(c) restricted $^{40}Ar/^{39}Ar$ step heating analysis of:
     Leakey I B1 pumice   2.50 ± 0.5 my
(d) $^{40}AR/^{39}Ar$ age spectrum I B2 gave an 'average
     plateau age' of   2.61 ± 0.26 my

The individual error figures for sample I B1 bracket the time range 1.42 my to 4.62, but 2.50 ± 0.5 was regarded as a minimum age.

The age spectrum analysis provided the best estimate of the age of the crystals extracted from the pumice, I B2. Clearly this value, 2.61 ± 0.26 million potassium argon years must be regarded as being technically an excellent determination of age.

The use of the $^{40}Ar/^{39}Ar$ age spectra technique minimizes some of the possible systemic errors that can lead to distorted ages (inherited argon, retained atmospheric argon, etc.); however, the ages obtained still refer to the time of crystallization or cooling from very high temperatures. Because the pumice became partially rounded, there must have been some time lag between eruption and deposition; but since the beds above and below the tuff horizon are devoid of pumice particles, it seems likely that any quantity of pumice that is associated with considerable volumes of fresh aeolian and stream-borne tuffs must have derived from eruptions that were 'contemporaneous' within the range of the experimental error figures.

At the time of writing the fossil fauna from the stratigraphic succession that includes this tuff and artefact occurrence has been examined but not studied in detail. There appears to be general agreement that the Koobi Fora IIA assemblage is of Lower Pleistocene character, though Cooke (personal communication) has expressed the opinion that there are features that make an age much greater than 2.0 million years hard to accept. The 95 per cent confidence limits for the date are 3.13–2.09 and the true value of the age is a matter that remains to be resolved.

The artefact assemblage described by M.D. Leakey (in R.E. Leakey *et al.*, 1970) and subsequently augmented by Isaac *et al.* (1971) appears to fall within the morphological range of the Oldowan assemblages known at Olduvai. Flakes and flake fragments are many times more frequent than the choppers or polyhedrons, which may also have served as cores. The core-tools show moderately intensive flaking, and many of the flakes have numerous ·dorsal scars and some have multiple platform facets. Edge damage is evident on some specimens but secondary trimming on flakes has not been recognized unequivocally.

Dates from other units of the Koobi Fora sequence are urgently needed, as well as further careful biostratigraphic work, but in the meantime FxJj 1 can reasonably be advanced as the oldest dated occupation site.

2. *The Shungura Formation (Ethiopia)*. (Howell in Bishop and Miller, 1972). Various occurrences of Oldowan industry.

K/Ar dating 3.75–1.8 my.

The stratigraphy, palaeontology and chronometry of the Omo Group, of which the Shungura Formation is a part, are discussed in other contributions to this volume [Bishop and Miller, 1972], especially those by Cooke and Maglio and by Howell. Available reports (Brown and Lajoie, 1971; Fitch and Miller, 1969) show that dates from a succession of tuffs make up a concordant sequence. Numerous hominid fossils have been recovered, but as yet no occupation site or other concentrated artefact occurrence has been found (Howell, personal communication; Chavaillon, personal communication). A vein quartz side chopper was found embedded in an outcrop of a stratum closely overlying Tuff E (Chavaillon, 1970), which would imply an age of *c*. 2.1 my. However, subsequent excavation has not revealed any concentration of material in the bed (Chavaillon, personal communication). Various scattered artefacts have also been found apparently *in situ* or in situations strongly suggestive of derivation from strata ranging from Member C to Member G, that is *c*. 3 my to 1.9 my (Howell in Bishop and Miller, 1972). Some of these occurrences may well be older than the Koobi Fora FxJj site, but archaeologically they are, thus far, less informative.

3. *Olduvai Gorge Bed I and Lower Bed II (Tanzania)*. Oldowan industries.

K/Ar dating for Bed I and Lower Bed II: 35 acceptable determinations averaging $1.82 \pm 0.13 \times 10^6$ (Curtis and Hay in Bishop and Miller, 1972). Fission track data: $2.0 \pm 0.25 \times 10^6$ (Fleischer, *et al.*, 1965). Palaeomagnetic evidence: $1.9–1.7 \times 10^6$ (Curtis and Hay in Bishop and Miller, 1972)

Careful reappraisal of the stratigraphy and geochronometric data from these strata has led Curtis and Hay (Bishop and Miller, 1972) to revise aspects of the chronology that had previously been accepted. It now appears from more than thirty dates and palaeomagnetic evidence that the time interval represented by the deposition of strata between the basalt lava flows and the 'aeolian tuff' (Tuff IIA) of Bed II was of the order of 100,000 years only. These beds must be regarded as amongst the most securely dated Early Pleistocene strata anywhere in the world.

The numerous archaeological occurrences from Bed I and Lower Bed II constitute the type series for the Oldowan Culture (Industrial Complex) (M.D. Leakey, 1966, 1967, 1971). They show a high degree of variation in their typological composition and in aspects of the morphology of the artefacts. There are no highly conspicuous trends of change through time within the series, but increasing incidence in spheroids and 'protobifaces' appears to be documented.

The excavated sites together indicate that by 1.8 million years ago the following behaviours were well established: (1) manufacture of stone tools: (2) consumption of meat (hunting); (3) food sharing (by inference): (4) organization of activity around the existence of a home base.

In strata closely overlying the Lemuta Member ('aeolian tuff') of Bed II, but separated from it locally by an unconformity, there occur the first sites containing large handaxes and cleavers. These signal the appearance of the extremely widespread and long-lasting Acheulian industrial complex.

Oldowan style industries also occur in the same strata of Upper Bed II and are termed 'Developed Oldowan'. Isaac (1969) has argued that the sharp distinction between these new Acheulian industries and the Oldowan or Developed Oldowan is related to the appearance in the former of large flakes which formed the blanks on which tools were made. A 'quantum jump' or 'invention' may well have been involved in this changeover. On the basis of the revised data, it seems that the earliest Acheulian sites (e.g. EFHR) are likely to be about 1.4 ± 0.2 million years old (Hay, personal communication). This figure could also be taken as an estimate for the beginning of what have hitherto been termed 'Middle Pleistocene' biostratigraphic entities in East Africa.

4. *Djetis beds (Java).* Hominid fossils but no artefacts.

    c. 2 million years (Curtis, personal communication).

Research into the age of the Pleistocene fossil beds of Java is currently being undertaken by Garniss Curtis. One determination on a sample associated with the Djetis beds has given an age of *c.* 2 million K/Ar years. Further determinations are awaited. This date would be in accord with the probable australopithecine character of '*Meganthropus palaeojavanicus*'; however, *Homo erectus* fossils are also said to derive from the beds and so early a date for these would require some revisions in human palaeontological interpretation. If the date is confirmed, then the stratigraphic relations of the Sangiran and Modjokerto *H. erectus* fossils will need to be checked. No archaeological associations have yet been established with certainty.

Middle Pleistocene artefact occurrences

Numerous archaeological sites are regarded on palaeontological and stratigraphic grounds as being of Middle Pleistocene age. As shown in Fig. 2 these cover a very wide geographic range and include at least one distinctive 'tradition' not recognizable in the Lower Pleistocene: the 'Acheulian industrial complex', as well as various less clearly characterized continuations of Oldowan kinds of tool-making practices. However, there are very few dated occurrences and the internal chronometry and chronology of this period is in many respects less well established than that of the Lower Pleistocene.

5. *Humbu Formation (Natron Basin, Tanzania).* Acheulian industry.

    K/Ar dating: Olivine basalt 1.4–1.6 million years (Curtis, 1967: 365).

        Olivine basalt 1.52 million years (KA 1745, a recalculation

          of the same measurements, Curtis personal communication).

This stratigraphic unit has yielded in addition to two Acheulian assemblages, a fossil fauna and a hominid mandible. The industry and fossil fauna indicate an age broadly comparable to that of Middle and Upper Bed II, Olduvai (Isaac, 1967a). A concordant sequence of three potassium argon age determinations has been obtained from the area (Isaac, 1967a: 231). Of these, the most recent is for the olivine basalt, bedded in the Humbu Formation at a level judged to be intermediate between that of the hominid mandible and that of the two

Acheulian sites. This flow has normal polarity, while the sediments within which it is stratified conformably overlie a lava flow with reversed polarity. Isaac (1965 and 1967a) concluded that this implied that the Humbu Formation spanned the changeover from the Matuyama reversed to the Brunhes normal epochs now dated at 0.69 million K/Ar years B.P., and that the date of the basalt was anomalous. However, since then, other minor normal events within the Matuyama epoch have been recognized, and Cox (1968, 1969) has predicted that numerous short-period polarity changes may have occurred. There is no longer any decisive anomaly in accepting a date of 1.5 million years for a lava with normal polarity, though there is only a very low probability that a hitherto undated magnetic episode is represented. Further age determinations are clearly needed and fresh samples have been collected for dating in G. Curtis' laboratory. The revised estimates at Olduvai for the age of the earliest Acheulian industries are not incompatible with an age of *c.* 1.4–1.6 for the Humbu Formation.

The Peninj mandible has been identified as belonging to an australopithecine (L.S.B. Leakey and M.D. Leakey, 1964; Tobias, 1965b). However, re-examination by R.J. Clarke and A. Walker (personal communication) has led them to suspect that it may in fact have belonged to a hominid comparable to Olduvai hominid 9 from LLK II, the so-called 'Chellean' skull. This possibility is under investigation.

The Acheulian industry (Isaac, 1965, 1967a and in preparation [1977b]) is closely similar to some occurrences in Upper Bed II at Olduvai (e.g. EFHR), and both sets of assemblages are markedly rougher and less elaborate than Upper Acheulian assemblages from Kariandusi, Olorgesailie, Isimila or Nsongezi (Isaac, 1969).

6. *Kariandusi beds (Kenya).* Acheulian industry.
   K/Ar dating: 0.928, 0.946, 1.1, 3.1 my (Evernden and Curtis, 1965; data nos. KA 965, 1035, 1061, 415).

The Kariandusi beds are exposed in a small upfaulted block of diatomites and volcanic sediments (Solomon in L.S.B. Leakey, 1931; Shackleton, 1955; McCall, 1957, 1967). From data in McCall, 1967: Fig. 16, the section can be summarized as follows:

Riverine silts ('Gamblian')
– – – – – – – – – – – – – – – – – unconformity
Upper pumice beds including fluvially reworked deposits with
    Acheulian occurrences   Up to 80 ft (24 m)
Upper diatomite (with tuff lenses)   0–40 ft (0–12 m)
Pumice and diatomite   20–35 ft (6–11 m)
Main diatomite   60–113 ft (18–35 m)
– – – – – – – – – – – – – – – – unconformity
Gil Gil trachyte.

The sediments certainly incorporate large quantities of contemporaneous pyroclastics; the lapillae, bombs and some of the tuffs are clearly primary, so that K/Ar determinations ought to provide some reliable dates. The clustering of three of the determined values around a mean of 0.991 could be taken to imply that this is a valid estimate of age. The anomalous value of 3.1 my (KA 415) does not detract from the significance of the cluster since it might well be due to the presence of derived pyroclastics, the entire basin being ringed by ancient tuff deposits.

The industry at Kariandusi was originally classified as 'Chellean' (Leakey, 1931); however, subsequent excavations greatly enlarged the sample and demonstrated the presence of numerous refined bifaces. All subsequent appraisals have rated the industry as typologically equivalent to, or more advanced than, those of Olorgesailie and Bed IV at

Olduvai (Leakey in the Olduvai Guide pamphlet; Kleindienst, 1961; Howell and Clark, 1963). That is to say, it is 'Upper Acheulian' in the sense of Isaac (1969: 16–18).

In evaluating the surprisingly early date, various factors need to be considered. Mitigating circumstances include the following: (a) the dated strata underlie the industry, which may therefore be younger than the volcanics dated, although the section does not imply any long time interval; (b) the most refined bifaces are made of obsidian and it is difficult to assess the extent to which the excellence of this material might have favoured an industry with an unusually refined aspect for its age.

In addition to there being archaeological grounds for scepticism, aspects of the regional geology also appear to weigh against acceptance of the dates without further investigation. McCall has claimed, without detailed substantiation, that the Kariandusi tuffs are laterally equivalent to a series of faulted remnants of volcanic cones south of Lake Elmenteita. Were these small cones a million years old, it seems geomorphologically inconceivable that they could still preserve their eminence and steep slopes.

The author has reservations with regard to the implied antiquity of the industry, but it must be admitted that the determinations are not demonstrably anomalous in relation to any other determinations, and the mean (excluding the 3.1 value) has therefore been included in Fig. 2 as a doubtful date.

7. *The Kabuh Beds and other strata containing 'Trinil fauna', Java.* Homo erectus but no clearly defined stone history.

   K/Ar dating:

(i) (a) Basalt 0.495 my (confidence limit 0.435–0.593) (Lippolt in von Koenigswald, 1962).

   (b) Basalt 0.500 my (KA 433 and 433 R) (Evernden and Curtis, 1965).

(ii) (a) Tektite 0.610 my (confidence limit 0.520–0.690) (Lippolt in von Koenigswald, 1962).

   (b) Tektite 0.73–0.05 my (Schaeffer, 1966).

(iii)   Pumice from the locality yielding *Pithecanthropus* II: *c.* 0.9 my ± 50% (Curtis, personal communication).

The two leucitic-basalt samples are splits of a specimen from the Muriah volcanic complex some 80 km north of Trinil. The lava specimen was collected in 1891 and is said to belong with 300 m of leucite-bearing breccias exposed around the Patihajam dome. The breccias contain a 'typical Trinil vertebrate fauna' (von Koenigswald, 1962: 116; van Bemmelen, 1949: 594). Neither details of the stratigraphic relationships between the samples and the fauna, nor details of the fauna itself, were presented with the date.

The dated tektites are samples from fairly numerous specimens which have been gathered from the Sangiran area and from the Patihajam dome, with which the basalt is also associated. Apparently no tektites have been recovered *in situ* but they are reported to be closely associated with the 'uppermost part of the Trinil layers' (von Koenigswald in Barnes, 1963). Van Bemmelen (1949: 567) reports that 'the tektites and palaeolithic implements collected by von Koenigswald in the Sangiran area are mostly found on the erosional surface separating the Kabuh layers and the Notopuro breccias'. The Kabuh layers contain the Trinil fauna and *Homo erectus* fossils. These tektites belong to a widespread shower which affected Indo-China, the East Indies and Australia (Barnes, 1963). More than thirty K/Ar determinations on these tektites cluster very closely around an age of 0.7 million years. Finds of micro-tektites in ocean cores are associated with the transition between the Matuyama reversed epoch and the Brunhes normal epoch also dated to 0.7 million years (Glass and Heezen, 1967). If the relationship between the tektites and the upper Trinil layers is confirmed, then 0.7 million years becomes a probable, or maximum, age for that part of the deposit; if they are associated with the overlying Notopuro beds or with the unconformity, then they provide a minimum age for the Trinil fauna and hominids. Until there is more certain information regarding the stratigraphic provenance of the tektites their significance for palaeoanthropology will remain uncertain.

The provisional age determination on pumice is from a sample collected by G. Curtis out of a bed stratified within the fossiliferous sediments. The age estimate has a very wide margin of uncertainty owing to large quantities of atmospheric argon in the sample. A suite of dating samples is currently awaiting processing (Curtis, personal communication).

8. *Olorgesailie Formation (Kenya)*. Upper Acheulian industry.
    K/Ar dating:

> Member 10, pumice (whole rock) 0.425 ± 0.009 my (J.A. Miller in Bishop and Clark, 1967: 367).
> Member 10, anorthoclase from pumice 1.45 my (Evernden and Curtis, 1965, #925).
> Member 4, anorthoclase from pumice, 0.486 my (Evernden and Curtis, 1965 #413).
> Member 4, anorthoclase from pumice, 1.64 my (Evernden and Curtis, 1965, #923).
> Member 4, anorthoclase from pumice, 2.9 my (Evernden and Curtis, 1965, #435).

The general features of the Olorgesailie stratigraphy are reported in Shackleton (1955), Baker (1958) and Isaac (1966a, 1968b). Dates in excess of 1 million years can be discounted on the basis of regional stratigraphy, since the Olorgesailie Formation definitely overlies a complex of trachyte lavas for which four dates by the Cambridge and Berkeley laboratories all lie in the range 0.72–1.76 million years. The question remains as to whether the two dates in the range between 0.4 and 0.5 million years have any significance.

Most of the sediments in the Formation include redeposited pyroclastic material and there are some fine, thin, primary ash-fall beds. At some horizons the streams entering the basin became charged with large volumes of apparently fresh pumice. It seems likely that these were being derived without undue time lag from the region to the north, where volcanoes such as Suswa and Longonot were forming. However, the basin is ringed with older pyroclastic deposits so that samples are liable to contain materials of various ages.

The fossil fauna from the Formation is of 'Middle Pleistocene' character but cannot be pinned down more closely than that (Cooke, 1963). The archaeological occurrences are a highly variable series that appears to be broadly equivalent to the range now being recovered by Dr Mary Leakey from Olduvai Gorge Bed IV.

The age values are two or three times greater than the age estimates that most archaeologists would have considered reasonable, but unfortunately there are no yardsticks by which their validity can be judged. All that can be said is that major tectonic deformation of the Rit Valley appears to have occurred since the time of the Olorgesailie Formation (Shackleton, 1955; Isaac and Shackleton, in preparation[4]). Further, previous estimates of dates in the Middle Pleistocene depended purely on guesswork and these two dates are not in conflict with any other reliable geochronometric determination in spite of their unexpected magnitude.

Attempts are currently being made to obtain further age determinations on the fresh pumices from Member 10.

9. *The 'Tuff with black pumices', Torre in Pietra (Italy)*. Underlying an Acheulian industry. K/Ar dating from various localities in the Rome area (Evernden and Curtis, 1965), all on sanidines.

KA	304	Rome area	0.431 my
	334	Torre in Pietra area	0.434 my
	345	Torre in Pietra area, same sample as 334	0.438 my
	1185	Torre in Pietra area, same sample as 334	0.431 my
	407	Cava del Cecio, N.W. of Rome	0.417 my
	408	Cava Nera Molinario	0.432 my
	1175	Cava Nera Molinario	0.422 my
		Mean	0.429 ± 0.007 my

The 'tuff with black pumices' was deposited 'at an advanced phase of the eruptive activity of the Sabatino group of volcanoes' (Blanc, 1957). The highly consistent results obtained from seven age determinations must give it rank as the most securely dated Middle Pleistocene stratum in any way directly associated with archaeological material. An account of the stratigraphy and industry is most readily available in Howell (1966: 170–4).

The artefact assemblage, which was regarded as Upper Abbevillian–Lower Acheulian (Blanc, 1957), but which is said to be clearly 'Middle Acheulian' by Howell (1966), occurs at the base of 'sands and fluviatile gravels (3.5 m) rich in volcanic elements and redistributed brackish molluscs' (Howell, 1966: 172). This stratum immediately overlies the dated horizon. While the section does not appear to give evidence of any major time gap, this super-positioned relationship is possibly a weak link in the dating of the industry. The deposits containing the industry and those overlying it yield evidence of intensive frost action and cold conditions. These are attributed to the regional climatostratigraphic entity the 'Nomentanian', which in turn is correlated with the 'Riss' glaciation of the Alps.

If, as seems likely, the Acheulian industry is of the same order of age as the 'tuff with black pumices', then the age determinations greatly exceed the estimates that would hitherto have been advanced by archaeologists and stratigraphers. These dates are also at variance with most estimates for the 'Riss' glaciation, except for those of Ericson and Wollin (1968). However, the technically excellent dates are not in clear conflict with any other line of chronometric evidence, so that there seems no reason to reject them out of hand. The practice of dating sites by assigning them to one of four glacial or three interglacial slots may well have been misleading in this case as in many others.

10. *Vértesszöllös (Hungary)*. Buda industry.

Age estimates have been based on the isotopic composition and ratios of travertine samples (Cherdyntsev *et al.* 1965).

	'Ionium age' × 10^6	'Radioactinium age' × 10^6
Sample (page 798) # 9	0.225 ± 0.035	> 0.110
# 10	0.250 − 0.475	−
# 11	> 0.300	> 0.110

Vértesszöllös has yielded rich archaeological evidence from several occupation horizons. The industry is an extremely delicate one involving minute core-tools that have somewhat misleadingly been termed 'choppers', and numerous small, refined but none the less *'ad hoc'* scrapers, borers etc. (Kretzoi and Vértes, 1965, 1966).

The associated microfauna and bone food refuse is regarded as being of 'Upper Biharian age'. This East European biostratigraphic unit is generally regarded as being partially equivalent to the Mindel glaciation. Portions of a hominid calvarium have been recovered and are assigned to *Homo palaeohungarica* by Thoma (1966).

Isotopic determinations on travertine clearly do not provide a very satisfactory basis for estimating age (cf. Rosholt and Antal 1963) and it is doubtful whether the figures listed ought to be considered as dates.

11a. *Strata belonging to the Anfatian marine transgression (Morocco).*
Th^{230}/U^{234} dating from Stearns and Thurber (1965).

L 841E	Sidi Abderrahman unit G1	$>0.200 \times 10^6$ yrs
L 841F	Sidi Abderrahman unit G2	$>0.200 \times 10^6$ yrs
L 841T	Rabat, ? Anfatian	$>0.200 \times 10^6$ yrs
L 841Z	Rabat, ? Anfatian	$>0.200 \times 10^6$ yrs

Various rich occurrences of Acheulian artefacts are closely associated with the Anfatian marine deposits at the Sidi Abderrahman quarries, Casablanca. These are assigned to stages IV–VI in the regional sequence (Biberson, 1961). On the grounds of artefact morphology, these occurrences could well be of equivalent age to the Olorgesailie and Torre in Pietra industries, but no great reliance can be placed in this as a basis for correlation.

Two subsequent strata on the Moroccan littoral have been dated (Stearns and Thurber, 1965).

11b. *'Pre-Ouljian'.*
L842D 'Gray-white calcarenite ... deposited on a surface originally bounded inland by a seaward-facing scarp cut in older, finer grained yellow brown calcarenite (Anfatian (?))'

$$0.145 \pm .01 \times 10^6 \text{ yrs}$$

L842B[5] Pre-Ouljian deposit thought to be equivalent to L842D

$$0.050 \pm 0.005 \times 10^6 \text{ yrs}$$

Biberson (personal communication) reports that 'Pre-Ouljian' refers to the Harounian transgression. Acheulian stages VII and VIII have been defined on the basis of occurrences in associated strata. These industries show Mousterian-like features, and have also been compared to the 'Fauresmith' of southern Africa.

11c. *Ouljian transgression (+ 5–8 m).*

L 841X[5]	Dar es Soltan area	0.095 ± 0.005 my
L 842C	Rabat area, overlying L842D	0.082 ± 0.005 my
L 842G	*Ostrea* shells from Agadir (coll. Choubert)	0.075 ± 0.005 my
L 842H	*Purpura* shells from Agadir (coll. Choubert)	0.050 ± 0.005 my

Unfortunately there are no clear-cut archaeological associations with the Ouljian strand line deposits, although Aterian industries are found in strata overlying them, as for example at the cave of Dar es Soltan where a C^{14} date of $> 30,00$ has been obtained (UCLA 678 A, B).

The dates for the Anfatian transgression and typical Acheulian industries are of limited value because they are open-ended determinations, but they are in general accord with the long chronology that may be implied by the Olorgesailie and Torre in Pietra determinations. The tentative date for Acheulian industries of Mousterian aspect is of great potential interest, but requires verification.

12. *Dallol, Afar (Danakil depression (Ethiopia)).* An Acheulian biface.
Th^{230}/U^{234} dating (Roubet, 1969, based on Lalou *et al.*, 1970):

Sample # 108	Coral	$0.140 \pm 0.030 \times 10^6$
109	Coral	$0.210 \pm 0.040 \times 10^6$
26	Coral	$0.200 \pm 0.030 \times 10^6$
88	*Tridacna* shell	$0.180 \pm 0.030 \times 10^6$

An Acheulian biface and one flake were found on exposures of marine deposits on the scarp surrounding the Afar depression, also known as the Danakil Rift. The presence of an encrustation of marine molluscs leaves no doubt about the provenance of at least the biface. While it is comparatively rough, the measurements and indices given for the specimen fall well within the range established for Upper Acheulian biface assemblages from sites such as Olorgesailie and Isimila. A count of between 40 and 50 trimming scars can be estimated from the drawings of the tool. This value is well outside the known range for Lower Acheulian industries (cf. Isaac, 1969: Fig. 3).

Madame Roubet accepts the three age determinations that cluster around a median value of *c.* 200,000 years as a valid date, and rejects the value of $0.140 \pm 0.03 \times 10^6$ as inconsistent with these.

The minimal nature of the associated archaeological material limits the significance of the chronometry, but it is of interest and is at least consistent with the chronological implications of other determinations.

Upper Pleistocene archaeological occurrences
Archaeological resolution is at present very poor for the earlier part of the Upper Pleistocene.[6] There are very few geochronometric determinations in the range 60,000–200,000 and for a number of areas the culture-stratigraphic situation is somewhat uncertain. This latter difficulty probably arises in part from the fact that, in Europe and the Mediterranean at least, this was a period of transition and the industries are consequently difficult to recognize and classify.

By contrast, the events of the last 30,000 to 40,000 years of Pleistocene time have been extensively dated by the C^{14} method. More than 1,800 dates in excess of 10,000 years have been published for the Old World and of these *c.* 530 relate to archaeological evidence.[7] Clearly it is not possible to deal with this corpus of data individually and it is treated by means of frequency distribution analysis.

In several cave sites, a succession of C^{14} dates in upper layers provides a basis for estimating the age of lower layers by extrapolation. Two examples are included in this list of geo-chronometric documents.

13. *The Kapthurin Formation, Lake Baringo area (Kenya).* Upper Acheulian.
     K/Ar date for the Baringo trachyte underlying the Formation 0.230×10^6 years
     (J.A. Miller, personal communication).
The date is said to be technically good, but to be close to the upper age limit of reliability of K/Ar dating (J.A. Miller, personal communication).

Within the Kapthurin Formation, a unit designed the 'Middle Torrent Wash' was found to contain a hominid mandible, part of an ulna and several other long-bone fragments. Samples of an Acheulian industry have been recovered by surface collection and excavation at two localities (Margaret Leakey, 1969). The industry is unique amongst other East African assemblages in showing elaborate development of the 'Victoria West' or Proto-Levallois technique. This technical feature is also known in Middle and Upper Pleistocene Acheulian assemblages from Morocco (Biberson, 1961) and the Vaal river valley (Sohnge *et al.* 1937) and consequently has no special chronological significance. Perhaps even more remarkable is the presence of extremely long delicate blades struck from neat prismatic cores. These range from 5 to 9.5 per cent of the 'waste', but appeared to be a distinct modality (Margaret Leakey, personal communication and personal observation). These blades are well outside the range of forms present in such well-known Acheulian industries as those of Olorgesailie, Nsongezi, Isimila and Kalambo Falls. The closest parallel known to me may be the blades associated and interstratified with late Acheulian industries in Palestine (Garrod and Bate,

1937; Rust, 1950; McBurney, 1967). Whether or not the blades have any chronological significance is unknown at present.

The hominid mandible is stated by Tobias (in Margaret Leakey, 1969) to fall within the range of variation predictable for *Homo erectus* and to be similar to the Ternifine mandibles in many aspects of morphology. No explicit comparison with *Homo erectus* material is discussed. Tobias defers a final taxonomic decision by assigning the mandible to *Homo* sp.

Only a small number of mammalian fossils were recovered and these, while being in some respects distinct from modern species, do not lend themselves to precise biostratigraphic correlations.

The assemblage is separated from the dated trachyte by between 200 and 300 feet of sediments, mainly cut and fill deposited alluvial beds. A moderately long but unknown time interval must be represented.

Margaret Leakey suggested that the material could be assigned to a 'date in the Upper Middle Pleistocene'. However, the Middle to Upper Pleistocene boundary is poorly defined in Africa and if comparability of geologic time terms between Africa and Europe is to be retained, then the assemblage is best regarded as Upper Pleistocene. Bishop (personal communication) intends to attempt to get C^{14} dates for overlying members of the Formation.

14. *Kibish Formation, Omo valley (Ethiopia).* Hominid fossils and somewhat nondescript stone artefacts.

Th^{230}/U^{234} and C^{14} dating, in relation to the sequence established by Butzer *et al.* (1969):

Member IV (C^{14})	b	$0.005,900$–$0.005,350$ B.P. $\times 10^6$
	a	$0.009,700$–$0.007,700$ B.P.
Member III (C^{14})	>	$0.026,000$ B.P.
	>	$0.037,000$
Member II		no dates
Member I Th/Ur		0.130×10^6

This last age determination seems very reasonable in relation to the number of lake-level oscillations and the thickness of sediments that separate it from the carbon-dated strata at the top of the Formation.

Fossils representing parts of three individuals were discovered by R.E. Leakey's Omo Research Party (Leakey, Butzer and Day, 1969), plus a small number of undiagnostic stone artefacts. The fossils form a varied series all assigned to the species *Homo sapiens*. It is unfortunate that so little archaeological material was recovered from the beds, since it might fill a critical gap in the African archaeological record.

15. *Grotte du Lazaret (southern France).* Acheulian industry.

Th^{230}/U^{234} dating: *Spondylus gaedoropus* shell $0.110 \pm 0.010 \times 10^6$ (Stearns and Thurber, 1965).

De Lumley correlates the uppermost deposits in the cave as Würm II. By counting weathering horizons affecting successively lower strata it is concluded that marine beach deposits at the base belong to Mindel-Riss and the inter-Mindel high stands. The validity of this procedure is unclear.

The sample comes from littoral deposits at *c.* + 20 m. These underlie a sequence of cave deposits with various Acheulian occurrences in them (de Lumley, 1969a). The industries are reported as 'Middle and Upper Acheulian'. By contrast with most African Acheulian industries and with earlier Acheulian industries from Europe (e.g. Torralba and Torre in Pietra), they are extremely refined and 'Mousterian-like'.

16. *Weimer-Ehringsdorf (Germany)*. Mousterian industry and 'unspecialized' Neanderthal skull.

Th^{230}/U^{234} and Pa^{231}/U determinations on travertine (Rosholt and Antal 1963); apparent age of uranium introduction: (minimum) 0.06×10^6, (maximum) 0.12×10^6.

Travertines and interbedded sediments have yielded an industry of Mousterian, or at least Mousterioid, character and mammal fossils including a hominid calvarium (Muller-Karpe, 1966: 308, plate 208). The palaeontological remains indicate an interglacial age, presumably Eemian.

Details of the provenance of the sample are not given and the authors indicate reservations about regarding their measurements as dates. They concluded that at this stage in the investigation of Pleistocene dating by uranium decay no really suitable type of material had been found that indicates an accurate dating potential. The age range indicated is in accord with expectations but is too uncertain and imprecise to be of great value.

17. *Haua Fteah (Libya)*. 'Pre-Aurignacian industry'.

Extrapolation from C^{14} dating: *c*. $0.080 - 0.050 \times 10^6$ (McBurney, 1967: 49).

The stratigraphy at this cave site in Cyrenaica appears to span an unusually large segment of Late Pleistocene time and consequently deserves mention apart from its representation in the frequency distribution patterns of C^{14} dates. About 5 metres of deposits were excavated below 'Mousterian' levels which have been C^{14} dated as follows:

W 85	Layer	XXVIII (Mousterian)	$0.034,000 \pm 0.0028 \times 10^6$
GrN 2564		XXVIII (Mousterian)	$0.0434 \pm 0.0013 \times 10^6$
GrN 2022		XXXIII (rest fraction)	$0.040 \pm 0.0015 \times 10^6$
GrN 2023		XXXIII (bone fraction)	$0.470 \pm 0.032 \times 10^6$

Extrapolation of the sedimentation rate down through the underlying strata gives a reasonable geochronometric estimate of at least 70 to 80,000 years for the base of the excavation. The small artefact sample from the lowest levels represents an idiosyncratic industry which includes fairly numerous blades (McBurney, 1967: 91), burins, Acheulian elements (*ibid*.: Fig. IV, 7:1, 2, 6), Mousterian elements (*ibid*.: Fig. IV, 1: 7; Fig. IV, 5: 4; Fig. IV, 7: 3), the oldest known fossil musical instrument (*ibid*.: 90; A.IV), and perhaps the oldest shell midden (*ibid*.: 99).

The sequence is also of interest inasmuch as palaeo-sea temperature indications by O^{18}/O^{16} and other methods have been obtained from samples at various points in the column. These suggest that the 'Pre-Aurignacian' strata were deposited during a warm phase of higher sea level; while the 'Mousterian' and Upper Palaeolithic layers were deposited during generally colder times corresponding to phases of the last glaciation.

18. *Shanidar Cave (Iran)*. Mousterian industries.

Extrapolation from C^{14} dating: $0.080 - 0.100 \times 10^6$ years (Solecki, 1963, 1964).

C^{14} dates for the upper levels:

W 667	Layer B1	(Mesolithic/Proto-Neolithic)	$0.0106 \pm 0.0003 \times 10^6$
W 179	Layer B	(Upper Palaeolithic Zarzian)	$0.0120 \pm 0.0004 \times 10^6$
		(hiatus)	
L 335H	Layer C	(Upper Palaeolithic Baradostian)	$0.0265 \pm 0.0015 \times 10^6$
W 654	Layer C		$0.0287 \pm 0.0007 \times 10^6$
W 178	Layer C		$0.0295 \pm 0.0015 \times 10^6$
W 650	Layer C		$0.0333 \pm 0.0010 \times 10^6$
Gr N 1830	Layer C		$0.0339 \pm 0.0009 \times 10^6$
Gr N 1494	Layer C		$0.0340 \pm 0.0004 \times 10^6$
Gr N 2015	Layer C		$0.0345 \pm 0.0005 \times 10^6$

W 180	Layer C		0.034
Gr N 2016	Layer C		$0.0354 \pm 0.0006 \times 10^6$
		(hiatus)	
Gr N 2527	Layer D	(Mousterian)	$0.0469 \pm 0.0015 \times 10^6$
Gr N 1495	Layer D		$0.0506 \pm 0.003 \times 10^6$

This long series of essentially concordant C^{14} age determinations spans *c.* $4\frac{1}{2}$ m of sediment and appears to provide a sound basis for Solecki's chronometric estimates of 80,000–100,000 for the age of the artefact-bearing deposits at the base of the section some 8 m lower down. Solecki (1963: 184) implies that the whole 8.5 m of the basal culture-stratigraphic unit (Layer D) contains Mousterian artefacts that include 'rather typical points, scrapers and knives made on unifacial flakes'. In addition, seven Neanderthal skeletons were found in Layer D.

19. *Frequency distribution of C^{14} dates in Europe and the circum-Mediterranean area.*[8]
The frequency distribution pattern of C^{14} dates in relation to gross culture-stratigraphic divisions (= techno-complex units of Clarke, 1968) is shown in Fig. 2.8. Almost half (132 out of 308) of the dates fall in the last 5,000 years of the Pleistocene, but determinations are sufficiently numerous for the pattern to be defined as far back as C^{14} will reach.

At the upper boundary of the Pleistocene three techno-complex categories are involved: 'Upper Palaeolithic', 'Mesolithic' and 'Neolithic'. Of these, the first two are merely arbitrary divisions within a continuum of hunter-gatherer economies, while the third represents the localized beginnings of the radically altered socio-economic systems consequent on farming. These early Neolithic dates are all from around the eastern end of the Mediterranean. More than 100 age determinations with values between 15,000 and 30,000 years B.P. indicate that the industries of this period are largely of the kind classified as 'Upper Palaeolithic'. C^{14} dates between 30,000 and 40,000 years B.P. are associated with both Upper Palaeolithic

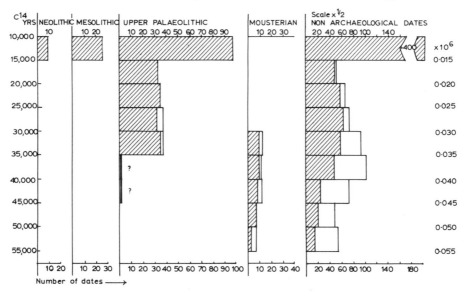

Fig. 2.8. The frequency distribution of C^{14} dates greater than 10,000 years B.P. for archaeological occurrences in Europe, the Middle East and the Mediterranean litoral of Africa. They are shown in relation to four gross 'techno-complex' divisions (see Appendix item 19). 'Greater than' dates are shown as unhatched segments of the histogram columns. The data have been obtained by sorting the edge punched cards issued by Radio-carbon Dates Association, Andover, Mass., based on *Radio carbon*, vols. 1–12 (1) (1958–1970).

and Mousterian industries. Within this span 'Mousterian' dates are relatively evenly distributed, while the 'Upper Palaeolithic' determinations are bunched within a few millennia of 30,000 years B.P. Only very few chronometric estimates for Upper Palaeolithic industries exceed 35,000 years B.P.; all of these are from the area around the eastern end of the Mediterranean, but whether this is a significant fact is as yet uncertain. It is also possible that they are part of an error scatter.

Most industries dated as greater than 35,000 or 40,000 years B.P. are of Mousterian aspect. Extrapolation from the C^{14} dates in sites such as Shanidar or Haua Fteah suggest that the 'Mousterian' extends back beyond the range of C^{14} dating, to at least 80,000–100,000 years ago, the preceding period being one involving unresolved cultural heterogeneity.

20. *Frequency distribution pattern of C^{14} dates in sub-Saharan Africa.*[9]
Fig. 2.9 shows the frequency distribution pattern of carbon dates associated with Pleistocene archaeological occurrences. The series is subdivided according to the gross culture-stratigraphic divisions that have hitherto been recognized (see J.D. Clark, 1970; Bishop and Clark, 1967). Many more dates are needed, but an interpretable pattern can already be discerned.

The Acheulian, at least locally, extended into the Upper Pleistocene without radical change from the characteristics of Middle Pleistocene occurrences. It appears just to reach the extreme limit of measurable C^{14} radioactivity, though it should be stressed that Vogel and Waterbolk (1967) point out that the Kalambo Acheulian 'dates' are really minimum ages.

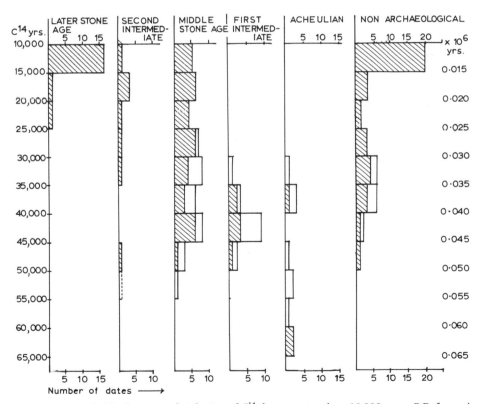

Fig. 2.9. The frequency distribution of C^{14} dates greater than 10,000 years B.P. for archaeological occurrences in sub-Saharan Africa. Relations to the gross culture-stratigraphic divisions hitherto recognized are shown (see item 20). Dates up to 1964 are drawn from J. Deacon, 1966, 1968; and since 1964 from *Radio carbon*, vols. 7–12 (2) (1965–1970).

The emergence of the geographically differentiated set of 'First Intermediate' industries is reasonably securely dated to the time span 50,000 or 60,000–30,000 years B.P. So-called Middle Stone Age industries which in some regions show involvement with Levallois stone technology are scattered over a wide range of time between 40,000 or more and about 10,000 years B.P. The scatter probably in part reflects the poor definition of this entity.

The so-called 'Second Intermediate' and 'Later Stone Age', which commonly involve backed microliths and some blade or bladelet technical elements in general, fall at the very end of the Pleistocene or in the Holocene, less than 10,000 years B.P. However, it now appears that industries showing some of these features have much higher antiquity in Africa than had hitherto been supposed.

21. *K/Ar dates from Europe that are not associated with archaeological occurrences but which have implications for the geological chronology used in this paper.*

Samples from two areas have been dated. One series has been used as a basis for calibrating a short chronology, the other implies a long time span for the Middle Pleistocene.

(a) *Laacher See volcanics (Germany)* are incorporated in Rhine terraces and are alleged to be correlatable with named climatostratigraphic entities (Frechen and Lippolt, 1965). Of 36 determinations shown in Tables 3–5, 17 are included in the summary (*ibid.* Fig. 8) as being applicable and acceptable. These can be summarized as follows:

Holstein warm period	2 dates	$0.150 - 0.140 \times 10^6$
Mindel II cold period	1 date	0.220×10^6
(? interstadial)	1 date	0.260×10^6
Mindel I cold periods	1 date	0.300×10^6
Cromer warm period	2 dates	0.320×10^6
Gunz I and II cold periods	9 dates	$0.420 - 0.340 \times 10^6$
Waal warm period	–	–
Older cold and warm periods	1 date	0.570×10^6

If these are meaningful age determinations and *if* the assignment of the earliest Acheulian (e.g. Torralba) and other important Eurasian artefact occurrences such as Vértesszöllös and Choukoutien to the Mindel climatostratigraphic divisions is a useful and valid procedure (Howell, 1966; Kurtén and Vasari, 1960), then the archaeological record in temperate Eurasia has a duration only 1/4 to 1/5 as long as that of East Africa, and the appearance of the Acheulian in Europe was retarded by at least half a million years with regard to East Africa. Since such gross chronological disjunction seems unlikely, re-examination of both African and European dating and of the basis of correlation seems to be called for.

(b) *The Auvergne (France).* Volcanics associated with fossiliferous formations (Bout, Frechen and Lippolt, 1966 (marked L); Bout, 1969 (marked B); Curtis, 1967 (marked C); Savage and Curtis, 1970 (marked S and C). The ages are given in millions of years.

(i) Associated with Middle Pleistocene (i.e. post-Villafranchian) faunas:

Basalt flow (normal polarity) overlying beds believed equivalent to those containing the Champeix-Coudes fauna.	$0.5 \pm 0.1 \times 10^6$	(L)
Basalt flow (reversed polarity) overlying beds 'correlated' on altimetric grounds with others at Malbattu near Issoire which have yielded a St Prestien mammal fauna.	0.8 ± 0.1	(L)
Basalt from Ceyssac above Le Puy, younger than stratum with Villafranchian fauna.	0.9	(C)

(ii) Associated with 'Villafranchian' faunas:

Two basalt flows of the Le Coupet volcanic complex:

Vazeilles (normal polarity) ⎧ overlying beds	1.84	(C)
Le Coupet (reversed polarity) ⎨ with the Le	1.92	(B, S, C)
⎩ Coupet fauna		

Roca Neyra ash (Perrier district) conformably underlying beds with the Roca Neyra fauna.	2.5	(B, S, C)
Ash underlying the Etouaires local fauna and the Roca Neyra fauna.	3.4	(S, C)
Roca Neyra basalt disconformably underlying the Etouaires fauna and the Roca Neyra fauna.	3.9	(C)
	3.5	(S, C)
	3.1 ± 0.2	(L)
Basalt correlated with pebbles underlying the Roca Neyra basalt.	3.4	(B)
Vialette lava associated with the Vialette local fauna.	3.8	(S, C)

There is a gap in determinations between 1.8 and 0.9 million years. During this hiatus 'Villafranchian' faunas gave way to 'Middle Pleistocene' faunas.

Resolution of the differences between the stated implications of the two sets of dates depends on (1) checks on the validity of the climatostratigraphic correlations of the Laacher See volcanics; (2) checks on the relationships of faunal divisions, climatostratigraphic divisions and geologic time divisions; and (3) checks on the validity of the K/Ar determinations. As already indicated the Auvergne chronology is more in accord with dating results in Africa and in North America.

Notes

1 Dates have frequently been given as decimal fractions of a million years (10^6). This has been done in order to achieve special emphasis with regard to the magnitude of the time span being discussed and of the great change in the degree of resolution required during the latter portions of the Pleistocene.

2 Note that in some terminological systems, the terms flake and blade are used in mutually exclusive senses with the boundary drawn on the basis of the breadth:length ratio (B/L of a blade being less than 0.5). However, this deprives us of a general term for the entire class of objects produced by conchoidal fracture and masks the fact that a blade is separated from a flake by gradational variables.

3 The various uranium decay series dating methods as applied to Quaternary calcium carbonate materials have proved less reliable than was supposed at the time of writing– see comments by Thurber in Bishop and Miller, 1972.

4 Geological map published in Bishop, 1978a: 171. It is attributed to Robert M. Shackleton only and titled 'Geological map of the Olorgesailie area, Kenya'. [Ed.]

5 Denotes dates suspect on account of laboratory checks on the suitability of the dating samples.

6 The time span designated 'Upper Pleistocene' is itself poorly defined. For those who trust the vagaries of glacial chronology it begins either with the Riss glaciation (e.g. Oakley, 1966: 16) or with the Riss-Würm (Eem) Interglacial (e.g. Kurtén, 1968). In sub-Saharan Africa it is exceptionally indistinct. Some workers have even taken to using the end of the Acheulian and the beginning of C^{14} dates of *c.* 60,000 as the boundary (e.g. Bishop, 1963).

7 These figures and the frequency distribution analyses are based on sortings of the edge punched cards issued by the Radiocarbon Dates Association, Andover, Mass., which in turn depend on the lists in the Radiocarbon supplement issued by *Science*.

8 Including the Fertile Crescent and the North African littoral, but not the Nubian Nile or the Sahara.

9 Frequency distribution patterns were first drawn up by J. Deacon (1966, 1968). These data have been brought up to date (1970) by abstracting dates > 10,000 from *Radio carbon*, vols. 7–12 inclusive.

3

Early hominids in action: a commentary on the contribution of archaeology to understanding the fossil record in East Africa[1]

The impression is sometimes given that physical anthropologists still have a stereotype of palaeolithic archaeologists as dedicated enthusiasts who spend their summers at the bottom of holes in the ground, and their winters poring over tables covered with small angular pieces of stone. For many people the study of palaeolithic archaeology is synonymous with the study of stone tools; however, this situation is changing steadily as archaeologists concerned with the Pleistocene broaden the scope of their studies. They are beginning to realize that for many aspects of research, the value of stone tools lies not so much in the details of morphology as in the fact that these objects are crucial markers of the places where early man was active. Even if archaeologists were to glance at each specimen they found, identify it merely as an artefact, and then without further ado throw it away, they would be able to carry out many of their most important research functions. A patch of artefacts, of whatsoever character, if associated with broken-up animal bones, tends to show that the bones were very probably food refuse. It is often reasonable to deduce that the patch in question was some kind of campsite or butchery site. Similarly, the distribution pattern of artefacts in an ancient landscape can be used as an indicator of the habitats that were frequented by hominid toolmakers; this inference can be made regardless of the meaning of the details of the artefact characteristics.

In this essay I want to offer a commentary on current researches into the archaeology of early man in East Africa; that is to say, the archaeology of the period spanning from some $2\frac{1}{2}$ million years to about 1 million years ago. I will show that archaeological researches concerned with this time range are no longer bound by exclusive preoccupation with the details of stone artefact morphology and technology. In fact, they are concerned just as much with questions relating to diet and land use, and hence with adaptation. In consequence, archaeological research is of direct relevance and importance for enlarging our understanding of the dynamics of human evolution.

The last few million years of this evolution have been characterized more by changes in behaviour than by changes in anatomy, and since archaeology is the discipline best placed to work out the trajectory of change, it has a crucial role to play in elucidating human origins. It is essential for archaeology and human palaeontology to be integrated into a comprehensive evolutionary biology of the Hominidae.

I am in a position to offer an essay on the integration of archaeological and palaeontological data on early man in East Africa by virtue of the cooperative research that I am currently doing at East Rudolf with Richard Leakey and many others. At the time of going to press [1976] the name Lake Rudolf has been changed to Lake Turkana and our research group will henceforth call it this. I shall draw on the work of this project as a source of examples in this essay, but it should be recognized that the East Rudolf Research Programme is itself only one of several projects that are currently elucidating the early stages of human evolution. What is attempted is only a commentary; for more detailed statements of the archaeological and other evidence the reader is referred to the volume *Earliest Man and Environments in the Lake Rudolf Basin, Kenya* (Coppens *et al.*, 1976).

East Africa as a source of evidence

The potential of East Africa as a source of early hominid fossils and archaeological traces might well have been predicted in advance of their discovery. There are good theoretical reasons for believing that our species had its origins over some tract of the Old World tropics (Weiner, 1973), and more specifically within environments that were neither forests or deserts. East Africa lies at the centre of the huge arc of tropical savannahs that surrounds the Congo river basin, and thus the region occupies a focal position within the ecological zone that one would regard as optimal for hominid differentiation. Researches over the past decade have shown that the early hominids were not particularly rare creatures. At East Rudolf, their fossils occur with the same frequency as those of the larger carnivores, and about half as commonly as ground-living cercopithecids (Leakey, 1975).

However, East Africa was only a part of the larger biogeographic zone that may have supported populations of early hominids, and it is an additional factor that gives it its present pre-eminence: over the past 10 or 12 million years there has developed a huge geological feature across the subcontinent – the Rift Valley system. During this time period sediments preserving fossils have accumulated in basins scattered along the length of a gigantic trough in the earth's crust. Tectonic activity insures that a proportion of what is preserved is pushed back up to the surface and exposed by erosion. The great potential of the area was first shown by the pioneer explorations of Dr Louis S. B. Leakey; and following his lead the scale of research has expanded greatly so that numerous institutions and nationalities are now involved in the enterprise. It has become clear that deposits of different ages occur in different localities along the Rift, and that with patience it will be possible for palaeontologists and palaeoanthropologists to piece together a composite picture of evolutionary events in eastern Africa that spans much of the past 10 million years. What we have at the moment is only a small sample of the total store of information that is preserved in the Rift system.

At the present time, most of the archaeological information relating to the first known stages of cultural development derive from three geological formations that are associated with the Rift: namely, the Olduvai Gorge formations, the Koobi Fora Formation on the east side of Lake Turkana, and the Shungura Formation in the Lower Omo valley. Other localities such as Chesowanja have been discovered but not yet investigated in detail, while areas such as the Peninj in the Natron basin present somewhat less complete archaeological records (Isaac, 1967a). For the purpose of this essay I will confine my attention to the record that derives from the three main localities just mentioned.

Figure 3.1 shows diagrammatically the time relations that are believed to prevail among available samples of archaeological evidence based on geophysical age determination data.

The best studied series of archaeological documents from the time range with which this essay is concerned come from Olduvai Gorge. This research was carried out and reported by Dr Mary Leakey (1971). The record spans a time range from just under 2 million years ago to about 0.5 million years ago. However, this essay is only concerned with the part of the record that ends about 1 million years ago.

Very early archaeological traces which are preserved in Member C of the Shungura Formation were recently announced by J. Chavaillon at a meeting in London. There are also somewhat younger traces at the Omo with an age of about 2 million years, and these have been investigated in recent years by Merrick *et al.* (1973) and by Chavaillon (1976).

The third area yielding important evidence is that on the eastern margin of Lake Turkana (formerly Rudolf), where I myself have been working since 1970 (Isaac, 1971a [this volume, ch. 10]; Isaac, Harris and Crader, 1976). The oldest of these sites have been dated by the ^{40}Ar/^{39}Ar step heating methods at about 2.5 million years (Fitch and Miller 1970); though there are now some new conventional K/Ar determinations that give apparent ages of around 1.6 or 1.8 million years. The geochronological questions involved in this matter remain to be resolved. The region also preserves a wealth of archaeological traces that belong unequivocally to the time range between 1 and 1.5 million years. These are being studied in detail by John W. K. Harris, of the University of California, Berkeley.

Results from any one of the three localities, Omo, Olduvai or East Rudolf, could be used to exemplify the research movement with which this essay is concerned; however, because of my own involvement in the study of the earlier group of sites east of Lake Turkana, I will draw on this work as the primary source of examples.

Lines of evidence

Figure 3.2 provides a diagrammatic representation of the interrelationships of archaeological research and other kinds of investigation. Traces of the presence of

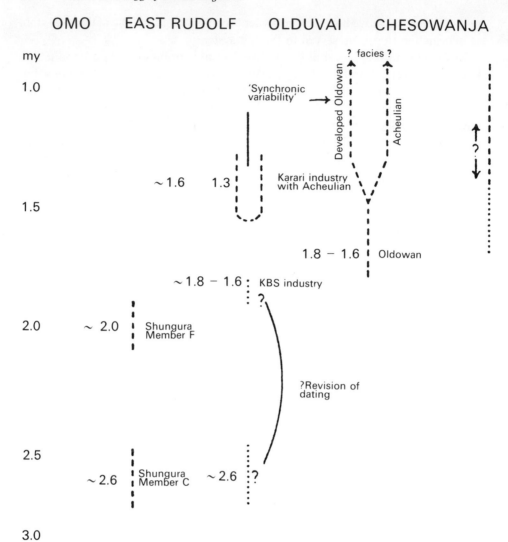

Probable distribution in time of the main sources of archaeological evidence from the 'Plio-Pleistocene'.

Fig. 3.1. Chronological relationships as determined by potassium argon dating. Two different K/Ar techniques have given divergent estimates of the age of the KBS Tuff. Note that after 1.6 my, at Olduvai some assemblages are dominated by handaxes and are called 'Acheulian', others are virtually without these tools and are called 'Developed Oldowan'. The Karari industry from East Rudolf also shows increased variability but the specifics are different. Archaeologists still debate the meaning of synchronic variety in these assemblages.

early hominids and of the characteristics of their way of life come in the form of hominid fossil bones and artefacts. The hominid fossil bones allow for the determination of the physical characteristics of various early hominids and estimates of their locomotor and other capabilities, while, on the other hand, the archaeologist treats with what hominids actually did. Thus skulls and cranial capacities provide a crude index of developing brain functions, while artefacts, skill in hunting and

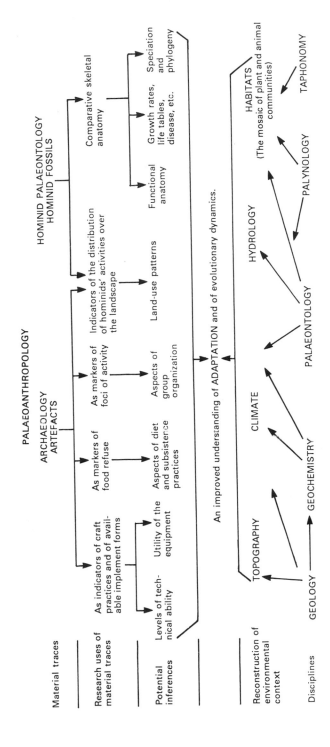

Fig. 3.2. Aspects of the structure of modern inquiry into the early stages of human evolution. The diagram attempts to illustrate (1) the combination of inferences possible from archaeological traces and hominid fossils; and (2) the convergence of palaeoanthropological and palaeoenvironmental information in understanding adaptation. (See Behrensmeyer in *Yearbook of Physical Anthropology for 1975*).

adaptability of economic patterning are the positive expressions of these potentials. The association of artefacts with broken-up bone can permit the identification of hominid food refuse, and therefore deductions regarding early hominid diet; patches of stone artefacts and broken-up bone demarcate campsites or home bases as we may call them, and these in turn have a variety of implications regarding developments in social organization. Still other kinds of information derive from the technological and design characteristics of the artefacts themselves, such as the possibility of assessing aspects of the cultural capabilities of the early hominids. In addition, the spatial distribution of both hominid fossils and artefacts over ancient landscapes gives rise to the possibility of working out land-use patterns of these early proto-human creatures. Investigation of these topics shown in the upper part of the diagram comprise the particular research activity of palaeoanthropologists; however, our curiosity about the life of early hominids goes beyond this in its extent. We want to know how dietary patterns, social patterns, and particular anatomical adaptive patterns were articulated with the larger realms of nature. This clearly demands that we attempt to reconstruct the habitats which were occupied and exploited by early hominids. The reconstruction of the mosaic habitats involves extensive cooperation with the research work of a broad range of natural science disciplines, notably geology, palaeontology and palynology.

Archaeological research at East Rudolf: an example

Eroding outcrops of the Plio-Pleistocene sediments occur over an area approaching 1,000 square miles in extent along the east side of Lake Turkana. The first step in any aspect of research is of course to search these outcrops for traces of hominid presence that are being exposed by erosion. During general exploration of this vast region, a number of localized areas were discovered that preserved a particularly promising series of archaeological traces. Up to the present time, research has been concentrated only on the most promising areas. The exposures are carefully combed and as many concentrated patches of artefacts or other traces of archaeological significance located as possible. From the range of sites discovered in the survey phase we select a series of sites for excavation, and we deliberately chose a varied set that is likely to be representative with regard to variations in geological and palaeontological context, and also to diversity of apparent archaeological characteristics. In this way, we hope to achieve information on a broad range of early hominid cultural activities. At each site that is selected for detailed investigation, excavation is carried out to determine something of the area which the patch of archaeological traces occupies, and to discover any internal spatial arrangements that exist there. The site is also subjected to careful microstratigraphic study, which in many instances can lead to a detailed reconstruction of the topographic and palaeogeographic setting that prevailed at the time that the site was occupied, and hence in turn provide a first step to assessing the habitat that was being used by the hominids who left the archaeological traces behind them. Ideally, each excavation results in the recovery not only of artefacts but also of broken-up bone, which is likely to represent part of the food refuse of the occupants.

Each of these classes of material is collected and taken to the laboratory for detailed analysis.

Over the past five years we have excavated some twenty Plio-Pleistocene sites. These must be seen simply as a sample of the total record of early hominid cultural activity. We will work steadily to enlarge the sample, to seek patterns and to extend the range of diversity represented. As our archaeological information grows it should also be possible to place the patterns of archaeological site characteristics in relationship with the larger palaeogeographic and palaeoenvironmental picture which the other natural scientists in the group are reconstructing. It should also be possible to relate the archaeological evidence to the extraordinarily rich hominid fossil evidence that is also being recovered from the east side of Lake Turkana.

Site location and characteristics

Figure 3.3 shows an imaginary landscape in which tool-using hominids have been active so as to leave discarded stone artefacts scattered over the terrain. It is from the disposition of the material of this kind that the archaeologist gets his most important clues as to the nature of early hominid behaviour. It can be seen in the diagram that some of the discarded material is concentrated in patches, while many other artefacts merely form a diffuse scatter over the landscape. The concentrated patches are commonly known to archaeologists as sites and are subject to the most intensive investigations. As I shall explain at the end of the essay, the mere

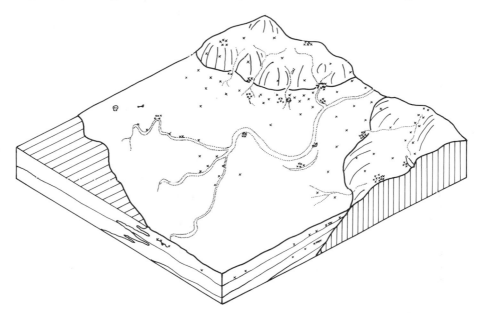

Fig. 3.3. A schematic representation of a portion of landscape frequented by tool-using hominids, with the locus of discarded artefacts marked X. The distribution pattern of discar ded items and of hominid bones is a potential clue to land-use patterns, except that material on the hills surrounding the sedimentary basin will not be preserved (Isaac 1972b). The existence of concentrated patches may be indicative of important aspects of social and economic organization.

existence of these concentrated patches has profound behavioural implications, and almost certainly denotes the existence of novel adaptive arrangements that were crucial in human evolution. Research on the scatter between the patches has also begun.

Let me use one particular part of the research as an example, namely the archaeology of Area 105, where sites occur in association with the KBS Tuff at the top of the Lower Member of the Koobi Fora Formation. In this area, geological research by Kay Behrensmeyer and myself, and later by other geologists, has demonstrated that the beds in question represent the deposits of a delta that was growing out into the lake. Across the floodplain of the delta there ran a series of distributary river channels. By fortunate chance, a volcanic eruption somewhere in the headwaters of the river system choked the rivers with volcanic ash, so that a series of the distributary channels have been preserved by being filled in with conspicuous grey tuff deposits (Findlater, 1975). Walking over the outcrops we can trace some of these ancient delta channels over some distance. In one case we can follow the course of the distributary channel for more than a kilometre. In 1969, Kay Behrensmeyer found stone artefacts in one of the outcrops of this volcanic ash at a site which was named KBS in her honour (Kay Behrensmeyer Site) (R. E. Leakey, 1970; M. D. Leakey, 1970a). Subsequently the archaeological team under my direction has subjected the entire area around KBS to a detailed search and survey. All along the distributary channels there was a very low density scatter of stone flakes and a very few core choppers. However, in three localities we found concentrations of artefacts also associated with the channels. Two of these have been excavated and their characteristics are now known in some detail.

At the site of KBS we have discovered that the artefacts occur in a patch of 15–20 m in diameter, and in among the artefacts are the broken-up bones and teeth of various animals. The stone artefacts are not distributed through any great thickness of strata on the site, but occur predominantly at an interface representing an old ground surface. It appears that the archaeological material in this instance represents only a short duration of occupation of the locality, perhaps even a single brief usage. The scatter of discarded material rests on the sandy bed of a stream channel and was covered over by fine grey volcanic dust and silt, for at the time of occupation the stream had already ceased to flow with any vigour. From the combination of archaeological traces and the microstratigraphic evidence, we can reconstruct the following chain of circumstances for the site. First, a winding distributary channel was established here across the floodplain. Probably along its banks there grew, as in many such situations in East Africa today, groves of trees that thrived on the well-watered and well-drained margins of the channel. Later, the stream shifted its course, leaving an abandoned series of meanders as depressions in the floodplain surface still shaded by their groves of trees. It appears that at this point a group of early hominids chose to use the locality for activities that resulted in the discarding of two or three hundred artefacts and a quantity of bone refuse on the sand. It seems probable that the sandy substratum of the abandoned channel and the shade provided by the trees were major reasons for the attractiveness of the locality to the hominids. Subsequently, the swale of the abandoned delta distributary was filled in by fine grey volcanic ash mixed with a little sand. This material was very probably a mixture of wind-borne dust blown in from the floodplain, plus material washed in by gentle colluvial action. It contains the impressions of leaves that augment the evidence for the existence of a grove of trees and bushes at this spot. Although they have not been specifically identified, it is amusing to report that they have been tentatively classified as the leaves of some species of *Ficus*, the African fig! The volcanic dust covered the refuse left behind by the hominids, with a minimum of disturbance. Some of the stone chips that were preserved there are so small that strong winds such as prevail in the area today would blow them away if we did not take great care over their recovery.

The second site in Area 105 to be investigated is HAS (Hippo and Artefact Site). This site is contemporary with KBS and about 1 km away, to the south across the former delta floodplain. The expedition was alerted to its existence when Richard Leakey discovered a number of bones from the carcass of a single hippo eroding out from the top of the tuff-filled distributary channel. Among the hippo bones was a series of definite stone flakes. Excavation at this site has shown that in some respects it resembles KBS, while it differs in others. Like KBS, it is associated with the abandoned course of a distributary stream channel. The hippo bones were con-centrated apparently in a depression along the channel, formerly some kind of pool or muddy wallow. On a slightly elevated adjacent bank or bar the main scatter of artefacts occurs. It is exactly adjacent to the patch of hippo bones and does not extend for any distance away from the bones. It differs from that of KBS by being somewhat smaller with only a diameter of some 10 m or less. We can estimate that fewer artefacts were discarded and those that were left here show less diversity of form.

Clearly, the artefact scatters show that each of these sites represents a focus of early hominid activity. Having established the characteristics and circumstances of each, we can turn to the details of the contents for clues to the nature of the activities carried out at each locality.

Food refuse

At HAS, the bone that is associated with the artefacts derives from the carcass of a single large animal, an extinct species of hippo (S. Coryndon in Coppens *et al.*, 1976). Sites with this kind of association are commonly termed butchery sites by archaeologists. About one-half of the bones of the hippo in question seem to have remained more or less intact and were perhaps left lying in the wallow where the dead animal lay. These bones were re-exposed by the erosion that enabled us to locate the site in the modern outcrops. Unfortunately, once washed out onto the surface the bone began to break up, so it has been difficult to make any detailed determination of original fracture patterns or the like. Among the stone artefacts on the adjacent small sandbank are more fragments of hippo bone. These appear to have been smashed into quite small pieces perhaps by the hominids who made and discarded the flakes. However, this elevated portion of the site was subjected to weathering and mild soil formation processes prior to the covering over of the site by silts. As a consequence, the bone in this area is too weathered for detailed determinations to be made. In summary, the site of HAS provides very strong circumstantial evidence for the butchery of a hippo carcass by a group of hominids who may have discarded some 100–150 stone artefacts at the locality in the process. There is no way for us to tell whether they killed the hippopotamus or found it dead. Equally, as I have indicated, the fine details of their butchery practice cannot be determined.

With regard to food refuse, the site of KBS presents a contrasting set of evidences. At this site, the bone that is scattered among the discarded artefacts derives from several animals. A list of species identified by Dr John Harris of the Kenya National Museum is shown in Table 3.1. It can be seen that these range from smallish animals such as a porcupine to medium-sized animals such as waterbuck and equids, and finally there are at least the tusks of hippopotami. The remains consist of smashed-up fragments of long bones with a few identifiable articular ends and teeth either as isolated specimens or small parts of tooth rows from upper or lower jaws. It seems that in this case the bone that accumulated along with the discarded artefacts derives from a number of different animal carcasses. It seems unlikely that all of these animals could have been killed or found dead at the spot, and one is therefore inclined to offer the interpretation that the same hominids that imported and discarded the stone tools carried in the bones and dropped them. I would surmise that the main reason for carrying in such a varied series of bones was that originally there was meat wrapped around them! At present there is no easy way to tell whether the animals from which the meat and the bones derive were killed by hominid hunters or were from carcasses scavenged by them. Elizabeth Vrba (1975) has begun to develop ideas for quantitative discrimination between the two processes, and we may eventually be able to make an informed guess. I think that the concentration of varied bone refuse has profound implications for our under- standing of the overall organization of their behaviour, a matter to which I shall

Table 3.1. *Taxonomic identification of mammals recognized among the broken-up bone on the KBS site*

Bovidae	*Antidorcas recki*
	Damaliscus sp.
	Kobus cf. *ellipsiprymnus*
Giraffidae	*Giraffa jumae*
Suidae	*Mesochoerus limnetes*
	Metridiochoerus andrewsi
Hippopotamidae	
Hystricomorpha	*Hystix* sp.

Note: All the material is fragmentary, and only a small proportion of the bone recovered is identifiable. Details will be published elsewhere. The identifications were made for the archaeology group by Dr J. M. Harris of the National Museum, Nairobi.

return later in the paper. Ultimately, the validity of these deductions depends on our ability to demonstrate that the concentration of bone that is specifically associated with the discarded artefacts is higher than the general background concentration of bone at this horizon in this area. We have good qualitative evidence to indicate that this is the case, but eventually we will need more rigorous quantitative testing of this proposition.

Other sites with early hominid food refuse are already known from Bed I at Olduvai Gorge (M. D. Leakey, 1971) and the foregoing paragraphs are presented largely as exemplification to non-archaeologists of the way in which such work is being done. Comparative studies are now possible (Isaac, 1971a [this volume, ch. 10]).

The meaning of sites

The fact that discarded artefacts tend to be concentrated in restricted areas is itself highly suggestive. It seems likely that such patches of material reflect the organization of movements around a camp or home-base, with recurrent dispersal and reunion of the group at the chosen locality. Among living primates, this pattern in its full expression is distinctive of man. The coincidence of bone food refuse with the artefacts strongly implies that meat was carried back – presumably for sharing. These behaviour patterns had crucial significance in human evolution, and cannot be deduced at all from the hominid fossils themselves.

All of the concentrated patches of artefacts that have been excavated to date and that appear to represent reasonably short-term hominid activity at a site are concentrations with a diameter of between some 10–20 m. They thus fall within the size range of the great majority of those Pleistocene open-air sites that are not complex palimpsests. It is not until the very late Pleistocene of some areas (Klima, 1962) and the post-Pleistocene that individual occupation sites show any important tendency to become enlarged beyond this range, a fact which may turn out to be an important clue in the reconstruction of long-term trends in social configurations.

Artefacts

I stated at the outset of this paper that Pleistocene archaeology is no longer exclusively preoccupied with the study of artefacts; however, artefacts do remain as important repositories of information about the early hominids. There are several lines of interpretation that palaeolithic archaeologists seek to make from them. First, artefacts can function as indicators of the level of technological sophistication of their hominid makers and as indicators of their capabilities for conceiving and executing elaborate designs. They are indicators only of the minimum level of capabilities that must have existed. Toolmakers in prehistory commonly had capabilities far beyond those that are expressed in their artefacts.

Second, artefact assemblages can be used as indicators of degrees of cultural affinity. This, of course, was the objective most emphasized in those palaeolithic studies that have become classics. Their aim was to determine the way in which strands of cultural tradition are woven through time and space. There are severe problems in doing this for the early periods, where the sample is small, the extent of time and space huge, and the phenomenon being studied of a rather simple character (Isaac, 1972a, e [this volume, chs. 1 and 2]).

Third, artefact studies seek to understand the function of the objects, that is to say, their role in the adaptation of the hominids who made them.

There seem to me to be two fundamentally important series of objects; on the one hand, there are blocks or chunks of stone from which pieces or flakes have been knocked by percussion so that their form is modified and so that in many instances they acquire sharp or jagged edges. These we may term core tools. The other series consists of thin slivers of stone that are flakes and flake fragments produced by percussion from the first series. The two series are necessary concomitants of each other. An important function of the first series of objects is probably simply the production of flakes that comprise the second series; and equally many of the second series may merely be by-products of sharpening blocks of stone, because the relatively massive core forms are also suitable for use as tools in their own right, for hacking and chopping and coarse scraping work. It seems most likely to me that they fulfilled roles both as cores and as heavy-duty tools. The second series of flakes and flake fragments come off their parent cores with a wide range of very sharp edges and angular points. An opportunistic selection from this series can provide objects suitable for use in cutting, whittling, shaving and scraping; in addition, others can be used without further modification for grooving or for piercing membranes and the like. They are extraordinarily handy and versatile implements without any elaborate secondary trimming.

Now, superimposed on this first basic morphological distinction between comparatively massive core tools and comparatively thin sharp-edged slivers of stone, is a second distinction that is more subtle in its character and perhaps is more often misunderstood by non-archaeologists. In one set, Palaeolithic archaeologists place those objects which are considered to have been deliberately shaped to a *particular* form, that is, which have had a specific set of design rules imposed on them. These objects are termed *tools* by prehistorians, who thereby arbitrarily give this English word a limited and restricted meaning in archaeological usage. Much confusion arises from continuing failure to distinguish between the technical and non-technical usage of the term *tool*. Probably a new unambiguous label should be developed. The other set consists of objects which do not seem to show this deliberate imposition of design and these are known by such other terms as *debitage* or *waste*. A third set is also often recognized: that of *utilized* or edge-damaged specimens. In this category are placed objects which are non-tools in the sense that they do not show careful designed modification of form, but yet which carry traces of chipping and damage believed to have been caused by the use of the objects as implements. It should be understood by all that come across these terms that it is simply not true that none of the items in the category debitage or waste were ever used. It now seems very likely that through the Stone Age the majority of actual utensils that assisted in the lives of Pleistocene men came from this category of objects.

Specimens representative of all these classificatory sets occur in the samples of early stone artefacts from Olduvai and from the Upper Member at East Rudolf. However, some of the categories are lacking from the Shungura samples and the East Rudolf Lower Member samples. It is not yet clear whether these differences are caused by the characteristics of the available raw materials or whether they are due to local differences in hominid habits (culture). It is also possible that the lack of some shaped-tool categories from some of the older samples may reflect the existence of a contrast between stages of technological development, but this is not by any means established yet.

Unretouched flakes and flake fragments, so-called debitage, predominate among the early stone artefacts, as indeed they do in almost all palaeolithic assemblages. (Percentages commonly range between 20 and 95 per cent with the mode perhaps at 80 and 90 per cent.) However, until the publication of Mary Leakey's monograph in 1971, the attention of the literature was exclusively confined to such core-tool categories as the choppers and so forth. Many classic archaeological monographs on the Lower Paleolithic do not treat the flakes at all. This pattern of emphasis not only hides the numerical preponderance of the flakes and flake fragments, it also obscures their functional significance. I would argue that the untrimmed, thin slivers of stone that comprise the so-called waste material are a far more versatile set of potential utensils than the more massive core-tool set (Isaac, 1975b). Even the least highly organized techniques of stone-knapping generate a great array of shapes with variously curved sharp edges, spurs and points. Without further ado, items can be picked out from among these that will be suitable for use in any task involving such basic operations as cutting, piercing, shaving, whittling, and so on. Opportunistic tool production of this kind remained important among some stone-using peoples right down to the ethnographic present (Gould, Koster and Sontz 1971; White, 1969). There is no reason to suppose that the objects used are appreciably less effective than the more elaborately shaped rule-bound forms that occur in other cultures (Isaac, 1974).

I have argued elsewhere (Isaac, 1977a) that the inception of stone toolmaking was very probably in part a threshold phenomenon. That is to say, there may not have been a long, gradual increase in the complexity of assemblages. The discovery by hominids that stone fractures in a predictable way when struck may well have given rise immediately to a wide range of forms. The two fundamental series are both unavoidable consequences of the discovery; there have to be cores, and there have to be flakes, and both are themselves potentially useful in hominid activities. Higher levels of technical organization are achieved when additional steps in manufacture are added. Among the artefact samples under consideration, some show the incorporation of two supplementary elements that are not present in all: (1) adjustment of the shape of the edge of flakes and flake fragments by secondary retouch, as in the making of a small scraper; (2) the imposition of arbitrary shapes.

In the Shungura samples (Merrick *et al.*, 1973) and the Koobi Fora Lower Member samples (Isaac, 1975), secondary retouch of flakes is so rare that the few doubtful specimens can probably be regarded as accidental. However, it is clearly represented in Olduvai Beds I and II (M. D. Leakey, 1971) and in the Upper Member of the Koobi Fora Formation (Harris and Isaac, 1976). This may or may not turn out to be symptomatic of a developmental sequence in which this practice was added to earlier stone-working habits that had lacked it.

What I am suggesting is that the initial discovery of conchoidal fracture was a quantum jump, which was perhaps followed by a slow process of elaboration through increased maximum levels of selectivity and purposiveness. The opportunity to test this threshold model may come through the discovery of very early archaeological records in the Hadar, Laetolil, or the Kubi Algi Formation east of Lake Turkana.

The decision as to whether or not an assemblage of flaked stones displays arbitrary design can involve partly subjective interpretation of subtle aspects of morphology. I think that most archaeologists would agree that the smashed quartz pebbles of Member F of the Shungura Formation do not show arbitrary design; similarly, I think most of us would recognize the arbitrary imposition of a simple preconceived design in the handaxes that start to appear in Olduvai Bed II (Leakey, 1971) and in the Karari industry of the Upper Member in the Koobi Fora Formation (Harris and Isaac, 1976).

These definitely designed biface forms date from at least 1.5 my (Isaac and Curtis, 1974). Other artefact samples lie between these two comparatively clear-cut extremes; the choppers, discoids and polyhedrons of the Oldowan of Bed I and of the KBS industry surely do represent the imposition of some degree of arbitrary design, but the extent of it is difficult to assess.

The archaeological sequences at both Olduvai and at East Rudolf show comparable shifts between the characteristics of the earlier and the later samples. The gross abundance of artefacts is much greater in the latter, and the variety of contrasting, organized forms is also greater. The largest shaped objects are five or ten times bigger than those in the older ones. It appears as though during the time between about 1.8 my and 1.4 my the toolmaking activities of at least some hominid toolmakers became more frequent, more habitual, more diverse, and more forceful. This impression will have to be checked as additional samples become available.

The foregoing changes in artefact characteristics probably relate to increases in the capabilities of hominids for technology and to the mounting importance of equipment as a part of a total economic pattern. However, an adaptive threshold as well as a technical threshold was involved. Even the simplest of the assemblages mentioned in this essay opens up a whole novel range of possibilities; a raw flake alone can be used to whittle the end of a stock to a sharp point so that it can be used as a digging stick, or as a spear, thereby enlarging the range of foods available to savannah-living primates. Hominids cannot readily penetrate and divide the carcass of an animal larger than themselves without implements – but even a small untrimmed flake will do the job admirably (Clark and Haynes, 1970; Gould, Koster and Sontz, 1971; Isaac, 1977a), and the chunks of portable food so generated can be carted off to be shared and eaten elsewhere. These simple stone tools can thus be seen as a crucial part of the nexus of evolutionary change.

Relationships to hominid fossils

For the most part in East Africa, hominid fossils and archaeological traces are not directly associated, the exception being Olduvai, where a fair number of direct associations do occur (M. D. Leakey, 1971). In the other sites, the fossils and artefacts form interdigitating series through the beds, but the nature of the connection between them is a matter of conjecture only. Even at Olduvai there is no sense of a guarantee that the hominid fossils on a site are all necessarily the bones of the toolmaking population.

However, the archaeological and hominid fossil records are critically intertwined in our sense of what happened in human evolution. The fossils show that before 3 million years ago some hominids were effective upright bipeds, presumably with their hands free to make tools, to use implements, and to carry things about (Washburn, 1960; Hewes, 1961). But we have to turn to the archaeological record for confirmation that by 2.5 million years ago some hominids were engaging in more intensive toolmaking than any living animal other than man. There is also evidence for the carrying of stone and meat. Similarly, the fossils attest changes in brain size and shape, and in tooth patterns, but it is archaeology that creates the possibility of assessing the meaning of these changes in terms of actual developments in technology, diet and economic strategy.

Kay Behrensmeyer's contribution to this volume [*Yearbook of Physical Anthropology for 1975*] illustrates another approach to the study of early hominid ecological relationships. Her taphonomic study of the habitats with which the remains of various forms of early hominid were associated parallels and complements the longstanding interests of archaeologists in site location. The studies which she has begun deserve to be extended, together with intensified archaeological research into man–land relations.

Several of the study areas in East Africa yield artefacts and fossils of two or three contemporaneous hominid taxa, and the question arises: which of these were the toolmakers? At the present time, archaeology does not contribute a direct answer to this query. One would presume that hominids on the line of descent leading to modern man did make tools, but whether or not any of the others did remains a matter for surmise (M. D. Leakey, 1971).

Building integrated models of hominid evolution

During the past decade archaeology has been convulsed by massive injections of concern with theory. The sluggish pragmatism of previous archaeological convention has been quickened by consideration of the hidden mechanics of interpretation, and enhanced by interest in explicit propositions concerning the processes of change. However, it should also be pointed out that our science, like many others, involves a restless alternation between exploration and investigation. Initial research commonly represents groping in the unknown with only a very vaguely defined theoretical position as a starting point. Subsequent work can, and should, deal with the formulation and testing of much more precise propositions. Field studies of the record of human evolution illustrate this very clearly. Darwin's enunciation of the general theory created incentives to the search for fossil and archaeological traces of proto-men, but at the outset it was not clear either where specimens would be found or what they would look like. Now one hundred years later, a widely scattered array of evidence can support an inductively derived scenario that in turn permits deductive hypotheses to be specified. These are then available for incorporation into the design of fresh research.

For the archaeology of very early man, the publication of Mary Leakey's monograph in 1971 represented just such a turning point. Here is a body of data that demonstrates for the first time the kinds of models that archaeologists can generate.

Following Washburn (1965), I have argued elsewhere (Isaac, 1969, 1972a, e [this volume, chs. 1, 2]) that the first step in organizing archaeological inquiry into the emergence of human behaviour patterns is to look at the contrast between the behaviour of humans, preferably non-agricultural humans, and that of our closest living relatives, for instance the chimpanzees. At the risk of gross over-simplification a list can be set out along the lines indicated below, which is not intended to be exhaustive. Men differ from chimpanzees in showing much more intensive involvement in the following modes of behaviour:

-   speech communication
*   manufacture and use of tools, equipment, and structures
+   food sharing and collective responsibility for subsistence
*   propensity to consume animal protein (importance of hunting and fishing)
-   division of labour among age, sex and other classes
*   organization of varied daily movements around a temporarily fixed location (home base or campsite)
-   existence of family units consisting of pair-bonded male(s)/female(s) plus children
*   involvement in symbols, ornament and art
+   observance of detailed rule systems and codes that regulate the mode of execution of almost all individual and social functions

Recent intensification of fieldwork on chimpanzees has shown that few, if any, of these are absolute distinctions, and this is interesting since the incipient behaviours may also have been present in the last common ancestor. However, most of them involve changes in scale that are so great that the contrasts can for ordinary purposes be treated as qualitative differences.

Behaviours on the list that leave clear-cut archaeological traces are identified with an asterisk, those that can be reasonably securely inferred, albeit indirectly, are marked with a plus sign, the others which are not yet definitely detectable in the Pleistocene are marked with a dash.

Now the question that evolutionary biologists can fairly ask is, in what order and with what dynamic interrelationships have these differences between the human and the chimp phyletic lines arisen? The study of the fossil record suggests that changes in the masticatory apparatus and in body posture and locomotor mechanics probably occurred first, being followed by progressive enlargement of the brain, plus other minor adjustments. This invites speculation on the behavioural concomitants of the changes, but palaeontology cannot document them and it is archaeology that takes over the inquiries.

Figure 3.4 suggests the main features of a model that should be of considerable interest to physical anthropologists, although it is based on archaeological data. The model is derived from the kinds of evidence outlined earlier in the essay. Its essential features have been presented and discussed in greater detail in other more technical papers (Isaac, 1969, 1972a, e [this volume, chs. 1, 2]. I make no pretence that the suggestions incorporated are being made for the first time; many aspects of what is envisaged are widely shared among numerous accounts of human evolution such as, for example, Campbell (1974), Pilbeam (1972), and Washburn and Moore (1974). However, I have included the figure here because it makes the role of archaeology more explicit than usual.

The model entails the concept that the present condition of mankind incorporates two tiers of evolutionary change: the first consists of an adaptive complex with the

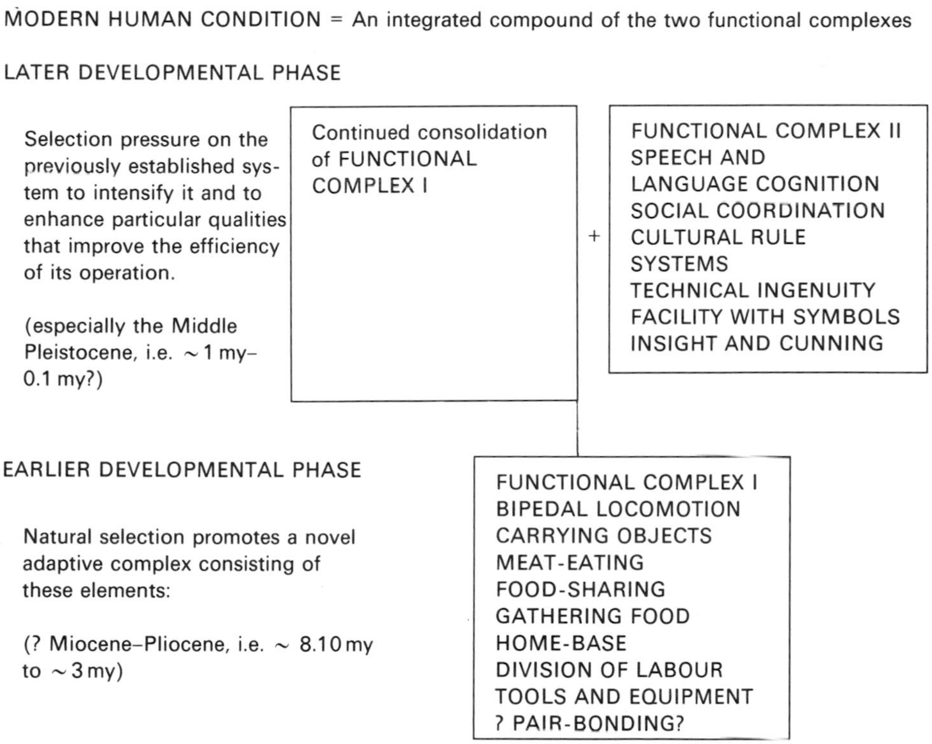

MODERN HUMAN CONDITION = An integrated compound of the two functional complexes

LATER DEVELOPMENTAL PHASE

| Selection pressure on the previously established system to intensify it and to enhance particular qualities that improve the efficiency of its operation.

(especially the Middle Pleistocene, i.e. ~ 1 my– 0.1 my?) | Continued consolidation of FUNCTIONAL COMPLEX I | + | FUNCTIONAL COMPLEX II
SPEECH AND LANGUAGE COGNITION
SOCIAL COORDINATION
CULTURAL RULE SYSTEMS
TECHNICAL INGENUITY
FACILITY WITH SYMBOLS
INSIGHT AND CUNNING |

EARLIER DEVELOPMENTAL PHASE

| Natural selection promotes a novel adaptive complex consisting of these elements:

(? Miocene–Pliocene, i.e. ~ 8.10 my to ~ 3 my) | FUNCTIONAL COMPLEX I
BIPEDAL LOCOMOTION
CARRYING OBJECTS
MEAT-EATING
FOOD-SHARING
GATHERING FOOD
HOME-BASE
DIVISION OF LABOUR
TOOLS AND EQUIPMENT
? PAIR-BONDING? |

Fig. 3.4. Diagrammatic representation of a two-tier model for the evolution of human behaviour. Of course the process was continuous and the evidence discussed in this essay probably derives largely from the transition between the two phases shown.

following set of mutually reinforcing ingredients – bipedalism, the carrying of food and implements, varied toolmaking and using, hunting, food collecting, food sharing, division of labour, organization of movements around a home base. The value of each of these behaviours is greatly enhanced when combined with the others, and it seems very probable to me that they arose in human evolution not one by one, but as a coherent set that was intensified collectively by natural selection. It is possible to deduce that a successful hominoid animal could be adapted by means of this kind of functional complex without the behavioural system being a human system as we know it (Lancaster, 1968). I offer as a working hypothesis the suggestion that in the archaeological record of 2.5 to 1 million years ago we are seeing traces of a non-human adaptive system that nonetheless incorporated the evolutionary foundations of humanness. To make this more explicit, let us imagine we could be transported back to observe the behaviour of the toolmaking hominids at KBS or at Olduvai in Bed I times. I suggest that we would first of all be impressed with the non-human qualities of what we saw. Speech might well have been lacking or so rudimentary as to be unfamiliar to us as such. Social coordination may have been weak, and a lack of emotional restraint and the like may well have been at levels far below expectation for humans. Yet, of course, the archaeological record tells us plainly that if we watched for a while we would see behaviours that nowadays are found only as a significant combination in mankind: varied toolmaking, meateating, food collecting and food sharing, and so on. Indeed, these behaviours may have been established at an intensity equivalent to the hunter-gatherers of ethnography. Now, while we can surmise that a system incorporating this functional complex could operate without language as we now know it, we can deduce that its operation would be greatly facilitated by cooperation and by exchange of information on the deployment of group members and on the location of resources. Here, the language of bees springs to mind as a distant parallel. The model set out in Fig. 3.4 envisages that, as the first functional complex became established and intensified, so selection pressure would come to bear on communication systems among the early hominids, and on their insight, cunning and capabilities for social coordination. So language systems and capabilities with symbols would be developed. With mounting complexity of these qualities, cultural codes of all kinds could and would become more elaborate. There are archaeological signs that modern capabilities in these regards were not achieved until less than 50 thousand years ago – but that raises questions far beyond the scope of this essay (Clark, 1970; Bordes, 1971).

In the study of human evolution, the distinctions between archaeology, human palaeontology and evolutionary biology are steadily breaking down. If this essay has helped to illustrate the way in which these once separate pursuits have become intermeshed, then it will have served its purpose well.

Acknowledgements

The specifics of research used in illustrations derive from the team efforts of the East Rudolf Research Project which is coordinated by Richard Leakey. Financial support comes from the National Science Foundation, the National Geographic Society, and several other sources in the USA and Britain. We work with the support and encouragement of the Museum's Trustees and the Government of Kenya.

I work jointly with my wife, Barbara, who has argued out many of the ideas with me, edited the scripts, and drawn the pictures and diagrams.

Note

[1] This essay represents an expanded and modified version of a lecture with the slides given at the 1975 Annual Meeting of the American Association of Physical Anthropologists in Denver.

4

Aspects of human evolution

Understanding the literature on human evolution calls for the recognition of special problems that confront scientists who report on this topic. Regardless of how the scientists present them, accounts of human origins are read as replacement materials for genesis. They fulfil needs that are reflected in the fact that all societies have in their culture some form of origin beliefs, that is, some narrative or configurational notion of how the world and humanity began. Usually, these beliefs do more than cope with curiosity, they have allegorical content, and they convey values, ethics and attitudes. The Adam and Eve creation story of the Bible is simply one of a wide variety of such poetic formulations.

We are conscious of a great change in all this, starting in the eighteenth and nineteenth centuries. The scientific movement which culminated in Darwin's compelling formulation of evolution as a mode of origin seemed to sweep away earlier beliefs and relegate them to the realm of myth and legend. Following on from this, it is often supposed that the myths have been replaced by something quite different, which we call 'science'. However, this is only partly true; scientific theories and information about human origins have been slotted into the same old places in our minds and our cultures that used to be occupied by the myths. The information component has then inevitably been expanded to fill the same needs. Our new origin beliefs are in fact surrogate myths, that are themselves part science, part myths.

It is also true that the study of human evolution is a meeting ground of science and humanism. We can and should seek to be rigorous in our testing of propositions and hypotheses so that we achieve an expanding corpus of secure information and orderly knowledge – but as I have already indicated, the meaning that people attach to these findings will surely be affected in subtle and complex ways by variations in individual experience of humanity and by the ethos of the times. Just as historians expect to have to rewrite continuously the comprehension of history, so will consumers of human evolution evidence want to re-evaluate the meaning of their 'facts'.

Clear examples of myth-making extensions of scientific information include the embellishment of the man-the-hunter theme. Archaeology does provide strong indications of early hominid involvement in the acquisition and consumption of meat from large animals. However, romantic and symbolic meanings that go far beyond the empirical information have commonly been attached to the evidence. In fact, themes that are common in folklore, mythology and the scriptures are unconsciously attached to the archaeological findings (cf. Morgan, 1972; Perper and Schrire, 1977). Similarly, in recent years, in order to redress the imbalances of years of unconscious male bias in versions of the story of human evolution, women writers have set forth female-gathering hypotheses as rivals. Various of these are perfectly plausible and deserve to be tested, but meanwhile they clearly have the same social function as legitimizing myths. Further evidence of the emotional charge that attaches to the form and content of interpretations of human evolution can be seen in the reception given to sociobiology. People clearly do want to be free to choose their evolutionary origin stories. Bear this in mind as you read this and other accounts of human evolution.

As a starting point, I am going to take a question: what has science learned about human evolution that was not known to Charles Darwin when in 1871 he wrote *The Descent of Man?* I shall then go on to look briefly at some points of current debate, and at lines of inquiry that are now getting under way.

In 1871 the Neanderthal and Gibraltar skulls were the only significant human fossils known. In his 1863 essay, *Man's Place in Nature*, Huxley had already shown that the Neanderthal form was effectively a variant of the human type rather than an evolutionary link, so that Darwin's concept of human evolution was of necessity 'fossil free' (cf. Pilbeam, 1980). Darwin based his ideas on comparative anatomy plus what little was known of the natural history of apes, plus a general knowledge of human behaviour patterns (augmented by his own ethnographic observations during the voyage of the Beagle). Darwin's notions were configurational rather than fully narrative (Fig. 4.1). He envisaged a series of interconnected ingredients which promoted or had been promoted by natural selection to produce humanity. The key elements were non-arboreal habitat plus upright bipedal stance with the hands free. Darwin perceived this condition to be helpless and defenceless, and he envisaged two concurrent lines of evolutionary solution – the use of the hands to make and wield tools and weapons plus the development of 'social qualities which lead him to give and receive aid from his fellow men'. To this mix was added 'the natural selection arising from the competition of tribe with tribe . . . together with the inherited effects of habit . . . which . . . would under favourable conditions have sufficed to raise man to his present high position in the organic scale'. Darwin wrote: 'The small strength and speed of man, his want of natural weapons are more than counterbalanced . . . by his intellectual powers, through which he has formed for himself weapons, tools etc.' One can thus read Darwin's writing as arguing both that the brain led the way in evolutionary change and also that it followed. For this reason the elements are best viewed as a configuration rather than a narrative. However, there is one storyline, namely that the process began with leaving the trees and adopting an upright stance.

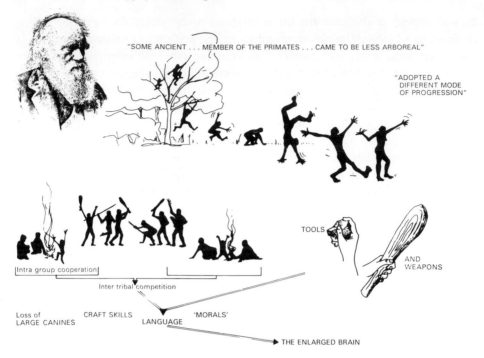

Fig. 4.1. Darwin's concept of human evolution involved an initial event, 'leaving the trees', followed by the adoption of a bipedal stance with hands free. Natural selection then acted on a system of adaptation that involved tools, weapons, social cooperation and tribal warfare . . . finally delivering an animal with an enlarged brain and a strong moral sense.

So, in *The Descent of Man*, there is a first approximation that brought a whole series of potentially important topics and issues up for consideration: habitat shifts, bipedalism, tool use and social systems involving reciprocal altruism . . . to say nothing of group selection. As I shall show, with the exception of group selection these elements are still part of discourse; they contend for pride of place in explanation, they are all subjects of active investigation and we have by no means yet succeeded in evaluating their interaction, or their relative importance. It might well be asked, what in that case is new? In reply one can best respond that since Darwin there have been surges of growth in several major fields of inquiry that relate closely to understanding human evolution:

1. Recovery of fossil hominoids and hominids.
2. Excavation of archaeological evidence covering two or three million years of co-evolution of brain and culture.
3. Field studies of primate behaviour and ecology.
4. Analytic studies of the ecology and social systems of human hunter-gatherers.
5. Effective inquiry into climatic and environmental changes over the past several million years.
6. Biochemical measurement of degrees of relatedness.
7. The growth of explicit theory concerning evolutionary ecology and concerning relations between social systems, ecology and population genetics.

Several of these lines have developed only in the last 10 to 20 years and their eventual implications for our understanding of human evolution have not yet been fully worked out.

My own research is on archaeological evidence for early stages in the differentiation of human-like behaviour patterns, and because a short review cannot be comprehensive I am going to focus on the study of the past, rather than on the implications of neontological studies.

Biochemical evidence

The rise of biochemistry and molecular biology has led to the development of rigorous, quantitative information on degrees of relationship (Fig. 4.2). This in turn

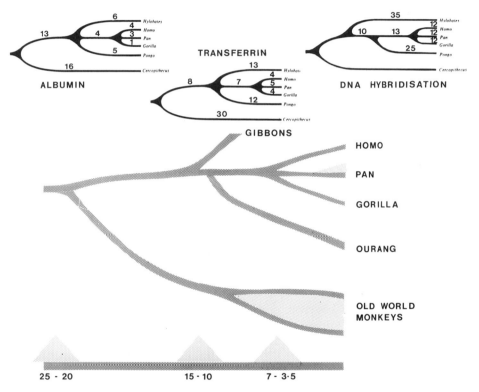

Fig. 4.2. Biochemical evidence concerning degrees of relatedness among the apes and Old World monkeys. Along the top are examples of a series of molecule types for which comparative matrices have been determined. From these matrices trees can be drawn showing branching sequence and quantitative estimates of differences attributed to each internode. Taken together, these and other biochemical determinations provide unambiguous evidence of the branching sequence shown below. Given strong evidence of stochastic consistency in the rates of cumulative change, estimates of divergence times can be offered. The time scale is a 'rubber ruler', which can be proportionately stretched or shrunk, but if this portion of the overall vertebrate phylogenetic tree were to be stretched beyond the limits shown, one would have great difficulty accommodating the estimates for divergence times in the rest of the Mammalia and Vertebrata. (Based on Sarich and Cronin. 1976; see also Wilson, Carlson and White. 1977 for a review and Bendall, 1983 for new confirmatory evidence.)

calls both for revisions to the family tree and for some careful thinking about interpretations of the fragmentary fossil record. There has been heated debate over both these issues, but, rearguard actions apart, the battle now appears to be over, in favour of the biochemistry.

Fig. 4.2 summarizes the evidence that the human lineage diverged from a common ancestor with African apes no more than four to six or seven million years ago. Chimpanzees and gorillas emerge as sibling species with humans.

If rather than molecules, the physiology and behaviour of humans is compared with that of their close living relatives, then particularly important contrasts can be seen in three, or maybe four, systems:

1. *The locomotor system* with modifications especially of the foot, pelvic complex, the back and the hands.
2. *The socio-reproductive system*, with human females losing conspicuous oestrus and concealing ovulation, and with the males investing in the feeding of offspring and mates.
3. *The brain–speech–technology–culture system*, involving an enlarged modified brain, prolonged infancy with an extended learning period, during which young humans must assimilate language, the making and using of tools and complex bodies of customs, rules and information.
4. *The food choice–masticatory and digestive system*. Modern humans tend to eat a rather different diet from apes with strong biases towards including more animal tissue and more starch. Relative to apes, humans have small front teeth and thick-enamelled back teeth. This was even more pronounced at an early stage in hominoid divergence.

Accepting these contrasts, students of human evolution are then confronted by a number of questions. What was the common ancestral condition? When did each of these systems start to become modified? Under what circumstances did change occur? What have been the selection patterns favouring these trends of change? We are thus facing a challenge first to determine the sequence of changes, which I shall term the narrative and second to inquire into the mechanisms, which can be called the dynamics. It is the first of these that has commanded most explicit attention during the century since Darwin, and indeed this is often treated as being synonymous with the study of human evolution. However, in recent years, curiosity about mechanisms has become steadily more conspicuous and in the last part of this chapter I shall argue that it is here that some of the most exciting growing points in research are to be discerned.

Narrative

For the past 100 years, most of the specific effort devoted to this branch of science has been in pursuit of missing chapters in the story. I will attempt, with the aid of diagrams, to provide a simplified summary of the sequence of changes as they are now known. However, before doing so, it is fun to be able to draw attention to a recent analysis of what goes on when scientists deal with origins.

Misia Landau (1981) has done a careful analysis of a series of accounts of human evolution starting with Darwin's own writings. She points out two main things: (1)

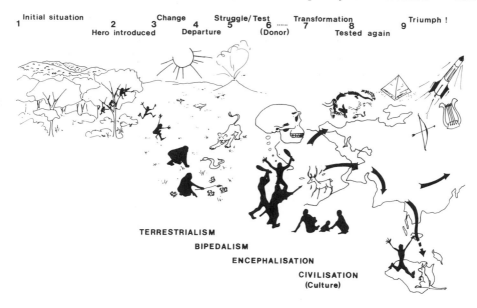

Fig. 4.3. Accounts of human origins are almost invariably cast as narratives that follow the format of hero tales in folklore (Landau, 1981). Here one common version is shown involving leaving the forest, struggling in the harsh savannah, being granted aid by a donor (natural selection), which promotes solutions in the form of brain enlargement, tools, hunting and social living. Final triumph takes the form of a spread across the globe and the development of art and civilization.

the same elements tend to recur in the accounts though they may be arranged in different order. These elements or episodes are 'terrestriality' (coming to the ground), 'bipedalism', 'encephalization' (brain and intellect enlargement), 'civilization' (technology, custom, tradition, social morals, etc.): (2) although the specifics and the order may vary, the accounts tend to a common structure, which under scrutiny emerges as the structure of folklore hero tales (cf. Propp, 1968). One version of this analysis is playfully suggested in Fig. 4.3. Misia Landau has called the literary genre of the narratives the 'anthropogenic'.

When I first read Landau's work, I became worried. Was there any way to present a sequential account that did not involve the hero-story structure? If not, did that disqualify study of the narrative of human evolution from being science?

I have got used to the idea now – and would counter-argue that provided the fit between the stories and empirical evidence is improvable through testing and falsification, then this is indeed science. (If any of the rest of the scientific community is inclined to snigger at the embarrassment of palaeoanthropologists over all this, pause and reflect. I bet that the same basic findings would apply to accounts of the origin of mammals, or of flowering plants, or of life . . . or even the big bang and the cosmos.)

One of the major developments since the time of Darwin has been the recovery of substantial numbers of hominoid and hominid fossils from all over the Old World. Our grasp of several phases of human evolution need no longer be fossil-free.

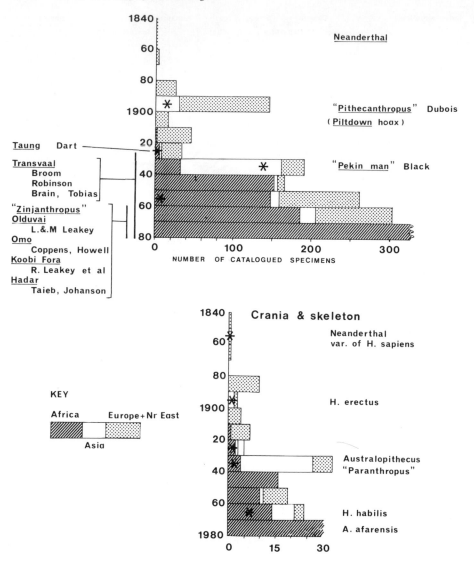

Fig. 4.4. The romance of discovery expressed as a histogram. Bars represent numbers of specimens recovered in each continent in each decade since 1840 (based on Oakley *et al.*, 1971–7). The upper frame shows all specimens, the lower shows only crania, maxillae, mandibles and ± whole skeletons. Major discoveries are indicated by place and person. The sequence is shown in which the various taxa were recovered. In general, the most human-like taxa were found first and this has affected interpretation (see Reader, 1980). Records for 1970–80 are incomplete.

Figure 4.4 provides histograms that give some idea of the distribution of finds shown in relation to sequence of discovery and to time and geography. This summary chart deals with the romance of exploration and discovery as far as I intend to take it in this review. The legitimate excitement which scientists and lay folk alike feel over the finding of missing links is thoroughly familiar from news-

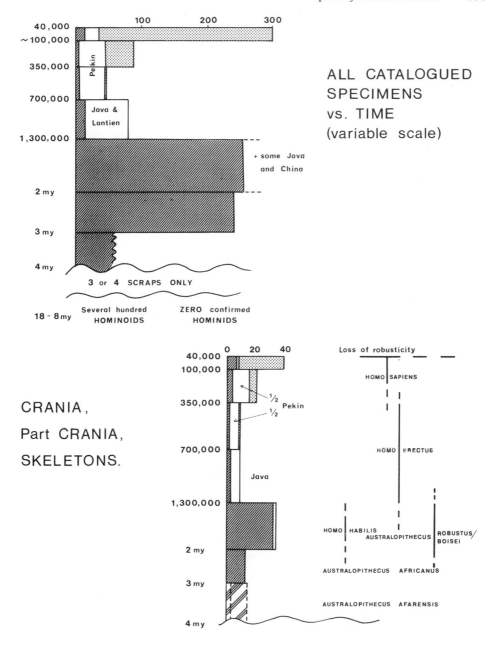

Fig. 4.5. As for Fig. 4.4 but with specimen numbers shown relative to variable divisions of a chronometric time scale. The time ranges of taxa in common usage are also shown (bottom right). Note: Before about 1–2 mya all material comes from Africa, while Europe dominates the Upper Pleistocene record because of the large number of caves which have been excavated there. These are mainly 'Neanderthal' fossils.

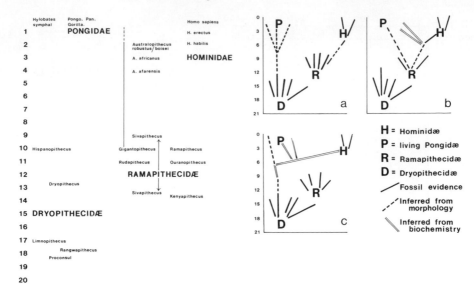

Fig. 4.6. Left: Described genera of fossil and living hominoids shown against a time scale with family groupings indicated (based on Pilbeam, 1980, with modifications). Right: Three alternative phylogenetic schemes of which (a) is incompatible with the biochemical evidence. The hominid species are widely but not universally accepted (see Tobias, 1980, White *et al.*, 1981; Leakey, 1981). Note: from biochemistry the living Pongidae emerge as a polyphyletic group.

papers and magazines – as is the existence of still another involvement of palaeoanthropology with hero mythologies. (As an aside, it is also apparent from this popular literature that bits of old hominid bone arouse excitement quite beyond their information content. Our field has unwittingly got mixed up in latter-day sacred-ancestor fetishism!)

Figure 4.5 shows that for the last 4 million years a useful if still somewhat patchy fossil record of members of the family Hominidae has been recovered. We need more, but what we have is a handy start. A similar useful but patchy series of hominoid fossils has been recovered from the time range from about 18 to 8 million years ago. In spite of loudly enunciated early claims to the contrary, a concensus is now emerging that none of these earlier hominoids can be classified as members of the family Hominidae.

Between the Miocene and the Pliocene to Pleistocene fossil samples there is a 4 to 5 million-year gap, a period for which we have as yet virtually no hominoid fossils of any kind. This is the period during which the biochemical evidence would indicate that hominids, chimps and gorillas separated. Although we know more than Darwin did about the range of skeletal organization patterns that existed before divergence, our interpretation of the divergence itself is still obliged to be fossil free.

Perhaps 95 per cent of the hominoid palaeontology literature deals directly or indirectly with taxonomy and naming. This is a necessary, but boring topic, and I propose to deal with it in diagrams (Fig. 4.6a,b). The genera represented here are

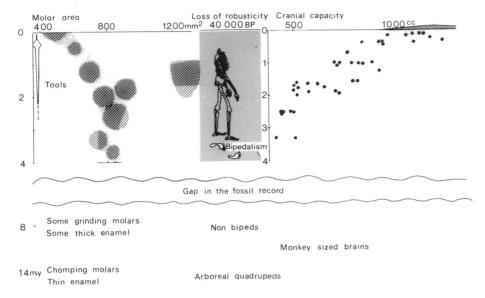

Fig. 4.7. A graphic summary of changes in anatomy of hominoid and hominid fossils shown in relation to the time scale. Left: teeth and jaws; centre: post-cranial and locomotor pattern which has been essentially unchanging over the past 4 my; right; cranial capacity. (For details and sources, see Figs 4.9, 4.10 and the text.)

clustered by Pilbeam into four families. Each of these can be thought of as a small-scale adaptive radiation. Drawing phyletic lines is much more speculative. Fig. 4.6b shows three schemes for deriving the later families (radiations) from the earlier ones. It should be noted that Scheme a. which has for a long time been confidently advocated by palaeontologists, is contradicted by the steadily strengthening corpus of biochemical evidence.

Note that while there is a four-million-year record of fossil hominidae there is no record at all for the chimp or gorilla. Pilbeam (1980) has rightly pointed out that securing such a fossil record would be a major contribution to understanding human evolution.

Fig. 4.7 presents a highly simplified summary of successive anatomical shifts that can be detected from the samples of hominid fossils which have so far been recovered. These span the time range 4 million years to the present. As I understand the record, it divides in two parts with the features of the first (4–2 mya) part being:

1. The earliest known hominids were fully bipedal (although their feet, hands and shoulders may still have been more adapted for tree-climbing than are modern human limbs and extremities). All subsequent hominids were fully bipedal (Lovejoy, 1978; McHenry and Temerin, 1979).

2. The earliest hominids had large cheek teeth with thick enamel plus relatively small anterior teeth. Canines were reduced relative to both dryopithecine apes and modern pongids, but in the very earliest sample series, *Australopithecus afarensis*, these projected further than those of subsequent hominids (Wolpoff, 1973, 1975; Johanson and White, 1979; Wood, 1981).

3. The earliest hominids had brains the size of modern pongids in bodies that were

probably a little smaller than modern ape bodies (Pilbeam and Gould, 1974; Holloway, 1981; Tobias, 1981).

4. Many workers feel that no known fossiliferous formation that dates to between 2.5 and 4 mya contains more than one sympatric species of hominid, though if this is true of the Hadar, then the early forms were as sexually dimorphic as gorillas. (For a contrary view see R. Leakey, 1981:70.)

At about 2 million years ago, the second part begins and the situation became more complex in interesting ways. Samples from all richly fossiliferous localities start to be differentiated into two (or perhaps more?) sympatric species. One of these forms shows a tendency to cheek tooth enlargement and to increase in body size (*Australopithecus robustus* in South Africa and *A. boisei* in East Africa). Others show some reduction in tooth size and a marked increase in cranial capacity (*Homo habilis*).

Between 2 and 1 million years ago in Africa, specimens of both species are often found in the same layers, but thereafter the ultra megadont form disappears from the record. The discovery of the existence of two species of hominid in the time range 2.2 to 1.2 mya is one of the exciting, original contributions of palaeontology. It could not have been predicted from any other class of evidence.

Dating from 2 million years to the present, fossil specimens have been found which are usually classified into three successive species of the genus *Homo*. If cranial capacities are plotted against time they show a tendency to increase until a levelling off occurs in the last few hundred thousand years. If cheek tooth size is

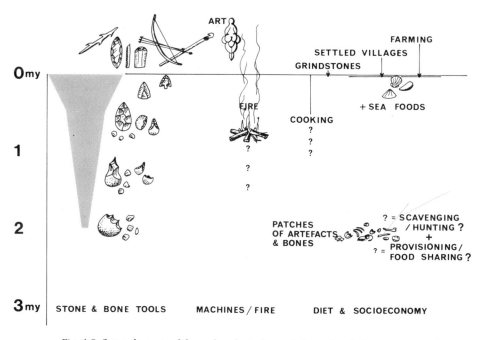

Fig. 4.8. Some elements of the archaeological record shown in relation to a time scale. Many familiar elements such as putting handles on tools, art, bows, spear throwers, villages, grindstones, etc. only appear very late in the known sequence. (See J. G. D. Clark, 1977 for a summary, and Isaac, 1972, [this volume, ch. 2] for a discussion of the tempo of change.)

plotted in the same way, it shows a decrease until in the recent past a size range equivalent to that of both dryopithecine and chimpanzee cheek teeth is reached.

A final anatomical shift occurs which is much less well known but which may be of fairly profound importance. Between about 50,000 or so and 30,000 years ago, with precise timing varying from region to region, all surviving human populations show a marked reduction in skeletal robusticity. Virtually all previous hominid fossils show a thickness of bone, plus muscular ridging that is outside the range that can be induced in modern humans even by extreme muscular training and stresses. There are also some subtle changes in skull architecture and pelvic form (Trinkaus and Howells, 1979). These are the major contrasts separating modern humans from Neanderthals, Neanderthaloids and 'archaic Homo sapiens'. The biological meaning of this loss of robusticity is as yet poorly understood (J. D. Clark, 1982).

One of the specific characteristics of the human evolutionary lineage has been the propensity to make tools – and to discard them. This has created a trail of litter that can be traced back some 2 to 2.5 million years. Archaeological study of this trail of refuse represents a major contribution to our knowledge of what has happened during the final 2 million years or so of the co-evolution of the brain and culture (Fig. 4.8).

Stone tools comprise the most widespread and persistent element of this record. The oldest known sets from sites such as Olduvai, Omo, Koobi Fora, Hadar, Melka Kunture and Swartkrans are all in East and South Africa. They are simple in terms of technology and design. Rocks were broken by conchoidal fracture so as to generate a varied set of sharp-edged forms. Experiment shows that these forms can be used effectively to cut off branches and to sharpen them as digging sticks or spears, or to cut up animal carcasses, ranging in size from gazelles to elephants. Newly developed techniques for determining use patterns from microscopically detectable polishes on the edges join other lines of evidence to show that some early examples were indeed used for cutting up carcasses, others for whittling wood and others for cutting plant tissue (Keeley and Toth, 1981; Bunn, 1981; Pott and Shipman, 1981). Thus, we begin to see that in spite of their simplicity these early artefacts had considerable importance in effecting novel adaptations. They are to be understood mainly as meat-cutting tools and as tools for making tools.

From the first appearance of stone artefacts, these occur both scattered over the landscape and in conspicuous localized concentrations which archaeologists call sites. These concentrations are often found to involve quantities of broken animal bones among the artefacts. This has led archaeologists to write into their narratives the early beginning of hunting (or at least, meat eating) and the early adoption of a socio-economic pattern involving 'camps' or 'home bases' and food sharing (e.g. M. D. Leakey, 1971; Isaac, 1978b). The validity of these interpretations is currently subject to testing and debate (Binford, 1981; Bunn *et al.*, 1980 [this volume, ch. 8]; Isaac, 1981a (see below)).

In Fig. 4.8. notice that the antiquity of control over fire is currently highly uncertain. It goes back at least half a million years, but may go back to 1.5 or 2 million years or more (Gowlett, Harris, Walton and Wood. 1981). Notice also that many material culture attributes of humans appear only in the last 1 to 5 per cent of the record. This wave of innovation occurs in the same time range as the loss of robusticity. This could be taken to mean that many of the familiar accoutrements of being human came only towards the very end of the narrative.

Hominoid fossils of the early and maybe the middle Miocene all come from some sort of tropical forest context. The late Miocene is more complex – some hominoids continued to live in forests, but others, including the ramapithecines which had somewhat hominid-like teeth, seem often to have lived in more open, varied woodland habitats (see Behrensmeyer, 1982 for review with references; and Butzer, 1976, 1977). This is interesting, but as we have seen it is quite uncertain whether or not this ramapithecine adaptive radiation is in any way ancestral to the Hominidae.

However this may be, faunal analysis and fossil pollen analyses combine to show that the earliest known fossil specimens of hominids between 4 and 2 mya all derive from strata that were laid down under non-forest conditions. The environments represented are very varied and range from open thorn-veldt grassland (Laetoli and some Transvaal layers) to complex mosaics of grassland, marsh, riverine gallery woods and lake margins (e.g. Hadar, Olduvai, Omo and Koobi Fora; see Jolly, 1978; Bishop 1978a).

This association of hominid fossils with relatively open country has commonly been taken as vindication of Darwin's narrative propositions that our early ancestors left the trees, an idea which has also become enshrined in our folk sense of human evolution. However, one of the surprising twists of discovery in recent years has been the recognition (1) that the hands, feet and shoulders of the early hominids may have been highly adapted for tree climbing (Susman and Creel, 1979; Vrba, 1979) and (2) that early archaeological sites commonly occur where groves of trees would have grown (Isaac, 1972b, 1976b). Perhaps bipedalism is yet another example of changing so as to remain the same with the new locomotor pattern being extensively used initially to move between widely spaced patches of trees. Maybe we left the forest a while ago but the trees only much more recently (cf. Romer, 1959; Rodman and McHenry, 1980).

After 2 million years ago, available evidence allows us to believe in the kind of success story we clearly love for ourselves–expanding geographic distribution, and expanding range of habitats used. Notice though, that the occupation of really extreme environments such as unbroken forests, deserts or tundra can only be documented inside the last 100,000 years.

Whether it had any influence or not, the last 2.5 million years of geologic time has witnessed global climatic oscillations of increasing amplitude. These invole the so–called ice ages. Following relatively stable, equable conditions in the Miocene and early Pliocene, there have been some 16 or 17 ice ages since the emergence of the genus *Homo* 2 million years ago (cf. Butzer, 1976; Shackleton, 1982).

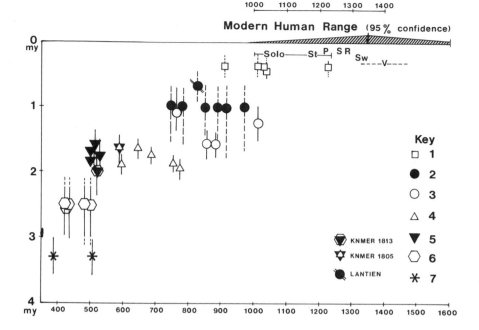

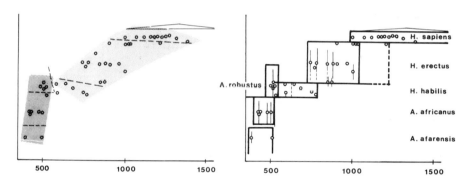

Fig. 4.9. (a) Endocranial volumes of hominid fossil skulls plotted against a time scale. The degree of uncertainty about age is indicated by the vertical bars. 7 = *Australopithecus afarensis* from Hadar; 6 = *A. africanus*; 5 = *A. robustus* and *A. boisei*; 4 = *Homo habilis*; 3 = *H. erectus* (E. Africa); 2 = *H. erectus* (Java and Lantien); 1 = *H. erectus* (Pekin). Early *H. sapiens* (the range for skulls): P = Petralona, St = Steinheim, S = Saldanha, R = Kabwe (Rhodesia man), Sw = Swanscomb, V = Vértesszöllös. (b) The same data (left) fitted to a phyletic gradualist model and (right) to a punctuated model. The species indicated at the right apply to both versions. (*Sources*: Holloway, 1981; Day, 1977; Howell, 1978a; Tobias, 1981; Cronin *et al.*, 1981.) For discussion of relation to body size see Pilbeam and Gould, 1974.

Dynamics

Thus it can be seen that over the past decade the outlines of a 4-million-year narrative of human evolution has emerged, and curiosity has begun to switch over to questions about the evolutionary mechanisms involved. Here, I can only touch hastily on aspects of a few selected topics.

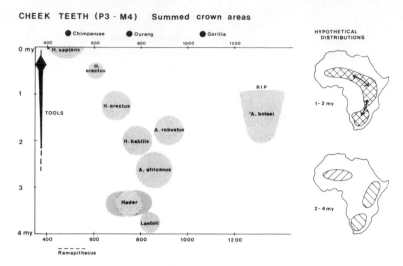

CHEEK TEETH (P3 - M4)   Summed crown areas

Fig. 4.10. The size (total area in mm^2) of mandibular cheek teeth plotted against a time scale with means for each taxon/sample shown schematically as a stippled zone. Mean values for the closest living relatives of man and for *Ramapithecus* are shown for comparison. If one bears in mind that hominids between 2 and 4 mya were smaller than *H. sapiens* and no bigger than chimpanzees, then it is apparent that they had proportionately large teeth (see Pilbeam and Gould, 1974). *A. boisei* was certainly not as large as a gorilla and was ultra-megadont. The maps at right suggest a scenario of allopatric speciation followed by the breakdown of isolation, range overlap and perhaps character displacement. Some authorities (e.g. Leakey, 1981) would split the Hadar sample between two taxa, others (Johanson and White, 1979) regard it as one highly dimorphic taxon. (*Sources*: Wolpoff, 1975; Tobias, 1981; White, Johanson and Coppens, 1982.)

One such is the question as to whether human evolution over the past several million years has proceeded by a process of cumulative genetic changes that pervaded populations over wide areas so that all went through evolutionary transformation, or whether successive species of hominids all exhibit stasis, with widespread change being accomplished by species replacement events (Gould and Eldredge, 1977). It should be noted in advance that these alternative models do not seem to me to be entirely mutually exclusive.

Figs 4.9 and 4.10 show data for two relatively simple measurable attributes of hominid fossils plotted against time. Contrary to the view of Cronin *et al.*, (1981). Fig 4.9b suggests that both gradualist models and punctuated equilibrium models can equally well be fitted to the available data. The best case for stasis in the record is the taxon *Homo erectus*. It can be argued that the first appearance of this taxon looks like a punctuation event and the taxon lasts a million years. However, at its later end many investigators seem to be reporting mosaic patterns of transition into 'archaic *Homo sapiens*' and this would not be compatible with a clear-cut punctuation event.

Numbers of workers, myself included, have tended to think of the loss of robusticity transition of 30,000–50,000 years ago as a possible example of a punctuation/ genetic replacement event. But this view would seem to be falsified by the new mitochondrial DNA data (Ferris *et al.*, 1981; Cann *et al.*, 1982).

Fig. 4.10 also illustrates a possible example within the hominid fossil record of the effects of the breakdown of barriers which had separated trivially differentiated allopatric species. According to one interpretation two species of Australopithecus came to have overlapping ranges, and responded by undergoing niche separation and character displacement (Schaffer, 1968; Swedlund, 1974). One of the resultant species (or species complex) is *Australopithecus robustus/boisei*, which underwent selection for enlarged body size, and perhaps, following the Jarman–Bell principle, a coarsening of diet. The other became *Homo habilis* and retained moderate body size and took to higher quality foods perhaps acquired in part through the aid of tools. Maybe this is indeed a fairy story, but it is fun and it may turn out to be at least partly true.

The peculiarities of the early hominid megadont phase presumably relates to diet, but what this was continues to baffle us. Scanning electron microscope (SEM) studies of tooth wear by Alan Walker (1981) and others suggest that non-siliceous plant tissues were being consumed – presumably fruits (*sensu lato*) or seeds. But what fruits or seeds? And why such large teeth? These questions call for studies of floristic communities and the feeding opportunities they offer as well as scrutiny of fossils.

A battery of new techniques for palaeodietary studies is being developed, includ-

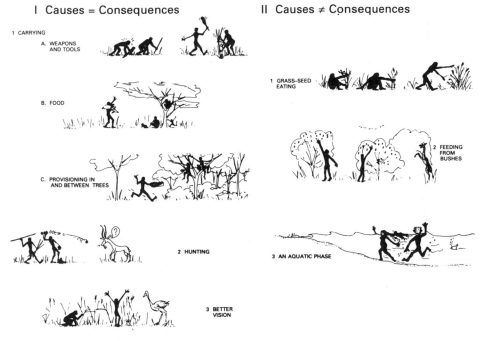

Fig. 4.11. Rival theories to account for the adoption of a bipedal gait. *References*: 1a, e.g. Darwin, 1871; Washburn and Moore, 1980; 1b, e.g. Hewes, 1961; Lancaster, 1978; 1c, e.g. Lovejoy, 1981; 2, e.g. Washburn and Lancaster, 1968; 3, various; 4, Jolly, 1970; 5, Pilbeam, 1980; 6, Hardy, 1960; Morgan, 1972, 1982. Note; Palaeoanthropologists in general judge the aquatic hypothesis to be highly improbable or impossible, but it cannot be formally eliminated yet, and it is fun to keep on the list meanwhile.

ing SEM studies and the analysis for the strontium and ^{13}C composition of old bones. A major onslaught on this fundamental problem seems to be getting underway (Walker, 1981).

As the outlines of the narrative of human evolution have emerged, two particularly intriguing puzzles have emerged with it. Under what selection pressures did, first, the two-legged gait and, secondly, the enlarged brain become adaptive? The first of these can be rephrased as: why did ancestral hominids become bipedal when all other primate species which have come to the ground have adopted some or other form of quadrupedal locomotion? Many thinkers on these topics, starting with Darwin, have tended to opt for an all-purpose explanation which might explain both bipedalism and brain enlargement, for instance, tool and weapon carrying. However, since specific evidence for the two evolutionary shifts is separated by at least 2 million years, it may be wise to uncouple the searches for explanations.

Fig. 4.11 playfully indicates some of the competing explanations which have been or are being discussed in relation to bipedalism.

More fossils, more palaeoenvironmental, and palaeodietary data will certainly help to advance understanding on this question, but it should also be clear that intelligent neontological/ecological work is called for. For instance, do potential feeding niches really exist that would make bipedalism adaptive?

The brain-culture system

We all share in some degree the conviction that our words, our intellect, our consciousness, our aesthetic and moral sense, constitute the quintessential characteristics of being human. Further we associate these qualities directly with the evolutionary enlargement and reorganization of our brains. The issue can be put like this: 'The brain is the organ of culture, and culture is the function of the brain.' The term culture refers to the intricate body of language, craft skills, social custom, traditions and information which humans learn while growing up and living in any human society. (For a good discussion of this, see Geertz, 1973.) Cultural complexity and flexibility of this kind is unknown in any other organism and would be impossible without the hypertrophied brain. It is also hard to make sense of the intricacy of the brain without supposing that the adaptive advantages that have brought it into existence have long involved culture of increasing complexity. However, to keep our topic from becoming dull and predeterministic, perhaps we should allow for the possibility that the enlarged brain, like bipedalism, might have been a pre-adaptive development that was favoured by selection for reasons other than culture. This point notwithstanding, for the time being I shall treat the brain and the culture it sustains as likely to have evolved as a single adaptive complex, that is to say as a co-evolution (see Wilson in Bendall, 1983).

We are rightly impressed with the biological success that seems to have followed from the development of the brain through some critical thresholds, but it must be remembered that enlarged brains require prolonged infant dependency and high-

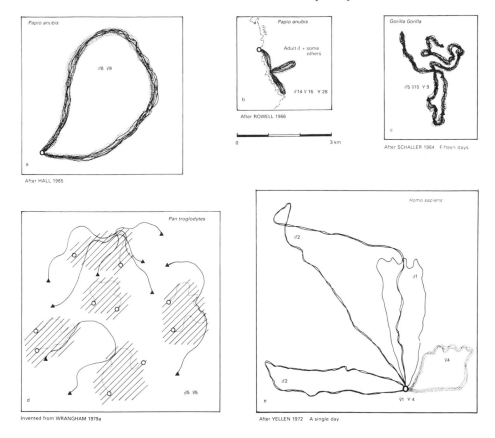

Fig. 4.12. The contrast between human ranging patterns and those of a representative sample of non-human primates (see Isaac, 1980 for sources and discussion). Note: Humans are represented by San hunter-gatherers, but the same basic pattern would be found if agriculturalists were represented, or modern city dwellers with offices and supermarkets as the endpoints of radiating movements.

quality nutrition (Sacher and Staffeldt, 1974; Martin in Lewin, 1982). Both of these are expensive commodities in the economy of nature. No other lineage has experienced selection producing such an extreme development. The central puzzle to understanding our origins, therefore, remains the problem of figuring out under what novel selective circumstances this trend was initiated, and under what conditions the selection was sustained.

Set out below is a list of some of the distinctive innovations which have been suggested and discussed as prime movers in the initiation of the trend towards elaboration of the brain-culture system:

1. The use of tools and weapons (e.g. Darwin, 1871; Washburn, 1960; Tobias, 1967, 1981).
2. Hunting (e.g. Darwin, 1871; Dart, 1925, 1953; Audrey, 1961; Washburn and Lancaster, 1968).
3. Gathering (e.g. Zihlman and Tanner, 1979; Tanner, 1981).
4. Generalized social cooperation with 'autocatalytic' feedback (e.g. Darwin, 1871; Lovejoy, 1981).

5. Adoption by small-brained hominids of a socio-reproductive system involving food sharing, provisioning and central-place foraging (e.g. Hewes, 1961; Washburn, 1965; Isaac, 1978b; Lancaster, 1978).

It should be noted that these competing explanations are not mutually exclusive, and future research will have to involve subtle assessment of their relative importance at different stages rather than simple Popperian falsification.

It should also be noted that the study of the fossil and archaeological record will not suffice by themselves to distinguish among hypotheses. It is all very well arguing that tool-use was a pivotal development that imposed novel selection pressure, but under what circumstances would tools be adaptive? As I argued in the paper *Casting the Net Wide* (Isaac, 1980), answering this kind of question calls for problem-oriented quantitative field studies of feeding possibilities and foraging strategies.

Over the past twelve years my own research has been focused first on developing and then on testing the predictions of the so-called 'food-sharing hypothesis' and its possible bearing on the initiation of selection for larger brain size. I shall briefly indulge myself by discussing aspects of this model and this work.

The first point to be made is that major changes have occurred in human ranging patterns and feeding behaviour (Fig. 4.12). These changes involve the collective acquisition of food, postponement of consumption, transport, and communal consumption at a home base or central place. These features are so basic in our lives that we take them for granted and very often they do not even appear on lists of contrasts between humans and non-human primates. However, if we could interview a chimpanzee about the behavioural differences separating us, this might well be the item that it found most impressive: 'These humans get food and instead of eating it promptly like any sensible ape, they haul it off and share it with others.'

The food-sharing hypothesis should be renamed the central-place foraging hypothesis. It incorporates tools and meat eating. It postulates that at some time before 2 million years ago, the behaviour of at least one kind of small-brained hominid was modified to include the elements shown in Fig. 4.13, namely the use of tools, the acquisition of meat, perhaps preferentially by males, the transport of portions of that meat to central places where it would be apt to be collectively consumed by members of a social group, some of whom, especially females and young, had not participated in its acquisition. At the beginning or at some subsequent stage, female gathering was surely included in the system. Conscious motivation for 'sharing' need not have been involved. The model works provided that radiative ranging patterns developed with transport of some food back to the foci of social aggregation.

For me, the interest of the model is not that 'humans' existed 2 mya, but that it promises to help explain how the non-human hominids of that time began to be modified into humans. Once food transport was initiated, novel selection pressures would come to bear on (1) ability to communicate about the past, future, and the spatially remote and (2) enhanced abilities to plan complex chains of eventualities and to play what one might call 'social chess' in one's mind. That is, the adoption

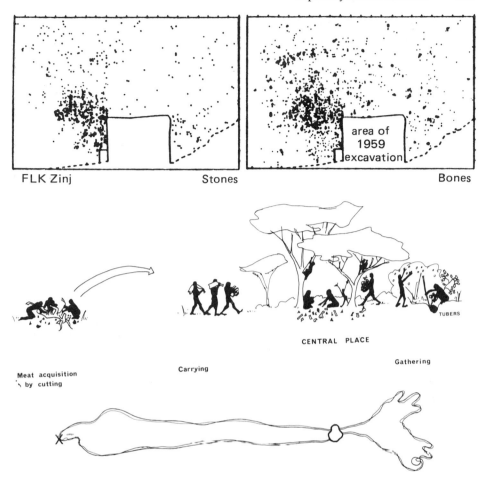

FLK Zinj   Stones   Bones

area of
1959
excavation

Meat acquisition
by cutting

Carrying

CENTRAL PLACE

Gathering

TUBERS

Fig. 4.13. (a) Two plans of an excavation which appears to be a well-preserved early central-place foraging base – the FLK Zinj site at Olduvai (based on M. D. Leakey, 1971). More than 2,400 stone artefacts and 40,000 bone fragments (right) occur within a radius of 10 m. Some 8 per cent of the identifiable bones show the marks of sharp stone tools (Bunn, 1983a) and these include damage due to dismemberment marks and to meat removal. (See also Potts, 1982, and Potts and Shipman, 1981 for detailed information and a more conservative estimate of cut-mark damage frequency.) (b) A hypothetical model of the processes involved in site formation. The transport of stones and bones (meat) is certain, the transport of plant foods is possible but unconfirmed. Whether sharing occurred at all is harder to judge – and whether it was incidental or 'deliberate' is impossible to tell.

of food-sharing would have favoured the development of language, social reciprocity and the intellect. Evolutionary strategy models should now be developed to explore the conditions under which food sharing might become an ESS (see Maynard-Smith in Bendall, 1983).

Clearly, part of the nutritional cost of brain enlargement and the costs of prolonged dependency during brain growth with extended learning would be taken care of by the provisioning/nurturing characteristics which in this scenario would already be part of the system.

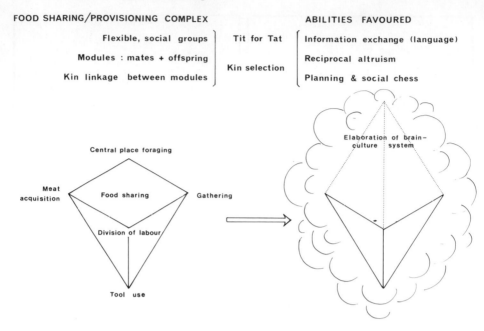

FOOD SHARING/PROVISIONING COMPLEX   ABILITIES FAVOURED

Flexible, social groups   Tit for Tat   Information exchange (language)

Modules : mates + offspring   Reciprocal altruism
                                Kin selection
Kin linkage between modules   Planning & social chess

Elaboration of brain–
culture system

Central place foraging

Meat
acquisition   Food sharing   Gathering

Division of labour

Tool use

Fig. 4.14. The 'food sharing' or 'central-place-foraging' hypothesis suggests a socio-reproductive milieu in which 'mental and emotional proclivities' could be selected that started to transform non-human hominid systems into human type systems. Communication, reciprocal help and planning ahead would all be favoured (left). Novel behavioural ingredients form structural members in a non-human system. These same elements now enveloped as core-components within highly elaborated, flexible, variable cultural systems (right); see text Isaac, 1978b; Maynard-Smith and E. O. Wilson in Bendall, 1983 for discussion of the issues and of the modes of selection that are indicated.

The model arose as a *post hoc* explanation of the existence of concentrated patches of discarded artefacts and of broken-up bones in layers between 1.5 and 2 mya. Having set it up, we have turned around and have been enjoying the sport of trying to knock it down, with the help of fierce critics (e.g. Binford, 1981).

The technicalities of this debate and this research go beyond the scope of this review (see Isaac, 1981a [this volume, ch. 12], 1983a; Bunn *et al.*, 1980 [this volume, ch. 8]; Bunn, 1981; Potts and Shipman, 1981). Suffice it to say that, in my view, we have obtained ample confirmation that hominids were indeed acquiring meat through the use of tools and were transporting this to favoured localities where the observed concentrated patches of bones and tools formed. Whether these places were 'home bases' or whether provisioning and/or active food sharing were going on is harder to judge. My guess now is that in various ways, the behaviour system was less human than I originally envisaged, but that it did involve food transport and *de facto*, if not purposive, food sharing and provisioning.

The food-sharing model has been widely misunderstood as implying that by 2 million years ago there existed friendly, cuddly, cooperative human-like hominids. This need not be so. The attractiveness of this model is that it seems entirely feasible for such a behavioural system to come into existence among non-human hominids that had brains no larger than those of living apes, and it is my strong suspicion that if we had these hominids alive today, we would have to put them in zoos, not in academies.

Clearly, this initial configuration can very readily be plugged into models involving kin-selection, and/or tit-for-tat selection patterns that would provide plausible, if hard-to-test models of the subsequent elaboration of brain–speech–culture–society systems (Fig. 4.14). Amongst other things, the provisioning and division of labour implied by the system would make bonded male–female reproductive modules highly adaptive, if they did not already exist at the outset.

In conclusion

No two people who undertook to review this topic would have tackled it in the same way. I have chosen to stress inquiries focused on stratified evidence from the past, while other writers would equally legitimately have emphasized the contributions made by studies of biochemistry, ecological dynamics or by comparative behaviour and sociobiology.

Following the pioneer descriptive phases of primate studies, various workers have begun to search out generalizations among non-human primates concerning relationships between food choice, ranging patterns, reproductive strategies and social format (e.g. Clutton-Brock and Harvey,1977; Wrangham, 1979, 1980; Milton, 1981). The results have not yet been fully assimilated into thinking about human evolution, but already it emerges that humans have distinctive ecological relationships and social configurations that are outside the range of other primate patterns. My hunch would be that this will prove to be connected with colonization of habitats where potential foods were more patchy and more widely dispersed than normal for primates. This in turn involved altered diets which focus on two distinctive and quite different things; first on plant foods that yield large numbers of calories per item (e.g. tubers and nuts), and second, significant feeding on the meat of large animals and/or fish. Acquisition of all of these is facilitated by tool use. It is at present uncertain when and by what stages these shifts occurred. Finding out is one of the major challenges that confronts palaeoanthropology.

Relative to other primates, humans have highly distinctive social patterns. In spite of tremendous variation this almost always includes reproductive units involving direct male investment in child rearing, and comprising one male and one or more females. These units are almost invariably integrated as modules into highly variable larger-scale social entities. I can see no way of predicting the human pattern from the primate patterns without introducing some novel elements into the mix of variables. One candidate for an influential novelty may well be the significant incorporation of dietary components to which one sex rather than the other had referential access. Clearly, meat is one such commodity, though it may not be the only one.

Lovejoy (1981) has argued that monogamous pair bonding and food transport preceded meat eating and the formation of bands. However, we need to retain as the alternative hypothesis that pair bonding occurred within multi-male, multi-female social groups and was associated with division of food acquisition labour. Recent examination of relations between mating system, body size and testis size in primates does not support a multi-male social group for *Homo* (Harcourt *et al.* 1981; Martin and May, 1981). However, if early ancestral hominids already had mated pair modules within the troop this objection might not apply.

Relating studies of the present to studies of the past will require changes of emphasis. Much of the literature on the stratified record of human evolution is devoted to the taxonomy of individual fossils and to arguments about whether particular ones are on the line or not. The topic is in its own way important, but with major taxa reasonably clearly established the younger generation of scientists is becoming more and more involved in inquiring into relationships between shifts in anatomical configurations and shifts in models of adaptation. This line of research can be pursued profitably even if we do not know which particular fossils are indeed on the line and which are off it. I would go on to predict that progress with this topic will involve much less narrow focus on fossils. Hominid palaeontologists and archaeologists will need to collaborate in assessing the adaptive significance of technology, subsistence patterns and socio-economic arrangements. For this, the archaeologists will have to give up the artefact typology fixation that has been their equivalent of fossil-philia. Both archaeologists and hominid palaeontologists are also going to have to work closely with ecologists. This has started: e.g. Schaller and Lowther, 1969, Peters and O'Brien, 1981, and J. Sept and A. Vincent (personal communication).

In summary, improvements in knowledge about human evolution require the acquisition of richly diverse classes of information. This includes both stratified evidence from the past and the elucidation of the intricate features of living behavioural and ecological systems. As is normal in science, hypotheses regarding both narrative and mechanisms need to be restlessly formulated, tested and revised. However, as indicated in the introduction, and as amply illustrated in Darwin's own treatment of the topic, the meaning that each of us finds in the growing corpus of secure, tested information, nonetheless remains a humanistic abstraction.

Acknowledgements

My being in a position to undertake this review stems from an appointment in East Africa, given me in 1961 by the late Louis Leakey. Since then my wife and I have been part of a goodly company of researchers in East Africa during a period of exciting discoveries. Many of my ideas surely derive from this participation. I recognize particularly strong influence from discussions with S. L. Washburn, D. R. Pilbeam, J. D. Clark, Vince Sarich and A. C. Walker. Also from the team that has worked with Richard Leakey and me at Koobi Fora. My wife is a part of the talking, the fieldwork and the laboratory work, and she draws the figures. For this paper, Jeanne Sept has done the light-hearted sketches (Figs. 4.1, 4.3, 4.11, 4.13). Stanley Ambrose encouraged me to think about the material in Fig. 4.10 and he is preparing a paper[1] on character displacement in hominids. I wish to pay tribute to three great scientists, recently deceased, who did much to foster the study of biological and cultural co-evolution – Kenneth Oakley, François Bordes and Charles McBurney. The last-named especially was my mentor during my student days and after.

NOTE

1 'The earliest archaeological traces: proximate and ultimate causes.' Lecture at a symposium on 'Glynn Isaac's legacy: lithic, land use, dietary, and actualistic studies', Annual meeting of the American Anthropological Association, Philadelphia, 5 December 1986.

5

The archaeology of human origins: studies of the Lower Pleistocene in East Africa 1971–1981

Introduction

East Africa has become the Klondike of palaeoanthropology, with the Rift Valley sediments as the mother lòde. As a result of feverish searches the area has yielded a sequence of fossil hominid specimens that span 5 million years. Claims and counterclaims regarding their interpretations have very properly caused ripples of excitement among lay and scientific communities alike. However, while the discovery of hominid bits and pieces has commanded public attention, another research movement has been more quietly getting under way, which may ultimately have quite as much significance for our understanding of human evolution. Archaeologists have been seeking potential lines of evidence bearing on the ways of life of early hominids. Now, after an initial phase of exploration, archaeologists have begun to focus their attention on a series of key questions and propositions that relate to the narrative and the dynamics of human evolution. This review is organized as an assessment of progress being made in dealing with these key questions.

There are two great landmarks in the modern archaeology of ancient hominids in East Africa: the first was the discovery by Mary and Louis Leakey in 1959 of 'Zinjanthropus' and the excavation of a dense patch of artefacts and broken bones with which the hominid skull was associated. The second was the publication in 1971 of some very early archaeological sites in Beds I and II of Olduvai Gorge. I treat this influential and important treatise as the point of departure, and as continuing stimulus, for the research movement under discussion.

The excavations and researches of Mary Leakey (1971) and co-workers in Beds I and II at Olduvai established an empirical situation that can be summarized as follows:

1. Stone tools had begun to be made by 1.8 million years ago (mya).
2. The stone tools sometimes occur in dense localized clusters in close juxtaposition with quantities of broken-up animal bones.
3. Two instances were discovered of juxtaposition of stone tools with the partial skeletons of very large animals.

4. The earlier assemblages consist of various core-tool forms, plus simple retouched flake scrapers and numerous unretouched flakes. This is the *Oldowan industry.*

5. More highly designed tool forms of the kinds designated as *Acheulian* first appear between 1.3 and 1.6 mya.

6. After the appearance of Acheulian tool forms, the diversity of penecontemporaneous assemblages increases and two categories of assemblages are recognized by Mary Leakey:

   a. The *Developed Oldowan industry,* which involves essentially the same forms as the Oldowan, plus some changes of emphasis, such as more spheroids, more flake-based tools (scrapers, etc.), and the addition of chunky, poorly made bifaces.

   b. The *Acheulian industry,* which involves simply but deftly made handaxes and cleavers. This dichotomous situation, with some subtle changes, has since been reported to continue on up through Olduvai Beds III and IV and the Masek and Ndutu Beds, that is from > 1 mya to < 0.5 mya (M. D. Leakey 1975, 1976). It links with a dichotomy previously recognized between Acheulian and sets of assemblages variously known as *Hope Fountain, Tayacian,* or *Acheulian Type B* (current evaluation of these terms is discussed in the section below on terminology and nomenclature).

7. Fossil hominids from Olduvai document the first known appearance by 1.8 mya of crania showing conspicuous relative and absolute brain enlargement (*Homo habilis*). By 1.4 mya the distinctive *Homo erectus* morphological suite had made its appearance and had superseded the *H. habilis* morphology. Robust australopithecines (*Australopithecus boisei*) have been shown to coexist with both of the two successive *Homo* species, but to become extinct sometime between about 1.4 and 1.0 mya.

The Olduvai researches of the 1960s produced a wealth of significant and detailed information to which this bald summary does not do justice. However, in my view these are the salient 'facts' that have emerged from this classic study and that have served as the inspiration and starting point of the researches done in the next decade.

In the first round of research the empirical observations just listed were interpreted without undue introspection. They were taken by all of us involved in the field research as an indication that by 2 mya there existed proto-humans who used and made tools, who obtained and cut up substantial amounts of meat, and who carried some of their meat and bones back to particular places for collective consumption (*food sharing*). The places were termed *occupation sites, living floors,* or *home bases,* and were regarded as fossil camps. These first impressions may turn out to be essentially correct, but starting in the mid-1970s there has been a growing recognition that if we were not simply going to do prehistory by projecting the present into the past, then these interpretations needed rigorous investigation and testing. As is explained below, such testing has been an important part of the second phase of research.

In the 1970s research continued at Olduvai (Hay, 1976; Jones, 1981; M. D. Leakey 1975, 1976), but it has also been extended to include other sedimentary basins such as the Omo, Koobi Fora, Melka Kunturé, Chesowanja, Gadeb and the Afar. (Each of these is briefly discussed and references given in the Appendix at the end of the chapter.) For each of these sedimentary formations the investigators

needed to engage in exploratory work comparable to the pioneer work at Olduvai
so as to determine the local character and configuration of early archaeological
evidences. Many of the empirical features listed above were found to be repeated
also at other places, thereby seemingly confirming the widespread occurrence of the
kind of pattern reported by Mary Leakey in 1971.

However, additional attention has been increasingly focused on a series of
questions that in some ways seem to arise as inductive propositions from the
observed pattern, though a little reflection shows that they are also being projected
into archaeology deductively from outside. Archaeological research concerning the
behavioural and adaptive patterns of early stone tool making hominids joins with
more general inquiries into human evolution. For instance the significance of
archaeologists' longstanding concern to discover the antiquity of food sharing is
now sharpened by Lovejoy's (1981) suggestion that *provisioning* (of females and
young by males) was an innovation that occurred early on in the differentiation of
the hominid clade. Equally, the interest that archaeologists have in assessing the
importance or not of meat eating, scavenging and hunting in the early Pleistocene
connects with behavioural reconstructions discussed by authors such as Nancy
Tanner (1981) and others.

The scope of this review

Figures 5.1 and 5.2 indicate the distribution in time and space of the strata that
over the past decade have been the sources of evidence. It will be seen that I am
restricting this review to the time period that extends back from the Bruhnes–
Matuyama geomagnetic polarity boundary to some 2.5 mya, which is the age of
the earliest serious claim for the antiquity of artefacts and hence for the beginning
of the archaeological record. As the chart also shows, there are a few sites elsewhere
in the world that belong in the later part of this time range.

An Appendix provides a very brief commentary on the East African sites and a
list of references. Further information is given as appropriate under the topical
headings that follow.

Early sites and their contents

Archaeologists have characteristically focused their attention on particular places
where relatively large numbers of artefacts occur concentrated within a relatively
small area. These particular places, which are the entities called *sites*, are usually
found by searching along outcrops until a cluster of artefacts is encountered that
has been exposed by erosion. Excavations then uncover artefacts and associated
materials still in place within the stratified sediments. The level and position of
objects and features are recorded before the material is lifted and sent to laboratories
for study.

Some of the sites have material scattered throughout a considerable thickness of
sediment (*vertically diffuse sites*), others have the material concentrated at a

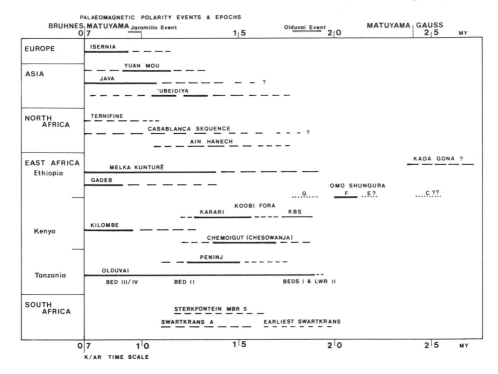

Fig. 5.1. The estimated time relations among well-dated archaeological occurrences judged to be older than 700,000 years. All sites covered in this review are shown. Selected sites in other areas are included. Reference sources for the sites in areas outside East Africa are as follows: Isernia, Coltorti *et al.* (1982); Yuan Mou, Zhou Mingzhen *et al.* (1982); Pope (1982); 'Ubeidiya, Bar Yosef (1975); Ternifine, Balout *et al.* (1967), Jaeger (1975); Sidi Abderrahman and the Casablanca Sequence, Biberson (1961), Jaeger (1975); Ain Hanech, Balout (1955), Jaeger (1975); Sterkfontein, Robinson (1962), Mason (1962a), Stiles and Partridge (1979), Vrba (1982); Swartkrans, Brain (1981, 1982), Vrba (1982).

For the East African sites, brief notes and a bibliography of sources are given in the Appendix.

sedimentary interface or within a zone of the sediments that is no more than 10–20 cm thick. Such a vertically concentrated occurrence is referred to as a *horizon*.

Most artefact concentrations so far excavated in the Lower Pleistocene sedimentary formations of East Africa appear to be patches of discarded materials with diameters between 10 and 20 m. The patches are apt to contain quantities of between 200 or 300 artefacts for the smaller, less dense ones and several thousands of artefacts for the larger and/or more dense sites. Some sites also contain animal bones and bone fragments. A very few actually contain hominid skeletal remains. More detailed information on studies of size, content and configuration are given in a subsequent section, along with references.

In recent years during the course of field surveys it has become increasingly apparent that, in addition to the concentrations, artefacts also occur scattered about in the ancient sedimentary layers as isolated items or in very small clusters.

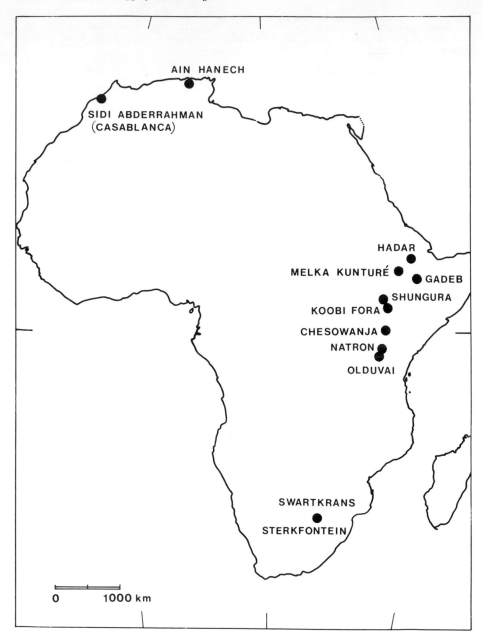

Fig. 5.2. Early sites in East Africa discussed in this chapter.

The isolated items have come to be known in the Koobi Fora project as the 'scatter between the patches' (Isaac and Harris, 1975, 1980), and the small clusters as *minisites* (Isaac *et al.*, 1981 [this volume, ch. 9]). Both are becoming subjects for active investigation and this is discussed briefly in the section below on Environments, site location and ecology.

Localized, relatively dense, vertically concentrated clusters of artefacts used to be informally classified as living sites, occupation sites, or home base sites if they contained substantial numbers of broken-up bones deriving from a variety of animal individuals and species. Other sites where artefacts were found with a bone assemblage dominated by the skeletal parts of a single large animal were termed *butchery sites*. Still others with large amounts of flaking waste are apt to be called *quarry sites* if close to stone sources, or *workshops* or *ateliers* if farther away. All these labels are convenient and doubtless in many cases are valid; however, because they do prejudge the functions of the sites, a more neutral system may be preferable for categorizing observations prior to interpretation (Isaac, 1978a [this volume, ch. 11], 1978b).

Sites of Type A are concentrations of artefacts without bone (or where bone is present at densities at or below normal background density). This configuration can arise because bones were never concentrated at the locality or because they were subsequently dispersed or were destroyed by weathering.

Sites of Type B are clusters of stone artefacts intermingled with bones representing substantial parts of the skeleton of a single large animal.

Sites of Type C are concentrations of artefacts that are interspersed among broken-up bones deriving from numbers of individual animals belonging to several species.

Since the original scheme was drawn up the existence of another significant category has been demonstrated:

Sites of Type M are concentrations of bones bearing artefact-inflicted damage, but yet lacking discarded artefacts in detected quantities. Only one such site, GaJi 5, is yet known (Bunn 1981b, 1982a), but more may well be found if searches are undertaken.

This terminology makes it possible to entertain a variety of hypotheses regarding ways in which the observed conjunctions and configurations formed, whereas it is not really feasible to engage in a discussion of whether butchery did occur at a 'butchery site' (Type B), or whether hominids really lived at a 'living site' (Type C). The neutral terminology should facilitate such discussions.

When did stone tools begin to be made?

As Fig. 5.1 shows, a number of localities have yielded archaeological assemblages that are reliably dated to between 1.5 and 1.9 mya. Of these, the Olduvai Bed I assemblages and the Koobi Fora Lower Member (KBS Tuff) assemblages are the most securely dated, with the age of the strata at both localities determined by numerous direct K/Ar measurements and by palaeomagnetic stratigraphy.[1]

Looking back to earlier time ranges the number of potential instances drops to two or three. Of these, in my opinion, only one is as yet sufficiently securely dated and documented to be treated as an established datum point. This is the group of artefact clusters that has been excavated by H. V. Merrick (1976) and J. Chavaillon

(1976) in Member F at the Omo. These consist largely of assemblages of smashed quartz, which, although not very aesthetically pleasing, are undoubtedly artefacts. They occur between two tuffs that, using new decay constants, are dated at 2.1 (Tuff F) and 1.98 (Tuff G) mya. These Omo Shungura assemblages are in my opinion the oldest confirmed artefact occurrences yet known anywhere in the world.

However, from strata that appear to be older there are several claims that deserve to be considered carefully. (1) At the Omo, from Member E, Jean Chavaillon (1970, 1971, 1976) has reported finding a chopperlike flaked and battered quartz cobble. This was collected from the surface of an outcrop of Member E at Site Omo 71. The piece was encrusted with limonite concretion like that found in the clasts encased in a thin gravel bed within the outcrop. Excavation did not yield any further stone artefacts but did yield some modified bone fragments, which may be artefactual. This stratum has an age of between 2.4 and 2.1 mya based on the K/Ar dates for Tuffs D and F (Brown and Nash, 1976).

In addition, 148 smashed artefacts have been recovered by excavation into an outcrop at Omo 84. There is no doubt about the artefactual status of these or their provenance. However, the outcrop from which they derive is within a small fault block that lacks any distinctive marker beds. J. Chavaillon and Boisaubert (1977), who excavated at the site, have suggested a correlation with Member E, which would imply an age of between 2.0 and 2.4 mya. J. de Heinzelin (in press) reports that although the outcrop was first assigned to Member C (age about 2.5 mya) one can no longer be sure of this. He also regards the Member E correlation as unconfirmed.

(2) The most recent claim for an artefact occurrence that is appreciably older than 2 million years comes from the Hadar area of Ethiopia. Hélène Roche and Jean-Jacques Tiercelin discovered four flakes and some eleven cobbles with fractures in lenses of conglomerate that crop out in the Kada Gona, which is a gully complex parallel to the better-known Kada Hadar and some 6 or 7 km south-west of it. These conglomerates are believed to be stratified within the Hadar Formation at the level of BKT II Tuff, which is dated by the fission-track method to 2.7 mya (Roche, 1980; Roche and Tiercelin, 1977).

Subsequently J. W. K. Harris found artefacts stratified in floodplain silts that outcrop at essentially the same stratigraphic level but a kilometre or so away from Hélène Roche's localities (Harris and Johanson, 1983). These findings were first of all reported informally (in *Lucy* (Johanson and Edy, 1980) and in the Research News column of *Science* (Lewin, 1981)). Seventeen artefacts were recovered from a 7–10 m^2 excavation and some 33 more from the outcrop. Three specimens are flaked cobbles (e.g. choppers) and the remainder are flakes and flake fragments. There is no doubt about the artefactual status of this assemblage.

These Kada Gona finds may well be the oldest-known stone tools with an age of between 2.5 and 2.7 mya. However, the discoveries were made just before field research in the area came to an end at the request of the new government of Ethiopia, consequently the kind of detailed follow-up study that is needed to clinch

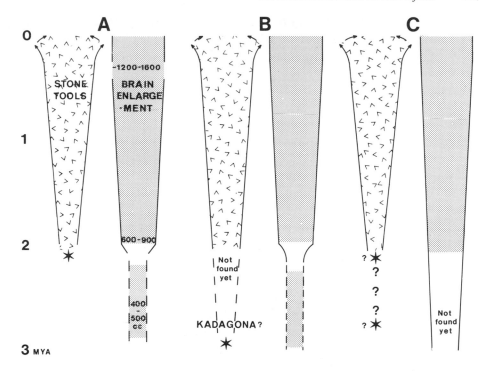

Fig. 5.3. Several possible sequential relationships between the beginnings of stone toolmaking and the start of a pronounced trend to brain enlargement. A, stone-tool invention and start of trend to brain enlargement coincide; B, stone toolmaking precedes marked brain enlargement; C, relatively large-brained hominids existed before stone-tool invention. If the Kada Gona assemblage is 2.7 my old, B or C fit best; otherwise A is the simplest, best-fit model.

the stratigraphic correlation and dating has not yet been done and reported. For the moment my own judgement is that the Kada Gona evidence for a very early start to stone tool making behaviour must be regarded as probable but not certain.

Given uncertainty over whether stone artefact making began 2.0 or 2.7 mya we will have to continue to entertain multiple alternative hypotheses regarding the placement of this innovation in human evolution. Fig. 5.3 represents three possible interpretations. We require further archaeological and hominid fossil evidences to distinguish among them.

There are other interesting uncertainties about the beginnings of stone tool making. Many early writings tacitly assume that the beginnings were gradual. This model implies that the first discovery enabled hominids to remove just a few flakes from one side of a pebble. Later it occurred to some genius that flakes could be removed from two opposite faces, still later three directions came to be involved, and so on. A moment's reflection and a little practical stone-flaking experience make clear the inherent implausibility of this kind of tacit gradualistic assumption. Awareness that stones can be fractured at will is a threshold, and as soon as one starts to do it, even in a simple-minded way, a wide range of possibilities is open. For instance, whether one likes it or not, one is going to produce two major classes of artefacts; sharp-edged stones from which flakes have been struck (cores, core tools, flaked pieces), and thin, sharp-edged flakes. As I argue in a later section, the composition of the earliest, well-reported stone-artefact assemblages does reflect just this basic pattern.

I have previously (Isaac, 1977b) contrasted the gradualistic model of stone artefact beginnings with the 'big bump' model. In Fig. 5.3, interpretation A is compatible with this latter version. It implies that the conchoidal fracturing of stone was invented about 2.0 to 2.2 mya and that by 1.5 to 2.0 mya stone artefacts were fairly common fossils in many different East African sedimentary basins (Omo, Olduvai, Koobi Fora, Chesowanja, Melka Kunturé) as well as in other parts of savannah Africa (e.g. Sterkfontein, Swartkrans, Aïn Hanech, and the Casablanca area).

In addition to questions about the date at which stone tools began to be made, questions arise as to which species of hominid were involved in making stone tools. At present all that can be said is that, with the possible exception of Kada Gona, all the early stone artefact assemblages come from a time interval that has also yielded both early fossils assigned to the genus *Homo* and fossils of robust australopithecines. There exist at least three possibilities as to the authorship of the artefacts: (1) the early forms of *Homo* made them, (2) the robust australopithecines made them, and (3) both species made them. At present I see no way of distinguishing among these possibilities, though one tends to favour the first and possibly the third. The issue is not further discussed in this review.

In writing about archaeological inferences concerning early culture and adaptations, I assume that the inferences refer to whichever of one or more species were active stone toolmakers. The relatively large-brained hominid fossils that are contemporary with the early archaeological sites of about 1.5 and 2.0 mya are generally given the label *Homo habilis*. After about 1.5 or 1.6 mya the distinctive *Homo erectus* suite of morphological traits starts to be represented and this species is assumed to have evolved out of, or to replace, *H. habilis*. This replacement–succession occurs at a point close in time to the appearance of Acheulian tool-making patterns and the events are often considered to be related, though positive evidence of this is not available. The taxon *Homo erectus* continues on well into the Middle Pleistocene, long after the period covered by this review. (For a thorough comprehensive review of the hominid fossils, their dating, and taxonomy see Howell, 1978a.)

It should be noted that the beginning of stone toolmaking was almost certainly preceded by a long phase of simple toolmaking and use involving non-fractured stone materials. It is also probably true that the discovery of stone fracture would not have become habit forming if there was not a prior need for sharp edges. For instance it is not clear to me that there is anything in the normal life of chimpanzees that would be greatly facilitated by access to sharp-edged tools. So part of solving the puzzle of the beginnings of stone toolmaking is figuring out what novel prior need they satisfied. This brings us to the question of the function of early tools. What role did they play in adaptation?

The functions of early stone tools

Until very recently our notions on the functions of early stone tools were almost entirely speculative. Information remains very incomplete but three new lines of inquiry are beginning to contribute some firm evidence. These are (1) the replication of artefact forms, followed by experimental assessment of the feasibility of performing a series of basic tasks with each artefact form; (2) microscopic study of use-wear polishes; and (3) the study of marks made by stone tools on other materials, notably bones.

Informal demonstration of the potential uses of stone artefact forms has long been a part of the repertoire of Palaeolithic archaeology. For instance, Louis Leakey provided clear demonstration that handaxes and cleavers make effective butchery tools (Leakey, 1954). J. Desmond Clark did experiments in the uses of core axes and other forms (in Howell, 1965:120–1). From these beginnings there has developed in recent years a move to engage in systematic experimentation. A series of controlled trials are made that allow the relative efficacy of the different forms for different tasks to be ranked, or, where feasible, measured. Working in association with Mary Leakey's researches at Olduvai, Peter Jones is conducting one such experimental programme (Jones, 1980), while within the Koobi Fora project Nicholas Toth has independently completed a first round of investigation (Toth, 1982, ch. 7; in press). Table 5.1 presents a simplified synopsis of Toth's preliminary results. It can be seen that plain unretouched flakes (débitage) emerge as among the most effective and versatile artefact forms in the Oldowan–Karari industry assemblages. They are of prime utility for hide slitting, dismembering, and the shaping of wood staves. The core forms 9choppers, discoids, core scrapers, etc.) can be of use for instance in hacking off branches or certain rough butchery functions, but they are less versatile. This raises the question as to whether or not the so-called core tools were actually more important as sources of flakes than as tools (cf. Chavaillon, 1976; Isaac, 1976b; M. D. Leakey, 1971:269; Toth, 1982). This will be discussed further in a section dealing with the categorization and nomenclature of artefacts.

Toth's stone experiments show that Acheulian tool forms, handaxes and cleavers also make efficient butchery tools if large animals are being cut up. In particular Toth (1982:296) has shown that the sinuous retouched edge of a hand-axe retains its meat-cutting efficacy longer than a plain flake edge. Toth has also shown that cleavers make very effective hide slitting tools and that they are the most efficient of all Lower Palaeolithic forms for chopping off branches and related woodcutting tasks. When they are used for this they acquire a characteristic damage pattern consisting of small scars scaling away from the edge (Toth, 1982:67, Fig. 5). Damage of this kind has been observed on ancient cleavers, though its significance in the absence of experiments could only be guessed at (cf. Gobert, 1950; Isaac, 1977b:88–9).

From these kinds of experiments it emerges that with a relatively simple, Oldowan-level assemblage of flakes and core choppers, a wide range of basic tasks could be accomplished; notably, skinning and butchering of animals, cutting off branches, sharpening them so as to form a point (for a spear or digging stick),

Table 5.1. *Synopsis of the feasibility of performing certain tasks with various artefact forms*[a,b]

	Severing a branch	Wood-shaping	Hide slitting	Dismembering small animal	Dismembering large animal	Meat division	Summary
Smallish flakes and flake fragments	0	2	1	1	1–2	1	Very useful for *all* cutting and whittling operations; not useful for heavy-duty wood hacking
Flake scrapers	0	1	2	2	2		The best form for wood shaping/whittling
Choppers and related forms (>300 g)	2	Var	0	0	Var		Moderately useful for hacking off branches; not very good for cutting up carcasses
Core-scrapers	2	1	0	0	Var		Hollow sectors of an edge make good spoke shaves (also true for some choppers)
Handaxes	3	Var	3	3	1		Good butchery tools for large animals. Serviceable also for branch severing and hide splitting (see also Jones, 1981)
Cleavers	1	2?	2	3	1		The best form for branch severing and excellent large-animal butchery tools (see also Jones, 1981)

[a] This is based largely on the results of Toth (1982: ch. 7, in press) and Jones (1981), together with my own more limited experimental experience. For details of experiments and of edge-angle characteristics, see Toth (1982). *Note:* this does not purport to state what was done with these forms, only what a modern experimentor finds them suited to do.

[b] 1 = tends to be the best form; 2 = serviceable but not usually optimal; 3 = possible but difficult; Var = varies with the individual piece.

scraping hide, cutting stems and fibre, and breaking open bones or nuts. As already mentioned for the cutting tasks, simple though they be, flakes are likely to have been more effective and more important than so-called choppers, discoids, or polyhedrons.

There are some functions missing; for instance none of the flaked stone artefacts can plausibly be regarded as 'weapons'. If the Lower Pleistocene tool-making hominids were hunting with equipment, they must have been using spears without stone tips (i.e. pointed staves or horns on staves), clubs, and, perhaps most important of all, thrown sticks and stones. Many assemblages include spheroids[2] and unmodified stones that would have been effective, lethal projectiles (A. B. Isaac, n.d.) [1987].

Important as these feasibility studies are, they indicate only what the early stone assemblages could and could not accomplish. Clearly what we really want to know is what was actually being done with the early tools and how often. One new technique is just beginning to yield results of that kind. As is now well known, Lawrence Keeley has shown (1980) that when flint is moved against different classes of substances, polishes develop on and adjacent to the edges. Under high-power magnification, contact with various contrasting substances produces distinguishable textures. So far this technique for identifying use is only known to be applicable to homogeneous, very fine grained or 'glassy' silicious rocks. At all the very early East African sites such rocks occur only as a minority component of the assemblages. But they do occur, and one such sample of 56 items from Koobi Fora has been examined and reported (Keeley and Toth, 1981). Of the 56, 9 showed definite traces of use wear, (in 2 or 3 more there were probable traces). Of the definite cases, 4 showed the kind of polish caused by cutting meat, 3 showed low intensity woodcutting or wood-whittling polish, and 2 showed the kind of polish induced by cutting plant tissues such as stems.

These are very interesting and important results inasmuch as they imply that already at the time when tools first appear in the geological record they were being used for a fairly broad range of functions. However, the sample is far too small to allow us to form any judgement as to the relative frequency of the various functions. Further work is in progress and eventually we may hope to have more quantitative indications. However, even with further work some limitations will remain, notably the fact that the majority of the artefacts are of materials that are not amenable to use-polish analysis (lava at Koobi Fora and Melka Kunturé; quartz at Olduvai and Omo).

Finally, there is a third new line of evidence regarding stone artefact function. This has been characterized by Diane Gifford (personal communication, 1979) as 'smoking gun' evidence. At Olduvai and Koobi Fora bones have been found that bear unmistakable marks where stone tools have sliced into or scraped against the bone when it was fresh (Bunn, 1981; Potts and Shipman, 1981). In most instances the marked bones come from concentrations of artefacts plus bone, but in other instances they come from layers in which artefacts and sites have hitherto been undetectable.

These discoveries effectively settle some long-debated aspects of the behaviour of Lower Pleistocene hominids and the role of stone tools in facilitating innovations in adaptation. It is now clear that (1) hominids were cutting up the carcasses of animals much larger than the known prey or protein food of any living non-human primate, and (2) that stone tools were integrally involved in this food-getting activity. The meat-eating aspects of these discoveries are discussed in the next section.

How important was meat in the lives of early toolmaking hominids?

The notion that in times before civilization men were mighty meat-eating hunters is deeply embedded in the folklore, sacred myths, and philosophy of West European cultures and perhaps other cultures as well (see Perper and Schrire, 1977 for an analysis of this). Presumably unconsciously moved by this underlying current of thought, hunting is a theme that has been incorporated into many accounts of human evolution starting with Darwin (1871) and going on through many subsequent writings (e.g. Ardrey, 1961; Dart, 1953; Gregory, 1922; Isaac, 1976b; Pfeiffer, 1969; Washburn and Lancaster, 1968).

The idea is that some ancestral, non-human hominoids turned to hunting as an ancillary mode of subsistence and that this pursuit in turn induced natural selection pressures favouring weapon use, tool use, cunning, foresight, cooperation and communication. Clearly the idea seems a plausible potential explanation for the evolutionary origins of many capabilities that have later become the hallmarks of mankind. However, plausible though it may be, we need to test for its validity by seeking to find out at what stage in human evolution hominids can be shown to have begun a significant involvement with hunting and/or meat eating. Inquiry into this matter has over the past decade been a major preoccupation of archaeologists studying the early period, and distinct progress has been made.

Until recently the best evidence for early hominid involvement in meat eating was the archaeological finding that early stone artefacts often occurred jumbled up with broken animal bones. The artefact concentrations were taken as marking 'occupation sites' or 'living floors', with the bones assumed to have been refuse left over after the consumption of meat and marrow. This line of interpretation is clearly set forth by Mary Leakey (1971) and previous review articles have discussed the evidence and the dietary and behavioural implications that follow if these concentrations are food-refuse accumulations (Isaac, 1971a [this volume, ch. 10]; Isaac and Crader, 1981). However, by the mid-1970s it was apparent that we needed to test the working hypothesis that bones found with concentrations of stone artefacts were necessarily hominid food refuse. As a result the mode of formation of artefact-plus-bone-concentrations became the focus of intensive inquiry. Publications and reports have begun to appear (e.g. Bunn, 1982a; Bunn *et al.*, 1980 [this volume, ch. 8]; Isaac, 1981a [this volume, ch. 12]; Potts, 1982). These show that the formation of the occupation sites involved a complex interplay of agencies and factors. I thus propose to leave open the question of bone refuse as

Table 5.2. *Incidence of cut marks on different animal taxa*

Species		Koobi Fora (c. 1.6 mya)	Olduvai Beds I and Lower II (1.85–1.7 mya)	
		Bunn (1982a)	Bunn (1982a)	Potts (1982)
Suids		X	X	
Antelopes				
Size 1	< 50 lbs (< 23 kg)		X	
Size 2	50–250 lbs (− 114 kg)		X	
Size 3	250–750 lbs (− 340 kg)	X	X	X
Size 4	> 750 lbs (> 340 kg)	X	X	
Equids		X	X	X
Giraffids		X	X	X
Hippopotamus (various species)		X		
Elephant (*Elephas recki*)		X	X	X

evidence of meat eating until the whole issue is dealt with in the next portion of this review. Meanwhile other new, unambiguous evidence needs to be considered.

In order to help settle controversial questions about early-hominid meat eating, two young research workers began searching the bone collections from early sites, looking for cut marks inflicted on the bones by stone tools. Henry Bunn worked with the Koobi Fora and with selected Olduvai collections, while Richard Potts (in collaboration with Alan Walker and Pat Shipman) worked with Mary Leakey's Olduvai collections. Independently, both made definitive findings (Bunn, 1981, 1982a; Potts, 1982; Potts and Shipman, 1981). As already indicated in the discussion of the function of stone tools, they discovered significant numbers of cut marks. Most of these were found on bones from archaeological sites, but Bunn and co-workers also found cut marks on bones deriving from scatters on the ancient landscape where direct association with stone artefacts was not detectable.

Table 5.3. *Incidence of cut marks on various body parts for Olduvai and Koobi Fora sites*

Body parts	Koobi Fora (c. 1.6 mya)	Olduvai Bed I and Lower II (1.85–1.7 mya)	
	Bunn (1982a)	Bunn (1982a)	Potts (1982)
Crania and mandibles	X	X	
Vertebrae		X	
Ribs	X	X	X
Pelvis	X	X	
Scapula	X	X	X
Humerus	X	X	X
Radius – ulna	X	X	X
Femur	X	X	
Tibia	X	X	X
Limb-shaft fragments	X	X	X
Cannon bones	X	X	X
Podials		X	
Phalanges			

Tables 5.2 and 5.3 summarize the results so far reported by Potts (1982) and Bunn (1982a). The salient points are these:

1. Cut marks[3] that have been carefully verified by SEM scrutiny, occur on specimens from both Olduvai and Koobi Fora.
2. The marks occur on a variety of taxa that vary in size from relatively small animals (e.g. gazelles) to very large animals (e.g. giraffes, hippos, and elephants).
3. Marks have been found on a wide variety of different anatomical parts (e.g. skulls, mandibles, vertebrae, humeri, femora, cannon bones and phalanges).
4. Although not indicated in the table, it has also been found that one can distinguish several possible functional modes for the cutting action that produced the marks:
   a. Slicing marks from the vicinity of joints that seem to relate to dismemberment and the detaching of segments.
   b. Slicing and scraping marks on the bone shafts and blades that seem likely to have resulted from muscle (meat) removal.
   c. Marks on portions that are devoid of meat. These probably relate to skin removal (e.g. on ungulate metapodial bones). Such marks could well result from skin removal so as to gain access to marrow.

On these salient qualitative characteristics of the cut-mark evidence Potts and Bunn are in agreement and the series of behaviours implied by these characteristics can be treated as having firm archaeological documentation. However, inspection of the table also shows that there are differences in the qualitative data reported. Most important for the bone accumulation at the Olduvai FLK *Zinjanthropus* site, Bunn reports finding that between 200 and 300 out of more than 3500 identifiable bones show definite cut marks; Potts reports finding many fewer, namely some 24 cut-, scrape-, and chop-marked bones from all the Olduvai sites together.

The technicalities of this difference remain to be resolved,[4] but meanwhile the results as they stand already have great significance. They seem to show definitely that by 1.5 to 2.0 mya some hominids were (1) using stone tools to gain access to meat and probably marrow from the carcasses of medium- to large-sized herbivores. This pattern contrasts qualitatively with the meat eating of contemporary non-human primates, such as chimpanzees and baboons, which are not known to feed on meat from prey larger than 10 to 15 kg, which they tear apart with their hands and teeth (Strum, 1981; Teleki, 1973). The hominids were also (2) removing portions of carcasses by severing joints. This means that useful parts could have been rapidly removed from even very heavy carcasses and carried away.

At Koobi Fora cut-marked bones have been found in one area (Area 103) that had yielded hominid fossils (KNM-ER-730, 1807, 1808, 1820, 1515) but in which artefacts deriving from the ancient layers have not yet been observed, despite searching. This constitutes a significant extension of the archaeological record. Henry Bunn (1982a) first searched through palaeontological collections from the area. He found a fossil pygmy-hippo femur with numerous cut marks around its proximal end and down the shaft. Subsequently, on visiting the locality from which the femur came (near KNM-ER-730), several other specimens were found, including several pieces within a cluster of bone fragments on one small outcrop (Site GaJi 5). No stone artefacts could be found. A small excavation adjacent to the surface cluster failed to reveal any more *in situ*, but the derivation of the pieces from the beds of the Koobi Fora Formation Upper Member is not in any way uncertain. The beds in question are lake margin, delta-front deposits. Further work at the locality is needed to get more information on the context and arrangement of the marked bones.

Subsequently, at Ileret Area 8, Barbara Isaac found a fossil pygmy-hippo humerus (shaft and distal). This had cut marks around the joint and along the shaft. A number of hominid fossils have been recovered from the same outcrop strip (KNM-ER-803, 806, 807, 808, 809, 733) and a few widely scattered lava flakes also occur. One small site, FwJj 1 is known at the same level a short distance away (Harris, 1978; Isaac and Harris, 1978; Isaac *et al.*, 1976).

But the areas where cut marked bones have been found outside sites are areas where stone artefacts are present at an undetectable level (Area 103) or at very low densities (Area 8). Palaeogeographic reconstruction (Findlater, 1978; Vondra and Bowen, 1976) shows that no stones of a size suitable for stone toolmaking would have been available within a radius of 10 to 15 km. The new evidence seems to imply that sharp-edged flakes were carried to such areas and used in butchery, but discarded only very sparingly. The evidence also implies that at times large portions of large animals, such as hippo legs, were detached and removed from the carcass.

I am not aware that cut-mark evidence has yet been searched for and recorded at early East African sites other than Olduvai and Koobi Fora, although artefacts in association with bones have been reported at Melka Kunturé, Chesowanja and Gadeb (see below).

In addition to the cut-mark investigations, some workers have studied bone fracture patterns in the hopes of discovering discriminants between specimens broken by deliberate hammer percussion and those broken by other processes. This has involved observations of bones chewed by carnivores, bones trampled by cattle, and experiments with hammer fracture (Bunn, 1982a; Potts, 1982; Toth, 1982). In some cases it seems possible to make distinctions, especially in cases in which conjoining pieces of the same bone can be put back together so as to reconstruct the fracture sequence. Bunn has reported on a number of longbones from Koobi Fora Site FxJj 50 and from the Olduvai 'Zinj' site that do seem to have been broken open by a series of hammer blows struck in succession along the shaft. The interpretation seems to me to be convincing, but tentative (see Bunn, 1982a; Bunn *et al.*, 1980 [this volume, ch. 8]).

The claim has been advanced that several early sites provide evidence for the butchery of very large animals by early hominids. These are the sites of Type B mentioned above, where a substantial portion of a single large animal is present and is associated with stone artefacts in such a way as to imply that the artefacts were discarded in the process of cutting up the carcass of that animal.

As far as I am aware, there are only three instances of this that have been published in sufficient detail for them to be evaluated. Two of these are at Olduvai (FLKN 6 and FLK *Deinotherium*), and one is at Koobi Fora ('HAS' or FxJj 3). Preliminary reports indicate possible instances at Melka Kunturé, but details are not yet available (Chavaillon *et al.*, 1979).

These cases were reviewed and discussed by Isaac and Crader (1981), who concluded that the butchery interpretation was plausible but not fully proven, especially in the case of the deinothere. Since that time Bunn (1982a) and Potts (1982) have done careful, independent studies of the bone from the FLKN 6 putative elephant butchery site. They both found cut marks on some of the elephant bones, which strengthens the case for carcass dismemberment activities by hominids. However, they also confirmed the existence of the bones of many other animals in the same archaeological layer, which would seem to complicate the simple butchery hypothesis. However, it should be borne in mind that the tops of the elephant bones stand at least 30–40 cm above the ground level on which they rest. There is abundant evidence of continuing artefact discard and bone accumulation at FLKN, so that these quasi-associated other bones (and some artefacts) may be accounted for by the operation of these accumulation processes during the time that it took for the elephant skeleton to get covered with sediment.

There is no new information on the FLKN deinothere site. However, Bunn has done more detailed studies of the Koobi Fora Hippo Site. The results of these studies might be taken to weaken the case for this site as a proven butchery site. Here too Bunn (1982a) has demonstrated the existence of what may be higher than background incidence of other non-hippo bones. Equally, as reported in the earlier writings, the bothersome fact remains that the well-preserved hippo bones lack cut marks and were found on the surface of the outcrop, whereas the artefact cluster occurred both among the bones and within the adjacent outcrop, along with a few very weathered hippo fragments that do not necessarily belong to the same individual. The evidence is thus circumstantial, leaving room for legitimate doubt. The site may well be a butchery locale, but the case is not proven. (See also Crader, 1983 for a discussion of modern pachyderm butchery in relation to the early sites.)

To some degree the issue at stake in the scrutiny of these cases has been rendered moot. The discovery (as reported above) of various bones from pachyderms with cut marks on them makes it absolutely certain that the early toolmakers did at times use tools to cut up the carcasses of very large animals. None of these sites or isolated bones gives any indication of whether the hominids killed any of the animals involved, or whether they scavenged their carcasses. I suspect that the latter is more probable. Nick Toth (1982) has shown that a simple quartz or basalt flake is fully capable of cutting open a pachyderm carcass. This is something that hyenas and other mammalian carnivores cannot do until decay is advanced. When hominids succeeded in being first into a pachyderm carcass they would have had access to prodigious quantities of meat. Sometimes they seem to have cut off whole limbs. As yet we have no idea how frequently these bonanzas occurred.

The findings of Bunn, Potts and Shipman allow us to eliminate models of human evolution that do not incorporate a shift to significant meat eating by at least the *Homo habilis* stage. However, cut-mark data, even when statistical problems have been resolved, do not readily allow one to assess the frequency of meat-getting behaviours. On average, did it occur once a week, once a month, once a year, or once in a lifetime? What proportions of food did meat from large carcasses comprise?

Other techniques such as bone-composition analyses will be needed if we are to get beyond mere speculation in our answers to these questions (see below).

These data also leave unsettled questions regarding the relative importance of active hunting and opportunistic scavenging as the means of access to carcasses. I return to this issue following the review of evidence from combined concentrations of artefacts and bones.

The cut marks indicate that carcass parts as large as the legs of hippopotami were being detached. However, these data do not indicate whether such parts, once severed, were transported far away from the source carcass, or, if so, to what kind of places they were carried. Possible evidence relating to these questions is taken up next.

How were dense patches of artefacts plus bones formed?

The formation of dense artefact-plus-bone patches has become the pivotal question in the archaeology of early man and an active group of researchers is at work tackling aspects of it. On the outcome there hinge crucial issues both in our knowledge of the narrative and our understanding of the dynamics of human evolution. These uncertainties give the current cycle of scientific involvement something of the atmosphere surrounding a poker table. The stakes seem high and everyone is watching each play with great attention. I report on the cards that have been turned so far, but the game is still in progress and the outcome is not yet known. Some historical background information is important for understanding the state of play.

When archaeologists began searching for evidence from Plio-Pleistocene sedimentary formations, they found that in numerous instances artefacts occurred in dense patches that also contained quantities of broken bones. This occasioned no sense of surprise. Familiarity with the structure of modern human behaviour had led us to expect this kind of configuration (Fig. 5.4).

In the first round of research these artefact-plus-bone patches were categorized without discussion as home bases, occupation sites, or living floors (J. D. Clark, 1970; Isaac, 1969, 1972b, 1976b; L. S. B. Leakey, 1963b; M. D. Leakey, 1971). These labels carried the clear implication that these sites had formed at places that were social and industrial foci in the lives of the early hominid toolmakers to which food was brought for collective consumption. This view of the sites and their anthropological meaning was then made highly explicit in papers by Isaac (1976b, 1978a [this volume, ch. 11], 1978b) in which it was argued that the early establishment of food sharing and home-base behaviours could be used in accounts of the dynamics of human evolution to help explain selection pressures leading to the later development of communication abilities (language) and of elaborate, long-range social foresight and cause–effect thinking (the intellect). As soon as these propositions had been clearly enunciated it became obvious that it was very important to have rigorous tests of the initial intuitive assumption that the artefact-plus-bone concentrations were indeed in some sense fossil home-base sites. Figure

First Interpretations...

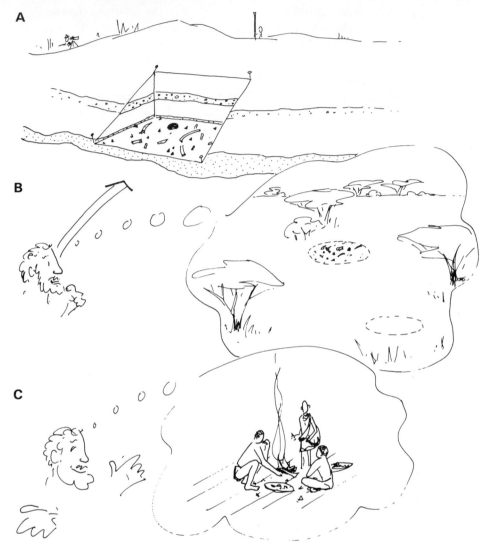

Fig. 5.4. First interpretations of sites. A, archaeologists, working in early Pleistocene sedimentary formations in East Africa, search along outcrops and excavate at places where surface indications imply a concentration of material. B, the excavation data plus the surface indications have commonly been taken to mean that a dense, localized patch of artefacts existed on what was formerly the surface of the ground. C, taking another step, it has seemed intuitively obvious that these patches are fossil campsites or home bases with many of the behaviours that characterize such places for modern humans. Some five years ago a research movement to check these assumptions began.

5.5 suggests how archaeologists had got drawn into the home-base line of interpretation. Figure 5.6 shows why it is crucial to make more tests of its validity.

In 1977 two groups of workers started taking up the challenge. Richard Potts, aided by Pat Shipman and Alan Walker, began, with Mary Leakey's encourage-

Starting with familiar home-base and food-sharing behaviours...

.... then finding Late Pleistocene cave middens

... mid-Pleistocene?

Then back to the 2-my-old patches of artefacts- -plus-bones at Olduvai and Koobi Fora

... this trail has been taken to imply continuity of basic behavioural organization back to the Plio-Pleistocene.

Fig. 5.5. Archaeologists have had a sense of following a trail of refuse back through the Pleistocene.

ment, a fresh round of research on the materials and records from the Olduvai excavations. At the same time, the Koobi Fora archaeology team tackled the problem by developing a problem-oriented set of inquiries that involved a combination of excavation, survey, natural history observation, and experimentation. Fieldwork was confined to Koobi Fora but collections from Koobi Fora and, with Mary Leakey's kind permission, Olduvai were subjected to comparative study. This group adopted a quasi-Popperian approach that actively attempts to overturn the initially favoured hypothesis (Bunn *et al.*, 1980 [this volume, ch. 8]; Isaac, 1981a [this volume, ch. 12]).

This research movement began quietly, with the aspect of a drawing-room card

Collective
feeding/sharing

Transport of
  food
Postponed
  consumption

WHEN?   HOW?

Normal primate feed-as-you-go subsistence mode.

Fig. 5.6. From an ape's-eye view it is clear that major reorganizations have occurred during the evolutionary differentiation of human ancestors.

game, but the recent entry into the stakes of a well-known player has brought the game to the attention of a much wider audience. In 1981 Lewis Binford published *Bones: Ancient Men and Modern Myths*, which effectively and dramatically challenged the home base, food-sharing line of interpretation. In due course I take up some of the important issues raised in that book (see also Bunn, 1982b; Grayson, 1982; Isaac 1983a [this volume, ch. 13]).

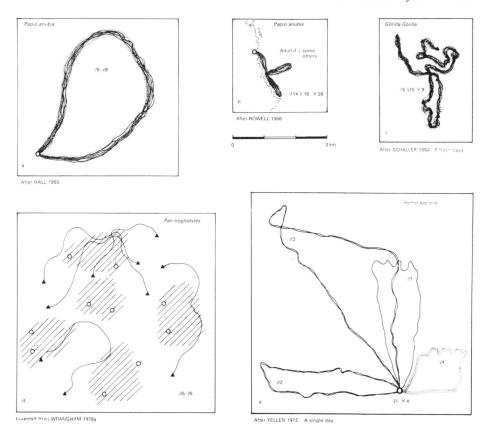

Fig. 5.7. The contrast between human ranging patterns and those of a representative sample of non-human primates.

The problem that is under scrutiny is an interesting one that involves inductive and deductive aspects. Archaeologists have found concentrations of artefacts plus bones.[5] These are empirical facts that demand explanation. Equally, comparative behaviour studies show that at some stage in human evolution human ancestors developed a distinctive ranging pattern and socio-economic system with central-place foraging as a key element (Fig. 5.7). The questions are: (1) do the Plio–Pleistocene artefact-plus-bone concentrations fit the deductive predictions of a central-place foraging model; and (2) can other, less anthropologically loaded explanations equally well account for the Plio–Pleistocene concentrations? My sense of rigour in science suggests to me that one needs to take both questions into account, but to tackle them in reverse order; that is, to start by considering the processes that govern the distribution of bones in a sedimentary formation, then also those that determine the distribution of stone artefacts. Different kinds of plausible intersections of these systems then provide potential explanations of the combined artefact-plus-bone patches. These are rival alternative hypotheses, each of which will carry different specific implications. Research can then proceed to collect the data necessary for testing. This is the kind of approach that began to be applied in the latter half of the 1970s.

As a result of the thought and inquiry pertaining to this research movement, one can offer a brief synopsis of the processes governing the distribution of bones and of artefacts considered separately.

   1. Processes affecting bones:
      a. The distribution of death.
      b. Patterns of initial carcass consumption by primary predators leading to total or partial bone destruction.
      c. The break-up and rearrangement of any residual carcass parts, with further ingestion of bones as a possibility.
      d. Transport of bones away from a carcass for consumption or use elsewhere (e.g. by birds, various carnivores, porcupines, and modern humans).
      e. Defecation or regurgitation of ingested bones.
      f. Transport and regrouping by flowing water.
      g. Destruction at different rates by chewing, digestion, weathering and so forth (with preservation by burial in some suitable sediment being the comparatively rare process that emplaces a very small fraction of the total annual bone yield in the fossil record).

Note that at the moment of death the bones of a skeleton are spatially concentrated. Most of the processes listed above tend to disperse and/or destroy bones. Only a few unusual variants of the processes produce secondary concentrations. These are (1) the existence of highly localized places where mass death or recurrent death occur, (2) recurrent transport of bones to a den or lair, (3) recurrently used defecation or regurgitation locales, (4) concentration by water transport of carcasses into drifts or of bones into gravel bars and so forth, (5) long-term cumulative build-up due to localized preservation in the midst of an otherwise destructive environment (see Behrensmeyer, 1983).

I would stress that bones are a hot commodity in the African bush, with many different organisms actively competing to feed on them if they can. As a consequence, concentrations tend to be unstable, dispersal usually wins, and even where a partial concentration does survive it is usually only as a residue that is a small fraction of the set that was originally present. (For more intensive treatment of many of these processes see Behrensmeyer and Hill (1980), Brain (1981), Shipman (1981a) and Binford (1981)).

   2. Factors affecting artefacts:
      a. The distribution of sources of flakeable stone.
      b. The distribution of needs for sharp edges.
      c. Different transport and logistic modes; for example, (i) continuous carrying in case of unpredicted needs, (ii) fetching when the need arises, (iii) transport to form stockpiles in convenient places (Potts, 1982), (iv) transport to secondary tool-manufacturing places.
      d. Discard patterns (e.g. dropping immediately after use, abandoning of flaking debris, eventual discard of a worn-out, long-term curated item).
      e. Differential destruction by weathering. This occurs but artefacts are stable over hundreds of years relative to bones, which in the tropics normally survive weathering for only 5–10 years unless buried.

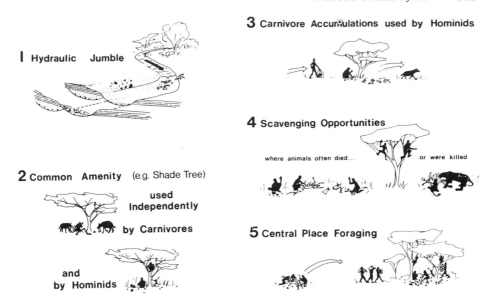

Fig. 5.8. A series of processes whereby coincident concentrations of bones and artefacts might form.

   f. Transport by flowing water, which normally disperses, but which can produce kinematic wave, gravel bar, or lag concentrations.

By contrast with bones, there are fewer dispersive agencies for stone. Stone flaking engenders local concentrations of items and in general it is only hominid transport, erosion or flowing water that will disrupt these.

Taking this general sense of the processes involved, the question of how the combined artefact-plus-bone concentrations could have formed can be addressed.

Fig. 5.8 indicates a set of five possible scenarios, each of which represents a distinctive intersection of processes affecting bones and those affecting artefacts. These particular combinations of processes can be thought of as multiple alternative hypotheses to be tested. Note first that the set of possibilities shown is not exhaustive: this is simply a series of the most plausible hypotheses currently envisaged. Restless deductive and inductive search for other plausible hypotheses should continue. Note also that the hypotheses are not mutually exclusive; each represents the operation of processes that could occur in complex combinations with all the other processes. This means that Popperian falsification can only be achieved in the sense that an explanation can be shown not to be complete and sufficient. Realistically, research comes down to the acquisition of information that will allow one to evaluate the *relative* importance of each process in any given case.

Five or six years ago archaeologists began to realize that they would need very varied data sets to evaluate these rival hypotheses. These would have to include precise and appropriate data from excavation and field survey; appropriate laboratory studies of excavated specimens; experimental studies of the properties of bone and stone under various treatments; knowledge of animal life and death patterns; precise knowledge of predator and scavenger behaviour; and an understanding of hydraulic transport and sorting processes. Researchers plunged in to start acquir-

Table 5.4. *Studies of site formation processes*

Geologic site formation processes	Non-human bone accumulations and relevant aspects of taphonomy[a]	Bone at human settlements	Stone artefact making and using	Plant communities and niches available for early hominids
Isaac (1967a)	Sutcliffe (1972)	Brain (1967b, 1976)	Leakey (1952)	J. D. Clark (1980)
Gifford and Behrensmeyer (1977)	Hill (1975)	Gifford and Behrensmeyer (1977)	J. D. Clark (in Howell 1965)	Peters (1979)
Gifford (1985)	Behrensmeyer (1978a)	Gifford (1977)	Jones (1979, 1980, 1981)	Peters and O'Brien (1981)
Kaufulu (1983)	Behrensmeyer et al. (1979)	Yellen (1977b)	Toth (1982)	Hatley and Kappelman (1980)
Schick (n.d.) [1984]	Behrensmeyer and Dechant (1980)	Bunn (1982a, 1983b)	Keeley and Toth (1981)	Sept (n.d.) [1984]
	Shipman and Phillips-Conroy (1976)	Crader (1981, 1983)		Vincent (n.d.) [1984]
	D. Boaz (1982)			
	Bunn (1983b)			
	Potts (1982)			
	Crader (1983)			
	Klein (1975, 1982)			
	Scott and Klein (1981)			

[a] A selected list only of the studies most directed to being of archaeological interest. See Brain 1982 for an excellent summary of South African work.

ing this information, as Table 5.4 shows, and reports are beginning to become available. However, at present many of the studies are either incomplete or so recently received that their full implications have not yet been grasped. In this review I can only indicate aspects of what is beginning to emerge and provide references for further reading.

I restrict attention to the sites where there exist dense localized concentrations of artefacts plus bones and conditions of preservation are optimal.[6] For the time period under discussion, the sites that best meet these conditions, and for which reports are available, are Olduvai – FLK Zinj, FLK NN3, FLK N1–6 (M. D. Leakey, 1971) – and Koobi Fora – FxJj 50, FxJj 20, FxJj 20E (Bunn *et al.*, 1980 [this volume, ch. 8]; Harris, 1978). Explanations developed and tested on these sites may well be found to fit less well-preserved sites, but the converse procedure would be inappropriate.

Given this restriction, one of the rival hypotheses can be effectively eliminated at the outset. A whole series of lines of evidence shows that none of these well-preserved sites is purely and simply a 'hydraulic jumble'. This can be shown most convincingly for some of the sites (FxJj 50, 20M, 20E and FLK Zinj) by the prevalence of refitting (conjoining) stones and/or bones and by the spatial configuration of fitting pieces (see Bunn 1982a; Bunn *et al.*, 1980 [this volume, ch. 8]; Isaac, 1981a [this volume, ch. 12]; Kroll, 1981; Kroll and Isaac in press [1984]; Schick n.d. [1984]). Equally, the sedimentary context at most of these selected sites makes extensive hydraulic concentration seem very unlikely. (See Hay (1976) and Potts (1982) for good information in regard to Olduvai, and Z. Kaufulu (1983) for comparable studies on Koobi Fora.) It should be noted that some early sites *are* hydraulic jumbles; for example, the Koobi Fora channel sites (Harris, 1978) and some Olduvai sites, such as BK II (M. D. Leakey, 1971). It is also true that virtually all the early East African sites were covered by silts and sands deposited by flood waters. Even when energy was low it was not zero and some rearrangement has taken place. Careful reanalysis of archaeological evidence, coupled with field experiments on stream action, is being undertaken by Kathy Schick (in Bunn *et al.*, 1980 [this volume, ch. 8]; Schick n.d.). This should facilitate assessment of degrees of disturbance.[7]

Having eliminated hydraulic concentration as a major factor in the formation of the test case artefact-plus-bone concentrations, it follows that the *artefact* concentrations were formed at the sites by hominid action; the focus of inquiry then shifts to the question of how the bones got there. Two major logical possibilities can be recognized:

1. The animals contributing bones died at the site in a mass death or in recurrent deaths over a few years.[8]
2. The bones were carried in and concentrated by organisms capable of and motivated for relatively large carcass or bone transport. In modern Africa this set consists of (a) porcupines, (b) leopards, (c) hyenas, (d) hominids.

If we use recently published reports by Gentry and Gentry (1978), Potts (1982), and Bunn (1982a) for information on the characteristics of the test case assemblages, and consider these in relation to information about taphonomic processes and the composition of non-humanly accumulated assemblages, then the range of possible interpretations can be further reduced.

First, disarticulated place-of-death assemblages tend to suffer dispersal and loss of limb elements with an accumulation lag of axial elements (Hill, 1975; Potts, 1982). All the test-case assemblages show converse characteristics, such as those that are characteristic of scavenger-transported assemblages (i.e. preferential accumulations of limbs rather than axial elements). Equally, if these were purely and simply place-of-death (or kill) assemblages involving a minimum number of individuals (MNI) between 15 and 50, and species diversities between 10 and 20, which all these are, it is difficult to envision circumstances that would restrict the concentrated bone patch to the very limited areas observed at these sites (between 10 and 20 m in diameter in each case). Mass deaths followed by flood concentration of carcasses at river bends can produce extreme concentration (see A. Root's film, 'The Year of the Wildebeest', and Dechant-Boaz, 1982). However, such cases would be liable to involve distinctive geological contexts for which there is no evidence at the test-case sites.

Among the four known non-hydrologic transport agencies that are possible means for concentrating macromammal bones, two can be swiftly dropped from consideration, namely, porcupines and leopards. Porcupines can be eliminated because they are not known to concentrate bones in open-air situations and they tend to leave characteristic gnaw marks on 20 to 80 per cent of the accumulation (the site assemblages under consideration never show percentage values that approach this at all. For other criteria that do not fit see Brain, 1981; Bunn, 1982a; Potts, 1982). Leopards are also improbable or impossible accumulating agents because they tend to prey on and transport a range of animals markedly smaller than the modal sizes at any of the sites (cf. Brain, 1981; Bunn, 1981; and discussion in Potts, 1982). Equally they are not known to produce highly concentrated discard patches in the kind of time span that the bone accumulations represent (1–5 or 6 years).

This leaves hyenas (or hyena-like animals) and hominids as the principle candidates for being the transporting and concentrating agents. There is strong positive evidence for the presence of both forms at the sites; unravelling who did what and with what frequency is a tough challenge. Final answers are not yet possible and they may prove to differ from site to site, but there are some relevant data available to report in this review.

Logically there are four important possibilities for combined hominid and hyena involvement in site formation:

1. Both hyenas and hominids use a common amenity independently (e.g. shade tree or edge of water hole). The hyenas accumulate bones that the hominids ignore. The hominids make and leave stone artefacts for reasons having nothing to do with the presence of bones.
2. Hyenas accumulate bones that hominids later exploit, at the same time making and leaving artefacts.
3. Both hyenas and hominids bring in and deposit bone, with the hominids also leaving artefacts.
4. Hominids bring in and use carcass parts (bones), and make, use, and discard artefacts. Scavenging carnivores come in afterward and chew, rework, and remove bones.

These rival hypotheses form a graded spectrum of possibilities and each site may have had its own mode within the series. At present, in my opinion, we cannot definitely settle which permutation of intensities was specifically involved for each site, but some can be eliminated in their purest and simplest form, whereas the relative probability of the others can perhaps be ranked.

For sites where cut marks are found on the bones (or hammer fractures if these can be recognized), Possibility 1, the 'common amenity' explanation, cannot apply. Cut marks have been found on bones at all the selected test-case sites except FxJj 20E.

Beyond this, ranking of the other possibilities depends on plausibility arguments. However, these are of sufficient strength to allow us a fair level of confidence.

First, all hyena accumulations so far studied consist of entirely defleshed, dry bones. Some unbroken bones presumably would contain marrow at the time of abandonment, but it is difficult to imagine how this could be a resource of sufficient scale to occasion production on the spot of thousands of artefacts (so one would have to combine Possibility 2 with either 1 or 3 to make it convincing). Further, the pattern of cut marks (Bunn, 1982a, Potts, 1982) is such as to imply that many of these were inflicted when the bones were still encased in skin and/or flesh. It has been suggested that the cuts were made so as to sever periostium (Binford, 1981). This could only be true of a minority of marks, and in my opinion this is a superfluous explanation. Our bone-breaking experiments gave no signs of any need to cut or scrape periostial tissue before extracting marrow.

These considerations narrow the acceptable explanations of the test case artefact-plus-bone concentrations to Possibilities 3 or 4. Given the present information, the inference seems inescapable that the hominids must have had an active involvement in carrying parts of carcasses that they had often detached using sharp stone flakes and that they further divided and broke up using flakes and hammers. They did this with sufficient frequency and/or intensity to create concentrations. Both of the two independent workers who have recently studied the pertinent collections reach this conclusion after trying hard to find other explanations (Bunn, 1982a; Potts, 1982).

Since gnaw marks and coprolites document hyena presence at the sites, it is possible that both hyenas and hominids introduced and deposited bones. However, once one has accepted that hominids were carrying bones to places where extensive flaking also was practised, then there are good reasons for regarding the postulation of this kind of combined action as superfluous and improbable. Contemporary African experience provides good evidence that if humans create bone refuse, albeit broken up and chewed over, then hyenas, jackals and other scavengers will certainly visit, chew, ingest, and remove parts of the refuse (see Isaac 1967b [this volume, ch. 6], 1983b for further documentation). There is thus no difficulty in understanding why considerable numbers of bones at most of the sites do show carnivore gnaw marks. Possibility 4 thus emerges as the most likely. However, it should be noted that this does not necessarily imply home bases and food sharing (see below).

This conclusion amounts in effect to a reaffirmation of the views expressed and implied by M. D. Leakey (1971). However it has been essential to lay out in some detail the logic and the lines of evidence involved in checking this interpretation because (1) it has been subject to legitimate challenge (especially Binford, 1981: ch. 6) and (2) if the inference is substantiated then it becomes a significant datum in our understanding of human evolution.

Before leaving this issue I should comment on Binford's (1981) suggestions in relation to the evidence and arguments just presented. Binford's book, *Bones*, does three things. First, it draws attention to the fact that Pleistocene archaeologists have tended to drop into the dangerous unquestioning assumption that bones found in spatial conjunction with artefacts are necessarily food refuse. This point is valid and important and, as I have shown, has over the past five years been increasingly anticipated. Second, Binford advocates the investigation of processes affecting bones and contributes useful studies of this kind, which he terms *middle-range analysis*. His emphasis on this is valuable. It articulates a movement that has been growing steadily and that previously had lacked a label (cf. Behrensmeyer, 1978a; Behrensmeyer and Hill, 1980; Brain, 1967b, 1976, 1981; Gifford, 1978; Hill, 1975; Isaac, 1967a; Shipman and Phillips-Conroy, 1976). Third, he re-analysed published data on the Olduvai sites and bone assemblages. Using arguments and criteria from his middle-range studies, Binford interprets the results of a multivariate analysis in terms of site-formation processes. He seeks to assess the degree to which the Olduvai archaeological bone assemblages meet predictions for kill sites, background-near-kill scatters, or carnivore den accumulations. He concludes that most of the Olduvai Beds I and II sites could perfectly well be regarded as examples of such non-hominid-induced bone aggregates. He infers only a very minor bone-handling role for hominids. The analysis is original and interesting and should be read by all who are concerned with this topic. However, many of its conclusions run counter to those for which logic and evidence have been laid out above. Specifically the following seem to be weaknesses in Binford's conclusions:

1. They are based on reworking and extrapolation from published data sets that were declared by their author M. D. Leakey (1971) to be incomplete and preliminary. The subsequent work of Gentry and Gentry (1978), Potts (1982), and Bunn (1982a) shows that detailed work has, as Mary Leakey predicted, resulted in many revisions and additions.

2. The middle-range data set used as a basis for establishing discriminants is very limited, involving mainly Alaskan data and only one hyena den set. Use is not made of other hyena den data or of data regarding African bone-refuse accumulations of undoubted human authorship.

3. The conclusions are presented as arising from a complex multivariate analysis that in many ways disconnects such clear discriminants as there may be from the outcome.

4. Binford's arguments largely leave out of account the fact that several of the bone assemblages come from tightly concentrated patches in which thousands of artefacts also occur. In my view, as already indicated, satisfactory explanation must cope with the combination of bone assemblage characteristics, spatial concentration, and the existence of a coincident artefact concentration.

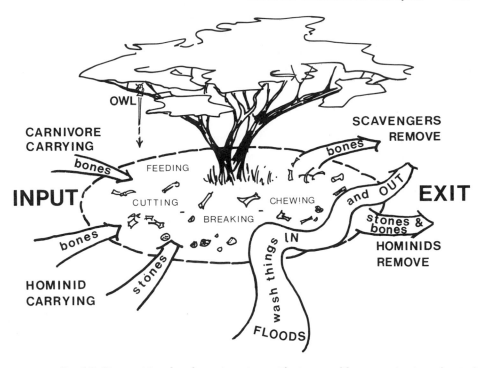

Fig. 5.9. Sites envisioned as dynamic systems with stones and bones moving in and out of them. Careful studies by Bunn, Kroll, Potts, Schick, Toth and others make it very clear that the sites sampled by excavations have been subject to the interaction of many different processes; the material recovered is a residue that dropped out of the flow. However, it is hard to avoid the conclusion that the initial reason for concentrations of artefacts-plus-bones was the localization of hominid activity.

Binford's main conclusion seems to be that, although hominids may have had some involvement in feeding off carcasses and bones, there is no evidence that they were the principal agents that formed the conspicuous concentrations that came to be known as living sites. Binford may well be correct in his strictures about many sites and in his view that for some of them hominid action may well have been only a minor factor. What I have attempted to show is that over the past five years the rigorous handling of carefully collected relevant evidence allows us to be confident that the bones of at least some concentrated patches of artefacts plus bones were indeed carried and concentrated by hominids. Note this is not the same as concluding that home bases and food sharing necessarily existed. I return briefly to this point toward the close of the review.

I have laid out recent findings so as to deal in effect with the question: did early hominids ever accumulate quantities of bones in particular places? The answer seems to be, yes, at least sometimes they did do so. This does not mean that all co-occurrences of artefacts and bones were so formed, and it also leaves us ignorant of how often and under what circumstances such behaviours occurred in the lives of early hominids. It should also be recognized that the studies that justify the conclusion have also served to show that the early sites excavated by archaeologists have to be understood as the fallout of complex flow systems by which both stone artefacts and bones were being transported, modified, and then further transported. Hominids were introducing both stones and bones and modifying them at these places, but other agencies also removed things. Conjoining studies inform us about both stones and bones that must have been present but that are missing. Many agencies, including flowing water, will have partially rearranged materials, and sites cannot be regarded as photographic imprints of discard behaviour. (See Schiffer (1976) and Gifford (1978, 1981) for examples of good discussions of this matter in general.) Figure 5.9 provides a visual representation of the complex interplay of processes involved. Bunn (1982a) and Potts (1982) provide thoughtful accounts of the bone-affecting processes involved in site formation at Olduvai and Koobi Fora, and Schick (n.d.) [1984] is doing a study that will provide experimental data on many aspects, including stone-flaking processes and the hydraulic effects of flood waters.

Fire

When Oakley (1955) did a major review of the evidence for the antiquity of fire, it appeared that the oldest evidence anywhere was of Middle Pleistocene age (i.e. Choukoutien, now dated at about 0.5 mya) and that evidence from Africa was even younger (i.e. Kalambo Falls, then taken as 0.07 mya, now revised to perhaps 0.18 mya). These views have been widely accepted and consequently most discussions of the Plio-Pleistocene in Africa do not include explicit discussion of hominid control of fire.

Outside Africa evidence for fire has repeatedly come to light in sites that document the spread of humans northward into the temperate zones with freezing winters. Early Eurasiatic sites such as Yuan Mou in south China, now dated to 0.7–1.0 mya (Pope, 1982), Choukoutien in central China, Vértesszöllös (Hungary, 0.3–0.6 mya), Terra Amata (0.25–0.4 mya), and Torralba (0.3–0.5 mya) all contain charcoal and/or charred bones. Clearly by the time humans expanded out of tropical and warm temperate areas they did control fire. The question is how much earlier than the 0.5–1.0 mya age of that expansion did this crucial innovation occur? Had it begun during the Lower Pleistocene (i.e. before 0.7 mya)?

For some time it has been recognized that charcoal does not survive in dry, open air, sedimentary deposits in tropical Africa and hence the absence of visible black hearths from early sites is not necessarily significant negative evidence.

During the past decade the issue has become the focus of research attention again and although the questions are not settled new potential evidence has come to light and new challenges have emerged.

First, in several sedimentary basins, burned earth materials, including conspicuous baked masses of hard reddened earth up to 30 or 40 cm in diameter, have been found. Sometimes these can be seen to be moulding the form of a root or stump, in other cases they erode out as more amorphous hard bosses. These have been observed at Olorgesailie (Isaac, 1977b), at Koobi Fora in the Upper Member

(Harris, 1978; Isaac, 1982), and most recently in the middle Awash around Bodo (J. D. Clark, personal communication, 1982). Disintegrating fragments of natural terracotta are fairly widespread in many layers, at least at Olorgesailie and Koobi Fora. It is very clear that these widespread knobs and bosses of baked earth are formed as a result of bush fires, which ignite stumps that may smoulder at high temperatures in contact with the ground. (See M. Wendorf (1982) for an account of larger-scale comparable phenomena in the coastal forests of California.)

In addition to these widespread bush-fire traces, specific evidence of fire or heating have been found on several Lower Pleistocene sites. The traces of fire include fragments of baked earth (Chesowanja (Gowlett *et al.*, 1981)), reddened patches of earth within a site (e.g. Koobi Fora site FxJj 20E (Harris, 1978)), artefacts showing signs of having been burned (e.g. Koobi Fora site FxJj 20E (Harris, 1978); FxJj 50 (Keeley and Toth, personal communication, 1980); and Gadeb (Barbetti *et al.*, 1980)).

Clearly these site-associated evidences may be indicative of at least occasional controlled use of fire by 1.5 mya as a part of a very early stage in cultural and technological development. Such claims have been put forward (e.g. Gowlett *et al.*, 1981).[9] However, the evidence for periodic widespread bush fires complicates the interpretation of the evidence for burning. The physicochemical tests that attest to burning do not commonly provide a basis for distinguishing a controlled fire from the effects of a bush fire that swept through the site after abandonment. As already indicated, we know that such bush fires did occur with detectable frequency.

In my view the repeated conjunction of indications of fire and artefact concentrations is suggestive but the question must be regarded as unsettled until the discovery of a recognizable hearth, or until geophysical work is done to establish criteria for recognizing controlled fire and apply them to sites.

The configurations of objects within concentrations

Archaeologists very properly collect detailed records of the positions of objects and features discovered during excavation. Characteristically these are presented as plots and as vertical projections. All this is done, presumably, in the faith that the plans can eventually be interpreted as evidence for particular behaviour patterns that were characteristic of the hominids that made the artefacts. However, until comparatively recently only a few *ad hoc* interpretations of aspects of individual site configurations had been offered. An example of this is the *Zinjanthropus* site at Olduvai where, it is suggested, one can discern a dense central concentration of small objects, a partial gap, and then a surrounding sparser scatter of larger artefacts and bones. Mary Leakey (1971:50), quoting J. D. Clark, discusses the possibility that 'this gap between the central and the outlying areas may have been caused by the presence of a wind-break surrounding the central part of the camp site, so that debris would either remain inside or be thrown out over the top.' In addition, another feature in one sector of the FLK Zinj site is discussed as having formed through the falling of a tree.

The Olduvai site of DK yielded the now famous ring of basalt blocks. Mary Leakey (1971:24) points out that this 'resembles temporary structures often made by present day nomadic peoples who build a low stone wall round their dwellings to serve either as a wind break or as a base to support upright branches which are bent over and covered either with skins or grass.' The DK stone circle remains a unique feature and, like all unique features, there are difficulties in formulating testable explanations. The hypothesis that the feature was constructed by hominids and that it represents some kind of shelter remains perfectly plausible, but unverified.

More than ten years of work at Melka Kunturé has resulted in painstaking excavation of numerous archaeological horizons. Excerpts from the detailed plans have begun to be published. Jean Chavaillon *et al.* (1979) report that the earlier, Oldowan horizons are associated with river banks, and river beaches where the material is intermingled with cobbles and boulders. It is suggested that some of the configurations of large stone blocks were formed by the toolmaking hominids. In one case (Gomboré 1B) there is a raised area largely devoid of artefacts, which may be a structure. Large boulders round which faunal remains cluster are also reported. Middle Acheulian sites seem to involve a shift away from stony river beaches, to the use of the floors of small tributary channels. Scooped out basins become a feature and distinct activity areas are said to be clearly in evidence.

The preliminary reports and partial plans make it clear that a major new corpus of information will be available when the detailed monographs are ready. Clearly, given the channel bed and channel bank context of many Melka Kunturé sites the application for criteria for recognizing the effects of flowing water will be important.

Up to now the only substantial published body of site plans available for comparative study has been that in the Olduvai monograph (M. D. Leakey, 1971). Using these plans a few scholars have made a start on systematic comparative consideration (e.g. Davis, 1976, 1978; Ohel, 1977), and some others have used the Olduvai records as data sets with which to explore the applicability of various analytic techniques (e.g. Hietala and Larson, 1979; Larson, 1975; Robert Whallon, personal communication, 1980). In his study Ohel suggests that in numbers of Olduvai sites elongate areas of concentration with relatively large items, especially bones, were food preparation areas and that circular concentrations of finely comminuted bones and debitage were food-consumption areas. Davis (1978) explored an interesting combination of quantitative and graphic methods by which he reached conclusions that are partly similar to and partly different from those of Ohel. He suggests that (1) various low-density areas were dwelling or sleeping areas; and (2) dense concentrations of small artefacts and bone fragments were 'kitchen' areas, whereas (3) peripheral areas of scattered, larger items were 'primary butchery and/or other subsistence "activity" areas'. Both Ohel and Davis' lines of interpretation are plausible. However, both take for granted certain aspects of recent human behaviour, the existence of which by 1.9 mya is in fact an important question for inquiry. Neither of these authors engages in a careful evaluation of alternative explanatory propositions.

It would seem to me that what is needed is, first, a searching consideration of the

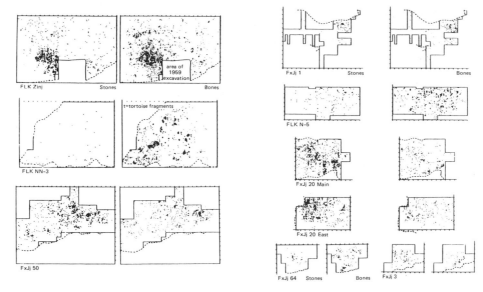

Fig. 5.10. A series of plots showing the basic intrasite spatial patterning at Olduvai and Koobi Fora sites. All are to the same scale, with stones on the left and bones on the right of each pair (from Kroll and Isaac, in press [1984]).

processes that are envisaged as forming intrasite patterns, and of how the action of each process will be recognized. Second, one needs to consider carefully what questions we have about the organization of early hominid behaviour for which separate spatial analysis might provide a basis of inquiry. Once these fundamental issues have been dealt with then they can serve to guide a comprehensive study that uses both qualitative and quantitative methods where appropriate.

Several people are exploring aspects of such an approach (e.g. R. Potts, 1982, and personal communication, 1980; K. Schick, n.d. [1984]), and, in particular, a major attack on the problem has been made by E. Kroll (1981, n.d.). Because Kroll and Isaac (in press [1984]), using both Olduvai and Koobi Fora plans, have prepared a fairly extensive review of issues, questions, and some indications of results, I do not attempt more than a very brief commentary here.

A first major point that needs to be recognized is that most excavations expose only a part of the site being studied. Commonly the trenches sample some sector with a relatively high density of material. However the spatial relation of the sector sampled to the rest of the 'site' is often not known, and information on the nature and positions of the edges of the artefact concentration is usually also lacking, or vague. The *Zinjanthropus* site at Olduvai comes closest to being an exception, in that the large cutting seems to expose an ultra-high density anomaly plus a surrounding lower-density fringe area. More recently other excavations also have sought to define site margins (Bunn *et al.*, 1980 [this volume, ch. 8]; Harris, 1978), but the problem remains.

A second major need for caution stems from the fact that one commonly does not know in advance whether the site formed during a single occupation, which often seems to be tacitly assumed, or whether it formed as a result of a sequence of usages, resulting in a cumulative build-up of discarded material.[10] Since bone in the African savannah does not last more than five or six years without beginning to show severe weathering, the well-preserved bone component at the sites must at least represent accumulations formed largely within five years or less. But five years leaves plenty of time for accumulative processes to operate and discussions of observed spatial patterns as though they represented the imprint of a single, integrated, organized system may well be wide of the mark. Getting more definite information on the number and duration of discard episodes represented at sites is an urgent need in the development of research.

Figure 5.10 shows a representative series of excavated portions of early East African sites with the distributions of artefacts and bones plotted. It can be seen that in almost every case artefacts and bones occur in localized clusters and in more diffuse scatters. In some instances there is, in effect, a single dense cluster and a variable peripheral scatter (e.g. the *Zinjanthropus* site). These sites can be thought of as clusters of clusters. It should be remembered that many more sites might emerge as clusters of clusters if our excavations had opened up much larger areas of ancient land surface.

In those instances where appropriate studies have been done (Davis, 1978; Kroll, 1981, n.d.), it has emerged that many very small flakes and flake fragments tend to occur within the conspicuous dense clusters. This probably implies that, among other things, stone knapping was done on the spot in these sub-areas. This has received further support from the distribution of conjoining pieces at FxJj 50 (Bunn *et al.*, 1980 [this volume, ch. 8]). The conjoining of bone would seem to imply that bone breaking also went on in or near these same spots (Bunn, 1982a; Kroll and Isaac, in press [1984]). As far as I am aware, stone knapping and bone smashing are the only two specific activities the localization of which can be identified with any confidence on the site plans. Sleeping areas or the equivalents of hearths, or any such organized feature, are not discernible. (This leaves the DK stone circle out of account as a unique, and hence hard to evaluate, instance.)

Where we have sufficient data on which to base estimates, most sites seem to range between 5 or 6 m and 15 or 20 m in diameter. They may be either roughly equidimensional or of irregular oval form. The dense intrasite concentrations range from 1 or 2 m to 6 or 7 m in maximum dimension. (See Kroll and Isaac (in press [1984]) for additional information.)

The Koobi Fora team has been deliberately seeking out several small clusters of artefacts for excavation. If the large, dense sites are composite, long-term palimpsests, then a series of mini-sites may eventually provide the best way of distinguishing the components that have become tangled up at maxi-sites (see Isaac *et al.*, 1981 [this volume, ch. 9]).

Some initial studies have been undertaken that seek interpretable pattern in the distribution of the various artefact classes recognized (e.g. Davis, 1978; Hietala and Larson, 1979; Larson, 1975). So far no strong, convincing associations have been found that indicate distinct tool kits or particular, localized intrasite activities. Part of the problem may lie in having to use categories that were set up for assemblage taxonomy purposes. New studies are in progress that employ attribute records made on the collections expressly for use in spatial analysis (Kroll, n.d.). Meanwhile it can be said that small objects are more highly clustered than larger ones. This may reflect the fact that (1) big items were tossed out of the way as secondary refuse, and/or (2) the bigger items were picked up and reused in various ways, thereby becoming scattered. My own view is that elaborate multivariate analyses are not wise until basic processes and patterns are better known than at present.

Eventually it should be very informative to compare the configurations found in well-preserved examples of very early sites with those of suitable later Pleistocene and recent sites to see if, besides the absence of visible fireplaces, there are any systematic differences. E. Kroll has started to do this, but results are not yet available.

Several methodological developments promise to transform spatial analysis. One is the use of conjoining as a way of linking (or separating) areas and stratigraphic layers – and as a way of charting the flow of flaking and breaking across the sites. The other is the application of computers to the analysis. By mapping different categories and attributes separately, these greatly facilitate qualitative study as well as making rigorous quantitative methods possible.

The existence of the concentrated patches of artefacts and bones is consistent with the notion that the toolmakers were central-place foragers. But as yet the details of configuration do not help in any way to prove or disprove the hypothesis. Equally, there is nothing in the distribution of material to indicate whether or not the toolmakers lived at these sites, or even slept there. Archaeology will need all the ingenuity it can muster to learn how to test propositions about the patterns of action and modes of use prevailing at these sites while they formed.

Stone artefact assemblages

Research over the past decade has resulted in three kinds of advance in the study of artefact assemblages dating from the 1–2 mya time range:

1. basic data have been added, with additional samples drawn from a wider geographic range and a more varied series of environmental contexts;
2. the approach to inquiry has changed, with assemblages viewed as partial expressions of systems rather than as sets of objects to be classified;
3. comparisons are beginning to be made that use the expanded data set and apply the systemic approach.

I use these as headings in setting out a brief review of the state of inquiry.

Additional data

At the time of its publication, Mary Leakey's 1971 volume provided the only corpus of systematic analyses of excavated lower Pleistocene assemblages from East Africa (or indeed virtually anywhere), the only other such assemblages previously published being those from Peninj (Isaac, 1965, 1967a). Since 1971 a series of reports have appeared extending the data on Olduvai (M. D. Leakey, 1975, 1976) and

Table 5.5. *East African sites as entries in a matrix of variables*

Time period (mya)	A								B		C			
	Olduvai (3°S)	Peninj (2°S)	Kilombe (0°)	Chesowanja (1°N)	K.F. (4°N)	Omo (5°N)	Gadeb (7°N)	M.K. (9°N)	Lava	Lava and quartz	Chert	Lake margin	Delta and floodplain	Fluvial beds
0.7	≥7		1					several	Kilombe	Olduvai[Q]				M.K. Olduvai IV
1.0		2			1			several	K.F. (M.K.) Gadeb	Olduvai[Q]			Peninj MHS	M.K. Olduvai II & III Gadeb? Peninj RHS
1.3	≈3			1	2 / 12		3	several	K.F. (M.K.) Chesowanja (EFHR)	Olduvai[Q]			K.F. Ileret	Olduvai II K.F. Karari
1.6	≈9				3	several minor locs		several	K.F. Lower (M.K.)	Olduvai[M]	Olduvai D.O.A.	Olduvai I–II M.K.?	K.F. Lower	
1.9									Omo					Omo
2.2						>5								

A = geography (latitude), with numbers of assemblages; B = predominant raw material; C = environment of deposition; D.O.A. = Developed Oldowan A sites; K.F. = Koobi Fora; M = mixed; M.K. = Melka Kunture; Q = mainly quartz-dominated.

adding data on excavated samples from other sedimentary basins. The largest additional data set has been that resulting from the work of J. W. K. Harris (1978) on samples from the Koobi Fora Upper Member. Comparable data are also being obtained and compiled for the Melka Kunturé sequence of sites; preliminary accounts are available (Chavaillon *et al.*, 1979; Piperno and Piperno, 1975), but so far detailed quantitative data have not been formally published. Full analytic data are also available for the Omo Member F assemblages (Chavaillon, 1976; Merrick, 1976; Merrick and Merrick, 1976) and for the Koobi Fora Lower Member (KBS) assemblages (Isaac, 1976c). Preliminary but fairly complete data are available for Chesowanja (Gowlett *et al.*, 1981; Harris *et al.*, 1981) and for Gadeb (Clark and Kurashina, 1979a,b).

Table 5.5 shows the coverage of the samples relative to divisions of time, geography, predominant raw material and paleogeographic context. It can be seen that although the data base is steadily growing, there are still many empty or sparsely filled cross tabulation cells. This should be taken into account in the planning of future research.

Approach

In the 1950s and 1960s the need for quantitative data on stone artefact assemblages came to be recognized (e.g. Bordes, 1950b). This in turn entailed setting up clearly defined categories (usually so-called types), that was done for different space-time sectors of the Palaeolithic by various authorities (e.g. Bordes, 1961b; Kleindienst, 1961; M. D. Leakey, 1966, 1971; Ramendo, 1963; Tixier, 1963). Explicitly defined systems of measurement were also introduced (e.g. Bordes, 1961; Isaac, 1972c, 1972a [this volume, ch. 1]; Roe, 1964). This movement also involved concern over precision and definition in the classification and nomenclature of cultures, or *industries* as they came to be designated (Bishop and Clark, 1967; Clark *et al.*, 1966).

During the late 1960s there was a strong if unstated sense that the first order of business for Palaeolithic archaeology was to amass a large series of quantitative analyses of assemblages from different times, places and contexts. All of us who were involved in this seemed to share a tacit assumption that what we wanted to know about early prehistory would in large measure emerge from comparative study of the quantitative data. It seemed that it would be possible to recognize *stages* (i.e. time-bounded sets), *regional variants* (i.e. culture-geographic entities), and *activity facies*, and that knowledge of the characteristics of these classificatory entities would be a basis for understanding technological development, adaptation, ecology and culture history. This aspiration is still inherently reasonable, but emphasis and priority have shifted in subtle ways. Because many researchers came to realize that what the standardized quantitative analyses were mainly producing was numbers rather than understanding, inquiry changed in two ways. First, much more attention was focused on the field context of artefacts as a source of information about activities and adaptation. Second, artefacts came to be thought of not as

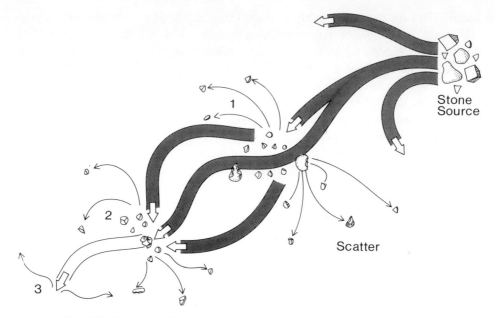

Stone
Source

Scatter

Fig. 5.11. Ancient artefact-production systems can be envisioned as a flow of stones over the landscape, with items being taken from one place to the next, then flaked there with some cores and some flakes removed from the products. Some items move on to another node, other items are taken out and discarded as items in a diffuse scatter.

sets of objects, but as the drop-out of a dynamic system. This clearly implied that in order to understand them and to devise useful counts and measures one would have to understand in some detail the processes by which they are produced, used, rejuvenated, and finally discarded (Figs. 5.11 and 5.12). It also became clear that the specifics of such understanding could only come from experimental studies. For the Olduvai research project this line of inquiry was taken up by Peter Jones (1979, 1981) and for the Koobi Fora project by Nicholas Toth (in Bunn *et al.*, 1980 [this volume, ch. 8]; Toth, 1982). The studies are still in progress and partial results have only recently begun to be available as papers and theses. I have already dealt above with studies of usage feasibility and I restrict myself here to giving some examples of the implications of experimental replication studies.

It has long been known that early assemblages of bifaces vary in the degree to which the handaxes, cleavers, and so forth have been trimmed. Specimens with many invasive scars appear 'refined' and it has been assumed that they would be later and more advanced. However, at Olduvai refined-looking assemblages are interstratified through the sequence with not-so-refined-looking sets. Peter Jones' (1979) experiments indicate that the differences are linked to raw material in a predictable way. Bifaces made of a brittle, readily flakable rock such as phonolite (or flint) tend to need trimming to stabilize the edges, whereas those of tough, flake-resistant rocks such as basalt can be used with their edges more or less unretouched. This may help to account for the surprisingly refined and intensively trimmed bifaces recovered from Kilombe (Gowlett, 1978), which is now known to be older than 700,000 years. These are made of phonolite.

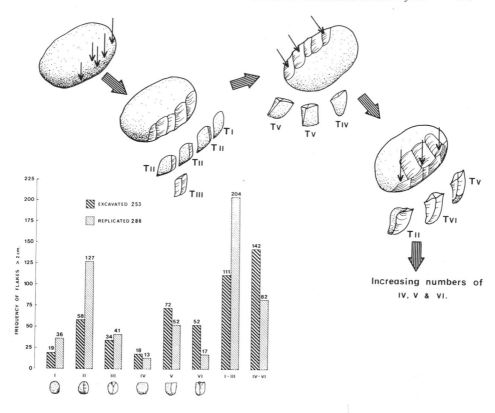

Fig. 5.12. One example of an analysis in which the artefact flow depicted in Fig. 5.11 has been demonstrated. N. Toth has defined six flake types depending on the amount of cortex on platform and dorsal surfaces of flakes. Using experimental replication as a basis for prediction, it can be shown that at FxJj 50 some items were introduced after being flaked elsewhere, whereas other items were flaked at the site and then taken away. (Based on Toth and Schick in Bunn *et al.*, 1980 [this volume, ch. 8].)

   A second useful example comes from the work of Nick Toth at Koobi Fora. Here, using the same raw materials (mainly basalt) and the same starting forms (mainly river-rounded cobbles), Toth copied the core and core-tool forms that were being recovered from the excavations. This allowed him to judge (rank) a variety of flaking strategies for ease of execution. This ranking can then be compared with the frequency of flaked pieces (cores and core-tools) in ancient assemblages. Further it was possible to study the flaking products resulting from different reduction sequences, and to compare them with the detached pieces (debitage) from the sites. From this latter it quickly emerged that most conventional flake attributes were not very informative about the flow of manufacturing acts, but a simple set of six categories for flakes could be used much more effectively to monitor what flaking procedures were being followed, and to determine what stages in them were best represented. The six categories and an application of the approach were published in Bunn *et al.* (1980) [this volume, ch. 8]. In the case of site FxJj 50 and others, it was possible to show that the flaking of cobbles had begun prior to their introduction to the site, and that very probably some pieces had been preferentially carried away after flaking. Thus the sites emerged as points through which artefacts flowed rather than as static repositories (see Fig. 5.10). More details and other instances are available in Toth's thesis (1982) and in several publications that are in preparation.

Toth's work also lends some support to previous speculations that many of the so-called tools of the early industries – choppers, discoids, heavy-duty scrapers – are just as likely to have had the provision of flakes as their primary *raison d'être*, that is to say that they were first and foremost cores rather than tools[11] (cf. Chavaillon, 1976; Isaac, 1976b; M. D. Leakey, 1971:269). This view has implications for the terminology to which I will return.

Interconnected with the development of these experimental middle-range studies has been the development of a fresh and more explicit logic in the pursuit of comparative studies. In seeking to account for variation among assemblages it makes good sense to use the method of residuals in the following order (see Isaac *et al.*, 1981):

1. Ascertain which characteristics of any assemblage are accounted for simply by the application of least-effort flaking procedures, given the particular forms of raw material used. Differences attributable directly to the simplest ways of flaking different raw materials do not enter into higher-order interpretation.
2. Residual differences not accounted for in step 1 can then be checked for being attributable to economy of effort in fetching replacement raw materials from a source that is not immediately to hand (e.g. intensive working-down of cores, repeated resharpening retouch, etc.).
3. Remaining variance, if any, can now be checked for interpretable connection to specific activities. That is, one would look for reduction in variance among members of sets that are grouped according to context variables such as palaeogeographic location, and amount and characteristics of associated bones. Such an apparent association becomes an activity facies hypothesis to be tested in other ways.
4. If there is any significant residual variance unaccounted for after step 3, the possibility can be entertained that it is due to arbitrary cultural differences of a stylistic nature.

Experimental studies of making and using artefacts provide the basis for informed judgements in steps 1, 2, and 3 above.

Formal application of a stepwise analysis of variance of the kind envisioned here requires reasonable numbers of assemblages in the cross-tabulation matrixes that are implied by each step. As yet we do not have enough entries to undertake formal analyses. However, it is useful to have the logic in mind as research proceeds and as interim assessments are considered.

In the foregoing I have stressed research that seeks to evaluate mechanical and functional contingencies and determinants. This does seem the place to start inquiries, but where a residuum remains unaccounted for it is clear that other factors need to be considered. Gowlett (1982, in press) [1984] has issued reminders that tools being made in regular habitual ways in itself implies the existence of unusual mental abilities and of a well-developed system of culture and culturally transmitted learning. He points to the existence by early Acheulian times at Kilombe and elsewhere (1.3–0.7 mya) of highly standardized forms with consistent shape proportions.

During the past decade there have been other experiments with different approaches. Hélène Roche (1980) has argued cogently the need to have the classification and comparison of early stone tools on typologically based criteria that distinguish different sequences and patterns of flake removal. Her approach and system is very carefully thought out and it will be interesting to see it applied to a more extensive inter-assemblage comparison. My own hunch is, as indicated above, that formal classificatory systems of analysis will prove less useful than flexible, experiment-based studies aimed at assessing flaking strategies as responses to particular forms of raw material. The distinction between such studies and the procedures advocated by Roche are not great.

Bower (1977) has experimented with the application of a very detailed attribute analysis of choppers, core-scrapers, and related Oldowan artefact forms.

In a more markedly contrasting approach, Stiles (1979:4) asked 'whether we can identify ethnic groups in the past through the study of stone tools'. He tackled this question by formulating a series of propositions and hypotheses and went on to discuss what data might be collected and what tests made in order to answer the ethnic groups question. Stiles' suggestions raise interesting questions of scientific strategy. In effect he starts with the most complex set of determinants of variability and then has to cope with subsidiary factors as complications, whereas the method of residuals proposed above attempts to start by seeing how much variation the relatively simple mechanical factors will explain before one ever gets into questions as subtle as 'ethnic' identity.

Wynn (1981) has taken the interesting step of seeking to apply to early stone tools the Piaget characterization of the stages of cognitive development through which modern human children grow. The approach is a promising one but I think that it will need to be applied not to the *objects* but to the design concept and motor patterns actually involved in making them. Once again direct experimentation is likely to be essential.

Comparisons: differences and changes

My own current judgement is that among the known very early assemblages the raw-material and least-effort factors account for most differences, leaving very little if any residual variance on which to base either activity facies or culture-historic kinds of interpretations.

Thus, for instance, the Omo Shungura Member F assemblages are clearly different from the Koobi Fora assemblages and the Olduvai assemblages. However, it appears that the most readily available stone materials on the Shungura floodplains of 2 mya were small, pigeon-egg-sized quartz pebbles. To obtain sharp edges, these were smashed, producing numerous slivers and splinters and very few recognizable core forms (Chavaillon, 1976; Merrick *et al.*, 1973; Merrick and Merrick, 1976). At Koobi Fora and Olduvai larger rocks were available and lavas were worked. The smash technique is difficult to execute on lava and does not tend to produce useful results, so that systematic uni- and bifacial flaking had to be done to produce cutting edges, with choppers and discoids being habitual easy-format cores. Quartz was also worked at Olduvai with larger, more angular starting forms inducing some size and shape differences relative to the Shungura, though the quartz debitage from FLK Zinj is in fact not unlike that from Member F of the Shungura.

The Koobi Fora and Olduvai series of samples show some interesting tendencies to differ that cannot at present in any simple way be attributed directly to raw material (Isaac, in prep[12]). Most notable among these differences are the following:

1. There is a larger proportion of large stones of all kinds in the Olduvai assemblages (i.e. manuports, choppers, polyhedrons, hammerstones, battered nodules, etc.).

2. Spheroids and subspheroids become prominent components of most Olduvai assemblages from upper Bed I onward. These particular forms do not occur at Koobi Fora for any stratigraphic level, and battered, pounded pieces in general are much rarer at Koobi Fora.

3. For any given category at any site at Olduvai, be it chopper, discoid, polyhedron, or plain flakes, the mean size is notably larger than the mean for almost any site at Koobi Fora. Only the values for channel-bed assemblages at Koobi Fora overlap at all the range of values for Olduvai assemblages (Harris, 1978).[13]

4. Smaller flake-scrapers and other retouched flakes are relatively rare at Koobi Fora, whereas they are fairly well represented in the Olduvai Bed I assemblages and become even more so in Beds II, III and IV. (This could be in part raw-material related because the Olduvai assemblages are predominantly made on quartz debitage.)

The data are not yet available to compare Melka Kunturé with other sites farther south, however Chavaillon *et al.* (1979) have offered a valuable preliminary commentary on comparisons between the assemblages in the sequence at Melka Kunturé. The sequence starts with relatively simple chopper and flake assemblages (Oldowan). These are followed by assemblages with more refined core forms, such as discoids and rare bifaces, fewer cortical flakes, and more retouched flake tools (Evolved Oldowan). Then about 1 mya Acheulian tool forms rise to prominence as choppers decline in frequency and become more acutely angled (Lower Acheulian). Subsequently, in the Middle Acheulian, the bifaces become more standardized and small tools tend to be more numerous and diverse. Obsidian from sources not immediately to hand comes to be more heavily used. These trends to refinement and elaboration continue into the Late and Final Acheulian, with the addition also of the Levallois method. From their data, Chavaillon *et al.* (1979) argues for a mosaic evolution of culture with technological shifts preceding changes in the organization of occupation sites. Clearly, when the specifics are available Melka Kunturé will be one of the longest archaeological sequences anywhere in the world. It will be interesting to see whether additional samples taken at the same horizon as these sampled so far introduce evidence for the kind of lateral variation previously found at Olduvai, Olorgesailie and Isimila.

As regards comparisons between time divisions, the most important and apparently most consistent feature is the appearance in several different basins of novel forms after about 1.3–1.5 mya. New data from Melka Kunturé, Gadeb and Koobi Fora tend to fit with the patterns previously observed at Olduvai and Peninj. In all cases very large (> 10 cm) flakes first appear in the record as consistent features of some assemblages. These are often the key starting forms for making Acheulian tool forms, such as handaxes, cleavers and picks. Isaac (1967a, 1969) has suggested that the seemingly abrupt initiation of the early Acheulian may relate to the discovery of how to strike large flakes consistently. What is not yet clear is whether bifaces at the moment of innovation represented *new tools* for performing long-standing tasks (such as butchery) or whether *new tasks* were added to the behavioural, adaptive repertoire. To resolve this we will need better information on function before, during, and after the beginning of the Acheulian.

Terminology and nomenclature

The system of categories introduced by Mary Leakey (1971) has become the standard basis for reporting the characteristics of assemblages and it continues to serve well. However there is one awkwardness in the labels used in the system. Specifically the use of the terms *tools* and *debitage* (or waste) for higher-order groupings of categories can cause misunderstandings and misconceptions. In the early industries most of the items designated as *tools* are larger pieces of stone from which flakes have been struck. That is to say they are also cores that served as the source of potentially usable flakes. In Olduvai Bed I many of these show signs of use damage and it is also often true that the majority of flakes in the assemblages are of quartz while the majority of core-tools are of lava, so it is reasonable to regard the items as tools. However at Koobi Fora they seldom show damage and often appear to have functioned mainly as cores.

Similar difficulties arise over the term 'debitage'. As has been shown in the section on the function of stone tools, there are good reasons for regarding plain flakes as the most important implements, as the critical items in entering a stone-tool-using mode of adaptation.

Thus we have a situation where the defined technical meanings of the terms *tools* and *waste/debitage* have almost perfectly inverted the common language meaning of these words. I have found myself explaining this situation as follows: 'many researchers now think that many of the specimens that we call *tools* are really not so much tools as cores, whereas the specimens that we call *waste* were actually the most important tools'. The situation poses few problems for practising Palaeolithic archaeologists because they are thoroughly familiar with the special meanings assigned to these words; however, discourse with scholars outside archaeology is hindered, and it would seem useful to shift to a series of less-interpretation-loaded labels (Isaac *et al.*, 1981 [this volume, ch. 9]), such as:

1. *Flaked pieces* – all stones from which significant flakes have been struck. This category would include both the cores and the trimmed or retouched tools of later industries. For the Plio–Pleistocene assemblages it is quasi-synonymous with tools. A flake that has been trimmed or retouched becomes a flaked piece.
2. *Detached pieces* – flakes, flake fragments, shattered angular fragments and core fragments. Quasi-synonymous with debitage minus the core category.

The most important archaeological taxonomic divisions that are in current use were set up by Mary Leakey (1966, 1971, 1975, 1976). They follow the 1967 Burg

Table 5.6. *Aspects of current usage in the taxonomy of early artefact assemblages from East Africa*

Time period (mya)	At Olduvai Gorge[a]		Elsewhere
	Acheulian Industrial Complex	Oldowan Industrial Complex	
0.7		Developed Oldowan C	
	Acheulian Industries		
1.5		Developed Oldowan B	
		Developed Oldowan A	Karari industry[b]
1.7		Oldowan	KBS industry[b]
2.0			'Shungura facies'[c]

[a] For definitions and explanations, see M. D. Leakey (1971, 1975, 1976).
[b] See Isaac (1976b), Harris and Isaac (1976), Harris (1978), and Isaac and Harris (1978). The KBS material is not particularly distinctive and this 'taxon' may be redundant. The Karari material is distinctive and deserves a label of its own, even if, as some of us suspect, the distinctive features are explicable as habitual, least-effort strategies given the form of raw material (see Toth, 1982).
[c] See Chavaillon (1976). He expresses reservations about putting the assemblages in the Oldowan and suggests the term *Shungura facies* as an interim designation.

Wartenstein recommendations (Bishop and Clark, 1967; Clark *et al.*, 1966). Assemblages with similar typological and technological characteristics are grouped into *industries*; higher-order groupings are designated as *industrial complexes*. At Olduvai the classification is as shown in Table 5.6. If the Oldowan Industrial Complex is taken to include all early stone industries that lack highly specific imposed designs, then the assemblages from several other sedimentary basins fit within this super-category. Several variants have been recognized and these are shown on the chart.

While the taxonomy and nomenclature are fairly straightforward and widely agreed upon, the meaning of the distinctive entities that are labelled is less clear and less widely agreed upon. For instance, Acheulian assemblages and the Developed Oldowan assemblages are interstratified in upper Bed II, Bed III and Bed IV at Olduvai and Gadeb. It remains uncertain whether two separate complete cultural entities (in the sense of coexisting tribes) are represented or whether the distinctly different assemblage types were the products of a single socio-cultural system that produced and discarded different artefact forms in different places (i.e. activities facies). Stiles (1979, 1980b) has argued strongly that the Early Acheulian versus Developed Oldowan distinction is not consistent in its expression and that it is not of a kind that could be taken to indicate the prolonged existence of stable ethnic groupings. More research will be needed to settle this, but meanwhile most researchers, myself included, probably favour some kind of activity variant hypothesis (see Binford, 1972; Clark, 1970; Isaac, 1972a [this volume, ch. 1]; M. D. Leakey, 1971 for discussion of this).

The anthropological meaning of other distinctive variants also remains to be settled. Applying the method of residuals that was outlined above, it would seem probable that the idiosyncratic features of the Karari industry are best regarded as due to stone-working *habits* that were adjusted to local raw material forms (Harris, 1978; Harris and Isaac, 1976). That is to say, it is simultaneously a minor local tradition transmitted across generations and a raw-material-induced response (Toth, 1982).

Faunal assemblages at sites of Type C

Mary Leakey (1971) presented extensive but preliminary data for the Olduvai sites. Since that time, Gentry and Gentry (1978) have reported in much greater detail on the Olduvai bovid remains, and two detailed zooarchaeological studies of selected Bed I sites have been reported (Bunn, 1982a; Potts, 1982). For Koobi Fora, until recently, only preliminary qualitative data have been available but detailed studies on all significant assemblages are now available (Bunn, 1982a; Bunn et al., 1980 [this volume, ch. 8]). The Omo Shungura sites did not contain significant quantities of bones, and only preliminary data are available for the other three early sites treated in this review; namely, Melka Kunturé (Chavaillon et al., 1979; Piperno and Piperno, 1975), Chesowanja (Gowlett et al., 1981; Harris et al., 1981), and Gadeb (Clark and Kurashina, 1979a,b). Isaac and Crader (1981) review all the published sources available to 1977 and present summarizing tables and charts, so this review is restricted to advances made since that time. Many aspects have already been touched on in dealing with evidence for the extent of meat eating, and in discussing how sites of Type C formed. All that remains is to indicate the implications of detailed analyses done in the past several years.

I report on the analyses as though the faunal assemblages of Type C sites had been accumulated largely by hominids because this seems the most plausible working hypothesis. However, readers should bear in mind that other agencies certainly were involved to some degree and in some cases they may eventually turn out to have been major factors at some sites.

Many of the features identified by Mary Leakey in her 1971 report have been confirmed for Olduvai and have also proven to recur elsewhere. For instance, at all sites the Bovidae predominate and at most sites this family contributes half or more of all individuals represented. The ratio of bones per individual also tends to be much higher for bovids than for any other group. Within the bovids fairly large animals (size 3) tend to be best represented – that is to say, animals in the size range between 115 and 340 kg (250–700 lbs.). The other recurrently represented taxa all tend to be of this size (e.g. large pigs or equids) or even larger size 5 and 6 animals (greater than 1,000 kg; e.g. giraffe, hippo, rhino and elephant). However, most of the very large animals at most of the sites are represented only by a very few scraps of bone and teeth, so that questions arise whether the incidence of these are significantly above normal background densities. The predominance of bovids could simply be a reflection of the fact that the Bovidae are the most numerous ungulates in almost all habitats, however the paucity of smaller Bovidae is probably not reflective simply of community structure. Differential preservation greatly favours the bones of larger over smaller animals and this may account for the persistent presence of the very big forms. However, bone is sufficiently well preserved at several of the sites for it to be more or less inconceivable that had quantities of remains of dik-dik or hare-sized animals been present, the remains would not have survived. This invites speculation as to why medium- and large-size animals preponderate. One major possibility that has occurred to various workers is that the assemblages formed as a result of scavenging activities. Smaller animals tend to be consumed so much more rapidly that their carcasses are minimally available for scavengers (see Binford, 1981; Bunn *et al.*, 1980 [this volume, ch. 8]; Clark, 1970; Isaac and Crader, 1981; Schaller and Lowther, 1969; and many other authors). Another possibility that has not been discussed is that for smaller animal carcasses a tear-apart-with-hands-and-teeth plus a feed-as-you-go consumption mode prevailed. This might have been comparable to that of chimpanzees so that no accumulation of bones with discarded artefacts would form. In contrast carcasses and carcass parts of animals too large to tear apart might have been transported to special places where they were cut up, and where their refuse accumulated along with discarded stone tools. Further discussion of both possibilities is reserved to the concluding section of the review.

Elizabeth Vrba (1975) has suggested some criteria for distinguishing bone accumulations formed primarily by scavenging from those formed by hunting, either by animals or hominids. The former should be marked by great variances in the sizes represented and by an under-representation of juveniles; the hunting-derived assemblages should be more sharply focused on a certain size of prey and should have an over-representation of the juveniles, especially juveniles of relatively larger prey forms. Without citing Vrba, R. Klein (1982) has elaborated on age profiles as a basis for distinguishing scavenged from hunted assemblages. The work of Potts (1982) and Bunn (1982a) provides for the first time estimates of the number of juveniles and sub-adults: there is no conspicuous over-representation of immature age classes. Equally, the size distribution spans a fairly wide range. These findings are consistent with derivation by scavenging, though they by no means prove it.

A variety of ungulate taxa are represented at most of the sites. Almost invariably the mix includes a fair number of grazing (grassland) bovids, such as the alcelaphini and the gazelles, but other grazers such as equids are generally less well represented than might be expected on the basis of present-day abundance (this is true both in terms of MNI and in terms of total numbers of specimens recovered). Most assemblages also include bush-loving forms (e.g. *Kobus, Strepciceros*, giraffe and some pigs) and, in the case of sites with primates such as colobus and mangabey (e.g. FxJj 20M and 20E), groves of gallery forest must have been sampled in the bone-accumulating process. These assemblages must have been accumulated by transport in from varied sectors of a mosaic of habitats or they must derive directly or indirectly from predation around water holes that drew together a range of species that are normally separated. This topic is discussed by Potts (1982).

The technicalities of body-part representation go beyond the scope of this review. Detailed data are provided in Potts (1982) and Bunn (1982a), and both works discuss this topic in some detail, as does Binford (1981), invoking the taphonomic work of Hill (1975), Behrensmeyer (1975, 1976a), Behrensmeyer *et al.* (1979), Shipman and Phillips-Conroy (1976), and others as a basis for interpretation. Suffice it to say here that broken-up limb-bones commonly form the great majority of bones that are in some degree identifiable. Ribs tend to be under-represented relative to the proportion that they comprise of intact skeletons, but two or three sites do have a fair number of rib fragments (e.g. Koobi Fora FxJj 50, Olduvai *Zinjanthropus* site). Vertebrae and pelves are relatively poorly represented. Teeth tend to be moderately well represented and figure well in taxonomic lists because of their high identifiability. However, as a fraction of the total number of specimens, teeth are not particularly numerous.

Highly fragmented bone is in the great majority at all sites where there is an abundance of artefacts. Fragments usually make up more than 90 per cent of any assemblage. In some cases where the bone has been scrutinized with this in mind, a plausible case has been made for the importance of hammer-smashing of the bones (Bunn 1982a; Bunn *et al.*, 1980 [this volume, ch. 8]). However, the distinction between hammer-smashed and jaw-crunched bones is a subtle one and further work is needed before anything definite can be said about the proportions of bones broken by hammer, chewing or trampling.[14] The effects of post-burial processes on fragmentation also need attention.

Meanwhile it can be said that the assemblages are consistent with the notion that detachable, food-rich portions of relatively large animals were removed from carcasses and carried in to the sites where they had tissue removed and where brain cases and long bones were broken up for food extraction.

As already indicated, cut marks have been recognized on bones from a number of sites. These include slicing marks seemingly caused by cutting muscle and tendons while detaching parts at joints. Other marks seem to represent muscle (meat) removal cuts and scrapes. Still others occur on distal limb bones such as metapodials and phalanges. These may represent cuts inflicted in skin removal prior to marrow extraction. Equally they may relate to skin removal that facilitated access to the carcass or secured the skin for use in its own right.

At most sites only a few cut-marked bones have been found (and none at some sites); however, in his study of the FLK Zinj site Bunn (1981, 1982a, 1983a) found some 300 bones with what he regards as clear stone-tool butchery marks. Potts and Shipman (1981) found many fewer, but a spot check on the reliability of Bunn's identifications seems to confirm a relatively high incidence at this site. Relative to identifiable bones, 300 specimens with cut marks represent between 4 and 5 per cent. This is a higher observed value than has been reported for the few African LSA sites where marks have been sought with great care (e.g. Prolonged Drift 2.9 per cent (Gifford *et al.*, 1980); Chencherere 1.4 per cent (Crader, 1981)). Bunn (1983a,b) has shown that these are distributed across joints and shafts in much the same way as are cut marks at more recent sites. Shipman (1983a) reaches a contrasting conclusion.

At a few of the Olduvai sites, notably FLK Zinj and FLK N 1–6, quantities of microfaunal remains were found, sometimes in small, localized concentrations.

These were reported by Mary Leakey (1971) with preliminary information on the taxa represented. Arguments were presented that these were not owl pellets, and that they might in fact be disintegrated hominid faeces (Napton in M. Leakey, 1971). Until recently no further work was done, but Andrews (1983) has now shown that the taxa represented are diurnal and that consequently the concentrations derive from the activities of a daytime predator. A number of small carnivores are known to mark territory by repeated defecation at one place. This is one patch-formation possibility, but hominid ingestion and defecation or regurgitation cannot yet be ruled out. At the *Zinjanthropus* site, large quantities of bird bones were recovered and these are currently under detailed study (Matthieson, n.d. [1982]). Several hundred waterfowl individuals are represented in this sample.

Environments, site location, and ecology

Over the past decade great progress has been made in gathering information on the palaeoenvironments of the early African sites, though a major synthesis has not yet been attempted. There are two aspects to the data. First, there is now a good deal of specific knowledge of local environmental conditions in the sedimentary basins that preserve the sites. This includes geological data on local palaeogeography (land forms, soils, hydrographic conditions, etc.), palaeolimnological data on the chemistry and biota of lakes; sometimes sparse pollen evidence for aspects of local and regional vegetation; and macromammal (and more rarely micromammal and bird) fossils indicative of the terrestrial faunal elements present. Second, there are sometimes indications that may relate to aspects of broader regional climatic conditions, though as yet these broader interpretations are much less secure than the reconstructions of local habitats and environments.

A full summary of the new information is beyond the scope of this review, but Table 5.7 presents in a highly simplified form some of the salient features of the context of the early archaeological evidence. References to the principal publications are given in the Appendix. See also Behrensmeyer (1982), Bishop (1978a), Bonnefille (1979), Butzer (1971; 1977), Coppens *et al.* (1976) for reviews on this topic.

Some salient features seem to emerge from all the disparate information. It appears that throughout the time span under consideration the Eastern Rift Valley and its surroundings had a mosaic of vegetation types not too unlike those of today. That is to say that a pattern in which various types of dry thorn savannah and open woodlands predominated, was interspersed with gallery forest along water courses and perennial rivers, respectively, and with evergreen forests on the major highland areas. Substantial areas of grasslands occurred on floodplains and probably on high plateaus. Large tracts of unbroken lowland forest probably did not occur. Studies of oxygen isotopes in carbonates (Cerling *et al.*, 1977) have been taken to indicate that before about 1.8 to 2.0 mya conditions were somewhat less dry. Various lines of biotic evidence can be taken as consistent with that interpretation but it cannot be regarded as proven. Also consistent with this hypothesis is the argument that

Table 5.7. *Palaeoenvironment and palaeogeography for each site*

Site	Mya		
	2	1.5	0.7
Melka Kunturé	A segment of the upper Awash valley, where a rising fault-block periodically ponded or impeded river flow. Fluvial and fluvial–lacustrine deposition. Fluctuating conditions with open high-altitude *Acacia* grassland. ⎯⎯⎯⎯⎯⎯⎯⎯⎯⎯⎯⎯⎯⎯⎯⎯⎯⎯⎯⎯⎯⎯⎯⎯⎯⎯→		
Gadeb		Ponded–low-gradient upland segment of the Webi Shebeli valley. High-altitude grasslands (2,350 m) just below montane forest. ⎯⎯⎯⎯⎯⎯⎯⎯⎯⎯⎯⎯	
Omo Shungura	Floodplain and upper delta of a major river flowing into Lake Turkana. Dry thorn savannah flanking river banks with gallery forest and back swamps. ⎯⎯ major transgression		
Koobi Fora	Floodplains between hills and proto-Lake Turkana, probably traversed by a perennial river, and certainly traversed by minor, local ephemeral streams. Dominant vegetation is dry thorn savannah with abundant grassland, some gallery forest, montane vegetation on hills. lake very fresh fluctuating brackish to fresh ⎯⎯ KBS ⎯⎯⎯⎯⎯⎯ KARARI		
Chesowanja		A small local sedimentary basin with a shallow lakelet or pond surrounded by seasonally inundated, low-lying ground. ⎯⎯⎯⎯⎯⎯⎯⎯	
Kilombe			Local colluvial and pond deposits in an upland area of impeded drainage. 2,000 m altitude. Probably *Acacia* savannah and edaphic grassland. ⎯⎯⎯⎯⎯⎯⎯⎯⎯⎯
Peninj	Stable salt lake showing one brief freshwater transgression. Perennial freshwater river ran in, forming a well-watered but mainly open grassland delta. ⎯⎯⎯⎯⎯⎯⎯ ⎯⎯⎯⎯		
Olduvai	Fluctuating salt lake with surrounding floodplains. Freshwater springs and streams producing local verdure in dry grassland surrounds. Forest on adjacent highlands.		Tectonics disrupt the basin, lake becomes a playa with dry surrounds traversed by seasonal streams.
	I	II	III/IV

changing characteristics for the large-mammal fauna indicate adaptation to progressively drier, more grass-dominated conditions (e.g. Coppens, 1978).

One feature in which the Plio–Pleistocene biota differed from the recent biota was
the much greater diversity of the macromammal fauna. For instance the number
of ancient species to modern species ratios were 4–5:2 for suids, 4:1 for giraffids,
3:1 for proboscideans, 3:2 for hyenids, 5 or 6:3 for large felids, 2:1 for baboons,
and 2:1 for hominids. What factors permitted this degree of diversity and what
changes reduced it are not yet clear. David Western (personal communication,
1982) has suggested greater stability of conditions as a possibility; perhaps less
pronounced wet/dry seasonality and perhaps less severe, less frequent drought
disasters. This suggestion is a challenge for future investigations.

There is evidence for fluctuations in Plio–Pleistocene conditions but the indications are often subtle and as yet there are few if any instances of a climatic event
or phase that can be securely recognized in more than one sedimentary basin.
Entirely gone are the days when a pluvial–interpluvial sequence could be offered as
the basis for correlation (see Cooke (1958) and Flint (1959) for the first demonstrations of the risks involved in such a scheme).

In only one case has it proven possible to scrutinize the changing frequencies of
some elements of a biota through a long sequence of strata. This is possible at the
Omo, and Boaz (1977) has presented plots for the percentage of alcelaphini-plus-
antilopini relative to other bovid tribes. An interesting quasi-cyclic pattern emerges,
but this remains to be checked against other data and in other sequences.

Against this general environmental background one thing that emerges clearly
is that our information about early hominid life comes from a highly biased sample
of habitats. Almost all the hominid fossils and archaeological sites come from
sedimentary basins with* low-flying flood plain and/or lake margin conditions
prevailing. The uplands, rolling hills, and dry plains that make up most of savannah
Africa were presumably lived in by early toolmaking hominids, but we have little
or no information on these landscape types. For an earlier time range the Laetoli
fossils and footprints and the sinkholes of the Transvaal attest to dry uplands as a
part of hominid range and the Olduvai upper Bed II, Bed III and Bed IV really pertain
to a proto-Serengeti-type dry environment.

Describing aspects of the setting of Plio–Pleistocene hominid life is only the start
of investigating environmental and autecological relations. There are formidable
difficulties in the way of going beyond this but in the past decade a start has been
made. Several lines of evidence can usefully be distinguished:

1. The distribution of hominid traces relative to the ancient habitat mosaics.
2. Evidence of diet.
3. Collection of relevant data from modern environments on the patterns of cost–
   benefit relationships prevailing for various possible food classes and various possible
   foraging strategies.

Distribution of traces

Traces consist of fossil hominid bones, stone artefacts, cut-marked bones, and

Table 5.8. *Estimates of the relative density of sites in different sedimentary facies at Olduvai*[a]

	Lake margin		Fluvial–lacu-strine		Fluvial		Alluvial fan and plain
	E	W	E	W	E	W	
III–IV	–	–	0.53		0.07	0.75 (1.5[b])	–
II	0.48 (1.05)[c]	0.30	0.88	0.30	0	–	0
I	1.3	0.16	–	–	–	–	0

[a] Distinction is made among three stratigraphic intervals and among seven lithofacies with palaeogeographic significance (from Hay, 1976:181).
[b] In main drainage way.
[c] In the Kelogi area.

footprints. Data have been compiled on the location of all these but the task of looking for interpretable regularities in the patterning is still underway.

The first substantial new statement was that of Hay (1976: ch. 12). Having reported in detail on the lithofacies and overall palaeogeography of the Olduvai sedimentary basin, he tabulated the number of metres of section traversed for each archaeological site encountered. Table 5.8 presents a simplified rearrangement of the data. It can clearly be seen that at any given time concentrations of artefacts (= sites) were not evenly distributed across the different sectors of the basin floor. In Bed I they were clustered on the eastern lake margin floodplain where freshwater pools and streams seem to have existed. As conditions changed, the lake became a playa with ephemeral streams running into it. Increasingly the artefact concentrations are found in the beds of these seasonal water courses and along their banks. Hay has also shown that in upper Bed II, sites with Developed Oldowan B type assemblages tend to be within a kilometre of the lake shore, whereas those with biface-dominated Acheulean assemblages are further out toward the margin.

Building on information provided by M. D. Leakey (1971), Hay also provides valuable data on changing patterns of redistribution by toolmakers of stones from different sources (1976:183).

The majority of artifacts at all excavated sites in Bed I and II are made of materials obtainable within a distance of 4 km, and at most sites the artifacts are less than 2 km from possible sources. However, sites with a large number of artifacts almost invariably contain a small proportion that are of materials available no closer than 8 to 10 km. As an example, lava from the volcanic highlands is present at most of the archeologic sites in the western part of the Main Gorge. The proportion of these materials from more distant sources in and near the basin appears to increase upward in the sequence, at least to the base of Bed III. A relatively few artifacts at various levels in the sequence are of material obtained from distant sources outside the Basin. Only in the Naisiusiu Beds (i.e. late Quaternary) do these exotic materials constitute an appreciable portion of the artifacts.

A study of one factory site at a palaeo-outcrop of chert and of the movement of material to other contemporary sites has been contributed by Stiles *et al.* (1974).

Hay (1976:186) concludes:

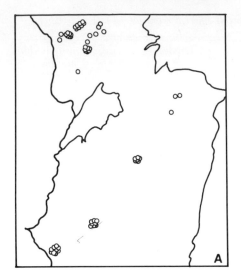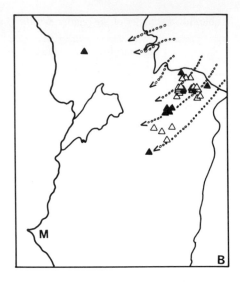

Fig. 5.13. At Koobi Fora, (A) hominid fossils are best preserved in the lake margins where stone was not available; (B) conspicuous clusters of ancient artefacts occur only in sectors of the sedimentary basin traversed by clast-bearing stream beds. O, Hominid sites; ▲, excavated archaeological sites; △, unexcavated archaeological sites; M, sites with cut-marked bones only; arrows represent stream beds.

Hominids ranged widely over the basin from Bed I upward, as shown by a small but significant proportion of materials from distances of at least 8 km at most sites yielding a large number of artifacts. The degree of human mobility seems to have increased through time, at least through the periods represented by Beds I and II, as based on the overall upward increase in proportion of raw materials from the more distant sources. Rare artifacts of materials from distant sources outside the basin may have been obtained from hominid groups with a territorial range bordering the Olduvai basin.

The evidence for increasing mobility is consistent with predictions from ecological theory. Lower population densities and wider-ranging patterns would be expected following the proven upper Bed II change to drier conditions with a sparser distribution of water and other resource patches.

At the Omo, Merrick and Merrick (1976) and Chavaillon (1976) have documented the existence of artefact concentrations both in association with small water courses (e.g. FtJi 1) and with floodplain and back swamp conditions (e.g. FxJi 3 and Omo 126). Jean de Heinzelin (personal communication, 1973) has suggested that the Omo archaeological sites of Member F are associated with local palaeogeographic conditions that were rather unusual for the Omo – namely, the existence of small, branching water courses at the head of a delta flood-plain, rather than a single, meandering main channel. I am not aware of specific published documentation for this.

At Melka Kunturé preliminary reports by Chavaillon and others (1979) comment that within the small, ponded, river-valley sedimentary basin the earlier, Oldowan sites tend to be associated with lake-edge situations, and the Acheulian sites with small, ephemeral stream channels.

At Koobi Fora the palaeogeographic distributions of both the hominid fossils and the artefacts have been examined. Kay Behrensmeyer (1976a,b, 1978a,b) has shown that the hominid fossils are best preserved in the lake margin and the shoreline floodplain sedimentary facies of both the Lower and Upper Members, but that they also occur in channel deposits back from the shore and as scattered and very rare specimens in fluvial floodplain silts. She has suggested that on the available data there appears to be some preferential association between *Australopithecus boisei* and channel deposits and between *Homo* fossils and lake margins. However, the association would effectively disappear if one channel in Area 105 with numerous *A. boisei* fossils were not a part of the sample. Further, unless *A. boisei* were the main toolmaker the distribution of archaeological remains gives contrary indications.

Isaac and Harris (1978) have compiled maps that show the combined pattern of hominid fossil find spots and the location of archaeological sites. This is reproduced here as Fig. 5.13. From it one can see that for Upper Member times (≈ 1.6–1.3 mya), most hominid fossils are found in the lake-margin facies toward the basin centre whereas most sites are in the fluvial beds close to the basin margin. It is probable that the hominids ranged fairly evenly over both sectors of the basin floor, but that detectable artefact concentrations only occurred in areas where cobble-bearing streams coming in from the margins provided plentiful close-at-hand stone sources. The fossil distribution, on the other hand, probably reflects conditions of preservation more than preferential lake-margin habitat use.

Information that tends to confirm this surmise and go beyond it has recently become available. Numbers of cut-marked bones have been found in two lake-margin areas where hominid fossils are well represented, but which yield few or no detectable artefact concentrations. Clearly stone tools were carried in but discarded only rarely. In addition, Kay Behrensmeyer found a short sector of a hominid footprint trail in lake-margin lagoon mud, implying that 1.6 mya some early hominids undertook activities that involved paddling or wading (Behrensmeyer and LaPorte, 1981).

Virtually all the Lower Member sites (1.9–1.8 mya) and the Upper Member artefact concentrations (1.6–1.3 mya) at Koobi Fora are closely associated with water courses, being on the banks or in the channel beds. Although some sites may represent secondary hydraulic concentrations, the majority do not, and it is very clear that the pattern is due to the recurrent localization of making and discarding artefacts along what are mainly seasonal stream courses with sandy beds (Isaac, 1972c, 1976b, 1981a [this volume, ch. 12]).

In recent years a new research approach has been tentatively developed by the Koobi Fora archaeology team. This has involved attempts to make a systematic study of the overall distribution of artefacts in the sedimentary basin. In the first round of fieldwork artefacts present were recorded along a series of transects running at right-angles to the outcrop lineations. Subsequently observations have been taken at sample points at stratified random intervals along the outcrop of particular beds that can be traced over a kilometre or more. Preliminary reports on the objectives, methods and some results have been published (Isaac, 1981b [this volume, ch. 7]; Isaac and Harris, 1975, 1980; Isaac *et al.*, 1981 [this volume, ch. 9]). These studies are in their early stages but they seem to reveal aspects of the configuration of evidence that were not apparent from the conventional find-and-excavate-dense-concentrations approach. It emerges that across the ancient fluvial floodplains of the Karari area there was a widespread but very-low-density scatter of artefacts deposited singly or in ones and twos. In addition, there are small clusters of artefacts with diameters of 5 to 10 m and with 10 or 15 to 100 or so artefacts that can sometimes be demonstrated by conjoining to result from the flaking of just two or three cores (e.g. FxJj 64; see Isaac *et al.*, 1981 [this volume, ch. 9]). These are informally called mini-sites. Then in some areas there may be an elevated background density over an area 300–400 m in diameter. Within the two best-studied such cases of elevated background density, a number of notably dense artefact concentrations occur. These are classic sites of the kind conventionally chosen for excavation (e.g. FxJj 20M, 20E, 20AB, FxJj 18NS, 18GS, 18IHS; see Harris, 1978).

From this perception of overall patterning, one of the possibilities that arises is that classic or *maxi-sites* are formed as the result of repeated superpositioning at the same spot of the same behaviours as form the mini-sites. If this is the case the study of numerous mini-sites may disentangle the behavioural components more readily than the study of maxi-sites where they are inextricably mixed (Isaac *et al.*, 1981 [this volume, ch. 9]).

Detailed interpretation of this new class of data would be premature but clearly it may eventually be interpretable in terms of ranging pattern, mobility, frequency of tool discard under different circumstances, and so forth. It may provide a much more balanced picture than would investigations that proceed exclusively by the excavation of dense concentrations.

A recurrent feature of major concentrations in all sedimentary basins and at all time levels is for them to be at or in close proximity to water courses. The only set that is a major exception to this are the Olduvai Bed I and lower Bed II sites, which were on a lake-margin floodplain. There are many possible reasons for the attraction of channels. Principal among these probably was the denser bush and tree growth along the drainage ways, which could provide shade, something to climb if predators approached, and presumably a variety of plant foods. Water may also have been obtainable in pools and by digging. This pattern of association continues right on through the Middle Pleistocene (Isaac, 1972c, 1977a). The anatomy of the hominids seems to give testimony that they did more tree climbing and were better adapted for it than are most modern humans (Jungers, 1982; Stern and Susman, 1983; Susman and Stern, 1982; Vrba, 1979).

Duration and seasonality

Some major shortcomings continue to hamper interpretation. First, we do not have unambiguous evidence on the number and duration of the usage bouts that led to the formation of the sites. As indicated above, bone-weathering data imply that they were open for at least a few years (Bunn, 1982a; Bunn *et al.*, 1980 [this volume, ch. 8]; Potts, 1982), but for not more than eight or ten years. Ecological and socio-economic interpretation of the sites will be noticeably affected by knowing whether they formed largely within the space of a year or so, or whether many years were involved. Seeking criteria in the micro-surface features of bones, and in other ways, is an important research need (Shipman, 1981b). Second, we do not know in any instance whether usage was sustained, erratically scattered in time, or markedly associated with a particular season. Speth and Davis (1976; Davis, 1978) have suggested that those Bed I sites where chelonian bones are abundant were wet-season sites. The specifics of this argument can probably not be sustained because the circumstances prevailing on the floodplain of a perennial lake and swamp may well have been very different from those found in the Kalahari thirstland to which they owe their main analogy. The conspecificity of the turtle and the constancy of its estivation–activity cycle are also open to legitimate doubt. However their paper is an important one in that it highlights the need for restless searches to be made that will reveal seasonality: for instance the sectioning of teeth and fish bones in search of patterned, incremental growth markings.

Diet

The archaeological evidence indicative of Plio–Pleistocene involvement in meat and marrow eating has already been discussed. That at least some of these hominids were sometimes involved in eating substantial quantities of meat from large animals can now be treated as settled. However, meat may have been an occasional rather than a regular food, and the characteristics of normal daily feeding patterns or of their regional or seasonal variation all remain unknown.

Most thoughtful scholars have long assumed that vegetable foods composed the main source of energy and the bulk of dietary intake,[15] but until very recently it was difficult to see how the importance of plant foods was to be directly documented or the specific components determined. Now, a few new techniques promise advances in this aspect of inquiry.

First, it has been demonstrated that teeth acquire different micro-scratch patterns that depend on the substances against which they move in chewing. In the first round of research it has been possible for Walker (1981) to demonstrate that the considerable sample of Miocene to early Pleistocene fossils examined by him do not include any hominoids that were eating grass leaves, grass stems, or grass seed-heads, or any that were chomping bones between their teeth. In addition all the specimens so far examined that are older than the first *H. erectus* at 1.5 mya lack the kind of damage that teeth acquire if food such as bulbs and tubers are dug out of the ground and eaten without careful preparation. By related kinds of study in South Africa, Grine (1981) has shown that the robust australopithecines were eating more tough foods than were the graciles. These results seem to indicate that foods in the fruit, pods, nuts, soft leaves, and insect range are the probable dietary components. However, the technique does not as yet help assess the question of the plants relative to meat proportion in the diet, nor does it do more than eliminate some plant foods; that is, grass, grains, and, for the earliest hominids, underground storage forms.[16] More can be expected as the technique is refined and applied to more specimens.

Two other techniques that are proving of great value in the late Quaternary may eventually be applicable for the early period. One of these is the determination of strontium/calcium ratios as an index of the position of an organism in the food chain (Schoeninger, 1982; Sillen and Kavanagh, 1982; Toots and Voorhies, 1965). However, there may be grave problems with diagenetic alteration in very old bones (Sillen, 1981). The other is the determination of stable carbon-isotope ratios. Relatively high $^{13}C/^{12}C$ ratios (less big negative delta values) are an indicator of the consumption of C4 (van der Merwe, 1982) tropical grasses or of grazing animals that eat such grasses. Ericson *et al.* (1981) have reported differences between a grazer and a browser that meet predictions, based on the stable carbon-isotope composition of bone apatite from the Omo. This is promising but further work on the effects of diagenesis will be needed.

Toward realistic ecological models

Access to increasingly detailed descriptive information about palaeoenvironments, combined with increasingly systematic information about diet and about the habitats in which early toolmaking hominids discarded tools, offers researchers the chance to develop and test various alternative models of subsistence and ranging patterns. However, it is becoming increasingly clear that we cannot develop realistic versions of such models without much more precise quantitative information on relevant characteristics of a range of modern environments that are analogous to those that early ancestral forms demonstrably used.

The logic is this: if we can measure the scale of various feeding and sheltering opportunities in appropriate present-day settings, we can seek to use some modern ecological theory, such as optimal foraging theory, to simulate possible feeding, grouping and ranging strategies. The spectrum of ecologically possible patterns will then be rival deductive hypotheses about the past and we will have to use our archaeological ingenuity in testing them.

This line of approach is being explored. The first, prescient paper of this kind known to me was that of Schaller and Lowther (1969), which made a preliminary assessment of the scavenging opportunities that would have been open to early hominids. Other more prolonged and more quantitative extensions of that study are now being planned (Blumenschine, 1983).

On the plant side, Peters (1979) and Peters and O'Brien (1981) have begun systematic work on what they term the *fundamental plant food niche*. This begins to lift this whole topic out of the realm of pure speculation. In addition field ecological studies are being done. Jeanne Sept has made systematic studies of the structure of vegetation communities that fringe the kinds of water courses with which many early artefact concentrations are associated. This study will allow a first assessment of the feeding and sheltering opportunities afforded by this much-used habitat type (Sept, n.d. [1984]). In another study, Anne Vincent is engaged in making a first field assessment of the abundance and patchiness of tubers and plant underground storage organs (USOs) in various floodplain and savannah environments. She will look at the extent of USO toxicity with and without cooking. This should facilitate cost-benefit analyses that will guide the formulation of models of the modification of the diet breadth of early hominids relative to non-human primates. The development of tools for digging up USOs could well have opened up this feeding opportunity, and we need to know its scale (Vincent, n.d. [1984]; and see also Hatley and Kappelman, 1980).

Conclusion and prospects

At the outset, the state of knowledge defined by Mary Leakey's 1971 volume on Olduvai was used as the point of departure. Following a question-by-question review of research activity over the past decade, it may be of interest to turn and ask in what way the overall situation differs as a result of ten years more work. Reflection shows that the cumulative differences in knowledge are subtle rather than sweeping. It is the state of *inquiry* more than the state of knowledge that has advanced.

If asked to make a summary statement about the essential characteristics of Plio–Pleistocene proto-human life now, most of the archaeologists involved in the research would not say anything very different from what would have been said ten years ago, though there are many more specifics and details to add. However, most wise archaeologists would probably be more cautious now than they would have been ten years ago. We still envisage small mobile groups that made stone tools of a very simple design but with varied useful forms. We believe that we have confirmed that they used these implements, among other things, to dismember carcasses, parts of which were repeatedly carried to particular places, which may have been central places, perhaps camps. The foci of tool discarding and bone accumulation tend to be at kinds of places characterized by tree and bush growth and/or by proximity to water sources.

What has changed is that (1) we now have many more cases from different times and places, still not enough but more than before; (2) we begin to have a much more process-conscious grasp of the characteristics of the stones and bones recovered in excavations. We begin to understand them not as a set of objects but as the remnants of complex 'flow' systems; (3) there are valuable new classes of information such as use polishes, cut marks, the patterns of conjoining pieces and the micro-scratches on teeth; and (4) there is a groping start on thinking in real ecological terms.

Most important of all, the acquisition of these much more varied bodies of information has been associated with liberation of thinking about very early proto-human ways of life. There is a growing realization that it may have been very

Hypothesis `X´

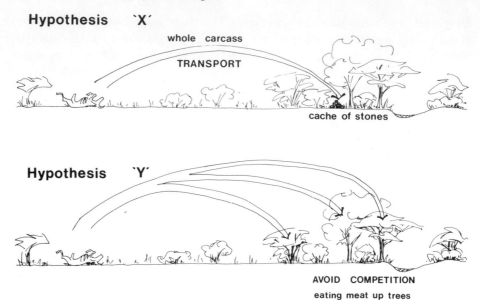

whole carcass

TRANSPORT

cache of stones

Hypothesis   `Y´

AVOID   COMPETITION

eating meat up trees

Hypothesis   `Z´

TRANSPORT

hominids
cut pieces off
Carcasses

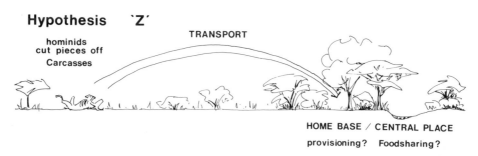

HOME BASE / CENTRAL PLACE

provisioning?   Foodsharing?

Fig. 5.14. Three rival hypotheses to account for the formation of artefacts plus broken-up animal bones. All involve active hominid transport of both the stones and the bones, but only one (Z) involves a central-place foraging (home-base) pattern. Hypothesis X from Potts (1982).

different from recent prehistory and modern times in its fundamental patterning. With that realization research is becoming an exciting exercise in archaeological exploration, with an alternation between leaps of imagination and rigorous testing.

In the past decade much effort has been spent testing time-honoured propositions such as the importance or not of meat as a food, or the existence or not of home bases. Superficially it may look as if the main elements of the initial consensus-interpretation have been sustained, but yet one can argue that in subtle ways many components have been more undermined than propped up. Let me give three instances. First, new research has confirmed that feeding on the meat of relatively large animals had begun to be a part of the proto-human behavioural repertoire by 2 mya, but we are now far more aware than we were that we do not know what fraction of diet or effort this represents. We do not know whether it was hunted or scavenged, and we have little idea what else was being eaten. Why did all the 2–4 mya hominids have such relatively large cheek teeth? What were they eating before our lineage began using stone tools? What differences did tools make?

Second, we can show that stone tools were carried to particular places where a good deal of flaking was done. Carcass parts were also carried to these places, presumably with edible tissues being eaten there. But does this mean that the places were campsites or home bases? Many workers now recognize that it need not mean this. The term *central-place foraging* is to be preferred over *food-sharing* but, although it may seem likely that many sites of Type C were some kind of central place, even that is not certain. Figure 5.14 shows three alternative hypotheses as to how the observed configuration of Type C sites could have formed. Further imaginative thinking might well reveal others that should be considered. We cannot yet eliminate any one or rank them objectively, so deducting testable distinctions between the expectations for each stands as a challenge to archaeological ingenuity in the next round of research. Moore (in press [1984]) has devised an interesting hypothesis for the start of meat transport and sharing that does not have the sentimental qualities of most previous models. He suggests that it involved seeking advantages in ranking and dominance.

Third, most writers on the early period, myself among them, seem tacitly to assume the existence of bandlike roving hominid groups that may have dispersed for periods of hours or a day or so but that would tend to reconvene at regular intervals, perhaps sleeping together. The patterning of remains with conspicuous clustering is certainly consistent with such a social configuration and ranging pattern. But if one shakes loose from simply projecting familiar human patterns back in time, then one can see that this is not the only ranging pattern that could have generated the observed pattern. What are the alternatives? Can archaeology be used to distinguish among them?

The realization has grown that the way of life of the earliest toolmaking members of the genus *Homo* need not have been merely a simpler prototypic version of recent human behaviour, nor need it have been, in a simple linear sense, intermediate between an ape pattern and a human pattern. There could well have been original configurations that nonetheless involved ingredients such as toolmaking and food transport.

It has also become clear that the record of the past – fossils, artefacts, arrangement, and context – does not provide us with all the information that we need in devising different models of proto-human adaptive systems and in distinguishing their goodness of fit with real evidence. As explained, palaeoanthropologists have to explore savannah Africa with the eyes of muscular but relatively small-brained hominids for whom toolmaking and perhaps social coordination were still relatively new and undeveloped tricks. We urgently need quantitative information on the scale and spacing of various feeding, sheltering, and life-support opportunities. This kind of work is just beginning.

It is uncertain how far we can ever go in figuring out what daily life was like between 1 and 2 mya, but we can go further than we have yet done and archaeologists are obviously going to have fun responding to the challenge.

APPENDIX

Notes and commentary on the key sites, with bibliographic references

The sites are arranged in geographic order from north to south: Kada Gona, Melka Kunturé, Gadeb, Omo Shungura, Koobi Fora, Chesowanja, Kilombe, Peninj and Olduvai.

Kada Gona (Ethiopia)

Kada Gona is a tributary gully complex a few kilometres south of Kada Hadar, in which the fluviatile gravels, sands, and silts of the upper part of the Hadar Formation are well exposed.

The potential palaeoanthropological significance of the whole area was first recognized by M. Taieb, with subsequent research by Taieb, D. Johanson and Y. Coppens. General accounts are available in Aronson *et al.* (1977), Johanson *et al.* (1978a,b), Taieb and Tiercelin (1979), and Chavaillon (1982).

The lower part of the formation is dated to 3 my or more and contains abundant faunal remains plus hominids that are attributed to a new species, *Australopithecus afarensis*. Artefacts have not been identified in the beds with the hominid fossils. However, in 1974 Gudrun Corvinus and Hélène Roche (1976) discovered artefacts in beds higher up in the sequence that seem to be interstratified with the BKT 2 Tuff, which has since been dated to 2.7 my (Walter and Aronson, 1982). These discoveries were followed up in 1977 by Hélène Roche, who found more localities (Johanson *et al.*, 1978b; Roche, 1980; Roche and Tiercelin, 1977). Subsequently J. W. K. Harris found and test excavated an additional site nearby (Harris and Johanson, 1983; Lewin, 1981).

The material consists of relatively simple flaked lava cobbles (cores and 'choppers') and the detached flakes and fragments. Discussion of the dating and significance of these important finds is set out in the main text (pp. 126–7).

Melka Kunturé (Ethiopia)

The Melka Kunturé site complex was discovered by a UN hydrologist, Dr G. Dekker. Initial investigations were carried out by archaeologist G. Bailloud (1965). Subsequently the direction and coordination of the long-term programme of investigation and excavation have been undertaken by Jean Chavaillon and are still continuing. Chavaillon and co-workers (1978, 1979) published very useful general summaries of the sequence, and Westphal *et al.* (1979) reported on stratigraphy and dating. More up-to-date information is contained in Chavaillon (1982).

At Melka Kunturé a small sedimentary basin formed and developed within the headwater catchment of the Awash river. The sites are at an altitude of 2,000 m. The total vertical range of exposure is approximately 30 m only, but because of complex cut-and-fill relationships, the section spans a large part of the Pleistocene. The lower units show reversed polarity and are certainly older than 700,000 years.

For the period covered in this review, the site of Gomboré is particularly important. An area of 200 m² has been exposed. Some 12,000 artefacts were recovered on the stony ancient channel bank. These are dominated by flaked-stone pieces with flakes themselves being fairly rare – either, as Chavaillon suggests, because the stones were flaked elsewhere, or because the flakes have been preferentially washed away by fluvial action. The artefacts are predominantly various sorts of choppers, core-scrapers (*rabots et grattoirs épais sur galet*) and polyhedrons. A few pieces seem to resemble thick, rough precursors of bifaces. The ensemble is regarded as representing an Oldowan industry (Chavaillon, 1982). Varied faunal remains occur within the site and are taken to be food refuse (Geraads, 1979). A part of a hominid humerus was also recovered. The age of this horizon is estimated as 1.7 my by Chavaillon (1982). The Garba IV site, which has also yielded more than 12,000 artefacts, is at a horizon estimated to be between 1.4 and 1.5 my old. The artefact forms are reported to be more evolved than those of Gomboré 1B. That is to say, the core-tool forms are better made and there is a greater development of flake-tool forms. Among the 12–13,000 artefacts there are three true handaxes and two cleavers. The assemblage has been identified as Evolved Oldowan (Chavaillon, 1982).

The site of Garba XII has yielded eight horizons believed to span the Jaramillo Event from about 1.1 to 0.8 my. The artefact assemblages include early Acheulian forms in reasonable numbers. It is suggested that an oval configuration of stones represents the footing of a simple shelter of poles or branches, and structural modifications have also been reported for the earlier sites. The contemporary site of Sumbiro III has been interpreted as a place where the large bovid form *Pelorovis* was butchered.

At Gomboré II two horizons have been excavated that are older than the Brunhes–Matuyama boundary with an estimated age of 0.84 my. The assemblage represents relatively advanced looking Acheulian industries with lanceolate, ovate, and cordiform handaxes, as well as a diversified flake-tool series that include *racloirs*, end-scrapers, backed knives, burins, awls, and so forth. A variety of faunal remains are also preserved at the site.

Other levels higher up the section document continuing technological development and a series of late Acheulian and Middle and Later Stone Age horizons have been studied.

Melka Kunturé is a site of the greatest importance. So far the reports available are mainly preliminary and do not provide full quantitative data, and for this reason Melka Kunturé does not figure as extensively as it should in the discussion of the main text of this review. Later, when the full reports are available, the site complex will clearly help to advance our understanding both of ways of life and of technological development.

Gadeb (Ethiopia)

High on the eastern shoulder of the Rift Valley at an elevation of 2,300 to 2,400 m, J. D. Clark and M. A. J. Williams have found and studied a sedimentary sequence that contains early Pleistocene artefacts. In the Pliocene a small lake formed with the deposition of diatomite layers. The lake was subsequently drained as a result of the headward erosion of the Webi Shebeli gorge. However, fluvial deposits continued to be laid down intermittently as cut-and-fill units within the sedimentary basin. The lower fluvial units show reversed polarity and contain mammal fossils plus Acheulian and 'Developed Oldowan' varieties of artefact assemblages (Williams *et al.*, 1979). Reports on the archaeology have been published by Clark and Kurashina (1979a,b).

The artefact assemblages include variable proportions of neatly made bifaces and small, rather opportunistic-looking flake-scrapers and other small tools. At one site (8F) the artefacts were found within channel deposits and were interspersed among a scatter of fossil hippo bones. This may represent a hippo butchery site, but cut marks have not been reported.

A number of welded-tuff specimens from excavation Site 8E were observed to show reddening such as might have been caused by exposure to the heat of a fire. Palaeomagnetic tests show that the stones may have been heated, though this is not certain (Barbetti *et al.*, 1980).

The Omo, Shungura Formation (Ethiopia)

Following up on the pioneer work of Bourg de Bozas and Camille Arambourg, an international scientific consortium was formed under the joint leadership of C. Arambourg, F. C. Howell and Louis Leakey. Subsequently the scientific direction of the research devolved on Y. Coppens and F. C. Howell.

The Shungura Formation is close to 1 km in thickness and spans a time range from about 3.3 mya to about 1 mya. A rich fossil vertebrate sequence is distributed through the full thickness of the formation and these fossils include numerous hominid specimens. The earliest form appears to belong to a gracile australopithecine (*Australopithecus afarensis* and/or *A. africanus*). In beds between 2 and 1 mya a greater diversity of hominids seems to have been sampled: robust australopithecines (*A. boisei*) plus two early species of the genus *Homo* (*Homo habilis*, followed by *H. erectus*). Good general summaries are available in Howell, 1976, 1978a,b.

So far archaeological sites have been discovered, excavated, and reported mainly at one level, Member F, which is dated to between 2.0 and 2.1 mya. As discussed in the main text, it is possible that there are artefacts also in Member E with an age of between 2.1 and 2.4 mya. Member G and other members in the upper part of the formation are reported to contain scattered artefacts, but no reports are yet available as to the characteristics of these.

The Member F archaeological occurrences consist largely of concentrations of flaked and smashed-up quartz pebbles. The site and the assemblages have been reported by Merrick (1976), Merrick and Merrick (1976), and Merrick *et al.* (1973), and by Chavaillon (1970, 1976) and Chavaillon and Boisaubert (1977).

Koobi Fora (Kenya)

The potential palaeoanthropological importance of this area was first recognized in 1967 by Richard Leakey. The first archaeological sites were found by A. K. Behrensmeyer and R. Leakey in 1969. From 1970 to the present, Glynn Isaac has worked in partnership with R. Leakey to coordinate the overall scientific programme at Koobi Fora. J. W. K. Harris joined Isaac as a partner in directing the archaeological research.

The Koobi Fora Formation spans the time range from about 4 to 1.3 mya. In the earlier stages of geological study it was assumed that there were a limited number of tuff horizons and that these could be used for correlation. It is now known that there are numerous tuffs in the lower part of the section and that the stratigraphic correlations that were proposed were seriously in error (Brown and Cerling, 1982). It is now clear that the early part of the stratigraphic section, much of which was formerly called the Kubi Algi Formation, ranges in age from 4 to about 3 mya. This portion of the section has yielded faunal remains but only a very few fragmentary hominid specimens and no artefacts. There are very few beds belonging to the interval between 2 and 3 mya, and in many sections there are one or more disconformities. Above the disconformities there occur a sequence of beds that range in age from about 2 to 1.39 mya. It is in this upper portion of the formation that all the archaeological sites and the great majority of the important hominid fossils occur. Although errors of tuff correlation have been found in the upper portion of the formation as well, these errors are fewer and less serious than those affecting the lower portions. This means that the published reports on the stratigraphic relations among the archaeological sites are in general still valid, though they must be used with caution.

The oldest archaeological sites occur within the KBS Tuff, which is securely dated to 1.88 ± 0.02 mya (McDougall, in press [1985]). Another major group of sites, the Karari industry sites, are stratified between the Okote Tuff, which is dated at 1.4 mya, and the Karari Tuff, dated at 1.38 mya. This group has been studied in detail by J. W. K. Harris (1978). The KBS Tuff sites and assemblages are reported in Isaac *et al.* (1976) and Isaac (1976c).

One early Acheulian site has been found and excavated and this has been judged to fall stratigraphically above the 1.38 mya Chari Tuff.

The KBS age sites are broadly contemporary with the KNM-ER-1470 skull and the other comparable hominid fossils that are put into the taxon *Homo habilis*, while there are early *Homo erectus* fossils in the beds contemporary with the Karari industry. *Australopithecus boisei* fossils are found scattered all through the layers between about 2 and 1.38 mya.

General accounts of the Koobi Fora stratigraphy, palaeontology and archaeology are available in R. E. and M. G. Leakey (1978). The hominid finds are summarized in Walker and Leakey (1978). Palynological studies are reported in Vincens (1979, 1982). Revised stratigraphy and dating are reported in Brown and Cerling (1982), Cerling and Brown (1982), and McDougall (in press) [1985].

Among the best-preserved sites at Koobi Fora is site FxJj 50 in the Okote Tuff complex. This has been the subject of a brief monographic report (Bunn *et al.* 1980 [this volume, ch. 8]). A full-scale compendium of site reports and assemblage analyses of all the Koobi Fora sites is in an advanced stage of preparation for publication by the Clarendon Press (Isaac, in prep.[17]).

Chemogoit Formation at Chesowanja (Kenya)

To the East of Lake Baringo, faults and a gentle anticlinal structure have led to the exposure of a small part of an early Pleistocene sedimentary formation. Unfortunately only a few thousand square metres of outcrop are available for study. Fossils, including two fragmentary robust australopithecine crania, and a series of stone-artefact occurrences have been found. Bishop *et al.* (1978) provide a general report on the locality and sequence based on the first rounds of work. Subsequently, in 1978 a team comprising John Gowlett, J. W. K. Harris and Bernard Wood resumed palaeoanthropological research in the area and some reports are now available (Blumenschine, 1983; Gowlett *et al.*, 1981; Harris *et al.*, 1981).

The exposed portion of the Chemogoit Formation consists of 25 to 30 m of tuffaceous silty sands, sandy silts and clays. The deposits are believed to have been laid down adjacent to the margin of a small saline Rift Valley lake. Artefacts occur scattered through the sediments but two sites have been located and trenched (GnJc 1/6E and GnJc 1/5). At the first site, 930 artefacts, plus > 85 bone fragments and more than 40 pieces of hard red clay were found forming a horizon within the fine-grained fill of an ancient gully, which had formed and then silted up in antiquity. The second site yielded 140 artefacts plus an unspecified number of bones. The artefacts are made of fine-grained lavas and consist of 5 to 10 per cent flaked pieces (choppers, discoids, polyhedrons, etc.) plus about 90 to 95 per cent detached pieces (flakes, flake fragments, etc.). In general aspect the material is equivalent to the Olduvai Bed I or Koobi Fora Formation assemblages and it has been designated as the Chemogoit Industry of the Oldowan Industrial Complex.

The Chemogoit Formation is overlain by a lava flow that has been dated to 1.42 ± 0.07 mya by the K/Ar method. A palaeosol horizon has developed on the lava and contains numerous small artefacts that are dated to the early Pleistocene and that have been designated the Losokweta Industry within the Oldowan Industrial Complex.

Chesowanja is important for providing additional stone-artefact assemblages from the time range 1.5 to 2.0 mya, and especially for the suggestive co-occurrence of artefacts and burned-clay fragments (see main text, p. 151 and note 9).

Kilombe (Kenya)

In 1970 within the Rift Valley at an altitude of 2,000 m an erosion gully complex was discovered that was exposing a rich assemblage of Acheulian handaxes and cleavers. William Bishop (1978b) prepared a geologic report and J. A. J. Gowlett (1978) undertook archaeological studies.

The 25 m-thick sedimentary sequence, which encases the archaeological horizon, consists of tuffaceous, colluvial, fluvial and swamp deposits that appear to have accumulated within a small localized depression at the western margin of the floor of the Rift Valley. Artefacts occur at several levels within the basal part of the sequence but there is one old land surface horizon that is littered with literally thousands of handaxes and cleavers, plus three or four times as many flakes. The horizon is exposed over an area in excess of 200×200 m. The original limits of the area are not known. Gowlett has made two test excavations, exposing sample areas of the archaeological horizon, of 25 and 14 m^2. The first yielded 127 handaxes, cleavers, and other bifaces, plus 36 choppers and cores, and 65 scrapers and trimmed flakes. There were 748 flakes and flake fragments. The second excavated area yielded similar material but with fewer cleavers and at a lower density.

The artefacts are made of fine-grained lava, probably mainly phonolite. The bifaces are neatly made forms that would be regarded as representative of middle or Upper Acheulian phases. It therefore came as something of a surprise that a waterlaid tuff overlying the horizon had reversed polarity, thus demonstrating an age in excess of 0.7 my.

Gowlett (1978, 1980, 1982, in press [1984]) has shown that the Kilombe assemblages include highly standardized, regular biface forms.

It would seem probable that the impressive dense litter of artefacts formed on a level ground surface adjacent to a small pond or swamp. The length of the time span during which the surface was stable and open for accumulation is not known. One supposes that it could be anything from a few decades to a few millennia. Bone is not preserved on the main horizon, but a few fossils have been recovered from underlying clays.

Peninj (Tanzania)

In 1964 R. E. Leakey and G. Isaac explored the area west of Lake Natron. A robust australopithecine mandible and two early Acheulian archaeological sites were found in beds dated to between 1 and 1.8 mya. The stratigraphy, chronology and archaeology were reported by Isaac (1965, 1967a) and Isaac and Curtis (1974).

New research has recently begun at Peninj but results are not yet available to be incorporated in this review.

Olduvai Gorge (Tanzania)

Olduvai Gorge is the classic locality for the study of Early Pleistocene archaeology in East Africa. The artefact-bearing sedimentary sequence at Olduvai spans from about 1.9 my at the base of Bed I to the Holocene deposits of the Naisiusiu Beds. The Brunhes–Matuyama boundary, which is used as the end point for this review, has been recognized within Bed IV.

Mary Leakey's 1971 monograph, which has been widely used as the point of departure for this review, covers the archaeology of Beds I and II, that is Oldowan and the early stages of the Acheulian–Developed Oldowan Complex. A monograph by M. D. Leakey on the Bed III, Bed IV and Masek Bed archaeology is in active preparation. Meanwhile some data on the post-Bed II archaeology is available in M. D. Leakey (1975, 1976).

The geology, dating, and palaeoenvironmental context of the Olduvai archaeology is reported in detail by R. L. Hay (1976).

Numerous other researchers have worked with and reported on aspects of the Olduvai evidence: bones – Andrews (1983), Bunn (1982a), Gentry and Gentry (1978), Matthiesen (n.d. [1982]), and Potts (1982); artefacts – Bower (1977), Jones (1979, 1981), Roche (1980), Stiles (1979, 1980a,b), and Stiles *et al.* (1974); spatial analysis and site characteristics – Davis (1978), Kroll (1981), Kroll and Isaac (in press [1984]), Ohel (1977), and Speth and Davis (1976).

Notes

1 The Koobi Fora KBS assemblages were initially dated as 2.7 ± 0.05 mya by the then new $^{40}Ar/^{39}Ar$ step-heating technique (Fitch and Miller, 1970). Palaeomagnetic results seemed, at first, to confirm this (Brock and Isaac, 1974). Problems over palaeontological correlation between Koobi Fora and the Omo then precipitated a major controversy that lasted for a few years (see Brown *et al.*, 1978; Fitch *et al.*, 1978). Further K/Ar dating by Curtis *et al.* (1975), Drake *et al.* (1980) and McDougall *et al.* (1980), together with new fission-track dates by Gleadow (1980) and additional palaeomagnetic data, has settled the debate conclusively in favour of an age of between 1.8 and 1.9 mya for the KBS Tuff.

2 Spheroids (and subspheroids) are lumps of stone that have been flaked and battered until they assume a roughly globular form with a rough texture. They are often, but not invariably, made of quartz. They occur in moderately high frequency in the Developed Oldowan at Olduvai, but do not occur at all in the contemporary assemblages at Koobi Fora. It is, at present, unclear whether they are by-products of stone flaking – perhaps repeatedly used hammers, since they show an inverse frequency correlation with hammerstones. Some other possibilities are that they were throwing stones, or pounders for some organic substance that needed to be pulverized (hides or tough plant material). Louis Leakey suggested that these items functioned as bola weights, but the great majority of them are far too large and heavy for this. The norm for diameters at Olduvai is 55–65 mm, corresponding to a weight of about 220 to 350 gms ($\frac{1}{2}$ to $\frac{3}{4}$ lb). Pamela Willoughby is carrying out a comparative and experimental study of this neglected class of tools [P. R. Willoughby, 1985].

3 The difference in cut-mark counts between Bunn (1981, 1982a), Potts and Shipman (1981), and Potts (1982) may be accounted for by the application of very conservative recognition criteria by Potts, and the insistence by Potts and Shipman of subjecting all potential cut marks to Scanning Electron Microscope (SEM) scrutiny before including them in their statistics. Bunn made the laboratory identifications on which his statistics are based using the naked eye, followed by low-power binocular microscope scrutiny where needed. However, he also took Xanthropren impressions of some 300 of the marked bones. Subsequently, in order to spot-check his results and to estimate percentage of confidence levels using a random-number table, he selected 15 of these for SEM study. Of these, 14 showed the clear internal score-mark features distinctive of stone-tool-inflicted cuts. The sector of the fifteenth that was subject to SEM scrutiny looks highly abraded and did not show internal striation. It is thus unconfirmed as a cut mark, but is not disproven. Other sectors of the same linear cut mark are said to show the diagnostic features of stone tool incision (Bunn, 1983a and personal communication, 1982). If these reliability tests are a valid indication, they imply that more than 90 per cent of Bunn's lab identifications would be confirmed if looked at by SEM, but further work on this will be needed.

4 Clearly, for resolution it is highly desirable either that Potts and Bunn confer over the differences between their findings with the specimens to hand for reference, or that other scientists make independent searches for cut marks and report on their results. It is also important for the community of scientists interested in zooarchaeology to undertake experiments that will establish discriminants between cut marks and non-cut marks (see

n. 14) and that formal tests be made of between method and between observer variances in degrees of quantitative consistency.

5 The inquiries under discussion involve the supposition that the so-called concentrations of artefacts-plus-bones are in fact localized anomalies that require special explanation. If this were not so, if relatively dense occurrences of bones and artefacts commonly covered wide areas, then the inquiry as just formulated would be inappropriate. However, I know from field experience in working on the East African Plio–Pleistocene sediments that artefacts have a very patchy distribution and the dense patches are of very limited extent. At Koobi Fora the same appears to be true of bones, especially broken-up bones. This perception is implicit in all writings on the subject, and the term *site* refers to such localized concentrations. However, formal data illustrating overall scatter pattern and patchiness are only beginning to be compiled (e.g. Behrensmeyer, 1976a; Isaac, 1981b [this volume, ch. 7]; Isaac and Harris, 1975, 1980). In my view, satisfactory explanation of the Plio–Pleistocene artefact-plus-bone occurrences have to cope with the fact that several of the sites are known to be highly localized combined artefact-plus-bone anomalies. Several otherwise promising lines of explanation prove deficient in this regard (e.g. Behrensmeyer, 1983; Binford 1981: ch. 6).

6 By optimal conditions of preservation I mean (1) situations involving minimal intersection of transport energy (i.e. non-channel context and fine-grained encasing matrix), and (2) with bone preserved sufficiently well for taxon and body-part identification and for scrutiny of surfaces for signs of modification. The logic of restricting consideration first to an optimal set is that if the hypothesis of predominantly hominid causation of the coincident dense accumulation of stones and bones proves superfluous in even these cases, then the hypothesis can be set aside altogether. On the other hand, if these sites require hominid bone–meat transport to account for their features, then one can look to see if further instances of the phenomenon can be found among the less well-preserved sites.

7 At the present time degrees of fluvial disturbance of materials are being judged in the following ways, based on various past and some current studies (Bunn *et al.*, 1980 [this volume, ch. 8]; Cahen *et al.*, 1979; Harris, 1978; Isaac 1967b [this volume, ch. 6], 1977b; Kleindienst, 1961): (1) preferred orientation of long axes; (2) departure of the size frequency distribution from those of undisturbed flaking bouts; (3) presence of any conjoining pieces in close proximity to one another; (4) existence of imbricate groupings; and (5) abrasion and rounding.

8 The instances of mass death known to me (1) are largely monospecific and, if highly localized, (2) tend to occur in topographically distinct sorts of places (e.g. mud wallows, the course of a river in spate, a playa lake). The test-case sites all contain a wide diversity of species and, with the possible exception of FLKN 1–6, occur under undifferentiated floodplain circumstances. We need to seek records or observations that extend the range of instances of mass death before this potential explanation can be finally eliminated.

9 The Chesowanja case reported by Gowlett *et al.* (1981) involves substantial-size fragments of baked earth in association with an artefact concentration dating to > 1.4 mya. The evidence is highly suggestive but is rendered less conclusive by the fact that both artefacts and baked earth fragments occur in the infilling of a small paleo-gully feature where they conceivably were swept together by sheet wash and channel flow processes. A small number of bone specimens were also recovered. These are reported in Blumenschine (1983) to contrast with the bone assemblages from several other early sites, such as Olduvai, FLK Zinj or Koobi Fora FxJj 50, and to resemble carnivore bone accumulations.

10 Many of the early sites have the archaeological materials distributed through some

noticeable thickness of sediment (10–30 cm being quite usual). We know from conjoining studies at Koobi Fora and elsewhere (e.g. the Meer site (Cahen *et al.*, 1979)) that such vertically dispersed material can be due to trampling, burrowing and other processes, and need not imply any great time lapse during site formation.

11 For Olduvai Beds I and II, Mary Leakey (1971) has been able to show that there are often disproportions in raw materials between core–tools (predominantly lava) and flakes (predominantly quartz). She argues very reasonably that the choppers were not primarily cores but were tools in their own right.

12 'Archaeology of the Koobi Fora area' (monograph), ed. G. Ll. Isaac assisted by A. B. Isaac.

13 Harris (1978) has shown that, at Koobi Fora, those sites where the artefacts are preserved in the sands or sandy gravel deposits of a channel bed have the frequency distribution curves displaced up the size scale. For flakes this can readily be explained as due to winnowing, but for core–tools (flaked pieces) this explanation fits poorly. The assemblages tend to include many items that are well beyond the maximum size found in floodplain sites. The initial assemblages, before winnowing, must have included many more larger pieces than are found on floodplains.

14 Bunn (1982a) reports an experiment in which a herd of cattle trampled partially weathered bone. This resulted in the production of numerous long, rectangular, ribbon-like bone splinters. The materials from the early sites do not resemble these.

15 Arguing that plant foods probably dominated early hominid diet is *not* the same as arguing that *gathering* was involved. Feed-as-you-go may well have been the prevailing mode. The term *gathering* ought to be restricted to the acquisition of foods, with postponement of consumption till after transport. We do not know when this began, the oldest putative direct documents being the 500,000-year-old hackberry seeds at Choukoutien. Great archaeological ingenuity and some good luck will be needed to detect early stages of this distinctive behaviour.

16 C. K. Brain (1982) has reported the discovery at Swartkrans Member I (estimated age, 1.5–2.0 mya) of a series of pointed bones with wear on the ends of a kind induced by digging up bulbs and corms on the local hillside.

17 See n. 12.

II

Site location and the use of land

6

Towards the interpretation of occupation debris: some experiments and observations[1]

Introduction

Archaeological studies of Pleistocene culture have undergone a marked change of emphasis during the past few decades. To an increasing degree, scholars are turning away from a narrow concern with artefact morphology and are making determined attempts to investigate the behaviour patterns of early man. The extent, content and patterning of debris and human disturbances discovered by excavation form the basis for inferences regarding aspects of culture such as size of resident groups, hunting practice, diet, duration of occupation, patterns of settlement and movement, craft practices, and tool usage.

Ambitious attempts to reconstruct accurately and systematically these aspects of behaviour demand an exceedingly fine exegesis of the excavated documents. The eager archaeologist frequently finds himself tempted, or even obliged, to invoke evidence from site features for which the determining processes have never been investigated. In this situation archaeologists must either run the risk of dependence on *a priori* reasoning and untested assumptions, or they must undertake the investigations of relevant processes by experiment or systematic observation.

Attention has recently been drawn to the value of such investigations by several authors, and their publications illustrate the diversity of phenomena and methods which are liable to be involved in such an approach to archaeological problems. The following serve as examples:

1. The experimental earthwork on Overton Down in England (Jewell and Dimbleby, 1966).
2. A detailed analysis of Hottentot bone refuse (Brain, 1967a,b).
3. Records of the contents and features of abandoned Bushman camps (Lee, 1965, 1968).

This paper reports on the preliminary stages of investigations which were initiated as a response to difficulties encountered in the interpretation of Acheulian sites at Olorgesailie in Kenya[2] (Isaac, 1966b, 1968a). The specific problems treated are:

1. Methods of discriminating between humanly determined site patterns and fluvial rearrangements of occupation debris.
2. The dispersal of bone debris from an area of concentration.
3. The proportional representation of skeletal parts in bone aggregates accumulating under known conditions

Effects of stream processes on Stone Age occupation debris

The majority of occurrences of Middle Pleistocene cultural remains have an alluvial sedimentary context. Even material stratified within formations loosely termed 'lake beds' tend to be associated with fluviatile silts and sands. Notable examples of important archaeological sites with such a sedimentary environment include Torralba and Ambrona (Butzer, 1965), Kalambo Falls (Howell and Clark, 1963), Isimila (Howell *et al.*, 1962), many Olduvai sites (Hay, 1963), Natron (Isaac, 1967a), and Olorgesailie (Isaac, 1966b). At all of these sites there are good reasons for inferring that the grouping and deposition of much of the occupation debris is due primarily to human activities: it is believed that the material is in 'primary archaeological context' (Kleindienst, 1961: 35–7). However, in all these cases there remains the possibility that the composition and disposition may have been affected to some extent by hydrological processes.

Criteria which have previously been employed for discriminating between anthropological and hydrological patterning include the following:

1. The size grade of the sediment in which artefacts are embedded. Gravels are regarded as clear evidence of movement and transport.
2. Bedding features such as conspicuous signs of erosion, scour and current bedding, are used to distinguish disturbance.
3. *Etat physique* of the material: abrasion and rounding may denote transport and hydrological rearrangement.
4. Orientation of elongate pieces: a preferred orientation is indicative of current or wave action (Howell *et al.*, 1962; Kleindienst, 1961:36).
5. The presence of groups of flakes from the same core, etc., would show a low order of disturbance.

In addition, evidence of sorting according to size might be applied as a discriminant on *a priori* grounds, but apart from mention by Isaac (1966b:139) I am not aware of its use.

These criteria are perfectly adequate for distinguishing extreme cases. Thus the position of artefacts dispersed within gravels can safely be regarded as primarily due to hydrological factors, while the arrangement of pieces on a level undisturbed palaeosol or clay horizon is usually preserved as an occupation pattern which has undergone a minimum of mechanical distortion. However, we have at present no way of evaluating marginal cases. For instance, we are uncertain of what reliance to place on the archaeological association and patterning of occupation debris resting on a surface with low relief, and covered by a sheet of fine alluvial or colluvial sand. We cannot afford to ignore such marginal cases because, as already indicated, they constitute a majority of the sites with promising palaeoanthropological evidence. Further evidence from site locations in basins of sedimentation suggests that Acheulian men frequently selected campsites on the sandy substratum of shallow ephemeral streams and washes (Clark, 1966:209; Isaac, 1966b:142, 1968a.). It is therefore clear that we require experimental data on such questions as the following:

1. The extent to which occupation debris can be moved and rearranged by water currents *without* showing any of the well-known stigmata.
2. The behaviour of large rock particles such as artefacts, artificially deposited in a *milieu* where the transported sediment is entirely of sand and silt grades.
3. The conditions under which material is either dispersed or concentrated by stream action.

While some of the data compiled by hydrologists and geomorphologists are very pertinent to these problems, it seems clear that the abnormal morphology and unusual composition of occupation debris coupled with the exacting demands of the archaeologist necessitate specially designed experiments and measurements.

A start on these problems was made by the instigation of field trials on the shore of Lake Magadi, Kenya (1° 55'S, 36° 15'E). The experimental material which was to be observed under more or less known fluvial conditions consisted of 100 concrete casts of five distinct forms of Acheulian handaxes and cleavers plus a quantity of rough lava flakes ranging from approximately 3–10 cm in greatest dimension. The casts weighed approximately three-quarters of the weight of the lava originals. During a period of a few months from November 1964 to April 1965, these casts and flakes were laid down in a series of five experimental plots. These were sited at points along the braided course of an ephemeral stream channel draining the Lendarut hills and passing down a narrow steep-sided fault graben. Observations suggest that the stream only flows in flash floods when a thunderstorm falls on the hills. During the period of observation this did not occur more than once or twice in a year, though unfortunately there is no means of recording the number and intensity of spates. As the watercourse approaches the lake, the valley widens and the channels become broader and more extensively braided (Fig. 6.1). Thus it can be predicted that variously placed experimental plots experience different intensities of current in the same flood. Up to the present only those plots (numbers 2 and 3) in the narrow channels have definitely been moved by water. When a very high intensity spate occurs, it is anticipated that the material on these plots will be swept away and lost, but the other plots should then respond to current action without complete dispersal.

At each of the plots (numbers 1, 2, 3, and 5), 24 to 25 concrete casts were laid out according to a rectangular grid pattern within a channel. Spacing ranged from 30 to 50 cm. Numbered specimens of the casts of the five variant biface forms were placed in series along the grid lines, with the long axes forming a regular, graded series around the points of the compass. Thus at the outset of the experiment each plot showed a regular orientation pattern without any preferred direction. The orientation of each piece was known (Fig. 6.6). The remaining plot (number 4) was prepared by marking out a 2 m square, and throwing pieces in from each side. At plots 2 to 5, a recorded number of rough lava flakes was placed in the spaces between the concrete casts.

Fig. 6.1. View southwards from the shore flats of Lake Magadi up the fault graben valley where the handaxe dispersal experiment was conducted. Plot 5 in the foreground; Plots 2 and 3 are in the distance where the valley narrows.

Return visits have been made at approximately one-year intervals. The results at the end of the first year, during which time probably only one mild flow had occurred, were as follows:

Plots 1, 4 and 5: All situated in broad, extensively braided channels with a sand/silt bed. No change apart from very slight settling into the bed.

Plot 2: Situated in a narrow channel with a sandy substratum. Showed the following changes:

1. Pieces had moved only trivial amounts from their initial position.
2. Many pieces were tilted and had sunk into scour hollows (Figs. 6.2, 6.3 and 6.4).
3. There was some increase in the number of pieces lying transverse to the current.
4. Twenty-one flakes out of an initial 48 flakes appeared to have been washed away. It is possible that some of these were buried in the sand, but this could not be checked without breaking up the experiment.

Plot 3: Situated in a narrow channel with a hard smooth substratum. Showed the following changes (Fig. 6.4):

1. All but 4 pieces had moved from their initial position or orientation. Mean distance moved 2.3 m; median 0.8 m
2. Three clusters had formed with 2 to 4 pieces lying in contact (Fig. 6.6).
3. Pieces had become partially reorientated with a preferred orientation transverse to the current (Fig. 6.5). A χ^2 test showed a probability of $c.5$ per cent only for the observed distribution of orientation given a nul hypothesis of no preferred orientation. All 10 isolated, transported pieces were transverse to the current, while pieces in clusters either lay transverse (3 cases) or axially (3 cases).

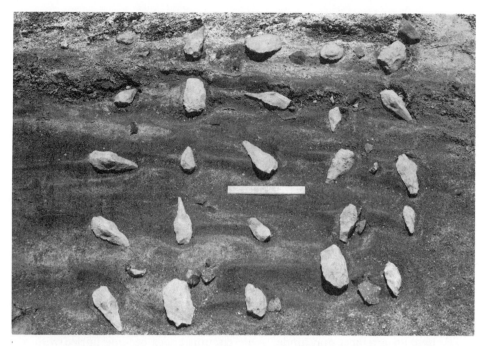

Fig. 6.2. Plot 2 after one year and the passage of possibly a single mild flood. Pieces are tilting and sinking into the sand.

Fig. 6.3. Oblique close-up of pieces in Plot 2, showing the upstream tilt as they subside into scour hollows.

4. Selective removal of flakes from the neighbourhood of the grid had occurred. The initial proportion, large pieces: flakes, was 24:45 and changed to 15:13.

After the lapse of another year, a visit by one of us (R. J. Clarke) indicated the following further changes:

Plot 1 and 5: Little change. Minor rearrangement of pieces may have been due in part to animal footfalls as indicated by the presence of dung at both sites.

Plot 4: Pieces were almost entirely embedded in sandy silt with little visible sign of movement.

Plot 2: Pieces were now almost entirely buried in the sand with little or no further movement or reorientation save for apparent (but not measured) increases in tilt. One piece lay *on edge* in the sand with its long axis sub-transverse to the current.

Plot 3: The pieces were now dispersed along *c.*75 m of the channel with only a small imbricate cluster of 4 pieces remaining near the grid. Seventeen specimens were recorded as lying transverse to the current and 7 were axial. Of these 7, 4 were lying on the sloping gravel banks bound by the channel. Actual orientations could not be measured in the time available.

Summary of indications

(1) Acheulian artefacts may under some circumstances become buried within a channel by silt and sand without appreciable disturbance (Plot 4, as observed on 20 October 1965 by R. J. C.).

(2) Large artefacts resting on sand appear to be very sensitive to current action and readily become embedded in the sand with *pronounced upstream tilts* (Fig. 6.4). One specimen even came to lie on edge with the long axis transverse to the current. This phenomenon has been observed on excavated Acheulian sites at Olorgesailie, Isimila (Howell, 1961:121), Latumne (Clark, 1966:209). Alignment transverse to the current or axial to it may also occur under these conditions, but was not proven. The observation of burial and rotation is corroborated by the results of flume experiments with cobbles and sand (Fahnestock and Haushild, 1962).

(3) Where Acheulian biface forms are dispersed by movement down a channel with a consolidated bed, they can be expected to show a strong preferred *orientation transverse* to the current (Fig. 6.5). There may be a less marked alternative alignment axial to the current. This observation is in accord with other records of the behaviour of elongate rock particles in streams (Kelling and Williams, 1967; Pettijohn 1956:250).

(4) Under both sand-bed and hard-bed conditions, flakes may be preferentially removed from an association of large artefacts and flakes.

It must be emphasized that the field trials here described are quite inadequate to form a secure basis for interpreting Pleistocene occurrences. However, the preliminary results serve both to demonstrate the value of such experiments and to indicate certain additional experiments and measurements which will be required before interpretation can be placed on a secure basis.

It is apparent that, in this experiment, entire ignorance of current velocities over

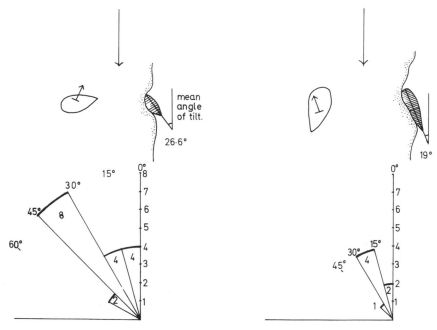

A. Specimens transverse to the current.   B. Specimens axial to the current.

mean angle of tilt.

26·6°

19°

Fig. 6.4. Frequency distribution of observed angles of tilt. Maximum tilt on the plain of maximum projection was measured. All tilts had a marked upstream component. (A) Specimens with long axes oriented between 45° and 90° to the current; (B) Between 0° and 44°.

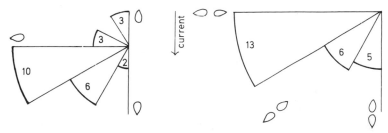

Fig. 6.5. Frequency distribution of orientation to the current. (Left) Orientation of apex distinguished. (Right) Orientation of long axis without reference to apex and butt.

the various plots make it impossible to discriminate between the effects of current and substratum in determining disposition and dispersal. Further, since this experiment was initiated the author has become aware of an important factor not previously taken into account, namely, the spacing of the large rock particles in the channel. It has recently been demonstrated (Leopold, Emmett and Myrick 1966:209–15; Langbein and Leopold, n.d. [1984][3]) that there may be important interactions between particles in a current, so that the competence of a given rate of flow to move large rocks decreases markedly when these lie in close proximity to one another. This interaction appears to result in the grouping of rocks along a channel into more or less evenly spaced gravel bars or stone concentrations which

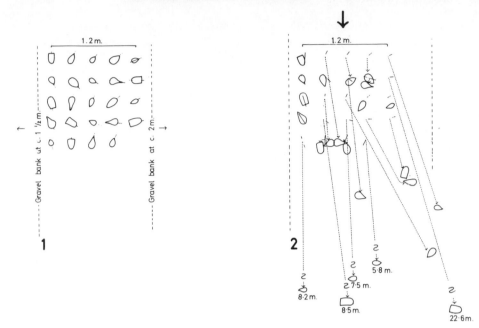

Fig. 6.6. (1) The layout used for Plot 3 and with minor variations for Plots 1, 2 and 5. (2) Disposition of pieces after current action (one flood?) during a year. Z denotes length of trajectory not shown to scale.

correspond to kinematic waves (Lighthill and Whitham, 1955a,b). It will clearly be necessary to compile field and laboratory data to permit discrimination between concentrations of stone due to the localization of human activities, and those due to the kinematic wave effect.

Leopold *et al.* (1966:213–14) have also reported that under commonly occurring conditions of transport in ephemeral streams, large rock particles tend to be deposited at the surface of sand and finer gravel beds. The distinguishing concommitants of this effect need to be described, because interpretations based upon it are directly opposed to those which would otherwise be indicated by the observations at Plot 2, or the data of Fahnestock and Haushild (1962).

Further investigation of the following aspects of this problem is required:

1. The threshold rates of flow needed to transport (a) bifaces, and (b) flakes in relationship to (i) substratum, and (ii) spacing of pieces; followed by field trials to discover under what conditions, if any, these two classes of artefacts might become partially segregated.

2. The effect, if any, of particle spacing on (i) orientation in relation to the current, and (ii) on tilting in cases where burial occurs.

3. The operation of the kinematic wave effect under the special circumstances where large particles are present only in limited quantities through the agency of man. Under what conditions does concentration as opposed to dispersal occur?

4. Determination of the effects of the trampling on concentrations of artefacts under alluvial circumstances.

The dispersal of bone debris from an area of concentration

The amounts of bone associated with artefact concentrations at Olorgesailie was found to vary greatly (Isaac, 1968a). At many sites only small quantities of splinters and a few teeth were preserved. Geological circumstances at the sites are so uniform that differences in post-burial preservation are unlikely to be of any importance. Hence it was necessary to evaluate the extent to which low densities of bone on sites might be due to natural dispersive and obstructive agents rather than to the virtual absence of meat from the diet of the occupants. Preliminary observations have been made on (1) the scattering of bone by wild scavengers in the Olorgesailie area today, and (2) on the breakdown of bone due to exposure and weathering.

(1) A locality was chosen in the comparatively undisturbed mixed *Acacia*-bush-land surrounding the Olorgesailie site. Domestic bone refuse, consisting of 23 'large' pieces and an unknown number of small splinters, was dumped at a peg during October and November 1964. By the end of December only three small splinters could be found in the vicinity of the peg (Fig. 6.7). Interpretation was complicated by the fact that the Masai had taken to driving herds of cattle across the selected area, so a new locality was selected and an area one yard square marked out. Fifty-five 'large' bones and bone fragments, plus more than 60 bone splinters were dumped during the period March to April 1965. The category 'large' bones and bone fragments consists of the chopped-off articular ends or decapitated shafts of cattle or pig bones, together with vertebra, pelvic fragments, rib fragments and phalanges. The greatest dimension of any piece was *c*. 20 cm, and the minimum for the category *c*. 5 cm. Fig. 6.4 shows the situation as it was recorded four months later in September. It can be seen that scavengers and various natural agencies had caused the major part of the refuse to be dispersed. In particular, all pieces of any appreciable size had been removed from the area. The limited size range of the chopped up bones employed in the experiment, and its limited duration, place severe restrictions on its value for archaeological interpretation; but it does seem clear that natural forces in Africa have considerable potential for dispersing bone and therefore that a presence of small numbers only of bone splinters on an excavated site does not preclude the consumption of fairly large quantities of meat. This conclusion has subsequently received corroboration from reports by L. S. B. Leakey (1965:98) and R. Lee (personal communication).

(2) An experiment initiated by M. Posnansky in 1958 indicates that bone weathering may also be a factor in the dissipation of evidence for diet and economy even in an area with alkaline soil conditions and a dry climate. The skeleton of a sub-mature goat and a few cattle bones were laid out on the ground for observation. After interference by a scavenging hyena, the surviving bones were protected within a low wooden frame, and covered with wire mesh. By September 1965, the condition of these (Fig. 6.8) had deteriorated to such an extent that the blades of both goat and ox scapulae had crumbled, leaving only the ridges, neck and articular surfaces. The unfused articular ends had fallen off the longbones. The cranium, mandibles, vertebra and many of the other bones were so cracked and friable that it seems certain that were they exposed to the normal accident of animal footfalls, nothing but small fragments would survive.

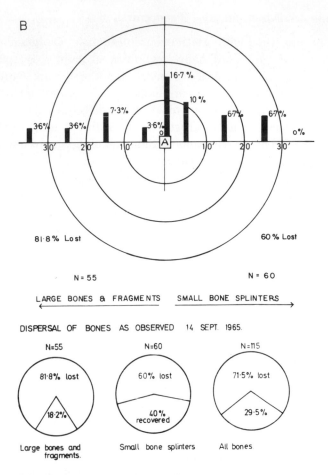

Fig. 6.7. (Top) Bar diagram from centre to left shows dispersal of large bones in the concentric divisions indicated. Bar diagram from centre to right shows data for small bones. (Bottom) Graphic representation of bone loss. All loss percentages are minimum values.

Observations on the composition of bone aggregates in the Suswa Caves

Interpretations of the composition of Pleistocene bone assemblages from Africa have given rise to an important anthropological and palaeontological controversy (e.g. Dart, 1956, 1957a,b; Washburn, 1957; Ardrey, 1961:195–9, 283–311; Brain, 1967b). This controversy arose because bone assemblages at australopithe-cine and other sites departed markedly in their composition from *a priori* expectations: the observed relative frequencies of specific anatomical parts of various mammal groups did not correspond to the relative frequencies with which these parts occur in the skeletons of the animals. Dart (1956, 1957a,b) claimed that the selective representation of certain bones could best be understood as a complex consequence of the use of bones as tools by the australopithecines. Washburn (1957) countered by reporting evidence from lion-kill sites and hyena lairs, showing that scavenging resulted in marked distortion of the proportions of skeletal

Fig. 6.8. August 1965: the bone weathering experiment at Olorgesailie initiated by M. Posnansky in 1958. The disintegration of some bones and the extremely fragile condition of most others is clearly visible.

parts to one another. Ultimately this particular controversy and wider problems in deduction of diet and behaviour patterns from archaeological bone assemblages depend on careful study of the composition of bone aggregates forming under known conditions

With a view to contributing to the development of this knowledge, a study of the bone assemblages in the Suswa Caves in Kenya (1° 9'S, 36° 22'E) was initiated in March 1964, following a pioneer study by Mrs S. C. Coryndon (1964). The work was undertaken by members of the staff of the National Museum and the Centre for Prehistory and Palaeontology, Nairobi (R. J. Clarke, G. Ll. and A. B. Isaac, A. MacKay, J. W. Simons). The writer was unable to continue the study beyond a four-day reconnaissance expedition; however, as there is no immediate prospect of a full report, some of the indications given by the reconnaissance are reported here. Simons (1966) has already given a useful description of baboon bones associated with leopard lairs, together with an analysis of patterns of damage caused by gnawing.

Mt Suswa is a dormant volcanic caldera in which certain lava flows are riddled with ramifying tunnels, some opening to the surface through collapse holes, and 'blow holes' (Glover *et al.*, 1964). The numerous caverns have served as shelters for human groups in recent times, possibly Mau Mau bands, and for various other mammals, including hyena and leopard (Coryndon, 1964; Simons, 1966; R. J. Clarke, 1966:91–2). Recent mammalian bones are widely distributed in the caves,

Table 6.1. *Summary of bone counts made in the field at Suswa*

	Man-made middens				Natural accumulations		
	No. per skeleton	Expected in 562 bones	Observed	Selective over (+) or under (−) representation	Expected in 158 bones	Observed	Selective over (+) or under (−) representation
Horn cores (equids are rare)	2	8.6	5		2.4	3	
Maxillae	2	8.6	18	+	2.4	12	+
1/2 Mandibles	2	8.6	99	+	2.4	12	+
Vertebra	42	181	50	−	51.1	13	−
Ribs	26	112	177[a]	+	31.6	13[a]	−
Scapulae	2	8.6	40	+	2.4	9	+
Innominate	2	8.6	23	+	2.4	10	+
Longbones[b]	12	52	142	+	14.6	47	+
Carpals/tarsals	16	70	5	−	19.4	19	
Phalanges	24	104	3	−	29.3	20	
Total	130	562	562		158	158	
Skulls & cranial fragments	−	−	7		−	8	
Loose teeth			75			4	

Man-made but scavenger-visited middens were recorded in caves 1, 2A, 2B, 10; natural accumulations in caves 6, 36, 14C. The expected numbers in the table are calculated from the cited number per skeleton. These numbers are generalizations for ruminant skeletons which form the vast majority of the series. The error introduced by including equids in the data seems likely to be less than that of excluding them on the basis of field identifications. Primate and carnivore bones have been excluded.

[a] Fragments were counted, making higher than expectation values understandable.

[b] See Table 6.2.

the densest accumulations, rodents excluded, always being in association with traces of human occupation. Other less dense accumulations occurred in dark recesses and 'lairs', and can safely be regarded as the leavings of carnivores and scavengers. Still other bones are scattered on the scree cones of openings, and along the tunnels. These too can in the main be attributed to non-human agencies. Hyena faeces are widespread, occurring both with man-made middens and also the other accumulations. Bones were counted and recorded at a number of localities in the caves; Tables 6.1 and 6.2 show summaries of findings for those localities with predominantly man-made middens and the predominantly natural accumulations itemized separately. The bone identifications were made rather cursorily in the field, so the table must be regarded as an approximation. For this reason also, the data presented have been restricted to the ungulates: antelopes and domestic stock including sheep; and no attempt has been made to subdivide this unusually comprehensive group.

Detailed interpretation of data compiled in this cursory fashion should not be attempted, but certain crucial points stand out very clearly: namely that the proportional composition of both the man-made midden and the natural accumulation differ markedly from the proportional composition of the skeletons which were the source of the bones. Bone-tool selection and use can be ruled out as a factor for both types of accumulation. The apparently reasonable assumption that

Table 6.2. *Analysis of totals for long bones*

	Man-made middens			Natural accumulations	
	No.	E	O	E	O
Humerus proximal			3		–
shaft			4		–
distal			19		6
	2	23.6	26	7.8	6
Femur proximal			–		2
shaft			2		3
distal			–		–
	2	23.6	4[+]	7.9	6[+]
Radius/ulna proximal			12		3
shaft			4		1
distal			3		1
	2	23.6	25[+]	7.8	7[+]
Tibia proximal			7		1
shaft			7		1
distal			16		6
	2	23.6	29[+]	7.8	10[+]
Metapodials proximal			40		11
shaft			6		–
distal			3		4
	4	47.5	55[+]	15.6	18[+]

[+] The difference between sums for portions of bones and the total representation of the bone is made up by intact bones.

bone assemblages ought to behave as random samples of the skeletons from which they derive is thus called into question. J. W. Simons (1966:67–8) showed that the baboon bones associated particularly with leopard lairs are also present in proportions radically different from expectation.

Since this study was carried out, Brain (1967a,b) has reported on a detailed investigation of Hottentot bone refuse, collected in South West Africa. This assemblage shows a very marked departure from primary anatomical composition, and Brain offers some explanation of this in terms of the structure, density and relative rate of maturation of the bones selectively over- or underrepresented. Gnawing by dogs and possibly jackals appear to be the principal agent of selective destruction. At Suswa, hyenas may well have been responsible for a similar process. Inskeep and Hendy (1966) have also reported an archaeological bone assemblage showing comparable though not identical patterns of selective distortion.

Discussion of these problems, and the mechanisms of selective destruction, is also to be found in Lubbock (1865:183–4). Lubbock reports observations by Steenstrup of disparities in the relative representation of skeletal parts in Danish kitchen middens, and that Steenstrup had experimented with his own dogs, showing gnawing as a probable cause of destruction. Steenstrup had also pointed out the correlation of durable bones and bone parts with early ossification during growth. These pioneer studies have been overlooked in the intervening century, and the patterns have now been rediscovered by Brain.

The morphology of fractured bones in the caves has not yet been carried out systematically, but during the fieldwork numbers of jagged dagger and apple-corer-like longbone segments were observed and collected.

It is not intended that this paper should be regarded as a refutation of the osteodontokeratic hypotheses of Dart. Data pertinent to the evaluation of the evidence for those hypotheses is merely presented, and the need for more rigorous studies stressed.

The Suswa bone accumulations deserve more thorough study; investigations of bone refuse surrounding contemporary habitation sites with various known dietary and butchering practices, settlement patterns and environmental conditions are also urgently needed. Comparable records of composition and fracture morphology in fossil bone assemblages from hominid-free contexts would also be of great value in assessing the meaning of patterns observed in both definite human and suspected hominid assemblages.

Conclusion

This paper has described a few simple experiments and systematic observations concerned with elucidating the processes involved in the formation of aspects of the archaeological record. It is to be hoped that such studies will become increasingly an important part of the archaeologist's and ethnographer's work.

Notes

1 With a contribution by R. J. Clarke.

2 The work reported in this paper was done while the author was employed by the Museums Trustees of Kenya in the Centre for Prehistory and Palaeontology, under the direction of L. S. B. Leakey. The freedom to engage in such studies, and the use of transport and facilities is gratefully acknowledged. The work was a by-product of the investigations at Olorgesailie, which were partly supported by a National Parks subvention, and by grants from the Wenner-Gren Foundation, Boise Fund, British Academy and British Institute of History and Archaeology in East Africa. Mrs A. B. Isaac assisted extensively with the work of all these experiments and observations, and prepared the diagrams.

3 River channel bars and dunes: theory of kinematic waves [1968].

7

Stone Age visiting cards: approaches to the study of early land-use patterns

Human or animal land use can be considered as comprising a web of pathways over a piece of terrain. The concept can be made more explicit if one imagines fixing a transmitter onto each individual of any species for which a land-use pattern is to be determined. Then, if a remote sensor high above continuously plotted the position of the transmitters, a map would form with lines marking the movements of the members of the species. For modern humans one would expect an image which was formed over several days to show criss-crossing networks of lines with clearly defined nodes at places to which people repeatedly returned. One set of nodes would involve the presence of groups of individual at particular locales for many hours, especially their presence at certain nodes each night. These overnight nodes would mainly be what archaeologists term 'settlements'. Many of the plotted movement trajectories would prove to be irregular loops extending radially from the settlement nodes (Fig. 7.1a).

If this hypothetical movement recording were carried out for the species which is the closest living evolutionary relative of mankind, a very different pattern could be expected (Fig. 7.1b, c). Nodes would be far less conspicuous features, and those which were represented would be found not to involve repeated overnight groupings of individuals, but only temporary aggregations at attractions such as groves of fruit trees in season. There would be no points in space that could be called 'settlements'.

Different human societies would imprint traces that would differ greatly in scale, density and detailed configuration, but all would be compounded of repeating modules rather like that shown in Fig. 7.1. If available, knowledge of movement patterns such as is envisaged here could be used to discern important intra-specific differences in human social and economic systems, and, as already indicated, differences in movement patterns are also indicative of major differences between species in their social organization and ecological relations.

Now, while we do not have movement and land-use plans compiled in the way just imagined, ethnographic and zoologic data often allow one to envisage at least the approximate character of the trace which would be obtained for living human

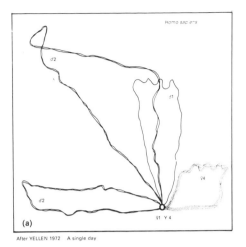

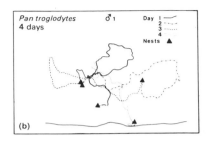

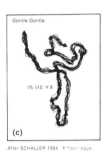

Fig. 7.1. A human pattern of movement in the landscape compared with patterns recorded for the closest living non-human relatives of mankind. (a) Zum/wasi (!Kung) hunter-gatherers over one day. (b) A chimpanzee over four days. (c) A gorilla troop over fifteen days. All are drawn to the same scale. Notice the relatively great area spanned by the human 'radial' pattern.

societies and for living animal species. But what of the past? What can be done if one's interest is in the evolutionary development of the distinctive human pattern and in the prehistoric land-use patterns of early humans and proto-humans? Our records of the past are meagre, but evidence does exist.

First, all animals possessing bodies which include hard, relatively imperishable parts leave a potential record of their trajectory at one point in their network of movements – the terminal point! At the moment of death, unless the carcass is transported, the position reached by the organism is marked by the presence of bones or a shell. Of these at least some may become fossils more or less at the point of death, thereby creating a partial record of points in the web of movement.

For a piece of terrain where conditions of fossil preservation without displacement are widespread, the aggregate of loci of the fossils may provide statistical indicators of the segments of the sedimentary basin which were most frequented by various fossil-forming organisms. Of course it must be borne in mind that if

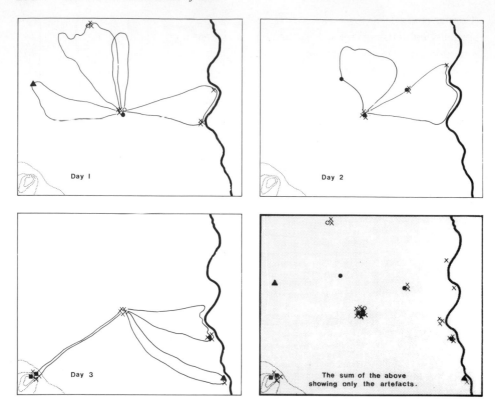

Fig. 7.2. The formation of scatters of different artefact forms over a landscape through daily movements from a single home base. A dense cluster of artefacts marks the home-base node in movements – other minor scatters mark activity loci or transient camps.

individuals tended to die more frequently in some portions of their range, or if the preservation rate was higher in some portions, then the fossil record of land use (habitat preference) would be correspondingly biased (see the taphonomic studies of Behrensmeyer, 1975, 1976b and in press [1980]; Hill, 1975 and in press [1980]).

Within this general framework the human species and its evolutionary antecedents constitute a special case. As with other vertebrates, humans may deposit their skeletal remains as markers at points scattered about the web of their movements, but they also mark their trajectories in other ways. At intervals throughout the life of each individual, distinctive objects, 'artefacts', may be discarded. As in the case of skeletal parts, if these discards are not secondarily transported they serve to mark points in the web of movements of the population that formed and abandoned them. Fig 7. 2 provides graphic representation of the way in which these familiar processes operate to produce the potential for an archaeological 'image' of human and proto-human land use.

We have already seen that for the human species a cumulative map of the lines of movement of individuals shows the existence of conspicuous nodes in which the pathways of many movement episodes tend to begin and end. As Foley shows

(Hodder *et al.*, 1981: ch. 6), the archaeological image provided by the location of artefacts exhibits analogous patterning: there are concentrated, localized accumulations of refuse which represent acts of discard repeated by numbers of individuals over a span of time. Common knowledge of contemporary human behaviour leads us to expect that many of these concentrated patches of material relicts are associated with 'settlement' nodes, but nodes which can be termed quarries, 'factories', butchery locales, etc. may also produce distinctive accumulations.

In idealized terms I have summarized the familiar process whereby archaeological configurations may be indicative of past human-use patterns. There are, of course, factors which complicate behavioural interpretation of the overall spatial patterns found in the real world.

1. Only those portions of human lines of movement along which durable artefacts are discarded will be represented in the imprint.
2. If the objects are transported after discard by natural agencies, they do not directly document points in the ancient web of movements.
3. Humans may deliberately transport discarded material away from its original place of discard. This process leads to the formation of 'secondary refuse' deposits (Schiffer, 1976) which, though part of the articulated set of evidence, have to be recognized and suitably interpreted.
4. Archaeologists have access only to a minuscule sample of the total number of artefact discard acts which originally formed the entirety of the potential record for the area and time period in question. Bias due to differential preservation, to differential re-exposure and due to imperfect recovery, all have to be assessed and allowed for.

It should then be very clear that the archaeological record as it comes down to us is in no sense a simple 'map' of where humans discarded things, much less a map of where they used things or of where they went. However, it is a partial image, albeit distorted and blurred, and with care and caution inferences can be drawn about the spatial configuration of daily life and about aspects of the use of the landscape.

This introduction has been concerned with generalities about the way in which human behaviour generates a record of aspects of spatial organization. The record for the last few thousand years is known in many areas to be rich and complex with intricate variations and permutations on the simplified themes indicated. However, in this essay I want to turn to the remote past and examine whether interpretational principles such as those outlined can help in the study of early stages of human life; stages in excess of half a million years; stages which might be termed 'proto-human'. More recent material is discussed by Foley (Hodder *et al.*, 1981: ch. 6).

My sense of the problems explored here has been greatly influenced by the work of David Clarke and he in fact read and commented on a draft of this paper a month before his death. I gratefully acknowledge this influence.

Empirical observations

Fig. 7.3 illustrates the kind of configuration which confronts archaeologists who

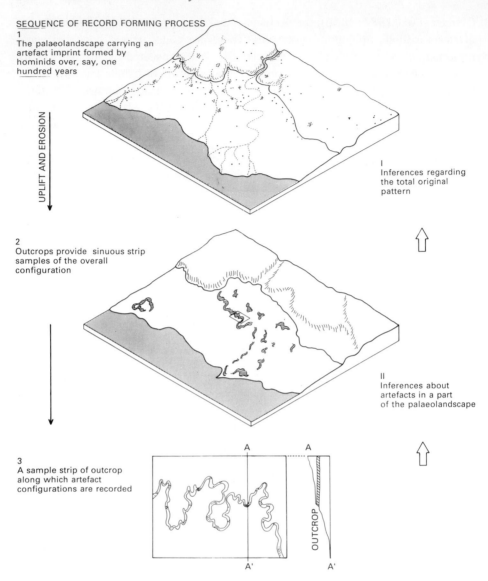

SEQUENCE OF RECORD FORMING PROCESS

1
The palaeolandscape carrying an artefact imprint formed by hominids over, say, one hundred years

UPLIFT AND EROSION

I
Inferences regarding the total original pattern

2
Outcrops provide sinuous strip samples of the overall configuration

II
Inferences about artefacts in a part of the palaeolandscape

3
A sample strip of outcrop along which artefact configurations are recorded

OUTCROP

Fig. 7.3. The processes which form the archaeological record of early hominid land use in sedimentary basins such as those of the East African Rift Valley. Reading the sequence from top to bottom shows the steps by which our sample of information becomes available to us. Reading from bottom to top, the sequence represents a chain of inferences. The diagram is based on Koobi Fora (Isaac and Harris, 1978).

study early human life using the record preserved in a large-scale sedimentary formation – such as that of Olduvai (Leakey, 1971; Hay, 1976), the Omo (Coppens *et al.*, 1976) or Koobi Fora (Leakey and Leakey, 1978). The record available for a given interval of past time represents a complex aggregate of samples. Each 'sample' is provided by the sinuous outcrop strip of one of a series of beds which can be determined to have been deposited within the time interval under study. By assembling the available data stepwise as shown in the figure, it may be possible to make an assessment of the characteristics of what was once the overall pattern.

The diagrams represent the sort of pattern which has been perceived in various early-man-bearing formations in East Africa, and notwithstanding the fact the methods for surveying, recording and measuring are still in very early stages of development, it is possible to report on the general characteristics. Over some parts of the floors of the sedimentary basins there existed, and was preserved, a low density scatter of discarded artefacts – isolated flakes or cores or small groupings of a few items. Very rough guesses of the minimum density of objects per unit area would be less than one piece per 10,000 m^2 and superimposed on this background scatter it is common to find some patches where objects occur in much higher densities (e.g. 1–100 per m^2). It is these patches or concentrations of materials that are commonly called 'sites' and archaeological attention has been focused almost exclusively upon them. Although the densities of the scatters between patches are often extremely low, the areas are very large and it is probable that for the early prehistoric period many more artefacts lie outside 'sites' than are contained within them.

There are two other aspects of the observed pattern to which attention should be drawn. First, both discarded artefacts and hominid skeletal remains constitute fossilized visiting cards. Their distributions are not necessarily the same and the two kinds of records need to be considered and interpreted jointly (Isaac and Harris, 1978; Fig. 4.2). Second, animal bones, like artefacts, were scattered over the palaeo-landscape and they, like 'artefacts', show a patchy distribution. The coincidence or non-coincidence of relatively dense patches of bone with relatively dense patches of discarded artefacts has given rise to an empirical classification of 'site' types (Isaac, 1978a [this volume, ch. 11]; Isaac and Harris, 1978; Isaac and Crader, 1981):

> Type A concentrated patch of artefacts only.
> Type B a concentration of artefacts coincident with numerous bones from the carcass of a single large animal.
> Type C coincident concentrations of artefacts and the bones of many different species of animal.
> Type O concentrated patch of bones only.

The recognition of the existence of a background scatter of artefacts, with superimposed concentrations and the recognition of variable patterns of association between clusters of bones and clusters of stone artefacts, are based on empirical observations; however, they have great potential importance in the interpretation of patterns of early proto-human life.

The structure of the spatial array: an hierarchic model

In the foregoing section and in Fig. 7.3 I have treated the archaeological record as a patterned array of points in space. If one is to build a theory or model that will allow the array to be interpreted one should perhaps start by asking what are these points? What are the irreducible units of spatial analysis? What is the archaeologi-

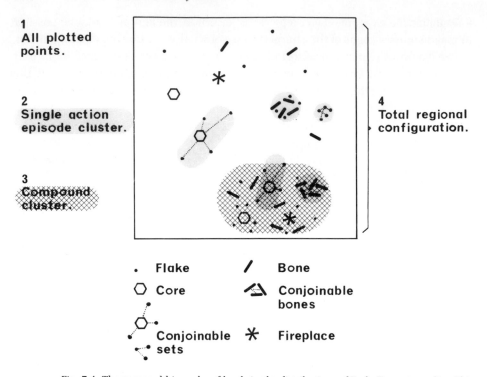

1
All plotted points.

2
Single action episode cluster.

3
Compound cluster.

4
Total regional configuration.

.	Flake	/	Bone
⬡	Core	◿◺	Conjoinable bones
⬡ (sets)	Conjoinable sets	✳	Fireplace

Fig. 7.4. The proposed hierarchy of levels in the distributions of Early Stone Age relics. This is a variant on the system of Clark (1977) that allows for the fact that houses and 'structures' are virtually absent from the record. Each plotted item in the diagram is a fundamental datum point (level 1). Some but not all of these are grouped into level 2 clusters. Compound cluster (level 3) may involve both groupings of individual datum points and internally recognizable action-episode clusters (level 2). The totality of the distribution of points over a given area, regardless of intermediate clustering, is level 4.

cal equivalent of a fundamental particle? For present purposes in palaeo-anthropological archaeology the fundamental particle should probably be taken as any individual discrete item that provides evidence of proto-human presence. Normally these will be individual artefacts however small and trivial, but they could include such items as a distinctively broken bone, a scooped-out pit, or whatever. The location of each of these irreducible items would constitute the points on the base plot of a comprehensive spatial analysis.

From our knowledge of the human way of life and from our acquaintance with the empirical features of the record, we would expect to find a hierarchy of linked sets, incorporating the 'fundamental points'. Pursuing the physics analogy, one can perhaps recognize the equivalent of an atomic particle. Perhaps in archaeology this is the set of objects representing a behavioural event which is in a sense indivisible. A set of conjoinable pieces from a single knapping episode might be one example. Others would be the job lot of bones from a single meal; a unified configuration of post holes and so forth.

The next level in the hierarchy, the equivalent of a molecule or compound, can, like molecules, be of very variable scale, but it would always be a complex cluster of archaeological datum points representing a number of episodes or a number of different actions. Most archaeological sites are entities at this level. Whether or not we can resolve the components, they are in fact clusters of clusters.

At still higher levels, 'sites' form a patterned set across the face of a region with their location determined by factors such as the distribution of resources, the density and organization of population and the network of communication and trade. This level is what is commonly referred to as a 'settlement pattern', a 'regional system', or a 'between-site system'. In a general way the hierarchy just outlined parallels that set up by David Clarke (1977), but for the purposes of analysis of patterns of very early land use a variant along the lines indicated is needed (Fig. 7. 4).

It should be noted that instances of levels 1 and 2 can either be independent entities or can exist as components of the next one or two hierarchical levels. Level 4 is that total array of all locations of hominid relics in a region. A level 4 array could in theory be made up entirely of unclustered fundamental datum points (level 1) without the existence in the particular case of any second or third order groupings.

It should also be noted that the single action-episode cluster is incorporated into the system because common experience of the organization of human behaviour establishes the fact of its existence. Manifestations of this level are sometimes recognizable as such in the archaeological record, but very often the distinction between sets of items comprising several individual action-episode clusters becomes blurred or totally obscured when they are grouped in a compound cluster (level 3).

Perhaps the foregoing account of a model and the hierarchic framework used to describe it can be made more explicit by reference to an actual example. While in Australia in 1976, I was privileged to be given a brief tour of the Lake Mungo area by Wilfred Shawcross and John Mulvaney. The configuration of archaeological relics that was shown to me there exemplified very clearly the structure we were groping to discern in our studies of much older, but apparently analogous materials in East Africa.

During part of the Upper Pleistocene, the 'Lake' Mungo depression, which is now a dry, saline playa, contained an extensive, shallow body of fresh water which was part of a whole system of lakes in the Willandra region (Bowler, 1971). From the downwing shore of the lake sand, silt and clay were continually blown so as to form a large crescent-shaped dune field of very low relief. Stone-using human inhabitants of the region came at intervals and used the dune area in various ways and left their marks on it. As time passed both the deposition of sand and human usage of the area continued so that the leavings of successive episodes tend to be separated from previous ones by small thicknesses of sand. Eventually the deposition of the Mungo Formation ceased. After a period of soil formation other deposits covered it; but in recent times the process has gone into reverse. Perhaps because of overgrazing, the ancient dune ('lunette') is being eroded by wind and rain and from wide relatively flat expanses the deposits are being stripped by the removal of successive thin 'skins' of sediment. As this natural excavation proceeds, relics of past human usage emerge at the surface. Initially the original configuration is preserved, but as time goes on material is let down and a lag concentrate forms, which is superimposed on the material *in situ*. Even so, walking about, it is possible to form an impression of the structure of the original arrays re-exposed.

The primary data points that are unequivocal human visiting cards consist of such traces as individual stone artefacts ('tools', cores and flakes), or the remains of a fireplace. These may occur as isolated items remote from any other visible human relict or they may occur as parts of clusters representative of a level 2 or 3 entity.

Clusters indicative of a single indivisible action episode are also visible – for instance, small clusters or flakes from a common core, burials or cremations and clumps of mussel shells, each apparently indicative of a single 'meal'. (An individual isolated mussel shell cannot readily be treated as a primary archaeological datum point, because it might just as well have been deposited by a bird or mammalian carnivore.)

Compound clusters of varying character also occur. They range from small-scale occurrences consisting of a fireplace and a clump of mussel shells, to scatters of stone artefacts, some broken bones and/or shells extending over many tens of square metres. The internal structure of these clusters could not be perceived in a brief tour such as I was given. Parts of some examples of such compound occurrences have been excavated by Shawcross (1975); by McBryde (n.d.); by Bowler *et al.* (1970) and elsewhere in the area by McIntyre (n.d.).

Clearly the interpretation of the configuration of the Lake Mungo archaeological array must be made by Shawcross and the others who are engaged in detailed, systematic studies, but this simple description of the configuration has perhaps indicated the potential of the framework set out in Fig. 7. 4.

Nowhere in the world has the total array of relics from any ancient non-agricultural society been preserved and then rendered available in its entirety through gentle erosion. What is available varies greatly between areas and between spans of time within an area.

The following are examples of low energy sedimentation mechanisms, which can cover extensive portions of a landscape preserving intact broadcast arrays of relics with all four levels observable and analysable: (1) aeolian sedimentation as in a dune field (e.g. Lake Mungo) or a loess mantle; (2) flood plain sedimentation on the valley floor of a big river (e.g. the Nile (Wendorf and Schild, 1976; Wendorf and Marks 1975)); (3) volcanic ash falls in the vicinity of volcanic vents (e.g. Eburru in Kenya (Isaac, 1972b), or Laetolil, Tanzania (Leakey and Hay, 1979)); (4) alluvial and lake-margin sedimentation in a lake basin (e.g. the Rift Valley study areas of Olduvai (Leakey, 1971; Hay, 1976) or Koobi Fora (Leakey and Leakey, 1978)).

At another extreme, only isolated nodes in the former array may be preserved – as for instance in the case of many cave sites or the Terra Amata open-air Acheulian site (de Lumley 1969b).

The manner in which nature has selectively preserved part of a once widespread configuration and then selectively, by erosion, made available a part of the past, has to be considered in designing research and interpreting results.

Possibilities for research designs

In relation to varying objectives and in response to differences in the preservation or recoverability of the array of relicts, several different approaches have emerged in attempting land-usage inferences from the configuration of 'Stone Age' archaeological remains.

(1) The first might be designated as the 'classic' distribution map study, as in Groube's contribution to this volume [Hodder *et al* 1981 (ch. 7)]. After a region has been explored extensively, the locations of all 'sites' are plotted on a map. In almost all cases 'site' refers to a 'compound cluster' in the terminology developed earlier in this essay. Another class of distribution map which plots find-spots of distinctive artefact forms or constituent materials (e.g. handaxes or bell beakers, obsidian, etc.) generally covers a far wider area than that envisaged here and has usually been used in studies of cultural geography or of trade networks rather than in studies of land-use economies (cf. Hodder and Orton, 1976: ch. 5).

Given a reasonably comprehensive plot of the locations of sites pertaining to a particular phase in land-use patterning, it is conventional to look for regular 'repeated' relationships between site loci and other geographic factors, for example, topography, water bodies, soil zones, vegetation zones, and specific localized resources. Sites with different characteristics may show different associations. Relationships may be assessed by 'inspection' (e.g. Fox, 1932) or may involve systematic quantitative measures of associations (cf. Hodder and Orton, 1976 for general treatment of such methods). Comprehensive distribution maps can also be analysed for information about the spacing of sites and about the geometry of differentiation amongst them (cf. Hodder and Orton, 1976: ch. 4).

(2) A second contrasting approach has achieved prominence under the designation *site catchment analysis* (Vita-Finzi and Higgs, 1970; Jarman, 1972), used by Parkington in Hodder *et al.*, 1981 (ch. 12). Instead of looking at a map in search of repeated relationships between a series of sites and some geographical factors such as was discussed above, this method takes a single site and maps or inventories the 'resources' accessible from that site. In the pioneer works of the Higgs school, 'accessible' was taken to refer to terrain lying within 5 km (for farmers) or within two hours' walking time for hunter-gatherers. More sophisticated work with site catchment techniques together with a critique of the whole approach is contained in Flannery (1976: ch. 4). In that work Zarky's study makes comparisons between the incidence of certain resources within each catchment and averages for the area as a whole. Flannery's own study attempts an empirical estimation of what the catchment area for various commodities actually was and shows that it may be best to think in terms of a nested series of enveloping catchments. Both these studies make explicit an aspect of site catchment analysis that has been too seldom stated. When applied to a single site the technique is simply a useful descriptive device. It is only when the catchment characteristics of a series of sites are examined statistically in search of one or more repetitive patterns that the technique serves to define systems of land use.

An important advantage of site catchment analysis stems from the fact that it does not demand the preservation and discovery of substantial parts of an articulated set of sites, as does distribution map analysis. Data for a series of 'isolated sites' that are believed to have been formed as nodes within the same or similar land-use systems can be compiled and the sample of catchment characteristics analysed for regularities.

(3) Another approach is to model the economic and social factors which might be expected to determine the placement of sites within a particular region and then either to do a graphic simulation of the distribution which could be expected or to predict in quantitative terms the character and placement of sites (Hodder, 1978). The goodness of fit between simulated or predicted patterns and the observed patterns is then taken as a measure of the closeness with which the socio-economic model does approximate the system which created the observed sites. Examples of this approach are the work of Thomas (1973, 1974) and that of Jochim (1976), while Hammond (ch. 8 in Hodder *et al.*, 1981) introduces one of the most advanced examples of this type of work. If this method is applied, alternative input configurations need to be tried, since similar resultant site location patterns may result from more than one combination of input variables.

(4) The fourth approach to be discussed might be seen as a special, intensive version of the distribution map method. It involves collecting information not simply about site distribution, but about the overall distribution patterns of fundamental datum points. Sites emerge in the analysis as compound clusters and inferences can be attempted regarding the behavioural and ecological meaning of scatters between sites as well as that of the sites themselves.

Clearly, spatial analyses that deal with the distribution of compound clusters (sites) alone are treating only a part of the total configuration. Often this is because only major nodes (sites) within the original system are preserved and detectable. However, where sediment blankets have preserved comprehensive articulated broadcast sets of remains it behoves us at least to try to find out whether studies of the overall pattern do add anything to conventional site location studies. Clearly it is seldom feasible to comb the whole of a large area in search of individual isolated discards so that this approach will have to use sampling techniques.

Robert Foley has independently been pursuing this line of research (Hodder *et al.*, 1981: ch. 6). He has termed the approach 'off-site archaeology'. I would prefer a designation that makes it clear that sites are concentrations of special interest within a broad-cast array. Following the title of a paper that I and John W. K. Harris wrote in 1975 ('The scatter between the patches'), I would suggest the interim rubric *scatters and patches analysis*.

For those segments of prehistory where the archaeological record consists mainly of small discarded artefacts and food bones, this fourth approach may prove a particularly important additional method and it is at problems in the Palaeolithic that this essay is directed. We are fortunate that many of the localities which preserve very early archaeological evidence do so under circumstances where 'scatters and patches' analysis is possible. The concluding portion of this essay provides examples of three of the four approaches as applied in investigating early hominid patterns of life and land use in East Africa. I have not yet been involved in simulation work. The figures and the discussion provide indications of the applicability of three of the approaches just discussed without attempting definitive interpretation.

Examples

The site distribution approach is illustrated in Fig. 7.5. This shows the known sites from Bed I at Olduvai Gorge (Leakey, 1971; Hay, 1976) plotted in relation to the detailed palaeogeographic reconstruction achieved through the meticulous work of Hay. Also shown are the outlines of the margins of the main and side gorges. Inspection of Fig. 7.5 reveals a marked clustering of sites in the area between the

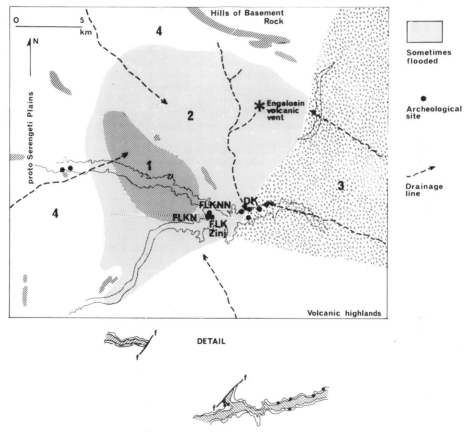

Fig. 7.5. An example of the 'distribution map' approach applied to studies of early land usage – the location of sites in Bed 1 Olduvai Gorge (after Leakey, 1971; Hay, 1976). The sites are shown in relation to environmental zones (as indicated by sedimentary facies). 1. Lake (permanently flooded). 2. Floodplain surrounds of the lake that was swampy and sometimes inundated. 3. An alluvial fan at the foot of the nearby volcanic highland. 4. The blank areas to the west and north were dry plains; those to the south are left blank for lack of information. The margins of the eroded gorge are shown superimposed on the reconstructed palaeogeography. The detail below serves to emphasize that the recorded distribution is only known from outcrop strips along the slopes of the erosion cuts.

margins of the perennial lake and the toe of an alluvial fan. Those reported were all on the lake margin floodplain with two lying to the east of the lake and the other nine (some of which are multi-level sites) to the east. How is such a map to be interpreted? The first point to recognize is that our information on the distribution of the sites does not cover the whole rectangular field represented in Fig. 7.5. Consequently, point pattern analysis techniques, such as those treated by Hodder and Orton (1976), are not applicable without modifications. Site locations can only be determined along the outcrops of the relevant sedimentary layers. Fig. 7.5 makes it explicit that what is available is in fact two irregular transects which sample the geography of the floor of a lake basin. The location of sites along the transect is determinable through systematic survey. Once understood in this light, various questions can be asked about the configuration of sites in this sample. First, is there a demonstrable tendency for the sites to be associated with some of the distinctive palaeoenvironmental sectors of the transect rather than others? An observed number of sites per length of outcrop can be compared with an expected number, given a null hypothesis of no preferred location for sites in any of the terrestrial environments. The permanently submerged lake floor needs to be excluded from this comparison since our expectation for number of sites there is zero! This is the classic formulation for a chi-square test of association, though the numbers involved are marginally adequate for such a formal test. The chi-square values, for what they are worth, do not run counter to the inferences drawn by Leakey (1971) and Hay (1976) that the Bed I sites are preferentially associated with the lake margin zone on the eastern shores of the palaeo-lake. They also indicate that the positive association may only be with some sectors of the lake margin zone, since the western sample sector has sites effectively at the expected incidence, and the sector in the side gorge has no observed sites against an expectation of about 4. Hay has suggested that the portion of the transect where the sites cluster was differentiated from the remainder of the lake margin zone by having a greater influx of water which formed relatively fresh pools and swamps around this edge of what was otherwise a saline lake (Leakey, 1971; Hay, 1976: 48).

A second series of questions that one might seek to ask relates to the spacing amongst sites considered as a system and without regard to habitat differences. Within a zone where sites occur, were they clustered or were they randomly spaced? How far apart were those nodes in the artefact-discarding activities of early hominids? Unfortunately the answers to these questions only have full meaning if the nodes under consideration are contemporary, and contemporaneity at the required level of resolution is hard to establish. However, interspersed in these beds are volcanic ash-fall layers which mark out time lines. These can be used to show which sites are not contemporary and from this it emerges that almost every one of the nine sites in the approximately 4 km long south-east lake margin sector of the transect can be excluded from being contemporaneous with any other. This negative finding is potentially interesting and suggests that at any given time the locales to which artefacts were transported and discarded were reasonably well spaced out. Archaeologists will need to work with mathematical geographers to

Table 7.1. *Relationship between section thickness and site frequency*

Facies	Total thickness measured	No. of sites (or levels) encountered	Metres of section per site
Lake	133	0	–
Lake margin (eastern)	139	18	7.7
Lake margin (western)	123	2	61.5
Alluvial fan	316	0	–
Alluvial plain (eastern)	97	0	–

learn how to model probable two-dimensional spacing from data collected along linear outcrops.

The foregoing analysis of spatial data for Olduvai Bed I is presented to exemplify the problems of applying the classic distribution map approach to 'buried' land-scapes such as are partially preserved in sedimentary basins. Other related approaches are possible; Hay tackled the problem of the association of archaeological sites with particular environments of deposition by analysing his field section logs to determine the average number of vertical metres of section surveyed in each

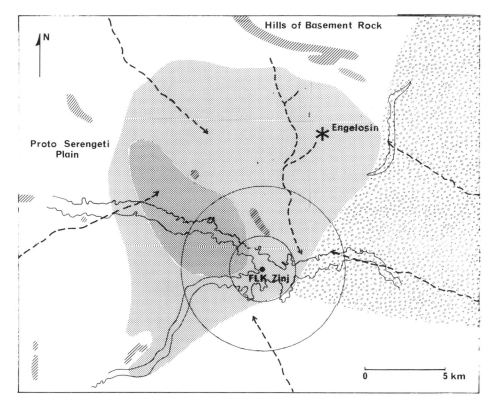

Fig. 7.6. An example of the site catchment approach applied to the study of early hominid land use. 2 km catchment circles drawn around the Bed 1 FLK *Zinjanthropus* site at Olduvai showing the palaeogeographic zones which were readily accessible from the site.

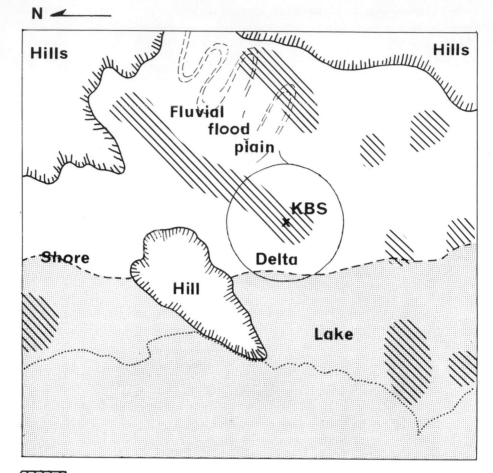

Outcrops of KBS horizon

Fig. 7.7. A 5 km site catchment circle drawn around the KBS site in the Koobi Fora area. The catchment area consisted predominantly of delta flood plain (presumably grassland and swamp traversed by ribbons of riverine bush) but also including lake shore environments and edge of better drained river floodplain environments. The hatched areas show schematically the areas of outcrop from which information on the KBS horizon derives (based on Behrensmeyer, 1975, 1976b).

facies for each site encountered (Hay, 1976, Table 32). For Bed I in the main gorge the results are shown in Table 7.1.

Clearly since the facies were differentially distributed in the palaeolandscape, this analysis is a form of spatial analysis and it is a method which deserves to be applied elsewhere. It facilitates incorporating the separate occupation levels of a multi-component site as distinct analytical entities. The section logs relate to a series of sample transects across the outcrop strips and further inferences about the spacing and associations of sites might well be obtainable through more extensive analysis of such data sets.

R. L. Hay's and M. D. Leakey's monographs make it clear that in addition to the concentrations called 'sites' or 'occupation floors' there are stray artefacts scattered through the sediments with the frequency being highly variable between layers and between areas. Measurements of this variability are not yet available so that the relations between the classic site distribution pattern and the 'scatters and patches' pattern are not yet determinable.

The Olduvai example has been chosen for presentation because the data are published and because of the unprecedented thoroughness of the geological and palaeogeographic information available. Related kinds of data are being assembled in other areas of eastern Africa, for instance at the Omo (Chavaillon, 1976; Merrick *et al.*, 1973; Merrick, 1976) and at Koobi Fora where J. W. K. Harris is pursuing palaeogeographic studies in conjunction with the geologist I. C. Findlater (Harris, 1978; Harris and Herbich, 1978; Isaac and Harris 1978; Harris and Isaac in press [1980]).

The site catchment approach is exemplified in Figs. 7.6 and 7.7. Clearly there are severe problems in doing such an analysis for very ancient sites where the environs of the site today are profoundly different in topography and biota from the environs that existed at the time the site was formed. The problem can be seen to be further complicated when one takes into account that our information about the surroundings of the site is based on an outcrop strip. In some cases (e.g. Fig. 7.7) this strip is sinuous and recurved so that it 'samples' terrain on every side of the site under study. In other cases the outcrops can form essentially a linear transect and the configuration of habitats and resources on both sides of the transect must be based on extrapolations.

These difficulties are formidable, but given that fairly detailed and reasonably reliable environmental reconstructions can be assembled in some cases, it does seem worthwhile to make tentative exploratory use of the approach and to test its utility.

As already explained, when site catchment analysis is applied to individual sites, it is simply a destructive device but, as Flannery (1976) has shown, if quantitative data is compiled from catchment data for a series of sites, then the method acquires potential as an analytical tool. Two types of quantification are readily envisaged; (1) the estimated percentage of certain habitat zones within 5 km of the site and (2) the minimum distance from the site to certain key resources or resource clusters. If such data are compiled for a large series of sites, then quantitative analyses would become feasible. The analysis should range from univariate summarizing statistics (frequency distribution, means and deviations), through bivariate correlations to multivariate approaches such as principal components analyses (cf. Wood, 1976).

The scatters and patches approach is one which has been relatively little developed – as yet. Examples known to me of work tending in the direction of treating the distribution of 'sites' and of isolated artefacts as parts of a single system include David Thomas (1973, 1974). Bettinger (1977) and Robert Foley (Hodder *et al.*, 1981: ch. 6). Since 1974 we have been attempting to incorporate this approach into the research of the archaeological segment of Koobi Fora Research

Project (Isaac and Harris, 1975, 1980). In order to provide an example, I will briefly summarize the procedures and the character of the results. Analysis is still proceeding and a full report by J.W.K. Harris and myself will be published elsewhere.[1]

The bottom diagram in Fig. 7.3 presents a plan of an erosion front cutting back through a stratified sequence of sediments such as characterize East African archaeological locales like Olduvai, Omo, Koobi Fora, Melka Kunturé etc. The erosion front is sampling parts of a sequence of superimposed palaeo-landscapes such as the one represented in the top diagram. Artefacts distributed at each 'horizon' are first exposed by the moving erosion front along a sinuous outcrop. Subsequently, gravity and erosional processes may move the pieces down slope where they may become mixed with other artefacts from other outcrops. Ultimately they will either disintegrate as a result of weathering or find their way into the deposits of the present-day rivers and streams. Clearly the series of freshly exposed objects along an outcrop is a sample of the contents of the layer taken along a sinuous transect that traverses a small part of the palaeo-landscape with which the layer was associated during the time of its formation. Equally, all post-exposure processes distort and bias this initial sample.

Given an interest in the overall distribution of artefacts on the palaeo-landscapes over which early hominids roamed, how is information to be collected? Sampling by excavation over tens of square kilometres of exposure is obviously impracticable. The question then becomes, can we use samples derived by the 'excavation' being done by 'mother nature'? Is the blurring and distorting process, the noise, strong enough to obliterate the signal? The only way to find out was to try! The results so far suggest that the signal can be discerned.

In our work we are mainly concerned with two kinds of archaeological variables: (1) the density of artefacts per unit area (or per unit volume of sediment); (2) the composition of artefact sets from different sectors of the palaeo-landscape (percentage of type, technique or raw material categories).

The investigation is predicated on the view that these archaeological variables are very possibly 'dependent' variables, the values of which will show predictable relationships to a series of 'independent' palaeogeographic variables. The two initially considered are: (1) distance of the sample point from the rocky hills of the basin margin; (2) topographic situation as reflected by lithologies indicative of different modes of deposition (e.g. conglomerate and sands indicate portions of stream channels, clays and silts indicate flood-plains). For the area under initial investigation, the Karari escarpment, some other potential variables such as distance from the lake shore are effectively constant and consequently did not enter into this particular inquiry. Other potentially significant independant variables may be added when more detailed geological work has been done. These would include distance between the sample point and a large perennial river or distance from the nearest conglomerate suitable as a source of raw material and so forth.

Since the horizons sampled are of progressively younger age as one ascends the series of outcrops, it is necessary to attempt to control for time in the analysis and the outcrops were divided into a series of stratigraphic levels.

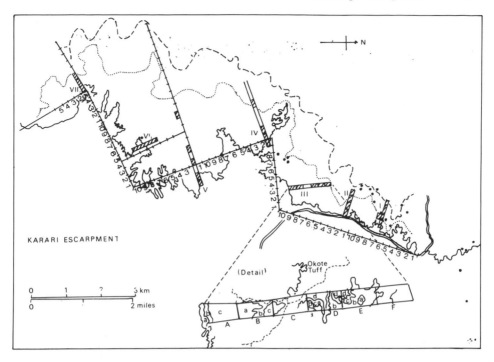

Fig. 7.8. An example of the scatters and patches approach: overall distribution patterns sampled by means of transects across the outcrops of a stratified sequence of layers each representing a palaeo-landscape. (From the work of Isaac and Harris, (1980) on part of the Upper Member of the Koobi Fora Formation.) The layout with transects placed by a stratified, random procedure is shown. Dots indicate dense patches of artefacts classifiable as sites. The detail shows the recording units used in one transect. Each unit is the outcrop of a distinctive lithology.

The first requirement was to secure a broad and reasonably representative coverage of information which could serve as a background for more refined and focused investigations. We attempted to acquire this by classifying and counting artefacts on each outcrop within a series of transect strips taken across the erosion front at stratified random intervals (Fig. 7.8) (see Isaac and Harris, 1980). There is great variation in both the density and the percentage data for the series of sample points. Given the complex interaction of variables, patterns of relationship will have to be worked out with caution, but there is every reason to expect that the spatial pattern being sampled will provide more balanced information of early land use than does site distribution analysis by itself.

The second step in developing this approach has been to take samples at intervals along the outcrop of a particular layer. In the first instance outcrops which contain an important excavated site (a concentrated patch) have been chosen. Fig. 7.9 illustrates this procedure, which is still in an early stage of application. Ultimately some way of acquiring a random sample of outcrops should be devised, since it is as important to know where material is not to be found as it is to know where it is found.

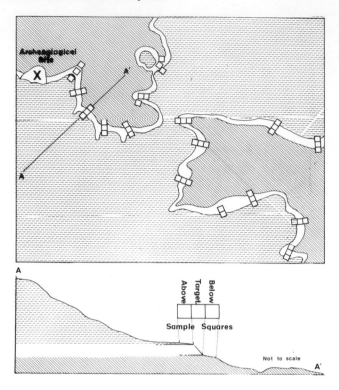

Fig. 7.9. The scatters and patches approach: the overall distribution pattern of stones and bones in a particular horizon is sampled by means of a series of squares placed at randomized intervals between 10 and 50 paces apart along the outcrop. The profile is a diagrammatic representation of the topographic configuration involved in one application of this method. At each sample point a central square measures the composition and density of items on the target outcrop. Control data are gathered from squares above and below.

Both these methods should allow us to address questions such as, was the morphology of the artefact sets in areas of high density (sites) the same as that of the set discarded as a dispersed scatter over the terrain?

The only explicit data known to me, relating to differences in stone discards between sites and non-site scatters, is that furnished by Gould (1977) on the basis of ethnographic observations in Australia. Here he did observe important differences. We became aware of his observations after embarking on our study and it reinforced our sense of the potential interest of the inquiry. During the course of the fieldwork, examples of all of the first three levels of the hierarchy set out in this essay were encountered; isolated artefacts, small clusters which range in scale from mini-sites with a few tens of pieces to mega-sites with thousands of artefacts.

Patterns within clusters

Detailed treatment of intra-site pattern analysis is beyond the scope of this essay. Another member of the Koobi Fora Research Project, Ellen Kroll, is currently

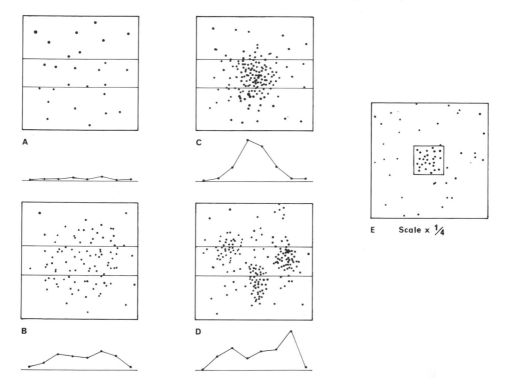

Fig. 7.10. (a)-(d) show diagrams of point pattern configurations which have already been recorded through the plotting of stones and bones at excavated early archaeological sites in East Africa. All are compound clusters but the hominid behaviours that formed each of them may have differed considerably as regards the number of site usage episodes, the duration of each episode, the number of individuals and the number of social 'modules' participating in any given episode. The nature of the economic and/or social usage pattern involved in each episode may also have differed. (e) shows the relatively diffuse frame (a) superimposed on a background one-tenth as dense; this illustrates that all of the compound clusters need to be considered in relation to their 'background' scatter configurations.

engaged in a careful investigation involving a variety of methodological experiments which she will report in due course.[2] However, there are some general points which need to be made about logical relations between intra-site analysis and the comprehensive study of the overall spatial configuration.

The point has already been made that sites are commonly 'clusters of clusters'. Even for the earliest-known sites we modern humans tend tacitly to assume that many of these are fossilized camping places, 'home bases', if you will, and all that that implies (Isaac, 1976b, 1978 [this volume, ch. 11]). This is a proposition that needs to be tested rather than assumed, hence intra-site analyses need to start at a fundamental level without taking for granted the basic behavioural meaning of the cluster and without plunging directly into the exegesis of detail such as the recognition of 'activity areas' and so forth (cf. Whallon, 1973, 1974). This is why it is so important that intra-site spatial analysis be conducted along with studies concerned with the overall array. It is especially important to know about the density of the background of discarded material, within which the concentrations are conspicuous anomalies.

Fig. 7.10 offers a simple classification of point pattern configurations which have already appeared in published plans of early sites. Clearly, it is entirely possible that the series represents accumulations which formed as results of quite different behavioural modes. Some sites may simply represent places in the landscape where actions that were commonly dispersed over the landscape recurred often enough to generate a concentrated patch of refuse. An example of this might be repeated individual feeding, with tool use, under a long-lived shade tree. Other patches may well represent special foci in hominid life that involved enactment of particular parts of the behavioural repertoire that were much less comonly performed outside of these special foci. (Modern human home bases are foci of this second kind.) In the former instance the material present and its arrangement might be expected to resemble simply a concentrated, mechanical aggregate of the low-density background materials. Examples of the second type might well differ from the background both in the composition of the leavings and in its arrangement. These are some of the problems to be dealt with in a comprehensive study. We need to work with the testing of as large a series of alternative hypotheses as our ingenuity allows.

Conclusion

Clearly all three approaches, which have been exemplified, hold promise of helping us to infer and understand early hominid ways of life. Surely the fourth, involving simulation, will also become important as more is known and as more relevant contemporary ecological data are collected. Research should proceed by trying out different variants of all these and comparing the results, searching for convergences.

For at least two reasons the scatters and patches approach may turn out to have particular importance in the study of the spatial configurations of the very early archaeological record. First, once recognized, the peculiar but inevitable 'outcrops-strip' character of the record places severe limits on the application both of normal site distribution map analysis and of site catchment analysis. Second, as we explore back into the remote past, it becomes more and more dangerous to assume that the basic organization of socio-economic behaviour was structured according to principles that are universal among humans today. If we wish to determine at what stages home-base nodes, food sharing and division of labour became established, we need to scrutinize with a minimum of prior assumptions the total arrangement of early archaeological datum points. We are fortunate that in addition to contributing their bones as markers, and sometimes footprints, early proto-humans dropped bits and pieces of modified materials in many places. The spatial configuration of all of these 'visiting cards' constitutes the most powerful clue we have to the beginnings of the human condition.

Acknowledgements

The ideas presented in this essay have been formed in the course of working with a team of colleagues and students in the archaeological segment of the Koobi Fora Research project – especially John W.K. Harris, Henry Bunn, Yusuf Juwayeyi, Zefe Kaufulu, Ellen Kroll, Nicholas Toth and Kathy Schick. Many of the ideas were clarified during a seminar series at Berkeley dealing with prehistoric land-use patterns. The seminar was taught jointly with J. Desmond Clark, to whom I owe much. While a visiting fellow in Peterhouse, Cambridge, in 1976, I discussed land-use patterns with David Clark, just before his untimely death, and with Rob Foley, with whom the dialogue continues. As a visitor to the School of General Studies at the Australian National University, Canberra, I was privileged to participate in seminars and field visits that helped me formulate the ideas in the paper. Participants to whom I am especially grateful include John Mulvaney, James O'Connell, Nic Peterson, Isabel McBryde and Wilfred Shawcross. Besides drafting the figures, Barbara Isaac constantly makes suggestions and valid objections.

Notes

1 This research was still in progress at the time of Glynn Isaac's death, and has not yet been written up. Certain aspects have been explored by Nicola Stern, of Harvard University, in her Ph.D. dissertation. [Ed.]

2 In her forthcoming Ph.D. dissertation for the University of California at Berkeley. [Ed.]

8

FXJj 50: an Early Pleistocene site in northern Kenya

Introduction: the site and its potential

Flying north-eastward from Koobi Fora, one leaves the shores of Lake Turkana and heads across low-lying country towards a sinuous line of hills. These hills form part of the rim of an ancient sedimentary basin into which river systems have been discharging loads of gravel, sand, silt and clay for several millions of years. In many places these layered deposits preserve a fossil record which includes both palaeontological and archaeological evidence relating to very ancient proto-human ways of life (for summarizing references see M. G. and R. E. Leakey, 1978; Coppens *et al.*, 1976; Leakey and Isaac, 1976; Walker and Leakey, 1978; Isaac 1978a [this volume, ch. 11]).

Looking out of the plane window at the part of the sedimentary basin that lies inland from Koobi Fora, one sees that today deposition has largely ceased, and the layered deposits that were laid down between 1 and 3 million years ago are being eroded. Under the semi-arid arid conditions which now prevail, areas of bush and scrub are interspersed among badlands where erosion gullies form intricate dendritic patterns. Some fifteen miles inland from the present-day lake shore lies an area where the sediments are predominantly fluviatile. These include lenses and tongues of gravels and sands that mark the alignments of ancient water courses, but the predominant sediments are extensive beds of brownish silts that were laid down on floodplains that developed alongside the water channels. These silts have become relatively hard, consolidated sedimentary rocks, and because they are more resistant, a slight escarpment has formed where the erosion front has reached their western margin. This is the Karari Escarpment (Fig. 8.1). The fluviatile beds contain the greatest abundance of artefacts found in the Koobi Fora area, and archaeological research has been concentrated here (Harris, 1978; Isaac and Harris, 1978).

From the southern part of the escarpment comes a seasonal water course – the Sechinaboro laga. If, while flying along this tree-lined streambed towards the scarp one looks out northward across the bush and scrub that grow at the foot of the scarp, one sees a small open space. A closer look would reveal this as a little

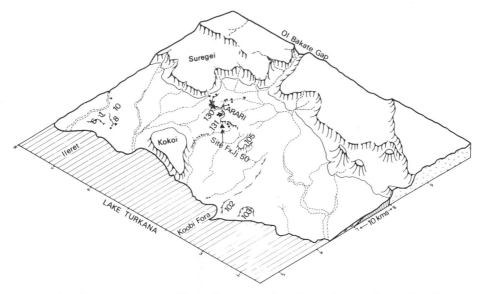

Fig. 8.1. Isometric view of the Koobi Fora area from the south-west. The numbers designate areas where hominid fossils have been found. Dots mark known archaeological sites of Okote Tuff age; triangles mark excavations already done (after Harris, 1978).

flat-topped ridge with trenches cut into its flanks (Fig. 8.2). The ridge is a small erosional remnant of the same fluviatile beds that form the escarpment half a mile to the east. The trenches are the marks of archaeological research at an early Stone Age site whose name is its catalogue number, FxJj 50. It is just one of many in the area, but because of the unusually good conditions of preservation that have prevailed there, we have singled it out for individual treatment in this paper.

The site was found by searchers working on foot, going through the bush from one isolated outcrop exposure to the next. It was first found by Dr Paul Abell in 1973, and then independently rediscovered by John W. K. Harris in 1974. Along the eastern margin of the ridge, a scatter of fossil animal bones and weathered stone artefacts showed that erosion had for some time been cutting into beds which contained archaeological evidence. However, the most exciting aspect of the discovery was one particular small embankment at the north-east corner of the ridge where numbers of artefacts and bones in very fresh condition were visible. These lay scattered just below the outcrop of a relatively well-consolidated tuffaceous silt layer, and this layer was clearly a promising one to dig. In April 1977, test trenches were excavated by John W. K. Harris. The site proved to contain such a well-preserved set of evidence that our team embarked on a programme of excavation which eventually involved four more seasons of work with a cumulative total of some nine months of digging by a 6–10 person crew of experienced Kenya National Museum excavators. The September to November season in 1977 was supervised by Glynn Isaac assisted by Ellen Kroll and Yusuf Juwayeyi, while the two 1978 seasons and the 1979 season were supervised by Henry Bunn.

Sites can be excavated just because they are there, but our reasons for devoting

Fig. 8.2. The FxJj 50 site and excavations: an aerial view from the north-east.

so much time and effort to this one were more specific. We needed sites where bone was well preserved. We had also decided that it would be interesting to excavate some more early sites where the material was not particularly abundant or dense, since sites with very dense masses of material may represent accumulations involving many events and activities that are hard to separate. FxJj 50 looked promising from both points of view.

Excavations at Olduvai (M. D. Leakey, 1971) and at Koobi Fora had led to the formulation of a series of propositions that needed to be tested. For instance, in both areas archaeologists had recovered concentrated patches of artefacts and broken-up bones. How had these concentrations been formed? Could they merely be hydraulic jumbles as Lewis Binford (1977a) strongly suggested, or did they indicate that by 1.5 to 2 million years ago some toolmaking hominids were eating substantial quantities of meat and marrow? Did the concentrations of bone imply that the toolmaking hominids were transporting meat (and other food) to special places (home bases or living sites) for sharing? The latter view was implicit in Mary Leakey's (1971) interpretation of her Olduvai sites and was offered as an explicit working hypothesis by Isaac (1976; 1978a [this volume, ch. 11]). Site 50 was excavated to test possible answers to such questions and also in the hope of obtaining further general evidence bearing on early proto-human ways of life.

Since 1977, archaeological research at Koobi Fora has involved division of labour among members of a team: the scope of the studies being undertaken by the team is far wider than the study of one site, but all members of the team have joined in studying this site and discussing its interpretation. What follows is truly a joint effort. Excavation at FxJj 50 did not end until late in 1979, so that this report must be seen simply as a preliminary account – an introduction to a wealth of well-preserved evidence. Some of the proto-human activities that led to the formation of site seem already to emerge incontrovertibly; other aspects of the evidence will require prolonged careful analysis for their interpretation.

Geology and palaeo-geography (AKB, ZK)

The site consists of a patch of stone artefacts interspersed with broken-up fragments of bone. These remains form a thin irregular lens within a bed of hard tuffaceous sandy silt. At the northern margin of the site, our excavation shows that the layer dips northward into the bed of an ancient watercourse. Equally, if the outcrop of the layer is traced round to the southern end of the little ridge, it can again be seen forming part of the eastern bank of a complex of river deposits that consists mainly of sands and gravels. Figure 8.3. is a simplified version of the contoured geological map surveyed by Zefe Kaufulu. Figure 8.4. is a reconstruction drawn by Kay Behrensmeyer of the topographic setting that the geology shows to have existed during the time when the site was formed. It is clear that the concentration of stone artefacts and broken-up bones accumulated on the floodplain of a river or stream just at a bend in the channel. The artefacts and bones were deposited on a substream of sandy tuffaceous silts, and as the channel aggraded they were covered with more sediment of the same character.

The archaeological materials at FxJj 50 are encased in tuffaceous sandy siltstones that form part of a widespread geological horizon known as the Okote Tuff (Findlater, 1978). Volcanic ash and pumice were evidently being erupted from vents some considerable distance away and then being washed into the Turkana basin by the flood waters of the big river that flowed down from the Ethiopian highlands. Pumices from the Okote Tuff complex have been dated by the potassium argon method. Fitch and Miller (1976:42) obtained dates ranging between 0.87 and 1.66 but preferred a value of 1.56 mya. Uncertainty about the reliability of an age picked from a scatter of values is in this case largely resolved by the fact that the Okote Tuff is stratified between two other tuffs for which extremely reliable, consistent age determinations have been made. The situation can be summarized as follows:

Karari Tuff (15–20 m. above the Okote)	1.4 ± 0.1 my	(Drake *et al.*, 1980)
Okote Tuff complex	1.56	(Fitch and Miller, 1976)
KBS Tuff (15–20 m. below the Okote)	1.8 ± 0.1	(Drake *et al.*, 1980)
	1.89 ± 0.01	(McDougall *et al.*, 1980)
	1.87 ± 0.04	(Gleadow, 1980)

The beds containing the site have shown reversed palaeomagnetic polarity wherever they have been sampled, so that the site certainly dates to the Matuyama Reversed Epoch. All in all, there can be high confidence that the site formed after the Olduvai Normal Event, some time about 1.5 to 1.6 mya.

Pollen has been found in only one sample of the sediments at the site – the layer just underneath the archaeological horizon (Vincens, 1979). The vegetation represented seems to have been fairly open, dry *Acacia-Commiphora* savannah or

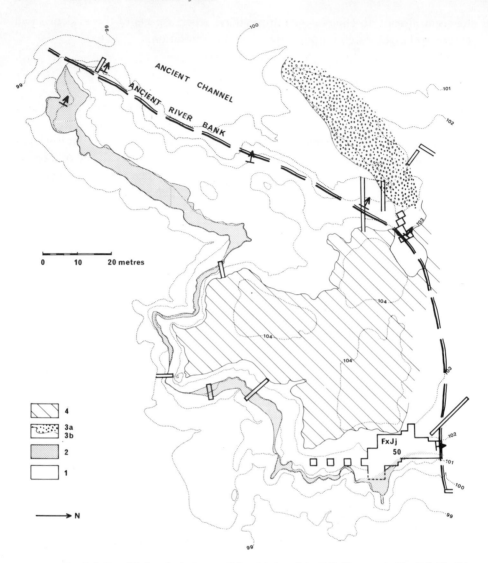

Fig. 8.3. Simplified geological map of the vicinity of site FxJj 50, surveyed by Zefe Kaufulu. Contour heights are in meters above an arbitrary datum. The sequence of layers is: (1) Undifferentiated beds underlying the site, principally brown floodplain silts. (2) A laterally variable grey tuffaceous silt intergrading with brownish sandy silts. The archaeological horizon is stratified in this unit. (3) (a) Brown sandy silt deposits with an interstratified tuffaceous unit; (b) channel sands and a gravel bar deposit, lateral to the upper part of 3 (a). (4) A lime-cemented, gravelly sandstone sheet, representing a minor disconformity within the Okote Tuff Complex beds. Arrows mark steep (8–15°) dÊepositional dips that delineate the position of the bank of an ancient water course that existed here during the time when units 2 and 3 were being deposited.

parkland, with about 80 per cent of the pollen being grass pollen. There is, however, a small quantity (0.4 per cent) of pollen from genera such as *Ficus* and *Ziziphus*, which grow along water courses. Judging both from root casts in the sediments and from the general features of analogous topographic situations in East Africa today, the banks of the water course would have been lined with groves of trees such as is suggested in the reconstruction (Fig. 8.4).

Geological studies show that at the time when early proto-humans came and flaked stones at the place where Site 50 formed, their activities took place in the midst of a vast floodplain. If some of these hominids had climbed a tall tree at the site and looked around, they would have seen flat, savannah terrain stretching away for some 15 km eastward to the rim of hills. Through a gap in the hills they would have seen a large river issuing out into the basin. Looking around they would have seen a ribbon of gallery forest marking the meandering course of this river as it wound its way across the floodplain to reach its delta some 25 km to the south-west of Site 50. We know that this delta and the adjacent lakeshores were familiar to these proto-humans or their neighbours, because in the silts that were being deposited there our expeditions have found both fossil hominid bones and ancient footprints (M. G. and R. E. Leakey, 1978; Behrensmeyer and Laporte, 1981). The hominid specimens from contemporaneous beds on the delta and elsewhere include remains of at least two species – *Australopithecus boisei* and *Homo erectus*. We tend to presume that the makers of the stone tools at our site belonged to the latter species, but there is as yet no way to prove this.

If the hominids in the tree-top had shifted their gaze to their immediate surroundings a scene something like that sketched in Fig. 8.4 would have met their eyes: a stream-bed curved its way through the floodplain. Along its course lay gravel bars

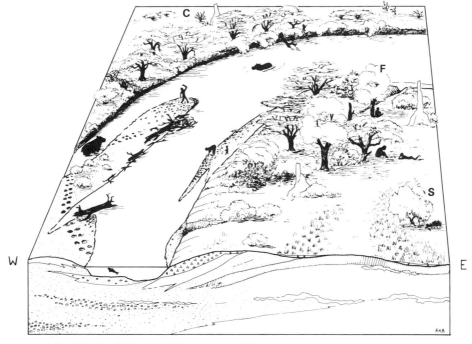

Fig. 8.4. Sketch by A. K. Behrensmeyer indicating the palaeotopography of Site 50 and the stratification that provides evidence for the reconstruction. The hatched layer is the tuffaceous sandy silt in the top of which the archaeological horizon is stratified. Examples of some tree genera represented in the pollen are shown and marked: C = *Commiphora*, F = *Ficus* and S = *Salvadora*. Other trees are three species of *Acacia*.

composed mainly of smallish lava pebbles, but with scattered larger cobbles and some siliceous rock fragments as well, making them convenient places to obtain material for flaking sharp-edged stone implements. The east bank of the channel here was steep, but on the flattish ground beside the bank were groves of trees providing shady places in which the hominids could flake their stones and pursue whatever other activities they had in mind. That they used this piece of floodplain fairly intensively is attested to by the accumulation of a patch of artefactual and other refuse.

The proto-humans who frequented this place would certainly have known whether this stream channel carried perennial water flow or whether it was seasonal, but we latter day geologists have not yet been able to determine this.

Excavations and the disposition of materials

The site has proved to consist of several dense clusters of material that interconnect with each other. Figure 8.5a shows the plan of trenches by which this configuration was discovered. The initial trenches located the two main clusters, and subsequent trenches attempted to locate the margins of the site and to sample the contents of its periphery.

The excavations revealed that there are occasional bone pieces scattered through all of the 3 m of silt beds sampled by our trenches. However, artefacts were virtually confined to a single, highly restricted zone within the beds and the great majority of all bone fragments also occurs in this zone (see Figs. 8.5b, c; 8.6 and 8.8). Over most of the site this artefact-bearing stratigraphic zone seems to form a relatively flat-lying thin lens, but in the most northerly trenches we found that the horizon dips down to the north-west and follows local irregularities in the floodplain surface. In this part of the site the silt and tuff deposits that encase the archaeological horizon could all be seen to have been draped over the banks of the channel that our geologists had already identified in the south-western outcrops (see Fig. 8.3). Artefacts and bones are scattered on the upper slopes of the channel bank which forms a northern limit to the site (Fig. 8.7). At the southern edge of our excavations, the density of materials diminished sharply. This was confirmed by the paucity of finds made in a series of 2 × 2 m sample pits. These yielded only a very low density of artefacts and bones which can be regarded as a part of the background scatter against which the high densities of the site centre stand out as strong anomalies (Kroll and Isaac, in press [1984]; Isaac, 1981b [this volume, ch. 7]). Our trenches seem effectively to have reached the western limits of the dense patch of artefacts and bones, but because we would have had to dig through more than 3 m of consolidated overburden to test this conclusion, it was not practical for us to do so. There may be outlying clusters in this direction. It is hard to judge the position of the eastern limits of the site, since this margin has been cut into by the gully erosion that had revealed the existence of the site in the first instance. Various aspects of the situation suggest that the patch of material did not extend very far in this direction. Within this area there are higher and lower density subsections, and

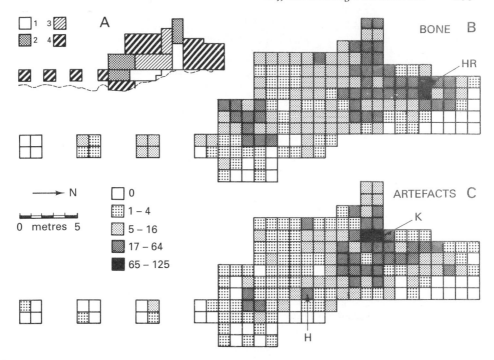

Fig. 8.5. (a). Plan of the excavation of FxJj 50 showing the increments by which the excavation was extended: 1 = 1977a test trenches; 2 = 1977b; 3 = 1978a; 4 = 1978b and 1979. The 1978b and 1979 excavations were undertaken mainly to define the limits of the site. (b) and (c) Plans showing the density of all bones and of all stone artefacts per square metre. These include small pieces recovered in the sieve (not shown in Fig. 8.6). HR, K, and H mark the positions of one bone and two stone clusters, as noted in the text.

these are discussed below. Figures 8.6 and 8.7 present profiles along the north-south axis of the site with the positions of all plotted finds projected on to them. In the southern part of the site the archaeological material forms a horizon that is only a few centimetres thick, while in the more northerly parts of the site the pieces are scattered through approximately 50 cm of deposit. This zone of greater vertical dispersal largely coincides with an area in which the silts are interpenetrated by the growth of calcium carbonate concretions with a very distinctive lobate morphology (Fig. 8.9), interpreted as the endocasts of subterranean termite nests which were tunnelled out by termites after the site had been covered over by silt layers. We are inclined to regard all or most of the observed increase in vertical dispersal as having been caused by the burrowing action of the termites.

Figures 8.10 and 8.11 show that lines joining the position of pieces that fit back together form an interconnecting web that links up all parts of the archaeological zone within the site, both horizontally and vertically (see discussion below). We are thus inclined to treat the entire occurrence as an indivisible archaeological entity. We suspect that nearly all of the material was laid down on a single irregular and gently sloping surface that was open and stable for some unspecified interval. Successive loads of overbank sandy silts then covered the stones and bones. Subsequently bioturbation processes, especially termite action, seem to have dispersed the

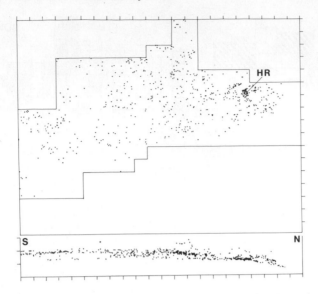

Fig. 8.6. The positions of plotted fragments of bone – a plan and a south-north profile. HR marks the position of a cluster of hippo rib-shaft fragments, as noted in the text.

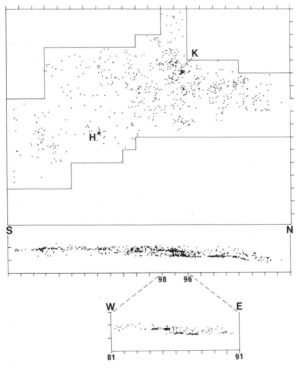

Fig. 8.7. The positions of plotted stone artefacts – plan and two profiles (south-north and west-east). H and K mark the positions of stone clusters as noted in the text.

Fig. 8.8. FxJj 50: trench at northern edge of site, with artefacts and bones defining the dip of the archaeological horizons as it passes over the rim of the river bank.

material to varying degrees in different parts of the site (comparable evidence for vertical dispersal of an archaeological horizon has recently been reported by Van Noten *et al.*, 1980). On the other hand, it is possible that in some parts of the site bioturbation has caused an upper (major) archaeological horizon to merge with a lower (minor) horizon, but this is not at all certain. We intend to test these hypotheses rigorously in future analyses of the material and its disposition.

The stone artefact assemblage (JWKH and GI)

Table 8.1 shows the typological composition of the assemblage of stone artefacts. The categories used are those established by M. D. Leakey (1971) with some modifications and additions (Harris, 1978). The analysis presented in this table allows comparisons to be made with assemblages from other early East African sites. In a subsequent section of the paper Nick Toth presents a technological analysis.

The table shows that, as at many other early sites, the artefacts are predominantly (94 per cent) flakes and flake fragments ('débitage'). The items classified as 'tools' in Mary Leakey's system of categories consists almost entirely of small cobbles and chunks of rock which have been flaked with varying but generally fairly low degrees of intensity. Under the rules of the typological system these items are classified as choppers, polyhedrons, discoids and core-scrapers. However, it should be noted that they also served as cores, and it is possible that the low

Fig. 8.9. FxJj 50: detail of calcium carbonate concretions in trench BB which seem to be casts of subterranean termite nests.

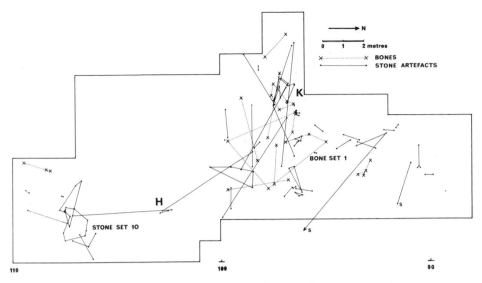

Fig. 8.10. The positions of conjoining pieces of stone and bone. For sets with 3 or more pieces, the lines are drawn around the outer perimeter of the set. H and K mark positions of stone clusters, as noted in the text.

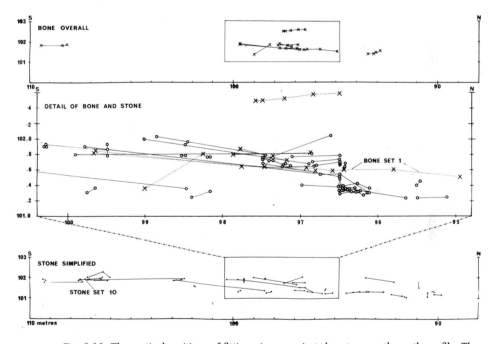

Fig. 8.11. The vertical positions of fitting pieces, projected on to a south-north profile. The upper frame shows all conjoining bone. The lower frame shows conjoining stone, with only selected pieces shown in the area of maximum density. The centre frame provides detail of the densest area drawn at a larger scale. The axes are marked in the metre units of the site grid system.

Table 8.1. *Typological composition of the artefact assemblage from FxJj 50* (analysis by JWKH)

		N	Percentage
A.	*Overall composition*:		
	Tools, core-tools and cores	59	4.2
	Modified/edge-damaged	33	2.3
	Debitage (flakes, flake fragments, etc.)	1313	93.5
	Total	1405	100.0
	'Manuports' (unshaped cobbles and split cobbles)	76	
B.	*Subdivisions of the 'Tools/core-tools/cores' class*:		
	Choppers	34	57.6
	Polyhedrons	6	10.2
	Discoids	4	6.8
	Core-scrapers	5	8.5
	Scrapers on flakes	4	6.7
	Flaked core/cobble fragments	6	10.2
	Total	59	100.0
C.	*Subdivisions of the 'Modified/edge-damaged' class*:		
	Modified battered cobbles	9	27.3
	Battered cobbles	12	36.4
	Hammerstones	6	18.2
	Edge-damaged flakes	6	18.2
	Total	33	100.1
D.	*Subdivisions of the 'Debitage' class*:		
	Whole flakes	534	40.7
	Broken flakes	193	14.7
	Angular fragments	440	33.5
	Core/cobble fragments	146	11.1
	Total	1313	100.0
E.	*Raw materials of the artefacts*:		
	Basalt		76.1
	Cryptocrystalline silica (chert, chalcedony)		10.4
	Ignimbrite		10.1
	Quartz		2.1
	Other volcanic rocks		1.3
	Total		100.0

percentage of so-called 'tools' in the assemblage reflects the fact that the flakes and flake fragments were functionally more important. Consistent with this notion is the observation that the edges of the choppers, discoids, etc. at the site show little evidence of damage or battering. In a few instances we know that a core/core-tool was taken away from the place where the flaking was done, leaving most of the flakes lying where they had fallen (see below). This could imply either use of the core as a tool or its reuse as a core.

The assemblage of 1,405 specimens contains only four instances of retouched flakes and six core or cobble fragments with trimmed edges. The retouch on these pieces is often inverse and has produced notched and denticulate edges. It is still uncertain whether or not these should be regarded as intentionally fashioned tools.

Only six flakes show macroscopic signs of edge damage such as might be attributed to use. However, utilization traces have been found on some items in a sample of the chert flakes submitted to Dr Lawrence Keeley for microwear analysis. This study is still in progress.[1]

There are fifteen cobbles with battering and minor fractures such as might be induced by pounding. Of these, six have localized bruising of the kind found on hammerstones.

All of the materials of which the artefacts are made occur in the gravels of the ancient channel complex adjacent to the site. The stones used for flaking tend to be smallish, and this is also true of the majority of clasts available in the gravels at this site (Harris, 1978).

The assemblage is technologically and typologically simple, in much the same way as the KBS industry (Isaac and Harris, 1978). The Site 50 and KBS assemblages fit well into the 'mode 1' category of J. G. D. Clark (1969); in their lack of more complex elements, they compare best with the series of assemblages from Olduvai Bed 1 which are the type series for the 'Oldowan'. However, it should be noted that the FxJj 50 assemblage is somewhat younger than the KBS and Olduvai Bed 1 assemblages (1.5 – 1.6 vs. 1.8 my) and that other assemblages including more elaborate tools are known to occur in the same Okote layers. These are the occurrences of the Karari industry (Harris and Isaac, 1976), in which well-made core-scrapers are conspicuous. We do not know yet why the FxJj 50 assemblage lacks forms present in the contemporary Karari assemblages, but one member of our team (N.T.) is investigating the possible influence of raw material on tool morphology. Another possibility of course is that different activities with correspondingly different tool-kits took place at the different sites.

The bone assemblage (HB)

Approximately 2,100 pieces were recovered, and these represent at least twenty vertebrate taxa. Table 8.2 summarizes the body parts present for each of a series of broad taxonomic categories; Table 8.3 provides a more precise taxonomic list along with other data. The assemblage shows a pattern common at archaeological sites in general, including other early sites in East Africa, namely that 65 per cent of the assemblage consists of non-identifiable pieces. The remaining 35 per cent is also highly fragmented, but it is identifiable at least to a general body part category (e.g. limb shaft) and broad taxonomic group (e.g. mammal or ungulate). Compared to material from other sites in the Karari area, the FxJj 50 bone assemblage is well preserved; however, much of the bone shows signs of post-depositional corrosion so that some specimens are leached, pitted and crumbly. The original surface of the bones, when visible, usually does not show the kind of cracking and flaking pattern which starts to develop after a few months to a year on bones exposed to equatorial weathering conditions. This would seem to imply that the majority of bones in our

Table 8.2. *Body-part representation for a series of broad taxonomic groups*

	Mammal, size indet.	Mammal, size 1–2	Mammal, size 3–5	Bovid, size 1–2	Bovid, size 3–4	Bovid, size 5	Suid	Equid	Giraffid	Hippo	Other mammal	Bird	Reptile
Teeth	5			1	3	8	8	4	2	8	5		7
Cranial		10	24	2	3	1				2			7
Axial		13	26		7	1							
Rib shaft		21	147	1	6					102			
Rib end		1	1							1			
Forelimb shaft			9	1	14				1	3			
Forelimb end		1	1		2	1	3			3			
Hindlimb shaft			10	3	13		1			6	1		
Hindlimb end				1	10	2			3	1		1	
Limb shaft		56	149										
Carpal, tarsal, phalanx, sesamoid		1	1	4	3		3		1	2	5	1	6
Unidentified	1,358												3

Numbers beside broad taxonomic groups refer to useful, arbitrary animal size groups (e.g. Klein, 1976), as follows:

1	< 50 lb	Thomson's gazelle size	4	750–2000 lb.	Eland, buffalo size
2	50–250 lb.	Impala, warthog size	5	> 2000 lb.	Hippo, rhino, giraffe size
3	250–750 lb.	Hartebeest, wildebeest, zebra size	6	> 6000 lb.	Elephant size

The very generalized body part categories shown here summarize detailed descriptions recorded using a system of alphabetic and numeric codes (Gifford and Crader, 1977).

Table 8.3. *Summary of animals, minimum number of individuals (MNI), age classes, and body-parts represented in the bone assemblage*

Common names	Taxon	MNI	Age	Body-parts
Small gazelle	Antilopini size 1–2	1	2	Tooth, femur, tibia
Impala	*Aepyceros* sp.	1	3?	Femur
Wildebeest tribe	Alcelaphini size 3	2	3	Tooth, radius, tibia
Wildebeest-size bovids	Bovid indet size 3	2	1, 1	Metatarsal
Size 4 alcelaphine	*Megalotragus kattwinkeli*	2	3?, 4	Mandible, vertebra, rib, humerus, metatarsal
Giant buffalo	*Pelorovis* sp.	2	1, 4	Tooth, vertebra, radius, tibia, metatarsal
Giraffe	*Giraffa* sp., size 3–4	1	?	Tibia shaft
Giraffe	*Giraffa jumae*	1	3	Tooth
Giraffe	*Sivatherium maurusium*	1	2	Tooth, ?tibia, ?metatarsal
Pygmy hippo	*Hippopotamus aethiopicus*	1	2	Tooth, mandible, humerus, pelvis
Large hippo	*Hexaprotodon karumensis*	2	3?	Tooth, rib, scapula, radius, ulna, carpal, femur, tibia, metapodial
Horse	*Equus* cf. *tabeti*	1	4	Tooth
Giant pig	*Metridiochoerus andrewsi*	2	3	Tooth, mandible, radius, ulna, metacarpal, fibula, phalanx
Giant pig	Suid indet.	1	1	Tooth
Baboon	*Papio* sp.	1	2?	Tooth, humerus, metatarsal
Porcupine	*Hystrix* sp.	1	2	Mandible, tooth
Bird	Aves	1	?	Tibia
Crocodile	*Crocodylus* sp.	1	?	Tooth
Crocodile	*Euthecodon* sp.	1	?	Tooth
Tortoise	Chelonia gen. et. sp. indet.	1	?	Carapace
Snake	Squamata gen. et. sp. indet.	1	?	Vertebra
Catfish	*Clarias* sp.	2	?	Cranial plate, pectoral spine, vertebra

Numbers under age refer to the following general age classes of individual animals:

1 = neonate	3 = prime adult
2 = juvenile, sub-adult	4 = very old adult

sample accumulated within a time span not exceeding a year or so. However, if there had been coverage by low vegetation, which we cannot fully detect archaeologically, this could affect such an estimate. After the assemblage had been sealed in by the deposition of sandy silts, soil processes, including ground water leaching and perhaps termite action, resulted in deterioration of some bone.

As Table 8.3 shows, a wide variety of animals is represented – practically every major group except carnivores, rhinoceroses, and elephants. Antelopes (bovidae) of a variety of sizes and forms predominate in the sample as they do in the modern East African fauna. Other grassland animals, such as equids and suids, are also represented. The presence of three types of giraffe lends credibility to our reconstruction of local environment, with a gallery of trees and bushes lining the nearby river bed. Large aquatic mammals are well represented by pygmy hippo and a large riverine hippo. Smaller animals occur in low frequencies: a baboon is the sole primate representative and, in addition, there are a set of articulated snake vertebrae, a small bird tibia fragment, and the lower jaws of a young porcupine. Scattered crocodilian teeth, and spines from a 10–15 kg catfish were also recovered.

With regard to parts of the body, a general pattern can be seen: limb shafts are much more common than limb ends. Likewise, rib shafts are much more common than rib ends, and vertebral processes, which are themselves uncommon, are much more abundant than vertebral centra. Teeth are moderately well represented. These features may in part reflect the fact that fragments of these bones are more readily identifiable even in small pieces. Some of the under-represented elements may have been missed because they are buried outside the area sampled by our excavation, but this would seem unlikely given the absence of evidence of marked spatial segregation of most body parts within the excavated area.

The differential representation of body parts raises questions about how the bones reached the site and what happened to them after they got there. Repeatedly, specific limb shaft pieces were assigned to animal size groups, and often even to a particular species of animal, only for us to discover that the adjacent limb epiphyses were not present. Could the abundant elements have reached the site as isolated fragments, perhaps washed in by fluvial activity, for example, as part of an over-bank deposit? This appears unlikely, since bones with many different transport potentials occur together in the assemblage. It seems more probable that whole bones were at one time present at the site.

The reconstructed humerus shaft of *Megalotragus* shown in Fig. 8.12 provides a useful example. In addition to the seven fragments which actually fit back together, three more pieces of humerus were identified as *Megalotragus*, a distal end (see below) and two shaft fragments. The distal end and one shaft fragment came from the same left side of the animal as bone set 1 and most likely are parts of the same bone; tiny, potentially linking fragments were not found, however, so the two pieces cannot be included in set 1 with absolute certainty.

The archaeological stratum at the site contains bones and artefacts at more than ten times the densities found in equivalent sediments outside the site. Clearly, particular processes operated at the site to create the combined concentration.

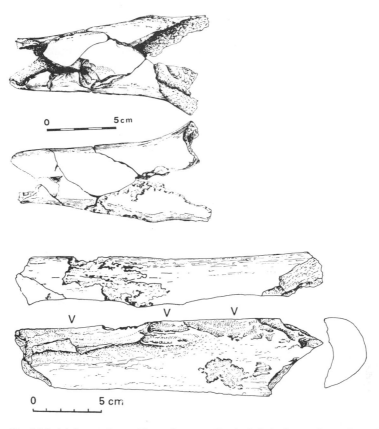

Fig. 8.12. (a) Seven pieces of bone (bone set 1) which fit back together to form the shaft of the humerus of a large bovid. The shaft seems to have been shattered by hammer blows. (b) A piece of radius shaft from a very large mammal, possibly a giraffe. Arrows mark points of impact.

While we readily tend to infer that the site must represent a place to which toolmaking hominids brought meat for consumption, the details of the evidence also show that a complex set of processes has interacted. For instance, in addition to the suggestive association of bones and artefacts, fossil dung gives clear signs that carnivores visited the locality, and gnaw marks attest to rodent and carnivore activity. Equally, the floodwaters which deposited silt over the horizon could have washed bones in and/or out. Our investigations have sought to determine as far as possible the relative importance of these various agencies. Only a preliminary outline of the evidence and interpretation can be given here.

In our inquiry we looked to see whether, in addition to juxtaposition to artefacts, any of the bones showed clear signs of having been processed by tool-using hominids. For the first time at any of the very early sites, we are able to report such evidence. Foremost among these evidences is the presence of what can best be described as cut marks – fine linear grooves scored into the bone surface by a sharp object. These linear marks are indistinguishable macroscopically from undoubted butchery marks, which are, of course, a common feature on archaeological bone debris from more recent periods. Fig. 8.13b shows a particularly well-preserved example of this kind of evidence on the medial side of the distal articular end of the humerus of a large antelope. Some of our own butchering experiments show that this is one place where cut marks are very likely to be inflicted when the radio-ulna is detached from the humerus. Ten or twelve other bones with probable cut marks have also been found – mainly on limb and rib shafts where detaching meat was the probable aim.

A second category of evidence comes from the fracture patterns evident on some bone fragments, especially from conjoining sets such as that illustrated in Fig. 8.12. A number of specimens show breakage patterns that closely resemble those induced experimentally by hammer blows, which differ from fracture patterns so far observed by us on carnivore-chewed bones. Our experience has shown that one very efficient method of breaking open a marrow bone involves resting the shaft on

(a)   (b)

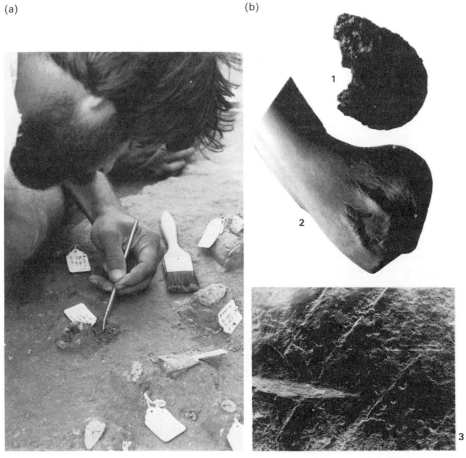

Fig. 8.13(a). FxJj 50: uncovering a typical scatter of bone fragments and small stone flakes. (b) (1) Fragment of distal end of humerus of a large antelope, showing cutmarks; (2) distal end of comparable modern humerus, indicating the anatomical position of the fragment (by courtesy of 1. Findlater); (3), a scanning electron microscope enlargement of the marks, × 16 (by courtesy of A. Walker and P. Shipman).

an anvil and then repeatedly hitting the exposed side with a hammerstone. If just the right amount of force is exerted, the shaft begins to split longitudinally. It is then advisable to shift the position of the shaft and hit it again where the longitudinal crack has not yet reached; otherwise, repeated blows in the same fractured spot simply have the undesirable effect of crushing sharp splinters of bone into the marrow. This method produces a line of characteristic impact marks along the bone shaft before it is sufficiently fractured for the bone marrow to be readily accessible. The hammerstone blows detach flakes of bone from the internal edges of the developing longitudinal crack in a manner similar to conchoidal fracture of stone. Broad internal flake scars on limb-shaft pieces and distinctive bone flakes are produced in this marrow processing activity. We have found numbers of broken bones at Site 50 which conform to this pattern (cf. Fig. 8.12b), and also several of the distinctive bone flakes.

The evidence of conjoining sets of bone fragments found close to each other strongly implies that bones entered the site more or less complete and were broken and/or chewed into pieces on the spot. In this connection the paucity of articular ends should be recalled: a feature that tends to characterize bone accumulations worked over by carnivores (Klein, 1975). The recovered sample may well be the residue of a dynamic system in which substantial amounts of bone were being consumed or removed by scavengers. There is much evidence to document the efficiency of scavenging animals in removing bones (e.g. Isaac, 1967b [this volume: ch. 6]), and the presence of both fossilized dung and gnaw marks from a medium-sized carnivore also supports this interpretation. It is much less clear whether the carnivores were introducing bone as well as disposing of it, but the close association with artefacts and the presence of butchery marks suggest that the toolmakers were the principal accumulating agency.

If this last point is correct, what can we say about how the hominids acquired bones and presumably meat in the first place? This point must, for the time being at least, remain in question form. The taphonomically complex and relatively small bone assemblage from Site FxJj 50 cannot by itself provide a definite answer. We are inclined to suggest that the wide range in animal sizes, with its bias towards large animals and low body-part representation, is consistent with Vrba's (1975) model for hominid scavenging. However, the presence of some neonate individuals and the apparent high frequency of young and very old animals compared to prime adults might perhaps suggest some hunting success by hominids. But these are mere guesses; we really need more information on modern social carnivores and modern hunter-gatherers, and more archaeological data from early sites like FxJj 50.

Fitting pieces back together

A major undertaking of our research team has been the conjoining of pieces of stone and bone. Figures 8.12 and 8.14 show examples of refitted bone and stone sets.

Table 8.4 summarizes the characteristics of the sets. Figures 8.10 and 8.11 present the horizontal and vertical distribution of conjoining sets. The search for refitting sets has been very time-consuming, but it has provided crucial information:

1. The distribution of members of conjoining sets demonstrates that, even though the archaeological material is dispersed through an appreciable thickness of sediment, the assemblage is an indivisible analytical entity that need not represent a very long time interval.

2. The members of sets commonly occur in fairly close proximity to each other, implying that post-fracture fluvial transport, at least in these cases, has been minimal. It also implies that bone breaking and stone knapping were done on the site at these precise spots.

3. The fact that some pieces are definitely missing helps to establish that the refuse at the site is only the partial residue of an input–output system that extends beyond the boundaries of the excavated clusters.

4. The refitted sets are informative regarding the procedures used in stone knapping

Table 8.4. *Composition of conjoining sets of stone and bone*

	Bas-alt	Other stone	All stone	Bone
Number of pieces	90	44	134	29
Percentage of assemblage[a]			9.5	3.9
Number of sets[b]	37	16	53	10
Size of sets				
2 pieces	32	11	43	7
3 pieces	1	2	3	1
4 pieces	2	1	3	–
5 pieces	–	1	1	1
6 pieces	–	–	–	–
7 pieces	1	–	1	1
⩾ 8 pieces	1	1	2	–
Vertical dispersion of sets[c]				
⩽ 10 cm			40	3
> 10 cm			12	7
Horizontal dispersion of sets[c]				
2 pieces:				
⩽ 1 m			30	2
between 1 and 3 m			7	3
> 3 m			5	2
3 or more pieces:				
⩽ 1 m			2	–
between 1 and 3 m			7	2
> 3 m			1	1

[a] The percentage for bone is calculated using the number of identifiable pieces.
[b] 8 stone sets involve the fitting of one or more flakes onto a core; 25 stone sets reconstruct a flaking sequence without the core; 20 stone sets consist of reconstructed individual flakes or parts of flakes.
[c] Exclusive of one set consisting of a conjoin between an excavated and a surface piece.

and in the breaking of bones. Reference to them also increases the proportion of securely classifiable pieces.

The spatial arrangement of stone and bone (EK)

Figures 8.5, 8.6 and 8.8 show the distribution of stones and bones within the excavated area, almost 200 m^2. The point pattern diagrams in Figs 8.6 and 8.8 show only those pieces for which coordinates were measured during excavation. The shaded density diagrams (Fig. 8.5) present the total number of pieces recovered, including pieces, mainly small, found during the screening of earth from excavation unit (1 m^2 × 5 cm). Fig. 8.13a shows a detail of a typical scatter.

The study of the arrangement of material at Site 50 is still in progress.[2] Ultimately, the horizontal and vertical distributions will be subjected to rigorous analysis, including the lane-by-lane dissection of the vertical dimension, further integration of the metre square data, and the computation of statistical measures of clustering intensity. However, even before these analyses have been undertaken, some parts of the pattern stand out as indicative of particular events on the site, affording glimpses of precise moments in early Pleistocene time.

In the southern part of the site there are two areas that seem to have been used for stone knapping. The southernmost of these involves seven overlapping sets of conjoining pieces (Fig. 8.10). Among them is set 10, which is illustrated in Fig 8.14. In this vicinity, about one-third of all debitage enters into the seven conjoining sets. For three sets, the cores are absent, having presumably been removed for use elsewhere either as cores again or as choppers. We cannot as yet determine whether the knapping episodes occurred during one visit or during a number of successive visits.

A second cluster (marked H on Figs. 8.5 (c), and 8.10) was found 4 m to the north. This consists of 36 pieces, many of which are minute chips, packed very closely together. The pieces are so small that conjoining has proved impractical. This cluster of minuscule pieces looks like the fine debitage that accumulates where sustained stone-flaking takes place; the extreme localization of the debris seems to imply that the patch represents a single episode. Two pieces from patch H conjoin with pieces from the other concentrations: a flake from patch H joins with a cobble in the southerly concentration, and a split flake from H fits with one in the northern concentration. We have not been able to identify the missing larger debitage from area H. Perhaps the larger flakes were taken away.

The northerly artefact cluster, some 7 m in diameter, is the largest of the site. It involves the same configuration as the southern sector, but there is much more material crowded together, including some 30 overlapping and contiguous conjoining sets. There is again at least one small patch with a dense of small debitage (marked K on the plans).

Each of the larger intrasite clusters seems to have formed as a result of a series of stone-knapping episodes which recurred in several sectors of the site, though in the northerly sector the process was either more intensive or more prolonged. We can only speculate what made the northern part of the site a favourite place to do things, but the observed pattern could, for example, imply the existence of a shady tree there. Perhaps the southern cluster formed in a smaller or less well shaded area. It may even have formed at a slightly different time.

The bone distributions also reflect specific episodes of which only a few can be discussed here. Particularly suggestive is the set consisting of the seven conjoining fragments of the *Megalotragus* humerus (Fig. 8.12), plus the cut marked articular end (Fig. 8.13b) which probably comes from the same bone. We do not know whether the antelope limb was dismembered at the place where the carcass lay or at the site, but the humerus certainly seems to have been broken at the site. The fragments are distributed in a patch with a diameter of about 5 m. Bone fragments do not normally fly apart when a bone is broken open for marrow, but if they were picked off and tossed aside as the marrow was extracted and eaten, one might expect them to have just such a distribution. Nearly all of the 21 *Megalotragus* bone fragments were found in the northern sector with two outliers further to the south-west.

On the northern edge of the main cluster, right on the stream bank, we found a cluster of bones in which fragments of hippo ribs predominate (marked HR on Figs. 8.5 and 8.6). Scattered pieces of hippo also occur through the site. It is not as certain as for the *Megalotragus* humerus, that these bones were carried in and discarded as food refuse, but it is a strong possibility. Spare rib of hippo would hardly be carried very far, so perhaps the original reasons for use of the site was the finding of a hippo carcass in the channel nearby.

The bone and stone plans show a dense distribution, especially in the northern sector, and we have wondered at times whether the concentrations might merely be dumps of refuse alongside the real activity areas (Schiffer, 1972). However, we gained valuable insight into this question when towards the end of our excavation we returned all the pieces from the northern area to their original horizontal positions (Fig. 8.15). It then seemed clear to us that given a substratum of loose, sandy silt, some leaf mould and a little grass, the hominids who made the tools and broke the bones here might have been blissfully unaware of the archaeological record they were creating underfoot. There is no need to suppose they needed to sweep it up or toss more than a few large pieces out of their way.

The question of post-occupation disturbance (KS)

It is clear that during the process of entering the geologic record all sites must undergo some distortion and rearrangement of their contents. Part of this post-occupation modification is due to differential decay. Changes are also induced by the processes that cover the site with soil or sediment, and by bioturbation of the encasing layers. All the early sites at Koobi Fora (and most elsewhere) have been covered by layers of sediment deposited from moving water, though at the best-preserved sites, such as FxJj 20, 18 IHS, 3(HAS) and FxJj 50, the covering consists

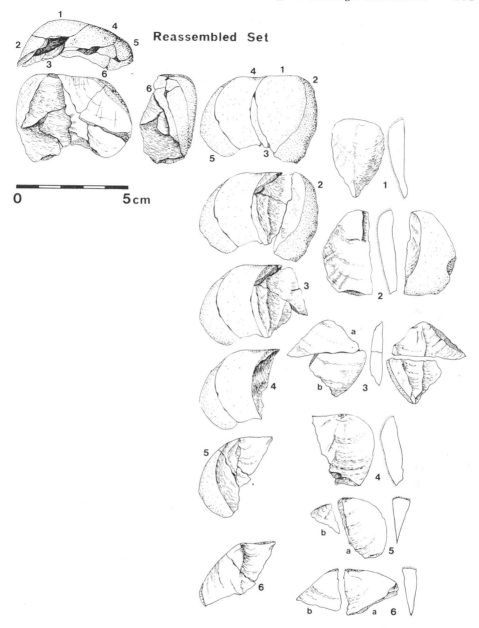

Reassembled Set

0   5cm

Fig. 8.14. One of the conjoining sets of stone (set 10 on the plan and profile). Top left are four views of the completed set; in the drawings below the set is progressively dismantled. The set derives from the flaking of a waterworn cobble. After these flakes were removed, the piece, which would have resembled a side chopper, was taken away from the vicinity. Drawn by Barbara Isaac.

of fine-grained material laid down under rather gentle flow conditions. Careful comparative and experimental studies of site-formation processes are necessary if we are to understand early sites where the series of processes to be investigated includes the effects of both human and geological agencies. Even the preliminary results of

Fig. 8.15. FxJj 50: artefacts and broken bones, replaced by horizontal coordinates on the floor of the northern sector of the excavation (photograph by courtesy of P. Kane).

the experiments which are in progress help with the interpretation of Site 50.

One way to assess the degree of fluvial disturbance to which a set of flakes from stone knapping has been subjected is to compare the observed frequency-distribution of artefact size, with that from experimental stone knapping, using the same materials and techniques. Extensive transport should result in size sorting (Isaac, 1967b [this volume, ch. 6]; Harris, 1978), and our experiments have shown that any flow strong enough to rearrange objects commonly produces a 'winnowing' effect, i.e. a selective removal of small pieces.

Figure 8.16 compares the frequency distribution for size in three sets of experimentally produced debitage with the debitage recovered from Site 50. It can be seen that while the modal values are similar, the percentage values for very small flakes are much lower in the excavated assemblage, and those for larger flakes necessarily somewhat higher. Two principal alternative explanations should be considered:

1. Smaller pieces have been selectively removed by water currents.
2. Smaller pieces may have been missed in the process of excavation even though the earth from the site was sieved.

We believe that the two processes have been jointly responsible. That members

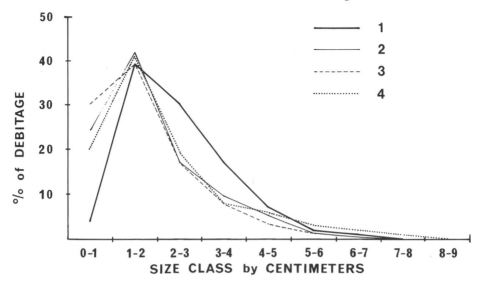

Fig. 8.16. Frequency distributions for maximum dimension of debitage from the FxJj 50 excavation, and from various knapping experiments: (1) FxJj 50 (n = 1324); (2) the replication of the Site 50 cores (n = 1128); (3) various flaking episodes with basalt (n = 1272); (4) flaking episodes with ignimbrite (n = 424).

of conjoining sets were found in close proximity argues strongly against very extensive transport. Since in digging in exceedingly hard sediments, where not all earth lumps could be broken up, we will have missed a fair number of very small pieces, we think that this cause of loss has been important. Further experimental work and screen-washing trials will be necessary to assess the relative importance of the two processes.

Experiments have also been carried out in order to assess the likelihood that some of the conjoining sets at the site may have been preserved lying exactly as they fell to the ground during episodes of stone flaking. In a series of tests the stone knapper worked by direct percussion with the core held in the hand, in some instances standing, in others crouching in one spot. In the resulting arrays, the diameter of the area of densest scatter (involving even very small fragments) is less than 1 m, the majority of the pieces are found in an area from 1.1 to 1.8 m in diameter, and the maximum extent of scatter has been 1.1 to 2.7 m. Of the ten conjoining sets with three or more pieces so far discovered at FxJj 50, eight are well within this range, with scatter diameters from 0.25 m. to 2.37 m.

The stone technology of FxJj 50 (NT)

The technology of the stone-artefact assemblage at FxJj 50 is very simple: only very elementary knowledge of the mechanics of stone fracture was required to produce these artefact forms. The majority of the cores began as small basalt clasts from river gravels near the site. The maximum dimension for cores made on cobbles or pebbles ranges from 3.1 to 9.0 cm, with a mean of 5.8 cm. A technological analysis of the FxJj 50 cores is given in Table 8.5.

A consistent feature of the assemblage is the predominance of unifacially flaked core forms, in which the cortical surface of the cobble or pebble has been used as the striking platform for the detachment of flakes. Interestingly, these types of unifacial cores were also prevalent in experiments done by novice knappers who had no previous experience in stone technology.

The majority of these cores could well be by-products formed during the deliberate manufacture of sharp-edged flakes and fragments. Such flakes would have been especially useful for animal butchery – an idea which receives some corroboration from the cut marks found on bones. Given this view, core morphology and therefore the incidence of typological categories would have been largely determined by the shape, size and raw material of the original piece selected for flaking.

An experimental replication of the entire population of lava cores from FxJj 50 (47 specimens) was undertaken, to compare the debitage produced by the experiment with that excavated from the site. This operation should help us to detect whether some classes of artefact were carried on to the site ready-made, and whether some classes have gone 'missing' through being carried off or through being washed away.

In the experiment, the set of replicated cores was made as nearly as possible identical to the set of excavated cores. The characteristics of the associated flakes could then be compared and for this purpose the flakes were divided into six categories, based on location of cortex (see Fig. 8.17). Flake types I–III would primarily represent unifacial flaking of cobbles and pebbles (having cortical butts),

Table 8.5. *Technological breakdown of the FxJi 50 cores*

	Basalt cobbles[a]	Basalt flakes/fragments	Ignimbrite cobbles	Vein quartz cobbles	Cryptocrystalline silica cobbles	Other	Subtotals	Totals
Unifacially flaked	21	10	2	2	1	1		37
around entire circumference	7			1			8	
around partial circumference	14	10	2	1	1	1	29	
Bifacially flaked	9	1	3	2		3		18
around entire circumference	1	1					2	
around partial circumference	8		3	2		3	16	
Polyfacial	2						2	2
Partly unifacial, partly bifacial	4						4	4
Totals	36	11	5	4	1	4		61

[a] Including both cobbles and pebbles.

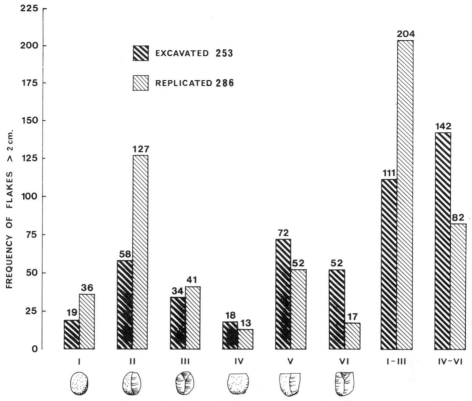

Fig. 8.17. Comparison of numbers of flake types recovered from the excavation with those produced during the experimental replication of the FxJj 50 cores. The six categories are defined on the basis of presence (I-III) or absence (IV-VI) of cortex on the butt and the dorsal face (as shown). Only flakes greater than 2 cm in maximum dimension are included.

while flake types IV-VI would primarily represent flaking another face (bifacial flaking) of a pebble or cobble, having non-cortical butts. Since the small size fraction from the site is in less than expected numbers, only lava whole flakes of length greater than 2 cm were used in this analysis. Figure 8.12 shows that there are fewer 'unifacial' flakes (types I-III) but more 'bifacial' flakes (types IV-VI) at the site than in the replicated series.

Assuming that the replications are fairly accurate, these results imply that the cores and flakes at FxJj 50 are not a complete and intact set. Various explanations seem possible: some cores may have been brought to the site after initial flaking elsewhere; some bifacial or polyfacial cores may have been removed from the site; or cortical flakes may have been selectively removed. We suggest that the behavioural patterns of early hominids at FxJj 50 were much more complex than simply bringing cobbles and pebbles on to the floodplain and flaking and using stone artefacts at one place. Substantial transport of materials involving areas outside our excavations probably occurred. We suggest that the primary agency was probably the toolmakers, though floodwaters may also have contributed to the dispersal of the material.

Discussion

During the excavation of Site 50 we have had a privileged sense of gaining glimpses of particular moments in the lives of the very early proto-humans who lived in East Africa 1.5 million years ago. More than anything else this attaches to the discovery of such things as cut marked bones and conjoining sets. Finding an articular end of bone, with marks apparently formed when a sharp-edged stone implement was used to dismember an antelope leg, cannot but conjure up very specific images of butchery in progress. Finding the fitting pieces of hammer-shattered bone shafts invites one to envisage early proto-humans in the very act of extracting and eating marrow. Hypotheses to the effect that such activities were a part of the adaptation of early hominids were already given wide credence before the excavation of FxJj 50, but they are reinforced and gain dramatic support from the evidence at the site. Equally, the discovery of clusters of conjoinable flakes establishes a sense of connection across time which one lacks in working with disconnected assemblages of debitage, even though it must have formed as the result of precisely similar flaking episodes.

FxJj 50 emerges as another instance in which the vicinity of a water course was a favoured location for activities leading to the accumulation of a concentrated patch of artefacts (see Harris, 1978 and Isaac, 1972a [this volume, ch. 1] for other instances). The popularity of such places probably stems from the existence in them of groves of shady trees, clumps of fruiting bushes, access to water, and sometimes, as here, access to stones for flaking.

FxJj 50 is also another instance of a place where a relatively dense cluster of stone artefacts coincides with a higher than background density of broken-up bones. In this case, particular places are detectable within the site, where flakes and fragments derived from stone knapping and bone breaking seem to lie more or less as they were dropped.

It is hard to tell the order of magnitude of time represented by the accumulation of material. All of the stone artefacts could be generated in less than an hour or so of knapping, but the bone set presumably represents items that were introduced in a spaced series of events. Nevertheless, the apparent absence of pre-burial weathering cracks on the bones seems to indicate that most of the bone component accumulated within the span of a year or so (see Behrensmeyer, 1978a). The site was sealed in by sandy silts deposited from flood waters that overflowed the banks of the adjacent water course. Experimental and comparative study leaves us with the working hypothesis that the site was not formed primarily by flood action, although material may have been partly rearranged and some small specimens may have been washed away.

Many of our observations will have relevance for testing hypotheses about the nature of early hominid behaviour (Biniford, 1977a; Isaac, 1981a [this volume, ch. 12]), but detailed discussion of this goes beyond the scope of this preliminary report. Suffice it to say that the concentrations of artefacts and bones, the cut marks and the conjoining sets are all consistent with (but not final proof of) interpretations that attribute meat-eating and food-transporting activities to the early toolmakers (cf. Isaac, 1978a [this volume, ch. 11]). Further, the characteristics of the bone assemblage invite serious consideration of scavenging rather than active hunting as a prominent mode of meat acquisition. This topic will be pursued in further analysis.

There are only a few other early, pre-Acheulian sites where substantial parts of a cluster of artefacts and bones have been removed by excavation in fine-grained sediments. Notable among the others are FLK Zinj, FLK NNI, DK ad HWK II at Olduvai (M. D. Leakey, 1971), Melka Kunture (Chavaillon and Chavaillon, 1971) and FxJj 20 at Koobi Fora (Harris, 1978). Each new site extends the data set in valuable ways, and it is through the rigorous testing of hypotheses against the mounting sum of observations that understanding of early proto-human patterns of life can be revised and refined. This task calls for prolonged, patient research, but the sense that Site 50 gives of providing vivid glimpses is in its own right an interim reward.

Acknowledgements

This study was done as a part of the Koobi Fora Research Project, which is an enterprise of the National Museums of Kenya. We thank the Museum and TILLMIAP staff for their participation and support during both field and laboratory work. The excavation owed much of its success to the skill and good humour of the crew of National Museum excavators. Muteti Nume served as site foreman with Kitibi Kimeu, Mukilya Mangoka, Musau Mangea and Bernard Kanunga as trench foremen. J. Speth helped supervise the completion of work, and at different times G. Dekker, B. Goerke, K. Harris, A. Kerr, J. Kimengech, F. Marshall, G. Mgomezulu, F. Musonda, J. Sept, W. Shawcross and A. Vincent all gave valuable assistance. Ian Findlater advised on geology. The report owes much to Barbara Isaac who worked tirelessly at drawings and graphics in the field and in the lab. Trudi Quinn has worked overtime to help us complete the text preparation. The preparation of a brief report on a site with such a wealth of data has involved generous forbearance on the part of all contributors. Richard Leakey and the National Museum provided logistical support, with aid from the National Geographic Society. The direct costs of the archaeological programme were covered by a grant to G. Ll. Isaac from the National Science Foundation.

Notes

1 Reported in an appendix to chapter 7 of the monograph (in preparation) on the archaeology of Koobi Fora (Isaac, n.d.; Keeley and Toth, 1981).
2 In her forthcoming Ph.D. dissertation for the University of California, Berkeley (Kroll n.d.). [Ed.].

9

Small is informative
the application of the study of mini-sites and least-effort criteria in the interpretation of the Early Pleistocene archaeological record at Koobi Fora, Kenya

The archaeological evidences that come down to us from the very early Pleistocene (1.5–2 mya), are meagre – even devotees such as ourselves have to admit this. What we have are broken stones, sometimes clustered into local concentrations that we call sites, and sometimes associated with a greater or lesser amount of broken-up animal bones. The broken stones are usually unmistakeably fractured by some kind of proto-human agency – they *are* artefacts, and they have the fascination of dating from the dawn of humanity; but if we are honest we have to admit that they are seldom very beautiful. Sometimes they show the elegance of simplicity (Fig. 9.1) but they are not works of art.

The broken animal bones too are full of interest, but it is sometimes debatable whether or not the toolmaking hominids had anything to do with the animals beyond sharing the landscape with them.

Perhaps because of the meagreness of the record, we archaeologists have sought unconsciously to compensate in various ways. We have habitually located our excavations, not in places that are representative of the ancient litter of discarded artefacts, but in places that are unusually crammed with material. In studying the artefacts some of us have taken a plethora of measurements and all of us have erected a multiplicity of typological categories.

In these ways our research on the archaeological evidence from Koobi Fora began; but fieldwork in a remote, arid area brings with it opportunities to sit under thorn trees and contemplate. Out of this there has emerged an interest in trying to develop alternative approaches to research that accept the meagreness of the record, and indeed move to recognize sparsity and simplicity as real reflections of the patterns of life and the states of mind that prevailed in remote prehistory.

In this paper we offer a tentative, preliminary report on attempts to develop methodologies that explore and take advantage of the meagreness of the record. We will deal briefly with three topics: (1) the overall scatter pattern of artefacts across ancient landscapes; (2) what might be gained by digging sites which contain very few remains; and (3) a simple minded approach to the study of very early artefacts.

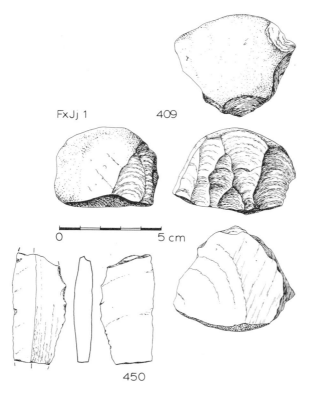

FxJj 1   409

0   5 cm

450

Fig. 9.1. Examples of early stone tools showing elegant simplicity of form. (409) A cobble with flakes removed along one margin. The piece could either be regarded as a core-scraper or as a single platform core. (450) A fragment of a blade-like flake (classified as an angular fragment). Both pieces from site KBS drawn by Barbara Isaac.

Scatters and patches

Walking over the eroded outcrops of the Koobi Fora Formation searching for dense clusters of artefacts that denote the existence of an excavatable site we have become aware that between the clusters there are many stray artefacts. These are pieces that appear to have been discarded one or two in a place or in small groups of one to a few dozen. Fig. 9.2 suggests the pattern and shows the mechanism whereby this record formed.

In 1974 we began to make systematic efforts to define overall distribution patterns. We threw a series of transects across the outcrops at a stratified random series of sampling points along a 14-km length of escarpment. This experiment has been reported in Isaac and Harris (1975) and in Isaac and Harris (1981).

In 1977 we reorganized our research strategy. Instead of making observations on the contents of transects that cross many outcrops, we began to sample along the outcrops of particular beds in the manner indicated in Fig. 9.3. In this way we are able to assess the pattern along what is in effect a sinuous strip sample of a portion of the ancient floor of the sedimentary basin. Aspects of this approach and

SEQUENCE OF RECORD FORMING PROCESS

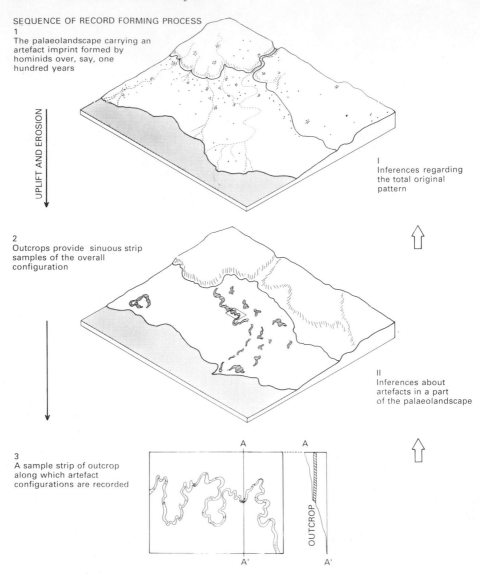

1
The palaeolandscape carrying an
artefact imprint formed by
hominids over, say, one
hundred years

UPLIFT AND EROSION

I
Inferences regarding
the total original
pattern

2
Outcrops provide sinuous strip
samples of the overall
configuration

II
Inferences about
artefacts in a part
of the palaeolandscape

3
A sample strip of outcrop
along which artefact
configurations are recorded

OUTCROP

Fig. 9.2. The processes which form the archaeological record of early hominid land use in
sedimentary basins such as those of the East African Rift Valley. Reading the sequence from
top to bottom shows the steps by which our sample of information becomes available to us.
Reading from bottom to top, the sequence represents a chain of inferences. The diagram is
based on Koobi Fora (Isaac and Harris, 1978).

methodology have been reported elsewhere (Isaac, 1981b [this volume, ch. 7]).
Here we will present a brief preliminary indication of some results.

We have sampled along the outcrops of the Okote Tuffaceous beds within the
Koobi Fora Formation in northern Kenya. (For background information on the
geology, palaeontology and archaeology of Koobi Fora see various chapters in
Leakey and Leakey (1978). The outcrops studied are of fluviatile sediments that
were deposited near the north-eastern margin of the Lake Turkana basin between

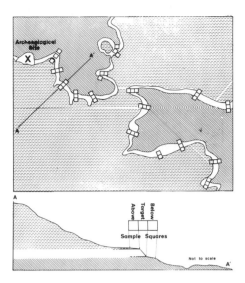

Fig. 9.3. The scatters and patches approach; the overall distribution pattern of stones and bones in a particular horizon is sampled by means of a series of squares placed at randomized intervals between 10 and 50 paces apart along the outcrop. The profile is a diagrammatic representation of the topographic configuration involved in one application of this method. At each sample point a central square measures the composition and density of items on the target outcrop. Control data are gathered from squares above and below.

1.3 and 1.6 million years ago. Individual beds of sandy silt between 50 and 200 cm thick can be traced in outcrop for distances of up to several kilometres along the Karari erosion scarp. The silt beds are interrupted laterally by tongues of sands and sandy gravels. The silt beds represent deposition over wide areas of floodplain and the sand tongues mark the courses of the drainage channels that traversed the floodplain. Very probably most of the channels represented in our sample traverses belonged to seasonal streams, running in off the nearby basin margin ridges, but this is not certain.

The sampling which we have done so far suggests that there were marked differences in the frequency that early proto-humans discarded stone artefacts in different parts of this ancient floodplain landscape. This translates into a configuration of artefact densities that is diagrammatically represented in Fig. 9.4. It is convenient to recognize three levels of density:

1. *Low background level.* Vast areas up to several kilometres in diameter accumulated only a very low density of discarded artefacts. Artefact recovery in $25 \, m^2$ sampling squares range from zero to two or three items, with zero being the most frequent observation. Small clusters of artefacts are rare but may occur.

2. *Intermediate levels.* Restricted areas, up to 500 m in cross section show a much higher average frequency of artefacts. Recovery from $25 \, m^2$ outcrop sample squares commonly ranges from 2 or 3 artefacts up to 10 or 20. There are signs that this higher average density is made up both of an increased density of isolated artefacts and through an increased frequency of small (30–100) clusters of artefacts.

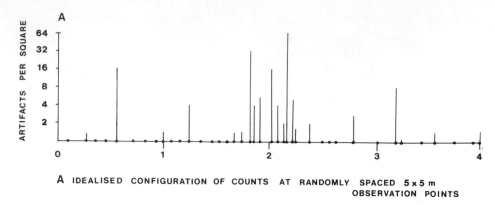

A IDEALISED CONFIGURATION OF COUNTS AT RANDOMLY SPACED 5 x 5 m
OBSERVATION POINTS

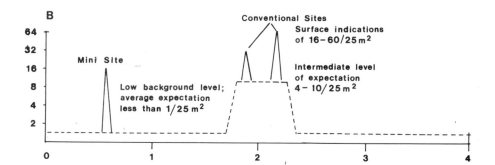

Fig. 9.4. Diagrammatic representation of variations in artefact densities observed along a 4-km strip of outcrop.

3. *Peak levels.* Highly localized concentration of artefacts occur which yield from 20 or 30 to more than 100 artefacts in a $25 \, m^2$ sample square, and where there is a cluster, involve a thousand or more artefacts in areas with diameters of 10 to 30 m. These are the classic 'sites' and it is these that have been the principal targets of excavation. Sites often occur as peaks of density within a wider zone of intermediate level, but they also occur as anomalies within low background density areas.

To translate these observations back into human terms, it appears that there were vast tracts of the ancient floodplain terrain where artefact discard occurred infrequently and at widely dispersed locales. However there were some sectors where discard events repeatedly took place in the same general vicinity. In addition there were some particular places only 10 to 20 m in diameter where quantities of artefacts were discarded.

There seems to be some tendency for the two higher levels to be associated with the banks and beds of channels – though the converse is not true and we have observed numerous sectors of channel where artefact density is low. That is to say the evidence is patterned as though there was 'something special' about some reaches of some channels. Determining what factors led to frequent artefact making and discarding in some areas rather than others remains a major challenge.

Ultimately we would hope to use the distribution patterns to test hypotheses about land use and foraging strategies, but this topic is not pursued here. (See Isaac, 1980, 1981b [this volume, ch. 7] for discussions of this.)

To return to the meagreness and sparseness of the record, what emerges is that in all probability the vast majority of discarded artefacts in the Okote complex do not occur in the dense site clusters that have until recently been the sole subjects of investigation. The site clusters are not representative of the total artefact forming/using/discarding system. It also emerges that frequently occurring elements in the total configuration are small clusters of artefacts, ranging from four or five to perhaps a hundred or so. These are what we are colloquially designating as '*mini-sites*'.

The configuration sketched above also suggests the possibility that one way in which sites showing the peak level of artefact density could form is through the repeated occurrence at one spot of the same kinds of behavioural events that otherwise formed the scattered, separate mini-sites. If this were so then the careful study of a whole series of discrete *mini-sites* (1) might inform us of some of the components of which early proto-human behaviour was made up and (2) might help us to understand the archaeological meaning of the macro-sites that have already been excavated.

Table 9.1. *Finds from mini-site FxJj 64*

A. Composition of stone artefact assemblage (based on analysis by F. Marshall)

	Excavated	Surface
Whole flakes (lava)	15	14
Broken flakes (lava)	11	4
Angular fragments (lava)	18	16
Miscellaneous fragments	1	4
Total	45	38

B. Conjoining sets: (searched by Marshall, Toth and Bunn; data compiled by Kroll).

	Stones	Bones
Size of sets: 2 pieces	3	1
3 pieces	1	
4 pieces		1
5 pieces	1	
Total	5 sets/14 items	2 sets/6 items

Number of pieces: 11/45 excavated; 3/38 surface stones; 6/578 all bones (1%)
          (24%)   (8%)   6/115 partial id. (5%)

Surface pieces conjoining with excavated pieces: 2 sets: 1 surface to 4 excavated; 2 surface to 1 excavated

C. Bones (analysis by H. Bunn)

	MNI	Notes
Mammal size 1–2	1	1 fragment
Mammal (bovid mainly) size 3	2	13 fragments
Hippopotamus	1	2 tusk fragments
Proboscidean (size 6)	1	75 small rib fragments
Catfish (*Clarias*)	1	8 fragments

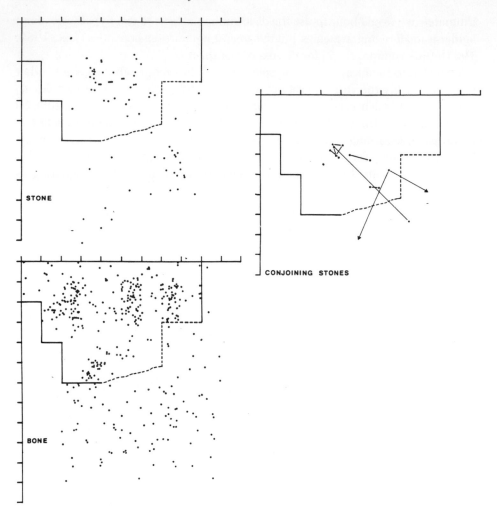

Fig. 9.5. Mini-site FxJj 64: distribution of artefacts, bones and refitting stones. The excavated area is at the top of each frame. Items exposed by erosion are shown in position below the outcrop line.

Mini-sites

This term refers to situations in which a cluster of up to a few dozen artefacts occurs in minimally disturbed context in an area with a diameter of only five to ten metres. In focusing our archaeological attention on such occurrences it is our hope that these may often represent the residue from a very restricted part of early proto-human life: perhaps at the scale of a single toolmaking bout, a single feeding event or some such.

By patient fieldwork and excavation we can collect a stock of instances for which we know (1) what artefacts were generated and discarded, (2) what other durable materials such as bones are associated, and (3) what the palaeo-geographic/palaeohabitat setting was. From this it seems reasonable to hope that we may encounter repeating patterns in the set of cases. It should be possible in due course to test hypotheses regarding early land use, tool use, and socio-economic behaviour.

Site FxJj 64 at Koobi Fora provides a specific example of a start on this approach. This mini-site was discovered and first excavated by A. K. Behrensmeyer during the course of palaeoecological investigations in August 1979. In October and November 1979 the excavations were extended under the field supervision of Fiona Marshall, who also analysed the artefacts in the laboratory (Table 9.1). Henry Bunn has provided us with a report on the bone specimens and Ellen Kroll has prepared plans which are presented in Fig. 9.5. Details of these analyses will all be presented by the investigators elsewhere.

From the figure and table it can be seen that this mini-site consists of a cluster of at least 83 artefacts which interpenetrates, but does not exactly coincide with a series of clusters comprised of 353 bone fragments. The bone fragments are dominated by pieces that come from segments of the rib or ribs of an elephant-sized animal. The combined artefact and bone clusters seem to have a diameter of about 7 m and to have formed on a sector of floodplain, probably at a distance of only about 10 or 15 m from the bank of a watercourse. The patch of material was covered by sandy silts that are presumed to have been deposited during a series of over-bank flooding episodes. Some flow-induced rearrangement of materials, and some washing in or washing out of objects may have occurred, but it seems unlikely that the occurrence was induced purely by hydraulic action. Fourteen pieces fit back together, and from this and other aspects it appears probable that the stone artefacts represent simply flaking products from the knapping of just a few water-rounded lava cobbles, such as occurred in the gravel banks of laterally equivalent channels.

The question arises, were the artefacts and the bones functionally connected or is the juxtaposition coincidental? No definite answer can be given, but it is important to report that Henry Bunn has found a cut mark on one of the fragments of elephant-sized rib.

A significant part of the rationale in pursuing the study of a series of mini-sites is that, while the behavioural interpretation of each individual instance may be ambiguous, the recurrence of some features may make certain lines of interpretation more secure. Site FxJj 64 has been reported here simply as an example of the kind of data that may derive from following this line of approach.

By contrast with site 64, major sites such as the FLK Zinj site at Olduvai (M. D. Leakey, 1971) or Koobi Fora sites like FxJj 20 (Harris, 1978) or FxJj 50 (Bunn *et al.*, 1980 [this volume, ch. 8]) involve thousands of stone and bone specimens packed into a limited area. Ultimately we hope to determine whether concentrations such as these could represent the additive combination of the materials found in a whole series of mini-sites, or whether there are some features or components that qualitatively distinguish major sites from all mini-sites.

Measuring simplicity

If the fractured stones recovered from our excavations and surface sampling of beds, ranging in age from 1.5 to 4.9 my in age, are laid out on tables in the laboratory, first it can be seen that within the set from each site the pieces vary considerably in size and shape. Secondly it can be seen that the sets from different localities differ from each other in the sizes and forms common in each sample. This is normal for artefactual materials of all ages, but for these very early assemblages some particular questions arise. Notably, differentiation informs us as to the level of complexity of most systems during the phase 1.5 to 2 million years. Does this intra- and inter-site variation of forms and assemblage composition imply a material culture system of considerable complexity? Can we use the patterns of differentiation as measures of complexity and as clues to adaptation during the oldest known phases of artefact manufacture?

Clearly these are problems which archaeologists of the Pliocene–Pleistocene share with all Palaeolithic archaeologists; however, as our studies have proceeded we have become aware of the possibility that our own procedures have tended to obscure the answers to the foregoing questions. In order to describe the diversity of forms and assemblages we have used numbers of typological categories, which at Koobi Fora may serve to make the system look more complex than it really was (Isaac, 1976c; Isaac and Harris, 1978).

One of the major stumbling blocks with which we have grappled is the time-honoured distinction between 'tools' and 'non-tools' or debitage. From the early Koobi Fora artefact samples we have formed the strong impression that obtaining sharp-edged, knife-like flakes was probably the main objective of the ancient stone knappers, and that the lumps of stone from which the flakes were detached were first and foremost important as the cores from which the flakes derived. However, prevailing convention would oblige one to formulate the above statement as follows: 'The flakes which belong in the archaeological category debitage, or "non-tools", were really the most important tools, while the lumps of stone from which flakes have been detached are put in the typological category "tools", but many of them may have been cores rather than tools.'

The truth of the matter seems to be that some flakes were tools, and that some flaked lumps were cores only while others were both cores and heavy-duty tools. This has been pointed out by M. D. Leakey (1971), and by J. Chavaillon (1976) for instance. However, the prevailing system of labels is undeniably confusing to scientists and lay-people outside the small circle of primary research workers.

In our own analysis we have decided to cut the semantic knot. We are continuing to use the typological categories of Mary Leakey (1971), but are regrouping some of them, and revising the labels of the higher-order groupings. Our macro-distinctions are as follows:

> *Flaked pieces* (Series FP): any piece from which significant flakes on chips have been removed. This includes (a) raw lumps of stone from which flakes have been detached, and (b) flakes or fragments which have had flakes struck off them, after their separation from a parent block.

Detached pieces (Series DP): flakes, flake fragments and shattered flaking products.
Pounded and battered pieces: relatively massive stone pieces that do not fit well within
   Series FP and which show signs of bruising and chipping. This includes such
   categories as hammerstones, anvils, modified battered cobbles, etc.

These categories do not semantically prejudge the complexity of the system or the
functions of the objects and we want to try and see if using these labels will allow
us to communicate more clearly.

Going on to the interpretation of inter-assemblage variation, after a good deal of
floundering around we have decided to follow a stepwise approach that attempts
to deal with potential explanatory factors in sequence. At each step one seeks to
judge how much of the morphological variation within and between assemblages
can reasonably be attributed to a specified influencing factor. Any residual unexplained variance is then carried forward for potential explanation by reference to
the next factor up the scale. The sequence we are exploring is as follows:

First we ask whether we could expect the observed features of an assemblage,
given the operation of *least effort* stone-fracturing procedures applied to the available forms of stone (pebbles, cobbles, screeblocks or whatever).

Second, if there are features not accounted for in Step 1, and if the assemblage
does not come directly from a stone source, then we ask – are some of the deviations
from simplest possible, least effort strategy, due to economy effort in carrying of
foregoing, then it is legitimate to consider the possibility that arbitrary differences
avoid having to go and fetch another piece of raw material?

Third, if there remain differences between assemblages that are not accounted for
by economy of effort strategies applied to varying forms and availabilities of raw
material, then we ask – could these differences be due to differences in the tasks
which the assemblages were intended to accomplish? This then involves us in
seeking repeated, regular relations between context and assemblage character.

Finally, if there remain significant features of variation not accounted for by the
foregoing, then it is legitimate to consider the possibility that arbitrary differences
between particular material culture systems are being observed; or, if the samples
span a significant time range that they document contrasting stages in the development of material culture systems as a whole.

It should be noted that the application of this system requires information from
outside of the conventional framework of artefact analysis:

1. For step one we need to know what constitutes a least effort stone fracture system
   for each variety of raw material used.
2. For step two we need to know what varieties of raw material were available and
   where.
3. For step three we need to know something about the relative feasibility of performing certain basic tasks, with the different early artefact forms. If possible we also
   need the evidence of use-wear studies as to the uses to which examples of contrasting forms were put (cf. Keeley, 1980; Tringham *et al.*, 1974; Keeley and Toth, in
   press [1981]).

These kinds of information are best obtained from experimental studies and these
have been undertaken for our research group mainly by N. Toth (this colloqium
and 1981) and for Mary Leakey's research group by P. Jones (1979, 1980).

The application of this approach, and the interaction between analysis and experiment is still in progress and will be reported in detail elsewhere. Suffice it to say here that it is our impression that the first two steps account for the great majority of fractured stone forms in the early Koobi Fora assemblages. If this view is sustained then it would imply that these assemblages represent rock-bottom simple material culture systems by which the early toolmaking hominids obtained a basic range of cutting and hacking implements.

The points we have made about three different aspects of the early archaeological record all have something in common. We have recognized in our own work the tendency to compensate for the meagreness, and probable simplicity of the record by focusing on its most intensive manifestation and by employing procedures which could be taken to imply complexity. Clearly the earliest tool-makers were not human, and if we are to understand them and their patterns of life better we'need to make deliberate efforts to step out of ourselves.

In this paper we are suggesting the possible advantages of thinking small as archaeology explores the most ancient spans of prehistory.

III Diet and foodsharing

10

The diet of early man: aspects of archaeological evidence from Lower and Middle Pleistocene sites in Africa

The habit of creating concentrated patches of food refuse and abandoned artefacts is amongst the basic features of behaviour that distinguish the human animal from other primates. The habit has created a trail of litter that leads back through the Pleistocene and can provide an extremely important source of evidence regarding the evolution of human behaviour. Systematic archaeological study of the long-term features of this garbage record is still in its infancy and yet it is already apparent that it is far from being a trivial pursuit.

Suppositions regarding the diet and subsistence activity of early men figure large in numerous writings that also treat broader questions regarding the qualities of human nature. For example Ardrey (1961) saw in the allegedly predatory behaviour of early hominids the origins of violent behaviour patterns that continue to be apparent in modern societies; Morris (1967) argues that many distinctive features of human behaviour and biology have arisen as a consequence of an evolutionary pathway that involved predation and led to important parallels with the biology of other social carnivores. Amongst others Washburn and Lancaster (1968) have stressed the importance of hunting in creating the selection pressures that have directed human evolution towards brain expansion and effective linguistic communication. Tiger (1969) argues that the widespread phenomenon of male bonding in human societies has its origin in social arrangements that were adaptive for early men that lived by hunting. The vegetable component of human diet has received less dramatic attention in discussion of human nature and human evolution, but recently a phase of seed-eating specialization has been suggested as having played a critical role in the differentiation of hominids (Jolly, 1970). This stock of examples is by no means exhaustive, but it serves to illustrate the interest in the feeding habits of early men and to indicate some of the implications that the findings of Pleistocene archaeologists have for anthropology.

While a number of general reviews of human evolution, including that of Howell (1965), do treat the topic of subsistence in general terms, they are not of a character where the relationships between evidence, the process of inference and legitimate conclusions could be critically discussed. What is attempted here is a brief, critical examination of the available stock of information and of the methods by which it can be evaluated. Special attention is given to the African evidence with which the author is most familiar.

Comparative considerations

In many evolutionary studies a first approximation of the historical problem of change can best be obtained from comparative considerations made prior to scrutiny of the fossil evidence. Amongst extant primates the human species is peculiar for the strength of its tendency to incorporate animal protein in its diet. We are, however, dealing with a difference in degree since it is now known from field studies that few of the anthropoid primates are exclusively vegetarians, while very few if any recent human communities are exclusively carnivorous.

The published symposium on 'Man the Hunter' includes a number of ethnographic essays on non-agricultural subsistence patterns (Lee and DeVore, 1968). It emerges that terms such as 'hunters' or 'carnivores' should probably only be applied to recent representatives of the human species with qualifications. The small available sample of studies from Africa and Australia suggest that in the tropics and warm temperate regions the meat component of diet may often have been appreciably less than 50 per cent. The data also imply possible latitudinal gradation in which the importance of meat and fish increases from equator to pole, with arctic and sub-arctic peoples as much as 80–90 per cent dependent on protein foods.

The occurrence of opportunistic hunting amongst baboons, chimpanzees and other anthropoids can probably be taken to indicate that this is a generalized anthropoid trait shared by an ancestral stock even prior to the evolutionary divergence of the hominids. Since we know that this tendency has been intensified in man, it is clearly worth attempting to determine the history of changes leading to the increased carnivorous proclivities that distinguish the species. However, in pursuing this evolutionary study it would seem wise to bear in mind the great variation found in ethnography. It seems likely that the evolution of human behaviour has involved not simply increasing intensity of predation but the unusual development of a flexible system of joint dependence on plant and animal food. Among many recent human communities, the retention of gathered food as a major dietary component constituted an 'insurance policy' that rendered hunting possible under marginal conditions. This ecological strategy made non-agricultural man unique amongst the large predators and appears to have depended on differentiation in the subsistence activities of the two sexes, probably partly genetically determined.

Comparison of extant human subsistence behaviour with primate behaviour in general reveals another set of contrasts which are functionally related to sexual division of labour and joint dependence on both hunting and gathering – namely the distinctive human practices of food sharing and the occupation of home bases. Repeated transport of food back to specific localities results in the localized accumulation of refuse which is what has made archaeological study of prehistoric life possible. However, as we trace the archaeological record back through time there must come a point where the integrated hunting, food-sharing and home-base pattern first appears, perhaps with only low intensity.

Studies of the early development of occupation sites in relation to their content of food refuse is clearly one of the important contributions that archaeology can make to the understanding of human evolution. Localities suitable for such studies have only recently come to light, but given suitable orientation of investigations it seems entirely possible that the evolution of these important aspects of human socio-economic behaviour can be worked out.

Traces, preservation factors, and other variables

Archaeological study of Pleistocene diet is a little like navigating in the vicinity of an iceberg: more than four-fifths of what is of interest is not visible. We do have some positive evidence of foodstuffs eaten but only in the form of certain minor by-products of a complex vanished system. Fig. 10.1 attempts to define the gross structure of the system as a flow diagram leading from an input of food to a residue of potential traces. Lines of evidence other than archaeological traces of food refuse and faeces do exist; for example, the morphology and wear patterns of hominid teeth; settlement patterns in relation to palaeoecology; artefacts with known functions in relation to subsistence. However, for the Early Pleistocene these are often ambiguous in their implications.

Fig. 10.1 shows that the extent to which diet is documented in an archaeological record is affected by selective factors at two main stages in the chain. First, *feeding habits* exercise a determining influence through (i) localization or dispersal of feeding activity; and (ii) the character of the food, especially the proportion and character of its durable refuse. Only the second of these two sub-factors is widely recognized. The normal primate type of dispersed foraging that does not involve

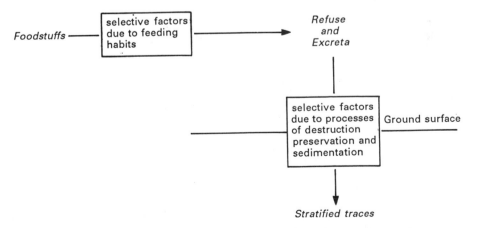

Fig. 10.1. The formation of an archaeological record of diet shown as a flow diagram. Interpretation should proceed in steps taken in reverse order.

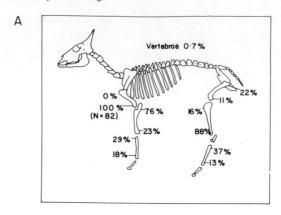

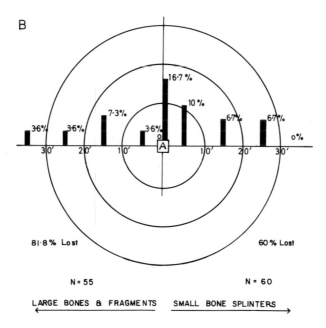

Fig. 10.2a.. Diagrammatic representation of a goat skeleton showing the great variation found in the relative frequency with which skeletal parts were preserved. (Modified after Brain, 1967b: Fig. 1.) Percentage values are relative to the minimum number of individuals involved as indicated by the most abundant part, the distal ends of humeri. The data were drawn from analysis of a collection of 2,373 specimens collected from the vicinity of eight Hottentot villages.

Fig. 10.2b. Experimental observation of the ability of scavengers to disperse and destroy bone in modern African savannah at Olorgesailie: 55 large (> 5 cm) and 60 small pieces of domestic bone refuse were dumped in a one-yard square at A over a two-month period. The diagram shows what proportion of each size category was recovered six months later. The percentage recovery is shown for each of the concentric zones drawn in the figure (after Isaac, 1967a: Fig. 4).

transport of foodstuff and food-sharing at a central locale would *not* be conducive to the formation of an archaeological record even when durable wastes were involved. For example, the absence of Lower and Middle Pleistocene shell middens could equally well be caused by the habit of consuming shellfish on the collection sites as by absence of sea foods from diet.

Differences in the ways in which carcasses of different sizes are treated provides another example of the effect of particular feeding habits on the formation of an archaeological record of diet. Smallish animals are likely to be carried back to camp whole; generally only selected parts of medium-size animals would have been transported. This will distort the bone refuse, but in a way that is often detectable. However, in the case of very large beasts, the bones are so heavy that if anything is moved it consists only of meat, so that its consumption at a remote home base would be archaeologically invisible. Fortunately for archaeology, other aspects of human behaviour probably often led to moving a campsite temporarily to the site of abundance – and such camps can be obvious archaeological sites. Perkins and Daly (1968) have coined the term '*schlepp* factor' for the way in which the composition of bone refuse is distorted by differences in transportability.

Schaller and Lowther (1969) have raised another notable point relevant to the reliability of the bone record formed during early phases of hominid adaptation to life as a diurnal, social carnivore. They suggest that the practice of accumulating bone at a home base would endanger the occupants by attracting nocturnal predators. Fortunately for archaeology, man's tendency to drop litter appears to have deep roots, and despite this hazard, bone refuse occurs at apparently domestic sites of almost 2 million years ago. In tracing the record further back, the factor of predator danger may need to be taken into account.

Secondly, *preservative factors* exert a controlling influence on what parts of the refuse and excreta that accrue do survive to be studied as palaeoanthropological documents. The most durable class of macroscopic food remains are of course vertebrate bones and mollusc shells. These survive in good condition in numerous Pleistocene sediments of all ages and constitute the great bulk of the positive dietary evidence of prehistoric archaeology. Careful study of bone refuse can lead to deductions concerning hunting and butchery practices, feeding habits and season of occupation.

Even where chemico-physical bone preservation conditions are ostensibly good, dispersal and destruction by scavengers may obscure or bias the record. Some current studies of the processes involved in the formation of fossil assemblages ('taphonomy') are of value in assessing this potential bias (eg. Brain, 1967b; Isaac, 1967b [this volume, ch. 6]). Figs. 10.2a and b are graphic excerpts from two such studies illustrating respectively relative destructability of body parts and the power of scavengers to disperse bone.

Given the great relative durability of bone, it can be seen that the archaeological record is liable to exaggerate the carnivorous proclivities of early men, unless deliberate steps are taken to counter the bias. Since macroscopic plant-food refuse survives in small quantities only at one or two pertinent sites such as Choukoutien

(Black, 1933; Movius, 1948) and Kalambo Falls (J. D. Clark, 1969a), more devious strategies for assessment will be required, as discussed below. Even where traces of plant foods do survive, such as hackberries at Choukoutien, and *Syzygium* fruits and *Borassus* palm nuts on Acheulian floors at Kalambo, it is very hard at present to gauge the dietary importance of these foodstuffs.

Even where feeding habits have led to the accumulation of refuse of which an interpretable proportion appears to be preserved, other variables also need to be assessed. Notably it is necessary to form some estimate of the numbers of hominids and the duration of time involved in refuse accumulation. Only at Terra Amata has any great precision yet been achieved in this direction and elsewhere we have to be content with assessments of orders of magnitude. Little systematic writing has been devoted to the matter, but it is probably widely assumed that crude proportional relations exist as follows: (a) Area of site $\propto$ number of occupants (see Cooke and Heizer, 1965; Isaac, 1969); (b) number of artefacts $\propto$ number of occupants and duration of occupation. Using these rough and ready assumptions we may perhaps start to sift available and incoming data by classifying sites according to size and by using the ratio of bone refuse to artefacts as a crude index of the abundance of meat in diet.

Some sites involving high intensities of occupation and low relative abundances of bone refuse may be those where diet consisted principally of gathered foods. This is one possible, if unsatisfactory, way of attempting to get around the non-preservation of vegetable refuse. Alternatives are of the greatest importance, and perhaps the most promising line of investigation of prehistoric diet that has not yet been extensively pursued is the analysis of chemical residues on occupation sites, given the extreme sensitivity of chromatographic techniques and the demonstrated persistence of a range of organic substances through geologic time.

Artefacts and subsistence activities

Stone artefacts are the commonest fossils that have any bearing on human evolution and yet, despite the fact that a good deal more than 90 per cent of the extensive literature on the 'Lower Palaeolithic' deals exclusively with artefacts, virtually nothing is firmly established about the way in which they functioned in the ecology and economy of their makers (Isaac, 1969: 12). It is probably true that cutting tools and simple weapons such as clubs and staves are an essential part of hominid adaptation to a partially carnivorous subsistence but adequate cutting edges are provided by a wide range of flakes and core tools and as yet we gain little additional information regarding economy from the diversity of forms common on most sites.

Some endeavours have been made to translate the results of elaborate quantitative analysis of stone artefacts assemblages into functional terms (e.g. Binford and Binford, 1966), though such attempts have been largely confined to Upper Pleistocene assemblages with their greater specificity of tool design and the approximation of forms to known ethnographic categories. Eventually the combination of such analyses with use-damage studies may bring stone artefact morphology to the point of contribution to our understanding of subsistence. Items such as cores, cobbles and manuports with signs of battering caused by use in pounding bone or vegetable foods are likely to be quite as informative as conventional shaped tools.

Richard Lee has pointed out in discussion that containers – baskets or animal membrane bags – are a very basic human invention, without which the division of labour between hunting males and female gatherers could not have arisen. Unfortunately no examples have yet been recovered from really ancient sites. Two sequences of behavioural evolution suggest themselves: either the use of containers preceded and hence facilitated the development of extensive food-sharing, and the organization of social life round the institution of a home base; or the home-base institution may have developed in conjunction with the transport and sharing of meat only, which does not require a container. Initially plant and insect foods would still have been foraged by each individual for himself in the manner of most non-human primates. Subsequently the invention of carrying equipment would have made it possible to diversify the adaptive potential of food-sharing by the inclusion of dispersed vegetable foods. Archaeology may eventually be able to resolve this question, but either sequence would be compatible with present evidence, though the second seems more likely.

Variation among sites

Undisturbed Pleistocene open-air sites are commonly referred to one of three main categories: occupation floors, kill (butchery) sites or workshop sites. These terms are reasonably well understood but have seldom been closely defined. Fig. 10.3 illustrates their meaning in relation to variations in the proportion of bone refuse to discarded stone artefacts. More subtle site classificatory schemes that take artefact character into account are discussed, for example, by Binford and Binford (1966) and Hole and Flannery (1967).

Since stone and bone are the most durable traces of Early Pleistocene behaviour, this classificatory scheme forms a convenient frame of reference for attempts to scan available archaeological and palaeontological data for patterns. In general, the diagonal defined by increasing artefact and bone densities represents increasing intensity of occupation. At one extreme, very low density sites which may be single occupation transit camps have only rarely been excavated; sites with abundant stone and bone have attracted more attention. These are liable to be regarded as home-base campsites that were occupied for some length of time or were reoccupied at intervals. Situated on either side of the diagonal in Fig. 10.3 are other classes of site. Occurrences with a relative abundance of bone and a paucity of stone are interpreted as 'kill' or butchery sites, especially where the bones of a single large mammal are involved (Clark and Haynes, 1970). However, in tracing the record back towards the beginning of the Pleistocene, it must be remembered that low artefact-to-bone proportions could also result from hominid behaviour patterns in

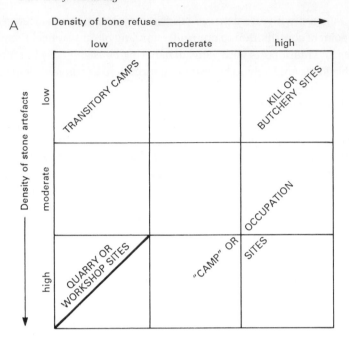

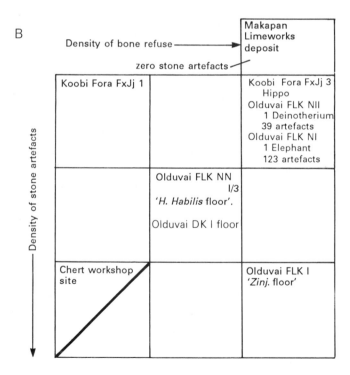

Fig. 10.3. (a) Sites classified according to their proportions of bone refuse to discarded stone artefacts. (b) Lower Pleistocene sites.

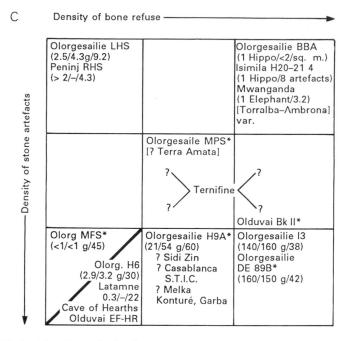

Fig. 10.3. (c) Acheulian and related industries associated with bone refuse.

which stone-tool manufacture played a lesser part. Other, complex factors can also lead to great variation in this regard (cf. White and Peterson, 1969).

Sites with favourable conditions of preservation and yet with small quantities of bone relative to abundant artefacts have commonly been regarded as workshop sites. However, the settlement patterns and distance from stone outcrops sometimes indicate that stone working cannot have been the primary function of the site. In these cases it is possible either that gathered foods formed a major component of diet or that the flensing of carcasses was carried out at kill sites resulting in a minimum importation of bones.

Following this potentially depressing review of factors which may distort the archaeological record of subsistence, it is necessary to ask whether the record is after all worth considering. Given that the history of subsistence is significant for understanding human evolution, and that refuse and excreta are the firmest documents likely to be available, continual research does seem essential, and research in turn requires the review of existing knowledge and the formulation of questions. The lasting contribution of archaeology in the matter is likely to come through the demonstration of pattern amongst numbers of carefully investigated instances chosen for their individual promise. Since feeding and preservation factors will vary from case to case, in a large sample we may be able to assess the overall preservation bias, and hence reconstruct something of the realities of original subsistence patterns. Meanwhile it is clearly unwise to base important evolutionary interpretations on selected cases that happen to suit a particular interpretation.

In order to tackle the evolutionary questions already raised, it is necessary to scan the archaeological record for signs of systematic change through time with regard to the following:

1. The gross abundance of bone on sites.
2. The gross and relative abundance of bone and artefacts.
3. The range and relative proportions of different animal species represented in refuse.

The review of evidence which follows makes use of the interpretation of Pleistocene chronology previously discussed by the author (1969). Available K/Ar dates and palaeomagnetic data indicate an age of *c.* 2.7 million years for the inception of major glaciation and hence of the Pleistocene according to many definitions. An estimate of 1.4–1 million years is more tentatively put forward as the age of the arbitrary boundary between Lower and Middle Pleistocene time-stratigraphic units in East Africa. Discussion of the connotations of the culture-stratigraphic terms 'Oldowan' and 'Acheulian', as used here, is contained in the same paper.

Evidence from the Tertiary

The date of the evolutionary divergence of hominids and pongids remains a controversial question and there is certainly no direct evidence as to the diet of Pliocene hominids, or of Miocene hominids if such there were. The claim made for a significant association in the Late Miocene of an alleged hominid, *Ramapithecus* (*Kenyapithecus*) *wickeri*, with traces of tool use and the breaking of marrow bones are intriguing but require fuller documentation before they can be incorporated as evidence in any discussions (L. S. B. Leakey, 1968).

Evidence from the Lower Pleistocene

From Africa, a series of undoubted hominid fossils spans the time from Late Pliocene (*c.* 3.5 million years) on through the entire Pleistocene. Archaeological evidence of tools and food refuse is well established from about 2 million years onward and current investigations at the Omo and the East Rudolf area are probing into earlier periods.

The only two sets of occurrences of Lower Pleistocene age that have yet been extensively investigated from a palaeo-dietary point of view are the occupation sites at Olduvai Gorge, Beds I and Lower Bed II, and the Makapansgat limeworks deposit.

At Olduvai, Dr Mary D. Leakey has carried out careful excavation and thorough analysis on an unprecedented scale. The monograph in which she reports on her work is in process of publication by the Cambridge University Press [M. D. Leakey, 1971]. When available, it will be a highly important source book for palaeoanthropology. The comments made here regarding the Olduvai evidence are based primarily on preliminary reviews (L. S. B. Leakey, 1960, 1961, 1963a and b; M. D. Leakey, 1967), on information acquired during visits to Olduvai and on numerous discussions with Drs L. S. B. and M. D. Leakey.

The australopithecine-bearing breccias at Makapansgat have come to be regarded as important sources of evidence regarding the evolution of human diet and behaviour. (See for example Dart, 1957a and b; Ardrey, 1961; Tobias, 1967; Howell, 1965; J. G. D. Clark, 1969; Wolberg, 1970.) However, through no fault of the investigators the situation is far from satisfactory; the site was largely destroyed by quarrying and the vast bone sample on which dietary and tool-usage hypotheses are based was obtained largely from the discard dumps of miners. Details of stratigraphic and archaeological context are consequently a matter in part of reconstruction and conjecture. If the australopithecines whose bones occur in the breccia were solely responsible for the accumulation of the bones then they were indeed, as Dart and Ardrey have contended, very effective carnivores. If, as seems likely, they were not the sole, or even the principal cause of accumulation, then it is hard to assess directly the extent to which meat figured in their diet. Pending further studies such as those of Brain (1970) at Swartkrans, the evidence must be set aside as ambiguous.

The evidence for osteodontokeratic tool use is similarly inconclusive. The data set out by Dart and elaborated by Ardrey and Tobias prove conclusively the existence of an assemblage showing a high degree of selectivity in body-part representation. The tool and weapon hypothesis was eminently reasonable when first set out, but, as Fig. 10.2a shows, subsequent research has demonstrated that natural and midden bone assemblages normally involve highly selective patterns of preservation and destruction of different body parts in circumstances where tool use can be ruled out as an explanation (Lubbock, 1865; Washburn, 1957; Brain, 1967b; Isaac, 1967b). Certain depressed fracture, breakage and damage patterns and the jamming of bones into one another remain as potential evidence of hominid activity, but much more systematic data are necessary regarding natural bone accumulations before decisions can be made even with regard to these features.

While the Makapansgat data do not offer satisfactory *proof* of australopithecine diet and behaviour patterns, the *supposition* that *A. africanus* was partially carnivorous and a tool user remains eminently reasonable.

The situation at Olduvai is very different. Active hominid involvement in the accumulation of concentrated patches of bone is attested not only by the occasional presence of hominid bones amongst the others, but by the presence of numerous artefacts and artificially introduced stones. It seems certain that hominids were the prime agency creating these concentrations. The sites document a behaviour complex that is fundamentally human: tool manufacture, a partly carnivorous diet achieved by hunting and/or scavenging, and the practice of bringing meat back to a home base for sharing amongst the members of a social group. In contrast to Makapansgat, the problem at Olduvai campsites is not to determine how many of the bones were introduced by non-hominid agencies, but how many may have been removed by scavengers.

Fig. 10.3b shows that Oldowan sites from the Lower Pleistocene at Olduvai (Bed I and Lower Bed II) cover almost the full classificatory range defined in Fig. 10.3c. Occurrences such as the 'Zinjanthropus' level at FLK I, the DK I floor and some levels at FLK N I involve moderately high densities of both stone artefacts and bone, and therefore rank as occupation floors or campsites. Others, such as FLK N I level 6 or

FLK N II, consist of numerous bones from single carcasses (an elephant and a *Deinotherium* respectively) and comparatively few artefacts or other bones. These can fairly be described as butchery sites (cf. Clark and Haynes, 1970:405). To complete the range, one recently discovered site in Lower Bed II was close to a contemporary chert outcrop, and has prodigious quantities of debitage with a minimum of other occupation refuse. This must be the oldest known quarry and workshop site.

Detailed consideration of the quantitative evidence for meat diet must await the appearance of Dr M. D. Leakey's monograph; however, certain features are already apparent in relation to the criteria listed on pp. 277–80.

1. Bone is at least moderately abundant on some of the Olduvai Bed I and Lower Bed II sites. How densities compare with those from the majority of Middle Pleistocene sites, remains to be determined.

2. Stone artefacts appear to be noticeably less abundant than on later sites. Compare the maximum figure of 2,659 artefacts at FLK I (Zinj) with 7,223 at BK II (M. D. Leakey, 1967) or with 5–6,000 artefacts on several comparable but somewhat smaller excavated areas at Olorgesailie (Isaac, 1968a: 257). The artefact-to-bone ratio is probably generally lower on Oldowan sites.

3. The full size range of African fauna is found in association with Lower Pleistocene Oldowan industries, but medium-size antelopes and pigs preponderate numerically as they do in the fauna itself. The remains of the largest animals such as pachyderms, giraffe or buffalo, though certainly present, may be less frequent than on later sites. There is no way of telling whether the butchered elephant and *Deinotherium* carcasses at FLK N were killed or found dead. The Olduvai evidence documents an established behavioural and dietary situation that had become distinctively human by virtue of the importance of meat.

4. There are as yet no reported instances of specialized or selective accumulations of large numbers of a single species such as the *Pelorovis* herd at BK II or the numerous baboons at Olorgesailie DE/89 (see below).

Reptile, frog, bird and rodent bones appear to be better represented in Bed I than in any African Middle Pleistocene site yet reported. This may partly reflect the lakeside site preference pattern and the excellent preservation conditions. At FLK N I concentrated patches of rodent and other microfaunal bones have been found. These do not closely resemble available samples of owl pellets and some may be residues from human faeces: if so, this would demonstrate that early hominids tapped the rich protein resources of the microfauna – a practice not unknown amongst more recent peoples in arid terrain.

The only site with numerous artefacts and very low bone density is the chert quarry site already mentioned. The absence of other such sites might be used as an argument against periodic or seasonal spells of dependence on plant food, but as yet the sample of sites is too small for this to have much force.

In summary, the available evidence shows clearly that a wide range of meat foods figured in Lower Pleistocene hominid diet at Olduvai and that the quantities involved were substantial. There is at present no real way to assess the relative proportions of the total diet that accrued from gathering, hunting and scavenging. All three were probably important activities. The observations of Schaller and

Lowther (1969) suggest that scavenging may only be feasible as a sole means of subsistence seasonally or in particularly favourable areas.

Research is proceeding in two areas where apparently earlier traces of hominids are preserved – namely the Omo delta (Arambourg and Coppens, 1967; Bonnefille *et al.*, 1970; Howell, 1968), and East Rudolf (R. E. Leakey *et al.*, 1970). At the Omo, hominid fossils are moderately abundant while artefacts are extremely rare, and nothing that can be called an occupation floor has yet come to light (Howell and Coppens personal communication). In the East Rudolf (Koobi Fora) area, artefact occurrences have been located in direct association with a tuff dated at 2.61 ± 0.26 my. At Richard Leakey's invitation the author commenced intensive archaeological investigation; the results of the initial excavation and survey work in 1970 suggest that at least one stratified scatter of artefacts and broken-up bone can be regarded as a low-density occupation floor (Site KBS or FxJj I). Surface indications imply that a hippopotamus butchery site may also be present (FxJj 3). If these preliminary results are confirmed by further work, then the Koobi Fora Formation will provide a backward extension of the known time range of the basic hominid behavioural complex of meat eating, toolmaking and the occupation of home bases.

Evidence from the Middle Pleistocene

Most Middle Pleistocene artefact occurrences in Africa can be assigned to the category 'Acheulian' *sensu lato* (see discussion in Howell and Clark, 1963; M. D. Leakey, 1967; Isaac, 1969). Fig. 10.3c depicts evidence for this period from a series of sites with a broad geographic range covering much of Africa and extending into Eurasia, where site complexes such as Torralba-Ambrona (Howell, 1966), Terra Amata (de Lumley, 1969b) and Latamne (J. D. Clark, 1966, 1967 and 1969b) provide comparable evidence for the Eurasiatic Acheulian. For the sake of comparison these sites are indicated on the chart in parentheses. Choukoutien, Vértesszöllös and Lehringen are important contemporary non-Acheulian sites with bone refuse, but they are not shown.

At present the various Olorgesailie sites comprise the largest single corpus of associations between Acheulian industries and bone refuse. Investigations at Olorgesailie were begun in 1942 by Louis and Mary Leakey (L. S. B. Leakey, 1952), and continued by Posnansky (1959) and Isaac (1966a and b, 1968a). A comprehensive report has been compiled as a thesis and, though unpublished, is available (Isaac, 1968b). A comprehensive report has been compiled as a thesis (Isaac, 1968b). A monograph is in preparation [Isaac 1977b]. Unfortunately at two of the other major site complexes in Africa, Kalambo and Isimila, bone is scarcely preserved owing to unfavourable geochemical conditions (Howell and Clark, 1963). Olduvai Gorge Bed IV can be expected to provide much critical evidence when current studies by Dr M. D. Leakey have been completed. The studies of melka Kunturé also are still incomplete (Chavaillon, 1967). Quantitative data are available only for Olorgesailie, the Natron sites (Isaac, 1967a), some of the butchery sites

(Clark and Haynes, 1970), Torralba-Ambrona (Howell, 1966, Freeman and Butzer, 1966) and Latamne (J. D. Clark, 1966, 1967, 1969b). The chart indicates these quantities as densities of bone by fragment number, and weight if available, and of artefacts by number, per square metre. Probable relative positions have been guessed for other important published sites even when quantitative data are not available. This is clearly unsatisfactory, but has been done to illustrate ways of thinking about the existing data and to stress the advantages of securing quantitative data in future. Fig. 10.3c makes it clear that there is wide variation with regard both to the gross and relative abundance of bone on Acheulian sites. At some there is spectacular evidence of success in hunting. The Torralba and Ambrona elephant butchery grounds are by far the most impressive of such sites, but the *Pelorovis* remains at Olduvai BK II (Leakey, 1957) and the mass of baboon bones at Olorgesailie DE/89 B are also notable in this regard. However, even when allowance has been made for distortions due to scavengers and poor preservation, it does appear that most Acheulian sites contain comparatively modest amounts of bone. Some, such as Latamne, Olorgesailie H/6, and the Cave of Hearths, contain only minor amounts of bone in spite of apparent favourable conditions for preservation.

If the spectrum of variation in bone abundance is confirmed by further research, it might indicate that the great variation also seen in the meat component of the diet of recent non-agricultural peoples has in fact been a consistent pattern throughout much of human evolution. Modern variation can be related within one culture to seasonal factors and to opportunism, and between cultures to technological and eco-geographic factors. Presumably the Middle Pleistocene variation was scarcely less complex.

Returning to the specific points set out on pp. 277–80:

1. Despite the great range of variation, the maximum values for gross densities of stone artefacts, and possibly also of bone refuse are apparently higher than in the Lower Pleistocene.
2. The full size range of African macro-fauna is represented on Acheulian sites, the medium size bovids and the equids being usually preponderant. No African sites yet document extensive exploitation of micro-fauna, but this might be a consequence of poor preservation. Rodent remains are numerous in the rich faunal assemblages of the non-Acheulian, Middle Pleistocene sites of Vértesszöllös (Vértes, 1966).
3. Sites such as Ternifine, Sidi Zin, Casablanca S.T.I.C., Olorgesailie H/9 A and I 3, and the Cave of Hearths show a fairly generalized bag of species, but, as already mentioned, two African sites and one European site are notable for the concentrated remains of one or a few species. These occurrences, detailed below, are of special interest for the light they throw on hunting methods and socio-economic organization; they are also the oldest cases for which scavenging can definitely be ruled out as the source of the meat and bone.

   a. At Olduvai BK II erosion and excavation exposed a transect across a broad channel (Leakey, 1957; M. D. Leakey, personal communication). Occupation in the vicinity was probably recurrent and abundant artefacts and broken-up bones are distributed through the channel-fill deposits. One bed of clay appears to represent a backwater or swamp and in it were found partially articulated remains of a number of ungulates, especially the extinct large bovid *Pelorovis*. In one case the lower extremities of all four limbs were found standing upright while the upper part of the carcass had been removed. The conformation of the remains and the presence of broken-up bones of the same forms in the refuse is strongly suggestive of drives on one or more occasion, of ungulate groups into the morass where they could be killed and butchered.

b. At Olorgesailie one major site, DE/89 horizon B, contained the comminuted remains of at least 40–50 adult and 13 or more juvenile baboons of the extinct robust species *Simopithecus oswaldi*. More than a thousand identifiable teeth and bones, plus 15 kg of bone splinters lay amongst a superabundance of handaxes and other artefacts (Isaac, 1968a and b; 1969).

c. At Torralba and Ambrona in central Spain there are preserved at several horizons stratified relics of former swampy valley-floor surfaces. These must frequently have been dotted with dismembered animal carcasses and the sparse artefactual refuse of the Acheulian men who butchered them (Howell 1965, 1966; Freeman and Butzer, 1966). Elephants predominate, but rhinoceros and various large ungulates are also represented. It seems probable that this was an area where animals could comparatively easily be waylaid and driven into swampy ground to facilitate killing and butchering, perhaps during seasonal migrations.

The remains at each of these three sites appear to indicate effective hunting practices that involved comparatively large groups of men in drives or in encircling movements. BK II and Torralba are probably of broadly similar age (early Middle Pleistocene); being somewhat older than Olorgesailie DE/89, they are the oldest positively documented cases of cooperative hunting. The elephant and hippo carcasses at FLK N I and II may conceivably have been scavenged rather than killed.

It is not clear whether the use of group hunting techniques was a new development and whether it led to meat becoming an abundant dietary staple during the Middle Pleistocene. The Olorgesailie and Olduvai instances may well document only occasional opportunism. The Torralba evidence clearly indicates regular repetition, but even this may have been of a seasonal character. It is of interest that this site complex, which is by far the most spectacular known instance of hunting success in the Middle Pleistocene, was occupied under cold temperate conditions.

The greatest resolution of behavioural detail yet achieved in the study of a Middle Pleistocene site is modestly claimed in a preliminary report on Terra Amata, a locality in France, near Nice (de Lumley, 1969). Eleven superimposed levels separated from each other by thin drifts of sand are thought to represent brief spring occupations in eleven successive years. Bone remains document deer as the major quarry, followed by elephant, boar, ibex, rhino and aurochs. Rabbits and other rodents are represented. Small numbers of marine shells and fish bones are present. Fossil human faeces were found, but only the presence in them of pollen indicating spring occupancy is reported so far.

Comparisons between the Middle and Upper Pleistocene

Studies of African Upper Pleistocene material have tended to retain culture-historic and technical preoccupations; consequently we have no corpus of Middle and Later

Stone Age sites excavated in the manner of Olduvai, Olorgesailie, Isimila or Kalambo. Various current research projects are geared towards rectifying this deficiency, but meanwhile some points of interest can already be discerned.

(1) Most African Upper Pleistocene and Holocene sites that have been excavated are cave sites. The abundance of bone varies but is in general probably low by European Upper Palaeolithic standards.

(2) At least two open air LSA sites are now known where the absolute densities of bone and artefacts far exceed the known African Lower and Middle Pleistocene range. Neither is published. Recent excavation by C. M. Nelson on a late Kenya Wilton site near Longs Drift in the Eastern Rift Valley revealed a bone and artefact accumulation where the estimated maximum density approaches 50,000 items per cubic metre (see Isaac *et al.*, 1970). This value may be higher than any Lower Palaeolithic values from Africa by a full order of magnitude; though photographs and descriptions suggest that some of the floors at Vértesszöllös in Hungary may show comparable high densities (Vértes, 1966). Preliminary descriptions of the Gwisho Springs sites in Zambia indicate similar very high densities (Gable, 1965; Fagan and Van Noten, 1966; Fagan personal communication). These higher densities are probably due to more sedentary habits rather than radical changes in hunting efficiency and diet.

(3) Shell middens and evidence of communities that were extensively dependent on aquatic foods are of wide occurrence in the Late Pleistocene and Holocene, but corresponding traces are unknown from Lower and Middle Pleistocene deposits. Fish and frog bones do occur on some African sites (e.g. Olduvai and Olorgesailie), but it is not always clear whether they derive from food refuse or are natural components of the waterside sediments. Minor quantities of fish bones and shell are reported as dietary traces at the Acheulian site of Terra Amata in France, but they do not appear to have been important gathered foods in spite of the proximity of the sea (de Lumley, 1969). Similarly, in spite of the proximity of many stratified Acheulian sites to former shore lines at Casablanca, there is no evidence of any shell middens (Biberson, 1961). The available evidence seems to indicate that during the Upper Pleistocene the range of human subsistence patterns was expanded amongst other things by localized extensive exploitation of aquatic resources. In cold temperate and sub-arctic Eurasia, hunters may well have reached new levels of predatory efficacy and dependence on meat, while in much of the tropics more generalized subsistence patterns persisted.

Geography and settlement patterns

Gross geographic distributions clearly do not give very precise palaeoeconomic indications. In Africa, known Lower and early Middle Pleistocene sites are confined to relatively dry regions, where subsistence by hunting and/or gathering is feasible, to judge by the contemporary examples of the Bushmen and Hadza. The distribution of late Middle Pleistocene Acheulian industries covers all of the African grasslands, savannahs and much of the woodland, but not extensively forested areas. This again is at least consistent with the variable, generalized hunting-gathering pattern envisaged for this time span in the tropics and warm temperate areas.

Various patterns are also beginning to emerge with regard to preferred locations for Pleistocene camps; for example, the Oldowan camps in Bed I and Lower II were all in lakeside floodplain situations, while Acheulian camps are generally away from the lake shores and along the courses of seasonal streams. When these patterns are known in more detail they may help to correct the distortions due to excessive reliance on the bone refuse record, by indicating the various eco-types that communities consistently sought to exploit. Considerable microenvironmental diversity is already apparent: for instance, the Olduvai and Natron basins included salt and fresh-water bodies, lake-side floodplains, arid steppe, stream courses presumably with riverine bush, and forest-clad volcanic mountains.

Conclusion

This review has been concerned almost exclusively with direct archaeological evidence for hominid diet, partly because, incomplete though it may be, this is likely always to be the most definite class of evidence available, and partly because the evidence has in recent years sometimes been abused. Various points with regard to human evolution and human nature have been backed by citation of *selected* items of archaeological evidence, whereas, in spite of its manifest imperfections, the implications of the whole corpus of archaeological data ought to have been considered.

Given the initial evolutionary proposition that man is descended from an ancestral stock that was much less extensively carnivorous, questions can fairly be asked as to whether archaeology documents initial stages in the evolutionary shift. This is not yet entirely clear, but available data suggests that at the outset of the known archaeological record, *c.* 2 mya, at least some hominids had a significant meat component in their diet. Investigations of the evolutionary antecedents of this situation should be fascinating, but localities have only recently been found where such studies can even be attempted.

Two recent studies of human evolution by B. Campbell (1966) and J. Pfeiffer (1969) suggested that the Lower Pleistocene could be characterized as a small game hunting phase while during the Middle Pleistocene a big game hunting phase led to the acceleration of mental, linguistic and social evolution. This is probably an over-simplification. Even during the Lower Pleistocene, the bones of big game animals are to be found in hominid refuse, though there may have been an increase in the proportion of large quarry during the Middle Pleistocene. Equally, while it is true that the first indications of effective cooperative hunting on a large scale are of Middle Pleistocene age, the sample of sites from the Lower Pleistocene is so small that the absence of a known instance is of uncertain significance.

The view is presented here that in Africa, which may well be representative of tropical and warm temperate regions in general, hunting has seldom if ever been in any exclusive sense the staff of hominid life. The archaeological record, such as it is, appears more readily compatible with models of human evolution that stress broadly based subsistence patterns rather than those involving intensive and voracious predation. Partial division of labour between male hunters and female gatherers constitutes an adaptive system that is unique to man and which should probably be more stressed as a feature of human evolution than mere predation. The archaeological evidence is at least consistent with the view that such an arrangement has been a prominent part of the behavioural milieu within which the last two million years of hominid development took place.

During the Middle and Late Pleistocene the geographic range of hominids was extended into cold-temperate and sub-arctic regions. This almost certainly led the hominids into new ecological conditions where protein foods had to be the dietary staples. The archaeological evidence for ensuing adjustments and considerations of the possible influences of more intensive hunting activity on the terminal phases of human behavioural evolution are clearly of the greatest importance but lie beyond the scope of this paper.

Acknowledgements

This review draws on a wider range of sources than can be indicated in the bibliography [of the original paper] or text; I am especially grateful to researchers in Africa such as Mary Leakey, and to Berkeley colleagues such as J. Desmond Clark and S. L. Washburn for the frankness with which they have shared their information and ideas in discussions over the past few years. J. Desmond Clark read and gave advice on a first draft of the manuscript. Barbara Isaac has given extensive help and comment at all stages in the preparation of the paper.

11

The food-sharing behaviour of proto-human hominids

Over the past decade investigators of fossil man have discovered the remains of many ancient proto-humans in East Africa. Findings at Olduvai, Laetolil, Koobi Fora, the Omo valley and Hadar, to name some prominent locations, make it clear that between two and three million years ago a number of two-legged hominids, essentially human in form, inhabited this part of Africa. The palaeontologists who have unearthed the fossils report that they differ from modern mankind primarily in being small, in having relatively large jaws and teeth and in having brains that, although they are larger than those of apes of comparable body size, are rarely more than half the size of modern man's.

The African discoveries have many implications for the student of human evolution. For example, one wonders to what extent the advanced hominids of two million years ago were 'human' in their behaviour. Which of modern man's special capabilities did they share? What pressures of natural selection, in the time since they lived, led to the evolutionary elaboration of man's mind and culture? These are questions that palaeontologists find difficult to answer because the evidence that bears on them is not anatomical. Archaeologists, by virtue of their experience in studying prehistoric behaviour patterns in general, can help to supply the answers.

It has long been realized that the human species is set apart from its closest living primate relatives far more by differences in behaviour than by differences in anatomy. Paradoxically, however, the study of human evolution has traditionally been dominated by work on the skeletal and comparative anatomy of fossil primates. Several new research movements in recent years, however, have begun to broaden the scope of direct evolutionary inquiry. One such movement involves investigations of the behaviour and ecology of living primates and of other mammals. The results of these observations can now be compared with quantitative data from another new area of study, namely the cultural ecology of human societies that support themselves without raising plants or animals: the few surviving hunter-gatherers of today. Another important new movement has involved the direct study of the ecological circumstances surrounding human evolutionary developments. Investigations of this kind have become possible because the stratified sedimentary rocks of East Africa preserve, in addition to fossil hominid remains, an invaluable store of data: a coherent, ordered record of the environments inhabited by these proto-humans.

The work of the archaeologist in drawing inferences from such data is made possible by the fact that at a certain stage in evolution the ancestors of modern man became makers and users of equipment. Among other things, they shaped, used and discarded numerous stone tools. These virtually indestructible artefacts form a kind of fossil record of aspects of behaviour, a record that is complementary to the anatomical record provided by the fossil bones of the toolmakers themselves. Students of the Old Stone Age once concentrated almost exclusively on what could be learned from the form of such tools. Today the emphasis in archaeology is increasingly on the context of the artefacts: for example the distribution pattern of the discarded tools in different settings and the association of tools with various kinds of food refuse. A study of the contexts of the early African artefacts yields unique clues both to the ecological circumstances of the proto-human toolmakers and to aspects of their socio-economic organization.

Comparing men and apes

What are the patterns of behaviour that set the species *Homo sapiens* apart from its closest living primate relatives? It is not hard to draw up a list of such differences by comparing human and ape behaviour and focusing attention not on the many features the two have in common but on the contrasting features. In the list that follows I have drawn on recent field studies of the great apes (particularly the chimpanzee, *Pan troglodytes*) and on similar studies of the organization of living hunter-gatherer societies. The list tends to emphasize the contrasts relating to the primary subsistence adaptation, that is, the quest for food.

First, *Homo sapiens* is a two-legged primate who in moving from place to place habitually carries tools, food and other possessions either with his arms or in containers. This is not true of the great apes with regard to either posture or possessions.

Second, members of *Homo sapiens* societies communicate by means of spoken language: such verbal communication serves for the exchange of information about the past and the future and also for the regulation of many aspects of social relations. Apes communicate but they do not have language.

Third, in *Homo sapiens* societies the acquisition of food is a corporate responsibility, at least in part. Among members of human social groupings of various sizes the active sharing of food is a characteristic form of behaviour; most commonly family groups are the crucial nodes in a network of food exchange. Food is exchanged between adults, and it is shared between adults and juveniles. The only similar behaviour observed among the great apes is seen when chimpanzees occasionally feed on meat. The chimpanzees' behaviour, however, falls far short of active sharing; I suggest it might better be termed tolerated scrounging. Vegetable foods,

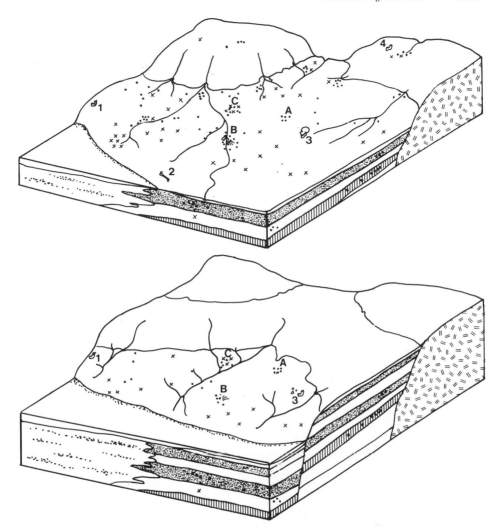

Fig. 11.1. Past and present landscapes in the Rift Valley region of East Africa, shown schematically, summarize the geological activity that first preserved and later exposed evidence of proto-human life. Two million years ago (top) the bones of hominids and other animals were distributed across hills and a floodplain (foreground) adjacent to a Rift Valley lake. Also lying on the surface were stone tools (black dots) made, used and discarded by the proto-humans. Layers of sediments then covered the bones and tools lying on the floodplain; burial preserved them, whereas the bones and tools in the hills were eventually washed away. Today (bottom), after a fault has raised a block of sediments, erosion is exposing some of the long-buried bones and clusters of tools, including the three types of site shown on the surface in the top block diagram (A–C). Sites of Type A contain clusters of stone tools together with the leftover stone cores that provided the raw material for the tools and waste flakes from the toolmaking process, but little or no bone is present. Sites of Type B contain similar clusters of tools in association with the bones of a single large animal. Sites of Type C also contain similar clusters of tools, but the bones are from many different animal species.

which are the great apes' principal diet, are not shared and are almost invariably consumed by each individual on the spot.

Fourth, in human social groupings there exists at any given time what can be called a focus in space, or 'home base', such that individuals can move independently over the surrounding terrain and yet join up again. No such home base is evident in the social arrangements of the great apes.

Fifth, human hunter-gatherers tend to devote more time than other living primates to the acquisition of high-protein foodstuffs by hunting or fishing for animal prey. It should be noted that the distinction is one not of kind but of degree. Mounting evidence of predatory behaviour among great apes and monkeys suggests that the principal contrast between human beings and other living primates with respect to predation is that only human beings habitually feed on prey weighing more than about 15 kilograms.

The gathering activities of human hunter-gatherers include the collection of edible plants and small items of animal food (for example lizards, turtles, frogs, nestling birds and eggs). Characteristically a proportion of these foodstuffs is not consumed until the return to the home base. This behaviour is in marked contrast to what is observed among foraging great apes, which almost invariably feed at the spot where the food is acquired.

Fig. 11.2. Desolate landscape in the arid Koobi Fora district of Kenya is typical of the kind of eroded terrain where gullying exposes both bones and stone tools that were buried beneath sediments and volcanic ash more than a million years ago. Excavation in progress (centre) is exposing the hippopotamus bones and clusters of artefacts that had been partially bared by recent erosion and were found by Richard Leakey in 1969. The site is typical of the kind that includes the remains of a single animal and many tools manufactured on the spot.

Still another contrast with great-ape feeding behaviour is human hunter-gatherers' practice of subjecting many foodstuffs to preparation for consumption, by crushing, grinding, cutting and heating. Such practices are not observed among the great apes.

Human hunter-gatherers also make use of various kinds of equipment in the quest for food. The human society with perhaps the simplest equipment ever observed was the aboriginal society of Tasmania, a population of hunter-gatherers that was exterminated in the nineteenth century. The inventory of the Tasmanians' equipment included wood clubs, spears and digging sticks, cutting tools made of chipped stone that were used to shape the wood objects, and a variety of containers: trays, baskets and bags. The Tasmanians also had fire. Although such equipment is simple by our standards, it is far more complex than the kind of rudimentary tools that we now know living chimpanzees may collect and use in the wild, for example twigs and grass stems.

In addition to this lengthy list of subsistence-related behavioural contrasts between human hunter-gatherers and living primates there is an entire realm of other contrasts with respect to social organization. Although these important additional features fall largely outside the range of evidence to be considered here, they are vital in defining human patterns of behaviour. Among them is the propensity for the formation of long-term mating bonds between a male and one or more females. The bonds we call 'marriage' involve reciprocal economic ties, joint responsibility for aspects of child-rearing and restrictions on sexual access. Another such social contrast is evident in the distinctively human propensity to categorize fellow members of a group according to kinship and metaphors of kinship. Human beings regulate many social relations, mating included, according to complex rules involving kinship categories. Perhaps family ties of a kind exist among apes, but explicit categories and rules do not. These differences are emphasized by the virtual absence from observed ape behaviour of those distinctively human activities that are categorized somewhat vaguely as 'symbolic' and 'ritual'.

Listing the contrasts between human and non-human subsistence strategies is inevitably an exercise in over-simplification. As has been shown by contemporary field studies of various great apes and of human beings who, like the San (formerly miscalled Bushmen) of the Kalahari Desert still support themselves without farming, there is a far greater degree of similarity between the two subsistence strategies than had previously been recognized. For example, with regard to the behavioural repertories involving meat-eating and tool-using, the differences between ape and man are differences of degree rather than of kind. Some scholars have even used the data to deny the existence of any fundamental differences between the human strategies and the non-human ones.

It is my view that significant differences remain. Let me cite what seem to me to be the two most important. First, whereas humans may feed as they forage just as apes do, apes do not regularly postpone food-consumption until they have returned to a home base, as human beings do. Second, human beings actively share some of the food they acquire. Apes do not, even though chimpanzees of the Gombe

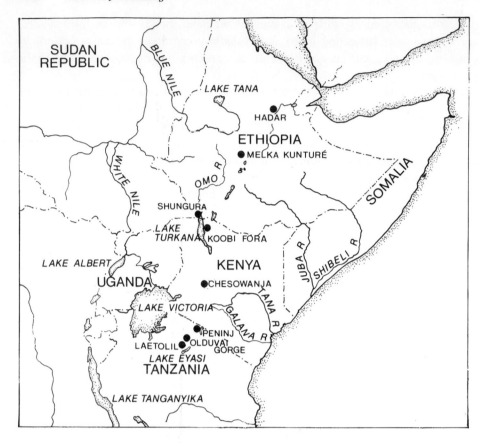

Fig. 11.3. Prominent sites in East Africa include (from north to south) Hadar, Melka Kunturé and Shungura in Ethiopia, the Koobi Fora district to the east of Lake Turkana in Kenya, Chesowanja in Kenya, and Peninj, Olduvai Gorge and Laetolil in Tanzania. Dates for clusters of stone tools, some associated with animal bones, uncovered at these sites range from 1 mya (Olduvai Upper Bed II) to 2.5 mya (Hadar upper beds). Some sites may be even older.

National Park in Tanzania have been observed to tolerate scrounging when meat is available.

From hominid to human

Two complementary puzzles face anyone who undertakes to examine the question of human origins. The first relates to evolutionary divergence. When did the primate stock ancestral to the living apes diverge from the stock ancestral to man? What were the circumstances of the divergence? Over what geographical range did it take place? It is not yet established beyond doubt whether the divergence occurred a mere 5 to 6 million years ago, as Vincent M. Sarich of the University of California at Berkeley and others argue on biochemical grounds, or 15 to 20 million years ago, as many palaeontologists believe on the grounds of fossil evidence. At least one factor is clear. The divergence took place long before the period when the oldest archaeological remains thus far discovered first appear. Archaeology, at least for the present, can make no contribution toward solving the puzzle of the split between ancestral ape and ancestral man.

As for the second puzzle, fossil evidence from East Africa shows that the divergence, regardless of when it took place, had given rise 2 to 3 million years ago to populations of smallish two-legged hominids. The puzzle is how to identify the patterns of natural selection that transformed these proto-humans into humans. Archaeology has a major contribution to make in elucidating the second puzzle. Excavation of these proto-human sites has revealed evidence suggesting that 2 million years ago some elements that now distinguish man from apes were already part of a novel adaptive strategy. The indications are that a particularly important part of that strategy was food-sharing.

The archaeological research that has inspired the formulation of new hypotheses concerning human evolution began nearly 20 years ago when Mary Leakey and her husband Louis discovered the fossil skull he named *Zinjanthropus* at Olduvai Gorge in Tanzania. The excavations the Leakeys undertook at the site showed not only that stone tools were present in the same strata that held this fossil and other

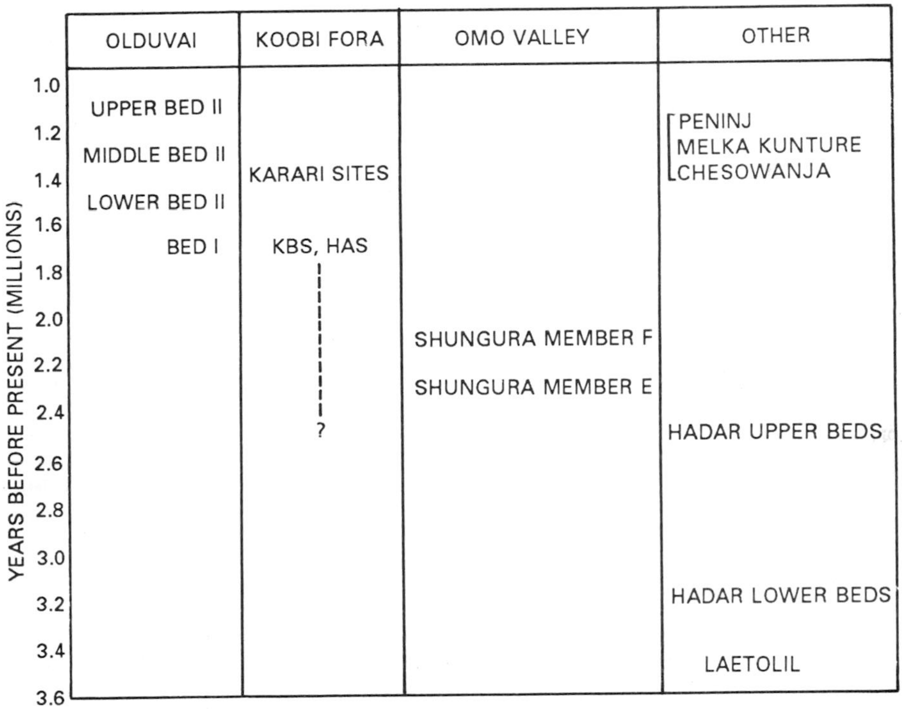

	OLDUVAI	KOOBI FORA	OMO VALLEY	OTHER
1.0				
1.2	UPPER BED II			⌈PENINJ
	MIDDLE BED II			MELKA KUNTURE
1.4		KARARI SITES		⌊CHESOWANJA
	LOWER BED II			
1.6	BED I	KBS, HAS		
1.8		¦		
2.0		¦		
2.2		¦	SHUNGURA MEMBER F	
		¦	SHUNGURA MEMBER E	
2.4		¦		HADAR UPPER BEDS
2.6		?		
2.8				
3.0				
3.2				HADAR LOWER BEDS
3.4				LAETOLIL
3.6				

YEARS BEFORE PRESENT (MILLIONS)

Fig. 11.4. Relative antiquity of selected sites in East Africa is indicated in this table. Olduvai Gorge Beds I and II range from 1.8 to 1.0 mya. The Shungura sites in the Omo Valley are more than 2 million years old. Two Koobi Fora locales, the hippopotamus/artefact site (HAS) and the Kay Behrensmeyer site (KBS), are at least 1.6 million years old. Initial geological studies of the Koobi Fora sites suggested that they might be 2.5 million years old (dotted line). Only hominid fossils have been found in the lower beds at Hadar and at Laetolil.

hominid fossils but also that the discarded artefacts were associated with numerous broken-up animal bones. The Leakeys termed these concentrations of tools and bones 'living sites'. The work continued at Olduvai under Mary Leakey's direction, and in 1971 a major monograph was published that has made the Olduvai results available for comparative studies.

Other important opportunities for archaeological research of this kind have come to light in the Gregory Rift Valley, at places such as the Koobi Fora (formerly East Rudolf) region of northern Kenya, at Shungara in the Omo Valley of south-western Ethiopia and in the Hadar region of eastern Ethiopia. Current estimates of the age of these sites cover a span of time from about 3.2 million years ago to about 1.2 million.

Since 1970 I have been co-leader with Richard Leakey (the son of Mary and Louis Leakey) of a team working at Koobi Fora, a district that includes the north-eastern shore of Lake Turkana (the former Lake Rudolf). Our research on the geology, palaeontology and palaeoanthropology of the district involves the collaboration of colleagues from the National Museum of Kenya and from many other parts of the world. Work began in 1968 and had the help and encouragement of the Government of Kenya, the National Science Foundation and the National Geographic Society. Our investigations yielded archaeological evidence that corroborates and complements the earlier evidence from Olduvai Gorge. The combined data make it possible to see just how helpful archaeology can be in answering questions concerning human evolution.

At Koobi Fora, as at all the other East African sites, deposits of layered sediments, which accumulated long ago in the basins of Rift Valley lakes, are now being eroded by desert rainstorms and transient streams. As the sedimentary beds erode, a sample of the ancient artefacts and fossil bones they contain is exposed at the surface. For a while the exposed material lies on the ground. Eventually, however, the fossil bones are destroyed by weathering or a storm washes away stone and bone alike.

All field reconnaissance in East Africa progresses along essentially similar lines. The field teams search through eroded terrain looking for exposed fossils and artefacts. In places where concentrations of fossil bone or promising archaeological indications appear on the surface the next step is excavation. The digging is done in part to uncover further specimens that are still in place in the layers of sediments and in part to gather exact information about the original stratigraphic location of the surface material. Most important of all, excavation allows the investigators to plot in detail the relative locations of the material that is unearthed. For example, if there are associations among bones and between bones and stones, excavation will reveal these characteristics of the site.

The types of sites

The archaeological traces of proto-human life uncovered in this way may exhibit several different configurations. In some ancient layers we have found scatterings

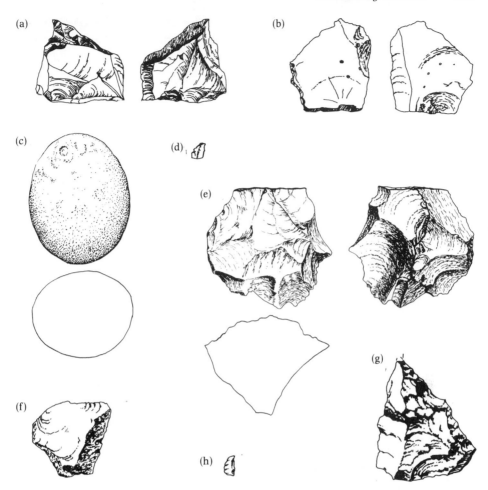

Fig. 11.5. Koobi Fora artefacts include four from the HAS assemblage (a–d) and four from the KBS assemblage (e–h). The stone is basalt. The HAS core (a) shows what is left of a piece of stone after a number of flakes have been struck from it by percussion. The jagged edges produced by flake removal give the core potential usefulness as a tool. The flakes were detached from the core by blows with a hammerstone like the one shown here (c). The sharp edges of the flakes, such as example (b), allow their use as cutting tools. The tiny flake (d) is probably an accidental product of the percussion process; the presence of many stone splinters such as this one in the HAS tool clusters indicates that the stone tools were made on the spot. At the same time the absence of local unworked stone as potential raw material for tools suggests that the cores were carried to the site by the toolmakers. The artefacts from the second assemblage also include a core (e) that has had many flakes removed by percussion and another small splinter of stone (h). The edges of the two flakes (f, g) are sharp enough to cut meat, hide, sinew or wood. As at the hippopotamus/artefact site, the absence of local raw material for stone tools at KBS suggests that suitable lumps of lava must have been transported there by the toolmakers.

of sharp-edged broken stones even though there are no other stones in the sediments. The broken stones come in a range of forms but all are of the kind produced by deliberate percussion, so that we can classify them as undoubted artefacts. Such scatterings of artefacts are often found without bone being present in significant amounts. These I propose to designate sites of Type A.

In some instances a layer of sediment may include both artefacts and animal bones. Such bone-and-artefact occurrences fall into two categories. The first consists of artefacts associated with bones that represent the carcass of a single large animal; these sites are designated Type B. The second consists of artefacts associated with bones representing the remains of several different animal species; these sites are designated Type C.

The discovery of sites with these varied configurations in the sediments at Koobi Fora and Olduvai provides evidence that when the sediments containing them were being deposited some 2.5 to 1.5 mya there was at least one kind of hominid in East Africa that habitually carried objects such as stones from one place to another and made sharp-edged tools by deliberately fracturing the stones it carried with it. How does this archaeological evidence match up with the hominid fossil record? The fossil evidence indicates that two and perhaps three species of bipedal hominids inhabited the area at this time, so that the question arises: Can the species responsible for the archaeological evidence be identified?

For the moment the best working hypothesis seems to be that those hominids that were directly ancestral to modern man were making the stone tools. These are the fossil forms, of Early Pleistocene age, classified by most palaeontologists as an early species of the genus *Homo*. The question of whether or not contemporaneous hominid species of the genus *Australopithecus* also made tools must be set aside as a challenge to the ingenuity of future investigators. Here I shall simply discuss what we can discover about the activities of early toolmaking hominids without attempting to identify their taxonomic position (or positions).

Reading the evidence

As examples of the archaeological evidence indicative of early hominid patterns of subsistence and behaviour, consider our findings at two Koobi Fora excavations. The first is a locality catalogued as the hippopotamus/artefact site (HAS) because of the presence of fossilized hippopotamus bones and stone tools.

The site is 15 miles east of Lake Turkana. There in 1969 Richard Leakey discovered an erosion gully cutting into an ancient layer of volcanic ash known as the KBS Tuff. (KBS stands for Kay Behrensmeyer Site; she, the geologist-palaeoecologist of our Koobi Fora research team, first identified the ash layer at a nearby outcrop.) The ash layer is the uppermost part of a sedimentary deposit known to geologists as the Lower Member of the Koobi Fora Formation; here the ash had filled in one of the many dry channels of an ancient delta. Leakey found many bones of a single hippopotamus carcass weathering out of the eroded ash surface, and stone artefacts lay among the bones.

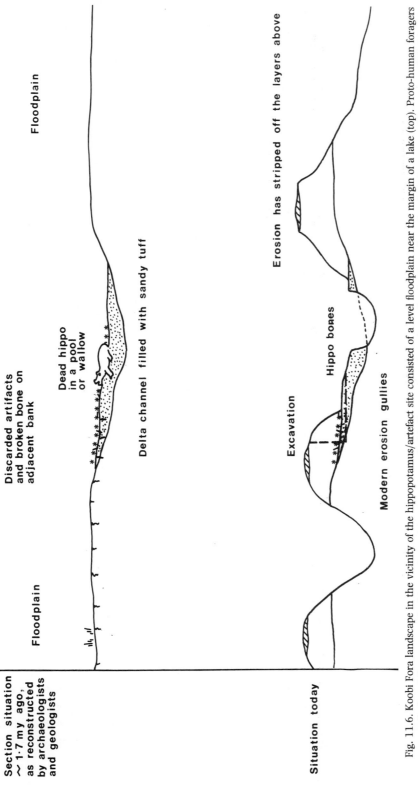

Fig. 11.6. Koobi Fora landscape in the vicinity of the hippopotamus/artefact site consisted of a level floodplain near the margin of a lake (top). Proto-human foragers apparently found the carcass of a hippopotamus lying in a stream-bed hollow and made tools on the spot in order to butcher the carcass. Their actions left a scatter of stone tools among the bones and on the ground nearby. The floodplain was buried under layers of silt and ash and was subsequently eroded (bottom), exposing some bones and tools. Their discovery led to excavation.

Fig. 11.7. Hammerstone unearthed at the hippopotamus/artefact site is a six-centimetre basalt pebble; it is shown here being lifted from its position on the ancient ground surface adjacent to the hippopotamus bones. Worn smooth by water action before it caught the eye of a toolmaker some 1.7 mya, the pebble is battered at both ends as a result of use as a hammer.

J. W. K. Harris, J. Onyango-Abuje and I supervised an excavation that cut into an outcrop where the adjacent delta sediments had not yet been disturbed by erosion. Our digging revealed that the hippopotamus carcass had originally lain in a depression or puddle within an ancient delta channel. Among the hippopotamus bones and in the adjacent stream bank we recovered 119 chipped stones; most of them were small sharp flakes that, when they are held between the thumb and the fingers, make effective cutting implements. We also recovered chunks of stone with scars showing that flakes had been struck from them by percussion. In Palaeolithic tool classification these larger stones fall into the category of core tool or chopper. In addition our digging exposed a rounded river pebble that was battered at both ends; evidently it had been used as a hammer to strike flakes from the stone cores.

The sediments where we found these artefacts contain no stones larger than a pea. Thus it seems clear that the makers of the tools had carried the stones here from somewhere else. The association between the patch of artefacts and the hippopotamus bones further suggests that toolmakers came to the site carrying stones and hammered off the small sharp-edged flakes on the spot in order to cut meat from the hippopotamus carcass. We have no way of telling at present whether the toolmakers themselves killed the animal or only came on it dead. Given the low level of stone technology in evidence, I am inclined to suspect scavenging rather than hunting.

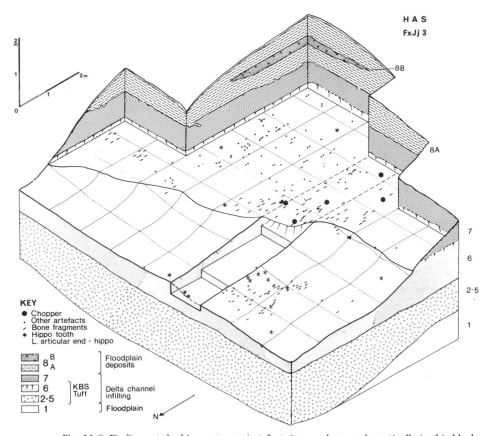

Fig. 11.8. Findings at the hippopotamus/artefact site are shown schematically in this block diagram; squares are one metre to a side. In the foreground are the objects that had been exposed by weathering. Trenching (across centre) and hillside excavation over a wide area exposed an ancient soil surface overlying a deposit of silty tuff. Lying on the ancient surface were stone cores from which sharp-edged flakes had been struck, more than 100 other stone artefacts and more than 60 additional fragments of teeth and bones. The scatter of tools and broken bones suggests the hypothesis that the toolmakers fed on meat from the hippopotamus.

The HAS deposit was formed at least 1.6 million years ago. The archaeological evidence demonstrates that the behaviour of some hominids at that time differed from the behaviour of modern great apes in that these proto-humans not only made cutting tools but also ate meat from the carcasses of large animals. The hippopotamus/artefact site thus provides corroboration for evidence of similar behaviour just as long ago as that obtained from Mary Leakey's excavations at Olduvai Gorge.

This finding does not answer all our questions. Were these proto-humans roaming the landscape, foraging and hunting, in the way that a troop of baboons does today? Were they instead hunting like a pride of lions? Or did some other behavioural pattern prevail? Excavation of another bone-and-artefact association, only a kilometre away from the hippopotamus/artefact site, has allowed us to carry our inquiries further.

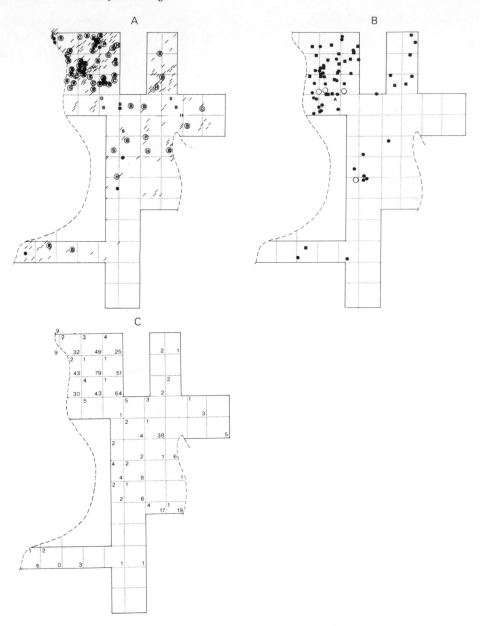

Fig. 11.9. Bones and stone tools were also found in abundance at the Kay Behrensmeyer site. As the plot of bone distribution (a) shows, the animal remains represent many different species. These are identified by capital letters; if the find was a tooth the letter is circled. Most are small to medium-sized bovids, such as gazelle, waterbuck and hartebeest (B). The remains of crocodile (C), giraffe (G), hippopotamus (H), porcupine (P) and extinct species of pig (S) were also present. Dots and dashes locate unidentified teeth and bone fragments respectively. The plot of artefact distribution (b) shows that three of four stone cores (open circles), most waste stone (squares) and flakes and fragments of flakes (dots) were found in 12 adjacent squares. Also found here was an unworked stone (A) that, like the cores, must have been carried to the site from a distance. Plotting of all tools and bones unearthed at the site was not attempted. Numbers in grid squares (c) show how many flakes and bits of waste stone *(upper left)* and fragments of bone *(lower right)* were recorded without exact plotting in each square.

The second site had been located by Behrensmeyer in 1969. Erosion was uncovering artefacts, together with pieces of broken-up bone, at another outcrop of the same volcanic ash layer that contained the HAS artefacts and bones. With the assistance of John Barthelme of the University of California at Berkeley and others I began to excavate the site. The work soon revealed a scatter of several hundred stone tools in an area 16 m in diameter. They rested on an ancient ground surface that had been covered by layers of sand and silt. The concentration of artefacts exactly coincided with a scatter of fragmented bones. Enough of them, teeth in particular, were identifiable to demonstrate that parts of the remains of several animal species were present. John M. Harris of the Louis Leakey Memorial Institute in Nairobi recognized, among other species, hippopotamus, giraffe, pig, porcupine and such bovids as waterbuck, gazelle and what may be either hartebeest or wildebeest. It was this site that was designated KBS. The site obviously represented the second category of bone-and-artefact associations: tools in association with the remains of many different animal species.

Geological evidence collected by A. K. Behrensmeyer of Yale University and others shows that the KBS deposit had accumulated on the sandy bed of a stream that formed part of a small delta. At the time when the toolmakers used the stream bed, water had largely ceased to flow. Such a site was probably favoured as a focus of hominid activity for a number of reasons. First, as every beachgoer knows, sand is comfortable to sit and lie on. Second, by scooping a hole of no great depth in the sand of a stream bed one can usually find water. Third, the growth of trees and bushes in the sun-parched floodplains of East Africa is often densest along watercourses, so that shade and plant foods are available in these locations. It may also be that the proto-human toolmakers who left their discards here took shelter from predators by climbing trees and also spent their nights protected in this way.

Much of this is speculative, of course, but we have positive evidence that the objects at the KBS site did accumulate in the shade. The sandy silts that came to cover the discarded implements and fractured bones were deposited so gently that chips of stone small enough to be blown away by the wind were not disturbed. In the same silts are the impressions of many tree leaves. The species of tree has not yet been formally identified, but Jan Gilette of the Kenya National Herbarium notes that the impressions closely resemble the leaves of African wild fig trees.

Carrying stones and meat

As at the hippopotamus/artefact site, we have established the fact that stones larger than the size of a pea do not occur naturally closer to the Kay Behrensmeyer Site than a distance of 3 km. Thus we know that the stones we found at the site must have been carried at least that far. With the help of Frank Fitch and Ron Watkins of the University of London we are searching for the specific sources.

It does not seem likely that all the animals of the different species represented among the KBS bones could have been killed in a short interval of time at this one place. Both considerations encourage the advancement of a tentative hypothesis:

like the stones, the bones were carried in, presumably while there was still meat on them.

If this hypothesis can be accepted, the Kay Behrensmeyer Site provides very early evidence for the transport of food as a proto-human attribute. Today the carrying of food strikes us as being commonplace but, as Sherwood Washburn of the University of California at Berkeley observed some years ago, such an action would strike a living ape as being novel and peculiar behaviour indeed. In short, if the hypothesis can be accepted, it suggests that by the time the KBS deposit was laid down various fundamental shifts had begun to take place in hominid social and ecological arrangements.

It should be noted that other early sites in this category are known in East Africa, so that the Kay Behrensmeyer Site is by no means unique. A number of such sites have been excavated at Olduvai Gorge and reported by Mary Leakey. Of these the best preserved is the '*Zinjanthropus*' site of Olduvai Bed I, which is about 1.7 million years old. Here too a dense patch of discarded artefacts coincides with a concentration of broken-up bones.

There is an even larger number of Type A sites (where concentrations of artefacts are found but bones are virtually or entirely absent). Some are at Koobi Fora; others are in the Omo Valley, where Harry V. Merrick of Yale University and Jean Chavaillon of the French National Centre for Scientific Research (CNRS) have recently uncovered sites of this kind in Members E and F of the Shungura Formation. The Omo sites represent the oldest securely dated artefact concentrations so far reported anywhere in the world: the tools were deposited some two million years ago.

One of the Olduvai sites in this category seems to have been a 'factory': a quarry where chert, an excellent tool material, was readily available for flaking. The other tool concentrations, with very few associated bones or none at all, may conceivably be interpreted as foci of hominid activity where for one reason or another large quantities of meat were not carried in. Until it is possible to distinguish between sites where bone was never present and sites where the bones have simply vanished because of such factors as decay, however, these deposits will remain difficult to interpret in terms of subsistence ecology.

What, in summary, do these East African archaeological studies teach us about the evolution of human behaviour? For one thing they provide unambiguous evidence that two million years ago some hominids in this part of Africa were carrying things around, for example stones. The same hominids were also making simple but effective cutting tools of stone and were at times active in the vicinity of large animal carcasses, presumably in order to get meat. The studies strongly suggest that the hominids carried animal bones (and meat) around and concentrated this portable food supply at certain places.

Model strategies

These archaeological facts and indications allow the construction of a theoretical model that shows how at least some aspects of early hominid social existence may have been organized. Critical to the validity of the model is the inference that the various clusters of remains we have uncovered reflect social and economic nodes in the lives of the toolmakers who left behind these ancient patches of litter. Because of the evidence suggestive of the transport of food to certain focal points, the first question that the model must confront is why early hominid social groups departed from the norm among living subhuman primates, whose social groups feed as they range. To put it another way, what ecological and evolutionary advantages are there in postponing some food consumption and transporting the food?

Several possible answers to this question have been advanced. For example, Adrienne Zihlman and Nancy Tanner of the University of California at Santa Cruz suggest that when the proto-humans acquired edible plants out on the open grasslands, away from the shelter of trees, it would have been advantageous for them to seize the plant products quickly and withdraw to places sheltered from menacing predators. Others have proposed that when the early hominids foraged, they left their young behind at 'nest' or 'den' sites (in the manner of birds, wild dogs and hyenas) and returned to these locales at intervals, bringing food with them to help feed and wean the young.

If we look to the recorded data concerning primitive human societies, a third possibility arises. Among extant and recently extinct primitive human societies the transport of food is associated with a division of labour. The society is divided by age and sex into classes that characteristically make different contributions to the total

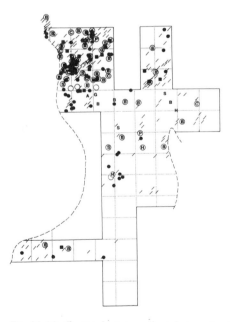

Fig. 11.10. Clustered mixture of artefacts and animal bones at KBS is evident when the stone and bone plots are superimposed. Combinations of this kind are sometimes produced by stream action, but such is not likely to be the case here, as is attested by the preservation of leaf impressions and other readily washed-away debris such as fine splinters of stone. It appears instead that the proto-humans who made and discarded their tools here were also responsible for the bone accumulation because they met here to share their food.

food supply. One significant result of such a division is an increase in the variety of foodstuffs consumed by the group. To generalize on the basis of many different ethnographic reports, the adult females of the society contribute the majority of the 'gathered' foods; such foods are mainly plant products but may include shell-fish, amphibians and small reptiles, eggs, insects and the like. The adult males usually, although not invariably, contribute most of the 'hunted' foodstuffs: the flesh of mammals, fishes, birds and so forth. Characteristically the males and females range in separate groups and each sex eventually brings back to a home base at least the surplus of its foraging.

Could this simple mechanism, a division of the subsistence effort, have initiated food-carrying by early hominids? One cannot dismiss out of hand the models that suggest safety from competitors or the feeding of nesting young as the initiating mechanisms for food-carrying. Nevertheless, neither model seems to me as plausible as one that has division of labour as the primary initiating mechanism. Even if no other argument favoured the model, we know for a fact that somewhere along the line in the evolution of human behaviour two patterns became established: food-sharing and a division of labour. If we include both patterns in our model of early hominid society, we will at least be parsimonious.

Other arguments can be advanced in favour of an early development of a division of labour. For example, the East African evidence shows that the proto-human toolmakers consumed meat from a far greater range of species and sizes of animals than are eaten by such living primates as the chimpanzee and the baboon. Among recent human hunter-gatherers the existence of a division of labour seems clearly related to the females being encumbered with children, a handicap that bars them from hunting or scavenging, activities that require speed afoot or long-range mobility. For the proto-humans too the incorporation of meat in the diet in significant quantities may well have been a key factor in the development not only of a division of labour but also of the organization of movements around a home base and the transport and sharing of food.

The model I propose for testing visualizes food-sharing as the behaviour central to a novel complex of adaptations that included as critical components hunting and/or scavenging, gathering and carrying. Speaking metaphorically, food-sharing provides the model with a kind of central platform. The adaptive system I visualize, however, could only have functioned through the use of tools and other equipment. For example, without the aid of a carrying device primates such as ourselves or our ancestors could not have transported from the field to the home base a sufficient amount of plant food to be worth sharing. An object as uncomplicated as a bark tray would have served the purpose, but some such item of equipment would have been mandatory. In fact, Richard Borshay Lee of the University of Toronto has suggested that a carrying device was the basic invention that made human evolution possible.

What about stone tools? Our ancestors, like ourselves, could probably break up the body of a small animal, as chimpanzees do, with nothing but their hands and teeth. It is hard to visualize them or us, however, eating the meat of an elephant,

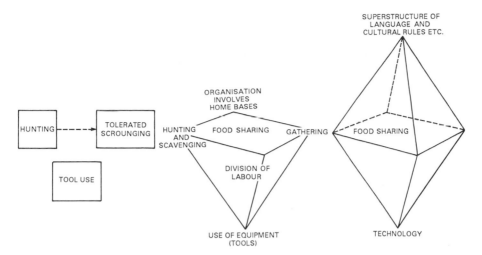

Fig. 11.11. Behaviour patterns that differ in degree of organization are contrasted in these diagrams. Living great apes, exemplified here by the chimpanzee, exhibit behaviour patterns that became important in human evolution, but the patterns (left) exist largely as isolated elements. Hunting occurs on a small scale but leads only to 'tolerated scrounging' rather than active food-sharing; similarly, tools are used but tool use is not integrated with hunting or scrounging. The author's model (centre) integrates these three behaviour patterns and others into a coherent structure. Food-sharing is seen as a central structural element, incorporating the provision of both animal and plant foods, the organization of a home base and a division of labour. Supporting the integrated structure is a necessary infrastructure of tool and equipment manufacture; for example, without devices for carrying food-stuffs there could not be a division of labour and organized food-sharing. In modern human societies (right) the food-sharing structure has undergone socio-economic elaboration. Its infrastructure now incorporates all of technology, and a matching superstructure has arisen to incorporate other elements of what is collectively called culture.

a hippopotamus or some other large mammal without the aid of a cutting implement. As the archaeological evidence demonstrates abundantly, the proto-humans of East Africa not only knew how to produce such stone flakes by percussion but also found them so useful that they carried the raw materials needed to make the implements with them from place to place. Thus, whereas the existence of a carrying device required by the model remains hypothetical as far as archaeological evidence is concerned, the fact that tools were used and carried out is amply attested to.

In this connection it should be stressed that the archaeological evidence is also silent with regard to proto-human consumption of plant foods. Both the morphology and the patterns of wear observable on hominid teeth suggest such a plant component in the diet, and so does the weight of comparative data on subsistence patterns among living non-human primates and among non-farming human societies. Nevertheless, if positive evidence is to be found, we shall have to sharpen our ingenuity, perhaps by turning to organic geochemical analyses. It is clear that as long as we do not correct for the imbalance created by the durability of bone as compared with that of plant residues, studies of human evolution will tend to have a male bias!

As far as the model is concerned the key question is not whether collectable foods – fruits, nuts, tubers, greens and even insects – were eaten. It is whether these proto-humans carried such foods about. Lacking any evidence for the consumption of plant foods, I shall fall back on the argument that the system I visualize would have worked best if the mobile hunter-scavenger contribution of meat to the social group was balanced by the gatherer-carrier collection of high-grade plant foods. What is certain is that at some time during the past several million years just such a division of labour came to be a standard kind of behaviour among the ancestors of modern man.

A final cautionary word about the model: the reader may have noted that I have been careful about the use of the words 'hunter' and 'hunting'. This is because we cannot judge how much of the meat taken by the proto-humans of East Africa came from opportunistic scavenging and how much was obtained by hunting. It is reasonable to assume that the carcasses of animals killed by carnivores and those of animals that had otherwise died or been disabled would always have provided active scavengers a certain amount of meat. For the present it seems less reasonable to assume that proto-humans, armed primitively if at all, would be particularly effective hunters. Attempts are now under way, notably by Elizabeth Vrba of South Africa, to distinguish between assemblages of bones attributable to scavenging and assemblages attributable to hunting, but no findings from East Africa are yet available. For the present I am inclined to accept the verdict of J. Desmond Clark of the University of California at Berkeley and Lewis R. Binford of the University of New Mexico. In their view the earliest meat-eaters might have obtained the flesh of animals weighing up to 30 kg by deliberate hunting, but the flesh of larger animals was probably available only through scavenging.

Tools as testimony

Of course, the adaptive model I have advanced here reflects only a working hypothesis and not established fact. Nevertheless, there is sufficient evidence in its favour to justify looking further at its possible implications for the course of human evolution. For example, the model clearly implies that early tool-making hominids displayed certain patterns of behaviour that, among the patterns of behaviour of all primates, uniquely characterize our own species and set it apart from its closest living relatives, the great apes. Does this mean that the toolmaking hominids of 1.5 to 2 million years ago were in fact 'human'?

I would surmise that it does not, and I have been at pains to characterize these East African pioneers as proto-humans. In summarizing the contrasts between living men and living apes I put high on the list language and the cultural phenomena that are dependent on it. We have no direct means of learning whether or not any of these early hominids had language. It is my suspicion, however, that the principal evolutionary change in the hominid line leading to full humanity over the past 2 million years has been the great expansion of language and communication abilities, together with the cognitive and cultural capabilities integrally related to language. What is the evidence in support of this surmise?

One humble indicator of expanding mental capacities is the series of changes that appears in the most durable material record available to us: the stone tools. The earlier tools from the period under consideration here seem to me to show a simple and opportunistic range of forms that reflect no more than an uncomplicated empirical grasp of one skill: how to fracture stone by percussion in such a way as to obtain fragments with sharp edges. At that stage of toolmaking the maker imposed a minimum of culturally dictated forms on his artefacts. Stone tools as simple as these perform perfectly well the basic functions that support progress in the direction of becoming human, for example the shaping of a digging stick, a spear and a bark tray, or the butchering of an animal carcass.

The fact is that exactly such simple stone tools have been made and used ever since their first invention, right down to the present day. Archaeology also shows, however, that over the past several hundred thousand years some assemblages of stone tools began to reflect a greater cultural complexity on the part of their makers. The complexity is first shown in the imposition of more arbitrary tool forms; these changes were followed by increases in the number of such forms. There is a marked contrast between the pure opportunism apparent in the shapes of the earliest stone tools and the orderly array of forms that appear later in the Old Stone Age when each form is represented by numerous standardized examples in each assemblage of tools. The contrast strongly suggests that the first toolmakers lacked the highly developed mental and cultural abilities of more recent humans.

The evidence of the hominid fossils and the evidence of the artefacts together suggest that these early artisans were non-human hominids. I imagine that if we had a time machine and could visit a place such as the Kay Behrensmeyer Site at the time of its original occupation, we would find hominids that were living in social groups much like those of other higher primates. The differences would be apparent only after prolonged observation. Perhaps at the start of each day we would observe a group splitting up as some of its members went off in one direction and some in another. All these subgroups would very probably feed intermittently as they moved about and encountered ubiquitous low-grade plant foods such as berries, but we might well observe that some of the higher-grade materials – large tubers or the haunch of a scavenged carcass – were being reserved for group consumption when the foraging parties reconvened at their starting point.

To the observer in the time machine, behaviour of this kind, taken in context with the early hominids' practice of making tools and equipment, would seem familiarly 'human'. If, as I suppose, the hominids under observation communicated only as chimpanzees do or perhaps by means of very rudimentary proto-linguistic signals, then the observer might feel he was witnessing the activities of some kind of fascinating bipedal ape. When one is relying on archaeology to reconstruct proto-human life, one must strongly resist the temptation to project too much of ourselves into the past. As Jane B. Lancaster of the University of Oklahoma has pointed out, the hominid life systems of two million years ago have no living counterparts.

Social advances

My model of early hominid adaptation can do more than indicate that the first toolmakers were culturally proto-human. It can also help to explain the dynamics of certain significant advances in the long course of mankind's development. For example, one can imagine that a hominid social organization involving some division of labour and a degree of food-sharing might well have been able to function even if it had communicative abilities little more advanced than those of living chimpanzees. In such a simple subsistence system, however, any group with members that were able not only to exchange food but also to exchange information would have gained a critical selective advantage over all the rest. Such a group's gatherers could report on scavenging or hunting opportunities they had observed, and its hunters could tell the gatherers about any plant foods they had encountered.

By the same token the fine adjustment of social relations, always a matter of importance among primates, becomes doubly important in a social system that involves food exchange. Language serves in modern human societies not only for the exchange of information but also as an instrument for social adjustment and even for the exchange of misinformation.

Food-sharing and the kinds of behaviour associated with it probably played an important part in the development of systems of reciprocal social obligations that characterize all the human societies we know about. Anthropological research shows that each human being in a group is ordinarily linked to many other members of the group by ties that are both social and economic. The French anthropologist Marcel Mauss, in a classic essay, 'The Gift', published in 1925, showed that social ties are usually reciprocal in the sense that whereas benefits from a relationship may initially pass in only one direction, there is an expectation of a future return of help in time of need. The formation and management of such ties calls for an ability to calculate complex chains of contingencies that reach far into the future. After food-sharing had become a part of proto-human behaviour the need for such an ability to plan and calculate must have provided an important part of the biological basis for the evolution of the human intellect.

The model may also help explain the development of human marriage arrangements. It assumes that in early proto-human populations the males and females divided subsistence labour between them so that each sex was preferentially tapping a different kind of food resource and then sharing within a social group some of what had been obtained. In such circumstances a mating system that involved at least one male in 'family' food procurement on behalf of each child-rearing female in the group would have a clear selective advantage over, for example, the chimpanzees' pattern of opportunistic relations between the sexes.

I have emphasized food-sharing as a principle that is central to an understanding of human evolution over the past two million years or so. I have also set forth archaeological evidence that food-sharing was an established kind of behaviour among early proto-humans. The notion is far from novel; it is implicit in many philosophical speculations and in many writings on palaeoanthropology. What is novel is that I have undertaken to make the hypothesis explicit so that it can be tested and revised.

Accounting for evolution

Thus the food-sharing hypothesis now joins other hypotheses that have been put forward to account for the course of human evolution. Each of these hypotheses tends to maintain that one or another innovation in proto-human behaviour was the critical driving force of change. For example, the argument has been advanced that tools were the 'prime movers'. Here the underlying implication is that in each successive generation the more capable individuals made better tools and thereby gained advantages that favoured the transmission of their genes through natural selection; it is supposed that these greater capabilities would later be applied in aspects of life other than technology. Another hypothesis regards hunting as being the driving force. Here the argument is that hunting requires intelligence, cunning, skilled neuromuscular coordination and, in the case of group hunting, cooperation. Among other suggested prime movers are such practices as carrying and gathering.

If we compare the food-sharing explanation with these alternative explanations we see that in fact food-sharing incorporates many aspects of each of the others. It will also be seen that in the food-sharing model the isolated elements are treated as being integral parts of a complex, flexible system. The model itself is probably an over-simplified version of what actually happened, but it seems sufficiently realistic to be worthy of testing through further archaeological and palaeontological research.

Lastly, the food-sharing model can be seen to have interconnections with the physical implications of fossil hominid anatomy. For example, a prerequisite of food-sharing is the ability to carry things. This ability in turn is greatly facilitated by a habitual two-legged posture. As Gordon W. Hewes of the University of Colorado has pointed out, an important part of the initial evolutionary divergence of hominids from their primate relatives may have been the propensity and the ability to carry things about. To me it seems equally plausible that the physical selection pressures that promoted an increase in the size of the proto-human brain, thereby surely enhancing the hominid capacity for communication, are a consequence of the shift from individual foraging to food-sharing some two million years ago.

12

Archaeological tests of alternative models of early hominid behaviour: excavation and experiments

Investigators of human evolution and cultural development tend implicitly to base their interpretation on the principle of uniformitarianism. That is to say they tend to explain as many features of early hominid adaptation as possible by constructing their models from some combination of the characteristics of modern apes and the characteristics of modern humans. This mode of procedure is surely the most convenient one to adopt in the initial stages of inquiry. However, it is very important also that its limitations be recognized. As Lancaster (1968), Freeman (1968) and others have pointed out, a major part of the fascination of the study of the early antecedents of the human way of life is that we are investigating systems that have no living counterparts. Since there are no proto-humans alive today and there are no societies with proto-languages we clearly need to bear in mind the possibility that some, perhaps many, features of early hominid adaptive systems were distinctive and original.

Since the behavioural systems of early hominids would have had profound influence on brain evolution, the topic, while fraught with difficulties, is one of considerable importance. This paper offers a preliminary report on research that is designed to make the interpretation of early archaeological data on hominid behaviour more rigorous by subjecting sets of rival hypotheses to carefully devised tests. The work is being done by a team for which I am co-ordinator and spokesman.

Figure 12.1 presents a timetable that indicates the first known appearance in the geological record of anatomical innovations that are a part of the human adaptive complex as we now know it. The figure presents, in a highly simplified fashion, minimum ages for important *anatomical shifts* in the human direction. What can be said about *behavioural* changes? For this, very largely we have to turn to archaeological evidence.

The ability of archaeologists to make a specific contribution to knowledge of early hominid patterns of life hinges on, but is not limited to, one particular innovation, namely hominid involvement in the making of recognizable implements from durable materials, most particularly stone. Once artefacts of stone began to be made

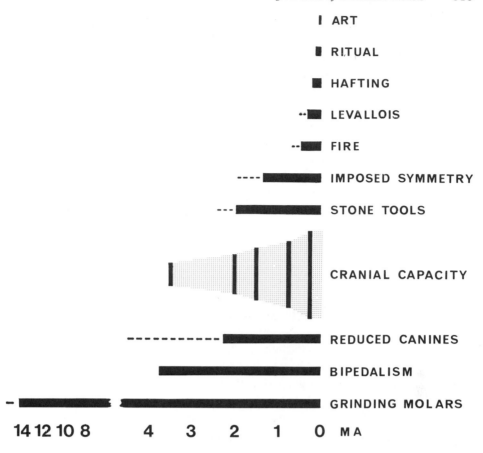

Fig. 12.1. A timetable showing the first known geological records of the appearance of human anatomical and behavioural traits. There is an almost complete gap in the record between 8 and 4 mya.

they became markers for the movements and activities of their makers and archaeological inference can go beyond technology.

The upper half of Fig. 12.1 provides a timetable of archaeological evidence for a series of significant technological, economic and cultural innovations.

The earliest known well-documented and securely-dated stone tools are those excavated by H. Merrick and J. Chavaillon from Member F of the Shungura Formation at the Omo. These are almost exactly 2 my old. Stone artefacts that may well be about 2.5 my old have been reported by Roche and Tiercelin (1977) from the Hadar, but we await further work for confirmation of the geological relationship and hence the age. The best studied and most informative set of very early archaeological occurrences are those of Bed I at Olduvai (M. D. Leakey, 1971), which are between 1.9 and 1.6 my old. Major features of the configuration discovered by M. Leakey are as follows: (1) stone tools were made; (2) the behaviour of the toolmakers was such that they discarded a scattering of artefacts here and there over the landscape, but also such that concentrated patches of artefacts formed in some places called sites by archaeologists; (3) some of these patches contain artefacts only, but others also contain quantities of the broken-up bones of a variety of animals, and in two cases the patch of artefacts coincides with the skeletal remains of the carcass of a single large animal. Subsequent research at Koobi Fora, Melka Kunturé, Chesowanja and Gadeb has shown that this configuration is not peculiar to Olduvai (see, for example: Isaac, 1978a [this volume, ch. 11]; Harris, 1978; Chavaillon, 1976; Bishop *et al.*, 1978).

The question then arises: what does this configuration mean? Can archaeological investigations of these material remains inform us about the adaptive patterns of early toolmaking hominids? The first round of research revealed the configuration, the second is attempting to probe its evolutionary meaning.

The overall timetable allows us to identify two grand puzzles that demand attention as we grope towards an understanding of the dynamics of human evolution. The first is the question of the circumstances surrounding the adoption of bipedal stance and locomotion and the second the nature of the selection pressures leading to a sustained trend towards brain enlargement and reorganization. From the timetable it can be seen that the archaeological record as we now have it can do little or nothing to eludicate the circumstances of the shift to bipedalism, which took place at least 1.5 to 2 my before the date of the oldest recognizable tools yet found. On the other hand the known record of marked brain expansion and the known archaeological record coincide rather closely and it has long seemed reasonable to suggest that these two phenomena were related. That is to say, it is widely believed that some of the novel behavioural ingredients that caused the archaeological record to start forming were also significant determinants of the trend towards brain enlargement.

Behavioural interpretation: hypotheses and tests

At first glance the configuration just indicated seems familiar and readily interpretable. Where we see artefacts among the bones of a large animal, we quickly conclude that this is a fossil butchery site indicative of meat-eating on a large scale (M. D. Leakey, 1971; Isaac, 1971a, 1978a [this volume, chs. 10 and 11]). Equally, the clusters of artefacts and broken bones from many different animals seem obvious to us as living sites (M. D. Leakey, 1971) or home bases (Isaac 1969, 1978a [this volume, ch. 11]). But one should ask, as critics have indeed begun to ask (see, for example, Binford, 1977a), whether these are the only possible explanations. In adopting them without further question might we not be guilty of simply projecting familiar human-ness backwards two million years. As I will briefly indicate at the end of the paper, the butchery, meat-eating, and home base interpretations are apt to get incorporated as components of far-reaching interpretations of the dynamics of human evolution. It surely behoves us to test these interpretations, to destruction if possible, before too much higher-order theory is based on them.

As E. O. Wilson (1975) has pointed out, writers on human evolution have tended to be passionate advocates of one particular explanation or interpretation.

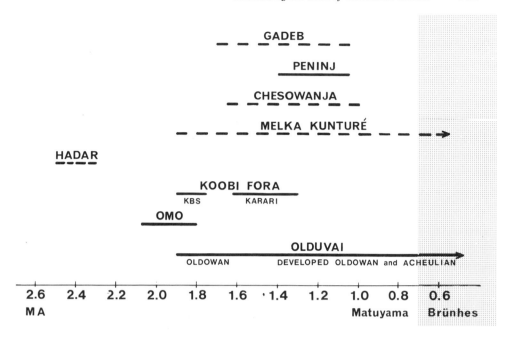

Fig. 12.2. The approximate time relations among localities in East Africa yielding early archaeological evidence. Dotted lines denote less certain age determinations.

However, in recent years the style has been changing in favour of the formulation of alternative or rival hypotheses, each with its own test implications that can serve to guide research. This not only turns out to be a constructive move, but also it is fun! What follows is a hasty portrait of how our research group is attempting to apply this approach. I will pose a series of problems as questions, then indicate two or more possible answers or rival hypotheses plus the predictions that follow from the hypotheses. Then I will indicate the kinds of research being done to test the extent to which the predictions are met. In most instances the research is still in progress by others and so I can only whet your appetites while you await fuller reports from the investigators themselves.

How did the clusters of artefacts and bones form?

Some possible explanations that have occurred to various people are as follows:
1. These are hydraulic jumbles in which artefacts and bones have been washed together by water currents.
2. Hominid activity caused the artefact concentration and another, independent, agency such as carnivore-feeding formed an overlapping bone concentration at some common amenity, for instance a shade tree, or a water hole.
3. That the hominids caused the observed configurations by carrying both stones and bones to particular places, where artefacts were sometimes made and dropped and where bones were broken up and discarded.

Each of these would predict the observed overall configuration, but each would

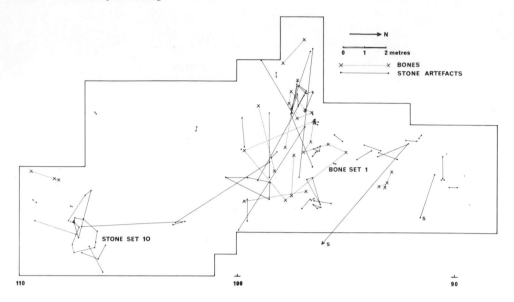

Fig. 12.3. A plan of the excavated area at FxJj 50 in the Koobi Fora area. The lines join up the find places of artefact and bone pieces that fit back together. The configuration strongly implies that the hydraulic jumble hypothesis should be rejected.

predict differences in detail. The hydraulic jumble hypothesis would carry the expectation that the concentrations and their matrices would have the size-sorted characteristics and sedimentary fabric of a water-lain deposit. Under the carnivore bone accumulation hypothesis the bones would resemble carnivore-chewed assemblages in their composition and damage patterns. The hominid stone-and-bone transport and discard hypothesis would predict that among other things some of the bones might show specific signs (such as cut marks) of having been processed with stone knives and breakage patterns caused by hammers rather than by jaws.

All of these suggested explanations need to be taken seriously, and it should be recognized that they are not mutually exclusive. Combinations may have acted to form individual sites. Almost all archaeological horizons in East Africa were covered over and preserved by sediments deposited from moving water, albeit in some cases very gently moving water which laid down only silts and clays. This means that, even where it seems highly improbable that the concentration of materials could have been caused by hydraulic forces, it is necessary to assess the extent to which the material has been moved about before interpreting the details of arrangement.

One member of the team with which I work, K. Schick, has embarked on a programme of experimental work designed to help archaeologists assess the degree to which an excavated assemblage has been transported, winnowed or rearranged. Her work involves a wide variety of controlled observations on the processes by which material accumulates and on the effects of geological and other agencies that could cause the materials to become stratified. The results of these experiments will be used to guide interpretation of archaeologically observed configurations.

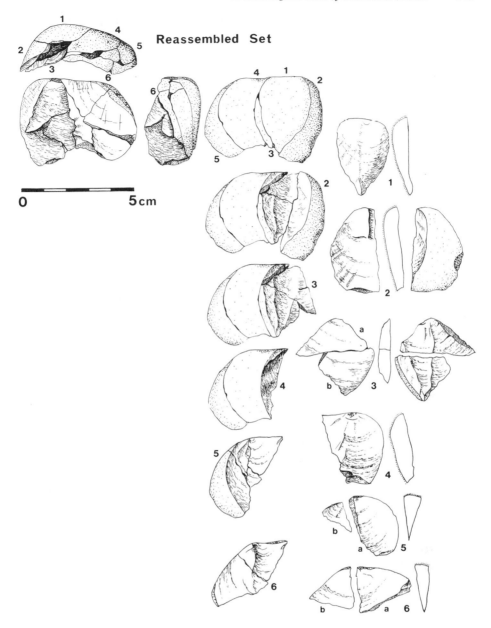

Reassembled Set

Fig. 12.4. An example of a set of flakes from site FxJj 50 that fit back together. The reassembled set is shown at the top and successive stages of disassembly are set out below. The flakes can be seen to have been struck from the margin of a water-rounded cobble. After the striking of the flakes, the cobble would have had the form of a chopper, but this had been removed from the vicinity where the flaking was done.

The bone assemblages from a series of sites at Koobi fora and Olduvai have been carefully studied by H. Bunn and those from Olduvai have also been studied by R. Potts. Both have independently looked for distinctive hammer breakage patterns and for modifications such as cut marks. At some sites the results of these searches have been positive and reports on these important new findings, which meet the predictions for hominid involvement with the bones, and which effectively falsify hydraulic or carnivore causation alone, will shortly be published [Isaac, in prep; Bunn, 1983].

Another new finding, which helps to distinguish the three rival hypotheses under discussion, has been the discovery by N. Toth, E. Kroll and K. Schick that at several sites numbers of stone artefacts and bones can be fitted back together again.

Preliminary plans by Kroll, who is doing detailed analyses of arrangement patterns, allow us to see that fitting pieces of stone and bone tend to be clustered in a way that would not be predicted if the artefacts and bones had simply been washed together.

What kinds of hominid behaviour patterns resulted in the formation of sites?

Given the working hypothesis that the site concentrations formed through active hominid manipulation of stones and bones, the question arises, what were the hominids doing at these places?

Many of the sites are located in stoneless terrain and it is very clear that stones were carried to the locality and flaked there. As the study of conjoining pieces shows, some artefacts were removed from the immediate vicinity in which they were made. However, the accumulation of bones is not so clearly attributable to proto-human transport, since bones, while in live animals, are independently mobile! Alternative hypotheses again need to be considered:

1. Artefacts were made and discarded at places where a variety of animal carcasses were periodically available for butchery and for breaking of bones, for instance the margin of a water hole, where animals recurrently died, or a bend in a river, where drifting carcasses washed up.
2. Bones and meat from many different carcasses were carried to a central locality at which the manufacture of stone artefacts was also carried out.

At the present time I cannot offer decisive evidence to prove false either of these alternatives. However, given the considerable diversity of species at some of the sites, and given their varied physiographic settings, such as floodplains on the shores of lakes for the Olduvai FLK Zinj site, and floodplains on channel banks for FxJj 50, one is inclined to regard the first explanation as less credible.

If the second hypothesis is adopted, then this implies the transport of food, a behaviour common in birds and bees but rare among mammals and almost unknown in primates other than humans. Whether the food was transported for sharing among an entire social group or simply for the feeding of the young would be an important follow-up question, to which we can as yet offer no answer, or even any potential tests.

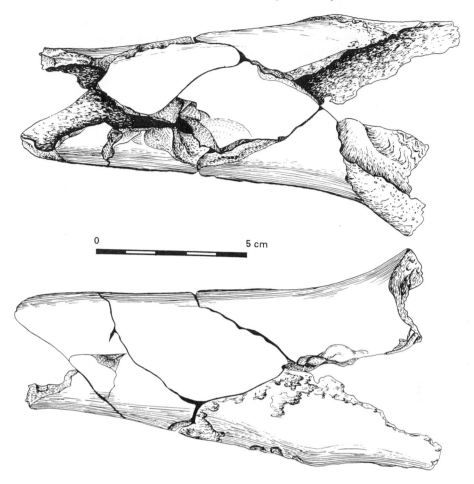

Fig. 12.5. An example of pieces of bone that fit back together. The reassembled set has been identified by H. Bunn as a humerus shaft from a large alcelaphine antelope. Experimental evidence strongly suggests that the fracture of the shaft was induced by a hammer blow. Part of what is almost certainly the articular end of this same bone was also found at the site and this has scored lines on it that seem to be cut marks inflicted by the sharp edge of a stone tool.

Another important question that arises as we pursue this chain of investigation is the matter of the amount of time and the number of site usage episodes that formed early sites. Were the assemblages of artefacts and bones at such living sites as the Olduvai FLK Zinj site or FxJj 50 and FxJj 20 at Koobi Fora deposited as refuse during a single sustained period of occupancy or did they accumulate as a result of a long-drawn-out series of short return visits, with each visit leading to the discard of an increment of refuse?

We know of no simple measures of duration and recurrence of occupancy, but patient work may help to put limits on the mode of accumulation. For instance, the degree of pre-burial bone weathering would allow one to distinguish bone assemblages that had taken many years to accumulate. H. Bunn has concluded that, at least at some of the early sites, sub-aerial weathering is not apparent on most bones, probably implying accumulation over no more than a year or so.

Another line of attack follows deductive logic. If at the majority of early hominid sites usage bouts were brief and short, there might also be many 'mini-sites' scattered about, places where activities lasted a few hours or a day or so and led to the deposition of just a few artefacts and other refuse items. We have begun to look for these and have indeed found some, but the sample areas searched and the series excavated need to be much enlarged before any judgement of the relative frequency of mini- and maxi-sites can be reached.

The early sites have been variously called occupation sites, living sites, home-bases and so on. All these are loaded terms that involve many tacit backward projections of the familiar forms of modern *Homo sapiens* patterns. For instance, even if food was carried to these places and if tools were made and used there, they need not have been sleeping places. In her spatial analysis of the sites, E. Kroll is seeking to formulate questions such as these and to seek discriminants between various possible modes of site usage and formation.

What do the early stone tools themselves teach us about the organisms that made them?

Within our team this problem is being studied in a variety of ways. J. W. K. Harris and I are testing for correlations between the characteristics of assemblages and the characteristics of the environmental context in which each variant set was discarded. This is being done in the hope of identifying distinctive habitat-specific activities. We have also looked for evidence of change through time (Isaac and Harris, 1978; Harris, 1978). In pursuing this work it became clear that we need to know whether the early artefact assemblages represent opportunistic least-effort solutions to the problem of obtaining sharp edges from stone, or whether, as in most late prehistoric and modern assemblages, there was a fairly elaborate set of culturally defined, arbitrary artefact forms. Different archaeologists can look at the same assemblage and come up with quite different judgements on this question. Approaches other than laboratory sorting were clearly needed to resolve this uncertainty.

In addition we realized, as did many other workers, that if we are to move towards an understanding of the adaptive significance of tools in early hominid life we need to ascertain first the uses to which they *can* be put, and secondly to seek evidence of how they actually *were* used.

Both the complexity of design problem and the problem of function called for a combination of experiments and close scrutiny of the sets of excavated ancient artefacts. A start on this large and important task has been made for the project by N. Toth, who has learned to replicate all of the artefact forms so far recovered from the early sites at Koobi Fora using the same raw materials as were used between 1.25 and 2 mya. He will be reporting his specific findings elsewhere, but it appears

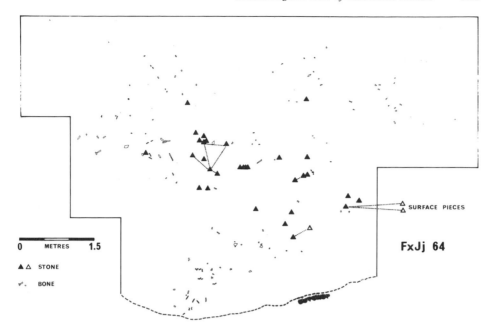

Fig. 12.6. An example of the disposition of finds at a mini-site of the kind that our research group is now searching out and excavating. At this one (FxJj 64) stone flakes, derived from the knapping of just three or four stones, form a cluster superimposed on a scatter of bone fragments. Such sites have the advantage that they may represent a single bout of activity during one visit to the locale, lasting from between an hour or so to a day or so. This example was found by A. K. Behrensmeyer and excavated by F. Marshall.

that the features of the early stone artefact assemblages can be accounted for as the application of an opportunistic, least-effort strategy applied to locally available forms of stone. Even such apparently fancy forms as the Karari scraper need be no more than this.

In the investigation of function, Toth and other members of our group have demonstrated that by means of simple flakes and core tools it is perfectly possible to perform all the most basic functions that in ethnography and later prehistory are necessary to the human way of life: branches can be chopped off and then sharpened so as to form a digging stick or spear; a simple carrying device such as a bark tray can be prepared; and animals, even very large pachyderms over which the non-human carnivores have great difficulty, can be cut up.

These experiments, together with those done by P. Jones and Louis Leakey (Jones, this symposium [1981]) and by others, go a long way to confirm the view that the discovery of how to obtain sharp-edged tools had great potential adaptive significance. Among others, they facilitate access to energy-rich food types such as meat and deep tubers.

However, what early tools might have been used for and what they actually were used for are not necessarily the same things. N. Toth has tackled this also, working with L. Keeley, a pioneer researcher on the distinctive wear patterns that are induced on stone by contact with such materials as wood, bone, hide, meat and plant tissue of various kinds. As Keeley and Toth will report in due course [1981], preliminary examinations seem to imply that several different varieties of use wear are evident on chert flakes from the Koobi Fora Formation.

The finding, by H. Bunn and R. Potts, of cut marks on bones represents still another important class of evidence regarding the function of some early tools.

In the preceding part of this paper I have given examples of the kinds of research question that our research group, among others, are pursuing. By way of conclusion I now want to deal briefly with how these kinds of archaeological inquiries connect with the overall interdisciplinary study of human evolution. As I mentioned in the introduction, two grand puzzles can be recognized, and it is to the second of these that archaeological data seem most relevant, namely the puzzle of how natural selection acted to initiate and sustain a prolonged trend in the human ancestral lineage towards the enlargement and reorganization of the brain.

Since the time of Darwin, a succession of more or less vague and speculative explanations has been advanced. Two stand out as particularly prominent, 'tool-using' and 'hunting'. The tool-using line of explanation, though widely invoked, is seldom stated very explicitly. Presumably it involves the notion that novel genetic configurations that endowed some small-brained, bipedal early hominids with superior abilities in making and using tools enabled the carriers of these genotypes to leave more surviving offspring. The argument runs on to the effect that, since many toolmaking and tool-using skills need to be culturally transmitted, the adaptive importance of tools led to the establishment and elaboration of culture in general (cf. Lancaster, 1968; Tobias, this symposium [1981]).

The hunting theory has been recounted in dramatic terms by writers such as Dart, Ardrey and Morris and in more restrained terms by, for example, Washburn and Lancaster (1968) and by Campbell (1966). It argues that, for savannah-living hominids, gaining increased access to a new food resource, meat, was the main selective advantage and that successful access was facilitated by mutations favouring the use of tools, enhanced foresight and cunning, and by mutations favouring communication and cooperation, especially among males.

Very recently, various workers, including myself (Washburn, 1965; Hewes, 1961; Lee, 1979; Lancaster, 1978; Isaac, 1978a [this volume, ch. 11]), have been involved in making explicit yet another line of explanation, food-sharing. This subsumes tools and hunting, adds some other components and then goes on to argue that it was the adoption of a whole integrated complex of behavioural innovations that in each generation gave individuals, or perhaps kin groups, with somewhat more versatile brains, a crucial advantage over their contemporaries.

The investigations outlined in the body of this paper are all aimed at helping to distinguish the relative credibility of these and other rival large-scale overarching theories of the evolutionary dynamics of human brain enlargement. The information that we now have does not make it seem that the earlier approximations, 'tool-using' and 'hunting' are wrong, only that they are seriously incomplete. For instance, use of stone tools could only have become important as a part of a whole series of social, reproductive and dietary changes (cf. Parker and Gibson, 1979).

Archaeological research has shown that many early artefacts occur jumbled up among the broken bones of edible animals. Does this circumstantial evidence really imply that the early hominids were hunting in a serious way? I have already indicated the existence of new evidence that tends to sustain the hypothesis that the toolmaking hominids were eating meat and marrow. However, there are more ways of obtaining flesh and bone than by hunting and killing. We need to consider scavenging as an alternative. There are aspects of the bone assemblages associated with early artefacts that would be more plausibly predicted under the scavenging hypothesis than under the hunting hypothesis (cf. Vrba, 1975; Schaller and Lowther, 1969). Most tropical modern human gatherer-hunters catch and consume quantities of medium to smallish animals, which size range it is unusual to obtain by scavenging. However, the archaeological bone assemblages from Olduvai (M. D. Leakey, 1971) and from Koobi Fora (H. Bunn, personal communication) are dominated by bones from medium to large animals, precisely the size range of carcasses that do provide scavenging opportunities (Vrba, 1975). The relative importance of these two alternatives remains to be explored in further research.

However, even if meat-eating and hunting are adopted as reasonably well-documented components of early hominid behaviour, the hunting hypothesis remains far from satisfactory as a comprehensive explanation of the basis for the evolution of the human brain–mind–culture complex. For instance, what were the females and children doing while males hunted?

The food-sharing hypothesis would predict the following as having been important: tools, transport of food, meat-eating, gathered plant foods, division of labour and the existence of places at which members of a social group would reconvene at least every day or so and at which discarded artefacts and food refuse would accumulate. The archaeological configuration observed at Olduvai and at Koobi Fora fits many of these predictions.

This line of explanation has important potential for helping us to understand the complex dynamics of the last 2 or 3 my of human evolution. It has already been adopted in such widely read popular books as *Origins*, written by Leakey and Lewin (1977). However, it is a hypothesis, not an established truth. This is why our research group has systematically sought to test it by attempting to prove its predictions false. However, there are important gaps: we assume that plant foods were the dominant source of energy and nutrition for the early Pleistocene hominids, but, beyond the preliminary findings of A. Walker in his studies of tooth wear (this symposium) [1981], we have few ways to test that assumption or to ascertain when gathering with postponed consumption of plant foods began. One member of our group, J. Sept, intends to attack an aspect of the problem by studying the feeding opportunities that are represented in modern analogues of the situations in which field evidence shows that early hominids lived, made tools and died.

Once the food-sharing system had been established the theory predicts that it would have produced steady selection pressure in favour of capabilities for developing social systems based on reciprocity. There are clear potential cross ties here between this theory and the recently enunciated theories of the evolution of social tendencies through the mechanism of kin selection (Hamilton, 1964; Trivers, 1971; Wilson, 1975).

The food-sharing line of explanation is not an entirely new suggestion, but until recently it was implicit rather than explicit. In 1975 I sought to rectify this by stating clearly the thesis that the early toolmaking hominids lived in social groups that manifested division of labour and practised food-sharing at home bases (Isaac, 1976a). Many people took this to mean that the early hominids must have been relatively placid, cooperative, gentle creatures who lived essentially human lives, less a few trappings of cultural elaboration. This does not necessarily follow, and I return to the point made at the outset: there are no living counterparts of the early hominids and we should expect that, as we refine our information about them, more and more distinctive and unexpected features may appear. To illustrate this let me close by pointing out that recent research on finger bones (Susman *et al.*, 1979) and shoulder joints (Vrba, 1979) strongly imply that the hominids of 2 mya, though adapted to bipedal locomotion, were also well adapted for tree climbing. It is entirely possible that they did not sleep at their so-called home-bases but that they slept in trees.

13

Bones in contention: competing explanations for the juxtaposition of early Pleistocene artefacts and faunal remains

Localized accumulations of discarded artefacts and broken animal bones have frequently been observed forming at the camp places of such hunter-gatherers as have survived into the era of ethnographic observation. Equally from the millennia just before the establishment of farming, the archaeological record in all five continents includes numerous examples of concentrations of stone tools, chipping waste and quantities of broken bone commonly mixed with charred materials.

Archaeologists have assumed that these commonplace accumulations are the residues of camps or settlements formed as the outcome of ethnographically observed processes that include as a quasi-universal behaviour the transport of food back to a 'home-base' for collective consumption. Whenever meat-on-the-bone forms a significant component of the transported food, a concentration of artefacts and broken bones is almost bound to form at the home base. This much is common knowledge and it has been possible and reasonable to base the fundamentals of interpretation on 'common sense'.

It has also long been known that apparently comparable concentrations of artefacts and faunal remains can be found in Upper Pleistocene deposits. Cave sites often contain spectacular accumulations, but open-air examples are also well known. Such Late Pleistocene 'middens' are widely assumed to have formed in the same essential ways as Holocene and ethnographic accumulations.

Although well-preserved examples become increasingly rare further back in time, similar configurations have been reported from both cave and open sites of Middle Pleistocene age. In some cases, the process at cave-sites seems to have involved bone-accumulating animals, as well as, or instead of, humans. Increasing numbers of the more ancient open-air sites involved fluvial deposition as at least one factor in their formation. However, in spite of these complications, most palaeoanthropologists have hitherto accepted that, throughout much of Middle Pleistocene time, toolmakers were engaging in hunting and food-transport behaviours.

In East Africa, when modern research began on fine-grained deposits of Early Pleistocene and Late Pleistocene age (i.e. 0.7 my to 2 my), a similar configuration was discovered. Artefacts occurred in localized concentrations and these commonly, but not invariably, contained quantities of broken-up animal bones. Having, as it were, followed an apparently uninterrupted trail of stone and bone refuse back through the Pleistocene, it seemed natural to all those involved in the first round of research to treat these accumulations of artefacts and faunal remains as being 'fossil home-base sites'.

However, if one comes at the issue from another direction one may see things differently. Meat-eating and food-sharing are very distinctive human behaviours, that are far more intensively developed in virtually all recent humans than in any other non-human primates. It is crucial to know when in evolution these behaviours began to be intensified and it is thus important not just to accept interpretations of the Early Pleistocene archaeological record that are backward projections of familiar modern human patterns. This point has been made recently with some vehemence by Binford (1981).

In response to a growing recognition of this need a new research movement has got underway over the past five years that seeks to investigate the processes whereby the Early Pleistocene archaeological and zoo-archaeological record was formed. This review will attempt to summarize the context of the inquiry and to introduce the overall rationale of the investigation to the archaeo-zoological community.

A key element in the new research movement is the concern to cope with multiple, rival hypotheses at levels of interpretation that range from the specifics of mode of deposition and details of damage and breakage patterns to more indirect constructs such as 'hominid meat-eating', 'food transport', 'sharing', and 'home-bases'. For each set of competing hypotheses a series of test implications must be defined. Appropriate evidence must then be collected and scrutinized for goodness-of-fit with the test implications. However, very often the rival hypotheses are not mutually exclusive and simple Popperian falsification is not possible. Research then winds up as the acquisition of data that can be used in assessing the relative importance of a series of interacting factors.

The inspiration for the recognition of items in the sets of rival hypotheses must in general come from observations of configurations and processes in the contemporary world, including those induced by human, animal and geological agencies. The working-out of test implications also involves experiments and ethnographic, taphonomic and geological observations.

Table 13.1 shows the distribution in space and time of sites in East Africa which date to more than 1 million years ago, and for which potentially important zoo-archaeological evidences have been reported. What follows is a brief summary of the logic of inquiries applicable to most of these Rift Valley sites. However, because I have worked for twelve years at Koobi Fora, I will tend to use this research project as the main source of examples.

Sites at all these localities have in the first instance been interpreted as 'camp-sites', 'occupation sites', and as fossil 'home-bases' (Fig. 13.1). This view has been based initially on the fact that quantities of broken bones are found intermingled with concentrations of discarded stone artefacts. As already indicated, the interpretation of these seems perfectly obvious to archaeologists familiar with recent

Table 13.1. *Early Pleistocene sites in East Africa which have yielded stone artefacts plus bone concentrations*

Locality	Age range (mya)	Reference
Tanzania		
Olduvai Gorge (more than 15 sites)	2–0.5	Leakey (1971)[a] Gentry and Gentry (1978) Potts (1982)[b] Bunn (1982a)[b]
Kenya		
Chesowanja	1.4–1.6	Gowlett *et al.* (1981)
Koobi Fora (more than 8 significant sites)	1.9–1.3	Isaac and Harris (1978) Bunn *et al.* (1980)[b] Bunn (1982a)[b]
Ethiopia		
Melka Kunturé (more than 10 sites)	1.5 to Holocene (discontinuous)	Chavaillon *et al.* (1979)
Gadeb (several sites)	≥ 1.0	Clark and Kurashina (1979a)

[a] Including relatively detailed tabulations containing taxon and body-part frequencies.
[b] Plus damage patterns.
For a general review, critique and bibliography written in 1976–77, see Isaac and Crader (1981).

sites. However, as I have also indicated, important issues in our understanding of the evolution of human behaviour are at stake, and rigorous testing is crucial. We need first to check whether the co-occurrence of artefacts and broken bones is a sufficiently definite phenomenon to call for careful archaeological attention, and then, if it is, we need to consider the various processes other than hominid actions that might serve to form such coincident concentrations.

The logic of inquiry can be set out as a series of questions: first, *how were stone artefacts and fragmented bones distributed in ancient landscapes occupied by early tool-using hominids? How often do patches coincide?* These questions are important because we would be misguided if we constructed special explanations for artefact-plus-bone concentrations if these merged simply as occasional quasi-fortuitous overlays of two essentially independent distribution patterns.

Fig. 13.2 and its caption indicates research oriented at defining distribution patterns. The work is in an early stage, but a reasonably clear assessment can be reached both from qualitative observations and from initial quantitative work. This is first that the distribution of artefacts and of concentrations of fragmented bones is highly patchy, and that the frequency with which the patches are found to be coincident far exceeds expectation, if both were independently stochastically distributed. In my view, Binford (1981) has seriously underestimated the strength of this relationship, and has underrated its significance.

Secondly, given that a non-random relationship between dense patches of artefacts and bone exists, the question becomes – *what processes might induce the formation of coincident concentrations of artefacts and bones?*

Fig. 13.3 suggests a series of rival hypotheses which we have begun to evaluate

First Interpretations...

Fig. 13.1. Archaeologists working in Early Pleistocene sedimentary formations in East Africa search along outcrops and excavate at places where surface indications imply a concentration of material (top). The excavation data plus the surface indications have commonly been taken to mean that a dense, localized patch of artefacts existed on what was formerly the surface of the ground (centre). Taking another step, it has seemed intuitively obvious that these patches are fossil 'campsites' or 'home-bases' with many of the behaviours that characterize such places for modern humans (bottom). Some five years ago a research movement to check these assumptions began.

in our research at Koobi Fora. The list is not exhaustive, but it has enabled us to get started. Notice that the various possibilities tend not to be mutually exclusive. Several may have been involved in forming one concentration.

A set of possible causes such as this serves to orient research activities. Clearly, once the problem is perceived in these terms one needs to learn to distinguish the differences between the detailed consequences of each of the processes envisaged. This in turn has called for investigations of the processes themselves and involves experiments and systematic observations in the modern world. This is effectively the same as the research strategy that Binford (1977b, 1981) calls 'middle range analysis'. The following are some of the studies undertaken so as to facilitate evaluations:

1. Studies of the effects of flowing water and other 'geological agencies' on artefacts, bones and on site formation (being undertaken by K. Schick).
2. Studies of the initial composition of fractured stone produced by simple flaking (size, manufacturing stages, etc.). This serves as a base line for assessing factors that have modified what is actually observed (Toth and Schick in Bunn *et al.*, 1980 [this volume, ch. 8]; Toth, 1982; also Jones, 1981).
3. The composition and morphology of broken-bone assemblages (e.g. experimentally induced fractures, carnivore lairs, ethnographic sites) (Bunn, 1982a; also Brain, 1981; Binford, 1981; Crader this volume [Clutton-Brock and Grigson, 1983]; Gifford and Behrensmeyer, 1977; Shipman and Phillips-Conroy, 1976; Yellen, 1977a and many others).

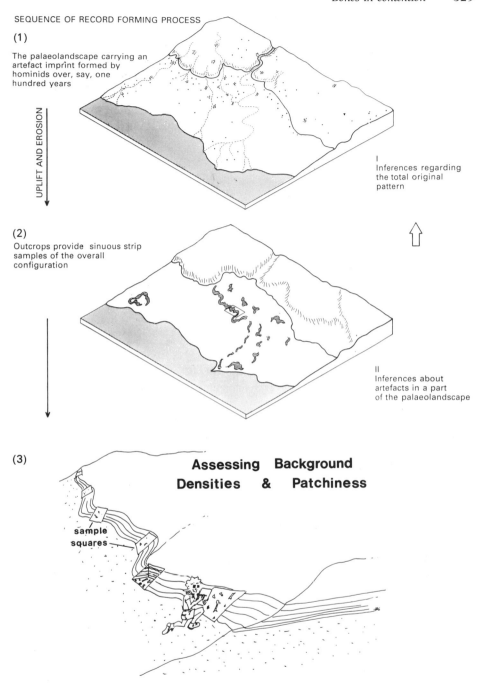

SEQUENCE OF RECORD FORMING PROCESS

(1)

The palaeolandscape carrying an
artefact imprint formed by
hominids over, say, one
hundred years

UPLIFT AND EROSION

I
Inferences regarding
the total original
pattern

(2)

Outcrops provide sinuous strip
samples of the overall
configuration

II
Inferences about
artefacts in a part
of the palaeolandscape

(3)

**Assessing   Background
Densities   &   Patchiness**

sample
squares

Fig. 13.2. The first requirement is to find out about the distribution of artefacts and bones in
the Early Pleistocene sedimentary basins of East Africa: (1) an idealized view of the situation
at some past moment, (2) the array is partially preserved by continued deposition of layered
sediments. Then following uplift, an erosion front cuts into the layers providing sinuous strip
samples of each horizon (3). Systematic samples along outcrops permit reconstruction of
aspects of the original configuration. It emerges that both artefacts and bones have a very
patchy distribution. The patches coincide more often than could be due to chance alone (see
Behrensmeyer, 1975; Isaac, 1981b [this volume, ch. 7]).

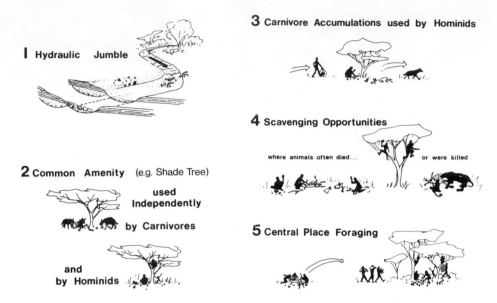

Fig. 13.3. A series of processes whereby coincident concentrations of artefacts and bones might form. The list is not exhaustive but has served to orient research over the past five years (see Isaac 1981a [this volume, ch. 12] for discussion).

4. The arrangement of objects within ancient sites considered in relation to process and in comparison with later sites and ethnographic examples (Kroll, 1981; Kroll and Isaac, in press [1984]).

5. The micro-stratigraphy and mode of burial of ancient concentrations of artefacts and bones (Hay, 1976, Kaufulu in preparation [1983]).

Most of these studies are in progress or only recently completed so that their results have not yet been fully drawn into disentangling the processes involved in forming early sites. However, a number of significant pointers already begin to emerge:

1. The best preserved sites (e.g. FxJi 50 and 20 at Koobi Fora, and FLK Zinj, the FLKN complex at Olduvai) do not have the characteristics of 'hydraulic jumbles', though some fluvial modification may have taken place (Bunn *et al.*, 1980 [this volume, ch. 8]; Isaac, 1981a [this volume, ch. 12]; Potts, 1982).

2. At several coincident artefact and bone concentrations, significant numbers of stone-tool cut marks on bones have been found (Bunn, 1981; Potts and Shipman, 1981, and the same authors in this volume [Clutton-Brock and Grigson, 1983]). These involve (i) marks indicative of *detaching a limb or other body part* while the joint in question was still encased in skin, flesh and sinews, and (ii) marks indicative of muscle removal. Neither of these observations would be expected if the tool-using hominids were acquiring food such as marrow purely by using bare bones which had been abandoned by large members of the order *Carnivora*.

3. Considerable numbers of the bones bear numerous carnivore tooth marks. This is consistent *either* with their being the primary residue of carnivore feeding, or with the carnivores taking advantage of fresh bone which had been abandoned by some other exploiting agency – meat eating hominids for instance. We know that if hominids did accumulate and eventually discard fresh bones, carnivores would chew on the bones. Fresh bones are a very hot commodity in the African bush. In 1964, as part of our Olorgesailie work, we dumped our domestic bone refuse for several months at a peg out in the wilderness. At the end of the experiment the

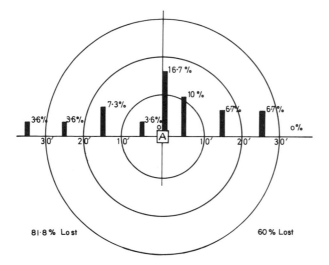

DISPERSAL OF BONES AS OBSERVED 14 SEPT. 1965.

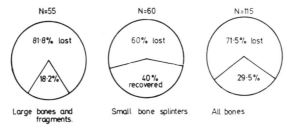

Fig. 13.4. Experimental test of the proposition that if humans concentrate fresh, defleshed bones, scavengers will rework and disperse a large proportion of the accumulations. At Olorgesailie, Kenya, domestic bone refuse was dumped at a peg in the bush over a 2-month period. Fifty-five large items (between 5 and 20 cm) were deposited and more than 60 small splinters (less than 5 cm). The upper graph records radial dispersal from the peg. The lower pie diagrams record total percentage loss from the site (from Isaac, 1967b [this volume, ch. 6]).

scavengers proved to have won game, set and match – only a few measly splinters remained (Fig. 13.4; Isaac, 1967b [this volume, ch. 6]). Similarly at Koobi Fora, Bunn tried to make a collection of experimentally fractured fresh bones. With the slightest relaxation of precautions, the local hyenas and jackals would slip into camp and remove the specimens! There is nothing hypothetical about carnivore reworking of hominid bone discards (see Brain, 1981; and Bunn, Potts, Shipman and Crader in this volume [Clutton-Brock and Grigson, 1983] for further information on carnivore action on bones, ancient and modern).

4. The numbers of individuals and the body parts present within several early artefact-plus-bone concentrations make it seem highly unlikely, if not impossible, that all animals represented had died within the site (Bunn, 1982; Potts, 1982 and both in this volume [Clutton-Brock and Grigson, 1983]). Almost certainly most of the remains had been *transported* and concentrated into a localized accumulation.

5. Keeley and Toth (1981) have examined flakes of siliceous rock types and have found that some 15–20 per cent of them show wear polishes with half or more of the polishes being meat polishes. It seems very probable that the basalt flakes that predominate in assemblages were also so used though the technique cannot be

applied to them. Toth and Schick (in preparation) [1983] and Jones (1981) have shown that simple flakes make very effective butchery tools with which even elephant carcasses can be opened and cut apart.

The sum of these findings make the following conclusions seem virtually inescapable (though we, and I imagine others, will continue to try to falsify them):

1. Early tool-using hominids were cutting up the flesh-covered carcasses of a range of large mammals (much larger than any reported consumed by chimpanzees, baboons or any non-human primates). One can only presume that they ate the meat that they cut.

2. The tool-using hominids transported parts of different carcasses to favoured places where substantial accumulations of artefacts and bones formed. At these places they surely broke bones, and presumably fed on the marrow thus exposed. We do not know precisely over what time span the accumulations form, but given the rate at which bone weathers in Africa no more than a few years is likely to have been involved, with ten years perhaps as an outside limit for the best preserved sites (Potts, 1982; Bunn, 1982a).

How do these findings affect judgement on the more general issues raised in the opening parts of this review? Do they settle questions regarding the antiquity of hunting and of food sharing? To this I would respond partly yes and partly no.

Meat-eating on a significant scale is indicated, but the existing data do not yet allow one to distinguish acquisition by hunting from acquisition by scavenging, though the assemblages from several sites are fully consistent with scavenging modes. Similarly, the recurrent *transport* of meat and bone to favoured locales is indicated, but does this imply active food sharing? Contrary to my earlier writings, I would now agree with various critics, Binford included, in admitting that while it may mean this, it need not necessarily do so.

Figure 13.5 provides graphic representation of several important aspects of the situation as I, in discussion with others including R. Potts, perceive it:

Fresh carcasses of medium to large animals, whether killed or found dead, would be periodically available in African savannahs (cf. Schaller and Lowther (1969) for pioneer work on this, though more studies are needed).

Such carcasses attract competing carnivores, many of which could be highly dangerous to hominids (e.g. hyenas and lions).

The use of cutting tools could have given relatively small-brained early hominids a competitive advantage (that is, it would have opened a new adaptive niche). They could have swiftly *detached* choice useful portions of carcasses).

These portions could then have been transported to places of comparative safety such as groves of climbable trees. The transport need not have been motivated by 'provisioning' or 'sharing' intentions, and it is entirely possible that although we archaeologists find the bones and artefacts on the ground, the feeding behaviours took place in trees (cf. Susman and Creel, 1979).

Now the existing record seems to document detachment and transport, but beyond this it is more ambiguous. What kind of social milieu existed? Did members of social groups other than the immediate acquirers get significant amounts of what had been transported? I confess we cannot yet answer these questions. We will have to think very hard about rigorous detectable criteria for distinguishing repeated, solitary, feeding-in-favourable places, from collective-social-feeding, which could in

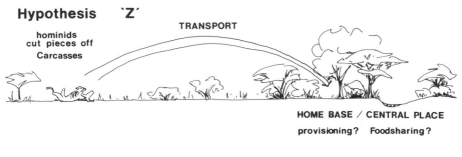

Fig. 13.5. Two variants of the hypothesis that early hominids were detaching portions of carcasses and transporting them. 'Y' – so as to provision young or share socially at a central-place site. 'Z' – so as to feed individualistically in a protected place, such as a grove of trees. (*Note*: the two are not mutually exclusive.)

turn be either provisioning (of infants), or tolerated scrounging, or active sharing (see definitions at the end of the paper). Perhaps different predictions can be made for the spatial patterns resulting from each of these possible behaviours. Then the predictions could be tested.

Meanwhile one can perhaps venture an opinion – the bone and artefact clusters often contain substantial numbers of items and are compact areas rather than very diffuse scatters. Perhaps this implies some kind of social focus – perhaps not. It could well be that whether or not sharing was 'intended', the recurrent transport of prime food to predictable, favourite places led to *de facto* dissemination of nourishment. This would constitute incipient central-place-foraging regardless of motivation.

I now recognize that the hypotheses about early hominid behaviour I have advanced in previous papers (e.g. 1978b) made the early hominids seem too human. It is important that we be as ruthlessly analytic as we can. I now favour relabelling the 'food-sharing hypotheses' as the 'central-place-foraging hypothesis'. This is a less emotionally charged label and surely implies components that are more readily testable.

Our studies are teaching us humility – it becomes increasingly clear, as Fig. 13.6 attempts to show, that the concentrations that we dig up represent only small fractions of materials that happened to drop out of complex, dynamic through-flow systems. Hominids, carnivores and other small creatures carried things into the places sampled by excavations and also took some away again. Flowing water did likewise. Given the complexity, one has to admit at some sites that a range of

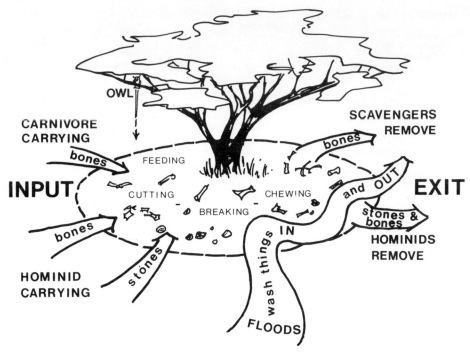

Fig. 13.6. Careful studies by Bunn, Kroll, Schick, Toth and others make it very clear that the sites sampled by excavations have been subject to interaction of many different processes with the material recovered as a residue which dropped out of the through-flow. However, it is hard to avoid the conclusion that the initial reason for concentrations of artefacts plus bones was the *localization* of hominid activity.

'*post-hoc* accommodative explanations' are all more or less equally plausible. However, fortunately, the evidences from some well-preserved sites such as FLK Zinj or FxJj 50 do constrain the range of possible interpretations more sharply. The existence of recurrent patterns also helps convert what in isolation would be *post-hoc* explanations into verifiable generalizations about processes. From all this emerges clear evidence of active bone acquisition, bone transport and localized concentration. The scepticism of Binford (1981) was salutary, but his specific conclusions that hominids were not significant meat transporters is in my opinion very probably wrong.

This account may appear to some as confirmation of the obvious and to others as a rearguard defence of a weak position. I would counter both reactions with the reminder that in pursuing the archaeology of the very remote past we are exploring behavioural *terra incognita*. If we are to avoid simply creating our origins in our own image, we have ruthlessly to expose all important propositions, however obvious seeming to potential falsification. Our research group and various colleagues have done this by seeking new lines of evidence. The early appearance of some human-like behaviours seems to be 'confirmed', others remain unconfirmed or untested.

Other papers have dealt with ideas concerning the possible evolutionary signifi-cance of an Early Pleistocene establishment of food-sharing behaviours, or, as I would now prefer to call it, 'central-place-foraging' (Isaac, 1978b, 1981a and b [this volume, chs. 12 and 7]; Isaac and Crader, 1981; Lancaster, 1978). Suffice it to say here that these papers argue that C–P foraging by small brained *non-human hominids* could well have placed novel selection pressures on abilities to communicate about the past, the future, and spatially remote places, and could have put selection on the development of reciprocation and intricate advance planning. All these could have been important in inducing the elaboration of brain function and brain enlargement. Clearly the arguments do *not* apply if central-place-foraging had not begun, so settling these questions really is important.

Zoo-archaeology has a major part to play in advancing understanding of early stages in the evolution of human behaviour. The outcome affects our understanding of long-term developments of human-animal relationships and of social relations among pre-human hominids.

Definitions

The English language takes distinctive human behaviour for granted and thus lacks vocabulary for behaviours that are normal in many animals. I offer the following explanations/definitions for terms relating to modes of feeding:

Individualistic-feed-as-you-go Self-explanatory term for what most primates do most of the time. Humans do it too at times, but we lack a good clear label. Barbara Isaac has suggested the medieval verb 'to pelf'.

Collective feeding Animals congregate at a single food source, but each feeds itself.

Tolerated scrounging Animals crowd round a single source controlled by one or a few who tolerate the acquisition of food by others. Well reported for chimpanzees with the term 'sharing' being used (e.g. Teleki, 1975). See Isaac (1978b), and Isaac and Crader (1981) for the introduction of the tolerated-scrounging term.

Provisioning Transport of food which is imparted to the offspring of the transporter.

Active-Sharing When food is transported to a social focus and imparted to other animals/humans, including other than the transporter's young offspring.

Acknowledgements

For the past twelve years I have been privileged to participate in the Kenya National Museum's field project at Koobi Fora. My understanding, such as it is, of the present state of inquiry derives in large measure from discussions with the good company of colleagues in this project and in neighbouring projects. In relation to the topic of this paper, I am particularly indebted to Henry Bunn, Richard Potts, Kay Behrensmeyer, John Speth, Pat Shipman and Alan Walker. Barbara Isaac joins in the discussions and draws many of the figures. For the light-hearted sketches for this paper, I wish to thank Jeanne Sept. The National Science Foundation has supported the work of our team.

IV

Technology

14

Squeezing blood from stones

Expectations about what information can be derived from stone tools has mounted in a series of leaps during the century or so that they have been studied seriously. When their existence was first rediscovered by Europeans in the golden days of Tournal, Boucher de Perthes, Falconer, Evans, and so on, everyone was delighted merely that they could be used as markers of man's geological antiquity. A short while later, with de Mortillet leading the field, it seemed that they could be used to define the rungs of the ladder of progress of humanity. Then as studies proceeded it became apparent to workers such as Breuil, Peyrony and Burkitt that the story was more complicated: stone tools varied in space as well as time – and they came to be used as the markers of palaeocultural entities each with its own geographic distribution and time range. For many, Stone Age prehistory became like a game of chess, with techniques and cultures weaving their way through time and space, with complex interactions. This approach can be characterized as 'culture historic', and in recent years there has been a reaction against it as the predominant goal of prehistory. Other schools of researchers have become convinced that stone tools contain information not only about culture history but also about the 'activities' of particular ancient societies. Interest in this idea arose gradually in various regions: in Africa I am aware of it in the 1950s in the writings of J. D. Clark (1959) and M. R. Kleindienst (1959, 1961). But it was the Binford and Binford paper of 1966 that dramatically caused attention to be focused on it. Since that time many prehistorians have entertained the conviction, or the hope, that suitable studies of stone tools could add spectacular new dimensions to our knowledge of the Stone Age past through the recognition of 'task forces', seasonal rounds, patterns of exploitation, and so on.[1] For ten years the feasibility of such inferences has been the cause of major debates among Palaeolithic prehistorians.

If one takes a dispassionate view of the mounting demands for information that we have made from stone tools, then it is clear that the temptation towards over-interpretation is very strong. They can be used in many ways – as markers of man's antiquity, as indices of 'progress', as symptoms of cultural differentiation in time and space and as indicators of the organization. However, we need to assess the limits to the amount of blood that can realistically be squeezed from these stones.

Fortunately, many prehistorians are now thoroughly aware that proper understanding will come not from artefacts alone but from artefacts in the context of distributions within and among sites and in relation to food refuse and other economic and ecological markers.

How are we to determine what information can realistically be obtained from stone tools and what the limits may be? Clearly this will have to be done by trial and error for each region and time period – we have to search for order and pattern among the artefacts and then see if we can find geographic, chronologic, economic, ecological, or sociological correlates of these patterns. However, when we work with the Pleistocene record we are in a way groping in the dark and herein lies the importance of Australia. It is only in this continent that we have direct observations on the lives of stone-using hunters living entirely in a world of hunters. In spite of the fact that stone tools have been a crucial agent of human adaptation for some 99.8 per cent of the 2.5 million years for which we have an archaeological record, in almost all other areas peoples, whether farmers or not, became involved in associated social, economic and technological complication. Australia is the only continent where the Stone Age archaeological record can be traced to the point where it merges with an ethnographic record of non-agricultured peoples dependent on stone tools. Thus, while Australian prehistory has its own intrinsic interest, it also has importance as a testing ground for ideas about the role of stone tools in the lives of people. It can also be a hone for methods of study.

In saying all this, I do not wish to imply that we can simply transfer chunks of Australian pattern and apply it to the Stone Age elsewhere. To do so would be to preclude the discovery of original, non-Australian patterns. However, we can use it to improve our insight into function and enlarge our imagination with regard to the processes involved in making, using and discarding stone tools. From this may come more realistic hypotheses for testing against the Pleistocene record, and alternative ideas about how particular configurations may have arisen in the past. Above all, our zeal to over-interpret may be tempered with constructive realism.

In Australia one can apply all the techniques and methods that are being developed by archaeologists who have nothing but archaeological evidence – but in Australia there is the unique opportunity of looking to see how the apparent results compare with 'ethnographic information'. The papers prepared for this conference show that this process is getting under way with great vigour and enterprise.

No two stone artefact assemblages are identical and it is common experience that any set of assemblages varies in a complex fashion with some distinctions being subtle and others being striking and conspicuous. In my understanding, the thrust of this conference was to discuss the interpretation of variation in stone tools as it bears on Australian data. The key questions can be paraphrased as follows: How well do stone tools work as markers of distinct cultural systems that changed, intergraded and interacted through time and space? How sensitive are stone tools as indicators of economic and ecological relationships? Can stone tools be used as clues to the differentiation of activities (seasonal or otherwise) within an individual socio-cultural system?

The contributions prepared for the conference range from case studies to tentative syntheses and exploratory generalizations – all of which bear on these questions whether or not there is explicit treatment of them. As an outsider to the specifics of Australian research, perhaps the most useful thing for me to do is to offer some commentary on methodology. In doing so I intend to point to the use of the ethnographic information which in Australia alone is available to serve as a kind of throwing stick to knock down unrealistic interpretations that the stones by themselves might tempt one to set up as theories.

Generalizations about material-culture history or about the economic relationships of stone tools must stem from the perception of recurrent patterns amongst a set of artefact assemblages. This necessarily involves comparative studies, and it is with aspects of that operation that this post-conference commentary will mainly be concerned.

The following steps are entailed in a comparative study:

1. Acquisition of a set of valid samples of assemblages relevant to the problem in hand.
2. Characterization of the assemblages (samples) in terms relevant to the questions that the inquiry seeks to answer.
3. Analysis – the assessment of patterns of resemblance and difference, plus search for regularities and order among the variables.
4. Projecting patterns discerned in the artefact evidence against external 'dimensions' such as time, space, habitat, site character, and so on.
5. Interpretation.

Fig. 14.1 presents a flow diagram of the process, and further comments are scattered through the text that follows.

The characterization of an assemblage

Stone artefact assemblages commonly show a range of forms that grade from specimens expressive of arbitrary, purposive design to forms that are merely determined by banal contingencies of simple stone-fracturing processes. The forms showing purposive design through trimming and retouch are by convention amongst Palaeolithic archaeologists termed 'tools', while the untrimmed flakes and chips are termed 'debitage' or 'waste'. This is a technical, morphological distinction that has nothing to do with recurrent judgements about whether individual objects in each series were or were not used. The two poles of the continuum intergrade through pieces in which the trimming or modification is minimal or highly irregular.

There exists also another axis of differentiation: items may display varying degrees of damage or wear resulting from use. Within an assemblage specimens will commonly range from those showing zero perceptible use damage to some showing comparatively conspicuous, intensive damage. Clearly items showing definite use

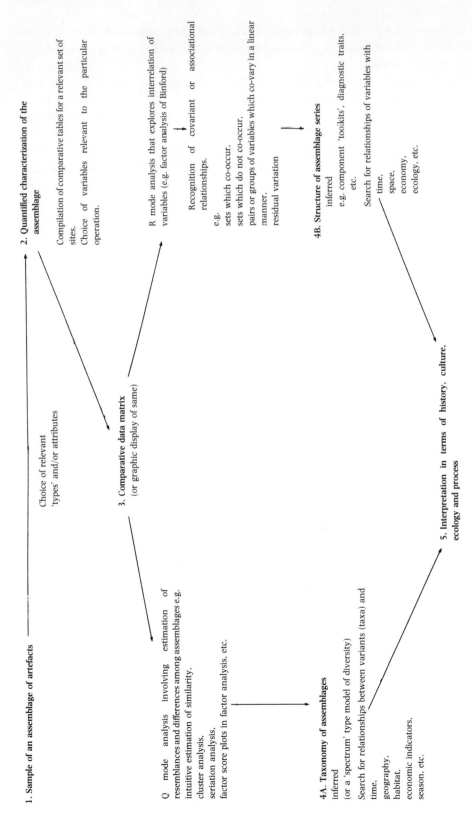

1. Sample of an assemblage of artefacts

Choice of relevant
'types' and/or attributes

2. Quantified characterization of the assemblage

Compilation of comparative tables for a relevant set of sites.

Choice of variables relevant to the particular operation.

3. Comparative data matrix
(or graphic display of same)

R mode analysis that explores interrelation of variables (e.g. factor analysis of Binford)

Recognition of covariant or associational relationships.

e.g.
sets which co-occur,
sets which do not co-occur,
pairs or groups of variables which co-vary in a linear manner,
residual variation

4B. Structure of assemblage series
inferred
e.g. component 'toolkits', diagnostic traits, etc.

Search for relationships of variables with
time,
space,
economy,
ecology, etc.

Q mode analysis involving estimation of resemblances and differences among assemblages e.g. intuitive estimation of similarity,
cluster analysis,
seriation analysis,
factor score plots in factor analysis, etc.

4A. Taxonomy of assemblages
inferred
(or a 'spectrum' type model of diversity)
Search for relationships between variants (taxa) and
time,
geography,
habitat,
economic indicators,
season, etc.

5. Interpretation in terms of history, culture, ecology and process

Fig. 14.1. Steps and procedures in the investigation of variation between assemblages.

damage were 'tools' in ordinary parlance, but they are not necessarily 'tools' in the technical sense.

Now it seems necessary to spell out these distinctions because changing practice in stone artefact analysis is causing confusion. The danger is particularly acute in Australia because of abundant ethnographic evidence that non-'tools' (in the technical sense) were in fact important 'tools' (in common parlance). One has to look at the history of method in Palaeolithic studies in order to understand the situation. In the early days of study in Europe it was customary only to collect and report the fancy trimmed forms which were designated as 'the tools'. Even amongst this selected series it was usual to base cultural classification of assemblages on particularly distinctive forms – *fossiles directeurs*. Now as time has gone on archaeologists have become more and more demanding with regard to the interpretation of stone tools and more and more conscientious over collecting and reporting complete assemblages. In Europe this movement culminated in the systematizations of typology and procedure that are associated with François Bordes (1950a, 1961b) and with de Sonneville-Bordes and Perrot (1954, 1955, 1956). These systems involve comprehensive reports on the technology of the assemblages including debitage, but cultural (industrial) taxonomy still depends largely on the composition of the trimmed tool series, which is commonly represented by the graphic display technique of a cumulative graph. That is to say, the features of the most highly designed segment of each assemblage remain the criteria for 'cultural' classification. Questions regarding aspects of the assemblages other than 'cultural affinity' must be answered by reference to other segments of the data.

During the past decade there has been greatly expanded interest in stone artefacts as indicators of 'activities' rather than as mere markers of culture historic patterns. This has led to the sense in some quarters that pieces for which use as utensils can be demonstrated as a result of use-marks are quite as important as trimmed tools, in the technical sense. This in turn is apt to lead to mixed characterization of assemblages and to comparative statements in which inferences based on specific 'design' elements and inferences based on potentially generalized use patterns become garbled up together.

In some regards it is regrettable that the upper Pleistocene stone artefact assemblages of western Europe have become, through the historical accident of priority, a standard of reference for the rest of the Stone Age world. It appears that they are more highly patterned than is the case in many other regions and as a consequence it has been easier to recognize the distinctions between 'tools', 'utilized' and 'waste'. There has thus been too little explicit discussion of the validity and practicality of these distinctions.

Because of this legacy of confusion, I would like to advocate that clear distinctions should be made in the presentation of artefact categorization data ('so called' typology).

These can be made to express the two axes of structure:

explicitly designed forms ↔ opportunistic untrimmed forms

perceptibly used items   ↔ items without traces of use

In my view a hierarchical layout along the following lines would promote clarity:

1. Gross composition of assemblage with percentages for A–D relative to the total sample: A. trimmed (designed) tools; B. utilized items; C. cores etc.; D. untrimmed flakes and flake fragments.

2. Detailed breakdown of sub-categories (≃'types') within each of the above categories – with percentages relative to the sub-sets A, B, C and D respectively.

3. Technological categorization – e.g. percentage of blades, of Levallois flakes, of bipolar flakes, etc. (This may cross-cut the A–D categories, with one specimen being simultaneously a 'tool' and a flake of a specific kind.)

4. Utilization-damage categorization, which may cross-cut A–D; i.e. if some items are simultaneously trimmed, designed 'tools' and show use damage of a kind also found on non-trimmed implements.

5. Other categorization data – e.g. raw material, fire damage, etc.

In many Australian industries, as with African and other stone industries, there is an important gradient within the trimmed 'tool' series from formalized, explicitly 'designed' forms to casually trimmed, opportunistic forms. In some instances this may justify splitting the 'tool' category between 'Formal' and 'Informal' divisions.

In addition to the categorization data discussed above, clearly there are many other qualitative and quantitative attributes which may be determined and reported. Some of these may be suspected to have primarily 'stylistic' significance (for example, scar counts on coeval Acheulian biface assemblages), while others may be suspected of having strong functional determinants (such as edge angles for scraper-like objects). The attributes selected for presentation should have definable relevance to questions being asked about the assemblages in question and they too should be presented in such a way as to facilitate clear thinking about implications for cultural affinity and for functional determinants.

This plea for orderliness in the gathering and presentation of data used to characterize assemblages for comparative purposes is made in all humility. There is no region where clarity of thought and presentation is yet common practice. The interest of Australian data and the fact of ethnographic information on function make orderliness of added importance. Mulvaney makes a similar plea in the closing paragraphs of his contribution to this conference.

Let me leave this point by rephrasing it in metaphoric terms: presentation of a meal as a series of discrete dishes does not prevent those who wish from making various kinds of amalgam – but it can be very hard to separate out the components of an Irish stew!

Recognizing pattern and order among assemblages

Once a series of samples has been characterized in a systematic and comparable fashion it is possible to seek to discover pattern and order amongst them. Once again procedure should be explicitly related to the questions that are being asked. If one is primarily concerned with culture as an information system operating within space and time, and if one wishes to measure degrees of interconnection and continuity, then most emphasis will be given to those aspects of surviving material culture that are sensitive to 'stylistic' and 'fashion' differentiation. Experience up to now suggests that the peculiarities of the most highly 'designed' components of stone-tool industries provide the best markers of idiosyncratic 'phases' and 'provinces' within the culture transmission system – and of continuity and interchange between phases and provinces. These objectives are of course closely allied to those involved in conventional 'culture historic' approaches. However, such an approach can perfectly well be concerned with 'process' and 'system' – as I have tried to show in my phrasing of these comments (see also D. L. Clarke, 1968, 1972).

Alternatively one may be primarily concerned with the role of artefacts as functional parts of an adaptive, economic system. Concern with generalizations regarding this aspect may be best rewarded by weighting sections of the data in which 'style' has minimal importance – for instance attributes that directly relate to edge character and mode of usage and so on.

It should be stressed that these two alternative lines of attack are not mutually exclusive, but in my opinion they are best kept separate until the integrative, interpretative stage of the investigation (step 5 of Fig. 14.1). If one feeds in an uncontrolled mixture of 'stylistic' and 'functional' data, then the patterns emerging from the analysis may be liable to more contentious and subjective lines of interpretation than are really necessary.

After acquisition of data on a set of assemblages for which comparative study is appropriate (for example, a set deriving from some geographic region and from a reasonably restricted time range), and after selection of variables germane to stated palaeoanthropological objectives, a 'data matrix' can be compiled (step 3 in Fig. 14.1). This is usually and most conveniently in the form of a table with the categories (types) and attributes (means, ratios and so on) labelled down the side and the assemblage samples labelled along the top. Each row then is comprised of all the expressions of a single 'variable' and each column is a list of the values determined for all the variables in one sample (Fig. 14.2).

The data matrix can often be so ordered as to facilitate direct perception of pattern. Thus if there is a question such as 'do samples from shore line locations (habitat I) differ from those on forested hilltops (habitat II)? – then it will be sensible to group these sets in the table so as to make a first judgement possible by scanning. Alternatively the columns can be grouped by time divisions, by geographic provinces and so on. Equally the variables can be grouped in relation to their supposed significance (such as 'style', 'technology', 'function').

The systematic analysis of a data matrix can proceed by two routes: one can compare assemblages (columns) assessing degrees of similarity and difference with regard to some or all variables. This is *Q-mode analysis* and it usually leads to a taxonomy of assemblages – or more rarely to a 'spectrum' type of ordering of assemblages as points along a continuum, as in seriation. Alternatively one may search for relationships between variables (rows) – this is *R-mode analysis*, which in Stone Age studies has been made known by the celebrated factor analysis of Binford and Binford (1966). (For good general accounts of the theory behind these

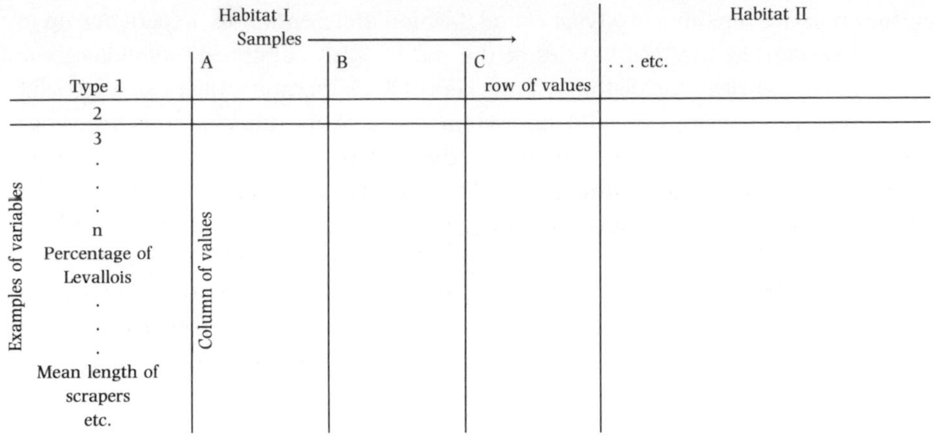

	Habitat I Samples ———————————————→				Habitat II
	A	B	C	. . . etc.	
Type 1			row of values		
2					
3					
.					
.					
.					
n Percentage of Levallois					
.					
.					
.					
Mean length of scrapers etc.					

Examples of variables (left axis) · *Column of values* (column A label)

Fig. 14.2.

terms, see Sokal and Sneath, 1963; Sackett, 1966; D. L. Clarke, 1968; Hodson, 1970.)

Both Q-mode and R-mode analyses can proceed by many different techniques, details of which fall outside the scope of this commentary. At the simplest, various graphic display devices can serve well, taking a few variables or a few cases at a time and projecting them. The *graphique cumulatif* of Bordes is one such technique – histograms, bivariate plots and ternary plots are others.

Alternatively more complex computation procedures can be undertaken. *Principal components analysis* and the closely related technique of *factor analysis* are capable of revealing either Q-mode or R-mode patterns and structures – though not every individual run will yield equally interpretable Q and R results. Other techniques include some form of cluster analysis, seriation, multidimensional sealing, and so on. Reviews by Cowgill (1968) and by Hodson and co-workers in *World Archaeology* provide good introductions to the application and relative merits of some of these techniques.

Multivariate techniques involve putting data into a hopper, letting them be processed in what for most of us is in some degree a 'black-box' and then getting a print-out suggesting certain patterns or relationships. It cannot be stressed too often that if bad or irrelevant data are fed in, then meaningless or misleading results will come out. Once a configuration or relationship has been suggested by a multivariate analysis, its archaeological reality and nature should be carefully scrutinized. Recent re-examination by means of bivariate plots of apparent covariant relationships with high correlation values in some early factor analysis studies has shown that peculiar distribution patterns for the pairs of variables can make Pearson r a misleading summary of the data – and hence brings the whole proceeding into question.

In this essay I am urging that the artefact data be analysed to discover its own intrinsic patterns and order. As already stated, I think that initially one should separate data relating primarily to 'design', to 'technology' and to 'function'. As patterns emerge in each analysis, the interrelationships which they may show can be explored and integrated.

Once pattern (taxonomy of assemblages) and structure (relationships between variables) have been established from the artefact data considered without regard to other non-artefact information, then these patterns and relationships should be projected against relevant external information. One must ask certain questions: To what extent do groupings within the comparative set coincide with time periods? To what extent with geographic regions or provinces? To what extent do they show direct relations with habitat or with non-artefactual evidence of activities? By asking and answering these questions the artefact study can make its contribution to understanding cultural history, cultural process, and to interpreting ecology and economy.

Synchronic and diachronic variation

Classic, culture historic approach to stone-tool archaeology is primarily concerned with change through time (diachronic variants) and differences between several regions at the same time (synchronic, allopatric variants). However, this approach makes little allowance[2] for the possibility that there could be markedly different stone-tool assemblages being generated in the same region at the same time (synchronic, sympatric variants).

Archaeological research in a number of areas has produced sets of assemblages that vary significantly, but for which the spectrum of variation may not be clearly associated either with geography or with time – within the limits of resolution of the latter. The most famous examples of this have been the patterns of variation reported in the Mousterian Complex (Bourgon, 1957; Bordes, 1961a; Bordes and de Sonneville-Bordes, 1970; Binford and Binford, 1966, 1969; Freeman, 1966; Mellars, 1970), or in the Acheulian and Oldowan complexes of Africa (Clark, 1959; Kleindienst, 1961; Isaac, 1969, 1972a [this volume, ch. 1]; M. D. Leakey, 1971; Binford, 1972). One possible solution to the dilemma that confronts a culture historian when he meets such a situation is to develop a model involving distinct co-existent traditions ('tribes') living in overlapping/interpenetrating territories. These kinds of solutions have been explored and advocated by various scholars (Bordes, 1961b; M. D. Leakey, 1971). Another solution which has had wide appeal is to explain large parts of the observed variation as being the artefactual expression of essentially the same people doing different things in different times and places. Thus, it is argued, they generate contrasting assemblages which are none the less *sensu lato* synchronous and sympatric. This is the 'activity differentiation model' made famous by Binford and Binford (1966).

Protagonists of these positions have stated them so clearly and so dramatically that, with all due respect, the palaeolithic intellectual scene has rather come to resemble the stamping grounds of rutting male antelope. However, there are other possibilities: all of the aforementioned positions assume persistent regularity in the determinants of stone artefact morphology through time and space – either as a consequence of stable 'tribal' tradition or as a consequence of persistent functional constraints. However, it is possible that *we should not assume such tight regularity and constancy*. What if a rather wide range of forms will fulfil the basic functions of stone tools equally well? What if the norms with regard to artefacts 'drift' about within broad limits? If we then draw samples whose time relations are not known in detail from assemblages representing such floating norms, would we not expect them to show sympatric and, at the low level of time-resolution, apparently synchronic variation? This is a possible way of explaining some of the bewildering variety that I have termed *stochastic* or *random-walk* patterning, and for which François Bordes in a letter to me used the phrase 'drunken man' progression. In people's eagerness to find grand designs, this possibility has perhaps as yet been too little considered.

It is important to stress that the random walk idea is *not* an explanation in its own right – it is the equivalent of residual variance in an analysis of variance. We must first seek to see how much of the variation in a given archaeological situation can be associated with time, space and independent evidence of activities, but we should not assume in advance that *all* variation has to be definably associated with these. I have developed these ideas in two recent essays and will not repeat them at length here (Isaac, 1972a, 1972b [this volume, chs. 1 and 2]).

Getting at activity differentiation

Over the past decade, concern with the relationships between 'activity' and the morphology of artefacts has clearly been a vital new development in Palaeolithic studies. Initially, the concepts involved were handled in part on the basis of the intuitive sense that assemblage character would necessarily express 'activities'. Many workers retained a certain sceptical reserve about the directness and simplicity of this relationship, but the objections were not often spelled out and forcefully stated. Now in the second round of studies the theoretical structure of the relationship between activity and assemblage characteristics is being explored, and also practical studies are yielding evidence about cases with ethnographic control. This symposium breaks important new ground in this regard and the material and discussions have importance far beyond Australia.

Ammerman and Feldman (1974) recently presented a discussion of the processes involved. From a purely theoretical point of view they point out that an archaeological occurrence incorporating artefacts is in fact generated by a complex series of processes, amongst which the following are conveniently separated as 'steps':

1. Manufacture of a given artefact or kit of artefacts.
2. Use of the artefacts for one or more purposes – with possible associated modification, resharpening or damage.
3. Discard of the artefact.

Now simple relationships between assemblage character and activity will only result from cases where usage and discard coincide spatially and temporarily and in which only one activity is represented. More usually one has to recognize that each of the three component processes has its own distinct spatial distribution – and its own rate of occurrence. That is to say, the total system involves complex differential mapping relationships between manufacture, use and discard. Ammerman and Feldman go on to show that such a system can generate 'correlations' between artefact forms used for different activities and mask correlation between forms used in the same activity.

This theoretical position had been formulated prior to the conference, but independently, direct observations of ethnographic situations were found at the conference to point in the same direction. The papers of Binford, Gould and Hayden constitute very important milestones in this regard. Binford introduces the verb 'to curate' to denote the carrying around of artefacts so that use occurs in many places and discard only in very few. Clearly explicit attention has to be given to this factor.

Both Gould and Hayden have provided estimates of the number of tools of each major variety made by the Aborigines of the Australian desert in the course of an average annual round of activities. This is extraordinarily valuable data of a kind that has not ever, as far as I am aware, been offered before for flaked stone tools. Lack of time prevented detailed discussion at the conference of these estimates and of discrepancies between them, but clearly the observations of the component processes involved have far more importance than the precise numerical values, which could not in any simple way be reapplied to other situations.

Gould also presents a clear account of spatial segregation between 'campsite' assemblages which occur in concentrated patches and special activity artefacts such as those for heavy woodcutting which occur dispersed over the landscape. This too is new and very important information. It immediately occurs to me that it may have relevance for the debate in African prehistory over whether the 'Sangoan' heavy duty assemblages are a 'culture' or a facies. It also establishes the importance for prehistory of studying dispersed and low density traces as well as the much more conspicuous and attractive dense patches on which attention has hitherto been focused.

A series of contributions also represents another line of attack on the important matter of the relationship between 'activity' and assemblage composition. These involve careful study of artefact assemblages from the recent past of areas for which ethnographic documentation exists. The objective in these studies is to gauge the extent of variability amongst assemblages that are reasonably regarded as deriving from the same land-use system, and then to seek to match archaeological data on assemblage variation with ethnographic information on the structure of daily and seasonal tool-using activities. Studies of this kind presented and discussed at the conference were those of Lourandos, McBryde and O'Connell, and similarly oriented research is also actively under way in Western Australia though it was not reported in detail (Sylvia Hallam, personal communication and in the Annual Reports of the Australian Institute of Aboriginal Studies).

O'Connell's study, of which a brief preliminary account is offered in this conference, involves his being shown traditional campsites by a group of Aborigines who abandoned a nomadic hunting and gathering life within living memory. The sites are identified by the informants as having been primarily used in wet or dry seasons and so on, and their proximity to significant food resources and raw materials can be determined. Collections of the stone artefacts lying around on these sites are then taken as a basis for attempting to determine the relationship between ethnographically determined site function and archaeologically determined assemblage characteristics. Clearly the research design involves risks and difficulties. The surface collection samples do not derive simply from the time span of ethnographic memory; the assemblages may have accumulated over centuries, even millennia, and they may incorporate items from much earlier, different material culture systems. In spite of these risks it seems possible that if a sufficient number of sites can be sampled any patterned differentiation that may have existed between artefact composition and site character will emerge. The interest of the propositions is quite sufficient to justify the continuation of O'Connell's experiment. As his paper in this volume shows [Wright, 1977], the most clear-cut patterning to emerge as yet relates to the relative availability of quartzite and chert at the sites. O'Connell was kind enough to allow me to examine the pilot series of samples collected to date. My impression was that variations, other than those associated with raw material frequencies, are rather subtle – they do not have the amplitude for instance of the much debated Mousterian variants in France or the Middle Pleistocene variants in East Africa. One must await the continuation of the experiment for more definite resolution of these matters.

McBryde has been engaged over the past decade in a careful archaeological and ethno-historical study of parts of northern New South Wales. Her contribution to this conference presents in miniature excellent exemplification of many of the questions discussed in this essay. Within her study area she appears to have differentiated both between subtly distinguished material culture systems ('microcultures') each appropriate to different subregions, and she seems to have assemblage differentiations within each subregion that are associated with specific habitats and economies ('activity facies'). This impressive body of archaeological information provides important opportunities for testing some of the analytical approaches discussed earlier, and for testing the results against ethnography.

Out of the discussions of 'activity facies' a proposition emerged at the conference – perhaps in Australia the archaeological expression of activity differentiation is weak because many crucial tools were carried about and used in many places where they were not discarded. By contrast, so the argument ran, perhaps in earlier segments of the Stone Age, such as the 'Mousterian' or the 'Acheulian', tools were more prodigally treated, being made for an immediate need and discarded on the spot immediately after use. This is a provocative hypothesis which should be tested. The Australian data cannot be used to prove or disprove the proposition, but it does enjoin caution.

Conclusion

Much of the current research reported to the conference seems likely to have a critical impact on our understanding of the relationship between stone tools and adaptation. Inasmuch as important studies remain uncompleted one should be careful to avoid premature judgement; however, some of the outcomes seem apparent already. In Australian prehistory, marked variations in stone-tool morphology and assemblage composition have complex time and space distributions. Attempts to find simple relations between the variants and economy, ecology or 'activity' do not seem likely to be successful, and prehistorians will have to continue to incorporate 'irrational' culture historic accidents in their treatment of the record. Also, if I judge the signs correctly, intra-cultural differentiation of assemblages in relation to 'activity' is detectable but it is far more subtle than many workers have supposed it would be. It seems to me that in general we are better off getting our inferences regarding 'activity', 'ecology' and 'economy' from food refuse, pollen analysis and the context of sites than from artefact studies alone.

Many facets of the information from past and present work in Australia are important for us all. Amongst the most important lessons are a series of warnings against the dangers of over-interpreting stone artefacts. It is clear that stone artefacts do provide a rich record of cultural transmission patterns ('culture-history') and that their characteristics are also related to economy and ecology. However, archaeology is not well served by unrealistic attempts to squeeze too much blood from stones alone. We need to concentrate our efforts on situations where the stones are only a part of a diverse record of mutually related traces of behaviour and adaptation.

Notes

1 Symptomatic of the urge for finer and finer exegesis of the record and of the concern with process has been the development of a remarkable vocabulary – our Stone Age hunters are now involved in 'extractive activities' and in 'procurement'. They 'maintain', 'curate' and 'utilize' their artefacts as they move about on 'maintenance' or 'monitoring' trips or as they do things at 'task specific localities' and so on. All of these terms cover concepts for which we need labels in our discussions but one also cannot help smiling at the way in which stone-using men have come to sound like operators in a Rand Corporation design for Pleistocene living.

2 Quarry sites and shell midden sites have long been recognized as liable to significant deviants from regional-phase norms.

15

Foundation stones: early artefacts as indicators of activities and abilities

The oldest known objects which were purposefully shaped by the hands of human ancestors came from geological layers in East Africa that can be dated as being between two and three million years old (Figs. 15.1 and 15.2).

What do we learn from these ancient artefacts about the course of human evolution? How far can we use the artefacts and archaeology to discover aspects of the way of life of the first stone-tool-making beings?

Evidence for toolmaking is often, and with good reason, used as signifying a watershed in the emergence of humanity (e.g. Lubbock, 1865; Darwin, 1871; Oakley, 1954; McBurney, 1960). And yet the use in the wild of tools by apes and

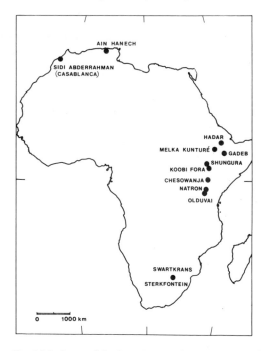

Fig. 15.1. Some of the important early sites in East Africa that are mentioned in the text.

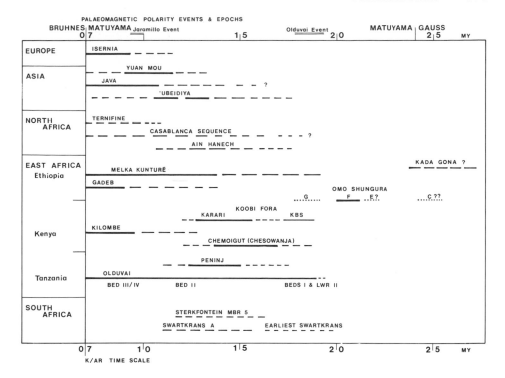

Fig. 15.2. Estimated chronological relations among the sites that yield early stone artefacts. (It is possible that the Kada Gona sample is as old as 2.5 or 2.6 mya but otherwise the record starts at about 2 mya.)

other animals is now well documented (e.g. Goodall, 1964; Hall, 1963; Jones and Sabater Pi, 1969. See Beck, 1980 for a comprehensive review). Equally, starting with the classic experiment of Wolfgang Kohler (1925), the tool-using abilities of chimpanzees and other animals have been tested. The data on animal involvement with tools do not diminish the distinctiveness of toolmaking as a characteristic of humanity, but they do make clear the need for comparative consideration of the earliest documented hominid tools. In particular (1) we need to assess the abilities that the early hominid toolmaking system reflects; (2) we need to inquire as to the extent of evidence for restructuring the behaviour and cognition of the earliest toolmakers; and (3) we need to ask what new patterns of natural selection were initiated that over the past two million years completed the evolutionary genesis of modern humans.

In 1959 when I first came to study in Cambridge, Charles McBurney sent me to read Kohler's *Mentality of Apes* and challenged me to think about the significance of this work for the archaeology of early hominids. Subsequently, for 25 years I have worked on stone tools and other archaeological traces of changing behavioural systems. In this chapter I want to look back and take stock of how we can now use archaeological inquiries to answer questions about stages in the development of human mentality. I overlap the coverage of John Gowlett's contribution to this volume [Bailey and Callow, 1986], but we approach the problem from different directions: he from the position that the early stone tools in themselves signify an essentially human mentality; I from the position that these tools may well have been formed by a non-human system which had within it the potential for evolutionary developments that would deliver the human condition as we now know it. The two essays converge on some issues and diverge on others. This dialectic should, in itself, be instructive.

Sequences of anatomical change

Before plunging into a consideration of the early stone tools and their archaeology, it is useful to pause and take note of relationships between artefacts and fossil hominids. (The record of the hominids themselves is treated in much more detail in Alan Bilsborough's chapter and I will focus only on the implications for archaeology of the conjunction of evidence.)

Figure 15.3 represents in highly simplified form some of the major features that have emerged from the fossil record of anatomical changes over the past four million years. The empirical situation that emerges can be summarized as follows:

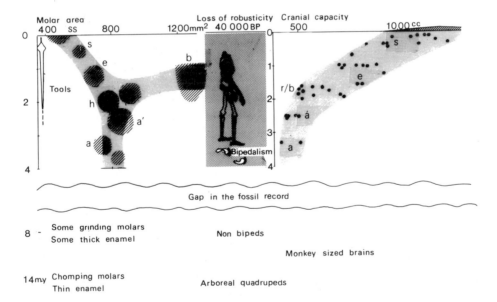

Fig. 15.3. The context of appearance of stone tools relative to anatomical changes; before about 4 mya there are no known significant specimens that can be identified as hominid. Between 2 and 4 mya upright bipeds existed with large teeth (samples and a′) and small brains. These are *Australopithecus afarensis* and *A. africanus*. No trends for change in brain size are evident and the teeth are all large, if variable. From 2 mya to the present a series of fossils exist that when placed against time show a trend toward reduced cheek tooth size (left) and to enlarged brain size (right). This is the *Homo* lineage. Tools appear at the point in time that these trends begin to be evident. (h = *H. habilis*, e = *H. erectus*, s = archaic *H. sapiens*, ss = modern *H. sapiens*, r = *Australopithecus robustus*, b = *boisei* (from Isaac 1983c, with permission of Cambridge University Press).

1. *Bipedal stance and gait* is evident in fossils representing the oldest-known members of the family Hominidae. These are the Laetoli and the Hadar fossils at 3.0 to 3.75 mya, with bipedalism evident both from the fossils and from the Laetoli footprint trail.

2. The fossils from between 4.0 and 2.0 mya are all variations on a single theme – they are all of small to moderate size and all have *small brains* (by modern standards) and *large teeth* (by any standard). This is the *Australopithecus* stage, with two species known, *A. afarensis* in East Africa and *A. africanus* in South Africa.

3. At about 2 mya there are several signs of change. Sedimentary layers of about this age and younger in many places contain remains of two hominid species. One of the species is larger in body size than earlier forms, has cheek teeth that are absolutely and relatively enlarged and retains a relatively small brain (these are the robust australopithecines *A. robustus* in South Africa and *A. boisei* in East Africa).

Specimens of the other species, when sufficiently complete, often show brain sizes that are significantly enlarged, absolutely and relatively (600–800 cc) and show molars that are somewhat reduced relative to earlier fossils. Body size is variable but not extremely small or large. These are the fossils classified as the oldest-known members of the genus *Homo* (*H. habilis*).

4. From two million years to around 0.1 to 0.2 mya one series of fossil hominid forms shows a trend of change involving brain increase and tooth reduction. Whether the trend of change is gradualistic or stepwise is still the subject of debate. Fossils in the middle sector of the time-range tend to be classified as *Homo erectus*. Those toward the recent end where brain size approximates modern, tend to be classified as archaic *H. sapiens*.

The robust australopithecines apparently became extinct around one million years ago.

The first point of particular interest in this consideration of the archaeological evidence is the fact that the oldest-known evidence of toolmaking appears at very much the same time as the evidence for the initiation of the two major trends of anatomical change (i.e. brain enlargement and tooth reduction). Coincidence is not sufficient to indicate causal connection but it does invite inquiry.

A second point of high importance for the issues being addressed is that the fossil forms in the time-range between two and four million years ago probably should *not* be regarded as human. These australopithecines had, from the neck down, the bodily form that today is exclusively characteristic of humans. At a distance of 100 paces with the light behind it, we would surely mistake an australopithecine for one of us, but on closer approach we would surely have found ourselves in the presence of a non-human being that happened to stand and to walk as we do. As already mentioned, atop their human form the australopithecines had essentially ape-sized brains, and they had very powerful jaws and big cheek teeth. It is my view that the australopithecines, gracile and robust alike, represent an adaptive pattern that has no living counterparts and that we do not yet understand ... However, this chapter is not about australopithecines, it is about using archaeology to try to understand aspects of the novel, new hominid form which appears in the stratified record around about two million years ago, namely *Homo habilis*. Being stone-tool-making hominids the representatives of this species perhaps qualify for the rubric 'human', but in some ways this begs the most important questions about them. The point at issue is whether we can use archaeology to assess their abilities and to understand aspects of their adaptive pattern. Such understanding will have to be sought through patient archaeological inquiry and if attained its features will surely be more subtle than the implications of assignment to one of a pair of opposing categories: human or non-human.

Archaeology

The archaeological evidence that comes down to us from two million years or so ago consists of the following: (i) flaked stones and the detached flakes; (ii) the distribution pattern of stone artefacts across ancient landscapes, with sparse scatters of artefacts in some areas, and with dense clusters in some places (sites); (iii) associations of artefacts and animal bones; and (iv) bones showing cut marks inflicted by stone tools (these occur both within sites and as scatters away from sites). This is essentially the material with which archaeologists must work in seeking enhanced understanding of the adaptive pattern of which the oldest-known, surviving tools were a part.

I have written elsewhere concerning aspects of the meaning of the association of artefacts and bones (Isaac, 1981a, 1983a [this volume, chs. 12 and 13]) and of aspects of spatial patterning (Isaac, 1981b [this volume, ch. 7]; Kroll and Isaac, in press [1984]). Here I will focus on the study of the artefacts themselves. I will address in sequence a series of questions for which research activity in the last few years is starting to provide answers. These are:

1. What are the morphological and technological characteristics of the earliest stone artefacts? How complex are they? How do they compare with later assemblages?
2. What role did early stone tools play in the lives of those who made them/ Why did they begin to be made some 2 to 2.5 million years ago?
3. What are the psychological, social and cultural implications of the early tools?

In addressing this nested series of questions, I will attempt, as Charles McBurney always did, to treat both substantive and methodological issues.

The range of artefact forms: intra- and inter-assemblage variation

The oldest-known artefacts that are definitely the result of purposive toolmaking activity are for the most part items formed when simple naturally occurring stones have been fractured according to the rules of conchoidal fracture. If stones are broken in this way two classes of objects immediately result: there will be thin, sharp slivers of stone (the flakes) and there will be larger pieces with concave scars and jagged edges. Though known by various names these two categories do indeed dominate the samples of early assemblages. In addition a third class sometimes occurs: lumps of stone which have been modified by being battered and pounded.

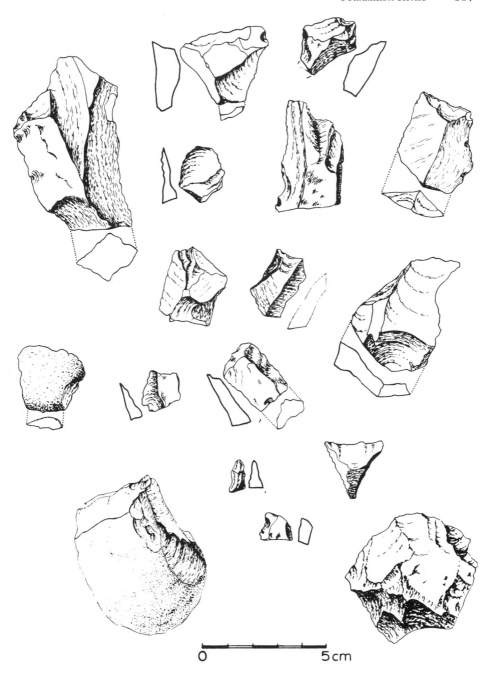

Fig. 15.4. A varied array of artefact forms from one early site (KBS at Koobi Fora). This sample series shows a wide range of shapes and hence of potential functions, but in terms of technology and deliberate design it is probably simple. The forms in the lower left and right corners are 'flaked pieces' (= cores = end chopper and discoid respectively), all the others are 'detached pieces' (= flakes and flake fragments). (Drawn by A. B. Isaac.)

A few rare examples of modified bones have also been reported (Robinson, 1959; M. D. Leakey, 1971; Brain, 1982).

Samples of fractured stones that are about 1.5 to 2 or more million years in age have been reported from Olduvai, the Shungura Formation at the Omo, Koobi Fora, Chesowanja, Melka Kunturé, Swartkrans and Kada Gona in the Hadar. (All of these very early assemblages tend to be classified as local variants of the Oldowan industry or industrial complex (M. D. Leakey, 1976)). For these Oldowan assemblages adequate quantitative information is available to me only for Olduvai, Shungura and Koobi Fora and in this part of the chapter I shall restrict attention to these samples. Some eleven or twelve assemblages have been reported for Olduvai (M. D. Leakey, 1971), some four for the Shungura and some thirteen or fourteen for Koobi Fora (Isaac, 1976c; Harris, 1978).

If all these samples of fractured stones were laid on laboratory tables, it would be seen that within the set from each site the pieces vary considerably in size and shape (for example, Fig. 15.4). Secondly it would be seen that the sets from different localities differ from each other in the sizes and forms common in each sample. This is normal for artefactual material of all ages, but for these very early assemblages some particular questions arise. Does this intra- and inter-site variation of forms and assemblage composition imply a cultural system of considerable complexity? Can we use the patterns of differentiation as measures of complexity and as clues to adaptation during the oldest-known phases of artefact manufacture?

Clearly these are problems which archaeologists of the Pliocene-Pleistocene share with all Palaeolithic archaeologists. However, as our studies have proceeded we have become aware of the possibility that our own procedures have tended to obscure the answers to the foregoing questions. In order to describe the diversity of forms and assemblages we have used numbers of typological categories, which at Koobi Fora may serve to make the system appear more complex than it really was (Isaac, 1976c; Isaac and Harris, 1978).

One of the major stumbling-blocks with which we have grappled is the time-honoured distinction between 'tools' and 'non-tools', or debitage. From the early Koobi Fora artefact samples we have formed the strong impression that obtaining sharp-edged, knife-like flakes was probably the main objective of the ancient stone-knappers and that the lumps of stone from which the flakes were detached functioned first and foremost as the cores from which the flakes derived. However, prevailing convention would oblige one to formulate the above statement as follows: 'the flakes which belong in the archaeological category debitage, or "non-tools", were really the most important tools, while the lumps of stone from which flakes have been detached are put in the category "tools", but many of them may have been cores instead of tools'.

The truth of the matter seems to be that some flakes were tools, and that some flaked lumps were cores only, while others were both cores and heavy-duty tools. This has been pointed out by M. D. Leakey (1971) and by J. Chavaillon (1976), for instance. However, the prevailing system of labels is undeniably confusing to everyone outside the small circle of primary research workers.

In our own analysis we have decided to cut the semantic knot. We are continuing to use the typological categories of Mary Leakey (1971), but are regrouping some of them, and revising the labels of the higher-order groupings. Our macro-distinctions are as follows:

> *Flaked pieces* (Series FP) – pieces from which significant flakes or chips have been removed. This includes (a) raw lumps of stone from which flakes have been detached; and (b) flakes or fragments which have had flakes struck off them, after their separation from a parent block.
>
> *Detached* (Series DP) – flakes, flake fragments and shattered flaking products.
>
> *Pounded and battered pieces* (Series PP) – relatively massive stone pieces that do not fit well within the series FP and which show signs of bruising and chipping. This includes such categories as hammerstones, anvils, modified battered cobbles, etc.

These categories do not semantically prejudge the complexity of the system or the functions of the objects, and we want to try to see if using these labels will allow us to communicate more clearly.

Going on to the interpretation of inter-assemblage variation, after a good deal of floundering around we have decided to follow a stepwise approach that attempts to deal with potential explanatory factors in sequence. At each step one seeks to judge how much of the morphological variation within and between assemblages can reasonably be attributed to a specific influencing factor. Any residual unexplained variance is then carried forward for potential explanation by reference to the next factor up the scale. This is the classic scientific procedure known as the Method of Residuals. Assuming that the object of the exercise was to get sharp edges, the steps are as follows:

Step 1. What kind of stone fracture forms would be predicted from the simplest possible 'least-effort' flaking strategy applied to the kinds of naturally occurring stones that were available? For instance, if a plentiful supply of lava cobbles were being worked this way we would predict unifacial so-called 'choppers' plus a range of flakes including many cortical flakes. If small quartz pebbles were the raw material, then the fragmentation products of bipolar smashing might be the prediction.

If a given assemblage largely meets the appropriate least-effort prediction, the analysis stops at that point. There is no need to invoke other explanations for the observed range of forms. If it does not and if, as is usually the case, it comes from a site away from the actual source of stones, we can proceed to step 2.

Step 2. What series of forms would be predicted in addition to least-effort flaking, if economy of transport were a factor? If instead of picking up another stone one kept on flaking the same stone then 'core-scraper', discoid and polyhedron forms plus many more non-cortical flakes would be predicted. Such assemblages look more complex.

Step 3. If there remain artefact forms or aspects of assemblage composition that are not accounted for in steps 1 and 2, then it may be legitimate to ask if the assemblage is biased in favour of forms that would facilitate a particular kind of task, e.g. cutting, boring, hacking or scraping or some such? Or conversely,

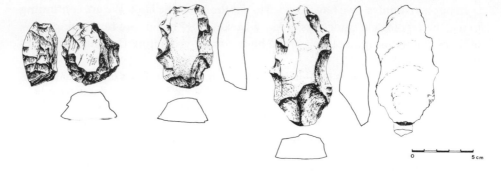

Fig. 15.5. 'Karari scrapers' (Harris, 1978). These are examples of relatively fancy-looking early stone tools. The series shows a regular form that might be taken as evidence of imposed design. However it is also possible that the flaking strategy that produces them is simply an orderly one that minimizes effort in the production of numerous flakes. If this is correct, these items should be understood as cores which are fossilized habits, rather than as carefully conceived and executed tools of a specific type. (Drawn by A. B. Isaac.)

Step 3 or 4. Are there unaccounted-for forms present which may represent the resharpening or rejuvenation of certain implements?

Finally (*step* 5), if there remain significant features of variation not accounted for by the foregoing, then it is legitimate to consider the possibility that arbitrary, stylistic differences between particular material culture systems are being observed; or, if the sample spans a significant time-range, that they document contrasting stages in the development of material culture systems as a whole.

The application of this type of logic is in its early stages, but it does seem to be helping us towards an orderly way of assessing the minimum levels of mental and cultural complexity that the early assemblages must represent.

In the early assemblages, at least at Omo and Koobi Fora, it appears to me that the great majority of pieces can be accounted for by steps 1 and 2. That is to say that *before* 1.5 mya there seems to have been a minimum of imposed design.

I am suggesting then that the early assemblages do not involve distinct, arbitrary imposed design. I am not intending to deny that they display orderly, purposive ways of flaking stone. They do display such features. A discoid is one neat, orderly way of getting a great many flakes from a single piece of stone. A Karari scraper is another such (Fig. 15.5). These can in fact be regarded as fossil habits, and like habitual skills in modern life they were presumably acquired and perfected during an individual's life-span, and presumably transmitted to others by teaching and the opportunity for imitation. However, insofar as they are predictable economy of effort strategies they cannot be treated as idiosyncratic markers of particular traditions.

Thomas Wynn (1981a and 1981b) has also tackled the problem of distinguishing assemblages that represent simple technology from assemblages representing more complex abilities. The logic of his study is not dissimilar in the sense that he formulates a stepwise series of theoretical predictions for successive levels. However, in his study the basis of prediction is not economy of effort in flaking but an analysis

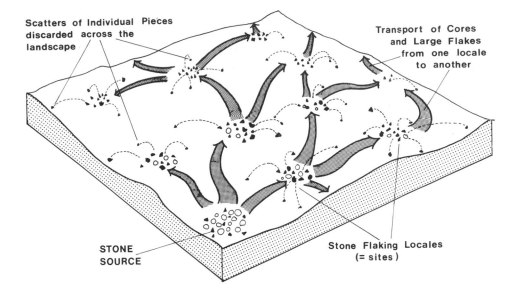

Scatters of Individual Pieces
discarded across the
landscape

Transport of Cores
and Large Flakes
from one locale
to another

STONE
SOURCE

Stone Flaking Locales
(= sites)

Fig. 15.6. In recent years it has become clear that early stone artefacts should be envisaged not as static items in fixed toolkits, but as the fallout of a complex system of extraction, manufacture, transport, use, resharpening, re-use, renewed transport and eventual discard. In this diagram the system is envisaged as a reticulate outflow from a source of raw material over a segment of landscape. The nodes of the system have conspicuous quantities of artefacts and are what archaeologists call sites. 'Sites' themselves also become potential secondary stone sources (Potts, 1982), with pieces moving between them and being reflaked at successive nodes. In addition pieces are spread out as a scatter over the landscape.

of organizational principles that follow the precepts of the psychologist Piaget. There are a number of points of convergence between the results of Wynn's analysis and those that we and other archaeologists are reaching by more conventional means. However, Wynn's study is focused on the geometry of flaked pieces, with the assumption that these are ends in themselves rather than byproducts.[1] As already indicated, this is an assumption that we regard as very uncertain. Further discussion of Wynn's work is deferred to the section dealing with assessment of ability and complexity.

When our research group at Koobi Fora groped towards developing this approach to analysis, it became clear that the predictions at each step necessarily involved experimental stone-flaking (see also Bradley and Sampson, this volume [Bailey and Callow, 1986], for replication studies). This work was taken on for the group by Nicholas Toth (in Bunn *et al.*, 1980 [this volume, ch. 8]; Toth, 1982). More detailed accounts of the applications of the method are in preparation for publication elsewhere. Toth's work also made us more aware of additional kinds of complexity in the early artefact-making/-using/-discarding system of which we were sampling the residue. It became clear that the fractured stone recovered from any given site cannot be regarded as an entire entity. It is simply the material which happened to drop out of a system of hominid acts that caused stone to 'flow' out over the landscape from natural sources, with progressive modification occurring as flow proceeded. Figure 15.6 illustrates this conception of early stone-tool production as a dynamic flow system. In Bunn *et al.* (1980: Fig. 12 [this volume, ch. 8]) Toth provided specific documentation of the dynamic character of the system by showing that some items had been brought in after they had been flaked elsewhere, and that other items had been flaked at site 50 and then removed (see Toth, 1982 for details).

Gauging complexity / recognizing simplicity

The notion that different stone-artefact assemblages show different degrees of complexity is itself a compound notion. I would suggest the following as some quantifiable attributes, each of which could measure some aspect of increasing complexity in a flaked-stone material culture system.

1. The number of flake scars removed between initial working and discard.
2. The number of strategically distinct steps involved (e.g. first striking a large flake and then trimming it into a handaxe).
3. The imposition of a standard, arbitrary form, which is repeated in numerous cases.
4. The presence in assemblages of an increasing number of distinct, arbitrary forms, each manifest by a series of standardized, repeating items of like form.
5. The existence of marked inter-assemblage differences, which are not determined primarily by differences in raw material assemblage.

Attributes 3 and 4 imply increased orderly intra-assemblage differentiation. This in turn makes possible more elaborate patterns of inter-assemblage variation and differentiation. These concepts are illustrated in Fig. 15.7.

In attempting to apply this kind of yardstick, Fig. 15.9 provides a schematic ranking of examples with criteria indicated. Tentatively I would suggest that what emerges is (1) that the Omo Shungura assemblages are the only ones that come close to being absolutely as simple as they could possibly be; (2) that those assemblages that are older than 1.5 mya are all towards the simple end of the scale by comparison with many (but not all) later assemblages.

Two things should at once be stressed about this tentative assessment. First, this is a ranking of complexity of design and execution. It does not necessarily reflect function and utility (that topic is taken up separately). Secondly, the ranked comparisons are with later, more elaborate human systems, not with animal systems. All these toolmaking behavioural manifestations are significantly more complex than any toolmaking procedure yet reported for a free-ranging non-hominid animal. Two separate wild chimpanzee tool-usage behaviours involve some of the elements: the making of termite fishing probes sometimes involves modification and short-term anticipation, while the use of nut-cracking hammers may at times involve long-distance transport and planning ahead. Oldowan toolkits required both to an even greater degree (Boesch and Boesch, 1981; Gowlett, this volume [Bailey and Callow, 1986]).

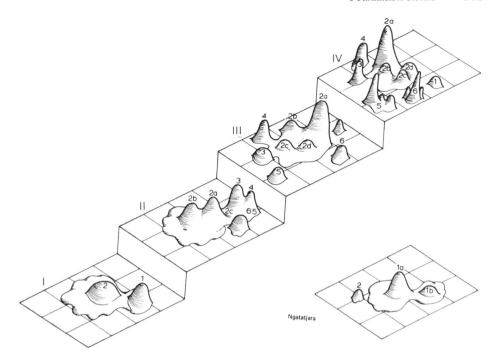

Fig. 15.7. The complexity of stone-tool assemblages certainly increased during the Pleistocene, and yet the total range of shapes does not change very much. This diagram provides an intuitive model of the pattern: the horizontal grid represents 'range of shapes'; the anthill-like mounds are intended to represent frequency distributions of shapes. In early industries there are many shapes but only very weakly developed, poorly standardized modal forms. In some but not all late Pleistocene industries there are relatively numerous highly standardized ('steep') modes. Key: I = Oldowan: 1 = core choppers, 2 = casual scrapers; II = Acheulian: 2a = scrapers, 2b = nosed scrapers, 2c = large scrapers, 3 = handaxes, 4 = cleavers, 5 = picks, 6 = discoids; III = Mousterian: 2a = racloir, 2b = grattoir, 2c = r. convergent, 3 = perçoir, 4 = point, 5 = burin, 6 = biface; IV = Upper Palaeolithic: 2a = grattoir, 2b = nosed scraper, 2c = raclette, etc., 3 = perçoir, 4 = point, 5 = burin, 6 = backed blade, etc. Th Ngatatjara frame represents an ethnographically reported recent stone toolkit from central Australia (Gould, Koster and Sontz, 1971): 1a = hafted adzes (purpunpa); 1b = scrapers (purpunpa), 2 = bec (pitjuru pitjuru). The figure is reproduced from Isaac 1976d, with permission.

Function

Notable effort went into transporting stone and making the early sharp-edged artefacts and this surely means that they helped to fulfil a significant need or needs in the lives of the early hominids. The question then arises as to what these needs were and how they affected the form of the first tools. Three lines of approach suggest themselves:

1. Consideration of aspects of the lives of extant non-human primates to ascertain whether there are significant activities in which using sharp-edged tools would be adaptive (i.e. where sharp tools would cut costs and/or raise benefits).

2. Experimental inquiry designed to ascertain what tasks the early artefact forms *are* capable of performing – and to measure how well the different forms work for different tasks.
3. The search for direct evidence regarding the actual usage of early artefacts.

Non-human primates

Food is the basic commodity in the economy of all animals, and modern evolutionary ecology strongly implies that in a search for the adaptive significance of a behavioural shift one should start with consideration of food acquisition.

Chimpanzees, along with gorillas, are the closest living relatives of *Homo* and the hominids. Detailed field studies of their lives and foraging strategies have been made in recent years (see various papers in Clutton-Brock, 1977, and in Hamburg and McCown, 1979). From these studies it emerges that chimps are predominantly fruit and leaf eaters, for which foodstuffs the use of sharp-edged tools would make little or no difference. This is even more true for gorillas which predominantly eat soft foliage. However, chimpanzees do take some foods where one could argue that cutting tools would reduce costs and raise benefits. (Throughout the discussion that follows I shall use the measures developed as part of optimal foraging theory as a yardstick for gauging adaptive significance. See Schoener (1971) for the basic concepts and Winterhalder and Smith (1981) for application to humans.)

Chimpanzee use of stems and sticks to fish and probe for termites and ants has become particularly well known and their use of stones for pounding nuts is also now well documented (see Beck, 1980 for summaries and a comprehensive bibliography). However, neither of these are tasks which would be assisted by sharp-edged fractured stones. Chimpanzees do go after honey and may use sticks to pry into and enlarge hive openings. A heavy-duty stone chopper or pick would presumably do even better at this task. Chimps also scratch in termite or ant mounds, a task for which a stone pick or a sharpened wooden stick would presumably be advantageous. Finally, chimpanzees are now known to hunt (Teleki, 1973) and even to scavenge (Hasegawa *et al.*, 1983). The most detailed data are available for Gombe Reserve where predation is normally restricted to smallish animals (2 or 3 to 10 or 12 kg). Once a prey animal is seized, clusters of chimps form with six animals as the modal number participating in consumption (range 4–15). The prey is pulled, pried and sucked apart by hands, fingers, teeth and lips. In spite of the large number of participants and the small size of the carcass, the average time taken for consumption is 3.5 hours (range 1.5 to 9.0 hours). Clearly this is a feeding activity which could be speeded up given the use of sharp-edged cutting tools.

All of the great apes at times feed on bark and cambium using their incisors and canines to strip and scrape. One imagines that under some circumstances sharp tools could facilitate this. They all, except gorillas, at times feed on insect larvae under bark or in rotting wood. Sharp tools might aid this also.

If the spectrum of primates considered is broadened beyond the apes, only one or two significant sharp-tool needs are added.

Underground foods such as bulbs and corms are much more important for baboons than for other apes. These are rooted up with hands and fingers and it often looks as though feeding would be facilitated by a tool – ideally a pointed stick or bone, though possibly also a pointed stone pick form could be used. However I am not aware that any significant cases of baboon digging-tool-use have been reported.

Feeding on seeds or beans within pods might sometimes be facilitated by use of a knife, but many primates process and disengage such foods very deftly with their incisors. Detaching or shredding bark is a feeding practice in which numbers of different primates engage (e.g. chimp, gorilla, orang), which well might be speeded up if appropriate tools were used.

Thus it emerges that there *are* a number of primate feeding modes for which the use of sharp-edged tools would reduce handling time and increase yield. This means that the adoption of fractured stone tools need not have been associated with the adoption of entirely novel foods. Intuitively I would guess that the primate data might be taken to indicate the following possible functions for early flaked-stone tools: (i) cutting up meat; (ii) scraping bark and cambium; (iii) getting at honey, insect nests and insect larvae; and, if one admits tools to make tools, (iv) sharpening digging-sticks for getting at bulbs and tubers.

None of the foodstuffs involved in this list is of prime importance in the lives of primates (with the exception perhaps of shallow bulbs for some baboons), and yet it should be noted that items 1 and 4, meat and tubers, are foods of great importance for most tropical humans (see Hatley and Kappelman, 1980; Isaac and Crader, 1981; Gaulin and Konner, 1977). This raises the strong possibility for consideration that sharp-edged tool-use made the human emphasis on these things possible.

What if one broadens the scope of potential primate tool needs to include *weapons?* Then intra-specific agonistic display and food acquisition all become possible functions. However, none of the early forms of stone artefact would be as effective in these uses as would be a thrown stone (Calvin, 1982; A. B. Isaac in press [1987]), or a brandished club or a pointed thrusting stick.

Feasibility and efficiency

In recent years formal programmes of experimentation have been initiated that have been designed to ascertain what can and cannot be done with stone artefacts of the kind recovered from Lower Palaeolithic sites. These formal experiments carry on an informal tradition begun long previously by many eminent prehistorians such as Breuil, Alfred Barnes (1947) working with Coutier, Louis Leakey, Desmond Clark, François Bordes, Jacques Tixier and others.

Working with Mary Leakey and the Olduvai research group has been Peter Jones (1979, 1980, 1981) and with the Koobi Fora group Nick Toth (in Bunn *et al.*, 1980 [this volume, ch. 8]; Toth, 1982, *in press*). The account which follows is based on the results reported by these scientists, tempered by occasional experimentation of my own or by participation in Toth's experiments. Those interested in the details of procedures should refer to the primary authorities.

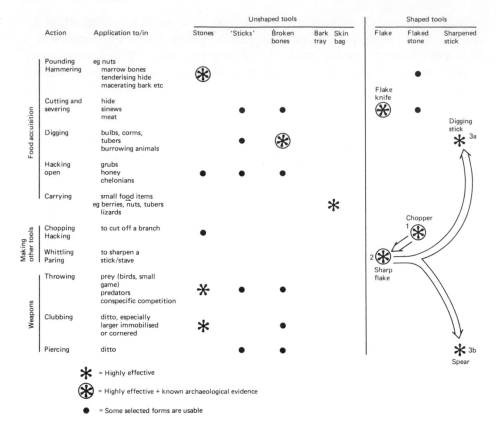

Fig. 15.8. A chart showing a series of basic tasks with potentially useful tool forms indicated. The series shown includes naturally available tool forms and shaped items.

The state of knowledge on this topic can perhaps be best represented by matrix configurations which cross-tabulate a set of potential complement forms against a set of basic tasks or functions. In Fig. 15.8 various natural object forms as well as fractured stone artefacts are represented. Only a binary distribution is made within the fractured stones: detached pieces (= flakes, etc.) and flaked pieces (= cores and core tools). Two levels of effectiveness are distinguished, namely 'very effective' or 'somewhat/variably effective'. In addition the chart identifies positive archaeological evidence for the performance of the particular task with a given form. In Fig. 15.9 finer distinctions are made among the various artefacts formed by conchoidal fracture processes. For each task the different forms are ranked in descending order of effectiveness.

As the charts imply, Jones' and Toth's work is starting to elucidate this whole question. It is now clear, first that a great many very important potential functions are well fulfilled by plain unretouched flakes. This includes cutting up animals, including animals ranging in size up to the size of an elephant (Toth and Schick, 1983; Jones, 1981 and *pers. comm.*). Equally such flakes can be used for scraping bark or for whittling a pointed end on a stick (though serrated/denticulate edges often accomplish this task more readily). Secondly it emerges that a great many

	Severing a branch	Wood shaping	Hide slitting	Dismembering small animal	Dismembering large animal	Meat division	Summary
Smallish flakes & flake fragments	0	2	3	3	2–3	1	very useful for *all* cutting and whittling operations, not useful for heavy-duty wood hacking
Flake-scrapers	0	3	2	2	2		the best form for wood shaping/whittling
Choppers and related forms 300 g	2	Var	0	0	Var		moderately useful for hacking off branches, not very good for cutting off branches
Core-scrapers	2	3	0	0	Var		hollow sectors of an edge make good spoke shaves (also true for some choppers)
Handaxes	1	Var	1	1	3		good butchery tools for large animals. Serviceable also for branch severing and hide splitting (see also Jones, 1981)
Cleavers	3	?2	2	1	3		the best form for branch severing and excellent large animal butchery tools (see also Jones, 1981)

0 = unsuitable; 1 = possible but difficult; 2 = serviceable but not usually optimal; 3 = tends to be the best form; Var = varies with the individual piece

Fig. 15.9. A chart showing the basic tool forms of the African Early Stone Age ranked in relation to serviceability in a series of basic functions. (Based on reports in Toth, 1982, Jones, 1980 and personal observation and experiment.)

flaked pieces (core tools such as choppers, core scrapers, polyhedrons, discoids, etc.) are not particularly useful for most tasks, though some can be useful for hacking off branches and so on, and others could serve in wood whittling, and I suppose in scraping bark. Thirdly, the larger forms that involve extra manufacturing steps and which come in at the beginning of the Acheulian (about 1.4 mya) often have fairly delicate edges and tips, and so far their only demonstrable highly effective function is in the butchery of very large animals (Jones, 1981; Toth, 1982). Cleavers are also very effective branch-severing tools but the rarity of conspicuous damage on their delicate edges suggests that they were not very often, if ever, used for this (exceptions being damaged cleaver edges recorded at Sidi Zin (Gobert, 1950) and at some Olorgesailie sites (Isaac, 1977b)).

What deserves to be stressed is the fact that *all* of the important functions or needs for cutting tools discussed in the section on non-human primates can be satisfied by the earliest-known stone-tool assemblages. The combination of knife-like flakes and stone lumps with jagged edges would certainly allow for

> cutting up carcasses
> hacking off a stick or club
> sharpening a stick
> widening the opening of a hive
> detaching and shredding bark or cambium
> hacking open logs to get at insect larvae

The sharpened sticks in turn could be used for digging or spearing. Under the right circumstances all of these abilities could serve to augment the rate of food acquisition – that is to say the sharp-edged tools could alter the diet breadth and dietary focus by changing the absolute feasibility and/or the benefit/cost ratio for certain foods.

Although not discussed up to this point, there are some other functions that are part of the basic tool repertoire of the non-human primates. These include the making of carrying devices such as trays and pouches. The early sharp-edged artefacts could perfectly well facilitate such fabrication, though we do not know whether or not they were so used.

It should also be stressed that although archaeologists have tended to emphasize the lumps of stone off which flakes have been struck (i.e. the so-called 'tools'), their adaptive significance is if anything less than that of the flakes (i.e. the so-called 'debitage'). Proposals for a new nomenclature that will be less ambiguous have already been set out.

In summary, the comparative consideration of the feeding practices and their limitations among non-human primates suggest possible 'openings' for an innovative primate that began to make and use sharp-edged tools. If meat from very large carcasses was becoming an important food, such tools would have been necessities not accessories.

The feasibility studies show that even the earliest, simplest flaked stone artefacts comprise versatile toolkits. The range of suggested uses overlaps heavily with speculative ideas that have been around for a century – but the basis for guessing and estimating is made more explicit. Finally, we begin to have specific evidence for some usages and this in part converges with the other two lines.

Hard evidence

During the past few years archaeologists have acquired the first firm, direct evidence regarding uses to which ancient fractured stones actually were put. There are two main lines of such evidence. The first has been called 'smoking gun' evidence and consists of the marks inflicted by stone tools on some substrate which so far for the very early period has always been bone.[2] The second line of evidence comes from the traces of use that are preserved on the edges of stone tools themselves, notably wear polishes of the kind first effectively studied by Keeley (1980).

Cut marks made by stone tools on bones of Lower Pleistocene age were first discovered by two young scientists, R. Potts and H. Bunn, who were working with the Olduvai and with the Koobi Fora archaeological bone collections (Bunn, 1981, Potts and Shipman, 1981). More detailed accounts have subsequently appeared, including some legitimate debate regarding criteria and procedures for tooth marks and other scratches (Bunn, 1982a, 1983a; Potts, 1982, 1983; Shipman, 1981b, 1983b). However, details of the debate notwithstanding, it is clear from the evidence that stone tools were being used to cut up carcasses. The positioning of marks ranges across the head, vertebrae, ribs, pelvic girdles and limb bones. Some are so placed as to imply the separation of joints. Others are along shafts and presumably relate to detaching muscle and tissue. Still others are at the distal extremities of limbs where skin and sinew removal are the most likely functions of the cuts. In these last cases it is unclear whether the stripping of skin or sinews as desired materials was intended or whether access to marrow was the objective. However this may be, the new evidence settles whatever doubt may have remained regarding the proposition that early stone tools were used in butchering animal carcasses. The carcasses with marks on them range in size from gazelle (about 20 kg) up to giraffe (< 1,000 kg), hippo (up to 2,000 kg) and elephant (up to 6,300 kg) so it is clear that at least sometimes stone tools gave their makers access to meat on a scale unknown in any non-human primate.

The second line of evidence is less dramatic but more versatile. On a sample of about fifty fine-grained siliceous flakes from the Koobi Fora Upper Member sites, Keeley and Toth (1981) found unambiguous use-wear polishes on nine, and probable but less definite traces on a few more. Applying distinctions developed for flint and checked in experiments performed by Toth with the same materials as the 1.5 my-old artefacts, Keeley and Toth report the following results:

> polishes of the kind induced by cutting meat – 4 specimens
> polishes of the kind induced by cutting wood – 3 specimens
> polishes of the kind induced by cutting plant stems – 2 specimens

An additional three or four specimens had probable meat polish.

The strong representation of meat in the series is consistent with the cut-mark evidence and other aspects of the archaeological record such as the co-occurrence of patches of artefacts and broken up bones. However the evidence for the *working of wood* is novel and potentially very significant. THIS IMPLIES THAT STONE TOOLS WERE BEING USED FOR MAKING OTHER TOOLS.

Also momentous is the indication that plant stems were being cut. For the moment we have no idea what the adaptive significance of this might be. Grass heads for food? Grass and vegetation for nesting/bedding? Pods to get seeds or beans? All possible but uncertain. I will also be curious to find the use-wear pattern that would result from cutting or stripping soft bark or cambium. These kinds of experiments remain to be done.

It should be noted that all of these traces of use are on *flakes*, which is consistent with the stress already laid on the great adaptive significance of flakes. However, since there are very few core pieces in these assemblages made of the fine-grained siliceous rocks, the point is not conclusively proven.

These preliminary and still scanty results need to be checked and the sample of observations needs to be enlarged. Meanwhile it is not uninteresting to note that Keeley's work (1980) on use-wear traces among artefact forms from Clacton and Hoxne also reveals meat-cutting and wood-working as well represented functions, with some use polishes and some hide-scraping added to the list.

Why increased complexity?

In the foregoing discussion I have indicated that almost all the basic needs for sharp edges that humans have can be met from the varied range of forms generated from 'Oldowan' patterns of stone flaking. The question then arises as to why many later stone-tool assemblages seem to show signs of being more organized and more complex? I use the terms to imply more deliberate design, more successive steps of manufacture and more careful control.

Experience of modern life makes us tend to assume that more complex equals better adapted, but such an assumption leaves the nature of the advantages, if any, undefined and unmeasured. So let me turn to examine what significant steps in rising complexity occurred after the time of manufacture of the Oldowan industries which have so far been discussed. Put another way, what was the adaptive significance of developments in stone craft since 1.5 mya?

In the 130 years of Palaeolithic archaeology since Boucher de Perthes, most archaeologists have tackled the task of describing and classifying so as to have an orderly sense of stone craft variation across geography and through time. There has been an underlying tacit assumption that change was commonly progressive – that it led to the development of superior, more effective toolkits. However, means for measuring that progress and for specifying its adaptive advantages have received scant attention. As a consequence, what follows is in the nature of a tentative formulation of some propositions.

The first post-Oldowan stone craft change is the appearance of Acheulian tool-forms. In artefact-bearing layers that are younger than 1.5 million years, large distinctive artefacts appear as components of some but not all assemblages. The large novel items span a spectrum of forms with the categories handaxe ('biface'), cleaver and pick being found useful by archaeologists seeking to distinguish among the shapes (Fig. 15.10). The addition of these forms can be assessed as representing

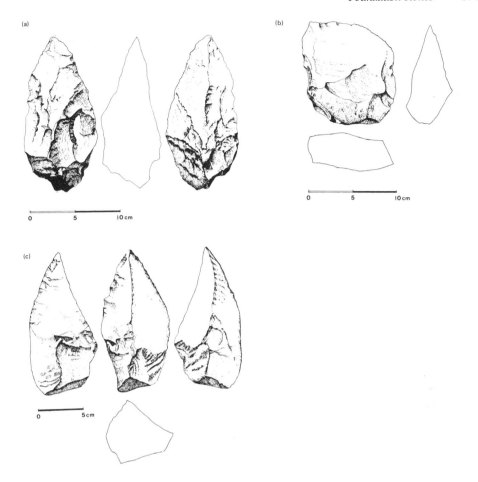

Fig. 15.10. Examples of the distinctive, novel forms that first appear around 1.4 mya and herald the start of the Acheulian. (a) A handaxe from the Humbu Formation, Peninj, Tanzania. (b) A cleaver from site FxJ 63, Koobi Fora. (c) A trihedral pick also from FxJ 63. All of these examples are made on very large flakes. This involves their makers in skilled, deliberate preparatory operations and it introduces elements of predictability and predetermination in the resulting morphologies.

a rise in the level of complexity because (1) an *extra step is commonly added to the manufacturing process* – namely the careful and deliberate striking of large flakes which commonly provide the blank from which the bifaces were made; and because (2) the innovation appears to involve for the first time in the archaeological record the *imposition of arbitrary, preconceived design norms*. This is manifest from the fact that the standard forms begin to be hacked out regardless of the size, shape and flaking properties of the initial raw material. Symmetry of the plan form and of the cross sections became a common but not invariable part of the designs which were imposed.

The question then arises as to what, if anything, was the adaptive significance of this innovation. And this question brings us to the embarrassing fact that, although for 50 years archaeologists have regarded the shift as important, we simply do not know what its functional significance was. It is still not clear today whether the new artefact forms represent new and better tools for some tasks that had previously been carried out with the Oldowan range of artefacts, or whether some new tasks were added to the behavioural repertoire at about 1.5 mya.

We cannot yet answer these questions but methods now exist for addressing them, and some preliminary indications are starting to be available. First, feasibility experiments imply that handaxes and cleavers are much more efficient tools for butchering very large animals (after initial incision through the hide with a flake) than are Oldowan forms on their own (Toth, 1982; Jones, 1981). Secondly, Keeley (1980) has demonstrated that at least some flint handaxes from the European Middle Pleistocene were used for butchery. Perhaps these forms just do provide much better ways of doing old tasks such as butchery. Another possibility is that, in addition to this kind of specific function, bifaces were also portable cores. That is to say that if bifaces were carried about, knife-like flakes could always be created by striking a few quick blows with a hammer, or the biface itself could be used as a larger implement.

We now know that the relatively early biface assemblages such as Kilombe (Gowlett, 1978) and Olduvai Lower Bed IV (both older than 0.7 mya) do include well-made refined looking bifaces. Peter Jones' experiments (1979) have shown that the refined, intensively retouched pieces are made of more brittle rocks and can be understood in part by reference to the raw material characteristics without the need to invoke a rapid early Acheulian rise in aesthetic sense. However, it is true that during the Middle Pleistocene the maximum degree to which symmetry and regularity is imposed increases. This seems to us like progress but at present, because we do not know much about the function of the forms that undergo refinement, we are in a poor position to assess whether the increased regularity made the tools more efficient or not.

Taking a different approach, John Gowlett (1982, in press) has demonstrated that some Acheulian industries that approach one million years in age show great precision in the execution of what seem to be standardized designs, and that they also show very regular proportion in the magnitude of their dimensions along three axes. Isaac (1977b) has obtained similar results for Olorgesailie. Gowlett uses this to argue that the materialist/economic approach that has been in vogue among Palaeolithic scholars in recent years may have led to underestimates of the mental and cultural abilities of Early Pleistocene hominids. He may well be correct in this and we need to seek methods for assessing the balance point between minimizing mechanistic indications and maximizing mentalistic ones.

A similar problem is apparent in the contrast between the analysis presented here and that of Thomas Wynn (1981a, 1981b) to which reference has already been made. There is agreement among Wynn, Gowlett, myself and many others over the fact that Acheulian industries do betoken greater craft complexity. I have characterized the shift in level as being manifest in the imposition of arbitrary design. Wynn makes essentially the same distinction but breaks the concept of arbitrary design into a series of Piaget conceptual categories as follows:

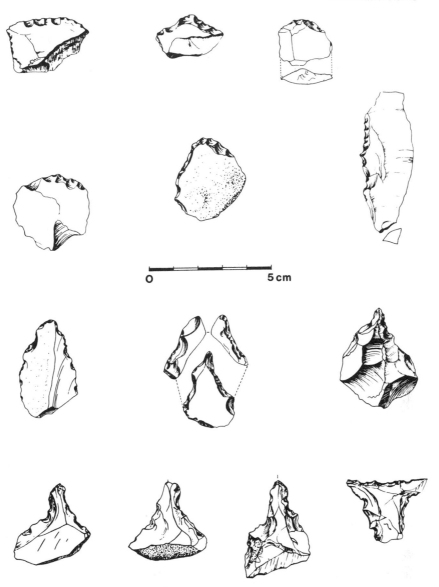

Fig. 15.11. Examples of relatively unstandardized Middle Pleistocene small flaked pieces ('scrapers') based on flakes. Many of the items have an opportunistic, *ad hoc* aspect, but in some sites series showing signs of what may be rule-bound design begins to appear. In particular, nosed and pointed forms (bottom row) have this aspect.

Whole-part relations – the variable deployment of trimming to achieve a standard form.

Qualitative displacement – in this case manifest by the ability to conceive and impose a straight-line format.

Spatio-temporal substitution – in this case the ability to adjust precisely an entire system of cross-sections even when the whole form cannot be seen at once.

Symmetry – the ability to perceive and impose one or more axes of symmetry.

Wynn goes on to argue that this set of abilities is indicative of what is designated in the Piaget system of analysis as operational intelligence. In modern primates this is characteristic only of human adults. Wynn may well be correct in this analysis, but I feel that the approach still needs to be tested in actual replicative stone-flaking and stone-flaking-instruction sessions (see note 1). Wynn goes on to argue that this also means that 'the thinking of these hominids [i.e. later Acheulian] was equivalent to that of modern humans'. I do not agree that this conclusion follows even if one accepts the first assessment. We will need to develop a far more searching framework of inquiry if such an important question is ever to be settled.

Two other post-Oldowan developments in stonecraft perhaps also deserve discussion in trying to assess what has been added since the time of the first stone tools. These are (1) the proliferation of small tool-forms and their eventual differentiation in some industries into a distinctive array of relatively standardized 'types'; and (2) the appearance of the Levallois method.

Mary Leakey (1971) showed that even in Oldowan assemblages some flakes have had their edge-form modified by the removal of smaller flakes. Characteristically the retouched flake forms are smallish scrapers without any very pronounced axis of orientation (i.e. they are not classic *racloirs* or *grattoirs* (Isaac, 1977b)). They also tend to have irregular or somewhat denticulate edges and spurs. In the early industries these look like *ad hoc* opportunistic adjustments to flake forms presumably to make them suitable for shaping and/or other materials; or alternatively perhaps some retouch served to rejuvenate knife-like flakes that had dulled or clogged in use from cutting meat or other tissue.

At Olduvai (M. D. Leakey, 1975, 1976) and at Melka Kunturé (Chavaillon *et al.*, 1979) the sequence of assemblages appears to show both a rise in proportional frequency within each assemblage and some increase in the number of clearly distinguishable forms. For instance, many Middle Pleistocene assemblages include small retouched pieces with pronounced nosed or beaked points (Fig. 15.11). As far as I am aware, this is not a feature of early Pleistocene assemblages. What does this rise in frequency and the addition of new forms mean? At present any answers that are offered are purely speculative, but one might guess that perhaps the importance of tools for making tools rose in the Middle Pleistocene with a wider range of wood- and fabric-working (hide and bark?) tasks being undertaken. This line of inference can presumably be checked by use-wear studies and by feasibility experiments.

If followed through the Middle Pleistocene, small retouched pieces appear to undergo similar changes to those already mentioned in connection with the increasing refinement of bifaces. Namely, there is some tendency for the *maximum* level of intensity of retouch to rise (length of retouched edge, number of scars per unit length, etc.) and for orderly preconceived designs to appear as a more conspicuous manifestation. This is in fact the same kind of trend that results in contrasts between Middle Palaeolithic assemblages and most early Lower Palaeolithic assemblages.

Another change which sets very early artefact assemblages apart from many later ones is the absence of the Levallois method. Disc cores, Karari cores, and so on show orderly flaking procedures in the early assemblages, but the specific elaborate cognitive structure that is evident in the Levallois method is absent. Prehistorians have long made a fuss about the emergence of the Levallois method as evidence of advances in development of mental ability. The validity of this seems clear enough, but like the increasing refinement and differentiation that has already been discussed, stressing the cognitive developments leaves unanswered the questions about adaptive significance.

Until we have much more use-wear information and many more local-adaptation studies, answers can only be tentative. My guess would be that many of these changes do not so much reflect changes in the mechanics and engineering of the artefacts, as that they reflect increases in the strength and pervasiveness of culturally ordained *rule systems*. That is to say that during the Middle Pleistocene the whole of the conduct of proto-human life became more and more governed by customs and precepts that specified with increasing exactitude what procedures were appropriate and socially acceptable. One way of thinking about this is to use a linguistic/cognitive metaphor and argue that behaviour in general, including toolmaking behaviour, was acquiring a deep grammatical structure for sociological reasons rather than engineering reasons, thus calling for an increase in orderliness and predictability (cf. Deetz, 1977; Glassie, 1975). The deep structural rules, and the specific artefact form-grammars generated from them, would be transmitted by teaching and imitation and would be subject to variation from region to region and in the same region through time. This model of change would predict that if cultural definition of appropriate conduct facilitated more and more efficient modes of adaptation, then the orderliness, symmetry and standardization among artefacts could be expected to tend to increase even if the same craft tasks could perfectly well be accomplished by simple, opportunistic toolkits.

All this may imply that the earliest toolmaking systems did lack extensive deep structure and grammatical complexity and that they could have been made by hominids with markedly subhuman mental and cultural abilities.

There is another point of difference between early and later industries, namely that tools were probably all held in the hand through most of the Lower Palaeolithic. At some point in time the *practice of hafting* some items entered into tool systems. Putting handles on stone working edges and putting stone armatures in long shafts would be facilitated by greater predictability and standardization of the components to be linked. It would seem possible that at least in some degree the rise to prominence of the Levallois method and the extra surge in orderliness that one seems to see around the end of the Middle Pleistocene (150,000 to 75,000 years ago) might be intelligible in relation to the increased prevalence of hafts. Hafting itself surely involves significant shifts in cognitive ability perhaps comparable to those implied by the Levallois method. However, except in Australia, where John Mulvaney (1966, 1969) has drawn attention to the possible effects on the overall format of stone tools, there has been little discussion of this innovation. Ultimately experiments and use-wear studies will be needed to ascertain how much of the relative simplicity of early stone-tool systems is a correlate of their being hand-held and how much is due as discussed above to intrinsically less rule-bound, less information containing cultural systems.

What are the social and cultural implications of early stone tools?

This is an important topic, but yet one on which it is difficult to turn speculation into testable, falsifiable hypotheses – so I will be brief.

Clearly even relatively simple toolmaking would have involved concepts and skills which would have to be learned during the process of growing up. This would be facilitated by a prolongation of infancy and juvenile dependence. As Parker and Gibson (1979) have pointed out, this almost certainly involved lengthened and intensified mother–infant bonding. Relative to other primates, chimpanzees show this kind of modification to the life cycle, humans even more so. It seems a safe speculation that shifts in this direction would have begun or have been intensified as tools became varied and important. Alan Mann (1975) has argued that the growth patterns of australopithecines in South Africa already show modifications in the direction of human-like prolonged, slow growth and delayed maturity.

Larger brains are costly in terms of nutritional requirements for growth and maintenance, and they also call for the birth of more than usually helpless young. At some stage or other in human evolution these factors may well have led natural selection to favour individuals who participated in social systems which provided childbearing females with some help in food acquisition and with protection. Such a social matrix would also facilitate the transmission of varied skills from generation to generation. If the social system which began to develop was from the start some kind of central-place foraging system, then communicating information about past encounters, future arrangements and the spatially remote, would have become more advantageous than it is in the lives of any living non-human primate. Natural selection could *begin* to favour the evolution of the mental abilities that make language possible.

The stone artefacts occur both as a scatter across the ancient landscape and in dense patches (so-called sites). Clearly there were some places where making, using and discarding stone tools was preferentially concentrated. whether this was through repeated activity bouts of solitary individuals or through usage by larger social groups is harder to tell. I am inclined to the view that these places were social foci, and that the accumulation of bones as well as stone artefacts at these places indicates that food was repeatedly carried in for consumption. In fact when these sites were first excavated it seemed intuitively obvious to us as modern humans that they were fossil camp-place, home-bases – or as I now prefer to designate the concept, 'central-place foraging loci'. But here we come to a point where it is clear that we may be reconstructing our ancestors in our own image. Ascertaining how these early dense concentrations of artefacts plus bones formed is perhaps the major challenge facing the archaeology of early man. It is a subject dear to my heart (Isaac, 1969, 1976b, 1978a, 1981a, 1983a and 1984 [this volume, chs. 11, 12, 13 and 5]) and since it has already been the subject of various papers I will not pursue it further here (see also Binford, 1981).

It is sometimes argued that toolmaking traditions such as we find in the Early Stone Age could only have been transmitted with the aid of language. I do not agree with this. One learns to make stone tools primarily by alternating watching with personal trial and error. The cognitive ability to conceive an elaborate design and execute it may or may not have been linked in evolution to the development of language abilities, but toolmaking *per se* does not call for this kind of communication. An orangutan has been taught to make simple stone tools (Wright, 1972).

Facing the challenge

Doing the archaeology of extremely remote periods can fairly be likened to a voyage of discovery. When we find two-million-year-old earth layers with archaeological remains in them, we have, like Columbus, traversed an ocean of time and arrived at the equivalent of a new world (Fig. 15.12). Our finds excite wonder and curiosity, but in the first instance we, like Columbus, are apt to interpret them in terms of our preconceptions. We may think we are in the Indies, when in reality we are at the edges of an unknown continent.

To shift to a different image of what is involved, let us imagine looking down a

Fig. 15.12. Christopher Columbus' landfall in 1492 (from an engraving by Theodor de Bry). Like Columbus, archaeologists carry numerous presuppositions in their heads when they travel across the 2-million-year sea of time and try to make contact with the first tool-making beings. *Photo*: Peabody Museum, Harvard University.

deep well-shaft. Beyond the dimly lighted upper rim is darkness extending away from the watcher ... but in these depths is the gleam of light on water. If the well is not too deep, by straining our eyes we perhaps see a figure – a figure set in an unfamiliar context, but yet a familiar figure – familiar, because it is our own reflection. Archaeological inquiry into the very remote past has recently experienced comparable moments of truth. Awareness is dawning that in part we have been using archaeology and the early evidence as a mirror by which to obtain more or less familiar images of ourselves.

In the first instance the realization that we might, as it were, be on a different continent, and the awareness that we were subconsciously seeking to find distant but definite reflections of ourselves in the remote past came as something of a shock, and as Binford (1981) has pointed out we tended to resist the change. Now many of the scientists involved are beginning to recognize that once we have faced up to the challenge our inquiry becomes an even more exciting voyage of discovery. Can our scientific imagination rise to the occasion? Can we conceive of patterns of behaviour and adaptation that could lead to the formation of familiar-looking patterns of archaeological evidence, and yet which were behaviours unfamiliar to us in that they were structured differently from recent and present-day human ones? Can we then figure out predictable differences in the archaeological evidence that will distinguish the various possible behavioural models?

To meet this challenge archaeologists will have to function rather in the manner of astronomical cosmologists who use physics and mathematics to imagine extraordinary phenomena such as 'black holes', and then predict the observable characteristics they would display if they existed. Our equivalent input will presumably have to be a knowledge of ecology and an understanding of alternative strategies for exploiting the economy of nature with and without technology, and with and without intricate information exchange (i.e. language). To these we must add an understanding of stone tools based both on experiments and perhaps on analytical and experimental studies of the cognitive processes involved in making stone tools.

The application of the method-of-residuals-logic to interpreting very early stone tools makes it clear that evidence for elaborate culture is at a minimum. The tools are opportunistic rather than made to a set socially prescribed pattern. To be sure, the tools do indicate socially learned behaviour which constitutes a simple level of culture, but there is little sign of arbitrary fixed designs, or of set rules or of style. These phenomena appear in the archaeological record only much later.

If I were to hazard a guess about the intelligence and mentality of the earliest toolmaking hominids it would be that it was definitely non-human, even though these creatures of two million years ago had begun to be involved in some behaviours which are now characteristic of humans alone among the primates.

What is important about the archaeological evidence for toolmaking, for meat-eating and perhaps for central-place foraging is not that these traits made the early enactors human, but that the traits helped to establish a situation in which individuals were exposed to natural selection patterns which transformed their descendants, over two million years, into the complex human beings that we now are.

Acknowledgements

In this chapter I have tried to consider early artefacts not as objects or types but as vestiges of ancient systems. On the one hand the systems must be understood in materialistic terms, as ones which began to fulfil needs in the lives of remote ancestors; and on the other hand the systems are expressions of early proto-human minds and must also be understood in terms of creative processes. The stimulus for me to begin to think about early artefacts in a broad behavioural context first came in 1959 when Charles McBurney took me on as a student. The stimulus continued as the relationship grew to be a friendship. He encouraged us, his pupils, to think restlessly about aims and methods in pursuing archaeology and his own work inspired me and others to avoid getting blocked into particular rigid typological frameworks. Charles taught us to enjoy thinking and arguing and I hope the chapter reflects this.

It also arises from long years of involvement in the archaeology of East Africa and the development of my thinking owes much to mentors in this work such as Mary Leakey, Maxine Kleindienst and Desmond Clark and to fellow diggers such as Jack Harris, Harry Merrick and John Gowlett. Latterly I have also been stimulated to think in many new ways about Early Stone Age tools by working with Nick Toth to develop an experimental programme within the Kenya National Museum's Koobi Fora project. The many other students in this team have helped one sharpen one's wits. Barbara Isaac has been a part of the work throughout, drawing tools and diagrams and arguing many issues.

A shorter version of this chapter was delivered as the 6th Kroon Lecture at the Instituut voor Prae en Protohistorie in Amsterdam in April 1982. I am grateful to my hosts in the Institute of Archaeology for their invitation to give this lecture in a series to which Charles McBurney had earlier contributed. Also some of the material has been included in a comprehensive review of Early Palaeolithic archaeology in East Africa (Isaac in press [1984]) but without full discussion of interpretation and intellectual context.

1 Wynn has attempted to analyse various stone-tool forms in terms of successive organizational abilities that are seen to develop during the growth of a human child, as demonstrated by Piaget. This is a pioneering lead that should surely be followed up, but I have a sense that further exploration will have to be done in conjunction with a programme of experimental replication and teaching of replication. Stone-tool-manufacturing operations that may seem simple in their 'logic' may in practice be difficult. For instance, Wynn picks on the polyhedron as the simplest Oldowan form when in fact this is a form that is very difficult to replicate. Equally Wynn suggests that a blade core is no more 'advanced' than a well-made biface. However, whatever the geometry, the sense of 'strategy' and planning in initiating, stabilizing and continuing the striking of blades takes far longer to master than does making a neat biface.

2 Wood with shaping marks is known from the second half of the Middle Pleistocene at sites such as Clacton (about 300,000 yrs?), Torralba (30,000 to 500,000 yrs) and Kalambo Falls.

16

Stages of cultural elaboration in the Pleistocene: possible archaeological indicators of the development of language capabilities

Asking an archaeologist to discuss language is rather like asking a mole to describe life in the treetops. The earthy materials with which archaeologists deal contain no direct traces of the phenomena that figure so largely in a technical consideration of the nature of language. There are no petrified phonemes and no fossil grammars. The oldest actual relics of language that archaeologists can put their hands on are no older than the first invention of writing systems some five or six thousand years ago. And yet the intricate physiological basis of language makes it perfectly clear that this human ability has deep roots, roots that may extend as far as, or farther back in time than, the documented beginnings of toolmaking some $2\frac{1}{2}$ million years ago.

However, to return to the simile: if the forest has been cut down and all that remains are the roots, then the mole may not be such an inappropriate consultant. So it is with the history of language development. Comparative studies can indicate phylogenetic patterns, while detailed understanding of the structure and physiology of modern human linguistic capabilities can suggest possible successive stages of pre-human development; however, beyond a certain point, historical understanding demands dated evidence for successive developmental stages. This record, if it is to be obtained at all, must be sought from palaeontologists and archaeologists. It is probable that the search is not quite as hopeless as it may look at first glance, but it is equally certain that there are no very simple answers.

In my mind there stand out two possible lines of approach to the problem. The first involves scrutiny of the record of developing proto-human material culture systems and consideration of its potential relevance to the problem in hand. Stone artefacts are the best and most persistent long-term markers, but during the last 5 per cent of the time span we can also deal with more fancy evidence such as burials, ornaments, art, notations, cult objects, structures, and so forth.

The second approach involves taking archaeological evidence which is indicative of the economic behaviour and the adaptive patterns of early hominids and then considering the potential effects of varying intensities of information exchange on the functioning of the systems. This second approach should contribute to an understanding of the selection pressures that have moulded the evolution of language abilities. PART 1 of this paper follows the first approach, and PART 2 the second.

Part 1. The evolutionary implication of the record of development in material culture[1]

In recent years our understanding of the early development of human culture has undergone several important changes: the known and measured time span of cultural traces has been extended by potassium argon dating and by new finds in East Africa from a grudging half-million years to at least 2.5 or 3 million years. This extension not only stretches the record; it affects our understanding of the evolutionary processes involved. We see now that the early stages of material culture were by our standards incredibly long-lasting and static. This has helped to jolt prehistorians out of the propensity to treat the whole archaeological record as a series of chapters in a conventional history, a narrative of events in which the human nature of the actors is tacitly assumed throughout. The long time scale makes us realize that we are dealing with non-human antecedents, rather than with quaint, archaic 'early men'. We have to grapple with the reconstruction of behavioural patterns that no longer have any living counterparts.

It is artefacts that normally function as the distinctive markers of human or proto-human behaviour in the geological record, and the earliest artefacts known at the present time have been found in East Africa at sites such as Olduvai, Omo and East Rudolf, where they can be geophysically dated to between 1.5 and 2.5 million years. Ancient as they are, they document definite purposive toolmaking activity: the formation of sharp edges by the organized and insightful banging of rocks together. The forms, however, are essentially opportunistic, involving empirical appreciation only of the fact that a suitable blow produces two potentially useful results: a sharp-edged flake of variable form, and a jagged-edged scar on the parent block. Either or both items could be, and seem to have been, used as tools. Modern humans can acquire an appreciation of the possibilities of Oldowan techniques in a few moments, and can produce examples of most of the forms with very little practice indeed. There was a minimum of design and control.

By a million years ago, some stone toolmakers were producing objects that impress us as much more refined. They involve more definite design and control. Balanced, symmetrical objects such as a handaxe are much harder to manufacture; they require a stronger sense of purpose, more example and instruction, and more practice. By 100,000 years ago, some stone-tool assemblages really begin to look elaborate, even to our technologically conscious eyes, and to learn to make them properly takes years of practice. By 30,000 or 40,000 years ago, a kaleidoscopic diversity of forms and techniques was being utilized, and changes began to be breathtakingly rapid by the standards of the early periods. Explicit traces of symbolizing and ritual become evident: burials with offerings, personal ornaments, engraved lines, representational painting and sculpture. By about 30,000 years ago, the archaeological record looked like a segment of ethnography. Presumably most of what happened since then has been the cumulative exploitation of the potential that had previously come into being. Another indication of rising levels of effective adaptability is provided by the expansion of hominid ecological range. Existing evidence suggests that hominids were confined to the tropics and warm, temperate zones until about 500,000–700,000 years ago; that is, for two-thirds of the time span of the total record (Bordes, 1968; Oakley, 1966).

The immediate question is: can we find in the archaeological record elements that will help us understand the genesis of human faculties other than technological ones? Do artefacts offer evidence that can help us discern changing levels of capability with symbols, rules and codes? I will report on the large-scale features of the archaeological record on the assumption that hominid capacity for conceiving and executing increasingly elaborate material culture designs has been connected with rising capacity for manipulating symbols, naming and speaking. I hope that this conference will stimulate active discussion of these interrelationships.

Gauging complexity

If we are to use the complexity of artefacts as an indicator, then we have to ask the technical question: What constitutes elaboration and complexity among artefacts? How is it to be measured? These are questions on which we all have intuitive sense, but I am not aware of much systematic work among either archaeologists or ethnographers. For the present purposes, I propose to use the following variables as yardsticks:

1. The number of distinct artefact classes, each with its own distinguishable set of rules. This has a connected but separate aspect.
2. The degree of latitude; that is, the amount of variation among representatives of a distinct class.
3. The number of operations involved in the production of an artefact. This may lead eventually to another quantum jump.
4. Compound artefacts; for example, stone-tipped spears, harpoons.
5. The extent of non-random differentiation in space and time; that is, the division of material culture into regional industries with successive distinct episodes or phases.

Palaeolithic prehistorians have hitherto made few explicit attempts to measure these qualities and to plot the trajectory of change through time.

There is one qualifying warning to which attention must be drawn at once: I am trying to deal with hominid capacity for, and capability with, the conception and execution of craft designs. In assessing this, positive features of the record, rather than negative ones, must be interpreted. Few, if any, of the assemblages have ever approached in complexity the limits of capability of their makers. Even the complex material culture of modern times has not presumably reached the extremes of which mankind is capable. Thus, lack of elaboration does not prove lack of capability; however, evidence for a particular level of complexity must reflect at least a minimum level of ability. If we look at ethnographic information on the artefacts of recent non-agricultural peoples, we find great differences in the degree of elaboration as measured in various ways, in spite of the fact that inherent capabilities are not known to differ. This view of the situation leaves me with the tentative model of change through time that is presented in Fig. 16.1.

I would argue that an assymptote in the minimum level was probably reached long ago. This involves such basic tool forms as digging sticks, spears, containers, cutting tools and chopping tools. The recorded equipment of the Tasmanians seems to have been quite close to this minimum. The maximum attainment of elaboration appears in the record to have gone creeping up through the whole span of prehistory. It was certainly not a linear growth pattern, but whether it was a simple geometric growth curve or one with a series of episodic surges remains to be ascertained.

The diagrams in Figs. 16.2 and 16.3 provide rough guides to what little data I have been able to put together regarding the growing complexity of material culture through time. Fig. 16.2 presents a tentative timetable for the incorporation of increasing numbers of elements. Simple artefacts such as digging sticks are included on a speculative basis. They are preserved so rarely in the record that the oldest-known examples almost certainly provide no real indication of the date when their use began. However, they are such basic agents of the adaptive strategy of tropical hunter-gatherers that I feel quite confident in guessing that their antiquity extends back at least as far as that of stone tools. Containers such as bags and baskets are essential ingredients of human behavioural organization, since without them reciprocal sharing of meat and vegetable foods is difficult, if not impossible. We do not know when they first came into use, but it could be argued that the presence on even the earliest sites of numerous small stone artefacts that were probably not made there implies the use of at least simple pouches or bundles. Certainly by 1.5 million years ago, the volume of artefacts at sites such as those of Upper Bed II Olduvai and of the Upper Member of the Koobi Fora Formation is so

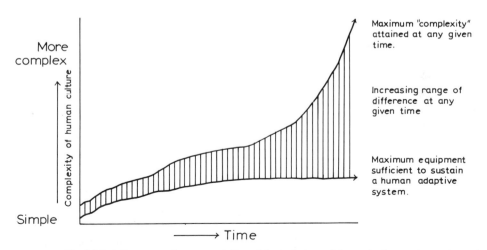

Fig. 16.1. A diagrammatic representation of the trajectory of change in the maximum (upper) and the minimum (lower) levels of complexity in material culture, during the course of human evolution.

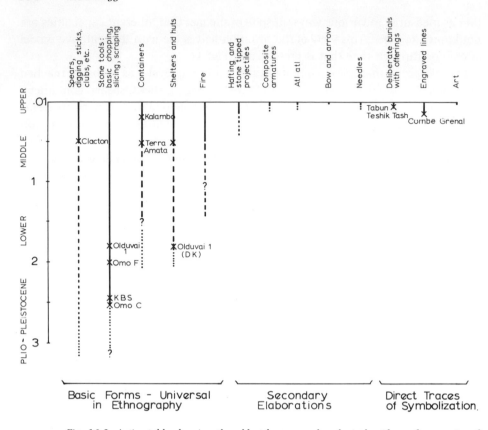

Fig. 16.2. A timetable showing the oldest known archaeological evidence for a series of important items of equipment. Dotted lines show conjectured time ranges (see text).

great that one feels certain that containers must have been in use. Mary Foster (personal communication) has suggested that appreciation of the properties of containers represents an important and formative step in hominid cognition and symbolizing abilities.

Figure 16.3 shows a tentative timetable for important conceptual steps in the development of methods of making stone tools (Bordes, 1968; Oakley, 1966; Leakey, 1934).

Differentiation

Stone tools, for all their limitations, constitute the best long-term record of changes in cultural systems that we have, and I think there are interesting features, as yet dimly perceived, that may be relevant to the problem in hand. One of these is a rise through time in the degree of differentiation shown by the most elaborate industry of any given period. Two factors are involved in the phenomenon as I perceive it: (1) the degree to which there were distinct target forms in the minds of the craftsmen as determined by cultural experience and neurophysiological capacity for

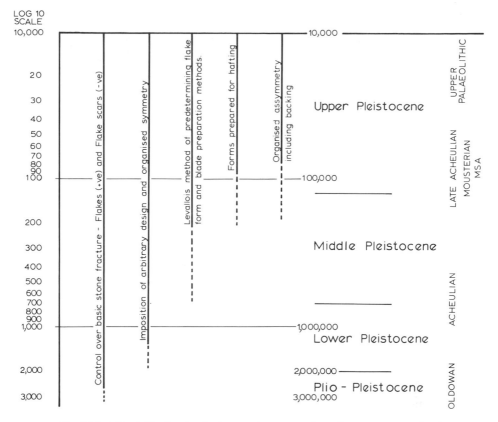

Fig. 16.3. A timetable showing the known time range of significant concepts and techniques used in material culture, especially as evident from stone tools (see text).

design conception; a metal template; and (2) the degree to which the craftsman can control his productions so that an orderly series of replicating forms results.

The two combine to make up what can be termed a 'rule system'; that is, an empirical code governing artefact form. In practice, of course, archaeologists study samples of artefacts and must try to recognize from them replicating patterns and hence infer the toolmaking habits, rules, and targets of an extinct population.

Differentiation, as I am using the word, is not the same as diversity. The fragments that are taken from a stone-crusher for use as road metal are diverse, but the wide range of forms are not patterned in a way that can be said to show intentional differentiation. In this respect, early stone artefact assemblages are much more like road metal than are many more recent stone artefact assemblages. Fig. 16.4 presents a diagrammatic expression of how I imagine increasing differentiation may have come about through a series of successive phases. At each stage, the maximum intensity of differentiation extended beyond that of previous phases. The convention of the diagram is such that in each frame a topographic surface is depicted so as to represent the pattern of differentiation. Location on the horizontal surface denotes morphology, whereas the vertical scale denotes relative

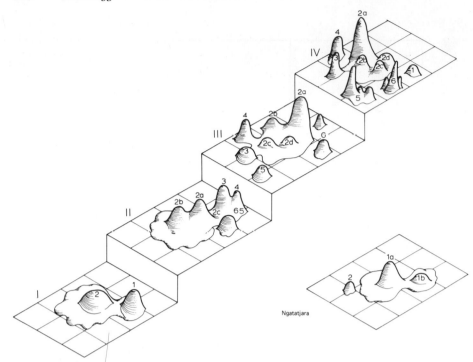

Fig. 16.4. A diagrammatic representation illustrating increasing degrees of stone-artefact elaboration and differentiation. The number of topographic humps denotes the number of distinguishable modalities; the height and pointedness of the peaks denote the degree of standardization within the modality. The recent Australian data (Ngatatjara) is based on the account of Gould *et al.* (1971).

1. e.g. Oldowan: 1 = core-choppers, 2 = casual scrapers; II, eg Acheulian (Olorgesailie); 2a = scrapers, 2b = nosed scrapers, 2c = large scrapers, 3 = handaxes, 4 = cleavers, 5 = picks, 6 = discoids; III, eg Mousterian; 2a = racloir, 2b = grattoir, 2c = r. convergent, 3 = percoir, 4 = point, 5 = burin, 6 = biface; IV, Upper Palaeolithic; 2a = grattoir, 2b = nosed scraper, 2c = raclette, etc., 3 = percoir, 4 = point, 5 = burin, 6 = backed blade, etc.

Ngatjara: 1a = hafted adzes (purpunpa), 1b = scrapers (purpunpa), 2 = bec (pitjuru pitjuru).

frequency. Each topographic hump represents what I regard as an intrinsic modality. Pinnacles represent very distinct replicative series; low mounds represent series sharing some features, but showing low overall morphological coherence. Very often these unstandardized forms have the air of opportunistic and casual tools. Properly, the volume of each feature should be scaled in proportion to relative abundance. Ultimately we should seek to map differentiation in some such way as this, but Palaeolithic archaeologists are as yet only groping toward such a conceptualization.

The earliest industries show only two or three distinguishable modalities, and within each there was little detailed rigour of design, either because the targets were vague or because the execution was imprecise and opportunistic, or both. To state this differently, the early assemblages seem to contain few really distinct artefact classes, and the degree of latitude in design was wide. By the end of the Pleistocene, many stone industries, particularly those outside tropical areas, showed extensive design differentiation and considerable fastidiousness in the execution and replication of particularities. Some industries of intermediate age show convincing intermediate states of differentiation. Notice that the last three frames involve progressively less time differences than the first ones: the process was speeding up dramatically toward the end. Note that the diagram also attempts to express the fact that the total range of forms does not change extensively through time. From the very beginning there were razor-sharp edges, bevelled edges, angular spurs, pointed projections, and so on; however, they occur in anarchic combinations with other variables of object form. In some later industries particular forms were picked out by custom and were carefully produced as a replicating series. Because the change is not so much in available forms as in the exactitude of the rules governing demand and production, the functional consequences cannot be regarded in a simple-minded fashion. It is not necessarily true that the increase in complexity reflects an increase in the number of tasks performed with stone tools, nor are the fancy tools necessarily more efficient in an engineering sense. This is a point that has seldom been recognized, and I will return to discuss it further.

Another aspect of differentiation is the propensity for all later Pleistocene industries to show marked regional idiosyncrasy, in a manner that one cannot help comparing with language and dialect. As we go back in time, variation among industries becomes less and less clearly patterned in relation to geography. There are problems in the resolving power of available samples, but I think that this aspect of changing cultural systems is real and important. The less internal differentiation there was, the less opportunity there was for arbitrary stylistic divergences. Perhaps the increase in differentiation reflects changing patterns of cultural transmission and increasing specificity of language variants.

Because I have discussed elsewhere the technical problems of measuring increasing intra- and interassemblage differentiation and have given tentative diagrammatic representations of such poor data as we have, I will avoid pursuing these issues here (see Isaac, 1972a, 1972e [this volume, chs. 1 and 2]).

That more and more exacting designs were imposed on materials is also apparent from the record. First, some $1\frac{1}{2}$ million years ago, we see the definite creation of symmetry, as in handaxes; then, about $\frac{1}{2}$ million years ago, into the repertoire there entered deliberate and highly organized techniques of core preparation, such as the Levallois method, and, later, prismatic blades.

One can see, as a culmination of this increase in conceptualization and control, the preparation of compound forms: stone-tipped spears, hafted scrapers and borers. The oldest examples known to me of stone forms showing deliberate modifications that I think indicate hafting are of late Middle or early Upper Pleistocene date, perhaps 100,000–200,000 years ago. However, recent peoples of Australia and New Guinea haft suitable unprepared stone fragments, so the practice may be much older than the first recognizable traces.

The fitting together of parts may well have important interconnection with cognition as a whole. At about the same time, pieces such as backed knives that show deliberate and organized assymmetry were differentiated, although they do not become very common until later.

Elaboration and adaptation

There is good evidence that a carefree stone knapper can generate a stock of chopping, slicing, scraping and piercing edges that are fully adequate to perform all the basic adaptive functions of a hunter-gatherer. Why, then, the increasing involvement with such qualities as symmetry and balance? Why the concern to produce series of objects that replicate each other in accordance to what must have been definite rule systems?

My intuition in this matter is that we see in the stone tools the reflection of changes that were affecting culture as a whole, and whose functional significance can only be understood in this light. Probably more and more of all behaviour, often but not always including toolmaking behaviour, involved complex rule systems. In the realm of communications, this presumably consisted more and more of elaborate syntax and extended vocabulary; in the realm of social relations, perhaps increasing numbers of defined categories, obligations and prescriptions; in the realm of subsistence, increasing bodies of communicable know-how. The elaborated systems as a whole may have conferred adaptive advantages on the practitioners, even when specific individual components such as fancy tools were not directly adaptive. Thus I envisage that once the capability existed, the elaboration of rules and categories could, in some societies, simply extend into various realms of material culture, whether differentiation was functionally important or not. Perhaps there is an underlying pattern of determinants such as that perceived by Mary Douglas in the relationships between social configurations, religion, and the elaboration of explicit ritual (Douglas, 1970). Certainly there seems to me to be a tendency to greater elaborations of Pleistocene rule systems in the cold and temperate zones than in the tropics. Meg Fritz (1974) has suggested that this may, in part, relate to social marking under conditions of stress.

Stages of development

In summary, then, I see in the record a rise in complexity and in capacity for design rules that comprises a continuum divisible into the following segments:[2]

Step 1 (2.5–1.5 mya). Simple tools, the form of which was determined by the mechanical properties of natural materials. The imposition of design was minimal. These tools are core-choppers and flakes, plus spears and digging sticks, at a guess. Apes can make and use simple tools, the forms of which are determined more by the material than by the ape (Koehler, 1927; Wright, 1972). It seems probable to me that the designing and symbolizing capabilities of Plio-Pleistocene hominids was not necessarily vastly beyond that of contemporary pongids.

Step 2: Middle Pleistocene (1.5–0.2 mya). Some but not all tools involve the imposition of arbitrary design rules and a new concern with symmetry and regularity – for instance, the handaxe. The repertoire of definite, arbitrary designs was always very small: one or two, to three or four. Technical systems show increasing insight and ingenuity, as in the Levallois preformation method. There was little tendency to systematic, stable, geographic differentiation in material culture rules. I would surmise that containers came into use early in step 2, if not before. This must be seen as the main formative phase for the more elaborate faculties of mankind. During this period changes in brain size resulted in a doubling of cranial capacity, whatever that means. Although there were few dramatic changes, the maximum expression of qualities such as differentiation and refinement had increased very conspicuously by the end of the phase.

Step 3: Late Acheulian, Mousterian, Middle Stone Age, etc. (0.2–0.04 mya). In hindsight, this phase appears as transitional between subhuman and fully human capabilities. The first burials, grave offerings, and traces of cult come in during this span, and the first engraved artistic squiggles (Bordes, 1972a). The first forms that are explicitly designed for hafting appear in this span, although this practice may have begun earlier. The maximum degree of differentiation of design increased sharply. Regional differentiation of rule systems became pronounced, but both are still at markedly lower levels than in step 4.

Step 4 (0.04 mya, upwards). The maximum level of design complexity and of differentiation again rose sharply. Explicit traces of representational and abstract art appeared in areas as far apart as Europe and Australia, and then became common. Traces of ritual and overt symbolism became more and more frequent, and the maximum scale of these increased. Regional differentiation of rule systems became increasingly conspicuous, and the turnover in design norms or style became increasingly rapid.

Step 4 material culture has long given archaeologists a feel of being organized on much more elaborate principles than step 3, and there is still heated debate over whether the change from 3 to 4 involved the spread of genes determining superior capabilities (Breuil, 1912; Garrod, 1938; Bordes, 1972a). Alternative hypotheses more recently advanced suggest the spread of cultural and/or linguistic innovations that put behaviour across a crucial organizational threshold, perhaps a cognitive and communications equivalent of the agricultural revolution.

The comparative richness of Upper Palaeolithic material culture, particularly in Europe, has stimulated a voluminous and varied body of literature. Most archaeologists familiar with the field seem to be convinced that they are dealing with the products of human societies in possession of the full biological capabilities of our species as it exists today. In other words, the archaeology of this period can be treated as a segment of ethnography. It appears that variety among cultures that have existed during the last 30,000 years is to be regarded as due to the differential accumulation and modification of traditions disseminated in a reticulate communications web, involving varying degrees of specific adaptation and partial isolation. Grahame Clark (1970) has discussed the humanistic significance of the dawn of self-consciousness and the growth of symbolic activity that the bodily adornment, burial practices, and art of the period would seem to indicate. Alexander Marshack's work has also stimulated renewed awareness of these aspects of the Upper Palaeolithic (Marshack, 1972a, 1972b). I find it hard to evaluate in detail the claims that some of the engraved bones of this period represent systematic notations of lunar cycles, and so forth. However, his work has shown clearly that the markings are organized in a much more complex fashion than had previously been realized. If prehistorians are correct in their supposition that the Upper Palaeolithic societies had modern levels of ability in cognition and organization, then Marshack's findings are perfectly credible. They affect the date that we put on the achievement of present levels of linguistic capabilities rather than the question of the stages and processes by which they originated. Many other workers are also pursuing careful analytical studies of social organization, style, symbolism and cultural marking for this time range, so that a much more detailed understanding must emerge in a few years time.

Part 2. Archaeological reconstruction of the behaviour of early hominids: the role of language

Another approach that has value for our present inquiries is to ask what we know about the way of life of early hominids. What were the influences that encouraged the development of language capabilities? Two lines of evidence can contribute: one is the morphology of fossil hominid bones which provide indications of changing appearance and physical capabilities; the other, which is probably more important for our purposes here, is the archaeological record of activities. It should be stressed that artefact studies of the kind to which the attention of Part 1 was devoted constitute only a small part of modern Pleistocene archaeology. In addition to serving as repositories of fossilized information, the stone implements serve as indicators for the location of hominid activities. Through association with artefacts, archaeologists can identify traces of diet, butchered carcasses and camp sites. Further, the location of the traces in a reconstructed palaeoenvironment gives important additional clues to the ecology and land-use patterns. It is to the interpretation of economy and activities that much of the attention of current research is devoted.

Details of the evidence are clearly beyond the scope of this chapter (see Leakey, 1971; Isaac, 1976e [this volume, ch. 3]), but I can offer a brief summary. Researches, mainly along the Rift Valley in East Africa at localities such as Olduvai, the Omo, East Rudolf, Chesowanja and Hadar show that by two to three million years ago the adaptation of at least some hominids involved the following ingredients:

Bipedal locomotion. The forelimbs were free of supportive and propulsive functions. This is clearly documented by postcranial fossils from South and East Africa.

Toolmaking. The purposive transportation of materials over at least several miles is most clearly documented by the quantities of flaked stone at archaeological sites that are often remote from sources of rock. Presumably sticks, fibres and skin were being shaped and carried, as well as stone.

Meat-eating. The hominids were consuming quantities of meat including flesh from carcasses of animals much larger than themselves. Examples include proboscideans at Olduvai (Leakey, 1971) and a hippo at East Rudolf (Isaac, 1971a, 1976e [this volume, chs. 10 and 3]). This aspect of diet and activity is evident from recurrent associations of artefacts at butchered carcasses, and the repeated presence of scatters of broken-up bone where discarded stone artefacts also occur (Isaac, 1971a [this volume, ch. 10], 1976b). Until now we have found it difficult to distinguish between bone refuse from hunted as opposed to scavenged carcasses, although Elizabeth Vbra, working in the Transvaal, has recently found some promising criteria (1975). It is clear that the early hominids were more strongly carnivorous than any other living primate, and one suspects that, like other large carnivores (Schaller and Lowther, 1969), they got their meat from an opportunistic combination of hunting and scavenging.

Gathering (?) As yet, we lack direct evidence regarding the consumption of plant foods by very early hominids, but everything we know about primates and about non-farming peoples in the tropics suggests that plant foods would have been of crucial importance, presumably at least 70 or 80 per cent of the diet. We do not know when the shift occurred away from the feed-as-you-go mode characteristic of primates to the common human pattern of gathering followed by preparation and quasi-collective consumption. As we have seen in Part 1, the quantities of stone may imply the existence of bags or baskets. I will return to comment on the probable importance of gathering in early socio-economic systems.

Home-bases. The existence of dense patches of discarded artefacts at specific localities in the palaeo-landscape is clear evidence that early hominid activities were at times spatially focused. The coincidence of food refuse at these sites seems to imply that in some degree the human institution of camps or home bases had come into existence. From such a focus, different members of a social group could have gone out and engaged in separate pursuits, returning later, confident of rejoining the band.

Food-sharing. The presence of scatters of broken-up bone in coincidence with scatters of discarded artefacts implies that meat was being eaten. When, however, as at Olduvai and Koobi Fora, the bones derive from several different carcasses which are unlikely all to have been freshly killed at the same spot, then the evidence also implies that foodstuffs were being carried back to the home base. Perhaps it was transported to feed infants, but it seems very likely that the archaeological evidence attests to the beginnings of a crucial evolutionary shift into food sharing and partial division of labour. We have direct evidence only of transport and sharing of meat foods, but if the sharing involved reciprocity between segments of the group, then gathered plant foods, which may well have been the staples, would have been as important, or more so.

Considered individually, these behaviours that archaeology shows were established by 1.5–2 million years ago are not exclusively human traits, but all of them have been developed to a much higher intensity and level of importance in man than in any other primate. If we look at them we see that they are a functionally interrelated set, such that each component reinforces the utility of the others; many of the traits are not possible in isolation. Thus bipedalism allows for the transport of equipment and of food for sharing; stone tools enable a primate to cut up a large carcass as effectively as a carnivore; digging sticks give access to additional underground food sources; bags and trays allow gathered foods to be carried, and so on. In addition, gathering and food-sharing served as an insurance policy that made it possible to engage in the quest for meat, even though that was an enterprise which might succeed only once in three attempts (Lee, 1978). Thus it can fairly be said that bipedalism, the transport of materials, and the manufacture and use of equipment, together with food-sharing, constitute an adaptive complex of great importance in the differentiation of men from apes. The archaeological evidence is consistent with the notion that these behavioural modifications and the bodily changes that made them possible are the foundations on which the superstructure of human evolution has depended.

But what has all this to do with the origin of language? It is entirely conceivable that this kind of adaptive strategy could be operated by creatures with apelike social behaviour patterns, but it is also clear that the adaptive value of food-sharing and division of labour would be greatly enhanced by improvements in communication; specifically, the passage of information other than that relating to the emotions becomes highly adaptive. This has proved to be the case also in other zoological phyla that have made the acquisition of food a collective responsibility, as is shown, for instance, by the development of the so-called language of bees and other social insects. Thus I would argue that archaeological researches on relics from the time range before one million years ago contribute in a crucial way to our understanding of the milieu in which capabilities for language were first important.

We can now look at the way in which the separate approaches of Part 1 and Part 2 of this paper fit together. I can best do this by offering an archaeologist's view of the stages in development.

Phase I. The establishment of the first proto-human adaptive complex (bipedalism, transport, toolmaking, food-sharing). We do not know when this evolutionary shift began, but its effects were sufficient for them to be archaeologically detectable by about two million years ago. However, hominids of those times may well not have been human at all, in our sense.

Phase II. The establishment of this adaptive system put selection pressure on the enhancement of communication and information exchange systems, which presumably began to develop even during Phase I, but which went on to mature during Phase II. Archaeologically, this finds expression in the long oscillating record of such Lower Palaeolithic entities as the Acheulian, which span the time from around 1.5 mya to 0.1 mya (i.e. 100,000 years ago). As we have seen, there were developments in the level of technique and design complexities, but by our standards they are not large in relation to the vast span of time involved. In spite of the somewhat monotonous character of this phase, it must have been the main formative period for human cultural and communications capabilities. On the basis of present evidence, I imagine that if we could observe the hominids of 1.5–2 million years ago, we would first of all be struck more by differences from our sense of what is human than by similarities; by the end of Phase II, a host of indicators imply a basically human grade of organization.

Much has been made of the evolutionary influence of big-game hunting on human development in this phase (Pfeiffer, 1969; Campbell, 1966). Hunting may have been influential to a degree, and doubtless the success of intensive hunting patterns such as those in evidence at Olduvai BK, Olorgesailie DE/89, or at Torralba did exert their own evolutionary influence (Isaac, 1971a [this volume, ch. 10]). However, I would surmise that selection pressure has in fact favoured all those qualities that facilitate varied and flexible ways of making a living, of which hunting was one when the need and the chance arose. Our evolutionary niche is probably best described as opportunism, and language is surely the foremost of the skills that make us such effective opportunists.

Phase III. The maturation of cultural and presumably linguistic capabilities during the Middle Pleistocene seems to have opened up new potentials. Between about 50,000 and 100,000 years ago the archaeological record documents a quickening of the tempo of change (Isaac, 1972e [this volume, ch. 2]; Clark, 1970). Finally, about 30,000–40,000 years ago, the record gives the appearance that a threshold was crossed with the emergence of much more complex and more style-ridden systems of material culture. From this same period, as we have seen, come the first surviving manifestations of art and of bodily adornment. At present we really cannot say whether the change of tempo and the apparent crossing of a threshold is due to some kind of discrete innovation that created a surge of change that looks like a discontinuity, or whether we are seeing simply the trace of a critical bend in a geometric or hyper-geometric growth curve. As far as I am aware, Kenneth Oakley (1951) was one of the first to suggest that crucial developments in language may provide the best explanation of the Upper Palaeolithic cultural spurt. This remains an untested, but, in my view, very plausible hypothesis.

The interpretations of Lieberman and Crelin (Lieberman, 1975) can be viewed as potentially related, but I feel that there will have to be a careful appraisal of their results by anatomists and speech physiologists before archaeologists should incorporate them in their arguments.

Much of what has been set out in both Part 1 and Part 2 of this chapter is necessarily speculative. It is certain, however, that the evolutionary enlargement of human language capabilities did take place as a concomitant of the technological and socio-economic developments to which the attention of archaeology is usually confined. I have sketched two aspects of the perception of human evolution that an archaeologist gains from evidence in the ground. I hope that this mole's-eye view can be brought into a profitable relationship with other patterns that are described by anthropologists, ethologists and linguists, each viewing the problem from a different stance.

Acknowledgements

The ideas in this essay have been developed over the years, especially in discussion
with Sherwood Washburn, J. Desmond Clark and Barbara Isaac, who also did the
drawings. The research into early hominid life on which Part 2 depends is an
enterprise I share with the East Rudolf Research group and other close colleagues
in Africa. In recent years my interest in the relationship between artefacts and the
origins of language has been stimulated by conversations with Mary LeCron Foster.

Notes

1 This section incorporates material from an unpublished review that I prepared for
  presentation in a symposium on Form and Formative in the Symbolic Process, organized
  by Mary LeCron Foster and Peter Claus, at the 73rd annual meeting of the American
  Anthropological Association, Mexico City, November 1974.
2 Steps 1–4 coincide fairly closely with modes 1–4 as defined by Grahame Clark (1970).

V

Approaches to archaeology

17

Whither archaeology?

V. Gordon Childe made a characteristically clear statement about the position of prehistoric archaeology within the realms of knowledge. He wrote: 'By the inclusion of prehistory the preview of history is extended . . . history joins on to natural history' (Childe, 1941:4). Archaeological studies are at their most significant when they attempt to elucidate the development of relationships both amongst men, and between man and the material world. Indeed it becomes increasingly clear that it is not possible to understand either kind of development independently of the other. Prehistoric archaeology is thus in its total aims not a natural science, a social science or a branch of the humanities; rather it is a distinctive pursuit in which all of these meet.

Archaeology can also be described as a worm's eye view of human behaviour. The archaeologist derives his information from the traces of men's activities which linger in the ground long after the death of the men themselves. These relics are extremely varied: they may be ruins, refuse, tools or works of art, or they may be soil erosion and modifications to living organisms and to plant and animal communities. However, most of the marks that man has left on the face of the earth during his 2-million-year career as a litterbugging, meddlesome and occasionally artistic animal have one aspect in common: they are things, they are not deeds, ideas or words. Thus for better or for worse archaeologists are involved along with natural scientists in the study of objects and materials. When archaeology is at its best, the things are studied in order to make possible insight into the functioning of the economic, social and ideological systems of prehistoric communities. However, the scope and penetration of our perception of extinct human orders is directly proportional to the extent and acuity of our primary observations of objects.

Given widespread appreciation of the need of archaeology to cast its net broadly, it is scarcely surprising that successive generations of archaeologists have sought help and inspiration amongst an ever expanding range of sciences and disciplines. In the first instances, as Jacquetta Hawkes recently pointed out, cooperation has been obtained from partially subservient specialists such as soil scientists, metallurgists and palaeontologists. Meanwhile the study of artefact design, the inner sanctum of archaeology, remained secure. More recently, however, the notion that archaeologists can profit even in the study of artefacts from the help and experience of biometricians, statisticians and experts in cybernetics has apparently caused widespread alarm.

This essay is a response to the editor's invitation to archaeologists under forty to offer alternatives to Jacquetta Hawkes' pessimistic survey of contemporary trends in archaeology. The opening paragraphs will have made it clear that I differ markedly in my view of what archaeology ought to encompass. I do not advocate that archaeology should sever its connections with history and the humanities, but I believe that it differs significantly from them in its character. Archaeology is used throughout this paper to mean prehistoric archaeology because the discipline is most distinctive when the process of reconstruction is unaided by writing or oral tradition. Since most aims and methods are held in common between studies of prehistoric and historic periods, I think that this simplifies discussion without invalidating the main arguments.

This essay is not written simply as a rebuttal, since that would contribute little to discussion of the issues confronting archaeology. Moreover, although several of the whipping boys attacked by Jacquetta Hawkes were in my view singularly ill-chosen, there is no doubt that some of her general criticisms are fair ones. Her essay deserves careful reading even by those whom it annoys, because the onus of demonstrating the value of the new concepts and methods which alarm some traditionalists does lie with those who are developing them.

As a preliminary to any consideration of contemporary archaeology, it is essential to stress the point that the subject has diversified enormously since its nine-teenth-century origins. It is safe to predict that branching and the establishment of liaisons with an ever-widening range of disciplines will continue to be one of the most conspicuous trends. This diversity is one of the causes of excitement for those who work in the field and for spectators, but it requires tolerance. The phenomenon of man is sufficiently complex to demand examination from many standpoints. Uniformity of training or approach are not desirable and fortunately there is no sign that archaeologists are getting more alike. *Quot homines, tot sententiae: suo quoque mos.*

Given the need for archaeology to incorporate scholars with educational roots in the sciences, I would argue that it is an unjustifiable conceit to suppose that these colleagues will be less sensitive to certain values than scholars trained in the humanities. Such great biologists as Julian Huxley, J. B. S. Haldane or Gaylord Simpson, by becoming concerned with man and nature, have shown the deep humanistic significance that the scientific approach can acquire.

The extent and scale of modern archaeology is prodigious. Research now spans two million years of prehistory and successive phases of cultural diversification over the faces of five continents. Most of this activity naturally consists of the application of established methods to the task of filling in the details of prehistory. On a global scale, current investigations of two critical prehistoric developments are proving particularly interesting. First there is the study of the roots of human behaviour patterns in the Lower Pleistocene. Secondly there is the elucidation of the processes by which human behaviour was transformed through intensive use of farming techniques in both the Old and New Worlds. Despite their interest, these are advances in knowledge and understanding rather than in method and concept; and consequently have limited relevance as a basis for guesses about the future characteristics of archaeology as a discipline. However, some aspects of the best early man or early farming studies do appear to indicate the shape of things to come. In a number of cases the problem to be studied has been carefully formulated and a team of investigators has been assembled, amongst which a variety of scientists interested in anthropological problems take their place as partners rather than as technicians. The range of past human behaviours reconstructed by such teams has tended to be much broader than it usually was in days when conventionally trained archaeologists often restricted their interests to tool typology and art history.

Cutting across the present dispersal and diversity of archaeological studies are two movements which tend particularly to have appeal for the younger generation of workers. These movements involve the kinds of changes in attitude which alarm Jacquetta Hawkes. Neither of them was actually started by young archaeologists but they have been vigorously espoused by them and are often loosely characterized as the 'new archaeology'. A great deal of unnecessary sound and fury has accompanied numerous declarations by angry young men, but it would be quite wrong to conclude from this that the commotion signifies nothing.

One of the movements is in response to a growing self-consciousness of archaeology as a thoroughly distinctive pursuit which, despite borrowing, is methodologically independent of all others. The growth of this awareness has been accompanied by a clamour for systematization of archaeological inference and for the development of a more explicit conceptual framework. The other movement is distinguishable, but closely related. It consists of a tendency to increasing use of quantitative data of all kinds in the documentation of archaeological reports and arguments; this is often felt to be an obligation rather than an option.

Archaeological inference

For better or for worse, archaeology has hitherto undergone a century of development without becoming highly organized as a discipline. At an empirical level artefacts and field data have commonly been described and classified in diverse ways indicated by experience, intuition and convenience. At an interpretative level, inferences concerning cultures, evolution, migration and diffusion are treated as realities demonstrated by this material. In most archaeological writing the process of deriving the interpretational level from the empirical level is tacitly treated as though it were self-evident or a matter of common sense. This split-level arrangement served well during much of the development of archaeological knowledge; in particular it was serviceable when the number of professional archaeologists was quite small and it was possible to form a personal understanding of the nuances of each scholar's use of words and concepts.

Two cumulative changes have combined to create the present sense of crisis with regard to archaeological reasoning. First, there has been a steady increase in the number of professional archaeologists all over the world; and in the years since 1945 the increase might almost be described as explosive. The luxury of unstated personal assumptions, and unexplained systems of nomenclature and inference, has become increasingly a barrier to communication. Secondly, as archaeology has grown through the pioneer phases of establishing in outline major divisions of prehistoric culture, there has arisen the opportunity and the demand for ever finer exegesis of the evidence. While the concepts and entities involved in the bold outlines may have been in large measure self-evident, this is not true for finer constructs: hence the tumult. This is not simply a phenomenon dividing generations of archaeologists: important attempts to cope with these problems have a long history.

To single out but a few examples of writings which have signposted developments in this movement one might mention V. G. Childe's essay 'Changing methods and aims in prehistory' (1935), his book *Piecing together the past* (1956) and Willey and Phillip's *Method and Theory in American Archaeology* (1958). More recently the volume *Background to Evolution in Africa*, edited by Bishop and Clark (1967), reports the deliberations of older and younger scholars at an international symposium. Discussion centred on the need for clarification of concepts and stressed the importance of well-defined terms to convey these concepts.

The difference between the generations is partly marked by an actual sense of revolt amongst many younger scholars and by a tendency towards excessive use of jargon by the same group. However, it would be unfortunate if distaste for a barrage of new terms, some necessary, some redundant, were to give rise to the delusion that the whole proceeding is contemptible. What is going on is a most lively process of exploration. Amongst the methodological forays in which the 'new archaeologists' engage, some are vain and ill-conceived or merely iconoclastic, others are well-conceived but will prove unproductive, yet others will surely lead to clearer and more explicit insight into the nature of archaeological patterns. It can be anticipated that the combination of such attempts will enable archaeology to integrate the split levels of operation and become a more mature discipline with more widely understood interpretative principles.

Two recently published books deserve mention as particularly important representatives of this movement. One, a symposium entitled *New Perspectives in Archaeology*, edited by S. R. and L. R. Binford (1968) contains a broad spectrum of reformist views. The other, *Analytical Archaeology* by D. L. Clarke (1968), makes valuable attempts at generalizations regarding order and pattern amongst artefacts and archaeological evidence. Amongst other things, Clarke has experimented with the application of concepts and methods derived from systems analysis and numerical taxonomy. The book shows extraordinarily broadly based scholarship, with material from archaeological, historical and ethnographic sources being considered in original ways. It does not make very easy reading because, at the present stage of understanding, simple formulations are probably inadvisable. Evaluation of

Clarke's work should be made in relation to the widespread sense of a need for exploration. Its importance probably lies not only in the wealth of apparently fruitful new lines of thought which are developed but in the stimulus his formulations should provide to constructive critics who view things differently.

Quantitative methods

There is wide agreement amongst younger archaeologists the world over that archaeology would be better off if certain kinds of *judgements and decisions* were made with due regard to *relevant* quantitative information. The phrase 'judgement and decisions' is italicized because some contemporary writers tend to imply that the use of numerical data deprives the investigator of the opportunity to judge and interpret. 'Relevant' is stressed because the usefulness of quantities in archaeology, or any other discipline, will always depend on the existence of a significant relationship between what is measured and the problem to be solved. It is true that precision with regard to quantities and frequency distribution patterns can sometimes spoil a good scholastic debate by settling it conclusively, but this can hardly be advanced as a serious argument for refusing to admit these as legitimate methods even in a humanistic discipline.

The use of some quantitative data is practically as old as archaeology, and during this century there has been an erratic tendency to increase in the systematic use of numbers. However the current situation is distinctive in that the preoccupation of many younger archaeologists with quantitative methods has become so intense that something akin to a cult of numbers has arisen in certain quarters. This flurry of interest is commonly associated with concern over the theoretical foundations of archaeology. Taking a long view it seems likely that quantitative methods will prove indispensable to aspects of archaeology, but present hyper-consciousness of numbers will probably subside when trial and error has resulted in the development of a more sound conceptual framework and when a stock of effective analytical methods has been established.

Meanwhile we have to put up with a partly tedious intermediate situation. Extensive and often dull explanations of method are at the present stage frequently necessary. Many authors understandably feel obliged to present their data both by orthodox verbal and illustrative exposition and by attempts at quantitative characterization. Further, many users of numbers are rightly or wrongly not sufficiently confident of the virtues of statistics to have the courage to replace hundreds of measurements by a few items of information such as the mean, median, standard deviation and range. In addition there are reports where numbers ramble like sacred cows: their contribution to the author's argument is not explicit and the likelihood that anyone else can use them may also be slender. In other cases valuable numerical data may be compiled and then in effect abandoned by a reversion to conventional classificatory systems which ignore the continuous property of numerical scales. It is also apparent that numbers create an illusion of purity and have a fascination of their own. Archaeologists should heed the warning provided by the barren years which craniometry spent in the wilderness searching for formulae which would make numbers the universal key to understanding evolution and race (cf. Washburn, 1969).

The deficiencies of the present situation cause as much concern amongst exponents of quantitative methods as they do amongst traditionalists. However, the difference lies in the fact that proponents advocate rendering the morass fertile by drainage, while traditionalists appear to be advocating mere retreat back into a forest where at least the mystique of half comprehension is familiar. This is not an appropriate place for a full parade of arguments in favour of the development and application of suitable quantitative methods. Suffice it to say that quantitative considerations have long played an essential but unspecified role in archaeological interpretations. Standard words, such as 'common', 'rare', 'typical', are all labels for inherently quantitative properties of the evidence.

Awareness of modes in artefact design is so much a part of our culture that mathematicians borrowed the word as their term for the phenomenon in general. We need hardly be shy of reintroducing the methods which they have devised for clarifying the concept.

There are some worthwhile perceptions of patterns in archaeological data which may only be possible through the use of quantitative analysis. Examples of this kind of pattern may prove to include really complex geographic or chronological seriation patterns, or the unravelling of complex interactions between stylistic and functional factors which determined the form of tools or the composition of toolkits. Some interesting studies have already demonstrated that subtle patterns with considerable sociological and humanistic significance can be detected in assemblages of archaeological materials by quantitative methods when normal inspection would have revealed little or nothing. An outstanding example of this is Richardson and Kroeber's (1940) study of cycles of European dress style and the apparent influence of social tension on degrees of variability. Deetz's work on relationships between aspects of the potter's craft and socio-economic changes amongst the proto-historic Arikara is another case holding out promise for this kind of approach (Deetz, 1965).

The advent of electronic computers provides important opportunities for those interested in developing the necessary knowledge to take advantage of them. These devices are capable of many varied operations which can cross-reference intricate records and which can express aspects of patterning in very complex data. It is safe to predict extensive contributions to archaeological theory and knowledge by investigations which would not be possible without computers.

Many archaeologists share the anxiety expressed by Jacquetta Hawkes (1968:258) concerning a 'vast accumulation of insignificant, disparate facts, like a terrible tide of mud, quite beyond the capacity of man to contain and mould into historical form'. However, brevity can be achieved in two ways: replacement of information by vaguely substantiated judgements or by the definition of patterns which can be demonstrated to be valid, significant orderings of the total complexity. In practice, of course, both processes are involved in preparing an archaeological report, but clearly pattern summary is less destructive of information than unspecified personal judgements, however sound. Statistical operations can often fairly be characterized as processes for making controlled generalizations from sets of otherwise disparate items of information. Clearly it is possible that statistics may prove to be one of the filters which can help to hold back the tide of mud while releasing a clear stream of water into the pool of knowledge.

If we are in a phase of trial and error searching for effective methods of quantitative analysis and pattern recognition then it is to be expected that parts of the work now being done will prove sterile, other parts will later appear as tentative gropings, while only a comparatively small proportion can be expected to provide the kind of elegant clarification of archaeological situations that we may fairly demand of quantitative methods if they are to become an established part of archaeological procedure.

The archaeology of living people

Archaeology has become fairly adept at reconstructing from flimsy traces significant aspects of otherwise unknown extinct human behaviour patterns. However, there is a growing conviction amongst many archaeologists that we could get some novel insights into our methods and perhaps added vitality for our reconstructions if we were to take the scarcely precedented step of observing closely potential archaeological traces amongst peoples whose economy, sociology and ideology is already known. I envisage observations of the relationships between refuse patterns, including chemical residues, and living habits; careful records of settlement size and form in relation to community size and social structuring. Also of crucial importance are observations of variation in artefact morphology amongst individual craftsmen, amongst communities and craft lineages, and amongst larger social units.

Observations of these kinds of material manifestations are made by archaeologists as a matter of course on sites, where exact behavioural significance is a matter for reconstruction, but the observations have no counterpart in classic ethnography where the behaviour and the material traces could both be determined. This kind of study has been dubbed action archaeology (Kleindienst and Watson, 1956), and there is now a small literature on the subject (e.g. Ascher, 1962; Brain, 1967; Foster, 1960), but further work is a matter of urgency since the expansion of mass-produced plastic and canned food will displace behavioural arrangements of the kind that prevailed through prehistory. It is conceivable that such studies may help to do for archaeology what genetics and primate behaviour studies have done for human palaeontology.

Conclusion

From the foregoing discussion, the view emerges that archaeology is currently engaged in experimentation with a vast range of new techniques and methods. Any attempt to hamper this process by deliberate revision to the situation which prevailed during the youth of established archaeological scholars would be stultifying and unsuccessful. The contributions of many of the great names cited by Jacquetta Hawkes as exponents of balanced humanistic archaeology have been incorporated into the foundations of modern archaeology. Their potential successors would hardly be worthy of the training they have received at these hands if they were content to devote their lives simply to more of the same.

There tends to be an inverse relationship between complexity of subject matter and the degree of maturity of the discipline engaged in its study. Physics has been characterized as the very complex study of comparatively simple processes; biology as the comparatively simple study of enormously complex processes. Anthropology is at the next remove up in complexity of subject matter, and at several steps down in the degree of penetration hitherto achieved by its methods. Because anthropology in its broadest sense subsumes archaeology and history, it is no discredit to archaeology that it has only now accumulated sufficient experience to organize an explicit conceptual framework for dealing with its particular complexity. It should also not occasion surprise that the transformation is proving in part to be traumatic and inelegant. However, if we follow Jacquetta Hawkes in her belief that 'it would be better not to put in the shop window this half cooked, unleavened dough' – then it is not clear how the body of archaeologists is going to find out which recipes are more promising than others.

It seems undeniable that the prime responsibility of any scholarly discipline must be to maintain its factual basis in good order. It is equally true that the superstructure of insight and understanding is what really interests most of the participant scholars and the rest of intellectual humanity. It would be a distressing discovery if it proved true that the pursuit of significant information is incompatible with the achievement of insight. Also, if the goals and values of humanistic studies really are irreconcilable with those of scientific studies, then archaeology would be condemned eternally to the present schizophrenia so well depicted by Jacquetta Hawkes. However, it seems equally probable that when the new stock of ideas has been sorted and allowed to mature, archaeology will be greatly enriched. New levels of precision in presenting data and in interpreting them can surely lead to briefer and more interesting technical reports as well as providing the basis for more lively literary portrayals of what happened in prehistory.

The goals of archaeology have been well defined over the past century and will require little change. Archaeology ought to be what archaeology already is. The problem is how can we improve our ways of doing it? This is a challenge that every generation faces afresh.

18

Ancestors for us all: towards broadening international participation in palaeoanthropological research

Introduction

Fossilized remains of human ancestors and archaeological vestiges of their handicrafts are being found in all the inhabited continents. Clearly, the narrative of human origins spans the globe, and the pursuit of knowledge concerning the events and processes of human evolution needs to be a cooperative venture shared among peoples of all nations. However, in the world as it is today, there are some important imbalances. To overcome these, thoughtful consideration by the scientific community is needed. After thought and discussion, deliberate action will be essential.

The discussion of the topic offered here is inspired and informed by the session that concluded the 'Ancestors' symposium in New York. The session was entitled 'Problems of sponsoring paleoanthropology faced by institutions in developing countries'. The issues were addressed by an international panel of scientists consisting of: P. K. Basu (India), J. D. Clark (USA), M. Day (Britain), H. de Lumley (France), A. Nkini (Tanzania), L. Osmundsen (USA), J. Radovčić (Yugoslavia), S. M. Raza (Pakistan), Wu Rukang (China), M. Sakka (France), S. M. I. Shah (Pakistan), E. Vrba (South Africa), and G. Isaac (USA), Moderator.

This brief report and commentary cannot pretend to represent fully the views of any one member of the panel, let alone the ensemble, but an attempt is made to convey the shared sense of the major issues. This report should be read in conjunction with the preceding paper [Delson, 1985] by Ibrahim Shah and Mahmood Raza, who eloquently summarize the past experiences and the aspirations of one country – Pakistan.

The situation

A situation of imbalance exists as a consequence of several intersecting historical circumstances. Notably, (1) the early ancestors of humankind lived only in the Old World tropics. Consequently, while later fossils are being recovered and studied all over the globe, fossils of the earliest stages can only be found in Africa and the southern portions of Eurasia. However, (2) over the last two centuries, the great international movement that we call 'modern science' has had its location of maximum growth and intensity in an almost exactly complementary sector of the globe – namely, first in Western Europe and then later also in North America, the Soviet Union, China and Japan. Consequently, the great majority of the world's trained scientists and the great majority of well-equipped laboratories and museums are situated in regions where the early fossils do not occur. This, in turn, has meant that over the past century, as scientific curiosity about human evolutionary origins rose in intensity, expeditions and colonial organizations reached out into the scientifically less developed countries of the Old World tropics and collected specimens that were often taken back to the industrial centres from which the expeditions emanated. Participation of the citizens of the fossil-homeland countries has often been restricted to non-scientific roles.

There has been a kind of inevitability to this pattern until recently, but now, with the emergence of independent, self-governing nation states over most of Africa and Asia, and with the steadily increasing numbers of university educated young scientists in these countries, such a situation is no longer appropriate or tolerable. Equally, with the rise of sovereign nation states around the world, the peoples of each country take pride in the heritage of the human past that is to be found within their borders. The fossils and artefacts from each country are legitimately expected to be appropriately housed and preserved within the country, and there is mounting concern that, while knowledge should be shared, members of each nation's own scientific community should be fully involved in the discovery, study and interpretation of evidence derived from the country itself.

The challenge confronting the international scientific community is clear. What can be done to broaden participation in the pursuit of knowledge about human origins? How can nations with large numbers of trained scientists and well-equipped institutions help with the development of proportionally equivalent levels of activity in those countries that have hitherto had lower intensities of involvement?

The panel at the 'Ancestors' symposium considered several lines of possible action: (1) recruitment and training of young scientists, (2) museum and research facilities, and (3) educating the public and informing governments. It was clear to all participating in the discussion in New York that these lines of action are highly interconnected. For instance, recruitment and training cannot proceed successfully unless the public and the government of the country in question are aware of, and interested in, the palaeoanthropological materials of the country. Similarly, training would be futile if no facilities are developed where research can be pursued and where specimens and records can be safely cared for. There are thus no priorities among these headings. All are vital from the outset.

Recruitment and training

There exist numbers of countries in which strata preserve important palaeoanthropological evidence that are already known and which are being found and studied largely by expeditions emanating from developed nations. For these nations, there was a strong sense that the first step is for the expedition scientists to form partnerships with colleagues in the most appropriate existing institutions of the host country – even if there are not perfectly matched counterparts. This commonly means partnerships with scientists in museums, geological surveys and universities. The second step is to encourage university students to participate in the field researches. For those students who show aptitude and enthusiasm, the visitors have an obligation to help arrange for further undergraduate – or more usually, graduate – education. Often this involves the securing of scholarship funds that will allow the student to go abroad to a well-established institution so as to secure a full and in-depth training. It is increasingly common for expeditions to participate in friendly reciprocation of this kind, but it does also depend on the sympathetic help of funding agencies in their countries of origin.

The training of technical personnel is also important. This too can begin with the apprenticeship of appropriate young men and women in the work of visiting expeditions. Further technical training can then proceed by having experienced personnel from developed nations come and work in the host country and simultaneously design and establish facilities and train apprentices in their operation. Alternatively, prospective technical personnel can go abroad for training and experience. Both can occur, which is what happened in the case of the excellent casting laboratory attached to the National Museums of Kenya, a laboratory that supplies the world demand for high quality casts of the numerous important fossils that have been discovered in Kenya and in Tanzania. Regional centres of expertise such as this can then help other neighbouring countries develop their capabilities. For instance, the Nairobi casting lab has helped train technical staff for the Malawi Antiquities Service.

Modes of recruitment are an important aspect of securing a vigorous, well-trained palaeoanthropological work force in developing countries. Palaeoanthropology, with its arduous fieldwork and its elusive fragmentary evidences, is a pursuit to which, regardless of ability, not all temperaments are equally well suited. How are countries to find the youngsters that have the particular flair and drive? One possibility that was discussed was that the organizers of research – both visitors and hosts – look for opportunities to run field schools as a part of their programmes. Such schools will have the combined effect of broadening well-informed public awareness of what is involved in palaeoanthropology and hopefully of intensifying educated enthusiasm for the subject. Many more students will participate in the schools than can become life-long professional palaeoanthropologists. Some among them are liable to become schoolteachers of biology, geography, history and other disciplines. Some will become agricultural officers, geological surveyors, and so on. Many benefits for palaeoanthropological discovery flow from having such members of professional communities be aware of and interested in prehistory. Last, but not least, from among the participants in field schools from time to time students with the aptitude and passion for archaeology, palaeontology and palaeoecology will emerge and go on to take further training.

At the panel discussion. Dr Mahmood Raza gave expression to several other important points:

What are the prospects that the well-trained, new returnee will be able to carry out research? It's quite common that when well-qualified people return they are involved in all kinds of office duties. They wear ties and suits, and do not get much time for research. Given the circumstances that they do manage to get away from these exercises, then there's not adequate comparative material, and often only very poor library facilities that they can use to keep in touch with what is happening in other parts of the world. One of the possible solutions, in addition to requesting their own institution or government for funds, would be to request funds from various international agencies to develop a modest library and raise a comparative collection. That could be done when people are about to finish their studies and want to go home. One could apply for that kind of support and could prepare a library which eventually will go to one's future institutional base.

The last point I would like to make concerns exchange among scientists. I personally feel that would be beneficial if scientists of developing countries could visit each other's institutions and participate in one another's field research projects. This would provide an opportunity to supplement each other's facilities and also help in broadening understanding of regional problems.

Laboratory, museum and research facilities

It is now widely agreed and recognized that fossils and antiquities recovered in any country are part of the heritage of that country and that such materials should, wherever possible, reside in their country of origin. Sometimes, where facilities do not yet exist for full-scale study in the source country, temporary export is appropriate, but for many reasons this should be avoided whenever possible. Prompt return is always desirable. However, this kind of policy entails the establishment of suitable, safe storage and study facilities such as are characteristic of well-designed modern museums.

Expeditions working as visitors in a country should be increasingly aware of the need and obligation to provide facilities, where these are lacking, for the safe housing and study of their collections. Clearly, it is irresponsible to collect irreplaceable antiquities from the field and then not be able to preserve them properly in the country to which they belong. To solve the problem by long-term export is equally unacceptable nowadays. This principle has had clear expression in the action, for instance, of the French and the American funding agencies in helping to develop storage and study facilities in Ethiopia and Kenya. Similar moves are under way to help Pakistan and other countries.

In addition to storage, research facilities and apparatus are essential – both to facilitate research activity by young, newly qualified scientists and to allow visiting scientists to work on materials that they are no longer permitted to take away for study.

The facilities that are needed minimally include such things as cameras, microscopes, X-ray machines, cast-making labs and libraries. Eventually, such things as scanning electron microscopes, dating laboratories and chemical laboratories will also be needed.

Quite as important as building and apparatus are generous terms of employment that enable young scientists to pursue research. Such terms need to include appropriate support staff (secretarial and technical); vehicles and fieldwork opportunities; funds and encouragement to attend appropriate conferences; periodic study leave so as to keep up to date; libraries and reprints, plus computer facilities. All this means substantial amounts of money, of which initially the host country can commonly supply only a part. The international palaeoanthropological community will need to work hard in securing the support of its sponsors to help develop such facilities where they are needed and where they will be well used.

Clearly, the cooperative development of a network of research facilities in countries where important palaeoanthropological evidence is found presupposes a spirit of common enterprise that simultaneously recognizes legitimate national pride along with the sharing of inquiry and new knowledge. It will be essential that protocols governing access to field sites and to collections be developed. These will presumably involve the normal etiquette of the reservation of access to recently recovered unpublished materials and the setting up of research clearance procedures to which would-be visitors can openly apply.

The interest of the specimens is also important. It is predictable that in ensuing decades the number of scientists and students interested in human evolution will steadily increase. If every member of this growing community handles and measures every fossil, the specimens will be worn out before the end of the century. Members of the panel reported on steps that curators are taking to keep access open when it is needed and yet preserve the fossils. Providing excellent casts, making available good, standard photographs, and issuing lists of standard measurements were all possible procedures that were mentioned.

The question of curation and access leads to the issue of the production, quality, and distribution of casts and replicas. The symposium in New York had the benefit of a report and commentary from Mrs Lita Osmundsen, Director of Research for the Wenner-Gren Foundation, which organization for many years pioneered in the production and circulation of high-quality casts. Mrs Osmundsen stated:

If techniques of mold and cast-making are thought of in the light of needs for wide distribution rather than in terms of occasional, individual needs and interests, new demands are placed on the production process. The leap from producing casts in a hit-and-miss way to one of developing a network of facilities for a maturing field of study is not a simple one. It requires not only finances and ongoing support but mutual collaboration on a global basis and the commitment of scholars, technicians, and administrators at the institutional, provincial, and governmental levels. We must also take into account the fact that despite the crying need this community feels for access to these materials, in mass-production terms the market is very limited, and the process, if well-designed for the control of quality, can be more costly than most people foresee. Furthermore, added to that cost is the factor of upkeep and update, which very few people think about . . .

The existence of casts of high and consistent quality can contribute to the protection, preservation, and interpretation of originals and the dissemination of knowledge. Much depends, however, on acquisition and on the integrity of the scholarly community at large to honor the standards of quality and respect the inherent rights of ownership. Copyrights attest to those rights and to the authenticity of product, but piracy does exist. It is the profession itself that must monitor these acts and prevent them primarily by moral pressure. Recipients of known pirated materials are equally responsible for undermining the total enterprise and rewarding such practices.

Issues that need to be further discussed include access, conceptualization, funding, appropriate methods of quality control, limits to fidelity and accuracy, and respect for the rights of ownership. These begin to set the agenda for a conference of the best and most responsible minds in the profession, who can develop the guidelines for managing a constructive and useful enterprise for disseminating reliable materials. The developing countries must play a major role. Developing such an enterprise offers a great opportunity.

Public education

We confront here a classic dilemma – a which-comes-first-the-chicken-or-the-egg situation! Public knowledge, interest, and pride are important as eggs to justify and secure support for inquiry into prehistory, but first one has to have a chicken in the form of trained personnel and effective museums! Dr Desmond Clark, as a member of the panel, put the matter well:

I was for 23 years a museum director in an African country [Zambia], and I fully appreciate the problems faced more recently by scientists starting up in independent nations. I had the same problems. The first is involved in educating the public, and that is bound up with educating the government to give you money! This is absolutely essential. It took us about 15 years to make my government [in colonial Northern Rhodesia] realize that a curator did not simply sit at the museum door and wait to show people around.

But after a lot of pushing and so on, once they realized the worthwhileness of what we were doing, then they gave us as much as they could afford, not only for conservation and display, but also for research . . . so I recommend first of all to educate the government for some funding, then also to encourage scientists from outside to come and collaborate so as to help provide collections and help provide the basic research that goes to understanding the collections. All this must be done in close collaboration. No longer is there any room for the hit-and-run expeditions of the past, where people descended from the sky, dug big holes, scooped up everything, took it away, and that was that. The people in the countries like to see the originals. They don't want to see casts in their national museums; they want to see originals and take pride in what it is that comes from their country.

Starting from scratch to disseminate knowledge and arouse interest clearly is not easy, but equally clearly it is important that scientific guests in developing countries put effort into helping their host scientists with this task, by giving classes and lectures, providing newspaper stories, and helping with exhibits. As already discussed, one possibility is the operation of field schools that cater to as wide a range of participants as possible – certainly more than just a handful of trainees.

Palaeoanthropology is mainly important for the answers that it provides about origins and history, but its researches also do bring practical benefits, and the scientific community needs to help developing countries realize and make use of those benefits. Among others, these include the links between comparative anatomical research and medical school anatomy training; or links between palaeoanthropology, stratigraphic geology, and the mapping of economic rock and mineral resources – to witness, diamond-bearing deposits in Angola, diatomites in Kenya, and gravels everywhere.

The 'Ancestors' exhibit has given the public of New York an extraordinary opportunity to become more interested and more informed. Should such exhibits of original specimens now go to capital cities all over the world in order to promote interest and support? Many scientists would join with Dr Mary Leakey, who argued at the symposium that New York's good fortune should not become a universal expectation, since if it were to do so, the irreplaceable fossils would be subject to repeated wear and risk of damage or loss. However, independent plans are already underway for carefully designed travelling exhibits involving casts. Such exhibits can surely go to cities all over the world and perhaps, if combined with the exhibition of originals from the host country can serve to arouse interest and to symbolize the international characteristics of human origins research.

The future

The panel adopted no resolutions and made no formal recommendations. However, some aspects of what should be done stood out particularly clearly. Most important is the development of a sense of partnership linking scientists in countries with well-established traditions of research and those where local involvement is just beginning. Whenever possible, research should be a joint collaborative effort. Happily, this is rapidly becoming common practice.

Members of such partnership enterprises then need to work together to foster interest and support in the developing nation, even if the support is modest in financial terms. The partners also need to work to educate the sponsors of palaeoanthropological research to recognize that it is no longer sufficient for them just to buy tents, jeeps and plane tickets. Funds must be included to facilitate the development of crucial facilities for the storage and study of the specimens that are found. Helping to secure scholarship funds for young trainees is also a crucial reciprocal responsibility. For example, the Baldwin Fellowships of the L. S. B. Leakey Foundation is a pioneer programme providing training for African nationals. All these kinds of changes for the better are already well underway, but they need all the help they can get.

The 'Ancestors' symposium as a whole and the session on problems for developing countries in particular gave ample evidence of the existence of a grand common esprit that links scientists from around the world as they share the pursuit of inquiry into human origins. Given the esprit, there are surely grounds for optimism about redressing current imbalances – optimism, yes, but complacency, no. Perhaps, the 'Ancestors' symposium can help us to start thinking about a formal international research and education drive modelled on the IBP – a decade of human origins research that, among other things, will organize funds to train personnel and develop facilities where they are most needed.

References

Ammerman, A. J. and M. W. Feldman. 1974. On the 'making' of an assemblage of stone tools. *American Antiquity* 39: 610–16.

Andrews, P. 1983. Small mammal faunal diversity at Olduvai Gorge, Tanzania. In *Animals and Archaeology: Hunters and their Prey*. Edited by J. Clutton-Brock and C. Grigson. Oxford: BAR International Services 163.

Arambourg, C. and Y. Coppens. 1967. Sur la découverte dans le Pleistocéne inférieur de la vallée de l'Omo (Ethiopie) d'une mandibule d'australopithécien. *Comptes Rendus des Séances de l'Académie de Sciences, Paris* 265: 589–90.

Ardrey, R. 1961. *African Genesis*. London: Collins.

Aronson, J. L., T. J. Schmitt, M. Taieb, D. C. Johanson, J. J. Tiercelin, R. C. Walter, C. W. Nasser and A. E. M. Nairn. 1977. New geochronologic and paleomagnetic data for the hominid-bearing Hadar Formation, Ethiopia. *Nature* 267: 323–7.

Ascher, R. 1962. Ethnography for archaeology: a case from the Seri Indians. *Ethnology*, 1, 360–9.

Bailey, G. N. and P. Callow. 1986. eds. *Stone Age Prehistory*. Cambridge: Cambridge University Press.

Bailloud, G. 1965. *Cahiers de l'Institut Ethiopien d'Archéologie*. 1. Addis Ababa: Institut Ethiopien d'Archéologie.

Baker, B. H. 1958. *Geology of the Magadi Area*. Report No. 42. Geological Survey of Kenya. Nairobi: Government Printer.

Balout, L. 1955. *Préhistoire de l'Afrique du Nord*. Paris: Arts et Métiers Graphiques.

Balout, L., P. Biberson, and J. Tixier. 1967. L'Acheuléen de Ternifine (Algérie), gisement de l'Atlanthrope. *L'Anthropologie* 71: 217–38.

Barnes, A. S. 1947. The technique of blade production in Mesolithic and Neolithic times. *Proceedings of the Prehistoric Society*. London.

Barnes, V. E. 1963. Tektite strewn-fields. In *Tektites*. Edited by J. A. O'Keefe. Chicago: University of Chicago Press.

Barbetti, M., J. D. Clark, F. M. Williams and M. A. J. Williams. 1980. Paleomagnetism and the search for very ancient fireplaces in Africa. *Anthropologie* 18 (2,3): 299–304.

Barthelme, John W. 1985. *Fisher-hunters and Neolithic pastoralists in east Turkana, Kenya*. Oxford: BAR International Series: 254.

Bar Yosef, O. 1975. Archaeological occurrences in the Middle Pleistocene of Israel. In *After *the Australopithecines.* Edited by K. W. Butzer and G. L. Isaac. The Hague: Mouton.

Beck, B. 1980. *Animal Tool Use.* New York: Garland STMP Press.

Behrensmeyer, A. K. 1975. The taphonomy and palaeoecology of Plio-Pleistocene vertebrate assemblages east of Lake Rudolf, Kenya. *Bulletin of the Museum of Comparative Zoology* 146: 473–578.

⸻ 1976a. Fossil assemblages in relation to sedimentary environments in the east African succession. In *Earliest Man and Environment in the Lake Rudolf Basin: Stratigraphy, Paleoecology and Evolution.* Edited by Y. Coppens *et al.* Chicago: University of Chicago Press.

⸻ 1976b. Taphonomy and paleoecology in the hominid fossil record. *Yearbook of Physical Anthropology* 19: 36–50.

⸻ 1978a. Taphonomic and ecologic information from bone weathering. *Paleobiology* 4: 150–62.

⸻ 1978b. The habitat of Plio-Pleistocene hominids in East Africa: Taphonomic and micro-stratigraphic evidence. In *Early Hominids of Africa.* Edited by C. J. Jolly. London: Duckworth.

⸻ 1982. The geological context of human evolution. *Annual Review of Earth and Planetary Sciences* 10: 39–60.

⸻ 1983. Patterns of natural bone distribution on recent and Pleistocene land surfaces: implications for archaeological site formation. In *Animals and Archaeology: Hunters and their Prey.* Edited by J. Clutton-Brock and C. Grigson. Oxford: BAR International Services 163.

⸻ 1980. The recent bones of Amboseli Park, Kenya in relation to East African palaeoecology. In *Fossils in the Making: Vertebrate Taphonomy and Palaeoecology.* Edited by A. K. Behrensmeyer and A. Hill. Chicago: University of Chicago Press.

Behrensmeyer, A. K. and D. E. Dechant. 1980. The recent bones of Amboseli Park, Kenya in relation to E. A. paleoecology. In *Fossils in the Making: Vertebrate Taphonomy and Palaeoecology.* Edited by A. K. Behrensmeyer and A. Hill. Chicago: Chicago University Press.

Behrensmeyer, A. K. and A. Hill. 1980. eds. *Fossils in the Making: Vertebrate Taphonomy and Palaeoecology.* Chicago: University of Chicago Press

Behrensmeyer, A. K. and L. F. LaPorte. 1981. Footprints of a Pleistocene hominid in northern Kenya. *Nature* 289: 167–9.

Behrensmeyer, A. K., D. Western and D. D. Boaz. 1979. New perspective in paleoecology from a recent bone assemblage. *Paleobiology* 5: 12–21.

Bemmelen, R. W. van. 1949. *The Geology of Indonesia* Vol. 1A, General Geology of Indonesia and Adjacent Archipelagoes. The Hague: Government Printing Office.

Bendall, D. S. 1983. *Evolution from Molecules to Men.* Cambridge: Cambridge University Press.

Bettinger, R. L., (1977). Aboriginal human ecology in Owens Valley: prehistoric change in the Great Basin, *American Anthropology* 42 (1): 3–17.

Biberson, P. 1961. Le Paléolithique Inférieur du Maroc Atlantique. *Publications du Service des Antiquités du Maroc* 17. Rabat.

Binford, L. R. 1963. 'Red ocher' caches from the Michigan area: a possible case of cultural drift. *Southwestern Journal of Anthropology* 19, 89–108.

⸻ 1968a. Archaeological perspectives. In *New Perspectives in Archaeology.* Edited by S. R. and L. R. Binford. Chicago: Aldine.

⸻ 1968b. Post-Pleistocene adaptations. In *New Perspectives in Archaeology.* Edited by S. R. and L. R. Binford. Chicago: Aldine.

1972. Contemporary model building paradigms and the current-state of Paleolithic research. In *Models in Archaeology*. Edited by D. L. Clarke. London: Methuen.

1977a. Olorgesailie deserves more than an ordinary book review. *Journal of Anthropological Research* 33 (4): 493–502.

1977b. *For Theory Building in Archaeology*. New York: Academic Press.

1981 *Bones, Ancient Men and Modern Myths*. New York: Academic Press.

1984. Bones of contention: a reply to Glynn Isaac. *American Antiquity* 49, 164–7.

1985. Human ancestors: changing views of their behavior. *Journal of Anthropological Archaeology* 4, 292–327.

Binford, L. R. and S. R. Binford. 1966. A preliminary analysis of functional variability in the Mousterian of Levallois facies. In *Recent Studies in Paleo-anthropology*. Edited by J. D. Clark and F. C. Howell. *American Anthropologist* Special Publication 68 (2), 238–95.

Binford, L. R. and S. R. Binford. 1969. Stone tools and human behaviour. *Scientific American* 220 (4), 70–82.

Binford, S. R. and L. R. Binford. 1968. eds. *New Perspectives in Archaeology*. Chicago: Chicago University Press.

1969. Stone tools and human behaviour. *Scientific American,* 220 (4), 70–84.

Bishop, W. W. 1963. The Later Tertiary and Pleistocene in eastern Equatorial Africa. In *African Ecology and Human Evolution*. Edited by F. C. Howell and F. Bourlière. Chicago: Aldine.

1978b Geological Framework for the Kilombe Acheulian site, Kenya. In *Geological Background to Fossil Man*. Edited by W. W. Bishop. Edinburgh: Scottish Academic Press.

Bishop, W. W. and J. D. Clark. 1967. eds. *Background to Evolution in Africa*. Chicago: University of Chicago Press.

Bishop, W. W. and J. Miller. 1972. *Calibration of Hominid Evolution*. Edinburgh: Scottish Academic Press.

Bishop, W. W., A. Hill, and M. Pickford. 1978. Chesowanja: A revised geological interpretation. In *Geological Background to Fossil Man*. Edited by W. W. Bishop. Edinburgh: Scottish Academic Press.

Black, D. 1933. Ed. Fossil man in China. The Choukoutien cave deposits with a synopsis of our present knowledge of the late Cenozoic in China. Contributions by D. Black, T. de Chardin, C. C. Young and W. C. Pei. *Memoirs of the Geological Survey of China* A (11). Peiping.

Blanc, A. C. 1957. On the Pleistocene sequence of Rome: paleoecologic and archeologic correlations. *Quaternaria* 4: 95–110.

Blumenschine, R. J. 1983. Taphonomy of faunal remains and site formation of Chesowanja archaeological locality 1/6E, Kenya. Manuscript on file, Department of Anthropology, University of California, Berkeley.

Boaz, D. D. 1982. Modern riverine taphonomy: its relevance to the interpretation of Plio-Pleistocene hominid paleoecology in the Omo Basin. Doctoral dissertation, University of California, Berkeley.

Boaz, N. T. 1977. Paleoecology of early Hominidae in Africa. *Kroeber Anthropological Society Papers* 50: 37–62.

Boesch, C. and H. Boesch. 1981. Sex differences in the use of natural hammers by wild chimpanzees: a preliminary report. *Journal of Human Evolution* 10: 585–93.

Bonnefille, R. 1979. Méthode palynologique et réconstitutions paléoclimatiques au Cénozoique dans le Rift Est Africain. *Bulletin de la Société Géologique, France* 21: 331–42.

Bonnefille, R., J. Chavaillon and Y. Coppens. 1970. Résultats de la nouvelle mission de l'Omo (3ème campagne 1969). *Comptes Rendus des Scéances de l'Académie des Sciences, Paris* 270: 924–7.

Bordes, F. 1950a. L'évolution buissonnante des industries en Europe occidentale. Considéra-tions théoriques sur le Paléolithique ancien et moyen. *L'Anthropologie* 54: 393–420.

1950b. Principes d'une méthode d'étude des techniques de débitage et de la typologie du Paléolithique ancien et moyen. *L'Anthropologie* 54: 19–34.

1953. Essai de classification des industries 'Moustériennes'. *Bulletin de la Société Préhis-torique Française*, 50: 226–35.

1961a. Mousterian cultures in France. *Science* 134: 803–10.

1961b. *Typologie du Paléolithique Ancien et Moyen.* Bordeaux: Imprimeries Delmas.

1968. *The Old Stone Age.* New York and Toronto: McGraw-Hill.

1971. Physical evolution and technological evolution in man: a parallelism. *World Archaeology* 3: 1–5.

1972a *A Tale of Two Caves.* New York: Harper and Row.

1972b ed. *The Origin of Homo Sapiens* Paris: UNESCO, INQUA.

Bordes, F. and D. de Sonneville-Bordes, 1970. The signifcance of variability in Palaeolithic assemblages. *World Archaeology* 2 (1), 61–73.

Bourgon, M. 1957. Les industries Moustériennes et Pre-Moustériennes du Perigord. *Archives de l'Institut de Paléontologie Humaine* 27.

Bout, P. 1969. Datations absolues de quelques formations volcaniques d'Auvergne et du Velay et chronologie du Quaternaire européen. *Revue d'Auvergne* 83: 267–80.

Bout, P., J. Frechen and R.-J. Lippolt. 1966. Datations stratigraphiques et radioch-ronologiques de quelques coulées basaltiques de Limagne. *Revue d'Auvergne* 80: 207–31.

Bower, J. 1977. Attributes of Oldowan and Lower Acheulian tools: 'tradition' and design in the early Lower Paleolithic. *South African Archaeological Bulletin* 32: 113–26.

Bowler, J. M. 1971. Pleistocene salinities and climatic change: evidence from lakes and lunettes in Southeastern Australia. In D. J. Mulvaney and J. Golson, eds., *Aboriginal Man and Environment in Australia.* Australian National University Press.

Bowler, J. M. R. Jones, H. Allen and A. G. Thorne 1970. Pleistocene human remains from Australia: a living site and human civilisation from Lake Mungo, Western New South Wales. *World Archaeology* 2: 39–60.

Braidwood, R. J. and B. Howe. 1962. Southwestern Asia beyond the lands of the Mediter-ranean littoral. In *Courses towards Urban Life.* Edited by R. J. Braidwood and G. R. Willey. Chicago: Aldine.

Brain, C. K. 1967a. Bone weathering and the problem of pseudo tools. *South African Journal of Science* 63: 97–9.

1967b. Hottentot food remains and their bearing on the interpretation of fossil bone assemblages. *Scientific Papers of the Namib Research Station* 32. Pretoria.

1970. New finds at Swartkrans Australopithecine site. *Nature.* 225: 1112–18.

1976 Some principles in the interpretation of bone accumulations associated with man. In *Human origins: Louis Leakey and the East African Evidence.* Edited by G. Ll. Isaac and E. McCown. Menlo Park, California: W. A. Benjamin.

1981 *The Hunters or the Hunted?* Chicago: University of Chicago Press.

1982 The Swartkrans site: stratigraphy of the fossil hominids and a reconstruction of the environment of early Homo. *Congrés International de Paléontologie Humaine* 1, Nice.

Breuil, H. 1912. Les sub-divisions du Paléolithique supérieur. Geneva: Congrés International d'Anthropologie.

1932. Les industries à éclats du Paléolithique ancien. *Préhistoire* 1 (2): 125–90.

Brock, A., and G. Ll. Isaac. 1974. Paleomagnetic stratigraphy and chronology of hominid-bearing sediments east of Lake Rudolf, Kenya. *Nature* 247: 344–8.

Brown, F. H., and T. E. Cerling. 1982. Stratigraphical significance of the Tulu Bor Tuff of the Koobi Fora Formation. *Nature* 299: 212–15.

Brown. F. H. and K. R. Lajoie. 1971. Radiometric age determinations on Pliocene-Pleistocene Formations in the Lower Omo Basin, Ethiopia. *Nature* 229: 483–5.

Brown, F. H., and W. P. Nash. 1976. Radiometric dating and tuff mineralogy of Omo Group deposits. In *Earliest Man and Environments in the Lake Rudolf Basin: Stratigraphy, Paleoecology and Evolution.* Edited by Y. Coppens *et al.* Chicago: University of Chicago Press.

Brown, F. H., F. C. Howell and G. G. Eck. 1978. Observations on problems of correlation of late Cenozoic hominid-bearing formations in the north Lake Turkana Basin. In *Geological Background to Fossil Man.* Edited by W. W. Bishop. Edinburgh: Scottish Academic Press.

Bunn, H. 1981. Archaeological evidence for meat-eating by Plio-Pleistocene hominids from Koobi Fora and Olduvai Gorge. *Nature* 291: 574–7.

    1982a. *Meat-eating and Human Evolution: Studies on the Diet and Subsistence Patterns of Plio-Pleistocene Hominids in East Africa.* Ph. D. dissertation, Department of Anthropology, University of California, Berkeley.

    1982b. Animal bones and archaeological inference: review of L. R. Binford 1981, *Bones, Ancient Men and Modern Myths. Science* 215: 494–5.

    1983a. Evidence on the diet and subsistence patterns of Plio-Pleistocene hominids at Koobi Fora, Kenya, and Olduvai Gorge, Tanzania. In *Animals and Archaeology: Hunters and their Prey.* Edited by J. Clutton-Brock and C. Grigson. Oxford: BAR.

    1983b. Comparative analysis of modern bone assemblages from a San hunter-gatherer camp in the Kalahari Desert, Botswana, and from a spotted hyena den near Nairobi, Kenya. In *Animals and Archaeology: Hunters and their Prey.* Edited by J. Clutton-Brock and C. Grigson. Oxford: BAR.

Bunn, H. T., J. W. K. Harris, Z. Kaufulu, E. Kroll, K. Schick, N. Toth, and A. K. Behrensmeyer. 1980. FxJj 50: An early Pleistocene site in northern Kenya. *World Archaeology* 12: 109–36.

Burkitt, M. C. 1933. *The Old Stone Age: A Study of Palaeolithic Times.* Cambridge: Cambridge University Press.

Butzer, K. W. 1964. *Environment and Archaeology.* London: Methuen.

    1965. Acheulian sites at Torralba and Ambrona, Spain: their geology. *Science* 150: 3704, 1718–22.

    1971. *Environment and Archaeology.* 2nd edition. Chicago: Aldine.

    1976. Pleistocene climates. *Geoscience and Man* 13: 27–44.

    1977. Environment, culture and human evolution. *American Scientist* 65: 572–84.

Butzer, K. W., F. R. Brown and D. L. Thurber. 1969. Horizontal sediments of the Lower Omo Valley: the Kibish Formation. *Quaternaria* 11: 15–29.

Cahen, D., L. H. Keeley, and F. L. Van Noten. 1979. Stone tools, toolkits, and human behavior in prehistory. *Current Anthropology* 20: 661–83.

Calvin, W. H. 1982. Did throwing shape hominid brain evolution? *Ethology and Sociobiology* 3: 115–24.

Campbell, B. G. 1966. *Human Evolution: an Introduction to Man's Adaptations.* Chicago: Aldine.

    1974. *Human Evolution: an Introduction to Man's Adaptations.* 2nd edition. Chicago: Aldine.

Cann, R., W. M. Brown and A. C. Wilson. 1982. Evolution of human mitochondrial DNA: molecular, genetic and anthropological implications. *Proceedings of the 6th International Congress of Human Genetics.* Jerusalem.

Cerling, T. E. and F. H. Brown. 1982. Tuffaceous marker horizons in the Koobi Fora region and the lower Omo valley. *Nature* 299: 216–21.

Cerling, T. E., R. L. Hay and J. O'Neil. 1977. Isotopic evidence for dramatic climate changes in East Africa during the Pleistocene. *Nature* 267: 137–8.

Cerralbo, Marquis de. 1913. Torralba, la plus ancienne station humaine de l'Europe? *Congrés International d'Anthropologie et d'Archéologie Préhistorique*, Comptes Rendus, XIV session. Geneva.

Chavaillon, J. 1967. La Préhistoire éthiopienne à Melka Kontoure'. *Archéologia* (Nov–Dec.): 56–63.

    1970. Découverte d'un niveau Oldowayen dans la basse vallée de l'Omo (Ethiopie). *Bulletin de la Société Préhistorique Française* 67: 7–11.

    1971. Prehistorical living floors of Melka Kontouré in Ethiopia (guide pamphlet). *VII Pan-African Congress of Prehistory and Quaternary Studies.* Addis Ababa.

    1976. Evidence for the technical practices of early Pleistocene hominids. In *Earliest Man and Environments in the lake Rudolf Basin: Stratigraphy. Paleoecology and Evolution.* Edited by Y. Coppens *et al.* Chicago: University of Chicago Press.

    1982. Position chronologique des hominidés fossiles d'Ethiopie. *Congrés International de Paléontologie Humaine* 1: 766–97.

Chavaillon, J. and J. Boisaubert. 1977. Prospection archéologique dans le Gemu-Gofa et la basse vallée de l'Omo. *Documents Histoire Civilisation Ethiopienne* RCP 230, CNRS Fascicule 8: 3–10.

Chavaillon, J., N. Chavaillon, F. Hours, and M. Piperno. 1978. Le Début et la fin de l'Acheuléen à Melka-Kunturé: méthodologie pour l'étude des changements de civilisation. *Bulletin de la SPF* 75: 105–15.

    1979. From the Oldowan to the Middle Stone Age at Melka Kunturé (Ethiopia): understanding cultural changes. *Quaternaria* 21: 87–114.

Chavaillon, M. J. and N. Chavaillon. 1971. Présence éventuelle d'un abri Oldowayen dans le gisement de Melka-Kontouré (Ethiopie). *Comptes Rendus des Séances de l'Académie des Sciences, Paris* 273: 623–5.

Cherdyntsev, V. V., I. V. Kazachevskiy and Ye. A. Kuz'mina. 1965. Dating of Pleistocene carbonate formations by the thorium and uranium isotopes. *Geochemistry International* 2: 794–801.

Childe, V. G. 1935. Changing methods and aims in prehistory. *Proceedings of the Prehistoric Society*, n.s. 1: 1–15.

    1941. *Man Makes Himself.* London.

    1956. *Piecing Together the Past.* London.

Chorley, R. H. and P. Haggett. 1967. *Models in Geography.* London: Methuen.

Clark, J. D. 1954. An early Upper Pleistocene site on the Northern Rhodesia–Tanganyika border. *South African Archaeological Bulletin* : 51–6.

    1959. Further excavations at Broken Hill, Northern Rhodesia. *Journal of the Royal Anthropological Institute* 89: 201–32.

    1966. Acheulian occupation sites in the Middle East and Africa: a study in cultural variability. In *Recent Studies in Paleoanthrolopogy.* Edited by J. D. Clark and F. C. Howell. *American Anthropologist*, special publication 68(2)2: 202–29.

    1967. The Middle Acheulian occupation site at Latamne, northern Syria (first paper). *Quaternaria* 9: 1–68.

    1968. Studies of hunter-gatherers as an aid to the interpretation of pre-historic societies. In *Man The Hunter.* Edited by R. B. Lee and I. DeVore. Chicago: Aldine.

    1969. Kalambo Falls Prehistoric Site, Vol. I: *The Geology, Palaeoecology, and Detailed Stratigraphy of the Excavations.* Cambridge: Cambridge University Press.

    1969. The Middle Acheulian occupation site at Latamne, northern Syria. Further excavations (1965): general results, definition and interpretation. *Quaternaria* 10: 1–71.

1970. *The Prehistory of Africa.* London: Thames and Hudson. 1975. Africa in prehistory: peripheral or paramount? Royal Anthropological Institute Huxley Memorial lecture (7 Nov. 1974). *Man,* n.s. 10: 175–98.

1980. Early human occupation of savanna environments in Africa with particular reference to the Sudanic zone. In *Human Ecology in Savanna Environments,* edited by D. R. Harris. New York: Academic Press.

1982. New men, strange faces, other minds: an archaeologist's perspective on recent discoveries relating to the origin and spread of modern man. *Proceedings of the British Academy.*

Clark, J. D. and C. V. Haynes. 1970. An elephant butchery site at Mwanganda's Village, Karonga, Malawi, and its relevance for Palaeolithic archaeology. *World Archaeology* 1, (3): 390–411.

Clark, J. D. and H. Kurashina. 1979a. Hominid occupation of the east-central highlands of Ethiopia in the Plio-Pleistocene. *Nature* 282: 33–9.

1979b. An analysis of earlier stone age bifaces from Gadeb (Locality 8E), Northern Bale Highlands, Ethiopia. *South African Archaeological Bulletin* 34: 93–109.

Clark, J. D., G. H. Cole, G. Ll. Isaac, and M. R. Kleindienst. 1966. Precision and definition in African archaeology. *South African Archaeological Bulletin* 21(83): 114–21.

Clark, J. G. D. 1954. *Excavations at Star Carr, an early Mesolithic site at Seamer near Scarborough, Yorkshire.* Cambridge: Cambridge University Press.

1957. *Archaeology and Society.* 3rd edition. London: Methuen.

1969. *World Prehistory: a New outline.* Cambridge: Cambridge University Press.

1970. *Aspects of Prehistory.* Berkeley, Los Angeles and London: University of California Press.

1977. *World Prehistory.* 3rd edn. Cambridge: Cambridge University Press.

Clarke, D. L. 1968. *Analytical Archaeology.* London: Methuen.

1972. ed. *Models in Archaeology.* London: Methuen.

Clarke, D. L. 1977. *Spatial Archaeology.* New York: Academic Press.

Clarke, R. J. 1966. Introductory notes on the use and habitation of caves by man south of the Sahara. *Bulletin of the Cave Exploration Group of East Africa* 1: 70–114.

Clutton-Brock, T. H. 1977. *Primate Ecology: Studies of Feeding and Ranging Behaviour in Lemurs, Monkeys and Apes.* London: Academic Press.

Clutton-Brock, T. H. and C. Grigson. 1983. eds. *Animals and Archaeology: Hunters and their Prey.* Oxford: BAR International Series 163.

Clutton-Brock, T. H. and P. H. Harvey. 1977. Primate ecology and social organization. *Journal of Zoology* 183: 1–39.

Collins, D. 1969. Culture traditions and environment of early man. *Current Anthropology* 10: 267–316.

1970. Stone artefact analysis and the recognition of culture traditions. *World Archaeology* 2: 17–27.

Coltorti, M., M. Cremaschi, M. C. Delitala, D. Esu, M. Fornaseri, A. McPherron, M. Nicoletti, R. van Otterloo, C. Perreto, B. Sala, V. Schmidt and J. Sevink. 1982. Reversed magnetic polarity at an early Lower Paleolithic site in central Italy. *Nature* 300: 173–6.

Commont, V. 1908. Les Industries de l'ancien Saint-Acheul, *L'Anthropologie* 19: 527–72.

Cook, S. F. and R. F. Heizer. 1965. The quantitative approach to the relationship between population and settlement size. *Reports of the University of California Archaeological Survey* 64: 1–97.

Cooke, H. B. S. 1958. Observations relating to Quaternary environments in East and Southern Africa. *Alex I. Du Toit Memorial Lecture* 5. Geological Society of South Africa (Annexure) 60: 1–73.

1963. Pleistocene mammal faunas of Africa with particular reference to Southern Africa. In *African Ecology and Human Evolution*. Edited by F. C. Howell and F. Bourlière. Chicago: Aldine.

Coppens, Y. 1978. Evolution of the hominids and of their environment during the Plio-Pleistocene in the lower Omo valley, Ethiopia. In *Geological Background to Fossil Man*. Edited by W. W. Bishop. Edinburgh: Scottish Academic Press.

Coppens, Y., F. C. Howell, G. Ll. Isaac and R. E. F. Leakey. 1976. eds. *Earliest Man and Environments in the Lake Rudolf Basin: Stratigraphy, Paleoecology and Evolution*. Chicago: University of Chicago Press.

Corvinus, G. and H. Roche. 1976. La Préhistoire dans la région de Hadar (bassin de l'Awash, Afar, Ethiopie): Premier résultats. *L'Anthropologie* 80: 315–24.

Coryndon, S. C. 1964. Bone remains in the caves. In *The Lava Caves of Mt Suswa, Kenya*. Studies in Speleology 1 (1). Edited by P. E. Glover *et al.*

Cowgill, G. L. 1968. Archaeological applications of factor, cluster, and proximity analysis. *American Antiquity* 33: 367–75.

Cox, A. 1968. Lengths of geomagnetic polarity intervals. *Journal of Geophysical Research* 73: 3247–60.

1969. Geomagnetic reversals. *Science* 163: 237–44.

Crader, D. 1981. *Hunters Alongside Farmers: Faunal Remains from Chencherere II Rockshelter, Malawi*. Ph. D. dissertation. Department of Anthropology, University of California, Berkeley.

1983. Recent single-carcass bone scatters and the problem of 'butchery' sites in the archaeological record. In *Animals and Archaeology: Hunters and their Prey*. Edited by J. Clutton-Brock and C. Grigson. Oxford BAR.

Cronin. J., N. Boaz, C. Stringer and Y. Rak. 1981. Tempo and mode in hominid evolution. *Nature* 292: 113–22.

Crook, J. H. and J. S. Gartlan. 1966. The evolution of primate societies. *Nature* 210: 1200–3.

Curtis, G. H. 1967. Notes on some Miocene to Pleistocene potassium/argon results. In *Background to Evolution in Africa*. Edited by W. W. Bishop and J. D. Clark. Chicago: University of Chicago Press.

Curtis, G. H., R. L. Drake, T. E. Cerling and J. H. Hampel. 1975. Age of KBS Tuff in Koobi Fora Formation, East Rudolf, Kenya. *Nature* 258: 395–8.

Daniel, G. E. 1950. *A Hundred Years of Archaeology*. London: Duckworth.

Dart, R. 1925. *Australopithecus africanus:* the man-ape of Southern Africa. *Nature* 115: 195–9.

1953. The predatory transition from ape to man. *International Anthropological and Linguistic Review* 1: 201–19.

1956. The myth of the bone accumulating hyaena. *American Anthropologist* 58: 40–61.

1957a. The Makapan Australopithecine osteodontokeratic culture. In J. D. Clark, ed., *Third Pan-African Congress on Prehistory (Livingstone 1955)*. Edited by J. D. Clark.

1957b. The osteodontokeratic culture of *Australopithecus prometheus*. Memoir of the Transvaal Museum.

Darwin, C. 1858. Extract from an unpublished work on species. *Journal of the Linnean Society, Zoology* 3(9), 45–62.

1859. *The Origin of Species by Means of Natural Selection or the Preservation of Favoured Races in the Struggle for Life*. London.

1871 *The Descent of Man and Selection in Relation to Sex*. London: John Murray.

Davis, D. D. 1976. Spatial organization and subsistence technology of Lower and Middle Pleistocene hominid sites at Olduvai Gorge, Tanzania. Ann Arbor, Michigan: University Microfilms.

1978. Lithic assemblage variability in relation to early hominid subsistence strategies at Olduvai Gorge. In *Lithics and Subsistences: The Analysis of Stone Tool Use in Prehistoric Economies.* Edited by D. D. Davis. Nashville, Tennessee: Vanderbilt University Publications in Anthropology 20.

Day, M. 1977. *Guide to Fossil Man.* Chicago: University of Chicago Press.

Deacon, J. 1966. An annotated list of radiocarbon dates for sub-Saharan Africa. *Annals of the Cape Provincial Museum* 5: 5–84.

1968. Supplementary list and index to an annotated list of radiocarbon dates for sub-Saharan Africa. Supplement to *Annals of the Cape Provincial Museum* 5.

Dechant-Boaz, D. 1982. Modern riverine taphonomy: its relevance to the interpretation of Plio-Pleistocene hominid paleoecology in the Omo Basin, Ethiopia. Ph. D. dissertation. Department of Anthropology, University of California, Berkeley.

Deetz, J. 1965. *The Dynamics of Stylistic Change in Arikara Ceramics.* Illinois Studies in Anthropology 4. Urbana: University of Illinois Press.

1977. *In Small Things Forgotten: the Archaeology of Early American Life.* Garden City, New York: Anchor Press Doubleday.

Delson, E. 1985. ed. *Ancestors: the Hard Evidence.* New York: Alan R. Liss.

Devore, I. and S. L. Washburn. 1963. Baboon ecology and human evolution. In *African Ecology and Human Evolution.* Edited by F. C. Howell and F. Bourléire. Chicago: Aldine.

Douglas, M. 1970. *Natural Symbols.* London: Barrie and Rockcliffe.

Drake, R. E., G. H. Curtis, T. E. Cerling, B. W. Cerling and J. Hampel. 1980. KBS Tuff dating and geochronology of tuffaceous sediments in the Koobi Fora and Shungura Formations, East Africa. *Nature* 283: 368–72.

Elliot-Smith, G. 1927. *The Evolution of Man.* 2nd ed. London: Oxford University Press.

Emiliani, C. 1958. Paleotemperature analysis of Core 280 and Pleistocene correlations. *Journal of Geology* 66: 264–75.

1963. The significance of deep-sea cores. In *Science in Archaeology.* Edited by D. Brothwell and E. Higgs. London: Thames and Hudson.

Ericson, D. B. and G. Wollin. 1968. Pleistocene climates and chronology in deep-sea sediments. *Science* 162: 1227–34.

Ericson, J. E., N. T. Boaz and C. H. Sullivan. 1981. Diets of Pliocene mammals from Omo, Ethiopia, deduced from carbon isotope ratios in tooth apatite. *Paleogeography, Paleoclimatology, Paleoecology* 36: 69–73.

Evans, J. 1872. *The Ancient Stone Implements, Weapons and Ornaments of Great Britain.* New York.

Evernden, J. F. and G. H. Curtis. 1965. Potassium argon dating of Late Cenozoic rocks in East Africa and Italy. *Current Anthropology* 6: 343–85.

Fagan, B. M. and F. Van Noten. 1966. Wooden implements from late Stone Age sites at Gwisho Hot Springs, Lochinvar, Zambia. *Proceedings of the Prehistoric Society* 32: 246–61.

Fahnestock, R. K. and W. L. Haushild. 1962. Flume studies on the transport of pebbles and cobbles on a sand bed. *Geological Society of America* 73: 1431–6.

Ferris, S. D., A. C. Wilson and W. M. Brown. 1981. Evolutionary tree for apes and humans based on cleavage maps of mitochondrial DNA. *Proceedings of the National Academy of Sciences* 78: 2432–6.

Findlater, I. C. 1975. Tuffs and the recognition of isochronous mapping units in the Rudolf succession. In: *Earliest Man and Environments in the Lake Rudolf Basin: Stratigraphy, Paleoecology and Evolution.* Edited by Y. Coppens *et al.* Chicago: University of Chicago Press.

Findlater, I. C. 1978. Stratigraphy. In *Koobi Fora Research Project. Vol. 1, The Fossil Hominids and an Introduction to their Context, 1968–1974.* Edited by M. G. Leakey and R. E. F. Leakey. Oxford: Clarendon Press.

Fitch, F. J. and J. A. Miller. 1969. Age determinations on feldspar from the lower Omo basin. *Nature* 222: 1143.

1970. Radioisotopic age determinations of Lake Rudolf artefact site. *Nature* 226: 226–8.

1976. Conventional potassium-argon and argon 40/argon 39 dating of volcanic rocks from East Rudolf. *Earliest Man and Environments in the Lake Rudolf Basin: Stratigraphy, Paleoecology, and Evolution.* Edited by Y. Coppens *et al.* Chicago: University of Chicago Press.

Fitch, F. J., P. J. Hooker and J. A. Miller. 1978. Geochronological problems and radioisotopic dating in the Gregory Rift Valley. In *Geological Background to Fossil Man.* Edited by W. W. Bishop. Edinburgh: Scottish Academic Press.

Flannery, K. V. 1976. *The Early Mesoamerican Village.* New York: Academic Press.

Fleischer, R. L., P. B. Price, R. M. Walker and L. S. B. Leakey. 1965. Fission track dating of Bed I, Olduvai Gorge. *Science* 148: 72–4.

Flint, R. F. 1959. On the basis of Pleistocene correlations in East Africa. *Geological Magazine* 96: 265–84.

Foster, G. M. 1960. Life expectancy of utilitarian pottery in Tzintzuntzan, Michoacán, Mexico, *American Antiquity* 25: 606–9.

Fox, C. 1932. *The Personality of Britain: its Influence on Inhabitant and Invader in Prehistoric and Early Historic Times.* National Museum of Wales.

1948. *The Archaeology of the Cambridge Region.* Cambridge: Cambridge University Press.

1967. In the beginning: aspects of hominid behavioural evolution. *Man* 2: 415–33.

Frechen, J. von and H.-J. Lippolt. 1965. Kalium-Argon-Daten zum alter Laacher Vulkanismus, der Rheinterrassen und der Eiszeiten. *Eiszeitalter und Gegenwart* 16: 5–30.

Freeman, L. G. 1966. The nature of Mousterian facies in Cantabrian Spain. In *Recent Studies in Paleoanthropology.* Edited by J. D. Clark and F. C. Howell, *American Anthropologist,* Special Publication 68(2): 2.

1968. A theoretical framework for interpreting archaeological materials. In *Man the Hunter.* Edited by R. B. Lee and I. DeVore. Chicago: Aldine.

Freeman, L. G. and K. W. Butzer. 1966. The Acheulian station of Torralba (Spain): a progress report. *Quaternia* 8, 9–21.

Frere, J. 1800. Account of flint weapons discovered at Hoxne in Suffolk. *Archaeologia* 13, 204–5 (quoted from G. E. Daniel. 1950. *A Hundred Years of Archaeology,* p. 27. London: Duckworth).

Fritz, M. 1974. Paper presented to the 73rd Annual Meeting of the American Anthropology Association. Mexico City. November.

Gabel, C. 1965. *Stone Age Hunters of the Kafue: the Gwisho A Site.* Boston.

Garrod, D. A. E. 1938. The Upper Palaeolithic in the light of recent discovery. *Proceedings of the Prehistoric Society* 4: 1–26.

Garrod, D. A. E. and D. M. A. Bate. 1937. *The Stone Age of Mt Carmel.* Vol. 1. Oxford: Clarendon Press.

Gartlan, J. S. and C. T. Brain. 1968. Ecology and social variability in *Cercopithecus aethiops* and *C. mitis.* In *Primates: Studies in Adaptation and Variability.* Edited by P. C. Jay. New York: Holt, Rinehart and Winston.

Gaudry, A. 1859. Haches trouvées dans le diluvium, prés d'Amiens. *Bulletin de la Société Géologique de France* 2(17): 17–19.

Gaulin, S. J. and M. Konner. 1977. On the natural diet of primates, including humans: In

Nutrition and the Brain, Vol. 1. Edited by R. J. and J. J. Wurtman. New York: Raven Press.

Geertz, C. 1973. The growth of culture and the evolution of mind. In *The Interpretation of Cultures.* Edited by C. Geertz. New York: Basic Books.

Gentry, A. W. and A. Gentry. 1978. Fossil Bovidae (Mammalia) of Olduvai Gorge, Tanzania, Parts 1 and 2. *Bulletin of the British Museum (Natural History) Geological Series* 29 and 30.

Geraads, D. 1979. La Faune des gisements de Melka-Kunturé (Ethiopie): Artiodactyls, Primates. *Abbay* 10: 21–49.

Geschwind, N. 1965. Disconnexion syndromes in animals and man. *Brain* 88: 237–94.

Gifford, D. 1977. Observations of contemporary human settlements as an aid to archaeological interpretation. Doctoral dissertation, University of California, Berkeley.

    1978. Ethnoarchaeological observations on natural processes affecting cultural materials. In *New Directions in Ethnoarcheology.* Edited by R. A. Gould. Albuquerque: University of New Mexico Press.

    1981. Taphonomy and paleoecology: a critical review of archaeology's sister disciplines. In *Advances in Archaeological Method and Theory,* Vol. 43, Edited by M. B. Schiffer. New York: Academic Press.

Gifford, D. P. and A. K. Behrensmeyer. 1977. Observed formation and burial of a recent human occupation site in Kenya. *Quaternary Research* 8: 245–66.

Gifford, D. P. and D. C. Crader. 1977. A computer coding system for archaeological faunal remains. *American Antiquity* 42(2): 225–38.

Gifford, D., G. Ll. Isaac and C. M. Nelson. 1980. Evidence for predation and pastoralism from a Pastoral Neolithic site in Kenya. *Azania* 15: 57–108.

Gifford-Gonzalez, D. P., D. B. Damrosch *et al.* 1985. The third dimension in site structure: an experiment in trampling and vertical dispersal. *American Antiquity* 50(4): 803–18.

Glass, B. P. and B. C. Heezen. 1967. Tektites and geomagnetic reversals. *Scientific American* 237: 32–8.

Glassie, H. 1975. *Folk Housing in Middle Virginia:* a Structural Analysis. Knoxville: University of Tennessee Press.

Gleadow, A. J. W. 1980. Fission track age of the KBS Tuff and associated hominids in northern Kenya. *Nature* 284: 225–30.

Glover, P. E., E. C. Glover, E. C. Trump and L. E. D. Wateridge. 1964. The lava caves of Mt Suswa, Kenya. *Studies in Speleology* 1(1): 51–66.

Gobert, E. G. 1950. Le Gisement paléolithique de Sidi Zin. *Karthago* 1: 1–64.

Goodall, J. M. 1964. Tool-using and aimed throwing in a community of free-living chimpanzees. *Nature* 201: 1264–6.

Gould, R. A. 1968. Chipping stones in the outback. *Natural History* 77, (2): 42–9.

    1977. Ethno-archaeology; or, where do models come from? a closer look at Australian aboriginal lithic technology. In *Stone Tools as Cultural Markers.* Edited by R. V. S. Wright. Australian Insitute of Aboriginal Studies.

    1980. *Living Archaeology.* Cambridge: Cambridge University Press.

Gould, R. A., D. A. Koster and A. H. Sontz. 1971. The lithic assemblage of the western desert aborigines of Australia. *American Antiquity* 36: 149–69.

Gould, S. J. and N. Eldredge. 1977. Punctuated equilibria: the tempo and mode of evolution reconsidered. *Paleobiology* 3: 115–51.

Gowlett, J. A. J. 1978. Kilombe–an Acheulian site complex in Kenya. In *Geological Background to Fossil Man.* Edited by W. W. Bishop. Edinburgh: Scottish Academic Press.

    1980. Acheulean sites in the central Rift Valley, Kenya. *Proceedings of the Eighth Panafrican Congress of Prehistory and Quaternary Studies.* Nairobi.

1982. Procedure and form in a lower Paleolithic industry: stone working at Kilombe, Kenya. *Studia Praehistorica Belgica* 2: 101–9.

1984. Mental abilities of early man: A look at some hard evidence. In *Human Adaptation and Community Ecology in the Pleistocene.* Edited by R. Foley. London: Academic Press.

Gowlett, J. A. J., J. W. K. Harris, D. Walton and B. A. Wood. 1981. Early archaeological sites, hominid remains and traces of fire from Chesowanja, Kenya. *Nature* 294: 125–9.

Grayson, D. K. 1982. Review of L. R. Binford. 1981. *Bones, Ancient Men and Modern Myths. American Anthropologist* 84: 439–40.

Gregory, W. K. 1922. *The Origin and Evolution of the Human Dentition.* Baltimore: Williams and Williams.

Grine, F. E. 1981. Trophic differences between 'gracile' and 'robust' australopithecines: a scanning electron microscope analysis of occlusal events. *South African Journal of Science* 77: 203–30.

Guichard, J. 1965. Un facies original de l'Acheuléen: Cantalouette (Commune de Creysse, Dordogne). *L'Anthropologie* 69: 413–64.

Hall, R. 1963. Tool using performances as indicators of behavioral adaptability. *Current Anthropology* 4: 479–94.

1965. Behaviour and ecology of the wild Patas monkey, *Erythrocebus patas* in Uganda. *Journal of Zoology* 148: 15–87.

Hamburg, D. and E. R. McCown. 1979. *The Great Apes. (Perspectives on Human Evolution,, vol. 5)* Menlo Park, CA: Benjamin/Cummings.

Hamilton, W. D. 1964. The genetical evolution of social behaviour II. *Journal of Theoretical Biology* 7: 17–52.

Harcourt, A. H., P. H. Harvey, S. G. Larson and R. V. Short. 1981. Testis weight and breeding system in primates. *Nature* 293: 55–7.

Hardy, A. 1960. Was man more aquatic in the past? *New Scientist* 7: 642–5.

Harnad, S. R., H. D. Steklis and J. Lancaster, *Origins and Evolution of language and Speech.* New York: New York Academy of Science.

Harris, J. W. K. 1978. The Karari industry: its place in African prehistory. Ph. D. dissertation. Department of Anthropology, University of California, Berkeley

Harris, J. W. K., J. A. J. Gowlett, D. A. Walton and B. A. Wood. 1981. Palaeoanthropological studies at Chesowanja. *X Congress Union Internacional de Ciencias Prehistoricas y Protohistoricas,* Mexico City.

Harris, J. W. K. and I. Herbich. 1978. Aspects of Early Pleistocene hominid behaviour east of Lake Turkana, Kenya. In *Geological Background to Fossil Man.* Edited by W. W. Bishop. Edinburgh: Scottish Academic Press.

Harris, J. W. K. and G. Ll. Isaac. 1976. The Karari Industry: Early Pleistocene archaeological evidence from the terrain east of Lake Turkana, Kenya. *Nature* 262: 102–6.

Harris, J. W. K. and G. Ll. Isaac. 1980. Early Pleistocene site locations at Koobi Fora, Kenya. In *Proceedings of the VIII Pan African Congress on Prehistory.* Edited by R. E. Leakey and B. A. Ogot.

Harris, J. W. K. and D. C. Johanson. 1983. Cultural beginnings: Plio-Pleistocene archaeological occurrences from the Afar, Ethiopia. *The African Archaeological Review* 1: 3–31.

Hasewaga, T., M. Hiraiwa, T. Nishida and H. Takasaki. 1983. New evidence on scavenging behavior in wild chimpanzees. *Current Anthropology* 24: 231–2.

Hatley, T. and J. Kappelman. 1980. Bears, pigs and Plio-Pleistocene hominids: A case for the exploitation of belowground food resources. *Human Ecology* 8: 371–87.

Hawkes, J. 1968. The proper study of mankind. *Antiquity* 42: 255–62.

Hay, R. L. 1963. Stratigraphy of Beds I through IV, Olduvai Gorge, Tanganyika. *Science* 139: 829–33.

1967. Hominid-bearing deposits of Olduvai Gorge. In *Time and Stratigraphy in the Evolution of Man.* Symposium sponsored by the Division of Earth Sciences, National Academy of Sciences, National Research Council, Washington DC.

1976. *The Geology of Olduvai Gorge.* Berkeley: University of California Press.

Heinzelin, J. de. 1961. *Le Paléolithique aux abords d'Ishango.* Institut des Parcs Nationaux de Congo et du Ruanda Urundi, Fascicule 6.

in press. The Geology of the Omo Group. Tervuren Museum Publications.

Heizer, R. 1969. *Man's Discovery of His Past.* Englewood Cliffs, N. J: Prentice-Hall.

Hewes, G. W. 1961. Food transport and the origin of hominid bipedalism. *American Anthropologist* 63: 687–710.

Hietala, H. H. and P. A. Larson. 1979. *SYMAP* analysis in archaeology: Intrasite assumptions and a comparison with *TREND* analysis. *Norwegian Archaeological Review* 12(1): 57–64.

Hill, A. 1975. Taphonomy of contemporary and Late Cenozoic East African Vertebrates. Ph. D. dissertation, University of London.

1980. Early post-mortem damage to the remains of some contemporary East African mammals. In *Fossils in the Making: Vertaebrate Taphonomy and Palaeoecology.* Edited by A. K. Behrensmeyer and A. Hill. Chicago: University of Chicago Press.

1984. Aspects of archaeological inference about bones. In *Human adaptation in the Pleistocene and Community Ecology.* Edited by R. Foley. London: Academic Press.

Hodder, I. 1978. ed. *Simulation Studies in Archaeology.* Cambridge: Cambridge University Press.

Hodder, I. and C. Orton. 1976. *Spatial Analysis in Archaeology.* Cambridge: Cambridge University Press.

Hodder, I., G. Isaac and N. Hammond. 1981. *Pattern of the Past.* Cambridge: Cambridge University Press.

Hodson, F. R. 1970. Cluster analysis and archaeology: some new developments and applications. *World Archaeology* 1: 299–320.

Hodson, F. R., P. H. A. Sneath and J. E. Doran. 1966. Some experiments in the numerical analysis of archaeological data. *Biometrika* 53: 311–24.

Hole, F. and K. V. Flannery. 1967. The prehistory of southwestern Iran: a preliminary report. *Proceedings of the Prehistoric Society* 33: 147–206.

Holloway, R. L. 1970. Australopithecine endocast (Taung specimen, 1924): a new volume determination. *Science* 168: 966–8.

1981. Exploring the dorsal surface of hominoid brain endocasts by stereoplotter and discriminant analysis. *Philosophic Transactions of the Royal Society, London* B 292: 155–66.

Hooijer, D. A. 1962. The Middle Pleistocene fauna of Java. In *Evolution and Hominization.* Edited by G. Kurth. Stuttgart: Gustav Fischer.

Howell, F. C. 1961a. Stratigraphie du Pléistocéne supérieur dans l'Asie du sudouest: age relatif et absolu de l'homme et de ses industries. *L'Anthropologie* 65: 1–20.

1961b. Isimila: a Palaeolithic site in Africa. *Scientific American* 205, 4: 118–29.

1965. *Early Man.* New York: Time-Life.

1966. Observations on the earlier phases of the European Lower Palaeolithic. *American Anthropologist* 68, 2(2): 88–201.

1967. Recent advances in human evolutionary studies. *The Quarterly Review of Biology* 42(4): 471–513.

1968. Omo research expedition. *Nature* 219: 567–72.

1976. Overview of the Pliocene and earlier Pleistocene of the lower Omo Basin, southern

Ethiopia. In *Human Origins: Louis Leakey and the East African Evidence.* Edited by G. Ll. Isaac and E. R. McCown. Menlo Park, CA: Benjamin.

1978a. Hominidae. In *Evolution of African Mammals.* Edited by V. Maglio and H. B. S. Cooke. Cambridge: Harvard University Press.

1978b. Overview of the Pliocene and earlier Pleistocene of the lower Omo Basin, Southern Ethiopia. In *Early Hominids of Africa.* Edited by C. J. Jolly. London: Duckworth.

Howell, F. C. and J. D. Clark. 1963. Acheulian hunter-gatherers of sub-Saharan Africa. In *African Ecology and Human Evolution.* Edited by F. C. Howell and F. Bourlière. Chicago: Aldine.

Howell, F. C., G. H. Cole and M. R. Kleindienst. 1962. Isimila, an Acheulian occupation site in the Iringa Highlands, Southern Highlands Province, Tanganyika. In *Actes du IVe Congrés Panafricain de Préhistoire* (Tervuren, Belgium). Edited by G. Mortelmans and J. Nenquin.

Huxley, T. H. 1963. *Evidence as to Man's Place in Nature.* London: Williams and Norgate.

Inskeep, R. R. and B. Q. Hendy. 1966. An interesting association of bones from the Elands-fontein Fossil Site. In *Actas del V Congreso Panafricano de Prehistoria y de Estudio del Cuaternario II.* Edited by L. D. Cuscoy. *Publicaciones del Museo Arqueologico Santa Cruz de Tenerife* 6: 109–24.

Isaac, A. B. 1987. Throwing and human evolution. *The African Archaeological Review* 5: 3–17.

Isaac, G. Ll. 1965. The stratigraphy of the Peninj Beds and the provenance of the Natron Australopithecine mandible. *Quaternaria* 7: 101–30.

1966a. The geological history of the Olorgesailie area. *Actas del V Congreso Panafricano de Prehistoria y de Estudio del Cuaternario.* Edited by L. D. Cuscoy. *Publicaciones del Museo Arqueologico Santa Cruz de Tenerife* 6(11): 125–33.

1966b. New evidence from Olorgesailie relating to the character of Acheulian occupation sites. *Actas del V Congreso Panafricano de Prehistoria y de Estudio del Cuaternario.* Edited by L. D. Cuscoy. *Publicaciones del Museo Arqueologico Santa Cruz de Tenerife* 6(11): 135–45.

1967a. The stratigraphy of the Peninj Group: early Middle Pleistocene formations west of Lake Natron, Tanzania. In *Background to Evolution in Africa.* Edited by W. W. Bishop and J. D. Clark. Chicago: University of Chicago Press.

1967b. Towards the interpretation of occupation debris: some experiments and observations. *Kroeber Anthropological Society Papers* 37: 31–57.

1968a. Traces of Pleistocene hunters: an East African example. In *Man the Hunter.* Edited by R. B. Lee and I. DeVore. Chicago: Aldine.

1968b. The Acheulean site complex at Olorgesailie, Kenya: a contribution to the interpretation of Middle Pleistocene culture in East Africa. Doctoral thesis, University of Cambridge.

1969. Studies of early culture in East Africa. *World Archaeology* 1: 1–28.

1971a. The diet of early man: aspects of archaeological evidence from Lower and Middle Pleistocene sites in Africa. *World Archaeology* 2(3): 278–99.

1971b. Whither archaeology? *Antiquity* 45: 123–9.

1972a. Early phases of human behavior: models in Lower Palaeolithic archaeology. In *Models in Archaeology.* Edited by D. L. Clarke. London: Methuen.

1972b. Comparative studies of Pleistocene site locations in East Africa. In *Man, Settlement and Urbanism.* Edited by P.J. Ucko *et al.* London: Duckworth.

1972c. Some experiments in quantitative methods for characterizing assemblages of Acheulian artefacts. *Vliéme Congrés Panafricain de Préhistoire et de l'Etude du Quater-*

naire, Dakar, 1967. Edited by H. J. Hugot. Chambéry: Imprimeries Réunies de Chambéry.

1972d. The identification of cultural entities in the Middle Pleistocene. In *Actes du VI Congrés Panafricain de Préhistoire et de l'Etude du Quaternaire, Dakar, 1967,* Edited by H. J. Hugot. Chambéry: Imprimeries Réunies de Chambéry.

1972e. Chronology and the tempo of cultural change during the Pleistocene. In *Calibration of Hominoid Evolution.* Edited by W. W. Bishop and J. A. Miller. Edinburgh: Scottish Academic Press.

1974. Form and design: aspects of rule systems in the Pleistocene. Paper delivered at the Annual Meeting, American Anthropological Association, Mexico City. Mimeo.

1975. Plio-Pleistocene artifact assemblages from East Rudolf, Kenya. In *Earliest Man and Environments in the Lake Rudolf Basin: Stratigraphy, Paleoecology and Evolution.* Edited by Y. Coppens *et al.* Chicago: University of Chicago Press.

1976a. East Africa as a source of fossil evidence for human evolution. In *Human Origins: Louis Leakey and the East African Evidence.* Edited by G. Ll. Isaac and E. R. McCown. Menlo Park, CA: Benjamin.

1976b. The activities of early African hominids: a review of archaeological evidence from the time span two and a half to one million years ago. In *Human Origins: Louis Leakey and the East African Evidence.* Edited by G. Ll. Isaac and E. McCown. Menlo Park, CA: Benjamin.

1976c. Plio-Pleistocene artifact assemblages from East Rudolf, Kenya. In *Earliest Man and Environments in the Lake Rudolf Basin.* Edited by Y. Coppens *et al.* Chicago: University of Chicago Press.

1976d. Stages of cultural elaboration in the Pleistocene: possible archaeological indicators of the development of language capabilities. *Annals of the New York Academy of Sciences* 280: 275–88.

1976e. Early hominids in action: a commentary on the contribution of archaeology to the understanding of the fossil record in East Africa. In *The Yearbook of Physical Anthropology for 1975.* Edited by J. Buettner-Janusch.

1977a. Early stone tools–an adaptive threshold? In *Problems in Economic and Social Archaeology.* Edited by G. de G. Sieveking, H. E. Longworth and K. E. Wilson. London: Duckworth.

1977b. *Olorgesailie: Archaeological Studies of a Middle Pleistocene Lake Basin in Kenya.* Chicago: University of Chicago Press.

1978a. The food-sharing behavior of protohuman hominids. *Scientific American* 238(4): 90–108.

1978b. Food-sharing and human evolution: archaeological evidence from the Plio-Pleistocene of East Africa. *Journal of Anthropological Research* 34: 311–25.

1980. Casting the net wide: a review of archaeological evidence for early hominid land-use and ecological relations. In *Current Argument on Early Man.* Edited by L.-K. Konigsson. Oxford: Pergamon Press.

1981a. Archaeological tests of alternative models of early hominid behaviour: excavation and experiments. *Philosophical Transactions of the Royal Society of London,* B, 292: 177–88.

1981b. Stone age visiting cards: approaches to the study of early land-use patterns. In *Pattern of the Past.* Edited by I. Hodder, G. Ll. Isaac and N. Hammond. Cambridge: Cambridge University Press.

1982. Early hominids and fire at Chesowanja, Kenya. *Nature* 296: 870.

1983a. Bones in contention: competing explanations for the juxtaposition of Early

Pleistocene artefacts and faunal remains. In *Animals and Archaeology: Hunters and their prey.* Edited by J. Clutton-Brock and C. Grigson. BAR International Series 163. Oxford.

1983b. Review of L. R. Binford 1981. *Bones: Ancient Men and Modern Myths. American Antiquity* 48: 416–19.

1983c. Aspects of human evolution. In *Essays on Evolution: a Darwin Centenary Volume.* Edited by D. S. Bendall. Cambridge: Cambridge University Press.

1984. The archaeology of human origins: studies of the Lower Pleistocene in East Africa, 1971–1981. In *Advances in Old World Archaeology* 3. Edited by F. Wendorf and A. Close. New York: Academic Press.

1984b. Review of *In Pursuit of the Past: Decoding the Archaeological Record* by L. R. Binford. *American Scientist* 72: 90–1.

n.d. *Koobi Fora Research Project.* Volume 4, *Archaeology.* Edited by G. Isaac, Oxford: Clarendon Press. Assisted by A. B. Isaac.

Isaac, G. Ll., and D. Crader. 1981. To what extent were early hominids carnivorous? an archaeological perspective. In *Omnivorous Primates: Gathering and Hunting in Human Evolution.* Edited by R. S. O. Harding and G. Teleki. New York: Columbia University Press.

Isaac, G. Ll., and G. Curtis. 1974. Age of early Acheulian industries from the Peninj Group Tanzania. *Nature* 249: 624–27.

Isaac, G. Ll., and J. W. K. Harris. 1975. The scatter between the patches. Paper delivered to Kroeber Anthropological Society Annual Meetings. Berkeley.

1978. Archaeology. In *Koobi Fora Research Project. Vol. 1, The Fossil Hominids and Introduction to their Context 1968–1974.* Edited by M. G. Leakey and R. E. Leakey. Oxford: Clarendon Press.

1980. A method for determining the characteristics of artefacts between sites in the Upper Member of the Koobi Fora Formation, East Lake Turkana. *Proceedings of the 8th Panafrican Congress on Prehistory and Quaternary Studies.* Edited by R. E. F. Leakey and B. A. Ogot. Nairobi: TILLMIAP.

Isaac, G. Ll., J. W. K. Harris, and D. Crader. 1976. Archaeological evidence from the Koobi Fora Formation. In *Earliest Man and Environments in the Lake Rudolf Basin: Stratigraphy, Paleoecology and Evolution.* Edited by Y. Coppens *et al.* Chicago: University of Chicago Press.

Isaac, G. Ll., J. W. K. Harris, and F. Marshall. 1981. Small is informative: the application of the study of mini-sites and least-effort criteria in the interpretation of the early Pleistocene archaeological record at Koobi Fora, Kenya. In *Las Industrias mas Antiguas.* Edited by J. D. Clark and G. Ll. Isaac. *X Congresso, Union Internacional de Ciencias Prehistoricas y Protohistoricas.* Mexico City.

Isaac, G. Ll., R. E. Leakey and A. K. Behrensmeyer. 1971. Archaeological traces of early hominid activities, east of Lake Rudolf, Kenya. *Science* 173: 1129–34.

Isaac, G. Ll., C. M. Nelson and H. V. Merrick. 1970. (unpublished). Preliminary report on the work of the University of California Archaeological Research Group in Kenya 1969–1970. Mimeographed copies filed with the National Science Foundation, Washington, and the Ministry of Natural Resources, Kenya.

Jaeger, J. J. 1975. The mammalian fossils and hominid faunas of the Middle Pleistocene of the Maghreb. In *After the Australopithecines.* Edited by K. W. Butzer and G. Ll. Isaac. The Hague: Mouton.

Jarman, M. R. 1972. A territorial model for archaeology: a behavioural and geographical approach: In *Models in Archaeology.* Edited by D. L. Clarke. London: Methuen.

Jewell, P. A. and G. W. Dimbleby. 1966. eds. The experimental earthwork on Overton Down.

Wiltshire, England: the first four years. *Proceedings of the Prehistoric Society* 32: 313–41.

Jochim, M. A. 1976. *Hunter-Gatherer subsistence and Settlement: a Predictive Model.* New York: Academic Press.

Johanson, D. C. and M. A. Edy. 1980. *Lucy: the Beginnings of Humankind.* New York: Simon and Schuster.

Johanson, D. C. and T. D. White. 1979. A systematic assessment of early African hominids. *Science* 202: 321–30.

Johanson, D. C., M. Taieb, Y. Coppens and H. Roche. 1978a. Expédition internationale de l'Afar, Ethiopie (4e et 5e campagnes 1975–1977): Nouvelles decouvertes d'hominidés et découvertes d'industries lithiques Plio-Pléistocénes à Hadar. *Comptes Rendus de l'Académie des Sciences, Paris* 289D: 237–40.

1978b. Geological framework of the Pliocene Hadar Formation (Afar, Ethiopia) with notes on paleontology including hominids. In *Geological Background to Fossil Man.* Edited by W. W. Bishop. Edinburgh: Scottish Academic Press.

Jolly, C. 1970. The seed-eaters: a new model of hominid differentiation based on a baboon analogy. *Man,* n.s. 5(1): 5–26.

1978. *Early Hominids of Africa.* London: Duckworth.

Jones, C. and J. Sabater Pi. 1969. Sticks used by chimpanzees in Rio Muni, West Africa. *Nature* 223: 100–1.

Jones, P. 1979. Effects of raw materials on biface manufacture. *Science* 204: 835–6.

1980. Experimental butchery with modern stone tools and its relevance for archaeology. *World Archaeology* 12: 153–65.

1981. Experimental implement manufacture and use: A case study from Olduvai Gorge. *Philosophical Transactions of the Royal Society, London B* 292: 189–95.

Jungers, W. L. 1982. Lucy's limbs: Skeletal allometry and locomotion in *Australopithecus afarensis. Nature* 297: 676–8.

Kaufulu, Z. 1983. The geological content of some early archaeological sites in Kenya, Malawi, and Tanzania. Ph. D. thesis, Department of Anthropology, University of California, Berkeley.

Keeley, L. H. 1980. *Experimental Determination of Stone Tool Uses: A Microwear Analysis.* Chicago: University of Chicago Press.

Keeley, L. H. and N. Toth. 1981. Microwear polishes on early stone tools from Koobi Fora, Kenya. *Nature* 293: 464–5.

Kelling, G. and P. F. Williams. 1967. Flume studies of the reorientation of pebbles and shells. *Journal of Geology* 75: 243–67.

Klein, R. G. 1969a. *Man and Culture in the Late Pleistocene.* San Francisco: Chandler.

1969b. The Mousterian of European Russia. *Proceedings of the Prehistoric Society* 35: 77–111.

1975. Paleoanthropological implications of the non-archaeological bone assemblage from Swart Klip I, South West Cape Province, South Africa. *Quaternary Research* 5: 275–88.

1976. The mammalian fauna of the Klasies River Mouth sites, Southern Cape Province, South Africa. *South African Archaeological Bulletin* 31: 75–98.

1982. Patterns of ungulate mortality and ungulate mortality profiles from Langebaanweg (Early Pliocene) and Elandsfontein (Middle Pleistocene), Southwestern Cape Province, South Africa. *Annals of the South African Museum* 90(2): 49–94.

Kleindienst, M. R. 1959. Composition and significance of a Late Acheulian assemblage based on an analysis of East African occupation sites. Dissertation submitted to the Faculty of the Division of the Social Sciences in candidacy for the degree of Doctor of Philosophy: Department of Anthropology. University of Chicago. Microfilm thesis no. 4706. Chicago, Illinois, August 1959.

1961. Variability within the Late Acheulian assemblages in Eastern Africa. *South African Archaeological Bulletin* 16(62): 35–52.

Kleindienst, M. R. and P. J. Watson. 1956. Action archaeology: the archaeological inventory of a living community. *Anthropology Tomorrow* 5: 75–8.

Klima, B. 1962. The first ground-plan of an Upper Palaeolithic loess settlement in Middle Europe and its meaning. In *Courses Towards Urban Life.* Edited by R. J. Braidwood and G. R. Willey. Chicago: Aldine.

Koehler, W. 1925. *The Mentality of Apes.* London: Routledge and Kegan Paul.

1927. *The Mentality of Apes.* Translated from 2nd rev. edition. International Library of Psychological, Philosophical and Scientific Method, London.

Koenigswald, G. H. R. von. 1962. Das absolute Alter des *Pithecanthropus erectus* Dubois. In *Evolution and Hominisation.* Edited by G. Kurth. Stuttgart: Gustav Fischer.

Kretzoi, M. and L. Vertès. 1965. Upper Biharian (Inter Mindel) pebble industry occupation site in western Hungary. *Current Anthropology* 6: 74–87.

Kroll, E. 1981. Spatial configurations of artifacts and bones at Plio-Pleistocene archaeological sites in East Africa. *Las Industrias mas Antiguas, Comision VI, X Congreso Union Internacional de Ciencias Prehistoricas y Proto-historicas.* Mexico City.

n.d. The anthropological meaning of spatial configurations at archaeological sites in East Africa. Ph.D. dissertation, Department of Anthropology, University of California, Berkeley.

Kroll, E. and G. Ll. Isaac. 1984. Configurations of artifacts and bones at early Pleistocene sites in East Africa. In *Intrasite Spatial Analysis in Archaeology.* Edited by H. J. Hietala and P. A. Larson. Cambridge: Cambridge University Press.

Kuhn, T. S. 1962. *The Structure of Scientific Revolutions.* Chicago: University of Chicago Press.

Kurtén, B. 1968. *Pleistocene Mammals of Europe.* Chicago: Aldine.

Kurtén, B. and V. Vasari. 1960. On the date of Peking Man. *Societas Scientiarum Fennica, Commentationes Biologicae* 23(7): 3–10.

Lalou, C., Nguyen Huu Fan, H. Fawre and L. Santos. 1970. Datation des hauts niveaux de covaux de la dépression de l'Afar. *Revue de Géographie physique et de Géologie dynamique.*

Lancaster, J. B. 1968. On the evolution of tool-using behaviour. *American Anthropologist* 70: 56–66.

1975. *Primate Behaviour and the Emergence of Human Culture.* New York: Holt. Rinehart and Winston.

1978. Carrying and sharing in human evolution. *Human Nature* 1: 82–9.

Landau, M. 1981. The anthropogenic: paleoanthropological writing as a genre of literature. Ph. D. dissertation. Yale University.

Langbein, W. B. and L. B. Leopold, 1968. River channel bars and dunes: theory of kinematic waves. *Geological Survey Professional Paper,* 422-L. U.S. Government Printing Office, Washington.

Larson, P. 1975. Trend analysis in archaeology: a preliminary study of intra-site patterning. *Norwegian Archaeological Review* 8: 75–80.

Leakey, L. S. B. 1931. *The Stone Age Cultures of the Kenya Colony.* Cambridge: Cambridge University Press.

1934. *Adam's Ancestors.* London: Methuen.

1935. *The Stone Age Races of Kenya.* Oxford: Oxford Unviersity Press.

1952. The Olorgesailie Prehistoric Site. In *Proceedings of the First Pan African Congress of Prehistory.* Edited by L. S. B. Leakey. Oxford.

1954. *Adam's Ancestor's* (2nd Edition). London: Methuen.

1957. Preliminary report on a Chellean I living site at BK II, Olduvai Gorge, Tanganyika Territory. In *Proceedings of the Third Pan African Congress of Prehistory, Livingstone 1955.* Edited by J. D. Clark. London.

1960. Finding the world's earliest man. *National Geographic Magazine* 118: 420–35.

1961. Exploring 1,750,000 years into man's past. *National Geographic Mazagine* 120: 564–89.

1963a. Adventures in the search for man. *National Geographic Magazine* 123: 132–52.

1963b. Very early East African Hominidae and their ecological setting. In *African Ecology and Human Evolution.* Edited by F. C. Howell and F. Bourlière. Chicago: Aldine.

1965. Comment on S. L. Washburn's contribution to the Symposium on the Origin of Man. Edited by P. L. Devore. New York: Wenner-Gren Foundation.

1968. Bone smashing by late Miocene Hominidae. *Nature* 218: 528–30.

Leakey, L. S. B. and M. D. Leakey. 1964. Recent discoveries of fossil hominids in Tanganyika: at Olduvai and near Lake Natron. *Nature* 202: 3–9.

Leakey, Margaret C. 1969. An Acheulian industry and hominid mandible, Lake Baringo, Kenya. *Proceedings of the Prehistoric Society* 35: 48–76.

Leakey, M. D. 1966. A review of the Oldowan culture from Olduvai Gorge, Tanzania. *Nature* 210: 462–6.

1967. Preliminary summary of the cultural material from Beds I and II, Olduvai Gorge, Tanzania. In *Background to Evolution in Africa.* Edited by W. W. Bishop and J. D. Clark. Chicago: University of Chicago Press.

1970a. Early artifacts from the Koobi Fora area. *Nature* 226: 228–30.

1970b. Stone artefacts from Swartkrans. *Nature* 225: 1222–5.

1971. *Olduvai Gorge, vol. 3. Excavations in Beds I and II, 1960–1963.* Cambridge: Cambridge University Press.

1975. Cultural patterns in the Olduvai sequence. In *After the Australopithecines: Stratigraphy, Ecology and Culture Change in the Middle Pleistocene.* Edited by K. W. Butzer and G. Ll. Isaac. The Hague: Mouton.

1976. The early stone industries of Olduvai Gorge. *Congrès IX, Union Internationale des Sciences Préhistoriques et Protohistoriques, Nice.* Colloque V.

Leakey, M. D. and R. L. Hay. 1979. Fossil footprints in the Pliocene deposits of Laetolil, Tanzania, *Nature* 278: 317–23.

Leakey, M. G. and R. E. F. Leakey. 1978. eds. *Koobi Fora Research Project, Vol. I: The Fossil Hominids and an Introduction to their Context, 1968–1974.* Oxford: Clarendon Press.

Leakey, R. E. F. 1970. New hominid remains and early artifacts from northern Kenya. Nature 226: 223–4.

1975. An overview of the Hominidae from East Rudolf. In *Earliest Man and Environments in the Lake Rudolf Basin: Stratigraphy, Paleoecology and Evolution.* Edited by Y. Coppens *et al.* Chicago: University of Chicago Press.

1981. *The Making of Mankind.* London: Michael Joseph.

Leakey, R. E. F. and G. Ll. Isaac. 1976. East Rudolf: an introduction to the abundance of new evidence. In *Human Origins: Louis Leakey and the East African Evidence.* Edited by G. Ll. Isaac and E. R. McCown. Menlo Park, CA: Benjamin.

Leakey, R. E. F. and R. Lewin. 1977. *Origins.* New York: E. P. Dutton.

Leakey, R. E. F., K. W. Butzer and M. H. Day. 1969. Early *Homo sapiens* remains from the Omo River region of south-west Ethiopia. *Nature* 222: 1132–8.

Leakey, R. E. F., A. K. Behrensmeyer, F. J. Fitch, J. A. Miller and M. D. Leakey. 1970. New hominid remains and early artefacts from Northern Kenya. *Nature* 226: 223–30.

Lee, R. B. 1965. Subsistence ecology of the !Kung Bushmen. Doctoral dissertation in the Department of Anthropology University of California, Berkeley.

1968. I. DeVore. What hunters do for a living, or, how to make out on scarce resources. In *Man the Hunter*. Edited by R. Lee and I. DeVore. Proceedings of a symposium sponsored by Wenner-Gren Foundation for Anthropological Research, Chicago 1966.

1979. *The !Kung San*. Cambridge: Cambridge University Press.

Lee, R. B. and I. DeVore. 1968. eds. *Man the Hunter*. Chicago: Aldine.

Leopold, L. B., W. W. Emett and R. M. Myrick 1966. Channel and hillslope processes in a semi-arid area, New Mexico. *Geological Survey Professional paper* 352-G. Washington.

Liebermen, P. 1975. *On the Origins of Language–an Introduction to the Evolution of Human Speech*. New York: MacMillan.

Lewin, R. 1981. Ethiopian stone tools are world's oldest. *Science* 211: 806–7.

1982. How did humans evolve big brains? *Science* 216: 840–1.

Lighthill, J. J. and G. B. Whitham. 1955a. On kinematic waves I. Flood movement in long rivers. *Proceedings of the Royal Society* 229A: 281–316.

1955b. On kinematic waves II. A theory of traffic flow on long crowded roads. *Proceedings of the Royal Society* 229A: 317–45.

Lovejoy, O. 1978. A biomechanical review of the locomotor diversity of early hominids. In *Early Hominids of Africa*. Edited by C. Jolly. London: Duckworth.

1981. The origin of man. *Science*. 211: 341–50.

Lubbock, J. 1865. *Prehistoric Times*. London: Williams and Norgate.

Lumley, H. de. 1969a. Une cabane acheuléenne dans la Grotte du Lazaret (Nice). *Mémoires de la Société Préhistorique Française* 7.

1969b. A Paleolithic camp at Nice. *Scientific American* 220(5): 42–50.

Lyell, C. 1863. *The Antiquity of Man*. London.

McBryde, I. n.d. Archaeological investigation in the Lake Mungo area. Paper presented at a symposium, Australian National University, July 1976.

McBurney, C. B. M. 1950. The geographic study of the older Palaeolithic stages in Europe. *Proceedings of the Prehistoric Society* 16: 163–83.

1960. *The Stone Age of Northern Africa*. Harmondsworth: Penguin.

1967. *The Haua Fteah (Cyrenaica) and the Stone Age of the South-East Mediterranean*. Cambridge: Cambridge University Press.

1969. *The Prehistory of Australia*. London: Thames and Hudson.

McCall, G. J. H. 1957. *Geology and Groundwater Conditions in the Nakuru Area*. Ministry of Works (Hydraulic Branch), Kenya, Technical Report 3.

1967. *Geology of the Nakuru Thomson's Falls–Lake Hannington Area*. Geological Survey of Kenya, Report 78.

McCall, G. J. H., B. H. Baker and J. Walsh. 1967. Late Tertiary and Quaternary sediments of the Kenya Rift Valley. In *Background to Evolution in Africa*. Edited by W. W. Bishop and J. D. Clark. Chicago: University of Chicago Press.

McDougall, I. 1981. ^{40}Ar/^{39}Ar age spectra from the KBS Tuff, Koobi Fora Formation. *Nature* 294: 120–4.

1985. K-Ar and 40Ar/39Ar dating of the hominid-bearing Plio-Pleistocene sequence at Koobi Fora, Lake Turkana, Northern Kenya, *Bulletin of the Geological Society of America* 96: 159–75.

McDougall, I., R. Maier, P. Sutherland-Hawkes and A. J. W. Gleadow. 1980. K-Ar age estimate for the KBS Tuff, East Turkana, Kenya. *Nature* 284: 230–4.

McHenry, H. and L. A. Temerin. 1979. The evolution of hominid bipedalism: evidence from the fossil record. *Yearbook of Physical Anthropology* 22: 105–31.

McIntyre, J. n.d. Archaeological investigations in the Willandra Lake area. Paper presented at a symposium, Australian University, July 1976.

Mann, A. E. 1968. The paleodemography of *Australopithecus*. Doctoral dissertation, University of California, Berkeley.

Mann, A. 1975. Some palaeodemographic aspects of the South African Australopithecines. *University of Pennsylvania Publications in Anthropology* 1.

Marshack, A. 1972a. Upper Paleolithic notation and symbol. *Science* 178: 817–28.

  1972. *The Roots of Civilization.* New York: McGraw Hill.

Martin, P. S. 1966. African and Pleistocene overkill. *Nature* 212: 339–42.

Martin. R. and R. May. 1981. Outward signs of breeding. *Nature* 293: 8–9.

Mason, R. 1962a. Australopithecines and artefacts at Sterkfontein. Part 2. The Sterkfontein artifacts and their maker. *South African Archaeological Bulletin* 17(66): 109–25.

  1962b. *Prehistory of the Transvaal.* Johannesburg: Witwatersrand University Press.

Matthieson, D. G. 1982. The contribution of the avifauna to the study of the early Pleistocene hominids from Olduvai Gorge, Tanzania. Paper presented to the 4th International Conference of Archaeozoology, London, April 1982 (abstract only).

Mellars, P. 1970. Some comments on the notion of 'functional variability' in stone tool assemblages. *World Archaeology* 2(1): 74–89.

Merrick, H. V. 1976. Recent archaeological research in the Plio-Pleistocene deposits of the lower Omo Valley, southwestern Ethiopia. In *Human Origins, Louis Leakey and the East African Evidence.* Edited by G. Ll. Isaac and E. R. McCown. Menlo Park, CA: Benjamin.

Merrick, H. V. and J. P. S. Merrick. 1976. Archaeological occurrences of earlier Pleistocene age from the Shungura Formation. In *Earliest Man and Environments in the Lake Rudolf Basin: Stratigraphy, Paleoecology and Evolution.* Edited by Y. Coppens *et al.* Chicago: University of Chicago Press.

Merrick, H. V. J. de Heinzelin, P. Haesaerts and F. C. Howell. 1973. Archaeological occurrences of early Pleistocene age from the Shungura Formation, lower Omo Valley, Ethiopia. *Nature* 242: 572–5.

van der Merwe, N. J. 1982. Carbon isotopes, photosynthesis, and archaeology. *American Scientist* 70: 596–606.

Milton, K. 1981. Distribution patterns of tropical plant foods as an evolutionary stimulus to primate mental development. *American Anthropologist* 83: 534–48.

Moore, J. 1984. The evolution of reciprocal sharing. *Ethology and Sociobiology* 5: 5–14.

Morgan, E. 1972. *The Descent of Woman.* London: Souvenir Press.

  1982. *The Aquatic Ape.* London: Souvenir Press.

Morris, D. 1967. *The Naked Ape.* London: Cape.

Mortelmans, G. and J. Nenquin. 1962. eds. *Actes du IVe Congrès Panafricain de Préhistoire,* Tervuren, Belgium.

Mortillet, G. de. 1883. *Le Préhistorique: Antiquité de l'Homme.* Paris.

Movius, H. L. 1948. The Lower Palaeolithic Cultures of Southern and Eastern Asia. *Transactions of the American Philosophical Society* 38: 329–419.

Movius, H. L., N. C. David, H. M. Bricker and R. B. Clay. 1968. The analysis of certain major classes of Upper Palaeolithic tools. *Peabody Museum, Bulletin* 26. Cambridge, MA.

Muller-Karpe, H. 1966. *Handbuch der Vorgeschichte,* Vol. 1. Munich: C. H. Beck'sche.

Mulvaney, D. J. 1966. The prehistory of the Australian aborigine. *Scientific American* 214: 84–93.

Neustupny, E. 1971. Whither archaeology? *Antiquity* 45: 34–9.

Oakley, K. P. 1951. A definition of man. *Science News* 20: 69–81.

1954. Skill as a human possession. In *A History of Technology*, Vol. 1. Edited by C. Singer and E. Holmyard. Oxford: Clarendon Press. (Reprinted with revisions in S. Washburn and P. Dohlinow, eds. *Perspectives on Human Evolution*, Vol. 2. New York: Holt, Rinehart and Winston.)

1955. Fire as a palaeolithic tool and weapon. *Proceedings of the Prehistoric Society* 21: 36–48.

1957. Tools makyth man. *Antiquity* 31: 199–209.

1966. *Frameworks for Dating Fossil Man.* Second edition. Chicago: Aldine.

Oakley, K. P., B. C. Campbell and T. I. Molleson. 1971. *Catalogue of Fossil Hominids.* London: British Museum (Natural History).

Ohel, M. Y. 1977. Patterned concentrations on living floors at Olduvai, Beds I and II: Experimental study. *Journal of Field Archaeology* 4: 423–33.

O'Keefe, J. A. 1963. Tektites. Chicago: University of Chicago Press.

Owen, R. C. 1965. The patrilocal band: a linguistically and culturally hybrid social unit. *American Anthropologist* 67: 675–90.

Parker, S. T. and R. Gibson. 1979. A developmental model for the evolution of language and intelligence in early hominids. In *The Behavioural and Brain Sciences*, Vol 2. Cambridge: Cambridge University Press.

Perkins, D. and P. Daly. 1968. A hunter's village in Neolithic Turkey. *Scientific American* 219(5): 96–106.

Perper, T. and C. Schrire. 1977. The Nimrod connection: myth and science in the hunting model. In *The Chemical Senses and Nutrition.* Edited by M. R. Kare. New York: Academic Press.

Perrot, J. 1966. Le Gisement Natoufien de Mallaha (Eynan) Israel. *L'Anthropologie* 70: 437–84.

Peters, C. R. 1979. Toward an ecological model of African Plio-Pleistocene hominid adaptations. *American Anthropologist* 81: 261–78.

Peter, C. R. and E. M. O'Brien. 1981. The early hominid plant food niche: insights from an analysis of human, chimpanzee, and baboon plant exploitation in eastern and southern Africa. *Current Anthropology* 22: 127–40.

Pettijohn, F. J. 1956. *Sedimentary Rocks.* New York: Harpers.

Pfeiffer, J. E. 1969. *The Emergence of Man.* New York: Harper and Row.

Piggott, S. 1959. *Approach to Archaeology.* London: Black.

Pilbeam, D. R. 1972. *The Ascent of Man.* New York and London: Macmillan.

1980. Major trends in human evoluton. In *Current Argument on Early Man.* Edited by L.-K. Konigsson. Oxford: Pergamon Press.

Pilbeam. D. R. and S. J. Gould. 1974. Size and scaling in human evolution *Science* 186. 892–901.

Piperno, M. and G. M. Piperno. 1975. First approach to the ecological and cultural significance of the early paleolithic occupation site of Garba IV at Melka Kunturé (Ethiopia). *Quaternaria* 18: 347–382.

Pope, G. 1982. The antiquity of the Asian hominidae. *Physical Anthropology News* 1982 (Fall): 1–3.

Posnansky, M. 1959. The Hope Fountain site at Olorgesailie, Kenya Colony. *South African Archaeological Bulletin* 16: 83–9.

Potts, R. B. 1982. Lower Pleistocene site formation and hominid activities at Olduvai Gorge. Tanzania. Ph. D. dissertation, Department of Anthropology, Harvard University.

1983. Foraging for faunal resources by early hominids at Olduvai Gorge, Tanzania. In

Animals and Archaeology. 1. Hunters and their Prey. Edited by J. Clutton-Brock and C. Grigson. BAR International Series 163.

Potts, R. B. and P. Shipman. 1981. Cutmarks made by stone tools on bones from Olduvai Gorge, Tanzania. *Nature* 291: 577–80.

Propp, V. 1968. *Morphology of the Folktale.* Austin: University of Texas Press.

Ramendo, L. 1963. Note sur un galet amenagé de Reggan. *Libyca* 12:43–5.

Reader, J. 1980. *Missing Links.* Boston: Little, Brown.

Renfrew, A. C. 1968. Models in prehistory. *Antiquity* 42: 132–4.

    1969. More on models. *Antiquity* 43: 61–2.

Reynolds, V. 1966. Open groups in hominid evolution. *Man* 1: 441–52.

Richardson, J. and A. L. Kroeber. 1940. Three centuries of women's dress fashions, a quantitative analysis, *Anthropological Records* 5(2). University of California Press.

Robinson, B. W. 1967. Vocalization evoked from forebrain in *Macaca mulatta. Physiology and Behaviour* 2: 345–54.

Robinson, J. T. 1959. A bone implement from Sterkfontein. *Nature* 184: 583–5.

    1962. Australopithecines and artefacts at Sterkfontein. *Part 1.* Sterkfontein Stratigraphy and the significance of the Extension Site. *South African Archaeological Bulletin* 27(66): 87–107.

Robinson, J. T. and R. J. Mason. 1962. Australopithecines and artefacts at Sterkfontein. *South African Archaeological Bulletin* 17: 87–125.

Roche, H. 1980. *Premiers outils taillés d'Afrique.* Société d'Ethnographie, France.

Roche, H. and J. J. Tiercelin. 1977. Découverte d'une industrie lithique ancienne *in situ* dans la formation d'Hadar. Afar central, Ethiopie. *Comptes Rendus de l'Académie des Sciences* 284-D: 1871–4.

    1980. Industries lithiques de la formation Plio-Pléistocéne d'Hadar Ethiopie (Campagne 1976). *Proceedings of the Eighth Panafrican Congress of Prehistory and Quaternary Studies.* Nairobi.

Rodman, P. and H. McHenry. 1980. Bioenergetics and the origin of bipedalism. *American Journal of Physical Anthropology* 52: 103–6.

Roe, D. A. 1964. British Lower and Middle Palaeolithic: Some problems, methods of study and preliminary results. *Proceedings of the Prehistoric Society* 30: 245–67.

    1968. British Lower and Middle Palaeolithic handaxe groups. *Proceedings of the Prehistoric Society* 34: 1–82.

Romer, A. 1959. *The Vertebrate Story.* Chicago: University of Chicago Press.

Rosholt, J. N. and P.S. Antal. 1963. Evaluation of the Pa^{231}/U-Th^{230}/U method for dating Pleistocene carbonate rocks. *Geological Survey Research 1962: Short Papers in Geology, Hydrology and Topography,* articles 180–239. Geological Survey Professional Paper 450-E. E108–E111.

Roubet, C. 1969. Essai de datation absolue d'un biface-hachereau paléolithique de l'Afar (Ethiopie). *L'Anthropologie* 73: 503–54.

Rowell, T. 1966. Forest living baboons in Uganda. *Journal of Zoology* 149: 344–64.

Rust, A. 1950. *Die Hohlenfunde von Jabrud (Syrien).* Neumunster: R. Wachholtz.

Sacher, G. A. and E. F. Staffeldt. 1974. Relations of gestation time to brain weight for placental mammals. *American Naturalist* 108: 593–614.

Sackett, J. R. 1966. Quantitative analysis of upper Palaeolithic stone tools. In *Recent Studies in Palaeoanthropology.* Edited by J. D. Clark and F. C. Howell. American Anthropologist Special Publication 68: 2; 2: 356–94.

    1968. Method and theory of Upper Palaeolithic archaeology in south-western France. In *New Perspectives in Archaeology.* Edited by L. R. and S. R. Binford. Chicago: Aldine.

Sampson, C. G. 1967. Zeekoegat 13: Later Stone Age open-site near Venterstad, Cape. *Researches of the Nasionale Museum* (Bloemfontein) 2(6): 211–37.

Sarich. V. and J. Cronin. 1976. Molecular systematics of the primates. In *Molecular Anthropology*. Edited by M. Goodman, R. E. Tashian and J. H. Tashian. New York: Plenum Press.

Savage, D. E. and G. H. Curtis. 1970. The Villafranchian Stage-age and its radiometric dating. *Geological Society of America, Inc. Special Paper* 124: 207–31.

Schaeffer, O. A. 1966. Tektites. In *Potassium Argon Dating*. Edited by O. A. Schaeffer and J. Zahringer. New York: Springer.

Schaffer, W. 1968. Character displacement and the evolution of the Hominidae. *The American Naturalist* 102: 559–71.

Schaller, G. 1963. *The Mountain Gorilla: Ecology and Behaviour*. Chicago: University of Chicago Press.

Schaller, G. and G. Lowther. 1969. The relevance of carnivore behaviour to the study of early hominids. *Southwestern Journal of Anthropology* 25: 307–41.

Schick, K. 1984. Processes of Palaeolithic site formation: an experimental study. Ph. D. dissertation, Department of Anthropology, University of California, Berkeley.

Schiffer, M. 1972. Archaeological context and systemic context. *American Antiquity* 37: 156–65.

1976. *Behavioral Archeology*. New York: Academic Press.

Schoener, T. W. 1971. Theory of feeding strategies. *Annual Review of Ecology and Systematics* 2: 369–404.

Schoeninger, M. 1982. Diet and the evolution of modern human form in the Middle East. *American Journal of Physical Anthropology* 58: 37–52.

Scott, L. and R. G. Klein. 1981. A hyena-accumulated bone assemblage from late Holocene deposits at Deelpan, Orange Free State. *Annals of the South African Museum* 86: 217–27.

Sept, J. M. 1984. Plio-Pleistocene hominid behaviour and East African vegetation: archeology, paleoenvironments and a study of modern habitats. Ph. D dissertation. Department of Anthropology, University of California, Berkeley.

Shackleton, N. 1982. The deep-sea record of climate variability. *Progress in Oceanography* 11: 199–218.

Shackleton, R. M. 1955. Pleistocene movements in the Gregory Rift Valley. *Geologische Rundschau* 43: 257–63.

Shawcross, W. F. 1975. Thirty thousand years and more, *Hemisphere* 19: 26–31.

Shipman, P. 1981a. *The Life History of a Fossil*. Cambridge: Harvard University Press.

1981b. Applications of scanning electron microscopy to taphonomic problems. *Annals of the New York Academy of Sciences* 376: 357–86.

1983a. Early hominid lifestyle: Hunting and gathering or foraging and scavenging. In *Animals and Archaeology: Hunters and their Prey*. Edited by J. Clutton-Brock and C. Grigson. Oxford: BAR.

1983b. 'Diagnostic criteria for recognizing various agents of bone breakage and accumulation'. In *Animals and Archaeology: Hunters and their Prey*. Edited by J. Clutton-Brock and C. Grigson, Oxford: BAR.

Shipman, P. and J. Philips-Conroy. 1976. Scavenging by hominids and other carnivores. *Current Anthropology* 17: 170–2.

Sillen, A. 1981. Strontium and diet at Hayonim Cave. *American Journal of Physical Anthropology* 56: 131–7.

Sillen, A. and M. Kavanaugh. 1982. Strontium and paleodietary research: a review. *Yearbook of Physical Anthropology* 25: 67–90.

Simons, E. 1972. *Primate Evolution*. New York: Macmillan.

Simons, J. W. 1966. The presence of leopard and a study of the food debris in the leopard lairs of the Mt Suswa Caves. *Bulletin of the Cave Exploration Group of East Africa* 1: 51–69.

Smith, P. L. 1966. The late Palaeolithic of northeast Africa in the light of recent research. *American Anthropologist* 68, 2(2): 326–55.

Sohnge, P. G., D. J. L. Visser and C. Van Riet Lowe. 1937. *The Geology and Archaeology of the Vaal River Basin.* Union of South Africa Geological Survey, Memoire 35.

Sokal, R. R. and P. H. A. Sneath, 1963. *Principles of numerical Taxonomy.* San Francisco: W. H. Freeman.

Solecki, R. S. 1963. Prehistory in Shanidar Valley, Northern Iraq. *Science* 139: 179–93.

  1964. Shanidar Cave, a Late Pleistocene site in Northern Iraq. *Report of the VIth International Congress on the Quaternary,* Warsaw 1961. Vol. 4. Archaeological and Anthropological Section: 413–23.

Sollas, W. J. 1911. *Ancient Hunters and their Modern Representatives.* London: Macmillan.

Sonneville-Bordes, D. de. 1960. *Le Paléolithique supérieur en Périgord.* Bordeaux: Imprimeries Delmas.

Sonneville-Bordes, D. de and J. Perrot. 1953, 1955, 1956. Lexique typologique de Paléolithique supérieur, outillage lithique. *Bulletin Société Préhistorique Française* 51: 327–35; 52: 76–9; 53: 408–12, 547–59.

Speth, J. D. and D. Davis. 1976. Seasonal variability in early hominid predation. *Science* 192: 441–5.

Speth, J. D. and K. A. Speilman. 1983. Energy source, protein metabolism, and hunter-gatherer subsistence strategies. *Journal of Anthropological Archaeology* 2(1): 1–31.

Stearns, C. E. and D. L. Thurber. 1965. Th^{230}/U^{234} dates of late Pleistocene marine fossils from the Mediterranean and Moroccan littorals. *Quaternaria* 7: 29–42.

Stekelis, M. 1966. *Archaeological Excavations at 'Ubeidiya 1960–1963.* Jerusalem.

Stern, J. and R. Susman. 1983. The locomotor anatomy of *Australopithecus afarensis. American Journal of Physical Anthropology* 60: 279–317.

Stiles, D. 1979. Paleolithic culture and culture change: experiment in theory and method. *Current Anthropology* 20: 1–2.

  1980a. The archaeology of Sterkfontein, A descriptive and comparative analysis of early hominid culture. Ph. D. dissertation, Department of Anthropology, University of California, Berkeley.

  1980b. Industrial taxonomy in the Early Stone Age in Africa. *Anthropologie* 18: 189–207.

Stiles, D. N., R. L. Hay and J. R. O'Neil. 1974. The MNK chert factory site, Olduvai Gorge, Tanzania. *World Archaeology* 5: 285–308.

Stiles, D. and T. C. Partridge. 1979. Results of recent archaeological and paleoenvironmental studies at the Sterkfontein Extension Site. *South African Journal of Science* 75: 346–52.

Strum, S. 1981. Processes and products of change: baboon predatory behavior at Gilgil, Kenya. In *Omnivorous Primates.* Edited by R. S. O. Harding and G. Teleki. New York: Columbia University Press.

Susman, R. and N. Creel. 1979. Functional and morphological affinities of the subadult hand (OH7) from Olduvai Gorge. *American Journal of Physical Anthropology* 51: 311–31.

Susman, R. L. and J. T. Stern. 1982. Functional morphology of *Homo habilis. Science* 217: 931–4.

Sutcliffe, A. J. 1972. Spotted hyaena: crusher, gnawer, digester and collector of bones. *Nature* 227: 1110–13.

Swedlund. A. C. 1974. The use of ecological hypotheses in Australopithecine taxonomy. *American Anthropologist* 76: 515–29.

Taieb, M. and J. J. Tiercelin. 1979. Sedimentation Pliocéne et paléoenvironment de rift:

Example de la formation à hominidés d'Hadar (Afar, Ethiopie). *Bulletin de la Société Géologique de France* 21: 243–53.

Tanner, N. M. 1981. *On Becoming Human.* Cambridge: Cambridge University Press.

Teleki, G. 1973. *The Predatory Behavior of Wild Chimpanzees.* Lewisburg: Bucknell University Press.

1975. Primate subsistence patterns: collector-predators and gatherer-hunters. *Journal of Human Evolution* 4: 125–84.

Thoma, A. 1966. L'Occipital de l'homme mindeléen de Vértesszöllös. *L'Anthropologie* 70: 495–534.

Thomas, D. 1973. An empirical test of Steward's model of Great Basin settlement patterns. *American Antiquity* 38: 155–76.

Thomas, D. H. 1974. *Predicting the Past: an Introduction to Anthropological Archaeology.* New York: Holt, Rhinehart and Winston.

Thomson, D. F. 1964. Some wood and stone implements of the Bindibu tribe of central Western Australia. *Proceedings of the Prehistoric Society* 30: 400–22.

Tiger, L. 1969. *Men in Groups.* London: Nelson.

Tixier, J. 1963. *Typologie de l'Epipaléolithique du Maghreb.* Paris: Arts et Métiers Graphiques.

Tobias, P. V. 1965a. *Australopithecus, Homo habilis,* tool-using and tool-making. *South African Archaeological Bulletin* 20(80): 167–92.

1965b. The early *Australopithecus and Homo* from Tanzania. *Anthropologie* 3(3): 43–8.

1967. Cultural hominisation among the earliest African Pleistocene hominids. *Proceedings of the Prehistoric Society* 13: 367–76.

1980. *Australopithecus afarensis* and *A. africanus:* critique and alternative hypotheses. *Palaeontologia Africana* 23: 1–17.

1981. The emergence of man in Africa and beyond. *Philosophical Transactions of the Royal Society. London B* 292: 43–56.

Toots, H. and M. R. Voorhies. 1965. Strontium in fossil bones and the reconstruction of fossil food chains. *Science* 149: 854–5.

Toth, N. 1982. The stone technologies of early hominids at Koobi Fora, Kenya: an experimental approach. Ph. D. dissertation, Department of Anthropology, University of California, Berkeley. Micro films Ann Arbor

in press. The implications of experimental studies, In *Archaeological Studies of the Koobi Fora Formation 1970–1979.* Edited by G. Ll. Isaac. Oxford: Clarendon Press.

Toth, N. and K. Schick. 1983. The cutting edge: an experimental elephant butchery with stone tools. *Interim Evidence: Newsletter of the Foundation for Research into the Origin of Man* 5(1): 8–10.

Trigger, B. W. 1969. More on models. *Antiquity* 43: 59–61.

1970. Aims in prehistoric archaeology. *Antiquity* 44: 26–37.

Tringham, R. E., C. Cooper, C. Odell, B. Voytek and A. Whitman. 1974. Experimentation in the formation of edge damage: a new approach to lithic analysis. *Journal of Field Archaeology* 1: 171–96.

Trinkaus, E. and W. W. Howells. 1979. The Neanderthals. *Scientific American* 241: 118–33.

Trivers, R. L. 1971. The evolution of reciprocal altruism. *Q. Rev. Biol.* 46, 35–57.

Van Noten, F., D. Cahen and L. Keeley. 1980. A paleolithic campsite in Belgium. *Scientific American* 242(4): 48–55.

Vertés, L. 1965. Typology of the Buda Industry, a pebble-tool industry from the Hungarian Lower Paleolithic. *Quaternaria* 7: 185–95.

1966. Des vestiges humains et des outils du Paléolithique Inférieur (450,000 av.J.C.) découverts en Hongrie. *Archaeologia* Sept.–Oct.: 66–71.

1968. Rates of Evolution in Palaeolithic technology. *Acta Archaeologica Scientiarium Hungarica* 20: 1–19.

Vincens, A. 1979. Analyse palynologique du site archéologique FxJj 50, Formation du Koobi Fora, Est Turkana (Kenya). *Bulletin de Société Géologique de France* 21(7): 343–7.

1982. *Palynologie, environments actuels et Plio-Pléistocénes à l'est du lac Turkana (Kenya).* Thése d'état, Faculté des Sciences de Luminy, l'Université d'Aix-Marseille 11.

Vincent, A. 1984. The underground storage organs of plants as potential foods for tool using early hominids. Ph. D. dissertation, Department of Anthropology, University of California, Berkeley.

Vita-Finzi, C. and E. S. Higgs. 1970. Prehistoric economy in the Mount Carmel area of Palestine: site catchment analysis. *Proceedings of the Prehistoric Society* 36: 1–37.

Vogel, J. C. and H. T. Waterbolk. 1967. Groningen Radiocarbon dates VII. *Radiocarbon* 9: 145.

Vondra, C. F., and B. E. Bowen. 1976. Plio-Pleistocene deposits and environments, East Rudolf, Kenya. In *Earliest Man and Environments in the Lake Rudolf Basin: Stratigraphy, Paleoecology and Evolution.* Edited by Y. Coppens *et al.* Chicago: University of Chicago Press.

Vrba, E. S. 1975. Some evidence of chronology and paleoecology of Sterkfontein, Swartkrans and Kromdraal from the fossil Bovidae. *Nature* 254: 301–4.

1979. A new study of the scapula of *Australopithecus africanus* from Sterkfontein. *American Journal of Physical Anthropology* 51: 117–29.

1982. Biostratigraphy and chronology, based particularly on Bovidae, of southern hominid-associated assemblages: Makapansgat, Sterkfontein, Taung, Kromdraai, Swartkrans; also Elandsfontein (Saldanha), Broken Hill (now Kabwe) and Cave of Hearths. *Congrès International de Paléontologie Humaine 1, Nice.*

Walker, A. 1981. Dietary hypotheses and human evolution. *Philosophical Transactions of the Royal Society B* 292: 57–64.

Walker, A. and R. E. F. Leakey. 1978. The hominids of East Turkana. *Scientific American* 239: 54–66.

Wallace, A. R. 1858. On the tendency of varieties to depart indefinitely from the original type. *Journal of the Linnean Society, Zoology,* III (9): 45–62.

Walter, R. C. and James L. Aronson. 1982. Revision of K/Ar ages for the Hadar hominid site, Ethiopia. *Nature* 296: 122–7.

Warren, S. H. 1926. The classification of the Lower Palaeolithic with special reference to Essex. *Transactions of the South-Eastern Union of Scientific Societies,* 38–51.

Washburn, S. L. 1957. Australopithecines: the hunters or the hunted. *American Anthropologist* 59: 612–14.

1960. Tools and human evolution. *Scientific American* 203: 3.

1965. An apes-eye view of human evolution. In *The Origin of Man.* Edited by P. DeVore. New York: Wenner Gren Foundation.

1967. Behaviour and the origin of man. Huxley Memorial Lecture 1967. *Proceedings of the Royal Anthropological Institute of Great Britain and Ireland* 21–7.

1969. One hundred years of biological anthropology. *One Hundred Years of Anthropology.* Edited by J. O. Brew. Cambridge, MA.

Washburn, S. L. and C. S. Lancaster. 1968. The evolution of hunting. In *Man the Hunter.* Edited by R. B. Lee and I. DeVore. Chicago: Aldine.

Washburn, S. L. and R. Moore. 1974. *Ape into Man: a Study of Human Evolution.* New York: Little, Brown.

1980. *Ape into Human.* 2nd edn. Boston: Little, Brown.

Weiner, J. S. 1973. The tropical origins of man. *Addison-Wesley Module in Anthropology* 44.

Wendorf, F. 1968. ed. *The Prehistory of Nubia.* Dallas, Texas: Southern Methodist University Press.

Wendorf, F. and A. Marks. 1975. eds. *Problems in Prehistory: North Africa and the Levant.* Dallas, Texas: Southern Methodist University Press.

Wendorf, F. and R. Schild. 1976. *Prehistory of the Nile Valley.* New York: Academic Press.

Wendorf, M. 1982. The fire areas of Santa Rosa Island: an interpretation. *North American Archaeology* 3(2): 173–80.

Westphal, M., J. Chavaillon and J. J. Jaeger. 1979. Magnétostratigraphie des dépots Pléistocénes de Melka-Kunturé (Ethiopie): Premiers données. *Bulletin de la Société Géologique de France 7e* 21: 237–41.

Whallon, R. 1973. Spatial analysis of occupation floors: the application of dimensional analysis of variance. In *The Explanation of Culture Change: Models in Prehistory.* Edited by C. Renfrew. London: Duckworth.

    1974. Spatial analysis of occupation floors II: the application of nearest neighbour analysis. *American Antiquity* 39: 16–34.

White, C. and N. Peterson. 1969. Ethnographic interpretation of the prehistory of Western Arnhem Land. *Southwestern Journal of Anthropology* 25(1): 45–67.

White, J. P. 1969. Typologies for some prehistoric flaked stone artifacts in the Australian New Guinea Highlands. *Arch. Phy. Anthrop., Oceania* 4: 18–46.

White, T. D., D. C. Johanson and Y. Coppens. 1982. Dental remains from the Hadar Formation, Ethiopia: 1974–1977 collections. *American Journal of Physical Anthropology* 57: 545–603.

White, T. D., J. C. Johanson and W. H. Kimbel. 1981. *Australopithecus africanus:* its phyletic position reconsidered. *South African Journal of Science* 77: 445–70.

Willey, G. R. and P. Phillips. 1958. *Method and Theory in American Archaeology.* Chicago: Chicago University Press.

Williams, M. A. J., F. M. Williams, F. Gasse, G. H. Curtis and D. A. Adamson. 1979. Plio-Pleistocene environments at Gadeb prehistoric site, Ethiopia. *Nature* 282: 29–33.

Willoughby, P. 1985. Spheroids and battered stones: A case study in technology and adaptation in the African Early and Middle Stone Age. Ph. D. dissertation. Department of Anthropology. University of California, Los Angeles.

Wilson, A., S. S. Carlson and T. J. White 1977. Biochemical evolution. *Annual Review of Biochemistry* 46: 573–639.

Wilson, E. O. 1975. *Sociobiology: the New Synthesis.* Harvard: Belknap.

Winterhalder, B. and E. A. Smith. 1981. eds. *Hunter-Gatherer Foraging Strategies.* Chicago: University of Chicago Press.

Wolberg, D. L. 1970. The hypothesised osteodontokeratic culture of the Australopithecinae: a look at the evidence and the opinions. *Current Anthropology* 11(1): 23–7.

Wolpoff, M. 1973. Posterior tooth size, body and diet in South African gracile australopithecines. *American Journal of Physical Anthropology* 39: 375–94.

    1975. Some aspects of human mandibular evolution. In *Determinants of mandibular Form and Growth* Edited by J. McNamara. Ann Arbor Center for Human Growth and Development.

Wood, B. 1976. *The Evolution of Early Man.* London: Peter Lowe.

    1981. Tooth size and shape and their relevance to studies of hominid evolution. *Philosophical Transactions of the Royal Society London B.* 292: 65–76.

Worthington-Smith, G. 1894. *Man the Primeval Savage: His Haunts and Relics from the Hilltops of Bedfordshire to Blackwall.* London.

Wrangham, R. W. 1979a. Sex differences in chimpanzee dispersion. In *The Great Apes*. Edited by D. Hamburg and E. R. McCown. Menlo Park: Benjamin/Cummings.

1979. On the evolution of ape social systems. *Social Science Information* 18: 335–68.

1980. An ecological model of female-bonded primate groups. *Behaviour* 75: 262–300.

Wright, R. V. S. 1972. Imitative learning of a flaked stone technology–the case of an orang-outan. *Mankind 8:* 296–306. Reprinted with better photographs in S. L. Washburn and E. McCown, eds., *Human Evolution: Biosocial Perspectives.* Menlo Park: Benjamin.

1977. ed. *Stone Tools as Cultural Markers: Change, Evolution and Complexity.* Canberra: Australian Institute of Aboriginal Studies.

Wynn, T. 1981a. The intelligence of Oldowan hominids. *Journal of Human Evolution* 10: 529–41.

1981b. The intelligence of later Acheulean hominids. *Man* 14: 371–91.

Yearbook of Physical Anthropology for 1975. 1976. Washington, DC: AAPA.

Yellen, J. 1972. Trip V. Itinerary May 24-June 9, 1968. Pilot Edition of *Exploring Human Nature.* Cambridge, Mass.: Education Development Center.

1977a. Cultural patterning in faunal remains: evidence from the !Kung. In *Experimental Archaeology.* Edited by D. Ingersoll, J. Yellen and A. MacDonald. New York: Columbia University Press.

1977b. *Archaeological Approaches to the Present: Models for Reconstructing the Past.* New York: Academic Press.

Zhou Mingzhen, Li Yanxian and Wanglinghong. 1982. Chronology of the Chinese fossil hominids. *Congrés International de Paléontologie Humaine 1, Nice.*

Zihlman, A. and N. Tanner. 1979. Gathering and the hominid adaptation. In *Female Hierarchies.* Edited by L. Tiger and H. M. Fowler. Chicago: Beresford Book Service.

INDEX

Page numbers in *italics* refer to illustrations